Praise for Alan M. Dershowitz...

CONTRARY TO POPULAR OPINION

"These short pieces, written with the concise to-the-pointness of legal briefs, present a commentator possessing a sharp mind, judicious judgment and sound principles."
—*The Jerusalem Report*

"Sometimes I agree, and sometimes I disagree, but I'm never bored for a minute...a great read."   —Susan R. Estrich

"An exciting, fascinating reflection of a brilliant mind."
—Arnold Forster, Human Rights Attorney

CHUTZPAH

"Fascinating...one of the most important and controversial books about American Jews since World War II."
—*Boston Sunday Globe*

"A bold, powerful book...[it] ought to be required reading for Jews, and on the suggested list for goyim. Everybody can use a little chutzpah."   —*The New York Times Book Review*

"Well worth reading."   —*San Francisco Chronicle*

"Enlightening, moving, and challenging."   —Elie Wiesel

CONTRARY TO POPULAR OPINION

ALAN M. DERSHOWITZ

BERKLEY BOOKS, NEW YORK

CONTRARY TO POPULAR OPINION

A Berkley Book / published by arrangement with
Pharos Books

PRINTING HISTORY
Pharos Books edition published 1992
Berkley trade paperback edition / June 1994

ISBN: 0-425-14147-0

BERKLEY®
Berkley Books are published by The Berkley Publishing Group,
200 Madison Avenue, New York, New York 10016.
BERKLEY and the "B" design
are trademarks belonging to Berkley Publishing Corporation.

PRINTED IN THE UNITED STATES OF AMERICA

10 9 8 7 6 5 4 3 2 1

To my daughter, Ella Kaille Cohen Dershowitz, who is already showing a wonderful ability to be contrary to her parents' opinions.

Acknowledgments

One of the great pleasures of a solitary writer is to have a great support team. Chief among my research team on this project was Daniel Eisenstadt. Eran Rephael, Stuart Slotnick and Rozella Oliver helped as well. Rosanna Cavallaro, Jack Zaremski and Joseph Lipner—my legal associates—provided much of the case research.

Typing and production of the book was overseen by my assistants, Mary Beth Johnson and Gayle Muello. Some typing and assistance was provided by Maura Kelly and Peggy Conant.

Appreciation as well goes to my literary agent, Helen Rees, and the people at United Feature Syndicate and Pharos Books—David Hendin, Rebecca Rhodin, Rebecca Shannonhouse and Kevin McDonough.

Thanks to my sons, Elon and Jamin, my nephew, Adam, my niece, Rana, my brother Nathan and my sister-in-law Marilyn who provided several ideas for columns.

A special thanks goes to Carolyn Cohen, who read every column and was lovingly critical.

Finally, a word of appreciation to my two-and-a-half-year-old daughter, Ella—to whom this book is dedicated—for showing me that being contrary is a natural human phenomenon.

Contents

Acknowledgments vi

Introduction xiii

Part One   JUDGES, JUSTICES, JURIES AND THE COURTS   1

1 // *Two Cheers for Our Legal System*   3

Today's Judges Fail to Make the Grade   //   Chief Justice Says He Is No Judge   //   Rhode Island Judge Inhibits Free Speech   //   Pitiful World of the Real Night Court   //   Unsung Heroes—Juries Offer True Justice   //   Juries Answer Only to Conscience   //   Brennan Vacancy Leaves Moderates Room   //   Let's Change the Way We Select Judges   //   Are Judges Privileged Characters?   //   Marshall's Resignation Ends an Era   //   Judge Thomas: Bush's Political Masterstroke   //   Is Clarence Thomas Ready for the High Court   //   "Street Justice" Ruled in the Rodney King Case   //   Double Jeopardy Should Bar Retrial of L.A. Cops   //   Demjanjuk and Coleman: A Comparison Between Israeli and American Justice   //   Could Salem Witch Trials Happen Today?   //   The Emergence of a Moderate Middle In The Supreme Court

Part Two   FREEDOM OF EXPRESSION AND THE RISE OF INTOLERANCE   39

2 // *Modern Challenges to the First Amendment*   41

Just "a Little Censorship" Goes a Long, Long Way   //   Take This Test for the First Amendment Club   //   A Way for Students to Fight the

CONTENTS

Censors // An Invitation to Murder? // Philip Morris Waves Flag
to Sell Death // Your First Amendment Right to Panhandle // To
Sue or Not to Sue? // Do Quotation Marks Guarantee Accuracy? //
New York Nudity Ruling Went Too Far

3 // *Intolerance on the Right*   60

Today's Censors: Conservative or Authoritarian? // Child Porn Laws
Threatens Free Expression // Law Protects Scorsese's *Temptation*
// O'Connor's Letter Aids Religious Bigots // Flag Burning in a
Flag-Waving Society // Censors Constantly Hunt for New Targets //
The Adultery Cops Are Watching // Relish Our Freedom to
Desecrate the Flag // Protect Rap Music and Flag Burning // Can
Town Officials Bump NC-17 Movies? // First Amendment Loses in
Obscenity Cases // Don't Censor Vanessa Redgrave // Souter's
Vote is a Foolish Fig Leaf

4 // *Intolerance on the Left*   88

The Road to Totalitarianism is Paved with Good Intentions //
Pornography Protest Has No Real Beef // First Amendment Protects
Right Wing, Too // Sitcom Vigilante Sends a Bad Message // Left
Says "No Comment" on China Massacre // Derrick Bell and Diversity
at Harvard // Is Crying Wolf OK for Blacks? //Does Press Have
Right to Expose Gays? // Chinese Leaders Scapegoat Pornography //
Put a Stop to Censorship by Death Threat // Can a Minority Be
Racist? // "Political Correctness" Endangers Freedoms //President
Bush Delivers Pomp, Hypocrisy // Multiculturalism Beats Bigotry //
Political Correctness Cops Strike on Campus // Thomas-Hill Satires
Test Free-Speech on Campus // Law School Parody Raises Free-
Speech Issue

Part Three   THE STATE, THE LAW AND THE RIGHTS OF INDIVIDUALS   125

5 // *The Limits of the Law*   127

Don't Blame the Law for Society's Ills // The Best Defense Stolen
Money Can Buy // The Last Thing We Need: A Plastic Pistol //
First, Let's Kill the Lawyers // TV Adopts a Law Enforcement

CONTENTS

Role // Misuse of RICO Laws Punishes "Pro-Lifers" // How Will
Court Rule on Police Intimidation? // Legal System Should Stop
Police Brutality // Is Homeless Person's Home His Castle? //
Court Ruling Encourages Police Coercion // Stop in the Name of
the Law // High Court Ponders Gang Members' Rights //
Castration Plea Bargain Smacks of Coercion // Obscenity Sting
Misuses Resources // Leona Helmsley: The Tax Scapegoat of
1992 // Revealing The Senate's Secrets

6 // *The Law and the Rise of the National Security State* 161

Court Turns North Accuser into Defender // Government Gives North
Too Much Sympathy // North Has Made Patriotic Crime Pay //
A Jury's Patriotism vs. Noriega's Rights // Taping Calls Violated
Noriega's Privacy // Noriega Tapes Fuel Dispute Over Amendments
// The Constitutional Power to Bluff // Should Saddam Hussein Be
Brought to Trial? // Will Civil Liberty Be a Gulf War Casualty?
// Why Caspar Weinberger Should Be Indicted // Caspar
Weinberger Gets No Special Treatment

7 // *The "War on Drugs" and the Rights of Individuals* 185

Drop Your Pants for a Drug-Free America // Trashing the Court's
Garbage Ruling // The Case for Medicalizing Heroin // U.S. Ship
Seizures Violate Liberties // End the Witch Hunt Against Pot Smokers
// Another Way of Solving the Drug Problem // Put That Cord Back
on Your Telephone // Was Marion Barry Entrapped? //Marion
Barry's Ignoble Defense Strategy // Let's Put an End to Those
"Bounty Hunter" Drug Arrests

Part Four THE LAW AND POLITICS OF SEX, LIFE AND DEATH 207

8 // *Women's Rights, Reproductive Freedom and the Politics of Abortion* 209

Mothers' Rights vs. Babies' Rights // When Abortion Leads to
"Femicide" // Overrule of Roe Would Injure Poor Women //

CONTENTS

Mothers Who Damage Their Unborn Children // Majority View on Abortion Will Prevail //Should Pregnant Women Be Denied Alcohol? // Unusual "Custody Dispute" Focuses on Eggs // More Than Ever, Law Focuses on Fetuses // Conceiving One Child to Save Another // Abortion Is the Wrong Litmus Test // No-Smoking Custody: How Far Can it Go? // Doctors Sing Government's Right-to-Life Song // Caution: Your Surgeon May Have PMS // Arguments Hint at No Abortion Overrule // . . . But it's Time to Overrule Roe vs. Wade // The Casey Decision // Is There a Right to Non-Paternity?

9 // *Capital Punishment* 244

Defense of Retarded Man Failed Him // Executions Embolden Fame-Seeking Killers // Seeking: A Hangman, Experience Preferred // Death Row Inmates Deserve a Lawyer's Aid // Technicality May Mean Death for Inmate // Don't Pull Plug on Televised Executions // Is the Death Penalty Rigged by Racism? // Court Distorts Justice in Death-Row Case

10 // *The Right to Die* 261

Tragic Mercy Killing Case Didn't Belong in Court // High Court Now Asks: When Does Life End? // Dr. Kevorkian and His Suicide Machine //Is Assisted Suicide First-Degree Murder? // Is it Murder if Life Support Extends Life? // Who Really Killed this Stabbing Victim?

11 / *Sex Crimes, Child Abuse and the Rights of the Accused* 274

The Tyson Case: Practicing Law in an Emotional Maelstrom // Child Abuse Case Defies Common Solutions // Should Rape Victims' Names Be Published? // Reasons to Publish Rape Victims' Names // The Rape That Never Happened // Protecting the Rape Victim—and Suspect // Child Is Missing, But Adults Have Rights // The Law Struggles with Sex Abuse Cases // Which Parents Abused Hilary Foretich? // Sacrificing Children to Religion // Punishing False Accusations of Rape // Should The

Media Identify Rape Victims? // Accuser's Identity Should Be Reported // Decide Rape Charge with Trial Not Politics // High Court Rules on Rape Shield Law // Explaining Pee-wee's Arrest to Your Kids //Facing the Accuser: Is the Smith Trial Fair? // Does the Smith Verdict Mean He's Innocent? // How *Not* to Televise Trials // When Women Don't Tell the Truth

Part Five OBSERVATIONS OF AN AMERICAN JEW 317

12 // *European Anti-Semitism* 319

Europe's Enduring Anti-Semitism // Old Anti-Semitism Taints "New" Poland // Auschwitz Dispute Sparks Slander Lawsuit // Auschwitz Nun Reveals Anti-Semitic Views // Anti-Semitism Rises in Eastern Europe // Come to the Synagogue, President Gorbachev // Will Gorbachev Denounce Anti-Semitism? // Be Wary of Investing Dollars in Poland // A Cardinal Cops a Plea // Fair Punishment for Lithuanians' Crimes

13 // *Embattled Israel* 341

The Case for Embattled Israel // Israel Is Still a True Democracy // Demjanjuk's Last Hope // Sentencing Ivan the Terrible // Patrick Buchanan's "Victim" Is No Hero // Indict Yasir Arafat for Murder // The World Should Not Honor Terrorists // Invasion Alters Israel's Occupation // Saddam Hussein's Israel Ploy // Why Is the PLO Still So Popular? // Israel Deports While Arabs Kill

14 // *American Anti-Semitism and Anti-Zionism: From the Right* 365

It Can Happen Here: American Right-Wing Anti-Semitism // Bush's Campaign Aide Supports Arab Cause // Pat Buchanan, the Jews, and the Nazis // Senators Advertising in a Racist Journal // A Cardinal Teaches by Example // Is Anti-Semitism on the Rise? // Should Newspapers Promote "Crackpot Idea," of Jew Hatred? // Buchanan Must Be Taken Seriously // The Moral Case Against Buchanan

CONTENTS

15 // *American Anti-Semitism and Anti-Zionism: From the Left*   386

The Socialism of Fools: Left-Wing Anti-Semitism   //   The Paper Alice Walker Shouldn't Have Signed   //   Half-Truths About Israel Pervade Media   //   Jackson's Silence Fuels Anti-Semitism   //How Can a Qaddafi Prize Honor Anyone?   //   Yom Kippur Exam Reeks of Anti-Semitism

Introduction

The 1990s promise to be a decade of dramatic change and dislocation. Already it has seen the breakup of the Soviet empire and of international communism. No one could have predicted this cataclysmic political event even a few years ago. Nor can anyone predict its long-term or even middle-term impact on the people of Eastern Europe or on the rest of the world. An enormous vacuum remains to be filled.

There are ominous danger signs all around. The foul odor of fascism can once again be detected in many parts of Europe. In the former Soviet Union, ultra-nationalist organizations such as Pamyat ("memory") are gaining power and legitimacy. In Romania, Hungary, Slovakia, Poland, and Croatia, neofascism, anti-Semitism, and xenophobia are on the rise even in the absence of sizable Jewish communities or an influx of immigrants. In France, Jean-Marie Le Pen is using antiimmigration hysteria to increase his support. In Italy, Benito Mussolini's granddaughter joined thirty-four other neofascists in Parliament and proudly claimed her grandfather's seat.

Perhaps most ominous is the growing power of a united Germany, coupled with a decreasing collective memory of the unparalleled evils of its Nazi past. Chancellor Helmut Kohl welcomed former Nazi Kurt Waldheim and condemned Jews who protested the meeting. In response to criticism from the World Jewish Congress, Kohl stated, "I don't need any advice," and then went on to accuse Jewish leaders of attempting to derail efforts toward German reunification.

Even here in the United States, where fascism has never gained a foothold, we are witnessing an increasing tolerance of the evils of bigotry and even fascism. Who could have imagined that less than half a century after our victory over the forces of Nazism there would be two significant American politicians with attachments to fascism. David Duke, a former Nazi party member and Ku Klux Klan leader, managed to win a majority of white voters in his unsuccessful race for U.S. Senator from Louisiana.

INTRODUCTION

Patrick Buchanan, a strong admirer of fascist dictator Francisco Franco, captured the votes of more than 30 percent of Republican voters in several presidential primaries. If we had a system of proportional representation, like France or Italy, fascist candidates would be well represented in our state and federal legislatures.

This is not to suggest that candidates like Duke and Buchanan attract voters *because* of their affinity with fascist dictators of the past or *because* of their racism or anti-Semitism. Many voters support them *despite* these perceived failings. What is new is that a decade ago, a candidate with fascist leanings would be rejected by virtually all voters. Today, such a background is widely ignored, even by people of goodwill.

A case in point is William F. Buckley, a conservative writer who in a cover article for his magazine, *The National Review*, reluctantly concluded that "I find it impossible to defend Pat Buchanan against the charge that what he did and said during the [recent] period under examination amounted to anti-Semitism." Yet within weeks of publishing this widely read and influential essay, Buckley himself told a television talk-show host that if he were a New Hampshire resident, *he* would vote for Patrick Buchanan in the upcoming presidential primary *as a protest* against the policies of President George Bush. The point, of course, is that even William Buckley, who recognizes that Patrick Buchanan expresses anti-Semitic views and who understands the danger of the growing tolerance for people with such views, is willing to ignore these evils in the interest of what for him is a larger issue—protesting the policies of President Bush.

Some voters also have other issues that permit them to ignore the bigotries of David Duke—issues such as opposition to racial quotas, busing, immigration, abortion, and secularization of American life. For many African-American voters of goodwill, there are issues that move them to ignore Louis Farrakhan's anti-Semitism or City College professor Leonard Jeffries's anti-white rhetoric.

All in all, the final decade of the second millennium threatens to be an unsettled period of dislocation, uncertainty, and searching. The appeal of extremism in such a time has been a recurring historical phenomenon, especially when the vacuum has occurred so quickly. The collective memory of any generation does not reach back more than a few decades. Our memory of World War II, of fascism, and of the Holocaust is quickly fading. More recent memories—of communism, of unwon wars such as Vietnam, of the civil rights movement—are somewhat sharper, though they, too, are blurring against the background of even more current realities, such as increasing unemployment, strident nationalism, and religious fundamentalism.

I approach this book with a wide lens on the larger, more international issues, and a more narrow focus on our own country and its unique problems, such as massive crime and the dangers it poses not only to our safety but to our liberty. Throughout, I try to look at our world—both large and small—from my own somewhat iconoclastic perspective. I represent no established point of view. I am difficult to chart on the conventional right-left, conservative-liberal, hawk-dove continua. I am a Jewish, American, academic, civil libertarian. But I disagree with much of what the Jewish "leadership" of this country stands for. I am out of sync with the current American leadership. I rarely agree with my academic colleagues. And I am a dissident within the American Civil Liberties Union. My views truly are contrary to popular opinion, even within those groups with which I most closely identify. I offer my perspective on a wide variety of issues in this volume for your consideration.   July 1992

P CONTRARY TO OPULAR OPINION

JUDGES,
JUSTICES,
JURIES AND
THE COURT

Part One

1 // *Two Cheers for Our Legal System*

TODAY'S JUDGES FAIL TO MAKE THE GRADE

I am certain that Winston Churchill would have evaluated the AngloAmerican legal system in much the same way he evaluated Anglo-American democracy: "the worst possible system—except for all the others!" Despite its considerable failings, both in theory and in practice, our legal system is better than all the others.

This is not, of course, to underestimate the failings of our system. Our judges, including our Supreme Court justices, are among the least qualified in the democratic world today. Many come from the ranks of the mediocrities, if not the dregs, of the legal profession. There are some very distinguished lawyers who ascend the bench, but they are way outnumbered by the mediocrities. Many judges are incredibly lazy, regarding their position as a kind of benign retirement from the rigors of law practice. Some are corrupt, although exchanges of cash are rare these days. The current currency of corruption is the exchange of favors and influence. Judges look more favorably on certain lawyers, law firms, and clients.

Some lawyers make it their business to cultivate the friendship of judges. They get themselves invited to "judicial conferences" where lawyers socialize with the judges before whom they practice. These lawyers manage to be photographed with judges and then hang these photos in their offices to attract clients. They try to serve on judicial selection, promotion, or evaluation committees. They attend dinners with judges. The appearance of impropriety coupled with the potential for impropriety would make such gatherings entirely inappropriate even if no actual improprieties occurred. But they do—and not infrequently. Lawyers solicit clients by boasting of their "close" friendship with judges. I have heard lawyers claim that they have certain judges "in their pocket." One New York lawyer, who serves on the judicial selection committee, once boasted to me that he "makes" judges and he can "break" them and they "know that" and "act accordingly" when he appears before them.

Some judges do everything in their power to avoid any complicity in this kind of corruption. Others encourage it by their overt favoritism toward friends, former colleagues, and potential future law partners.

But judges alone cannot always determine the outcome of a case at the trial level. The unique Anglo-American institution of the lay jury serves as a powerful, if incomplete, barrier to corruption. The jury is independent, anonymous, and unaccountable to anyone except themselves. That is both its virtue and its vice. In a case like the Rodney King acquittals, these attributes produced what most Americans regarded as an unjust verdict. No judge would have acquitted the defendants. He or she would have feared widespread criticism, peer condemnation, the impossibility of promotion, and perhaps even removal from office.

Our legal system, which employs both judges and jurors, is an attempt to strike a balance between the dangers of too much jury independence and the dangers of too much political and other influence on judges. It would work a lot better if the quality of our judges was higher. There is no excuse for our present system of judicial selection, which focuses so heavily on rewarding political hacks. We are entitled to better.   June 1992

CHIEF JUSTICE SAYS HE IS NO JUDGE

Well, Chief Justice William Rehnquist finally acknowledged what many Supreme Court observers have suspected for a long time. "I'm not a judge," he reminded Patricia Unsinn, a public defender from Chicago who was arguing on behalf of a criminal defendant. Unsinn had made the unforgivable mistake of addressing the chief justice by the lowly title "judge." That was too much for the usually unstuffy Rehnquist, who proceeded to publicly humiliate the nervous lawyer by glaring down from his lofty perch behind the Oak Bench and declaring: "I'm the chief justice. I'm not a judge."

Unsinn had no choice but to apologize, since she was representing a client whose liberty might turn on a single vote—though not likely a favorable vote by the chief justice. The press reported that the argument, which had just begun, continued with "a chill in the air." Rehnquist asked her no further questions. A law student who attended the argument reported to me that the shaken lawyer had difficulty recovering her composure. The lawyer says that at the moment of the rebuke she "felt like dying," but that she thinks she went on to make a creditable argument—at least to the other judges. (Whoops! Justices. Well, Excuuuse me.)

Some judges give women lawyers a particularly hard time, though there is no evidence that Rehnquist's put-down was motivated by sexism. But his schoolmarmish insistence on proper etiquette does remind me of Ph.D.s who insist on being called "doctor" and TV evangelists who demand the title "reverend." Most self-confident professionals I know are perfectly comfortable with their names and do not need elitist titles to make them feel secure. Many, though certainly not all, judges insist on being called "Your Honor" and demand that lawyers begin their argument with the reverential preface "May it please the court."

Rehnquist's predecessor, Warren Burger, used to complain when he was introduced merely as the "chief justice of the Supreme Court." "I am the chief justice of the *United States*," he would insist.

Beyond the obnoxiousness of his uncalled-for put-down, Rehnquist was wrong as a matter of constitutional law. Article II of the Constitution expressly provides for the appointment of "judges of the Supreme Court," not "justices." As a staunch advocate of literal interpretations of the Constitution's words, he should insist on being called by his constitutional title: "judge."

Rehnquist is also wrong as a matter of dictionary usage. The *Oxford English Dictionary* defines "judge" as the generic term for persons occupying any judicial office, except for "persons presiding judicially in *inferior* courts who are usually called 'justices' or 'magistrates.'" In the United States, the dictionary adds, the title judge is also applied to "a justice of the Supreme Court."

But perhaps there is some subtle truth to Rehnquist's insistence on not being called "judge" despite the plain words of the Constitution and the dictionary. Rehnquist is widely regarded by defense lawyers as a prosecutor in robes. He nearly always sides with the government and he often helps the prosecution make its case. Many defense lawyers do not regard him as a "judge"—in the sense of a neutral arbiter of constitutional rights— in criminal cases.

Indeed, it was precisely *because* both Richard Nixon, who originally appointed him to the Supreme Court, and Ronald Reagan, who elevated him to chief justice, believed that he would *not* be a neutral judge in criminal cases—that he would side with the prosecution—that he is where he is today. Nixon appointed him because of his reputation as an extreme-right-wing ideologue, a lawyer who had recommended declaring "qualified martial law" during antiwar demonstrations in Washington. Reagan promoted him to chief because of his consistent record of voting against the rights of criminal defendants—a record of one-sidedness unequaled by any other then-sitting justice. He was clearly not promoted or elevated because of his qualities as a neutral "judge."

In the profession of doing justice, there is no more noble title than that of judge. In some parts of the country, great lawyers who do not sit on the bench are called by the honorific title "judge." It is a title that has to be earned by respect, not mandated by political appointment. Justice Hugo Black, one of the greatest Supreme Court justices in our history, preferred to be called "judge" rather than "Mr. Justice" precisely because it was an earned accolade rather than a formal title.

Even religious literature refers to God as "Sovereign and Judge." The title may be good enough for God but not quite sufficient for William Rehnquist's elevated ego. (This will surely suggest the following variant on the old joke about the Angel Gabriel sending for the heavenly psychiatrist because God was having delusions of grandeur—he believed he was the chief justice of the United States.)

William Rehnquist is the chief justice. He should be called by that formal title—though he needn't interrupt nervous lawyers while they are arguing on behalf of their clients. Perhaps some day, if William Rehnquist continues the movement toward the court's center reflected in some decisions since his promotion to chief justice, he will actually deserve the noble title "judge."   October 1988

RHODE ISLAND JUDGE INHIBITS FREE SPEECH

Here's a current events quiz: He hadn't even read the book, yet he condemned the author and called for his destruction and banishment. He also urged his colleagues and followers to participate in attacks on the writer. He gave the offending author no opportunity to defend his book. Who is he?

There are two correct answers to this quiz: The first is the Ayatollah Khomeini of Iran; the second is the federal district court judge of Rhode Island, Ronald Lagueux. We all know the outrageous story of the Ayatollah Khomeini's threats against author Salman Rushdie for his book *The Satanic Verses*. Judge Lagueux's conduct is less well known, though it is equally outrageous, especially since it comes not from a Third World tyrant but from a U.S. judge who took an oath to support the Constitution.

Several years ago I wrote a book on the Claus von Bülow case, which had been tried in Rhode Island. I was von Bülow's lawyer on the appeal, which we won. While litigating the case, I observed some disturbing things about the Rhode Island justice system. Following von Bülow's acquittal, I wrote a book about the case, in which I documented some specific criticisms of certain Rhode Island judges. Before the book was published, a local Rhode Island newspaper carried a story about the criticisms it leveled.

At that time, Ronald Lagueux was a Rhode Island state judge who had just been nominated by President Reagan to become a federal judge. I had never even heard of Judge Lagueux; he had played no role in the von Bülow case, and I did not mention him in my book.

But when he read the newspaper account of my criticism of his state, the ayatollah of Rhode Island hit the ceiling. Without even reading the book, he announced to the press that I would be forever banned from practicing in his courtroom. He added: "I don't think there's a judge in Rhode Island who would allow him in their courtroom now." Judge Lagueux subsequently formalized his judicial excommunication of me by including it in a prepared opinion he delivered from the bench. When asked whether he would even discuss the issue with me, his injudicious response was: "There's an old saying that you don't get into a urinating contest with a skunk because you'll end up smelling the same as the skunk and that's what I think of Dershowitz."

To date, Judge Lagueux has not put out a contract on me, but he has tried to impose the judicial equivalent of a death sentence on my right to practice law in his state. He has made it abundantly clear that no Rhode Island clients can take the risk of retaining me to be their lawyer. All this because I dared to write a book that offended the ayatollah of Rhode Island and some of his followers.

Certainly no Rhode Island lawyers will ever dare to write books or articles that offend Rhode Island's judicial avenger, now that they realize the fate that awaits them. Nor will they come to the defense of others who defy the wrath of Judge Lagueux.

When some Massachusetts lawyers came to my defense—indeed, to the defense of the First Amendment—Judge Lagueux lashed out against them with equal fury. He held one of them in contempt, called another one a liar, and threatened criminal charges against the imagined "conspirators" who were ganging up on the Rhode Island judiciary.

Two of the lawyers had to drop out of a case they had before Judge Lagueux, at least in part for fear that their presence might hurt their client, which indeed it did. The court of appeals eventually reversed Lagueux and sent the case back for a retrial in front of an unbiased judge. But the lawyers who came to my defense were effectively banished from practice before the Rhode Island federal court. They, too, had committed the crime of judicial blasphemy by criticizing Judge Lagueux for his high-handed attempts at censorship.

Finally, after watching Lagueux threaten not only the lawyers who had criticized the Rhode Island judiciary but the very fabric of the First Amendment, I filed a formal complaint against him with the judicial conference—the federal judges who oversee the conduct of other federal judges.

I wish I could tell you the outcome of my complaint, but just last month I received word that the judicial conference was handling the matter in secret and that the public would not be informed of the outcome.

That result is unacceptable in a democracy. The consumers of justice are entitled to know how judges respond to well-founded complaints against their peers. Unless the public is informed about the judicial conference's response to Judge Lagueux's blatant attempt to punish an author for writing a controversial book, we will be taking a significant step toward becoming the kind of society that Iran has tragically become.

Lagueux has the power to disclose the outcome of the proceeding against him. If he refuses to, the public is entitled to draw whatever inferences seem appropriate about his unconscionable attempts to censor a book and punish its author.   March 1989

Judge Lageux was formally reprimanded for his statements by the Federal Judicial Conference. The panel of judges that issued this reprimand called the judge's action "glaringly injudicious." The panel explained the decision saying "the robe a judge wears as he sits upon the bench is not a license to excoriate lawyers or anyone else." (See page one of The New York Times, *July 14, 1989).*

PITIFUL WORLD OF THE REAL "NIGHT COURT"

In my twenty-five years of practicing criminal law, I have been to courts throughout the world. But until last week, I had never been to "night court." I went to watch my son, who is a legal-aid lawyer, at work in New York City's night court. I saw justice administered as I have never seen it before.

The justice to which I am accustomed is administered *retail*. Every case is considered *individually*. In a bustling night court, justice is administered wholesale, by category.

When I arrived in court, I had difficulty understanding the proceedings. Everything was said so quickly and so routinely that I could not separate the words. Gradually, I adjusted to the night court talk.

The categories of crime included such violations as "token sucking," a common crime in New York. A "token sucker," I learned, is someone, generally a homeless person, who earns his sustenance by sticking a wad of chewing gum or a paper clip into the token receptacle in the subway turnstile. The tokens become backed up in the receptacle and the nefarious criminal, according to a written complaint that I saw, "sucks them out by placing his lips around the opening and inhaling."

The paper clip he had used was described as a "burglar's tool," thus enhancing his criminal liability. Repeat token suckers get thirty days in jail. The defendant I saw had sucked $3.45 worth of tokens—twelve cents per day behind bars.

Another common crime in New York's night court is shoplifting. A young woman suffering from AIDS had stuffed a blouse and slacks under her jacket in Manhattan's fashionable Saks Fifth Avenue. The disparity between New York's extraordinary wealth and its equally extraordinary poverty was brought home to me when the price tag for the two pilfered items was announced—$1,200!

She stole the items, her court-appointed lawyer argued, in order to sell them for money she needed to buy some AZT, an experimental drug used to suppress the symptoms of AIDS. Her shabby garb gave credibility to the lawyer's claim. She was no walking advertisement for Saks's designer salons. Indeed, her un-Saks-like clothing was the reason she was observed by the security guards in the first place. The woman pleaded not guilty, but the judge set her bail at $1,000, thus assuring that she would have to remain in jail until her trial date. The judge ordered "medical attention" for her AIDS—a euphemism for segregation.

One of my son's cases involved a man who was accused of "robbing" someone of $100. The client is apparently a "shell man," an urban hustler who bets with passersby that they can't find the pea under the shell. Sleight-of-hand makes it virtually impossible to guess correctly, and the "mark" in this case had wised up to the scam and grabbed for the money he lost. The shell man declined to return it, and the mark called the cops.

My son argued that rather than it being a robbery, this was a dispute over a gambling debt. He declined to plead his client guilty and requested that the defendant be released on his own recognizance pending trial. The judge granted the request, and the con man gave my son an appreciative smile.

Then there were the prostitutes, dressed not in the gaudy tights they wear on TV's "Night Court" but rather in the shabby uniforms of the homeless. There is nothing even remotely sexy about them or about the quick, clinical acts they perform in dark alleyways to earn money for crack. They are sentenced to "time served"—the number of hours or days they have already spent in confinement awaiting their night court appearance. Their real sentence is being sent back to the streets to ply their pathetic trade.

The most exasperating cases are those involving defendants who are sentenced to jail for thirty or sixty days because they can't pay a $50 fine. Then there are the unlicensed street vendors—the people who sell merchandise from cardboard boxes—who are put in jail for trying to earn a living in precisely the way my own grandfather did a hundred years ago.

The judge presiding over this turnstile justice seemed competent and fair. But despite her judicial robes, she appeared more an administrator than a judge. Her superiors evaluate her performance, and her possible promotion out of the criminal courts, not by the *quality* of the justice she dispenses but rather by its *quantity*. The number of final dispositions— guilty pleas—is crucial to keeping the process moving.

The legal-aid lawyers are part social worker, part advocate, and part facilitator. They are idealistic young men and women who could be making triple their salaries chasing paper at uptown corporate law firms. But they understand, better than some leaders of the legal profession, that the emergency wards of our legal system must be attended to before we assign all the doctors to perform cosmetic surgery.   February 1990

UNSUNG HEROES—JURIES OFFER TRUE JUSTICE

The American jury, one of the great bastions of liberty, is under increasing attack. Many lawyers regard it as, at best, a necessary evil. It slows the process of adjudication. Its outcomes are unpredictable. It is inexpert at deciding complex issues. It is subject to emotional, even bigoted, appeals. Its verdicts lack consistency, since different juries arrive at different conclusions in cases with similar facts. It seems anachronistic in our age of efficiency and specialization.

In England, where the jury originated, it has been all but abolished in civil cases. In the United States, where our Constitution forbids its abolition in most cases, it has been limited wherever possible. Moreover, the traditional size of juries has been reduced from twelve to six in many cases, and the requirement of unanimity has been changed in many states to a two-thirds majority.

At an even more fundamental level, the cumbersomeness of juries has resulted in relatively few cases actually being tried: The vast majority are settled before trial, in criminal cases by a plea bargain and in civil cases by a financial compromise. The expense and unpredictability of jury trials have also driven many institutional litigants such as stock brokerage firms to demand that their customers waive trial by jury and accept the more streamlined mechanism of arbitration.

In sum, it's fair to say that if our Constitution did not mandate the right to trial by jury in most criminal and civil cases, the jury would be in danger of becoming an endangered species of adjudication.

It's ironic, though not at all surprising, that as we Americans unappreciatively chip away at the right to trial by jury, reformers in several Eastern European nations are calling for its transplantation onto their foreign soil. Having experienced totalitarian judicial and political systems, they are searching for mechanisms that promise some popular checks on the abuse of governmental power.

They have seen enough of Communist efficiency, predictability, expertise, and objectivity. They understand, as some Americans seem not to, that making the judicial "trains run on time" is not the sole criterion by which to judge a legal system. For a trial to be fair, the adjudicator must be *independent* of the powers that be, willing and able to stand up to pressures to do the government's bidding.

The American jury has passed that difficult test with flying colors, from the colonial period when it acquitted John Peter Zenger of politically inspired charges of libel to recent juries that have ruled in favor of such unpopular defendants as John Hinkley, Peggy McMartin Buckey, Imelda Marcos, and John DeLorean.

Juries, unlike judges, do not become routinized: Every case is their first and only case. It is their opportunity to do justice, and most jurors take their role quite seriously.

Many judges, especially some who have been on the bench for years, regard criminal defendants as presumptively guilty, since most who have come before them have pleaded guilty or been convicted. Juries, on the other hand, really seem to believe in the presumption of innocence and require the prosecution to prove each case beyond a reasonable doubt.

Nor can anyone *whisper* to a jury. Everything said to them is said openly and on the record. They hear only the evidence that is properly admissible. They do not learn that the prosecutor believes that the defendant is a bad or dangerous man—unless there is admissible evidence to support these assertions. The jurors are umpires, not fans.

The very independence and unaccountability of juries also make them a potentially dangerous institution in some settings. Racist juries in the pre–civil rights South routinely acquitted white killers of African-Americans. Some contemporary jurors, who regard themselves as foot soldiers in the war against drugs, seem willing to convict anyone with a Colombian passport of drug charges.

But the jury is simply one part of our system of checks and balances. It, too, must be kept in check by other institutions of government, such as trial and appellate judges.

In addition to recent efforts at limiting the role of juries, there is another serious danger on the horizon. Sophisticated social scientists are becoming increasingly involved on behalf of wealthy litigants in trying to select jurors who will favor their side. Since the average litigant cannot afford this expensive luxury—he can barely scrape up the money for exorbitant legal fees—only the most powerful plaintiffs or defendants will be able to manipulate jury selection to their advantage. These "designer juries" threaten to skew the randomness of the jury and destroy its objectivity.

In the end, the jury system, like democracy itself, is the worst mechanism for achieving justice, "except," as Winston Churchill said about democracy, "for all the others." Even with its imperfections, the American jury serves as a powerful check on the abuses of governmental power.

Our system of checks and balances may not be the most efficient mechanism for governing. But it is the envy of all who treasure liberty and believe in government by the people. American jurors are the people administering justice.   March 1990

JURIES ANSWER ONLY TO CONSCIENCE

The American jury has been much in the headlines of late. As Oliver North's prosecutors and defense team try to pick a jury, the judge has made noise about holding a journalist in contempt for allegedly making that task more difficult. Joel Steinberg, whose illegally adopted daughter was beaten to death, was convicted of manslaughter by a jury, several of whose members were then interviewed on television. Richard Ramirez, who is accused of a series of sensational California killings, began facing a jury that will almost certainly know they are sitting in judgment of the notorious "Night-stalker."

The jury, an institution virtually unknown outside of Anglo-American law, is the heart and soul of our legal system. Yet few people understand how juries really operate. Volumes of folklore have been written about juries. Speculation abounds about their secret deliberations. Lawyers spend hundreds of hours and thousands of dollars trying to psyche out juries. A whole new discipline—professional jury experts—has sprung up in recent years to help lawyers gain some edge in jury selection.

The Oliver North case illustrates the games lawyers play in selecting juries. North's very clever lawyer is attempting to make it impossible to find a jury sufficiently unbiased and untainted by exposure to North's immunized congressional testimony to actually try his client. Every potential juror who heard North's televised congressional show is being struck. Yet any experienced trial lawyer will tell you that North would be far better off with jurors who watched his Emmy-quality performance.

Why is North's lawyer trying to rid the jury of precisely those citizens who would be most likely to vote for an acquittal? Therein lies the gamesmanship of the jury selection process. If the case goes to trial at all, North's lawyer would almost certainly prefer precisely the kind of jurors he is now having struck. But his present tactic is to try to prevent a trial before *any* jury. A dismissal of the prosecution in hand is worth far more than an increased chance of an acquittal in the bush (or, if I dare pun, "a pardon from Bush").

But this gamesmanship carries considerable risk for North. If, in the end, the judge rules that the case can be tried, the resulting jury may indeed consist exclusively of jurors who never saw North on television. That would produce a jury composed of the least educated, least politically interested, and economically most disadvantaged citizens of the District of Columbia. Such a jury would spell deep trouble for North's defense. When his lawyers argue, or if he testifies, that he accepted a gift of a security fence to protect his children from Abu Nidal, at least some of these jurors will say "Abu who?"

To demonstrate the difficulty of selecting a jury, ABC law correspondent Tim O'Brien showed nine seconds of news clips from the North testimony and suggested that anyone who saw that might well be disqualified. This provoked Judge Gerhard Gesell into threatening a contempt citation and into forgetting that he has no power to dictate to the media what they can report.

Under the Constitution, Judge Gesell has his job (selecting a jury) and correspondent O'Brien has his job (informing the public). O'Brien's is at least as important as—Jefferson thought it more important than—Gesell's. And O'Brien did his job very well: He put the viewers into the story by making them think about whether their viewing of the clips would bias them as jurors. We'll see how well Gesell does his job. [*Oliver North was convicted in May, 1989 but his conviction was overturned in July, 1990.*] In the last analysis, there is no scientific way of assuring a fair jury. What seems fair to the defense often seems lenient to the prosecution and vice versa.

The Steinberg jury demonstrated that common sense often prevails over legal jargon. Steinberg was charged with several possible degrees of homicide. Legal concepts like "intent," "depraved indifference," "recklessness," and "negligence" were charged. It is unlikely that even the most sophisticated jurors comprehend the legal jargon used by judges—even good judges—in their instructions. The Steinberg jury seems to have cut through that jargon and arrived at a compromise that essentially said: "On a scale of one to four, this defendant's culpability certainly wasn't as low as a one, but it also wasn't as high as a four." They agreed on a "three"—the third most serious verdict out of a possible four. This sort of commonsense assessment of culpability is what a jury does best.

What jurors do worst is to decide on innocence or guilt when they are personally frightened of the accused. In the "Nightstalker" case, many of the jurors probably remember the terror they, or their loved ones, have experienced while serial killers have been on the loose. When jurors begin to personalize their verdict by asking whether they would feel safe if the defendant goes free, they compromise their objectivity.

The American jury is far from perfect. We trust jurors because they have no accountability other than to their conscience. No government official can tell them what to do, or threaten them if they don't follow orders.

February 1989

BRENNAN VACANCY LEAVES MODERATES ROOM

It is difficult for me to imagine the Supreme Court without Justice William Brennan. He has been the most consistent liberal and civil libertarian on the high court for a third of a century.

Brennan's imprint on the First Amendment will likely endure for the life of this nation. He defined the parameters of our freedom of speech, ruling early in his career that obscenity is not protected; in the middle of his career he held that honest mistakes, if they defame public figures, are protected; and at the end of his career that flag burning, obnoxious as it is, is also protected. His free-speech and press opinions were always controversial, but they nearly always carried the day.

In other areas, such as criminal justice, he was generally in dissent, especially in the past decade. But he continued to write for history. Perhaps someday, though not someday soon, his interpretations of the Fourth, Fifth, and Eighth amendments will again become the law.

Among Justice Brennan's most enduring legacies is his opinion in *Baker* vs. *Carr*, which required legislatures to end the most blatant forms of undemocratic malapportionment. Ironically, this decision and its progeny may prove to be the salvation of this nation, as the Supreme Court becomes less protective of our basic rights. Thanks to reapportionment, we can now win at least some of the battles for choice, equality, and basic fairness in the legislatures without having to rely on increasingly conservative courts.

On a more personal level, I have known Bill Brennan for thirty years. I first met him while I was still a law student. His son was my classmate.

I worked in the office next to his while I was a law clerk in the Supreme Court. He has remained a valued teacher, an inspiration, and a friend ever since. He has also inspired generations of law students to enter those areas of law that help the downtrodden, disenfranchised, and disadvantaged.

Justice Brennan has had quite a career, starting as he did as a New Jersey lawyer and ending his career as one of the handful of justices— along with Thurgood Marshall, Oliver W. Holmes, Louis Brandeis, and John Marshall Harlan—whose impact on the legacy of the law will endure well beyond their own tenures on the high court. When he was appointed by President Eisenhower, no one could have foreseen that he would emerge as the most influential voice for civil liberties in the post-McCarthy era. Part of his influence came from his interpersonal skills: He was every justice's best friend. He knew precisely which buttons to press to shape consensus. He has well-earned his retirement. May it be long and healthy.

Two questions arise immediately from the Brennan resignation. Will it precipitate other resignations from Justice Marshall or Justice Blackmun, who are both octogenarians? Neither is in good health, and both have been holding on to prevent a precipitous shift in the direction of the Supreme Court. If either or both were to retire, the court would be left without even a liberal minority. All that would be left would be three Republican-appointed conservatives, one Kennedy-appointed moderate, and two Republican-appointed moderates.

Even if the other two liberals remain, President Bush can shift the direction of the court on certain issues by his nominee.

The Constitution provides for the president to nominate justices with the "advice and consent" of the Senate. But recent presidents have not sought the advice of the Senate, especially when the Senate has been controlled by the opposite party. That may explain the relatively high number of failed nominations in recent decades.

President Bush would be wise to seek the advice of the Democrat-controlled Senate before he decides on his short list of potential nominees. The Senate has the right, as well as the power, to reject a nominee who would, for example, overrule *Roe* vs. *Wade*. The nomination and confirmation process is just that, a process. It has already begun, since the White House has been preparing for a possible vacancy over the past several months. Among the names on the list are Solicitor General Kenneth Starr, a conservative with a moderate bent, and circuit judges John Minor and Ralph Winter, who also fit that description. Several other circuit judges— Stephen Trott and Alex Kozinski—will probably also be considered. None of these distinguished jurists would likely face Senate rejection. But if President Bush were to repeat his predecessor's mistake and nominate a reactionary like Robert Bork, that nominee would face stiff resistance. And that would be entirely appropriate. As an early commentator on our Constitution put it: "A party nomination may justly be met by party opposition."

The best interests of our country would be served by a moderate nomination that would strengthen the Supreme Court and the nation.

July 1990

Justice David Souter has since filled the vacant seat left by Justice Brennan's departure.

LET'S CHANGE THE WAY WE SELECT JUDGES

The nomination of David (who?) Souter to become the swing justice on our nation's highest court raises general questions as to how our judges are picked throughout this nation. U.S. judges—both federal and state—are the most powerful in the world. Unlike their counterparts in virtually every other country, U.S. judges decide momentous political issues of life and death, including abortion, capital punishment, termination of life support, surrogate motherhood, freedom of speech, separation of church and state, as well as the more mundane conflicts between individual litigants.

Yet despite the important role they play, the processes by which our judges are selected are often sloppy, uninformed, accidental, nepotistic, and even corrupt. When I was growing up in New York during the 1940s and 1950s, the system was simple: Any lawyer who had not been disbarred could become a judge by simply "donating" two years of his projected judicial salary to the political party in power (which was the "Tammany Hall" Democrats). There was virtually no quality control, and the resulting judiciary was loaded with hacks, ne'er-do-wells, and occasional crooks. Although New York may have been at the extreme of corruption in picking judges, it was not alone. Most large cities with political machines did not do the judiciary proud. Cash may not have been the medium of exchange in purchasing judgeships, but loyal party service—often coupled with a promise that it would *continue* while on the bench—was the price of a judgeship.

Over the past quarter century, there have been significant reforms in the selection of judges, but serious problems remain. A federal judge is still likely to be a lawyer who knew a senator, and a state judge is more often than not a lawyer who was friendly with a governor. Sometimes even the "reforms" have backfired. In New York, for example, the two U.S. senators have appointed "committees" to propose candidates for the federal bench. The problem is that these committees include practicing lawyers who make their livings arguing before the judges they have helped to pick. One such lawyer, who had a case in front of a judge he had helped to nominate, let everyone know that he had "picked" the judge, that he could "make or break" him when it came to promotion, and that he had the judge "in his pocket." He terrified the other side into settling, despite the fact that his case was extremely weak. I have no idea whether he, in fact, had the judge in his pocket, but frightened litigants do not have the luxury of taking a chance.

This reminds me of the true story of the corrupt law clerk who would separately approach the litigants in a high-stakes case and make them the following offer they couldn't refuse: "I think I can get to the judge on your behalf; give me $10,000; if I get to him and you win, I keep it; if you lose, you get it back." The clerk never even tried to get to the judge. He just kept the money from the winning party and returned the losing party's $10,000.

In Rhode Island, the supreme court is picked by the state legislature. Not surprisingly, most of its judges are former legislative leaders without much legal experience. Also not surprisingly, a recent chief justice was forced to step down amid charges of corruption.

In Massachusetts, we have a dinosaur called the Governor's Executive Council, which must confirm all judicial nominees. One of its members is a convicted felon with alleged organized crime associations. He has threatened to blackball the nomination of a former prosecutor with an excellent record of convicting some of this councelor's buddies. The nominee is a woman, and the councelor refers to her as this "girl" and "honey" and says he is going to "bury" her. The threat is not idle, since the councelor's regular job is running a funeral parlor.

Finally, President Bush recently nominated his own first cousin to the nation's second-highest court despite the fact that there were far more qualified candidates.

All this brings us back to the "process" by which Judge David Souter was nominated for the U.S. Supreme Court. We have no idea what that process consisted of. Souter's opponents blame the nomination on the always unpopular John Sununu. His proponents credit New Hampshire's senator Warren Rudman. The public simply doesn't have a clue. The best that can be hoped for is that Souter will "turn out" to be "not so bad." As one of his proponents put it, "What is conspicuous by omission is [the] failure to identify a single case that says 'look, this guy is brilliant.' " His proponents point to other obscure nominees who have "turned out" to be good justices. We are entitled to better than this from the justices of our higher court.

In some parts of the world, judicial selection is based entirely on merit. The ablest lawyers and judges—as measured by peer review *excluding* lawyers who practice before the judge—are selected. It is time to consider a change in the way our justices are picked.   August 1990

ARE JUDGES PRIVILEGED CHARACTERS?

An important test case in New York is challenging the conventional wisdom that judges are somehow immune from the kind of criticism to which other public officials are routinely subjected. The case grows out of a Brooklyn rape trial in which the alleged victim was asked to get down on the floor to reenact the rape scene.

The district attorney of Brooklyn, former congresswoman Elizabeth Holtzman, publicly accused the trial judge of humiliating the woman by asking her to get down on the floor. At that point, the defense attorney and several court officers rushed to the judge's defense, claiming that it was the accused rapist's defense attorney, and not the judge, who had asked the alleged victim to get down on the floor. But whoever *initiated* the request, it was the judge who had control over the trial proceedings. It was his job to see to it that the alleged victim was not humiliated by the defense attorney or anyone else. This is especially so because victims do not have their own lawyers to protect them, and defense attorneys often try to humiliate rape victims in a tactical effort to discourage them from proceeding with their complaints.

District Attorney Holtzman has now been officially reprimanded for her criticism of the judge, and she is challenging that reprimand in New

York's highest court. (In the meantime, the judge was removed from office for unrelated misconduct.)

If the person against whom District Attorney Holtzman had publicly complained were anything but a *judge*, there would be no conceivable basis for any disciplinary action against Holtzman. After all, in the United States, any citizen has a right to vilify any public figure. Indeed, there is a long tradition of such vilification going back to pre-Revolutionary years. And in 1964, the Supreme Court ruled that public officials may not bring libel suits even if false statements were made about them, unless they can prove that the false statements were made with malice. And malice is defined as publishing a statement known to be false or with reckless disregard for whether it is true or false. In other words, U.S. citizens have a constitutional right to criticize public officials, even if their criticisms turn out to be wrong, so long as they were made in good faith.

But the legal profession has established different rules for lawyers who criticize judges. A lawyer may be disciplined, even disbarred, for daring to criticize a judge if the criticism turns out to be false, even if it was made in good faith. The disciplinary authorities in New York, which are dominated by—you guessed it—*judges*, ruled that a criticism directed against a judge may not be made by a lawyer unless that lawyer "first determine[s] the *certainty* of the merits of the accusations." In other words, before lawyers may criticize judges, they must be *certain* that they are absolutely right in every respect. This rule turns judges into privileged characters who are above criticism from those who know them best.

This special rule for judges is doubly troubling because even when the criticism directed against them is absolutely correct, other lawyers will rush to the judge's defense. Many lawyers specialize in currying favor with judges, hoping that the favor will be returned by the grateful judge in a subsequent case. Thus, we can never know for sure what role the judge in this rape case really played in the victim's humiliation.

Furthermore, lawyers are naturally reticent in publicly criticizing judges, even when the judges have behaved abominably. Judges can and do retaliate against lawyers who have the temerity to criticize them. The public interest demands more, not less, public criticism by lawyers against judges. Yet the rules of the legal profession are deliberately calculated to discourage such criticism.

The reason given for this special rule protecting judges is that judicial officials cannot respond to criticism, since they are bound by their own cannons prohibiting them from commenting on cases outside of the courtroom. But this reason does not justify the privileged status of judges. In the first place, the special rule is not limited to criticism against judges for their decisions in particular cases. It applies as well to general criticisms of their competence, diligence, and even honesty. Moreover, even if judges themselves cannot respond to certain criticisms, there is never a shortage of robe-stroking lawyers climbing all over each other to be given the privilege of publicly championing the judge.

The issue of how rape victims are treated in our courts is an extraordinarily important and controversial one. We need public debate about this issue—and the people who have an impact on it. If the reprimand against former district attorney Holtzman is upheld by the New York Court of Appeals, a deep chill will descend on the already too-uncritical bar. Lawyers, who are in the best position to criticize judges, will be frightened away from legitimate criticism. And the public, the consumers of justice, will be the ultimate victims of a conspiracy of silence.   February 1991

The New York State Court of Appeals upheld the reprimand against former D.A. Holtzman.

MARSHALL'S RESIGNATION ENDS AN ERA

Thurgood Marshall's resignation from the U.S. Supreme Court marks the end of one era and the beginning of another. The Marshall era was characterized by a vindication of the rights of the downtrodden, the underdog, the minority, and the unpopular. It was personified by the only justice in American history whose entire distinguished career at the bar was in the service of the poor, the disenfranchised, and the victims of discrimination.

Thurgood Marshall was the only real lawyer on the current high court—the only courtroom advocate who practiced his profession in the trenches and the emergency rooms of our legal system. As a lawyer for the National Association for the Advancement of Colored People, he was a driving creative force against racial and economic injustice and in favor of equality. Almost single-handedly, he leveled the playing field of law politics and even public opinion.

His was an era of checks and balances, when the judiciary stood tall against discriminatory practices mandated by the legislative and executive branches of both the state and federal governments.

The era that will almost certainly begin with President Bush's appointment of Justice Marshall's successor may witness the suspension, at least for a generation, of our valued system of checks and balances. If President Bush replaces Justice Marshall with a doctrinaire reactionary, such as Judge Edith Jones of the U.S. Court of Appeals for the 5th Circuit, the high court statist majority will have been solidified. I say "statist" because the emerging majority is neither conservative nor judicially restrained in any meaningful sense of those terms. It is an activist majority eager to centralize power in the elected branches of government, particularly in the executive branch of the federal government.

Big government is beginning to win nearly every case in which the rights of individuals are pitted against the power of governments. This is especially true in criminal cases, in which the defendant rarely even gets his petition for review granted and almost never wins on the merits. Virtually the entire criminal justice "revolution" of the Warren Court has now been overruled. And we are seeing a return to a time even before the Frankfurter-Vinson Court of the 1940s and early 1950s. Nor will the rights of criminal defendants be vindicated by legislative action, as the rights of those denied abortion advice may soon be.

The structural changes on the horizon transcend particular political issues or even judicial philosophies. They endanger the basic protections long afforded by our system of checks and balances. If the high court sees its "constituency" as identical with those of the elected branches of government, it will cease to exercise its proper constitutional function of checking and balancing those branches. It will instead simply rubber-stamp the expressed wishes of the majority and soon find itself of marginal relevance in American life.

If this scenario were to prove true, who would then vindicate the constitutional rights of minorities who lack the political power to have their rights enforced by the popular branches?

It is a mistake to see the emerging court as the right-wing mirror image of the Warren Court, or as the result of the inevitable swing of the pendulum. The Warren Court was countermajoritarian. It enforced desegregation against the wishes of popularly elected legislatures and governors. Indeed, it changed the very process of electing legislatures by demanding equal voting power for all voters. There was never a danger that the Warren Court could run amok, because it was always checked and balanced by the other branches. Nor could its views run roughshod over majorities or minorities that disagreed with them. The current court does not check and balance nor is it checked and balanced.

There is but one recourse. The Senate, which is controlled by the party in opposition, must exercise its power to check and balance by participating more fully in the constitutionally mandated process of selecting justices. It must do more than "consent" or refuse to consent in the president's selection. It must "advise" as well. And its advice should be for the president to appoint a moderate or a true conservative who will remain true to the high court's mission: as a tribunal of last resort—for Americans who have constitutional rights but who lack the political power to enforce these rights through political or economic means.

June 1991

JUDGE THOMAS: BUSH'S POLITICAL MASTERSTROKE

My Harvard colleague Derrick Bell fell right into the trap laid by President Bush's appointment of Judge Clarence Thomas to replace retiring Supreme Court Justice Thurgood Marshall. Bell complained that Thomas may "look black," but he "thinks white." He accused President Bush of "gross tokenism" in appointing "a black who is conservative." Bell's main criticism of Judge Thomas is that when Thomas was chair of the Equal Employment Opportunity Commission, he opposed racial quotas and other race-specific affirmative action programs.

Consider the irony. Bell favors explicit racial quotas that look *only* at a person's color in placing him or her in a group for favorable treatment. Regardless of how wealthy or privileged an individual black may be, that person deserves special preference *just* because he is black. Thomas opposes such racial grouping, advocating instead that each person be judged as an individual and be evaluated by reference to their own experiences.

Yet despite his advocacy of racial quotas, Bell insists, in this instance, on excluding Thomas from consideration for the "black seat" on the Supreme Court because he disagrees with Thomas's politics. The irony is multiplied because Thomas himself is the perfect affirmative action appointment; he is not only black, but he also comes from a deprived economic background and has overcome individual and familial hardship.

Professor Bell simply cannot have it both ways. Either candidates should be judged by the color of their skin, because all blacks have suffered discrimination as a result of their race. Or candidates should be judged by the individual merits of their personal situation, including, but not limited to, their race.

By appointing a black opponent of racial quotas, President Bush has confounded his critics, denied them the moral high ground, and invited them to fall into the trap of espousing what will surely appear to be hypocritical arguments.

The honest argument against the Thomas appointment is that it is a race-specific affirmative action appointment made by a president who purports to be against such appointments. The president's assurance that he picked Thomas because he was "*the* best man" for the job will not pass the giggle test. Surely he could have found at least one lawyer in America to whom the American Bar Association had given its highest rating, instead of a recently appointed appellate court judge who had only just been rated as "qualified" last year.

Judge Thomas is qualified to be a justice, certainly by the standards reflected by the appointments of Justices David Souter and Anthony Kennedy. None of these recent appointments are regarded by their peers as superstars or even stars. In the rankings of the legal profession, they are utility infielders with .250 batting averages. They are B+ students selected from a class that includes many A+ students, such as Robert Bork, who have disqualified themselves by the outspokenness of their controversial ideologies. These "stealth candidates" are nominated specifically because the president thinks he knows more than the public knows about how they are likely to vote on agenda issues. So far the president has been correct in his predictions.

Thomas, too, has been outspoken, but unlike Bork, he has limited his public rhetoric to one major issue: racial quotas and affirmative action. This is an issue on which the vast majority of Americans, especially those who vote Republican, agree with him. A Senate confirmation battle that focuses on racial quotas and that has Democrats defending them will inure to the political fortunes of President Bush and his party. In that respect, the Thomas nomination—hypocritical as it is—was a political masterstroke. It is an affirmative action appointment with deniability, a quota appointment that will place the blame for quotas on the doorstep of those who oppose the nomination.

The question remains whether President Bush will, in the end, be satisfied with Justice Thomas's performance on the high court, in the likely event that he is confirmed. I have my doubts about that. Clarence Thomas is no William Rehnquist. Thomas has experienced discrimination, poverty, and suffering at firsthand. He participated in antiwar demonstrations and worked for Senator John Danforth, a moderate Republican. He is not a reactionary statist, like the current chief justice and some of his colleagues. I predict that Clarence Thomas will situate himself more toward the center of the court on most issues. It is impossible to prophesy, of course, how he will come out on specific cases involving abortion, separation of church and state, criminal justice, and freedom of speech.

President Bush nominated Judge Thomas to make a point: that an African-American judge who made it to the top of his profession can be a strong opponent of racial quotas. Having made that point, the president may find that Justice Thomas is his own man on other important issues.

Only a probing confirmation hearing will let the public in on how Clarence Thomas thinks about nonracial issues. We are entitled to that information before Thomas is confirmed to the highest court of our diverse nation.   July 1991

IS CLARENCE THOMAS READY FOR THE HIGH COURT?

As Judge Clarence Thomas's record begins to unfold, the picture of a conflicted, confused, and unformed man emerges. Putting aside all issues of ideology, the question arises as to whether Judge Thomas, who has served on the bench for only fifteen months, is ready to be elevated to the high court now, or whether he should remain a lower court judge for several more years, until he works through his identity crisis and decides who he really is.

Few nominees to the Supreme Court have shown so many changes in fundamental attitudes in so short a period of time as has Clarence Thomas in the twenty-something years since he was in college at Holy Cross.

ALAN M. DERSHOWITZ

From a student who smoked marijuana and participated in antiwar demonstrations, Thomas quickly became an arch-conservative. He flirted with the racial separatism of Louis Farrakhan and then became a relatively assimilated member of the white establishment and of a predominantly white church.

He strongly opposed race specific affirmative action programs, then he strongly supported them, then he said they "don't amount to a hill of beans," and then he strongly opposed them once again. Later he said that he will "abide by the Supreme Court, whether I like it or not." But now he has been nominated to the Supreme Court, where he may become the swing vote on racial quotas, and he will not be able to pass the buck.

Thomas claims to be a judicial conservative who believes in judicial restraint and in simply interpreting the words of the Constitution, yet he also believes in expansive notions of "natural law" that are not constrained by the "positive law" of constitutional text.

As a summary article in the *New York Times* about Thomas's views on affirmative action put it: The record suggests a man "often torn by conflicts inside himself and with others." There is nothing wrong, of course, with introspection and reevaluation of one's views, but in Thomas's case the swings seem rather extreme, suggesting a person who is so unformed in his basic outlook toward life as to deny those who must vote on his confirmation even the most elementary basis for deciding whether he merits a lifetime appointment to the most powerful court in the world.

There is, of course, an alternative explanation for Thomas's radical changes in outlook and identity. He may simply be an opportunist whose views shift with the political winds and the environment he finds himself in at any particular time. What appear to be inexplicable swings in his world view may instead be careful calculations of political advantage. But this is sheer speculation, since we know so little about the internal dynamics of this latest stealth candidate.

Thomas's relative youth—at forty-three, he would become the court's youngest member and one of the youngest ever nominated—is seen as an advantage by President Bush, who would like his own imprint on the high court to last as long as humanly possible. But beyond that crass argument for power enhancement—for allowing the dead hand of a long-departed president to continue to influence the life and law of this nation well into the next century—there is a strong case for not appointing judges who are too young both in years and in relevant experience.

First, the promotion of lower court judges who were only recently appointed to the bench and who have no judicial records hurts the morale of other sitting judges who have labored long and hard in vineyards of justice. These seasoned veterans resent being bypassed by a rookie, especially one with no reputation for prodigious brilliance sufficient to overcome his lack of experience.

The experience necessary to become a good Supreme Court justice need not, of course, be on the bench. Some of our greatest justices have been nominated directly to the Supreme Court from nonjudicial positions. But virtually every great justice in history has been a great person—an accomplished professional in some sphere of legal life—before their elevation to the high court. Legal mediocrities generally become judicial mediocrities, though there have been a handful of exceptions to that rule.

The recent trend in Supreme Court nominations—toward younger candidates appointed not because of their distinction but because of their ideology and the brevity of their paper trail—threatens to further diminish the quality of our highest court. Ideology aside, the U.S. Supreme Court is already among the least distinguished high courts in the Western world. Most of the members of our Supreme Court do not hold a candle to their judicial brothers and sisters on the Canadian, English, Israeli, New Zealand, and Australian high courts, where merit, experience, and professional distinction are the primary considerations for appointment.

The time has come for a return to these criteria in our country. By these standards, Judge Clarence Thomas requires several more years of seasoning and testing in the Triple-A Minor League before he is promoted to the Major League for the rest of his life. July 1991

"STREET JUSTICE" RULED IN THE RODNEY KING CASE

The jury verdict in the Rodney King case reminds us once again that we pay a high price for our constitutional protections. Millions of people around the world who saw the videotape will wonder how the California jurors could have acquitted the police officers of assault charges. (There was a hung jury as to one count against one defendant.) It seemed like an open-and-shut case, especially to those who don't understand the dynamics of jury deliberations.

The American jury is not merely the finder of fact. It is also the conscience of the community. But it is a quixotic "conscience" that sometimes reflects the best of what we stand for—and at other times the worst.

During the civil rights marches in the 1960s, all-white juries repeatedly acquitted Klansmen who murdered civil rights workers. In recent years, predominantly black juries in some urban areas have acquitted, or rendered compromise or deadlocked verdicts, in what appeared to be open-and-shut cases against black defendants who have killed white policemen.

But the most common manifestation of what has come to be called "jury nullification" has always been in cases where policemen were charged with the use of excessive force, especially when that force was directed against so-called undesirable elements. Juries are rarely willing to side with the "bad guys" against the "good guys," even when the good guys have gone too far. Tough cops are supposed to teach the bad guys a lesson they will not soon forget, and we love them for that. The public trusts "street justice" more than court justice.

When the Rodney King video was first made public, it was widely believed that this case would be different. It toppled the old order among the police hierarchy, including the police commissioner. Surely a jury viewing the video would quickly convict the offending policemen.

But that prediction neglected the racial element in the case. Rodney King is black. The indicted policemen were white. The chief prosecutor was black. The defense attorneys were white. And the jury included no blacks.

The jury's acquittal in the face of the video does not necessarily mean that some or all of the jurors were overtly racist. It does mean that the jurors viewed the evidence through the prism of their own experiences. Jurors are more likely to sympathize with the arguments of those with whom they most closely identify. And many jurors identify on the basis of race, class, religion, gender, and ethnicity.

I recall a debate several years ago on "Nightline" between me and the attorney general of Georgia over whether the death penalty in Georgia was being administered in a racially discriminatory manner. I cited statistics showing that blacks who kill whites are ten times more likely to be sentenced to death than whites who kill blacks. The attorney general responded that Georgia juries have found that blacks who kill whites do so more violently and in more aggravated fashion than whites who kill blacks. I'm sure the attorney general is correct, in the sense that white jurors *see* black-on-white crime as more violent. White jurors identify with the victims of such crime.

Similarly in the Rodney King case, the white jurors could more easily identify with the white policemen, whom they see as their protectors against black criminals. They have more difficulty identifying with a black "criminal," who was "resisting" arrest. Their minds are more open to listening to the defense arguments than to the prosecution arguments. A juror told Ted Koppel that "King controlled the action," and that he could have stopped the beating at any time by simply submitting and not resisting. I doubt that many black jurors would have seen the evidence that way or accepted this "blame the victim" defense.

This leads to the obvious question of why the jury in the King case included no blacks. The answer lies with the very videotape that gave rise to the case. Because the tape was played and replayed, especially in Los Angeles, the defendants demanded, and received, a change of venue from Los Angeles, which has a substantial black population, to Simi Valley, which has few blacks and is home to a large number of white police officers. A fairer balance could have been struck between the rights of the accused policemen and the interests of the prosecution. Perhaps a city far away from Los Angeles but with a population more reflective of that city's racial diversity would have been a more appropriate venue for this trial.

In the last analysis, the constitutional right to a trial by a fair and impartial jury is a double-edged sword. In an attempt to avoid the Scylla of a jury biased against the defendants, we sometimes confront the Charybdis of a jury biased against the prosecution. Our Constitution demands that we err on the side of the defendant. It is a good rule that sometimes produces bad results.   May 1992

DOUBLE JEOPARDY SHOULD BAR RETRIAL OF L.A. COPS

As a civil libertarian who believes in the Bill of Rights, I cannot be enthusiastic about the prospect that the four policemen who were acquitted by a California state jury of assaulting Rodney King may now be tried for the same acts by the federal government. The Fifth Amendment to the U.S. Constitution provides that no person shall "be subject for the same offense to be twice put in jeopardy of life or limb." To place the four policemen on trial again in the federal courts would seem to violate both the letter and spirit of the "double jeopardy" clause. (The cop who had a hung jury on one count may be retried without compromising the protection against double jeopardy.)

But the Supreme Court has eviscerated the protection against double jeopardy, much as it has eviscerated other safeguards of our Bill of Rights. A majority of the high court has ruled that the federal government may retry a defendant who has been acquitted in a state court of identical conduct. The technicality upon which it has seized is the word *offense*. Since that word has a legal rather than a factual meaning, the court has lamely argued that the framers of our Bill of Rights intended it to be defined in the narrowest possible legal sense. And since the identical conduct—for example, robbing a federally insured bank—can give rise to two different offenses, both the state and federal governments can try the offender. The state can try the alleged bank robber on state charges of robbery, using the security video as its primary evidence. If the jury were to acquit on the ground that the video was unclear, the federal government could try the same robber on federal charges of robbing a federally insured bank and use the same security video to try to prove the same case a second time.

In the Rodney King case, the videotaped beating can also give rise to different offenses. Under state law, each allegedly excessive blow constitutes an assault. Under federal law, these very same blows might constitute a civil rights violation. The primary evidence in both cases would be the same infamous videotape, though a federal prosecutor would have the additional burden of proving that the police, in striking King, intended to deprive him of his civil rights. But at bottom, any federal prosecution of the acquitted police officers would be a transparent attempt to get a second bite at the apple—that is, to place the acquitted officers in jeopardy for the second time.

For those of us who believe that the Simi Valley jury was unfairly stacked in favor of the defense and that their verdict was clearly wrong, there is a strong temptation to compromise with constitutional principles and join the widespread demand for a second prosecution. "What is wrong," I hear people asking, "with getting a second bite at what was a rotten apple?" This time, the jury, more fairly selected, may get it right. But in succumbing to that understandable temptation, we would be contributing to the further evisceration of the Bill of Rights.

Some civil libertarians argue that the damage to the double-jeopardy clause has already been complete. Since the law now allows a second trial in the federal court, we might as well take advantage of that bad law to achieve a good result in the King case. I understand that argument, and a part of me even agrees with it. (It reminds me of the argument I hear every Christmas from some Jews who favor separation of church and state, but who press for the state-sponsored display of Hanukkah menorahs on the grounds that the courts have already approved state-sponsored displays of Christian religious symbols.) But it is not an argument that I can make with any degree of enthusiasm. In the end, it boils down to an "ends justifies the means" rationalization.

Whenever I consider these kinds of dilemmas—in which my politics comes down on one side and my commitment to the Bill of Rights comes down on the other—I remember a discussion I had with Justice Arthur J. Goldberg when I was his law clerk on the Supreme Court. The case before the high court involved the segregationist governor of Mississippi, who had defied a court order to desegregate the university. He was facing a long prison term for criminal contempt and demanded a jury trial. The federal government argued in favor of a trial before a judge on the grounds that an all-white Mississippi jury surely would acquit the governor. Justice Goldberg ruled in favor of trial by jury despite his strong view against segregation. He explained that "politics are for today, but the Bill of Rights are forever."

I feel the same way about the protection against double jeopardy. It needs to be strengthened forever, even if that means the erroneous acquittal of four obviously guilty policemen. May 1992

DEMJANJUK AND COLEMAN: A COMPARISON BETWEEN ISRAELI AND AMERICAN JUSTICE

The Israeli Supreme Court will almost certainly vacate the death sentence imposed on John Demjanjuk, who was convicted of atrocities against Jewish death camp inmates during the Holocaust. In vacating the death sentence— the second ever imposed in Israel, the first having been against Adolph Eichman—the Israeli High Court will not be declaring Demjanjuk innocent. It will be saying that doubts have been raised about whether Demjanjuk was "Ivan the Terrible" of Treblinka. In fact, his supporters acknowledge that Demjanjuk was a guard at Sobibor, the notorious death camp at which a quarter of a million Jewish babies, grandmothers and parents were murdered. Indeed that is what his alibi boils down to: he could not have been murdering Jews at Treblinka, because he was too busy helping the Nazis murder Jews at Sobibor. As his most vocal supporter, Patrick Buchanan, put it: "Authoritative Soviet sources insisted he served at Sobibor . . . where he was known as 'Ivan the Bloody.' "

The new evidence that will probably cause the Israeli Court to vacate Demjanjuk's sentence comes from recently opened police files from the former Soviet Union. These files show that Demjanjuk did indeed serve as a death camp guard at Sobibor—an allegation he has persistently and perjuriously denied since he fraudulently entered the United States shortly after World War II. They also show that there was another guard named Ivan Marchenko who was known as "Ivan the Terrible" of Treblinka.

The defense is now arguing that these documents provide reasonable doubt about whether Demjanjuk was Ivan the Terrible of Treblinka. The prosecution has responded by pointing out that Sobibor was only a few hours by train from Treblinka and thus Demjanjuk could easily have worked at both death camps—as many guards did. The prosecution also argues that there may have been more than one "Ivan the Terrible" at Treblinka. Ivan is the most common Ukrainian name, and any cruel death camp guard with that name would naturally be called "Ivan the Terrible." Moreover, when Demjanjuk was asked on his American visa application what his mother's maiden name was, he wrote "Marchenko"—the name of the other "Ivan the Terrible" of Treblinka. Demjanjuk now explains this remarkable coincidence by claiming that he forgot his own grandmother's last name and wrote a common name that just popped into his mind. It is certainly plausible that the name "Marchenko" popped into his mind because he worked alongside the other Ivan the Terrible at Treblinka for a period of time, thus lending support to the prosecution's "Two Ivan the Terribles" theory.

The prosecution also points to the hearsay nature of the new evidence that Ivan the Terrible was Marchenko. All the newly revealed evidence comes from the written statements of Treblinka guards who were executed many years ago. These statements were elicited by the KGB and are themselves as suspect as any information elicited by the KGB during the Stalin period. Moreover, the statements contradict one another and were never subject to cross-examination. They certainly would not be enough to convict Ivan Marchenko, were he to be found alive and now prosecuted. But they are enough to cast doubt on the certainty that should be required before Demjanjuk is subjected to the death penalty.

The United States Court of Appeals in Cincinnati has just reopened the case under which Demjanjuk was extradited to Israel for trial. They reopened the case not on the basis of any action brought by Demjanjuk's American lawyers or any new evidence presented in affidavit form. They reopened it—quite remarkably—on the basis of *newspaper and television accounts* of what is now transpiring in Israel. And they did so on their own motion, years after the matter was no longer within their jurisdiction. This judicial action is in striking contrast to a recent decision by the United States Supreme Court in refusing to consider the merits of a possibly innocent Virginia death row inmate's claims because the condemned man's lawyer had missed a filing deadline of *one day*.

It would be hypocritical in the extreme for the United States Courts to demand a higher standard of justice from the Israeli judiciary than it demands from our own courts. In any event, the Israeli Supreme Court seems to have the Demjanjuk case well under control. It has given Demjanjuk far more rights than our courts currently give death penalty inmates. And it will almost certainly reverse Demjanjuk's death penalty and conviction—without the intervention of the American judiciary.

Indeed, it is fair to ask whether our current Supreme Court would permit an American death penalty case to be reopened on the basis of hearsay statements by dead co-conspirators. Our Supreme Court can learn much from the manner in which the Israeli Supreme Court is carefully considering Demjanjuk's newly discovered evidence.   July 1992

COULD SALEM WITCH TRIALS HAPPEN TODAY?

Last week in Salem, Mass., they commemorated the 300th anniversary of the notorious Salem witch trials. "Honorable" and "distinguished" judges sentenced 20 witches to death, employing the forms of the law to legitimate the public demand for scapegoats. It got me to thinking about how our current Supreme Court and lower courts would react if an hysteria comparable to the witch trials were to occur today.

There is, of course, some relevant history to look to for guidance as to how the courts could behave. The Salem travesty was neither the first nor the last of its kind. The Spanish Inquisition, whose 500th anniversary we are currently commemorating, also employed the forms of the law and the legitimation of judges. Even in Hitler's Germany and Stalin's Soviet Union, "good" and "decent" judges went along to get along. During the McCarthy period in our nation, many judges willingly participated in the red-baiting and career-destroying paranoia of the time. Some of these judges even believed in the "justice" of the cause they were serving. But most were motivated by simple opportunism, careerism and a need to please those in power.

It is possible, of course, that even without the complicity of the judiciary, they would have hanged witches, burned heretics, gassed Jews, shot "cosmopolitans" and fired fellow-travelers. But the imprimatur of the judges was essential to giving an aura of legitimacy to entirely illegitimate undertakings.

Some judges had the courage to stand up to the abuse of the legal system. A few paid with their lives, others with their careers. In some instances, most notably McCarthyism, the dissenting judges actually had an impact on slowing down and finally halting the evil. But too few judges were prepared to take the risks of going against powerful and popular tyrants.

When I look at the current chief justice, William Rehnquist, and his predecessor, Warren Burger, I see judges in the mold of those who went along with the excuses of past tyrants. Oh sure, today's judges would find some contemporary rationale for their unwillingness to intercede on behalf of the victims of tyranny: judicial restraint, executive and legislative prerogative, separation of powers, original intent and many other catchwords that can be selectively invoked to justify inaction. But the real reason why the Rhenquists and Burgers of today's judiciary would not interecede is because they are *statists*, rather than true conservatives. Conservatives believe in limited governmental power over individuals. Statists believe in virtually unlimited governmental power and limited individual rights (except, in some instances, when it comes to property rights).

To garner some clue as to how former Chief Justice Burger would have responded to a modern-day witch trial, consider what he had to say in 1986 about the "crime" of private homosexual activity between consenting adults. In the case of Bowers v. Hardwick, Chief Justice Burger quoted approvingly Blackstone's characterization of " 'the infamous crime against nature' as an offense of 'deeper malignity' than rape, a heinous act 'the very mention of which is a disgrace to human nature,' and 'a crime not fit to be named.' " The judges in Salem might also have quoted Blackstone on the evils of witchcraft, had he written a century earlier: "The civil law punishes with death not only the sorcerers themselves, but also those who consult them;

limitating in the former the express law of God, 'thou shalt not suffer a witch to live.' And our own laws (rank) this crime in the same class with heresy, and condemning both to the flames."

I can picture Rehnquist—who, as a Stanford law-school student just after World War II, outraged Jewish classmates by imitating Adolph Hitler and goose-stepping around the campus with brown-shirted friends—as a German judge during the 1930s and even early 1940s. The German judges who were tried at Nuremberg included several distinguished jurists and professors with an authoritarian bent not so different from Rehnquist's.

I have little confidence that most current Supreme Court and other federal court judges would act courageously and independently in the face of modern-day witchcraft trials, especially if the atmosphere of the country were such that it would require personal and career risks to do so.

It seems more likely that several of the justices and judges would become part of the problem, going out of their way to lend an imprimatur of legitimacy to the evil at hand, as Chief Justice Burger did in the homosexuality case.

Former Justice Robert Jackson, who took a leave from the Supreme Court to serve as our nation's chief prosecutor at the Nuremberg Trials of Nazi War Criminals, explained the role of judges and law in legitimating tyranny: "(t)he most odious of all oppressions are those which mask as justice." In saying that, Jackson was echoing the caution of Lord Coke, expressed even before the Salem witch trials, "It is the worst oppression, that is done by colour of justice." We should keep these words in mind as we recall the judges of Salem and as we assess our own Supreme Court.

June 1992

THE EMERGENCE OF A MODERATE MIDDLE IN THE SUPREME COURT

The theory underlying the life tenure of Supreme Court justices is that they will be independent—independent of the president who appointed them, of the Senate which confirmed them and of the citizens whose rights they determine. Their own consciences, the traditions of the judiciary and peer acceptance are supposed to be the only constraints on their decision-making. Of course, they are not entirely free to make the law suit their personal or political preferences. They are bound by the constitution, the statutes and the prior cases which form the precedential base of our legal system. But within those loose constraints and wide bounds, there is enormous room for individual discretion.

This term of the Supreme Court—which ended in the last week of June—illustrated both the virtues and vices of such nearly untrammeled discretion. It also illustrated the old saw that presidents can appoint justices, but they cannot control them once they have taken their seats.

Most of the High Court's decisions during the 1991–1992 terms— terms run from the first week in October to the last week in June—were entirely predictable. The Court has moved radically to the right, and on most issues, the Court's decisions favored governmental power over individual rights. Especially in the criminal law area, the Court's rightward movement was palpable. In the criminal law area, this is not a conservative Court, but rather a *STATIST* Court, siding almost always with the prosecution and against those accused of crimes.

Consider, for example, the case of Dr. Humberto Alvarez-Machain, a Mexican doctor who the United States suspected of being involved in the torture and murder of Drug Enforcement Administration (DEA) agent. Although Mexico and the United States have an extradition treaty which provides for detailed legal procedures for bringing a Mexican citizen to our country for trial, our DEA agents arranged for gun-toting Mexican bounty hunters to kidnap Dr. Alvarez from his medical office in Guadalajara and slip him across the border so that he could be tried here. Both the trial court and the court of appeals ruled that Dr. Alvarez had to be returned to Mexico and extradited properly under the treaty. But the Supreme Court approved of the kidnapping, arguing that there was nothing in the extradition treaty which explicitly forbids one country from kidnapping citizens of the other country to bring them to trial. If a first-year law student made that argument, I would recommend that he transfer to auto repair school.

Of course, the treaty doesn't specifically forbid kidnapping. Nor does it forbid murdering or torturing suspected criminals. The treaty, like all treaties, presupposes that each country will obey the law—including the law against kidnapping. It provides for how extraditions should proceed *lawfully*, not *lawlessly*.

The Alvarez case was all too typical of the cavalier attitude the Supreme Court majority has shown toward the rights of persons charged with crime, though even in that area there were a handful of moderate decisions.

The real surprises this term came in the areas of speech, religion and abortion. The Court struck down a "politically correct" hate-speech ordinance which mirrored speech codes on many university campuses. And it did so by a 9-0 vote. This unanimity was especially surprising in light of the closeness—5-4—of the vote striking down as unconstitutional flag burning statutes. Surely burning a cross on a specific person's front lawn is at least as offensive as burning a flag. But the reality that flag burning is more a liberal-conservative issue than hate speech may explain the difference in the votes.

Perhaps the most surprising decision involved a relatively non-sectarian prayer given by a reform rabbi at a junior high school graduation. The High Court reaffirmed the separation of church and state, ruling that even so benign a prayer could not be imposed on young students at an important public school event.

The most significant decision was, however, saved for the High Court's last day. In the abortion case, a 5-4 majority reaffirmed *Roe* v. *Wade*, while allowing the states to impose conditions on abortion, so long as they do not create an "undue burden" on a woman's rights to choose. But even more profound than the substance of this decision was the remarkable opinion jointly authored by the Court's emerging centrist plurality—Justices O'Connor, Kennedy and Souter. That opinion focused on the "institutional integrity" of the Supreme Court and its obligations to adhere to precedent unless there are compelling reasons for overruling it. It is an opinion that foreshadows the potentially moderate future of this Court on issues that go beyond abortion—unless, of course, there are changes in personnel. As Justice Blackmun, the Court's oldest member, lamented: "I am 83 years old. I cannot remain on this Court forever, and when I do step down, the confirmation process for my successor well may focus on the issue before us today." That will almost certainly be the case—regardless of who is elected our next president. And it is a tragedy. The focus of any confirmation process for a Surpeme Court justice should be on broad issues of judicial philosophy, professional excellence and a commitment to the values of our Constitution, and especially its Bill of Rights.　　　　　July 1992

FREEDOM OF EXPRESSION AND THE RISE OF INTOLERANCE

Part Two

2 // *Modern Challenges to the First Amendment*

JUST "A LITTLE CENSORSHIP" GOES A LONG, LONG WAY

Almost everyone supports freedom of speech—in theory. But most would insist on some "limited" exceptions to complete freedom of expression. "Just this itsy-bitsy exception wouldn't cause any harm" is the argument I hear all the time. The problem is that everyone has a *different* itsy-bitsy exception, and in a nation of equal protection, it is difficult to pick and choose among the proferred exceptions. If we were to accept them all, there would be little left of the First Amendment.

I recall an incident at Harvard several years ago that illustrates this principle of "ism equity." A feminist instructor circulated a memorandum objecting to the fact that the Harvard library contained "*Playboy* magazine." She was "offended" by that particular item and could not understand why Harvard's money should be used to subscribe to an item that offended her. I wrote a tongue-in-cheek response in which I applauded her proposal and suggested taking it to its logical extreme: Every member of the Harvard community should have the power to demand that the library not carry one genre of material that he or she found offensive. I submitted my own particular favorite: books and articles that call for censorship. I argued that if every member of the Harvard community got to veto one offensive genre of writing, we could close down the costly library system, move the few remaining volumes to a few file cabinets, and convert Widener Library into squash courts—unless, of course, someone was offended by squash.

In a nation—or university—committed to equality, there can never be just "a little" censorship. The choice is between what I call "the taxi-cab theory of free speech" and a "system of censorship." Just as a taxi cab must accept all law-abiding passengers who can pay the fare without discriminating on the basis of where they are going or why they are going there, so, too, a government or university may not pick and choose between what books or magazines may be offensive. Once it gets into the business of picking and choosing among writings, then it must create a fair and equitable *system* of censorship based on articulated principles. If it decides that items offensive to some women can be banned, then it will have difficulty rejecting the claims of offensiveness made by blacks, Jews, gays, fundamentalist Christians, atheists, vegetarians, antifur proponents, and other politically correct and incorrect groups. I used to be able to argue that under such a system the only book left would be *Little Red Riding Hood*. But recently that children's classic was banned on the grounds that it promoted the killing of animals by glorifying the hunter as well as the drinking of wine by elderly grandmothers. June 1992

TAKE THIS TEST FOR THE FIRST AMENDMENT CLUB

Do you really believe in the freedom of speech guaranteed by our First Amendment? Or do you just support the speech of those with whom you agree? Nearly two hundred years ago, the French philosopher Voltaire articulated the fundamental premise underlying true support for freedom of speech: "I disapprove of what you say, but I will defend to the death your right to say it."

Defending "to the death" may be a bit strong and "disapprove" a bit weak, but the core of Voltaire's point is crucial. It is easy, and rather self-serving, to rally 'round the flag of the First Amendment on behalf of those whose speech you admire or enjoy. But unless you are prepared to defend the freedom to speak of those whom you despise—those who make your blood boil—you cannot count yourself as a member of that rather select club of true believers in freedom of expression.

I call it a select club because most people, even most who claim adherence to the First Amendment, favor some censorship. Deep down, nearly everyone wants to censor something. I have Jewish friends who support freedom of expression for everyone—except for Nazis who want to march through Jewish neighborhoods like Skokie, Ill. I have African-American friends who support freedom of speech for everyone—except those who would try to justify South African apartheid. I have women friends who support freedom of speech for everyone—except for those who are in the business of selling sexist pornography. And the list goes on.

The other day I spoke at a rally of artists, museum curators, and gallery owners protesting the prosecution of the Cincinnati museum curator who had exhibited the Mappelthorpe photographs of naked children and homosexual adults. It was a very self-serving rally. Of course, artists, museum curators, and gallery owners would protest the censorship of art! Art is their business, after all.

When I represented the musical *Hair*, which had been "banned in Boston" back in the sixties, of course we got the support of the theater crowd. No one should be surprised that the leader of the rock band 2 Live Crew has now become a First Amendment maven, since his rap lyrics have now been censored. When the Palestine Liberation Organization (PLO) was prevented from opening an information office in Washington, it was predictable that Arab-American supporters of the PLO would cry "First Amendment foul."

And what about that classic of self-serving promotion of the Bill of Rights: the Philip Morris sponsorship of TV ads praising the First Amendment at a time when Congress is considering further limitations on cigarette advertising. You don't have to be a supporter of freedom of speech to protest when your own ox is being gored. You do have to be a supporter of freedom of speech to protest when the government tries to censor the speech of those who are goring your ox.

Some examples from my personal Hall of Fame of true First Amendment believers:

• Women against Pornography and Censorship is an organization that tries to educate the public about what they perceive to be the sexist evils of pornography. But at the same time, they try to educate about the evils of censorship, reminding their listeners that if the government is given the power to censor pornography today, then tomorrow it may demand the power to prohibit the publication of information about birth control and abortion.

• Action for Children's Television strongly opposes much of the daily fare to which our children are exposed on the boob tube, but they also oppose censorship of television by the Federal Communications Commission.

• Those Jews, including some Holocaust survivors, who defended the rights of the Nazis to march through Skokie and who now defend the rights of hateful Holocaust deniers to publish their garbage.

• Those pro-choice activists who refuse to call the cops when right-to-lifers picket in front of abortion clinics.

One group that is in danger of being drummed out of the First Amendment Hall of Fame is the American Civil Liberties Union (ACLU). Until recently, it was a charter member. But over the past few years it has gotten soft on the First Amendment when it comes to racist, sexist, and homophobic speech on college campuses. It has also refused to defend the rights of the CIA to recruit on campus. And it was nowhere to be seen when Dartmouth University disciplined members of the right-wing *Dartmouth Review* for engaging in "vexatious," "aggressive," and "confrontational" speech against an African-American professor. As of now, the ACLU is still a member, but it is getting close to being placed on probation.

If you want to join the First Amendment Club, you must attend at least one free speech rally in support of views that you thoroughly despise. I mean really hate! It is not enough to say, as some do about the Mappelthorpe photographs, "Well, that's really not my taste, but I don't see why others who enjoy that kind of thing shouldn't be free to see it." That's cheating. You must find something that really disgusts, angers, or offends you to the core. Go out and defend its right to be expressed. Then come and claim your First Amendment membership card. July 1990

A WAY FOR STUDENTS TO FIGHT THE CENSORS

Dear High School Editor,

I know how disappointed you must be in the U.S. Supreme Court's recent decision authorizing school principals to censor your school newspaper. Many concerned citizens are upset at the negative message this sends to high school students about freedom of speech and journalistic responsibility. We are also concerned about the message it sends to high school principals: that they are relatively free to impose their own views about controversial subjects, such as divorce, birth control, and sex, on a captive audience of public school students.

We should all be proud of the student editors of the Hazelwood, Mo., *Spectrum*, who took their censorship complaint all the way to the nation's highest court. If ever student journalists proved they could act responsibly, Cathy Kuhlmeier and her fellow editors certainly did by the manner in which they responded to their principal's heavy-handed censorship. Even though they lost, it was a good civics lesson.

The Supreme Court's decision does not mark the last word about the freedom of high school students to publish uncensored newspapers. This open letter is intended to encourage you to take a somewhat different path from the one taken by most high school papers today. Do what real newspapers do: become independent! Form a journalism club outside the formal structure of the school. Start small—perhaps a one-page typed and photocopied newsletter. Try to get a few local merchants to place small ads. Charge a nickel a copy. Compete with the school's "official" paper. That's how Thomas Paine and John Peter Zenger began.

The school cannot censor outside newspapers—it would be good journalism and good education. It will teach you about the real world of newspapers. You must sell your product, cultivate readers, find advertisers. You must compete in the open marketplace of ideas. If you are to succeed, your paper must be better than the principal's paper.

There has always been something anomalous about officially sponsored school newspapers. It is difficult to expect those who pay the piper not to try to call the tune. This is especially true when the official newspaper is a monopoly.

Even independent newspapers have piper-payers who try to call tunes: large advertisers, subscribers, conglomerate owners. But at least they are not government officials. And let there be no mistake: School principals are government officials, answerable to school boards and other politicians.

My advice is to try to capitalize on the widespread outrage of many educators, journalists, and civil libertarians over the Supreme Court's decision. Try to get some seed money—a few hundred dollars for start-up costs—from those who believe in freedom of the press. Approach local newspapers, television stations, and magazines with a proposal and a modest request.

I hereby offer $500 of my own to any group of responsible students at the Hazelwood East High School who are prepared to continue in the tradition of Cathy Kuhlmeier and her fellow editors who challenged censorship. If you want to start an independent newspaper reporting on matters of interest to the students, my small contribution will probably cover the printing cost for two or three issues. Then you're on your own. I will not demand the right to see copy in advance. I am confident that you will exercise your freedom responsibly.

There is no assurance that the principal will approve. Few of those in power like to be criticized by those whom they cannot control. He may even try to stop you from distributing it on the campus. And the law is unclear about whether he can. The Supreme Court, in the Hazelwood case, went out of its way to leave that issue open. Test the issue: Try to distribute your independent newspaper within the school grounds. If the principal tries to stop you, sue him. Or distribute the paper outside the school gates.

There is no doubt that the current Supreme Court majority is seeking to cut back on the rights of high school students. The majority of justices seem to have more faith in the exercise of power by the authorities than in the exercise of rights by students. The American way is to fight back when your rights are being curtailed—even against school principals, and even against the Supreme Court.

The independent school newspaper is one way to do it in a civilized, mature, and constructive manner. The eyes of the nation will be upon you. Show the American people that high school students can exercise their First Amendment rights responsibly, in good taste, and with journalistic integrity. Show the world that censorship—of a high school newspaper in Hazelwood, Mo., or anywhere else—is not the American way.

January 1988

AN INVITATION TO A MURDER?

The case is a civil libertarian's nightmare. A murder victim's family is suing *Soldier of Fortune* magazine, claiming that an advertisement it ran led directly to the killing of Sandra Black. That macho journal of guns, guts, and gore used to run classified ads such as the following, which is the subject of the lawsuit: "Ex-Marines. 67-69 Nam Vets. EX-DI, weapons specialist—jungle warfare. Pilot. M.E. High Risk Assignment. US or overseas."

When Robert Black read that ad, he wrote to its author, John Wayne (what else?) Hearn, and inquired about seeing his gun collection. One thing led to another and soon the two gun fanciers were talking business: Black would pay Hearn $10,000 to murder Black's wife. (Black was having an affair with another woman.) This was nothing new for killer Hearn. It would be his third murder for hire in nineteen days. The assassination business, it appears, was thriving now that there was a place to advertise one's lethal talents.

The crime was quickly solved. Black was sentenced to death and is awaiting execution, while Hearn, the trigger man, is serving a life sentence. Suing either of them would do the victim's family little good, since neither has any money. But *Soldier of Fortune* and its parent company, Omega Group Ltd., have what lawyers aptly call "deep pockets."

The magazine is defending itself on First Amendment grounds, claiming that the ad, which does not specifically mention any illegal activities, was constitutionally protected free speech. "The ad is a very plain vanilla ad, the kind you would expect to find in a magazine of that type," says the magazine's lawyer, apparently missing the irony of his own admission.

On the contrary, responds the family's lawyer: It was "an unequivocal offer to commit domestic criminal services." Indeed, he says, he will prove that the magazine was aware of the ad's implications, and that more than twenty felonies in a two-month period can be connected to classified ads run by *Soldier of Fortune*.

The reason this case keeps civil libertarians awake at night is that the suit is over words that are claimed to have caused violence—a concept that has broad implications beyond this suit. Not all words in all contexts are, of course, constitutionally protected: A Mafia boss who orders one of his soldiers to "fire" at a rival gangster is no more protected than a hooligan who falsely and maliciously shouts "fire" or sets off a fire alarm in a crowded theater. Their words are not protected in these contexts because they are stimuli to immediate, almost automatic, actions that the government may lawfully seek to prevent.

An advertisement is quite different, especially when it is the magazine and publisher that are being sued rather than the author of the pregnantly ambiguous ad.

To illustrate the problem, imagine the following situation: Husband hires killer to murder his wife; they agree that the murder is to take place when husband is in Europe with an alibi; killer will be informed of the day by a coded ad in the local newspaper that says "Happy Birthday Gwendolyn"; the day after that ad appears, killer murders Gwendolyn. Surely the newspaper is not responsible for the murder, even though its ad led directly to it. A newspaper or magazine cannot be held responsible for unanticipated misuses of its advertising columns.

But the issue in the *Soldier of Fortune* case is precisely whether the magazine should have anticipated that its not-so-vanilla ads would be used by professional assassins and criminal clients who would make use of such ignoble and illegal services. If the victim's family can prove that the magazine was, in fact, on notice that these ambiguous "high-risk assignment" ads were invitations to assassinations, they may very well be able to collect from the magazine.

If *Soldier of Fortune* is held responsible for the Black murder, the implications—both civil and criminal—for other magazines could be staggering. Will magazines that run "personal" ads be held responsible for rapes committed—or for venereal diseases contracted—during dates arranged as a result of the ads? Will magazines that run ordinary gun advertisements be responsible for deaths or injuries committed with weapons sold to criminals or crazies?

The courts have already struck down as unconstitutional several attempts to hold publishers of alleged pornography responsible for assaults purportedly committed by those who have been exposed to offending smut. The fear is that if porn publishers can be sued by rape victims today, publishers of revolutionary tracts may be held responsible tomorrow for violence caused by those who read, and act on, the writings of Lenin, Hitler, Jesus, Malcolm X, or Meir Kahane. And if publishers are responsible, why not booksellers, libraries, and universities?

Unless it can be shown that *Soldier of Fortune* was aware that the ad in question was a coded invitation to assassination, the safer thing for the First Amendment would be for the court to limit responsibility to the killers themselves, and let the magazine, which is no longer running these ads, off the hook.   February 1988

PHILIP MORRIS WAVES FLAG
TO SELL DEATH

During the 1930s, 1940s, and 1950s, the American cigarette industry perpetuated a deadly hoax on our citizens. With growing knowledge of the carcinogenic nature of tobacco, it set out to con Americans into believing that smoking was medically desirable.

I become enraged when I go back and read the cigarette ads of the pre-surgeon-general-warning days. "More doctors smoke Camels than any other cigarette," says the large print in one 1946 ad. Its text goes on to assure the smoker that the "doctor is a scientist," obviously suggesting that he must know what he is doing to himself.

Another Camel ad takes this theme even further. It shows a "life expectancy" chart, with the average life span increasing "thanks to medicine's men in white" and to "modern medical science." And guess what these scientists do for pleasure? Why, of course, they smoke Camels. If you smoke Camels, you, too, can extend your life, is the not-so-subtle message.

Not only could you live longer by smoking, but you could also become a star athlete. Joe DiMaggio told his fans in 1942 that he smoked Camels for eight years, and implied that cigarettes gave him the release of energy necessary to become a champion baseball player.

Nor was Camel the only, or even the worst, offender. Other brands featured opera singers, actresses, socialites, even the president of the Child Welfare Committee of America assuring Americans of the "mildness," "relief from fatigue," and "lift" that a good smoke will give you, along with "protection—against irritation [and] cough." One ad had a prominent socialite urging smokers not to "worry about how many [they] smoke," even when they are smoking a lot.

Following the enactment by Congress of mandatory labels warning of cigarettes' relationship to cancer, the message changed. There were no more overt claims about good health or long life. Now the association was subtle. The Marlboro Man became the image of the era. Brand names were changed to suggest the great outdoors, coolness, crispness, virility, and success.

Then came the congressional ban on television advertising, which made it difficult for the cigarette industry to keep its brand names in the consciousness of our TV watching public.

So now Philip Morris had come up with a new shell game. It has begun a $60 million, two-year advertising campaign that focuses on TV ads extolling the Bill of Rights and especially the First Amendment, which, in its view, protects the right of the cigarette industry to advertise its lethal product. It is a sleazy and disgusting ad campaign, reminiscent of past associations with doctors, child-welfare advocates, sexy women, and macho men.

This time it has co-opted the National Archives. In exchange for a paltry payment of $600,000, the Archives, which houses our Bill of Rights and other national treasures, has rented its good name to a bad product and has authorized the following tie-in: "Join Philip Morris and the National Archives in celebrating the 200th anniversary of the Bill of Rights."

Can we next expect to see pictures of Thomas Jefferson, Alexander Hamilton, and James Madison lighting up a cigarette as they draft the text of the First Amendment? What about adding sculptured cigarettes to the lips of Washington and Roosevelt on Mount Rushmore in exchange for a contribution to the park service to fight forest fires caused by careless smokers? What other national symbols can we now expect to see with "for rent" signs?

We know how much it cost the Japanese to rent a former American president. How much will Congress charge to fly a Marlboro banner from the Capitol flagpole? It's enough to drive a patriot to drink. And Philip Morris wouldn't mind that, so long as we all drank Miller beer, another one of its products.

Philip Morris is within its legal and constitutional rights in sponsoring the Bill of Rights campaign. Although the First Amendment probably did not protect the kind of deliberately misleading and hazardous advertising engaged in by many cigarette companies in the bad old days, it almost certainly does protect the kind of subtle product identification that Philip Morris is currently perpetrating. It relies on the marketplace of ideas and the good sense of the American public not to be taken in by hucksters.

The U.S. Supreme Court is likely to rule early next year that the Bill of Rights also protects the "right to die." Now *that's* an association I hope the American public will make whenever it sees the Bill of Rights sponsored by a purveyor of killer cigarettes. November 1989

In June 1992 the Supreme Court decided to allow certain types of damage suits by smokers against the cigarette industry. (Cipollone v. Liggett)

YOUR FIRST AMENDMENT RIGHT TO PANHANDLE

If not one of the oldest or most noble occupations, begging surely has roots deep in the history of humankind. The beggar reflects both the failings of the society that has been unable to incorporate him—or, increasingly, *her*—into its productive work force, as well as the kindness of those members of society willing to share sustenance with those most in need.

The number and treatment of beggars in any society speaks volumes about the condition of that society. The beggar has been the subject of literature, religious homily, song, and humor in virtually every culture. Now the beggar has become the subject of an important constitutional law decision that may expand the meaning of our First Amendment.

A federal judge in New York recently ruled that "begging can be expression protected by the First Amendment." The lawsuit had been brought by two homeless men who beg for sustenance in the New York subway system. They complained that under the policy of the New York City transit system, all begging and panhandling was prohibited and that homeless people who violated this blanket prohibition could be ejected into the cold night air.

The homeless plaintiffs argued that begging is a form of speech—a request for help. The transit authority responded that begging is not speech at all, but rather an act—and an offensive one to many subway riders.

Judge Leonard Sand agreed with the beggars: The simple request for money by a beggar or panhandler cannot but remind the passerby that many people in the city live in poverty and often lack the essentials for survival. Even the beggar sitting in Grand Central Station with a tin cup at his feet conveys the message that he and others like him are in need. While often disturbing and sometimes alarmingly graphic, begging is unmistakably informative and persuasive speech.

Judge Sand cited Supreme Court cases concluding that organized charities that solicit for others do have a First Amendment right to send their message. He reasoned that no constitutional distinction can be drawn between the more refined entreaties of the professional fund-raiser and the "more personal, emotionally charged" face-to-face importuning of the subway beggar.

The judge recognized that begging is disturbing to many citizens. But he rejected the argument of the transit authority that government has the power to protect its citizens from being forced to confront the cruel reality of homelessness and poverty. The principal effect of the prohibition against begging, he said, was to keep "a public problem involving human beings out of sight and therefore out of mind." Indeed, the judge found that it was "the very unsettling appearance and message conveyed by the beggars that gives their conduct its expressive quality."

Having ruled that beggars have a constitutional right to ask for help, the judge then went on to offer some protection to those who are solicited.

Obviously, any citizen has a right to say no to a beggar's plea. The citizen also has a right to be protected from being harassed, accosted, touched, or threatened by a beggar—or anyone else, for that matter.

The judge made it plain that government does have the power to enact reasonable rules regulating the manner by which begging takes place, the specific locations at which begging may pose a danger and other limitations on the constitutional right to beg. Indeed, existing criminal statutes already prohibit most of the legally objectionable aspects of aggressive begging, such as physical touching or threatening.

The problem with the New York subway regulation was that it was an absolute ban to all begging: It prohibited even the most polite request directed at the most willing giver. The New York authorities must now either appeal Judge Sand's decision or enact new regulations that strike a constitutionally appropriate balance between the rights of beggars and other subway riders. In the meantime, New York beggars can continue to seek sustenance without fear of legal consequences.

The New York decision will obviously have an impact on prohibitions against begging that currently exist in other cities and towns across the country. Legal organizations representing the homeless are gearing up for litigation in several target cities. Judge Sand's decision, if it is eventually upheld, may become a Magna Carta for our poorest citizens.

In his conclusion, Judge Sand wrote eloquently about the rights of the homeless: "A true test of one's commitment to constitutional principles is the extent to which recognition is given to the rights of those in our midst who are the least affluent, least powerful, and least welcome. . . ." Judge Sand passed that test with flying colors.

It remains to be seen whether the Supreme Court, which in recent years has received flunking grades in regard to protecting the poor and the disenfranchised, will understand that freedom of speech includes the right of the homeless to beg for sustenance on the subway, as surely as it includes the right of corporate executives to lobby for tax breaks in Congress.

February 1990

In June 1992 The Supreme Court upheld a ban on panhandling in airports, but ruled that handing out informational leaflets cannot be prohibited. (See Krishna v. Lee)

TO SUE OR NOT TO SUE?

At least once a month, I get a call or letter from a citizen who feels aggrieved by something written about him or her in the press. They ask my advice as to whether they should sue for libel. I generally begin by quoting the great jurist Learned Hand, who once said: "I must say that as a litigant, I should dread a lawsuit beyond almost anything else short of sickness and death."

Lawsuits are, indeed, to be avoided whenever possible. They are disruptive of one's life, intrusive on one's privacy, and threatening to one's emotional equilibrium. This is especially true of libel suits, because it is difficult for a defamed citizen to win, especially if he is a public or quasi-public figure. Moreover, even if a plaintiff can prove that he was libeled, the jury must place a price on his reputation. It can be extremely destructive to be confronted with the reality that one's reputation is worth only a few thousand bucks.

There are other good reasons, of constitutional policy, to avoid unnecessary libel suits. Journalists need breathing room to report on controversial issues. In the competitive enterprise of beating deadlines, even the most careful reporters make honest mistakes. If the courts were to allow large damage awards for honest mistakes, even for simple negligence, the economic realities would dictate that only the most carefully checked and least controversial stories would be published. Investigative journalism of the kind that led to Watergate would be stifled. (Indeed, Woodward and Bernstein made some honest mistakes in their initial stories about the Watergate break-in.) That is why the Supreme Court has made it difficult, especially for public figures, to bring libel suits. In order to win, a public figure must prove that the false statement was not the product of an honest mistake or even of negligence but resulted from a reckless disregard for the truth.

Thus, if the reporter (or the editor) could easily have checked a critical defamatory fact but failed to do so, that defamation might not be protected by the First Amendment and the libeled citizen, even a public person, could win the lawsuit. The easiest case, of course, is where the reporter knows that the defamatory story is false and prints it nonetheless.

Over my quarter-century career as a lawyer, I have been defamed on several occasions, but I never seriously considered suing. Recently, however, a columnist put words in my mouth that I never uttered.

The background of the story is as follows: I had accused a judicial nominee of having made an ethnically biased statement. Mike Barnicle, a columnist for the *Boston Globe*, who I had met only once but who had written several nasty items about me, wrote a column attacking me for my accusations. In it he claims that I once "told him and a friend as we stood by the Out-of-Town News Stand that, in Al's [Dershowitz] exact words, 'I love Asian woman, don't you? They're . . . they're so submissive.' "

When the column appeared, I called Barnicle and asked him whether he intended that story as a joke, since he knew as well as I did that I had never made any such statement. He responded, "Well, I think it happened." Barnicle agreed that we had met only once, and that our brief and cool exchange of greetings—perhaps sixty seconds—had taken place nearly ten years earlier, when the owner of the Out-of-Town News Stand had introduced us. The owner remembers that I never made any statement about Asian women. Barnicle's "friend," who he said was with him, is now dead, according to Barnicle.

Shortly after Barnicle's column ran, I began to receive calls from other people who claimed that Barnicle had made up stories about them over the years. I learned that in 1981, Barnicle had been sued by a local Jewish merchant on the ground that Barnicle had made up a story about a racial slur that the merchant had allegedly made in Barnicle's presence. The courts found that "the things attributed" to the merchant by Barnicle "were not said by him." The record of the case also showed that Barnicle had "interlineated" his notes in an effort to lend credibility to his made-up story, but that the courts did not fall for it. Barnicle was found to have libeled the merchant and had to pay approximately $40,000.

My lawyers have told me that I could win a libel suit against Barnicle and that I could collect a considerable amount of money from him. Yet a part of me is reluctant to bring the case to court, since I generally disapprove of libel suits. But I would not be suing someone who merely made an honest mistake. This case would be directed at a columnist who has a record of making up at least one similar story. Surely the First Amendment was not intended to encourage deliberately false reporting.

To sue or not to sue, that is the question. I am still not certain of the answer.   December 1990

Barnicle eventually issued a public apology.

DO QUOTATION MARKS
GUARANTEE ACCURACY?

When you see quotation marks around a statement in a newspaper or a magazine, do you believe that the quoted words are the exact ones used by the person being quoted? Or do you assume that the writer or editor took some liberties in paraphrasing the actual language of the quoted speaker? Do journalists have literary license to change the words actually spoken in order to clean up their grammar or jazz up their syntax?

These are the kinds of questions ordinarily debated in classes on journalism and at conventions of editors. But last week these and other questions about journalistic integrity were at the center of impassioned arguments before the U.S. Supreme Court.

The case that raised these questions was a lawsuit brought by a psycho-analyst named Jeffrey Masson against a journalist named Janet Malcolm. Malcolm had written a critical profile of Masson for *The New Yorker* maga-zine. In the course of the profile she purported to quote Masson at length. Masson damned himself by his own—or were they?—words. Masson claimed that he never said several of the most damaging things attributed to him in quotation marks. Malcolm's forty hours of tape recordings of their conversations did not include the disputed passages, but Malcolm claims Masson said them off tape.

Masson sued for libel, alleging that Malcolm had deliberately mis-quoted him in order to make him look bad. He argued that such deliberate misquotation constitutes the "malice" required for a public figure to win a libel suit. (An ordinary private person can win a libel suit by simply proving that he or she was defamed, even negligently; but a public figure, a person whose life or career have become a matter of public interest, cannot win without proving that the defamation was malicious, in the sense that there was a reckless or knowing disregard for the truth.)

The lower courts dismissed Masson's suit on legal grounds without allowing the jury to decide whether he had made the quoted statements or whether he was defamed. They ruled that even if Malcolm had deliberately put words in Masson's mouth, that alone would not be enough to constitute malice, so long as the substance of the quoted words was not significantly different from the words actually spoken.

The Supreme Court granted review of the case in order to decide what weight the lower courts should give to misquotations in deciding whether malice was present. If Masson now wins, he gets the jury trial he was denied by the lower courts' dismissal of his lawsuit. If Malcolm wins, the case is over.

Whichever way the high court decides the case, its decision will almost certainly have a palpable impact on the rules of journalism. Prior to the case, journalists, even good ones, felt free to make changes in quotes so long as their changes did not alter the substance of the spoken words. Poor grammar by the speaker was sometimes, though not always, corrected. Simple, more understandable words were often substituted for complex terms. Long quotes were shortened and summarized. In the process, meaning was sometimes changed.

For example, Malcolm quoted Masson as having described himself as an "intellectual gigolo." Masson denied having used that term, and there is no reference to it on the tapes. Malcolm claims that Masson did use the term but argues that even if he did not, he certainly did use words that are fairly summarized by the quoted language. That will be a difficult argument to sustain in front of a jury, since the word *gigolo* is a uniquely self-damning characterization. A gigolo is after all a male prostitute, a person who exchanges sex for money and is utterly promiscuous in his sexual activities. No self-respecting doctor would describe himself as an "intellectual gigolo." It is not a term that can be properly used as an accurate shorthand for a longer quote that does not include a sex-for-hire analogy.

Although the Supreme Court is not the Pulitzer Prize Committee and is not empowered to decide what constitutes good or bad journalism, its decision in this case will likely have an important impact in the editorial rooms of the American media. If it decides that misquotation is evidence of malice, editors will insist that journalists use the exact words spoken by the person quoted, and may well require contemporaneous notes or even tape recordings. If, on the other hand, the high court affirms the lower courts' dismissals of the lawsuit, editors may continue to allow their reporters to tinker with quotes.

Regardless of how the case turns out, the reading public has now been alerted to the reality that quotation marks are not and have never been a certification that the words quoted are not necessarily the ones spoken by the person who was interviewed. Readers of newspapers and magazines have now been advised that the concept of caveat emptor is as applicable to the competitive enterprise of reporting as it has long been to the selling of used cars.   January 1991

In June 1991 The Supreme Court decided that fabricated quotations could be considered libelous and reinstated Masson's lawsuit.

NEW YORK NUDITY RULING WENT TOO FAR

I'm no prude, and I'm certainly not a censor. I've defended theater owners who want to show pornographic movies to consenting adults, nudists who want to cavort naked on specially designated beaches and gay adults who wish to have sex with other gay adults. But the recent decision of the New York Court of Appeals allowing women to "expose their breasts" in a Rochester public park went too far even for me.

The court ruled that since the New York nudity statute prohibited only the exposure of a woman's breast but not of a man's chest it raised serious equal protection concerns that could be avoided by interpreting the statute so as not to "cover"—whoops!—the female breast.

Two concurring judges went even further, apparently accepting the argument of the women who bared their breasts as part of a protest against sexist laws that eroticize women's bodies. They argued that the fact that some men in our society "may regard the uncovered female breast with a prurient interest that is not similarly aroused by the male equivalent . . . ," is itself a reflection "of prejudice and bias toward women." In other words, men who are turned on more by women's breasts than by men's chests are sexist bigots, rather than typical heterosexuals. The concurring judges thus found that the statute violated the women's right to equal protection of the laws. Under this approach, the state must now either require all men to cover their chests or permit all women to bare their breasts.

The lawyer for the "Topfree Seven"—as the women who bared their breasts call themselves—said that this decision meant that women in New York state may now "sunbathe topless or even walk down the street without a top." Well, sunbathing topless at the beach is one thing, since people who go to beaches—especially beaches in certain parts of the Northeast and California—expect to see an occasional bared breast. But strolling down Broadway, Main Street or the local neighborhood thoroughfare is something quite different.

Civil libertarians have always distinguished between what adults may do in private or among other consenting adults, on the one hand, and what they may inflict on unconsenting citizens, on the other hand. This is a sensible and obvious distinction that goes back to John Stuart Mill. It explains why we have different standards for what may be shown inside a movie theater and outside on its marquee. It also explains why sex is a constitutionally protected activity in the bedroom, but not in the middle of the town square.

Women should certainly have the right to remove their tops *and their bottoms* in front of any adult who chooses to view them—whether in the bedroom, on the beach or at the theater. But those who do not want to see the breasts of strange women also have rights, including the right to walk down Main Street without having to avert their eyes. Moreover, children walk down Main Street as well as adults, and their parents certainly have the right to decide whether their teen-age boys should or should not be exposed to the naked breasts of protesting women.

But what about discrimination between women's breasts and what the court called "the male equivalent." That, of course, begs the question: Is the male chest the "equivalent" of the female breast? Culturally, it is not—certainly not in most parts of this country or even in most parts of New York state. Is it really sexism to believe that men and women are anatomically different? Would the Topfree Seven protest against a law that distinguished between a stranger feeling a woman's breast and touching a man's chest? Would they support a law that *required* all competitive swimmers—male and female—to wear only Speedo bottoms? After all, if it is wrong to eroticize the female breast, should any woman have the *right* to insist on covering her breasts in situations where men did not have that right? If this is really about choice—a woman's right to choose what to wear—should we not also consider the choice of the majority of people not to be exposed to naked female breasts on Main Street?

We endanger freedom and equality when we trivialize it. The Supreme Court of the United States trivialized freedom last year when it upheld an Indiana statute that required topless dancers to wear "pasties" over their nipples when they danced in front of people who wanted to see them nude. And the New York Court of Appeals trivialized freedom and equality when it ruled that women have the right to walk down a busy street with their breasts exposed. That is why when I was asked, several years ago, to bring this kind of a lawsuit challenging the Massachusetts nudity law, I turned down the case. But I will continue to defend the rights of any woman or man who wants to expose any part of his or her anatomy to any other willing adults.   July 1992

3 // *Intolerance on the Right*

TODAY'S CENSORS: CONSERVATIVE OR AUTHORITARIAN?

Censorship from the right is as old as recorded history; yet in some respects it is surprising. To the extent that the right is associated with true conservatism, its adherents should favor limited government and freedom for the individual. Indeed, the libertarian branch of the right has, in general, opposed governmental censorship. And today, on many university campuses, it is the libertarian right that is defending politically incorrect speech. Although this defense may, for some, be nothing more than self-serving "free speech for me!" it has played a significant role in preventing censorship from the politically correct left.

Most right wingers in this country are not libertarians. Led by such reactionaries as Chief Justice William Rehnquist, they are not even conservatives. They are authoritarian statists. They support the *power* of the state over the *rights* of individuals. While this is a perversion of true conservatism, these statists often purport to speak for conservative voters.

It is difficult to imagine anything less conservative than a system of state mandated censorship or a system of compelled state prayers or pledges of allegiance. Yet these authoritarian proposals have become part of the mainstream "conservative" agenda.

Nor can the radical left be counted on these days to oppose censorship. To be sure, it opposes the censorship from the right—that advocated by the Jesse Helmses, the Reverend Jerry Falwells, and the Dan Quayles of the world. But the radical left has its own censorship agenda. It would simply substitute the William Kuntslers, Gloria Steinems, and Noam Chomskys of the world as the authorized censors.

Surprising as it may sound, free speech and censorship is not, and historically has never been, a right-left dispute. The reactionary right and radical left, which have always shared much in common, especially when it comes to liberty, have always been on the vanguard of censorship. Any group that believes it has a monopoly on knowledge is likely to be intolerant of dissidents and difference. The case for freedom of speech and against censorship has always come from a coalition of principled centerists—true liberals and conservatives—and whichever fringe group is being censored at any point in history.

Thus, during the McCarthy era, the radical left consistently joined the principled center in advocating free speech. Today, the reactionary right on university campuses is joining the principled center in a campaign against censorship by the left.

On the censorship side, coalitions are also evident. Many from the radical feminist left have created a censorial coalition with the reactionary religious right to censor "pornography." These groups, which are at each others' throats on issues such as birth control, abortion, gay rights, extramarital sex, and women's rights, have jumped into each others' beds against the common evil of "pornography."

The struggle against censorship, like the struggle for liberty in general, never stays won. Yesterday's allies may become tomorrow's enemies, and yesterday's enemies may become tomorrow's unlikely allies. What must always be remembered is that freedom of speech—indeed, freedom in general—is not the natural condition of humankind. Historically, censorship and authoritarian control have always been the norm. That is why it always is a mighty struggle to keep freedom alive and keep the censor, with his and her voracious appetite, at bay. July 1992

CHILD PORN LAWS THREATEN FREE EXPRESSION

Justice Oliver Wendell Holmes once cautioned us that hard cases make bad law. Well, emotional cases make even worse law. And few issues are more emotional than child pornography. That is why the U.S. Supreme Court's recent announcement that it will review a Massachusetts child pornography case is so worrisome to people concerned about freedom of expression.

In an effort to confront the evils of child pornography, Massachusetts enacted an extremely broad and general law making it a crime for any person to encourage or permit any "child" under eighteen "to pose or be exhibited in a state of nudity" for the purpose of a photograph or other visual reproduction, whether for private or commercial use.

Read literally, the statute would authorize a twenty-year prison term for any parent who posed a naked infant on a bear rug for the family album. It would make a felon of Brooke Shields's mother for permitting her daughter to pose naked when she was ten or to appear in the movie *Pretty Baby*.

It would prohibit the publication of illustrated teenage sex manuals such as the critically acclaimed national best-seller *Show Me*. And it would outlaw the work of prize-winning photographers who happen to take pictures of young men and women in the nude.

The Massachusetts Supreme Judicial Court read the statute literally and declared that it was unconstitutionally overbroad. Its language, ruled the court, "makes a criminal of a parent who takes a frontal-view picture of his or her naked one-year-old running on a beach or romping in a wading pool." The Massachusetts court reasoned that "photography is a form of expression which is entitled to First Amendment protection."

The court further observed: "Photography as a means of communication and expression can be strikingly informative, as in the works of Mathew Brady and Margaret Bourke-White. It can be inspirationally expressive, as Ansel Adams demonstrated. Although not every picture may be worth a thousand words, in a First Amendment sense, a picture is worth at least one."

It then concluded that a statute regulating photography must be narrowly drawn to prohibit only the kind of obscenity or pornography that is outside the protection of the Constitution.

The facts giving rise to the Massachusetts case were neither the innocent family bear-rug photo that any parent might take nor the X-rated child pornography that can be bought under the counter of some combat-zone sleaze emporiums. The case now before the Supreme Court involves a man named Douglas Oakes who was given a ten-year prison sentence for photographing his partially nude fifteen-year-old stepdaughter in the family room of their home. She was wearing shorts and a scarf, but her breasts were exposed.

Both the majority and dissenting Massachusetts opinions agreed that the photographs were neither obscene nor pornographic, that the girl had consented to pose for them, and that they were not intended for commercial use. But there the agreement ended. The dissenting judges characterized the pictures as "sexually provocative," argued that the consent of a fifteen-year-old was meaningless, and concluded that Oakes's conduct "constituted the abuse, exploitation, and degradation of a child," rather than the exercise of free speech.

The stage is thus set for what promises to be a major Supreme Court decision on the issue of what constitutes child pornography and exploitation. The case is scheduled for argument in the fall, and we are likely to see briefs submitted by major publishing houses, film studios, child-protection agencies, and others who may be affected by the outcome and language of the ruling.

The usual rule in First Amendment cases is that any statute that criminalizes expression must be narrowly drawn to cover *only* the unprotected evil and may not overbroadly include protected conduct. A defendant in a First Amendment case need not show that *his* particular expression is protected by the First Amendment. It is enough to show that the language of the challenged law *could* be applied to *someone else's* protected expression.

The reason for this rule is that the First Amendment needs breathing space, and the courts will not tolerate the existence of statutes that criminalize constitutionally protected expression, even if prosecutors elect not to prosecute such expression.

The possibility that people will censor themselves because of the implicit threat of selective prosecution is thought to be enough to invalidate such overbroad laws.

The Massachusetts appeal, brought by its generally liberal attorney general James Shannon, directly challenges this entire salutary approach to the First Amendment. It argues that defendants should not be able to avoid prosecution under the Massachusetts law by conjuring up other hypothetical cases that might be brought under the wording of the statute.

If the Supreme Court accepts that dangerous argument and does not limit the law's application, this case could change the court's entire approach to First Amendment cases and could overrule decades of established constitutional law. A great deal is thus at stake in this hard and emotional case.

In the meantime, at least until the Supreme Court renders its decision, make sure your baby is wearing a diaper when you snap the traditional bear-rug photo for the family album.   May 1988

In June 1989 The Supreme Court sidestepped the free expression question and sent the case back to the state court to determine whether Oakes could be a tried under a newly ammended statute requiring lascivious intent.

ALAN M. DERSHOWITZ

LAW PROTECTS SCORSESE'S
TEMPTATION

For years I have argued—often to doubting audiences—that if we compromise the right of free speech in one area, it will be more difficult to resist the voracious appetite of the censor in other areas. Morality in Media and other far-right religious organizations that have over the years issued shrill calls for censorship of sexual material seem determined to prove my point. The current target of their censorial scissors is the film *The Last Temptation of Christ*. The self-appointed guardians of our morality claim that Martin Scorsese's movie is "blasphemous."

Though I have not seen it—and I doubt that I will, because the handful of chains that control virtually all of Boston's movie theaters may capitulate to religious pressures—I am certain that the would-be censors are right. Indeed, any controversial depiction of a deity, prophet, or religious leader is apt to be blasphemous to at least some of the faithful. Blasphemy is in the soul of the beholder. And that is precisely why it should never be used as a basis for censorship, whether by government or monopolistic movie chains, in a heterogeneous, secular society.

Consider the consequences of allowing a judge or jury to decide what constitutes blasphemy! Who would be called as expert witnesses? What would be the criteria for deciding? Would they vary, depending on "local community standards"? Would the court have to accept the divinity of the particular deity as a matter of fact?

For centuries the tenets of Protestantism were blasphemy to Catholics, and those of the Catholics blasphemous to Protestants. Judaism, which denies the divinity of Jesus, was blasphemy to both. And atheism, which has as much standing under our Constitution as any religion, is blasphemy to all organized religions. (A recent ad by the American Society for the Defense of Tradition, Family and Property solemnly declares that "The divinity of Our Lord Jesus Christ is a sufficiently proven fact.")

Some of the greatest literary, political, and scientific writers—Dante, Galileo, Moore, Paine, Spinoza, Darwin, Freud, and Marx—were considered blasphemous.

This is not to deny that blasphemy is painful to some believers. Most writers and filmmakers are sensitive to the feelings of religious readers and viewers. Indeed, that is why so few contemporary books and films deal with controversial religious issues. Self-censorship has always been a more powerful inhibitor of expression than the law.

In this case, Scorsese and Universal Films did not self-censor, because they do not regard the film as blasphemous. Neither do some prominent Christian church leaders. But that is beside the point. Even if it were intended as blasphemy, the film would be entitled to the full protection accorded to freedom of speech in our country, as would the criticism of the film.

The point is that if our government is not empowered to "establish" a particular religion or religion in general, then it is not empowered to appoint official "protectors of the faith." Even democratic governments with established religions—Great Britain, for example—do not censor blasphemous films. Surely there is no room for religious censorship in the United States.

Some leaders of the religious right argue, in the context of mandatory school prayers, that any child whose religion is offended by the content of the official prayer can simply walk out of the classroom. Why can't these leaders tell their followers simply to "walk out" of the movie theater if their religious sensibilities are offended?

Apparently aware that they will not win their case in court, some religious groups have tried to buy off the producers. The Campus Crusade for Christ has offered Universal a big bundle of cash if the studio will turn all prints over to the Crusade for a "big bonfire." To its credit, the studio told the Crusade what it could do with its money. Imagine the implications of a studio or publisher capitulating to a cash offer in exchange for censorship. No critical biography of any wealthy person or institution would ever come to light.

Other fundamentalists have threatened Universal, the chairman of whose holding company is Jewish, with anti-Semitic and anti-Israeli reprisals. These extortionate threats are beneath contempt and should be denounced forthrightly by responsible church leaders. To his credit, the Reverend Jerry Falwell has denounced "every statement or action that in any way fans anti-Semitism," while also condemning the film. But to their everlasting shame, most other Christian leaders have not condemned the anti-Semitism of those who purport to speak in the name of their religions. Their silence in the face of bigotry is a greater blasphemy than anything contained in a fictional film.

The Campus Crusade for Christ has a viable option. Since it was prepared to put up several million dollars to destroy a film, why does it not use that money to produce a film of its own? If it can make a more reverential movie about the life of Jesus, a movie that depicts their Savior in a light more acceptable to them, let them do so. If God is indeed on their side, it will be a better film than Scorsese's. That is what the marketplace of ideas is all about. That is what America is all about.   August 1988

O'CONNOR'S LETTER AIDS RELIGIOUS BIGOTS

"A bunch of kooks," as conservative Barry Goldwater calls them, are determined to have the United States officially declare itself to be "a Christian nation . . . based on the absolute laws of the Bible." The First Amendment, of course, precludes such a declaration, since Congress may not establish any religion.

This sounds obvious enough to any rational reader of our Constitution and the Supreme Court decisions interpreting its words. But the kooks seem oblivious to our traditions of diversity and freedom of religion. It should surprise no one that a small number of bigots would be trying to turn the United States into a theocracy like the Ayatollah Khomeini's Iran. But it should surprise, and outrage, most Americans that these reactionary do-badders seem to have an ally in Supreme Court Justice Sandra Day O'Connor.

The leader of the group wrote to O'Connor last year, asking the justice for a letter to be used as part of their campaign to have the United States declared a Christian nation. This is how Justice O'Connor replied: "You wrote me recently to inquire about any holdings of this Court to the effect that this is a Christian nation. There are statements to such effect in the following opinions: *Church of the Holy Trinity* vs. *United States; Zorach* vs. *Clauson; McGowan* vs. *Maryland.*"

Were Justice O'Connor a law student she would have received a D-minus for her answer. The last two cases contain no statements to the effect that this is a Christian nation. Their thrust is entirely to the contrary. If a lawyer practicing before the Supreme Court were as sloppy with his citations as Justice O'Connor was with hers, he would be properly rebuked. The first case, which does use that term in passing, did not involve an interpretation of the First Amendment.

Further, that case was decided in 1892, when the voting population of this country was comprised almost exclusively of white Protestant males. In that decision, the Supreme Court, deciding whether an anti-immigration statute applied to a Protestant church that had contracted with a minister from England, ruled that since "this is a religious people," it would not assume that Congress intended to make it difficult for churches to secure ministers.

In support of its observation that "this is a religious people," the court pointed to historical documents that referred to God, to Jesus, and to "public Protestant teachings." It quoted a New York opinion declaring that followers of "Mahomet or the Grand Lama" were "imposters." (Thank God, the Ayatollah Khomeini wasn't around to get wind of that opinion.) In the course of its historical discussion, the court made the passing comment that various "unofficial" and "organized utterances" demonstrate that "this is a Christian nation."

The phrase was correct as a demographic but not a constitutional description of our population. The word *Christian* was used in those days interchangeably with *Protestant*. Indeed, delegates who voted against ratification of our Constitution complained that "a Papist or an infidel were as eligible for office as Christians." The term *Christian* did not, in those days, include Catholics.

From 1892 to the present time, the nature of our nation has changed dramatically. The influx of non-Protestant immigrants during the past century has transformed us into the most heterogeneous nation in history.

Modern Supreme Court decisions have recognized this change in our national character. Since 1892, the Court has not referred to this nation as "Christian" or "Protestant." Indeed, the justices have gone out of their way to be inclusive. For example, when Justice William O. Douglas sustained a New York program permitting public school students to be released for an hour each week for religious instruction, he specifically gave as an example of religious accommodation "a Jewish student [asking] his teacher for permission to be excused for Yom Kippur." Yet this was one of the decisions miscited by Justice O'Connor as containing statements to the effect that "this is a Christian nation."

When her letter was disclosed, Justice O'Connor issued a statement regretting that it had been "used in a political debate," and the Supreme Court media office said that O'Connor "had no idea" that the letter would be used politically. But the request to Justice O'Connor made it clear that she was being asked to write her letter specifically for use in the campaign:

"Republicans are making some interesting advances in this heavily controlled Democratic area. Some of us are proposing a resolution which acknowledges that the Supreme Court ruled in 1892 that this is a Christian nation. It would be beneficial and interesting to have a letter from you."

Justice O'Connor's letter was circulated as part of that campaign. Indeed, her miscitation of cases was relied on in the resolution enacted by the Arizona Republican party, which begins, "Whereas the Supreme Court of the United States has holdings to the effect that this is a Christian nation . . ." It then cites the three decisions provided by O'Connor and goes on to declare that we are "a Christian nation," and that the Constitution created "a republic based upon the absolute laws of the Bible, not a democracy."

The kooks are happy. The Ayatollah Khomeini must be smiling. Justice O'Connor should be ashamed of herself for aiding and abetting religious bigotry.
April 1989

Justice O'Connor's decisions on church-state matters have generally favored separation—see for example Lee v. Weisman.

FLAG BURNING IN A FLAG-WAVING SOCIETY

President Bush is seeking to amend the Bill of Rights to overrule the Supreme Court's recent 5–4 decision holding that burning the American flag is protected symbolic speech. The overwhelming majority of Americans are understandably appalled by the burning of our flag. I certainly am. I was brought up to love and respect the American flag and what it stands for. I was also brought up to believe that one of the most important principles it stands for is embodied in the First Amendment's guarantee of freedom of speech—even obnoxious speech.

President Bush declared that burning the American flag is "wrong." He is right. So is racist speech "wrong," along with sexist speech and anti-Semitic speech. (So, too, is "indecent" telephone sex, which the high court also ruled was constitutionally protected if it's not "obscene.") But just because speech is wrong—even disgustingly wrong—is not a proper basis for banning it by law.

There is nothing novel about the view that even appalling speech should not be censored. As Voltaire put it more than two hundred years ago: "I disapprove of what you say, but I will defend to the death your right to say it." The First Amendment to our Constitution was premised on that libertarian article of faith, and under the protection of the First Amendment, we have become the freest nation in history. Winston Churchill once observed: "The United States is a land of free speech. Nowhere is speech freer—not even here [in England], where we sedulously cultivate it, even in its most repulsive form."

Flag burning may well be among the most repulsive forms of speech, but it *is* speech. Just because it is not uttered in words does not deny it the protection of the First Amendment. "Symbolic speech," or communication by symbols, whether that be a black armband to protest a war or the picture of a dead fetus to decry abortion, is powerful communication. No one would seriously argue that a state could constitutionally ban the *waving* of a flag just because no words were used. No words are needed if the symbol is powerful enough.

One of the transforming events in our early history involved symbolic speech. Would we remember the colonists who protested the tax on tea if they had simply given speeches condemning it? They made their point by dumping tea into Boston Harbor. I can imagine King George ordering the arrest of the tea dumpers and arguing, in the words of dissenting Chief Justice William Rehnquist, that the protesters still had "a full panoply of other symbols and every conceivable form of verbal expression to express [their] deep disapproval of national policy." But in a free society, a government should not dictate the form or content of communications critical of its policies.

Burning the flag, obnoxious as it seems to us when the flag is ours, is one of the most powerful and universal forms of symbolic speech. Throughout the world, dissidents have burned flags to protest their countries' policies. During World War II, Americans proudly desecrated the German flag with its symbol of evil, the Nazi swastika. If I owned a Chinese flag today, I would be tempted to burn it in outrage at the recent massacres and executions.

Justice John Paul Stevens in his surprising dissent suggests a false analogy between burning one's own flag and spray painting "graffiti on the Washington Monument." Of course, no one has the right to burn another person's flag, or to spray paint another person's house, but one's own property is different, whether that property is one's flag, one's personal edition of the Constitution, one's copy of Salman Rushdie's novel, or one's picture of the Ayatollah Khomeini.

If the flag is to be exempted from symbolic derision, where would symbolic censorship stop? Would it become a crime to burn our president in effigy, to treat a Bible with disrespect, to fly a flag upside down? If we begin to amend the First Amendment, every special pleader will present his or her pet candidate for exclusion.

The First Amendment has served this country well for nearly two hundred years. It "ain't broke" and we shouldn't try to fix it. Instead, we should heed the wise counsel of Justice William Brennan: "We can imagine no more appropriate response to burning a flag than waving one's own, no better way to counter a flag-burner's message than by saluting the flag that burns, no surer means of preserving the dignity even of the flag that burned than by, as one witness here did, according its remains a respectful burial.

"We do not consecrate the flag by punishing its desecration, for in doing so we dilute the freedom that this cherished emblem represents."

June 1989

In 1990 the Supreme Court, in a 5-4 vote struck down flag burning statutes, and in 1992 the High Court in a vote of 9-0 reversed the hate speech conviction of a "skinhead" who had burned a cross in a black family's front yard.

CENSORS CONSTANTLY HUNT FOR NEW TARGETS

So now the Cincinnati censors are going after museums. The director of the Contemporary Arts Center, which is displaying the photographs of Robert Mapplethorpe, has been indicted, along with the museum itself, on charges of pandering obscenity. The bust was made by the vice squad, which herded out visitors and collected evidence by photographing the photographs. The defendants have pleaded not guilty, and the stage is now set for yet another precedent-setting trial, pitting the forces of censorship against the patrons of art.

It was inevitable that censorship would eventually reach into the museums, and it was all but inevitable that the confrontation would take place in Cincinnati. That divided city is home to both the darkest forces of repression and the most enlightened artistic sensibilities. That is the city which prosecuted Larry Flint for publishing *Hustler* magazine. And it is a city which boasts that it closed down X-rated movies theaters and adult bookstores.

When the target of the Cincinnati censors was tawdry smut, few complaints were heard from the artistic community. Indeed, some prominent feminists joined the campaign against pornography, which they regard as sexist. The success of that campaign laid a firm foundation for a more general regime of censorship. The indictment of the museum is merely the current focus of that regime.

It is not a particularly compelling argument to try to distinguish Mapplethorpe from *Debbie Does Dallas*. Once the door is open to censorship, the alleged artistic merits of a photograph, book, or film is only a matter of degree. Whether it is art, pornography, or both is in the eye of the beholder.

Some of the photographs in the Mapplethorpe exhibit involve nude children. Under the laws of several states, such photographs constitute child pornography. Earlier this month, the U.S. Supreme Court accorded the states enormous power to "protect the victims of child pornography" by destroying the "market for the exploitative use of children." In that case, *Osborne* vs. *Ohio*, the high court ruled that the states could criminalize private possession of child pornography in one's own home.

Nor did the court limit the definition of what a state could consider child pornography. In some states the definition is so broad as to include, in Justice William Brennan's dissenting words, pictures of "teenagers in revealing dresses" or "even of toddlers romping unclothed." Moreover, it is not always possible to know the age of the model or actor. For example, it was recently revealed that film star Traci Lords, currently featured in *Cry-Baby*, had made several X-rated videos before her eighteenth birthday. Under the Supreme Court's decision, a state could punish anyone in possession of those videos.

A state could also extend the law to museum exhibits. After all, even talented artists are capable of exploiting young children. And if the state has the power to censor in order to prevent the exploitation of children, does it not also have the power to prevent the exploitation of women? Many feminists argue that it should.

The point is that the appetite of the voracious censor knows no bounds. Give them the power to ban the worst form of smut, and they will soon be rummaging through our libraries, museums, and homes. Those patrons of the arts who come to the defense only of "true" artists do not understand how censorship works. It works by starting with the worst offenders, establishing precedents in those unchallenged cases, and then moving on to more controversial erotica. The American Civil Liberties Union, which purports to be our last bastion of protection against censorship, seems to be having some difficulty understanding this: It did not file a friend of the court brief in the Osborne case—one of the most significant First Amendment cases in recent memory.

As usual, Justice Brennan did understand. As he put it in his dissent: "When speech is eloquent and the ideas expressed lofty, it is easy to find restrictions on them invalid. But were the First Amendment limited to such discourse, our freedom would be sterile indeed. Mr. Osborne's pictures may be distasteful, but the Constitution guarantees both his right to possess them privately and his right to avoid punishment under an overbroad law."

When I defended porn star Harry Reems, the male lead in *Deep Throat*, against an obscenity conviction, a famous Broadway stage actress drew snickers during Reems's defense fund rally when she warned "Today, Harry Reems. Tomorrow, Helen Hayes!" If you don't believe that, ask the new president of Czechoslovakia, playwright Vaclav Havel, who spent years in a Communist prison for writing words that are now performed all over the world.

For censorship to succeed, all that is required is apathy of the kind shown by the ACLU in the Osborne case and by some patrons of the arts in Cincinnati in earlier disputes. The road to the Contemporary Arts Center begins in Clyde Osborne's basement.   April 1990

THE ADULTERY COPS ARE WATCHING

Our statute books are full of "crimes" that are committed every day by good citizens who consider themselves law-abiding. For example, it's illegal to eat ice cream in public in one New York town. Another city will bust you for jogging topless—even if you're a man! In Boston, they can fine you for shouting "impure language" at an umpire, and in more than half of our states it's a crime to commit adultery.

Recently, one of those states, Wisconsin, decided to get tough on adulteresses. A woman named Donna Carroll was charged with engaging in sex with a man to whom she wasn't married, although at the time she was separated and seeking a divorce from her husband. Her lawyers say she denies making an admission of an extramarital affair.

It happens that this case may be dismissed now that Mrs. Carroll, with no admission of guilt and no criminal liability, has agreed to perform forty hours of community service and attend two months of counseling for parents. If all the adulterers in Wisconsin were put to work for their communities, there'd be no need for paid public servants.

Studies suggest that a very high percentage of married people have sex outside of marriage. An even greater percentage commit technical adultery during the lengthy separations that often precede a final divorce. Indeed, whatever social stigma attaches to adultery during intact marriages certainly does not apply to affairs after the marriage has been terminated in every sense but the legal.

Yet state laws that continue to criminalize adultery make no distinction between intact marriages and those in the process of legal dissolution. The notion seems to be that a person seeking a legal divorce must come into court with clean hands and unsoiled sheets. Or, as some judges have put it, "you may not litigate by day and fornicate by night."

The attempted prosecution in Wisconsin generated a constitutional challenge. The American Civil Liberties Union (ACLU) was assisting Donna Carroll in her defense, arguing that adultery laws invade the sexual privacy of the individual. But I doubt that argument would have prevailed as a matter of constitutional law, since the Supreme Court has generally limited sexual privacy to the marriage bed.

The high court refused, for example, to extend the right of privacy to consenting, adult homosexuals in their own homes. Nor has it ever struck down any of the several state fornication statutes that criminalize all sexual encounters between unmarried adults, thus mandating virginity on the wedding night.

Even in liberal Massachusetts, the state's highest court recently upheld an adultery prosecution against a couple found romping in the back of a van. They were married, but not to each other. The Supreme Judicial Court of Massachusetts solemnly ruled that since "adultery is a ground for divorce," it follows that it can also be made a crime. But consider the implications of that argument: Impotence is also grounds for divorce! Could that be made a crime?

ALAN M. DERSHOWITZ

In Wisconsin, adultery is no longer grounds for divorce. This led the ACLU to argue that it must now follow that adultery can no longer be made a crime. That argument is as silly as the opposite one made by the Massachusetts court. Rape is also not grounds for divorce in some states, but surely it should be a crime, even when committed by a husband against his wife. There is simply no correlation, certainly no direct correlation, between grounds for divorce and criminal conduct.

Adultery should not be a crime because private sexual conduct between, even among, consenting adults, is simply none of the state's business. One does not have to believe that adultery is desirable to support this libertarian approach. Many undesirable acts should not be criminalized in a secular, heterogeneous society. The criminal code is not the Ten Commandments!

Nor do adultery laws work, as evidenced by the high rate of sex outside of marriage. Indeed, it can fairly be said that adultery is the marijuana of marriage. Both adultery and marijuana laws criminalize conduct that is engaged in by millions of otherwise law-abiding citizens. These criminal prohibitions generate a sense of cynicism and hypocrisy about law in general.

No marriage has ever been saved by a law making adultery a crime. And few people have been prevented by law from experimenting with marijuana. The criminal law has enough trouble trying to stop people from killing, raping, and maiming each other. Every law hour wasted trying to enforce one group's personal morality against other adults who disagree with that morality is an hour that would be better devoted to preventing predatory crime.

The courts, especially the Supreme Court, are unlikely to set matters right, so legislative reform is the way to go. But that, too, is uncertain, since many legislators like to posture about sexual morality, especially when their own posture is often prone in the boudoir of a paramour. Even if the votes of adulterers could be marshaled in support of repealing adultery laws, repeal would probably fail.

The righteous hypocrite vote in this country has always been stronger than the vice vote.   May 1990

RELISH OUR FREEDOM TO DESECRATE THE FLAG

During my recent visit to Eastern Europe, I thought a lot about the American flag and liberty. Nothing makes an American prouder of our special heritage than a visit to distant nations struggling to unchain themselves from tyranny and to emulate the United States.

From the balcony of my hotel room in Bucharest, Romania, I saw many flags. They were being waved by students, dissidents, and ordinary citizens. The remarkable thing about these flags was that they had all been desecrated: A large hole had been cut into each to remove the hammer and sickle, the hated symbol of communism. Nicolae Ceausescu, the former dictator of Romania, had been appalled by such desecration.

Now in post-Ceausescu Romania, it is regarded as desecration to place the symbol of communism back onto the Romanian flag. As one student put it: "The Communists desecrated the Romanian flag, and we removed the desecration."

In Moscow, Riga, Vilnius, and Tallinn, flags are being altered, burned, and trampled by some, while others wave them defiantly. The real news is that for the first time in many years, no one is being arrested in the Soviet Union for these attitudes, or even actions, toward the flag. A few short years ago I represented a Soviet woman who faced imprisonment for waving a banner simply requesting that she be allowed to emigrate so she could join her family.

Today in China, Cuba, North Korea, and other bastions of totalitarianism, no one dares to burn a flag or wave a banner of protest. They saw what happened to the students who dared to create a goddess of liberty in Tiananmen Square just a year ago.

Here in America, flag burning was virtually unheard of until opportunistic politicians, led by our president, began to wrap themselves in false patriotism by demanding a constitutional amendment to overrule a recent Supreme Court decision including desecration of one's own flag as within the protection of the First Amendment. A few radical showoffs, seeking their fifteen minutes of fame, responded to this flagomania just as we could expect: They burned a few flags.

Now the Supreme Court has yet another flag-burning case before it. There is no good legal reason why this case should come out any differently from the last one. The facts are exactly the same. The justices are the same.

And the Constitution hasn't changed. Although the new statute is somewhat different from the one declared unconstitutional, the changes are not significant.

But the Supreme Court is a political institution, despite disclaimers to the contrary. I can easily imagine a justice who voted with the 5–4 majority in the last case thinking that a constitutional amendment would be even worse than a Supreme Court decision allowing flag burners to be punished. After all, Supreme Court decisions can be overruled in years to come. But constitutional amendments are generally for keeps.

That kind of "judicial Realpolitik" has determined the outcome of several cases during our constitutional history. Several justices switched their votes on the constitutionality of the New Deal to blunt the pressure for President Roosevelt's "court-packing" plan. The plan would have increased the size of the high court above the traditional nine in order to allow the president to appoint enough new justices to determine the outcome of his New Deal cases. This drastic turnabout in the voting of several justices has been called "the switch in time that saved nine."

It would be a tragic mistake for the justices to allow their votes to be influenced by some calculation about the relative harms of a constitutional amendment versus those of a bad decision. The constitutional amending process is an explicit part of our political system. We have resisted many phony political amendments over the years, and it is certainly possible that we can resist this one as well. But if the forces of censorship and imposed patriotism are to prevail, it is far better that they prevail as part of an explicitly political process than as a result of a cynical manipulation of the judicial process.

Before our justices or politicians vote to criminalize the desecration of the flag, they should visit Eastern Europe. Then they should ask themselves whether it is better to live in a country where people want to burn the flag but cannot, or in a country where people are free to burn the flag but do not. At a time when America is rightfully demanding that other countries free their political prisoners, it would be a hypocritical tragedy if we began to make political prisoners out of American flag burners.　　　May 1990

PROTECT RAP MUSIC AND
FLAG BURNING

I detest rap music, and I despise flag burning. Yet I believe that both should remain constitutionally protected forms of expression.

I find rap deliberately confrontational, often violent, sexist, racist, anti-Semitic, and scatological. It is poor poetry set to even worse music—if that's what the sing-song beat purports to be. Rap music gives me a headache and gets me angry.

But then, I am not its intended audience. Rap music appeals largely to young, alienated, urban black males. Part of its appeal to that audience is that it is supposed to frighten people like me.

It is no coincidence, therefore, that the Florida censors are going after 2 Live Crew, a particularly scatological rap group. Earlier, there were efforts to stop the sale of anti-Semitic recordings made by Public Enemy, another rap group.

There are no laws against anti-Semitic or racist speech. But there are statutes that criminalize "obscene" publications or performances. That is why 2 Live Crew has become the first group in recent memory to have its recordings seized and two of its members arrested.

But attempting to apply obscenity laws to rap music is somewhat racist. The language of rap is certainly no dirtier than that heard nightly by millions of Americans on cable comedy shows and clubs around the country. Like it or not, dirty words have become the staple of stand-up comedy. As with comedy, rap is both entertainment and politics. And the use of dirty words can be an attention-grabbing way of enhancing the political message.

In 1971, the U.S. Supreme Court decided a landmark case involving an antiwar protester who decided to make his political statement by wearing a jacket with the words *F---the draft*.

The opinion reversing his conviction was written by one of the high court's great conservative justices, John M. Harlan, Jr.—a stuffy man of prissy tastes and proper upbringing. His words have particular application to the current controversy over rap: "While the particular four-letter word being litigated here is perhaps more distasteful than most others of its genre, it is nevertheless often true that one man's vulgarity is another's lyric."

Why, then, are the censors picking on the rap musicians rather than the equally dirty comedians? I believe it is because there is something frightening to many whites about the very genre of rap music. It has a quality of "in your face" provocation. Whites worry that the largely black audience will act on the "dangerous" messages contained in the lyrics. It is "their" music, and it is directed against "us."

There is no comparable fear of dirty comedians. "We" are their audience—if not we ourselves, then our children. We may not like dirty comedy, but at least we understand it. And by understanding it, we can dismiss it as mere entertainment, not to be taken seriously.

But "we" don't understand rap music, because it's not our genre. And because we don't understand it, it frightens us. We don't quite know how to deal with it. And so we try to censor it.

Of course, censorship almost always backfires. Since the arrests of the 2 Live Crew band members, my son and my nephew have bought the banned CD. They, like numerous others who don't ordinarily listen to rap, want to know what all the fuss is about. "Banned in Boston" was always more of an advertisement than an effective means of censorship.

But the dangers of governmental censorship are real. The voracious appetite of the censor is never satisfied. If rap musicians can be legally prosecuted, the comedians may well be next. And then the Broadway playwrights and novelists who use dirty words.

The history of censorship shows that the censor always goes after the most offensive stuff first. Having then established a precedent, he (and, increasingly, she) then goes after less offensive but equally "obscene" material. If you don't like 2 Live Crew, don't listen to their rap. Prosecuting them only gives the music more listeners and the censor more power.

This brings us to the flag burners. Fortunately, we live in a country where nobody—except a tiny number of fringe lunatics—wants to burn our flag. Old Glory, unlike the flags of some other nations, has *earned* the respect of our citizens. We don't *need* legally enforced patriotism. I hope that our legislators, who are under pressure to amend the First Amendment on the eve of its two hundredth birthday, will appreciate how much better it is to live in a country, like our own, where people have the right to burn flags but choose not to, than in a country like China where people want to burn the flag but have no right to.

As political prisoners are freed all over Eastern Europe and even in South Africa, it would be a tragedy for our nation to begin to imprison misguided dissidents who burn flags and outrageous musicians who use dirty words.   June 1990

CAN TOWN OFFICIALS BUMP
NC-17 MOVIES?

When the Motion Picture Association of America came up with its movie rating system back in 1968, it tried to make it clear that its ratings were not designed as an aid for governmental censorship. The sole function of the ratings is to "offer advisory cautionary warnings . . . so that parents can make their own decisions about what movies their young children should or should not see."

Indeed, the Supreme Court has ruled that a rating system that employs vague criteria such as the ones used by the Motion Picture Association cannot constitutionally be used as a basis for governmental censorship. The government may censor *only* films that meet the rigorous criteria for legal obscenity.

Despite the Supreme Court's ruling, several cities have insisted that their theaters not show X-rated films. Until recently, the X rating was given by the Motion Picture Association to films with heavy sexual content, such as *Last Tango in Paris*. Occasionally, the X was given to films with unusually graphic violence.

In the public mind, however, the X rating has long been associated with hard-core pornography. Indeed, pornographers advertise that their films are X or even XXX, without even submitting them for an official rating to the association. This is possible because the Motion Picture Association, which had received copyright protection for their other ratings—G, PG, PG13, and R—had failed to copyright the X rating. Anyone is free to use it, and the pornographers do.

Several weeks ago, I was asked to represent the film *Henry and June*, which had received an X rating from the association. That rating threatened to be a box-office death sentence for an artistic film about literary life in pre–World War II Paris, which had received wonderful reviews. Because of the X rating, many theaters would refuse to show it. Television stations and newspapers would refuse to advertise it. Some video-rental stores would refuse to stock it. And many patrons would be frightened away by the prospect of seeing hard-core pornography, despite the reality that there was no close-up portrayal of sex or even frontal nudity.

I was asked to appeal the X rating within the Motion Picture Association of America. In our brief, we argued that an X rating for this film would misinform viewers and that the film should either get an R rating or that the association should come up with a new rating for adult films that were not pornographic. Throughout Europe, *Henry and June* has received ratings enabling it to be seen by general audiences.

As our appeal was being submitted, the Motion Picture Association decided to add a new rating—NC-17, which means that no children under the age of seventeen will be admitted. In response to our appeal, the association announced that *Henry and June* would be the first film to receive that new rating.

As a result of this change of rating, most theaters have decided to show the film, and most television stations and newspapers are advertising it. But two selectmen in the town of Dedham, Massachusetts, were not satisfied. A local theater was scheduled to show the film to adults-only audiences. The two selectmen pressured the theater to cancel the showing on the grounds that the theater had "an agreement" with the town that it would not show X-rated films, and that since *Henry and June* had originally received an X rating, it was covered by the agreement.

Although their town councilors had not themselves seen the film, they were convinced that it would not be suitable for viewing by adults in their town. Other town councilors disagreed, and a majority sent a letter to the theater disclaiming any desire to censor. But the theater still refuses to show the film, thus relegating the adult citizens of Dedham to movies that are suitable for children only. (Ironically, the theater substituted the violent movie *Darkman* or *Henry and June.*)

No town—or town official—has the constitutional right to pressure a theater into canceling the showing of a constitutionally protected film. Any theater has the right, of course, to decide on which films it will and will not show. But neither the town nor its officials may place the heavy thumb of government on the theater owner's decision.

If the town believes that a film is legally obscene, it may seek protection from the courts. If a town concludes that a film is unsuitable for children, it has legal recourse as well. But no city or town may use the advisory rating system of a private association—and the Motion Picture Association of America is a private association of major movie studios—as a basis for governmental censorship.

It remains to be seen how other cities and towns around the nation deal with the NC-17 rating. Thus far, most seem to be complying with the intent of the Motion Picture Association of America: denying admission to children under seventeen but allowing adults to make their own decisions about whether to see the film.   October 1990

FIRST AMENDMENT LOSES IN OBSCENITY CASES

First Amendment supporters are applauding the jury verdicts in the 2 Live Crew and Mapplethorpe cases. A jury in Broward County unanimously acquitted the rap band of obscenity charges growing out of an adults-only concert in the Fort Lauderdale area. And another jury unanimously acquitted the director of Cincinnati's Contemporary Arts Center of obscenity charges for exhibiting photographs of the late Robert Mapplethorpe, which were homoerotic in nature.

A collective sigh of relief could be heard throughout the entertainment and art communities, following these verdicts. But the headlines should have been of the good news/bad news variety.

The good news was that two juries, composed of ordinary Americans whose tastes did not veer toward rap music or homoerotic photography, understood that freedom of speech includes the freedom of adults to choose to listen to and view material that most Americans dislike and many find offensive. The bad news is that these cases were submitted to juries at all.

The freedom of Americans to read, listen, view, speak, sing, or tell jokes should not be subject to the majority vote of anyone: not a jury, not a legislature, not even a plebiscite of all the people. The First Amendment is essentially an undemocratic—indeed antidemocratic—restriction on majority power. If any Americans wish to satisfy their intellectual, emotional, or artistic needs by exposing themselves to expression that all other Americans despise, that should be their right under the First Amendment.

Obviously, my right to swing my fist ends at the tip of your nose. No American has the right to exercise freedom of speech in a manner that directly harms another. But "harm" does not include merely being offended by the knowledge that someone else is enjoying art or literature that offends you. Although we began as a Puritan nation, our Constitution does not incorporate H. L. Mencken's definition of Puritanism as "the haunting fear that someone, somewhere, may be happy." Under our First Amendment, we may not concern ourselves with how other people enjoy themselves, unless they harm us in the process.

One unfortunate exception to this constitutional rule is obscenity. Under a series of Supreme Court rulings, the government has the power to prevent its citizens from enjoying obscenity. Even when it comes to adult obscenity, however, the government may not enter the home of its citizens and tell them what they may read or see in the privacy of their libraries or video-rooms.

But public performances are different, even if they are limited to consenting adults—hence the obscenity prosecutions against 2 Live Crew and Cincinnati's Contemporary Arts Center, which resulted in jury acquittals. But these cases reflect a dangerous precedent: namely, that it is constitutionally permissible to subject controversial art to the vagaries of a jury. This time the juries acquitted. Next time, they may convict. Indeed, another jury in Broward County did convict a record-store owner of selling the 2 Live Crew record that formed the basis for their concert. And who knows how the Cincinnati jury would have ruled if the same Mapplethorpe photographs had been exhibited in a gay sex shop rather than an elitist art museum.

The jurors who acquitted 2 Live Crew and the museum director are not the type of Americans who frequent rap concerts or erotic art exhibits. Why should they be the ones to decide whether other Americans—with different tastes, backgrounds, and values—should be allowed to hear and see what they have chosen as their forms of entertainment or stimulation?

Jury verdicts do not establish legal precedents. They are like limited train tickets: for this day and this train only. Any future jury is entirely free to ignore the acquittals in Florida and Ohio. What does establish a legal precedent is the decision of the two judges to allow the cases to reach a jury. And those are dangerous precedents under our First Amendment.

The paradox of our First Amendment is that it is intended to be an undemocratic check on majority rule, and yet it often relies on the democratic check of trial by jury. That places enormous responsibility on prosecutors not to abuse their power and trust by bringing cases that should never have been brought. Prosecutors such as those in Broward County and Cincinnati often use sensational obscenity prosecutions as reputation makers with conservative elements in the community. The appropriate check on such prosecutorial abuse should be the judges. But judges, too, especially when they are elected, often lack the courage to dismiss improper prosecutions, thus leaving it to the anonymous jury to protect the First Amendment.

In addition to prosecutors and judges benefiting politically from obscenity prosecutions, those who are subject to censorship often benefit as well: 2 Live Crew increased its sales dramatically as a result of these prosecutions, and attendance was way up at Cincinnati's Contemporary Arts Center after the prosecution was announced. The real loser in these cases is the First Amendment and the American citizens who depend on it for their freedoms.   October 1990

DON'T CENSOR VANESSA REDGRAVE

Vanessa Redgrave is once again the victim of political blacklisting. According to news reports, the talented but politically controversial actress has been dropped from a national theatrical tour of the British comedy *Lettuce and Lovage* because of statements she made in support of Saddam Hussein and against the presence of "U.S., British, and all imperialist troops" in the Gulf.

Back in 1982, the Boston Symphony Orchestra canceled a scheduled performance of Stravinsky's "Oedipus Rex," in which Redgrave had contracted to perform the role of narrator. The cancellation came after several musicians in the orchestra refused to perform with her, and after numerous subscribers and board members threatened to cancel their season tickets and contributions. Redgrave sued the Boston Symphony and eventually lost, but many civil libertarians were upset with the orchestra's decision to mix art and politics.

It is ironic that Vanessa Redgrave should be the focal point of a debate over blacklisting and over the propriety of mixing art and politics, since she herself has urged artists to engage in blacklisting and to mix art and politics. In 1978 and again in 1986, Redgrave tried to get the British Actors Union to blacklist Israeli artists and to boycott Israeli audiences. She approved as "entirely correct" the blacklisting of Zionist speakers at English universities. And she has even justified the political assassination of Israeli artists, because they "may well have been enlisted . . . to do the work of the Zionists."

Redgrave's political views are extremist and border on bigotry. She has described the American film industry as "Zionist dominated"—an obvious euphemism for controlled by "the Jews." She has called Zionism a "universal threat," comparable to "Nazism." And she has said that there is no "room for a state of Israel."

Redgrave has also expressed hatred for the United States and for our form of government, preferring a radical Marxist vision of violent revolution. She is one of the leaders of the Trotskyite Worker's Revolutionary Party, which has received significant financial support from Libyan leader Muammar Qaddafi and from the Palestinian Liberation Organization. In exchange for these payments, her party has agreed to provide intelligence information to Libya on the activities of Jews in the British government, industry, and communications. Her party, which purports to be on the left, has also collaborated with extremist right-wing groups, such as the National Front, in joint anti-Jewish and anti-Zionist activities.

It is not surprising, therefore, that Vanessa Redgrave's politics would not receive curtain calls from American audiences familiar with her activities off-stage. But her performances on-stage generally receive rave reviews, and she does fill the theaters in which she performs. The decision to cancel her national tour cannot therefore be justified as a purely economic one. It is primarily a political decision based on strong disapproval of her politics.

Those who canceled her tour will argue that there were economic considerations as well. But that is always the argument in blacklisting cases. During the McCarthy years, the movie and television blacklisters justified their censorship on economic grounds, arguing that audiences would stay away from shows featuring "Fifth Amendment Communists" or "fellow travelers." And there may even be some truth to that argument, though it is largely a self-fulfilling prophecy. But the principles of artistic and political freedom are too important to be compromised on the altar of box-office grosses.

Let the marketplace operate. Those, like me, who cannot abide Redgrave's politics are free to stay home when she speaks or even when she acts. But as long as there are those willing to fill the theaters in which she appears, they should not be denied that right.

Vanessa Redgrave's political views should be debated, rebutted, and defeated in the marketplace of ideas. But she and her audiences should not be punished artistically for the absurdity of her political ideas.

Nor is it a persuasive argument to point to Redgrave's own hypocrisy in calling for blacklisting, censorship, and the punishment of other artists for their political views. People who love freedom should not want to live by Vanessa Redgrave's totalitarian vision of Big Brother and Big Sister. The true test of liberty is our willingness to grant it to those who would deny it to us. But as we grant it, we should not make heroes of all those victimized by censorship, unless they are deserving of such status—as Redgrave is surely not. H. L. Mencken once observed that fighting for freedom requires the defense of some of the worst people. That is the spirit in which I defend Redgrave's right to perform.

Vanessa Redgrave is a naive fool, a nasty hypocrite, and a great actress. The American public is fully capable of distinguishing between her enormous talent in reciting lines written by others and her inability to write intelligible political speeches or programs. We do not need private or public censors keeping Redgrave off the stage or soapbox in order to protect us from her views.   February 1991

SOUTER'S VOTE IS A FOOLISH FIG LEAF

Supreme Court Justice David Souter has apparently discovered how to put the oldest profession out of business, prevent one of the most heinous of crimes, and discourage other assorted criminal behavior. The panacea for prostitution, rape, and other crimes is so simple! How could the rest of us have been so oblivious to it over the millennia? It is also so cheap—as might be expected from a fiscally frugal New Hampshirite. All it takes for a community to address these serious evils is to dress its local strippers in pasties and G-strings. For those of you not old enough to remember Gypsy Rose Lee and the golden age of the striptease, these accoutrements are the teeny-tiny bits of sequin strategically fitted over the otherwise naked female body to cover the "dirty" parts. (The biological fact that these are life-giving and nurturing parts has not changed the legal conclusion that their display, even to consenting adults, may make the difference between obscenity that can be banned and constitutionally protected expression.)

The occasion for Justice Souter's essay on crime prevention was a case from South Bend, Ind., whose town mothers and fathers decided to require their ecdysiasts to don G-strings and pasties before they were permitted to express themselves at local bars, strip joints, and other places of adult entertainment.

Three of the dancers challenged the Indiana law, complaining that it violated their constitutional right of free expression. Telling them what to wear, even if it was as *de minimis* as the dots and strings required by the law, denied them the right to convey the emotional and erotic message that total nudity allowed them.

The women won their case before the U.S. Court of Appeals. That should have been the end of the matter, since the Supreme Court routinely declines to hear about 98 percent of the cases brought to it for review. This case was a perfect candidate for leaving matters as they stood. Surely no great issue of constitutional principle need turn on whether a lower court was right or wrong in refusing to draw a constitutional distinction between total nudity and near-total nudity. The foundations of the republic would not crumble if pasties were required in some states and not in others. But something motivated the justices to allocate their valuable high court time— they are always whining about how overcrowded their docket is—to an adolescent schoolyard debate over whether pasties make a stripper more or less erotic.

In the course of this demeaning debate, three justices—led by Chief Justice William Rehnquist—concluded that nude barroom dancing is only "marginally" within "the outer perimeters" of the First Amendment. Thus marginalized, nude dancing could be regulated to protect the state's interest in protecting "morality."

Justice Antonin Scalia had even less of a problem upholding the Indiana pasty law. For him, nude dancing is strictly conduct and not at all speech. I wonder what he would have said to the American patriots who dumped tea into Boston Harbor, believing they were expressing, in a uniquely dramatic manner, their political opposition to the British tax on tea. Moreover, it is enough for Scalia that there is a "traditional moral belief that people should not expose their private parts indiscriminately, regardless of whether those who see them are disedified." What will he say to a ballet or modern dancer who expresses his or her art sans leotard, as is the fashion among some great choreographers? And what about the naked—and silent—sculptures in museums across the country: Are they not speech, and will Senator Jesse Helms be allowed to cover up their marble genitals with marble fig leaves and pasties?

Four other justices—White, Marshall, Blackmun, and Stevens—

agreed with the lower court and found the Indiana law an unconstitutional restriction on erotic expression. That left the new justice, Souter, as the deciding vote.

Drawing on his vast experience as a man of the world, the quiet New Hampshire bachelor wrote his first exegesis on the First Amendment. He concluded that the display of "specified anatomical areas" may well "produce" such crimes as prostitution and rape. Nor is the state required to produce any "proof" of this rather dubious connection It is certainly possible, he opines, that "the higher incidence of prostitution and sexual assaults in the vicinity of adult entertainment locations results from the concentration of crowds of men predisposed to such activities"—a very likely explanation. But it is also possible, he continues, that these crimes are caused by "the simple viewing of nude bodies . . ."

Justice Souter does not address the question of how either of these alleged causal links would be broken by dressing the women in sequin pasties and G-strings. The high court's conclusion that states may require strippers to cover up "specified anatomical areas" will not change anything. But its illogic may be dangerous to your liberties.   July 1991

It is noteworthy that Justice Souter joined the majority which subsequently reversed the conviction of a "skinhead" who burned a cross on a black family's property.

4 // *Intolerance on the Left*

THE ROAD TO TOTALITARIANISM IS PAVED WITH GOOD INTENTIONS

It is so easy to fight against censorship by bad people who seek to use it to bring about bad results. And it is so difficult to fight against censorship by good people who seek to use it to bring about good results.

This is particularly true of the current battle for the hearts, souls, and minds of college and university students. Lacking a historical memory, many young students are impatient with falsity. They *know* that racism, sexism, homophobia, anti-Semitism, and other forms of bigotry are false and evil. Why then must these evils be tolerated on the altar of some abstraction labeled freedom of speech? I see the sincerity on the faces of students as they ask this question. But it is no different from the sincerity on the faces of religious zealots who cannot understand why we tolerate the evil falsity of atheism, evolution, or abortion, which they *know* are wrong.

The marketplace of ideas is an uncomfortable and wasteful metaphor for those who *know* the difference between true ideas and false ones. Yet the alternatives are so self-evidently dangerous to all sides. Once the state or the university arrogates to itself the power to define what is true and false—what is politically correct and incorrect—a static inertia settles in. That is why those who have a strong stake in whatever status happens to be quo at any given time are often tempted into making the case for censorship.

But the good intentions of the censors should not lull us into inaction. Some of the worst abuse comes from those with the best of intentions. Not only is the road to hell paved with such intentions, but so is the road to the gulag and the gas chamber. As Justice Louis Brandeis put it sixty-five years ago:

. . . Experience should teach us to be most on our guard to protect liberty when the Government's purposes are beneficent. Men born to freedom are naturally alert to repel invasion of their liberty by evil-minded rulers. The greatest dangers to liberty lurk in insidious encroachment by men of zeal, well-meaning but without understanding.

Little seems to have changed since 1927 when it comes to the need to defend freedom of speech from men and women of zeal, well meaning but without historical understanding.   July 1992

PORNOGRAPHY PROTEST HAS NO REAL BEEF

After years of picketing, distributing leaflets, and demonstrating against others, I myself have finally become the object of a protest. Each Sunday morning a group called Women's Alliance Against Pornography parades in front of a kosher delicatessen in Harvard Square called Mavin's Kosher Court.

Now what, you may be asking, does a kosher delicatessen have to do with pornography? I wondered about that myself, until I saw the leaflet that was being handed out by the picketers. "Can a Pig Serve Kosher Meat?" was the probing question posed by the protesters. You see, I am a partner, along with a dozen or so others, in this newly opened establishment, and the protest is being directed against me.

I am the "pig" because I have been the lawyer for people charged with pornography offenses. Everyone is entitled to a defense, say the protesters, except those charged with pornography.

The leaflet describes me as "Pornography's Pal." If I am pornography's pal because of those whom I have represented, then I suppose I am also the "pal" of Nazis, Communists, the Palestine Liberation Organization, Holocaust deniers, the CIA, Vanessa Redgrave, the cigarette industry, pro- and antiabortion activists, Louis Farrakhan, and other assorted kooks and causes whose right of free speech I have advocated for a quarter of a century in and out of court.

I am, in fact, the "pal" of the freedom of American adults *to choose*—

what to read, what to listen to, what to do with their bodies, and what to do with their lives. I am the "pal" of the freedom of choice that allows a woman who wants an abortion to have one, and the woman who does not want an abortion to refuse one. I am the "pal" of the freedom of choice that permits every adult to choose a homosexual, heterosexual, or nonsexual life-style. I am the "pal" of the freedom of choice that allows everyone to practice their religion or irreligion.

I am the enemy of governmental coercion, especially in the areas of expression and belief. I know that if we submit to the demands of any censorship group, whether it be feminist censors, Jewish censors, black censors, gay censors, or fundamentalist censors, it will become far more difficult to mount a principled opposition to the equally righteous demands of others who would be censors.

Deep down, nearly everyone would like to censor something. Our First Amendment protects us from becoming a nation in which every offended group gets a veto over speech and the power to shut down offending stalls in the marketplace of ideas. It used to be said that if every group got to censor even one item of offensive speech, nothing would be left except Mary Poppins; but recently a group in San Francisco came out against Mary Poppins because it reflects "colonialist" attitudes.

Those who are picketing our deli do not seem to realize that even the right to picket is recognized by comparatively few nations. In many parts of the world, protesters, even dignified, peaceful protesters, go to jail for expressing their beliefs. Several years ago, I was part of the legal defense team assembled on behalf of a courageous woman named Ida Nudl, a Jewish refusnik in the Soviet Union who was sent to the gulag for displaying a sign that read "KGB, let me join my family in Israel."

Some of those in the recent Pastrami Protest were not even dignified. They were shouting the word *pimp* at me, as I asked the leaders to debate the issue of censorship and pornography. Again, I explained that in most countries, including such civilized ones as Canada, falsely shouting "pimp" would be a punishable offense. I assured them that I would defend their right to call me anything they chose or to urge potential patrons to boycott our deli, as they were doing.

The leader of the protesters, who refuses to debate on grounds that "pornography is not a debatable issue," has acknowledged that her group is "using" the occasion of our newly opened deli. It is resuming its moribund campaign in favor of a Cambridge referendum that would give women the power to go to court and secure legally enforceable injunctions against sexually explicit material that, in the view of the judge, "subordinates" women. Such a referendum was defeated in a previous election. A similar referendum, enacted in Indianapolis, was struck down as unconstitutional by a unanimous Court of Appeals and a unanimous Supreme Court—both composed of several Reagan appointees.

But neither the will of the Cambridge voters nor the voice of our highest courts has discouraged the zealots of censorship. They continue to march, though not a single patron has apparently been persuaded to boycott our pastrami.

Our patrons, like most Americans, seem to realize that the price of liberty is the right of some adults to choose to read or see "offensive" material, and that offensiveness is in the eye of the beholder. Those who choose not to be offended have a relatively simple option: to mind their own business and not read the magazines or see the movies that so upset them. No one has the right to force anyone to read, see, or perform pornography, just as no one has the right to force anyone to eat pastrami, corned beef, or hot dogs.

So long as consenting adults wish to indulge either in pornography, pastrami, or the picketing of either, I will be there defending personal choice.   June 1988

Maven's deli has since closed—but not because of the picketers.

FIRST AMENDMENT PROTECTS RIGHT WING, TOO

The *Dartmouth Review* is a right-wing, highly opinionated, and racially insensitive—some say racist—journal published off-campus by Dartmouth College students. A few of its reporters and editors have engaged in provocative, even outrageous, behavior in the name of adversarial journalism. To professors with long memories, their style is reminiscent of some radicals of the left who made life miserable for college administrators in the late sixties and early seventies.

Not surprisingly, Dartmouth College was finally provoked to the point of suspending several students associated with the *Review*. The specific incident leading up to the suspension was also reminiscent of left-wing activism of a generation ago: There were allegations of harassment, shouting, pushing, and shoving—in addition to claims of "vexatious," "aggressive," and "confrontational" speech. As is usual in such cases, there is agreement over the broad outlines of what happened but disagreement over specifics, such as who pushed whom first.

The agreed-upon facts are as follows: In February, the *Dartmouth Review* published a scathing criticism of the teaching of a black professor of music named William Cole. The article included allegedly verbatim quotes from the professor, which a student had taped during the class. To put it mildly, the professor's own words on tape were pretty damning. They included the use of derogatory terms against white students, women, and others.

Much of the class seemed to be devoted to amateurish political ranting against the various evils of society. I'm sure some of the students love this kind of "teaching," but others feel they are wasting their tuition, paying for what they could learn for free from Phil Donahue and Oprah Winfrey. Surely a student journal should be free to report critically on a controversial professor's teaching.

Shortly after the publication of the article, four members of the *Dartmouth Review* entered a classroom in which Professor Cole had just finished teaching his course. Their ostensible purpose for confronting the professor was to give him an opportunity to respond to the article and to apologize to *Review* members for obscenities he had called them. It would not be unreasonable to infer that they also intended to provoke the professor and to rub salt in the wound recently opened by their article. They came into the class armed with the tools of ambush journalism: a tape recorder and a camera.

The rest of the story is disputed, as these stories often tend to be. The *Review* editors claim that the professor started the shouting and shoving. The professor claims that the editors harassed him and violated his privacy.

The students were disciplined by the college's committee on standards, and three of them were suspended from school. One was found guilty "because he initiated and persisted in a vexatious oral exchange" with the professor after class. Another was suspended "because he was repeatedly aggressive, confrontational, and particularly vexatious in demanding an apology from Professor Cole in a raised voice."

The third was punished "because he repeatedly photographed Professor Cole, despite Professor Cole's repeated objections to being photographed and repeated requests to leave his classroom." (The class was over at the time.) One was also found guilty of tape recording a portion of the exchange between the students and the professor, though he turned off the recorder when Professor Cole asked him to. (The suspended president of the *Review* was hired to work in Senator Dan Quayle's Washington office.)

Not surprisingly, the students have not taken their suspensions sitting down. They and the *Dartmouth Review* have filed a lawsuit. The students sought support for their free-speech claims from the American Civil Liberties Union, but the New Hampshire branch of the ACLU declined to get involved in the case.

In contrast, the ACLU has repeatedly come to the aid of left-wing students who have been disciplined by private colleges under similar circumstances. In nearly all of those cases, there have been claims of harassment, invasion of privacy, and other misbehavior ancillary to the speech itself. The college invariably denies that the students are being punished for their speech alone.

Generally, the ACLU takes no position on the nonspeech aspects of such cases, but it does become involved, either as attorney or friend of the court, in opposing the punishment of speech. And in this case, the students were suspended, at least in part, because of their speech.

I have no doubt that if these were left-wing students being suspended on identical grounds, the ACLU would be in this case—Bill of Rights in hand—arguing against the punishment of students on such vague grounds as "vexatious," "aggressive," and "confrontational" speech. Both the ACLU and the Bill of Rights lose credibility when a double standard is applied, depending on the politics of those whose speech is punished.

Many of those who have come to the defense of the *Dartmouth Review* are also applying a double standard: They actively support censorship of speech with which they disagree. But the First Amendment does not protect only those who would apply it equally to others.

Now when my right-wing friends tell me that "a conservative is a liberal who's been mugged," I will be ready with a new rejoinder: "And a civil libertarian is a conservative whose magazine has been censored."

September 1988

ALAN M. DERSHOWITZ

SITCOM VIGILANTE SENDS A BAD MESSAGE

I used to like the TV sitcom "Designing Women" until I watched a recent episode that presented one of the most irresponsible civic lessons about self-righteous vigilantism I have ever seen on prime-time TV.

The premise of the episode was that Julia Sugarbaker, the oldest and most "responsible" member of the group of Southern women designers, became offended by a poster exhibited at the local newsstand. The offensive poster (which wasn't visible to the audience) apparently showed a woman dressed in rubber wearing some sort of dog collar. It was supposed to be a promotion for a *Playboy*-type magazine published by a woman who claimed to be a feminist.

The show was boringly preachy about the evils of "pornography," making it sound as if magazines like *Playboy* are not as fully protected by the First Amendment as sitcoms are. It misinformed its viewers about the scope of the First Amendment, suggesting that freedom of speech does not cover visual and photographic expression, but only verbal ideas.

And it wasn't very funny, apparently having decided to sacrifice comedy for propaganda. But that is hardly my complaint, since many current sitcoms have taken to moralizing instead of entertaining.

My complaint is about the message conveyed by the episode. Julia decides that the appropriate response to the poster is not to try to persuade the newsstand owner to remove it, or even to bring legal action. Instead, she deliberately crashes her car into the poster (and the newsstand)—not once, but three times—causing significant damage.

For this malicious destruction of property and vigilante censorship, she is lamely criticized by one of her co-workers but widely applauded by the studio audience.

I wonder how many women in the audience would have cheered had an offended right-to-life vigilante driven her car into the lobby of an abortion clinic or knocked down a poster for Planned Parenthood. Julia surely was offended by the offensive poster. But so are those who sincerely believe that abortion and birth control are immoral. So are Cat Stevens and Ayatollah Khomeini by Salman Rushdie's novel.

The difference between a heterogeneous democracy like ours and a conformist tyranny like Iran's is that, in America, being offended is not a justification for vigilante censorship. Members of the Ku Klux Klan are offended by interracial marriage. That does not allow them to disrupt an interracial wedding as an act of civil disobedience.

We must learn to live with a certain level of offensiveness as the price for our heterogeneity and our democracy. Of course, everyone supports freedom of speech when they agree with the message. The true test of one's adherence to the First Amendment is tolerance of speech that is offensive.

The lesson of intolerance taught by the "Designing Women" episode will surely have an impact on viewers. Both the preachy writer who scripted the episode and I agree on one thing: Speech, whether visual or verbal, does affect attitudes and conduct. Sexism and violence in pornography, as well as in mainstream and Main Street media, may well have an impact on the attitudes and actions of some viewers. But so might vigilante sitcoms.

It would not surprise me to learn that some viewers of the episode now feel justified in their desire to burn, or otherwise destroy, pornographic or other material that offends them.

Several years ago in my town, Cambridge, Mass., an antiporn vigilante fired a bullet through the window of one of our finest book and magazine shops to protest the sale of *Playboy* and *Penthouse*, and to frighten away readers. That fanatical censor probably was among those cheering most loudly for Julia. I hope our armed Cambridge Crusader doesn't again aim her gun (or her car) at the bookstore after being egged on by Julia's antics and the positive audience response to them.

In a neighboring town, Brookline, the powers that be have decided to file a RICO (Racketeer Influenced and Corrupt Organization) lawsuit against Operation Rescue, a group of antiabortion fanatics who have repeatedly engaged in acts of civil disobedience in an effort to prevent women from securing abortions.

Under a theory similar to that concocted by the Brookline town fathers and mothers, Julia could also have been guilty of violating the RICO law, since she repeatedly engaged in violent conduct to extort the newsstand owner to stop exhibiting the offensive, but constitutionally protected, poster.

Julia had many alternatives available to demonstrate her criticism of the poster. She could have handed out leaflets criticizing the newsstand or tried to organize a consumer boycott of the magazine—thus exercising her own freedom of speech. She even could have tried to change the zoning laws to move the newsstand out of her neighborhood (though that would invite right-to-lifers to zone abortion clinics out of their neighborhoods). But Julia did not have the right to engage in vigilante lawlessness.

I have no wish to censor any episode of "Designing Women," though

I was as offended by Julia's vigilante censorship as Julia was by the poster. My response is this column. It's a lot more constructive and more consistent with American traditions of tolerance than crashing a car into a newsstand.

The best answer to bad speech is good speech, not vigilante censorship.

June 1989

LEFT SAYS "NO COMMENT" ON CHINA MASSACRE

As most of the civilized world reacted with horror, and condemnation, to the Chinese massacre on Tiananmen Square, a resounding chorus of silence came from much of the extreme left, both American and international.

On the Wednesday and Thursday following the weekend massacre, I had my associate call a number of those who are most vocal in condemning the United States, Israel, and other Western democracies whenever they deviate even slightly from the highest norms of human rights. Not surprisingly, several of these perennial democracy-bashers were unavailable for comment: They were indisposed, incommunicado, incognito, incoherent, in the bathroom, or in Timbuktu.

But my associate did reach a fairly representative sample of the usually irrepressible and cacophonous left. Not a single one was prepared to condemn the Chinese government for shooting down and running over hundreds of unarmed students who died for democracy.

Countercultural lawyer William Kunstler, who has repeatedly condemned the United States and our allies, had nothing to say about the Chinese crackdown. His office told my associate that he would have no comment. This is entirely consistent with Kunstler's long-expressed policy of never condemning "socialist" regimes, lest his condemnation lend support to the "red baiting" of the reactionary right.

Similarly Noam Chomsky, the linguist who immodestly describes himself as a defender of all "underdogs," apparently does not consider unarmed students to be underdogs when they are supported by the running dogs of the fascist right. Chomsky, who rarely sees a day go by without some joyful condemnation of Western democracies and who has defended Holocaust deniers against charges of anti-Semitism, has been silent about China.

The Palestine Liberation Organization, which does not hesitate to intrude into the internal affairs of Israel by violence, refused to take sides on the Chinese massacre. Its U.N. delegation spokesperson told my associate: "It is an internal problem. We are not going to get involved."

The extreme left press—the *Guardian*, the *Workers Vanguard*, the *Revolutionary Worker*, and other Marxist weeklies—were busy trying to fit the events of China into their political orthodoxies. The Workers World Party condemned the students as counterrevolutionaries and commended the army for its decisive action, thus following the party line of such bastions of democracy as Cuba, Nicaragua, and Vietnam.

Even *The Nation*, whose June 12 issue must have gone to press before the massacre, was trying to figure out how to avoid crediting "Western values" for the students' desire for democracy. In a convoluted editorial, they managed to argue that the student movement vindicated "Gorbachev's main thesis" rather than "imported Western values." Conveniently, they ignored the students' Statue of Liberty, their references to Patrick Henry, and repetition of American freedom slogans.

Finally, the National Lawyers Guild, which offers simpleminded, left-wing solutions to all capitalist-versus-socialist conflicts, has decided that the Chinese situation "is too complex and too fluid" for immediate comment. It refuses to condemn the naked aggression of the Chinese army against unarmed students without "more information and discussion" about the student movement and its goals. I guess they are awaiting the arrival of the official Chinese newspapers, which now claim that no one except soldiers were killed in Tiananmen Square. The guild, which has adamantly refused to condemn Soviet political trials, has issued repeated condemnations of American and Israeli "repression."

Most of these democracy-bashers were also silent about the recent gassing of more than twenty women and children by Soviet troops, the use of poison gas against Kurdish civilians by Iraq, the systematic execution of entire villages by Syria, and the attempted genocide of the Bahais by Iran. For these hypocrites, human rights violations are committed only by the Western democracies they despise and never by the leftist tyrannies they support.

Nor does all the hypocrisy over human rights emanate from the extreme left. There is more than enough on the extreme right as well. Senator Jesse Helms was quick to proclaim that the events in Tiananmen Square demonstrate that we cannot trust any Communist government on any issue.

Helms, who would be the first to call for lethal force if American leftist students had occupied the Capitol grounds in Washington, condemned the Chinese not so much for what they *did*, but for who they *are*.

This all goes to show that for many on the extreme left and right—who are more similar in this respect than they are different—human rights is a phony tactical argument in their overall political campaign. They each selectively condemn human rights violations when committed by their political enemies, and justify, or are silent about them, when committed by their friends.

The next time you read or hear condemnation of the United States, Israel, or other Western democracies from the likes of Kunstler, Chomsky, the PLO, and the National Lawyers Guild, remember their selective silence in the face of one of the most inexcusable human rights violations in recent years.

Human rights will never become a reality until the world insists on a single standard of compliance, regardless of who the perpetrators and the victims are.   June 1989

Kunstler, Chomsky and The Lawyers Guild eventually issued ambiguous criticism of the Chinese action, while the PLO wired congratulations.

DERRICK BELL AND DIVERSITY AT HARVARD

My colleague, Professor Derrick Bell, has shaken the law school world by demanding leave without pay from his teaching duties at Harvard Law School, an act he characterizes as "a sacrificial, financial fast," until the school appoints a black woman to a tenured professorship. Although Harvard Law School has had, and will have, several black women as visiting professors, none has been granted tenure.

Bell, who earned his reputation as a first-rate lawyer during the civil rights activism of the 1960s, has been a law professor for the past twenty years. He is a popular teacher who has been a pioneer in developing new courses on racial issues. His decision to take an unpaid leave from teaching will have a real impact on students who have already registered for his classes next year. It will also have a potentially devastating impact on him and his family, who have to find alternate means of earning the approximately $125,000-a-year salary of professors at law schools like Harvard.

One can admire Bell's passion and self-sacrifice without, however, necessarily agreeing with what he is demanding. I don't know a member of the faculty who would not be genuinely pleased if several black women—as well as Hispanic, Asian, and other "diversifying" professors—were added to the permanent faculty. Indeed, substantial efforts have been made in the past decade to diversify the faculty, and a significant percentage of recent appointments, nearly half over the past ten years, have been minorities or women.

But Bell is apparently not satisfied with the *politics* of some of the black law professors who have recently been appointed. This is how he put it in a recent speech at a rally: "Most of [the law school faculty] support diversity. But the ends of diversity are not served by people who *look* black and *think white*. . . ."

A similar argument was made several years ago when the appointments committee at Harvard Law School recommended a particular woman for tenure. A majority of the male faculty voted for the appointment, but every single female member of the faculty voted against her, thus causing the appointment's defeat. Several of the women voiced an objection similar to the one raised by Bell about blacks who "think white." These women argued that the candidate, though a woman, was not a feminist.

The Bell argument, and the similar one made by some of the women several years ago, suggests that, at least for some faculty, "diversity" may be a code word for something very different. Those who would impose a political litmus test on blacks and women want to be certain that new faculty members of their race or sex think as *they* do. They do not want the widest possible diversity among the blacks or women on the faculty; they want a relative uniformity of viewpoint.

If that is true, it certainly undercuts some of Bell's most powerful rhetorical claims. For example, Bell argues that black students need role models, and that black men and white women cannot serve as role models for black women. But it would follow from that argument that conservative blacks and nonfeminist women also need role models.

Moreover, real diversity should not exclude blacks or women with atypical views. It would be the ultimate discrimination if only white males had the right to be different, while blacks and women had to swear an oath of allegiance to "thinking black" or "thinking feminist."

In the end, Bell's financial fast is not only a quest for racial and gender diversity. It is also a struggle for political power. Some on the left believe that more blacks and women will enhance their power, because blacks who think black and women who think feminist tend to support the left. But blacks who think white and women who aren't feminist tend to be conservative or unpredictable and will not enhance the power of the left. This is not to deny that power politics also play a role in why some right-wing faculty members demand that minority candidates think and write the way they do.

The entire legal profession needs a greater proportion of lawyers, whatever their race or gender, who are willing to serve the legal needs of the poor, the disenfranchised, the disabled, and the dispossessed. Derrick Bell is right when he says the color of one's skin alone does not tell you how a person thinks. It also does not tell you much about what kind of a lawyer or law teacher that person will become.

The best way to achieve real diversity within the student body, faculty, and the profession is to reject exclusively racial or gender quotas, as well as political litmus tests. Instead, we should recruit aggressively from within those segments of the community that are not even aware that a career in law is a realistic option. May 1990

IS CRYING WOLF OK FOR BLACKS?

Remember the case of Sabrina Collins, the Emory University student who was allegedly the victim of racist harassment, death threats, hate mail, and graffiti? Well, it turns out that she probably did it all herself. That is the conclusion of the local and university police who investigated the matter.

According to the county solicitor, "There certainly is some direct evidence and a great deal of circumstantial evidence that would cause one to believe that Sabrina was the only person involved in these matters." This evidence includes a fingerprint analysis, as well as proof that Collins first submitted her reports of racial harassment shortly after she was formally accused by the school of cheating on a chemistry test.

If this is true, then Sabrina Collins is a sick and pathetic young woman who deserves sympathy and needs treatment.

But what about Otis Smith, the president of the Atlanta chapter of the National Association for the Advancement of Colored People (NAACP)?

This was Smith's reaction to the disclosure that the Collins story was a deliberate hoax: "It doesn't matter to me whether she did it or not, because of all the pressure these black students are under at these predominantly white schools. If this will highlight it, if it will bring it to the attention of the public, I have no problem with that."

What exactly is Smith's message to black students in predominantly white schools? He seems to be saying that it is OK for black students to manufacture false claims of racial harassment, if such hoaxes "will bring to the attention of the public" the actual pressures these students experience.

Remember that Otis Smith is no peripheral figure who is just shooting off his mouth. He is the official spokesman for one of the most important chapters of the major mainstream black organization in this country. What he says matters. And when his organization speaks, black college students listen.

Smith's not-so-subtle incitement to obstruction of justice brings back memories of the Tawana Brawley case, in which a black teenager made up a gruesome story about how she had been raped by a gang of white policemen. Brawley, like Collins, was apparently a pathetic victim of her own internal demons. But her adult advisers—two lawyers and a minister—egged her on.

Eventually, they falsely accused an entirely innocent white policeman of the crime that never happened. A grand jury concluded that the physical evidence left no doubt that Brawley had contrived the entire matter and that the white policeman was entirely innocent. One of the lawyers has now been suspended from the practice of law, while the other faces disciplinary charges. Despite the grand jury finding that Brawley made up the entire story, the president of the Boston chapter of the NAACP, Louis Elise, recently stated on television that he believed that Tawana Brawley had, in fact, been raped by the white policeman.

At least Sabrina Collins never charged anyone in particular with the acts she apparently perpetrated against herself.

But the "ends justifies the means when it comes to racism" mentality reflected by Otis Smith's outrageous statement will inevitably lead to false accusations being directed at innocent people. Just as nature abhors a vacuum, the police abhor unsolved crimes, especially when they are highly publicized racial crimes. Phony victims who start by making up false crimes, generally end up by fingering innocent suspects, as the Brawley case demonstrates.

There are few crimes more destructive of our legal system than falsely accusing another of a heinous crime. Bearing false witness has been a sin, as well as a crime, in every civilized society, and for good reason.

Tyrants throughout history have manufactured phony crimes in order to stimulate public outrage against the alleged perpetrators. Hitler's burning of the Reichstag, Nero's torching of Rome, and Stalin's accusations against the doctors are but a few notorious examples of this phenomenon. The infamous "blood libel," by which Jews were falsely accused of murdering Christian children in order to use their blood for the baking of unleavened bread, provoked thousands of retaliatory pogroms throughout European history. And in the bad-old-days of segregation in our own country, black men were often falsely accused of raping white women in order to terrorize blacks and "keep them in their place."

There is no end so noble that it justifies the ignoble means of manufacturing false crimes. Otis Smith may "have no problem" with Sabrina Collins having made up a false charge of racial harassment, but all decent Americans—black and white—should have big problems with Smith's apparent lack of concern for the truth. I hope that Otis Smith does not speak for the NAACP on this issue, any more than Tawana Brawley's advisers spoke for any significant segment of the black community. The NAACP should immediately disassociate itself from Smith's cynical efforts to justify the bearing of false witness.   June 1990

DOES PRESS HAVE RIGHT TO EXPOSE GAYS?

Should the media have a legal right to disclose the fact that a public figure—a film star, politician, journalist—is gay? This question is being widely debated not only within the gay community, where such public disclosure is known as "outing," but also by the mainstream media.

Some tawdry magazines, such as the *Star*, *National Enquirer*, and *People*, have printed the names of celebrities alleged to be gay. But since nobody really believes what they read in these rags—as Jay Leno sarcastically quips, "It was in *People*, so it *has* to be true!"—little harm has been done. But now some respectable journals, such as *Newsweek*, *USA Today*, *Los Angeles Magazine*, and *Daily Variety*, have begun to print stories dealing with the alleged homosexuality of celebrities, and this trend is likely to spread, since "outing" has itself become news. As one editor put it: "How are you going to write about what other publications are doing without explaining what it is they're doing—and who they're doing it to . . . ?"

"Outing," which began in the gay community, is now extremely controversial among gay activists. Some refer to it as the new McCarthyism while others defend it as necessary to increase the power and visibility of gay political activism. There is also a middle-ground position, espoused by some gay newspapers: They will only "out" a closet gay who "is a homophobic who is effectively hurting gay people either in politics, the church, or society."

Thus far, no lawsuits have been brought by "outed" celebrities, but inevitably one of the tabloids will get sloppy and make a mistake. If the falsely "outed" celebrity then sues, a difficult question will be raised: How could the courts assess damages for falsely being called gay? If the courts believe that being gay is not "bad" or "immoral," and they must believe that in states or cities with civil-rights laws prohibiting discrimination against gays, how will they be able to conclude that the "outed" celebrity was harmed in any legal sense?

This problem is reminiscent of one that was experienced in the South during Jim Crow days. In those bad old days, closet blacks who were passing as white were occasionally "outed." In at least one case, a white man was erroneously identified as black. (The wire story had described him as a "cultured gentleman" and the newspaper printed "colored gentleman.") The Southern court found no difficulty assessing damages, since, in an age of segregation, being black was *legally* worse than being white. That is true today of being gay in those states that still punish homosexual acts as criminal. But it is not true in the growing number of jurisdictions that accord legal rights regardless of sexual preference. It will be interesting to watch how the courts deal with this delicate conundrum.

But what if a celebrity is accurately "outed"? Does he or she have any right of privacy that would be violated by public disclosure of private sexual activities? In most states, the answer is no. There is no right of privacy that protects public figures against truthful disclosures, even if the disclosure material involves very private matters.

But the law is not static. It changes as journalistic practices change. It is not impossible that some courts—particularly in states like California, which recognize some right of privacy—may find that some media have gone too far in disclosing sexual secrets.

Nor is "outing" limited only to homosexuality. Some feminists have argued that it would be proper to disclose that an antiabortion activist has herself had an abortion. And then, of course, there is the hotly disputed question of whether the names of rape victims, such as New York's Central Park jogger, should be published.

The issue is similar, in at least some respects, in each of these circumstances: In the public mind, there is still a stigma attached to being gay, having an abortion, and being raped. There should be no stigma attached to these statuses or actions, but the reality is that there is, at least among some members of the public. The theory of "outing" is that the act of publishing the names of famous people who are gay, who have had abortions, or who have been raped will itself help to reduce the current stigma. Balanced against that good is the violation of the "outed" person's privacy.

Our laws have generally resolved conflicts between disclosure and privacy in favor of disclosure: The First Amendment protects freedom of the press, and there is no explicit right of privacy in relation to the media. But this resolution carries a heavy price. In general, the press has exercised reasonable restraint by not going as far as the Constitution may allow it to go. But in journalism, as in other competitive enterprises, a Gresham's law seems to operate, which often pulls the best down to the level of the worst. To paraphrase Jay Leno: If it was in *People*, we better print it also.

September 1990

CHINESE LEADERS SCAPEGOAT PORNOGRAPHY

What does the Chinese Communist party have in common with the Moral Majority, radical feminists, Ed Meese, and Norman Podhoretz? They all believe that pornography is responsible for many of society's greatest evils.

The devil "porn," according to a new campaign by Chinese leaders, is the West's latest weapon designed to titillate the prurient interest of the Chinese people in order to subvert the Communist party: "They cannot succeed with guns, [so they] plot to win without firing a shot, and one of their methods is to distribute pornography and other corrupt materials."

President Bush must be surprised to learn that the Chinese regard him as the Manuel Noriega of smut. I doubt that they will send their army to abduct and put him on trial for poisoning the minds of the Chinese proletariat, but the Chinese government does want to apply the death penalty to porn kingpins, much like some of our politicians want to see drug kingpins executed. (If anyone thinks there is no basis for comparing the evils of pornography with those of drugs, let me tell you about a federal judge who recently proclaimed that if he had a choice between having his children exposed to heroin or to pornography, he would choose heroin, because drugs eventually leave the body, while the effects of porn last a lifetime.)

Every society, especially closed ones, needs "devils" or scapegoats to blame for the failures of their leadership. Pornography is a perfect candidate for China, especially after the student uprisings of last year and the government's murderous response to it. The students were stimulated not by genuine grievances against the corruption of the Chinese leadership but by the evil elixir of dirty thoughts, put into their heads by "hostile forces at home and abroad," says the Politburo member in charge of ideology. The cure follows from the diagnosis. Instead of addressing the real problems of Chinese society, all that is necessary is to "clean up pornography" and institute the death penalty for those who "use pornographic material" to carry out criminal and subversive activities. Already one woman has been sentenced to life imprisonment for selling romance novels of the kind available in every family supermarket in America. Oh how simple—and simpleminded—it is. It is also essential to the survival of the Chinese nation: "This struggle [against pornography] is linked to the very survival or collapse of the cause of Chinese socialism, indeed to the fate of the Chinese nation and people."

The fact that there is virtually no pornography available in China is a minor detail. Since when does ideology, especially totalitarian ideology, have to reflect reality? After all, there are hardly any Jews in Poland, and yet right-wing ideologists have little difficulty scapegoating the "devil" Jews for all of Poland's problems. At least the Chinese have picked an impersonal devil. Burning books, bad as it is, is a lot better than burning witches, though the former sometimes leads to the latter.

What do the Chinese authorities mean when they use the term *pornography*? We don't really know, since there are no "skin" magazines or films available in China. We do know that the last time the Chinese government conducted an "antipornography campaign," it closed down many newspapers, social science periodicals, and publishing houses that did not even dabble in the erotic. As one reporter put it: "The campaign was used to close publications that exposed provocative ideas as well as too much flesh."

But that is almost always what happens when any government or group targets the devil porn. Since pornography cannot be defined with any degree of objectivity—recall Justice Potter Stewart's famous quip about knowing it when he sees it—it is defined very differently by those with different agendas. Radical feminists define it to exclude egalitarian erotica but to include sexist subjugation. Moral majoritarians, who practice and preach sexist subjugation, define it to include anything inconsistent with "family values," such as nudity, homosexuality, and positive portrayals of promiscuity. Some limit it to violence, others to "abnormal" sexuality. The point is that each of these definitions is ideological and political.

All of art, whether pornographic, erotic, homoerotic, violent, racist, or sexist, contains ideas. And those who would ban pornography are offended or frightened by the *ideas* reflected by the genre of pornography they seek to ban. Sometimes it takes a campaign as transparent and absurd as that currently being conducted by the Chinese government to make us look at our own equally absurd campaigns against pornography.

You may not like dirty books, explicit videos, filthy rap lyrics, homoerotic photographs, or sexist magazines. You may even believe, despite the absence of any scientific data, that pornography "causes" certain evils. But please don't be so simpleminded as to blame all, or even most, of society's ills on what appears to be emerging as one of the world's most popular scapegoats: the devil porn.   November 1990

PUT A STOP TO CENSORSHIP BY DEATH THREAT

As President Bush vows that Saddam Hussein's violent aggression will not be rewarded, another group of Islamic extremists has proved that violent lawlessness will indeed be rewarded in a world unwilling to stand up to barbarous threats. The late Ayatollah Khomeini's contract hit against author Salman Rushdie has finally succeeded in bringing Rushdie to his knees. After nearly two years in hiding, Rushdie has announced that he has "converted" to Islam—a paradigmatic instance of medieval conversion by the sword—and that he would not authorize a paperback edition or further translations of his heretical novel.

George Bernard Shaw once called assassination the ultimate form of censorship. Khomeini and his zealous followers understand the meaning of this dictum and its corollary that the threat of assassination is a penultimate means of censorship. When Khomeini issued his contract for the murder of Rushdie—promising a million dollars and eternal salvation to his killer—the world responded in impotent horror. It complained loudly but did almost nothing. Not even the United Nations, which can convene at a moment's notice at the first sign of a deportation by Israel, was moved to act by a gangland contract issued by a head of state and formally backed by a member government.

Great Britain engaged in a gesture by breaking and then quickly restoring diplomatic relations with Iran. Most of the rest of the world continued business as usual with the Khomeini regime, as it has with terrorist groups such as the Palestinian Liberation Organization and nations that sponsor them, such as Syria and Libya. The message to bigots, zealots, and killers is clear: Violence will be rewarded if it is directed against the right people.

No one can blame Salman Rushdie for capitulating. He could not be expected to stand alone against an international gang of hit men. It must be humiliating for Rushdie to have to say that he does not "agree with any statement in my novel . . . uttered by any of the characters who insults the prophet Mohammed or casts aspersions upon Islam or upon the authenticity of the Holy Koran or who rejects the divinity of Allah." This negotiated mea culpa is certainly at odds with Rushdie's defiantly agnostic statements of the past. Nor can Rushdie be happy that his novel will not now be released in paperback, since he had previously said that unless a paperback edition is published, "in a few years the book simply won't be there for anyone who wants to read it. It will, for all practical purposes, have been suppressed."

Suppression is, of course, the goal of this entire "Godfather" scenario. "Until the book is completely removed our campaign goes on," threatens one zealot. Rushdie was made an interim offer he could and did not refuse. But still the death sentence and the contract hit have not been lifted, because the offending book remains in circulation.

Notwithstanding the continuing death sentence, Rushdie said that he feels "a lot safer" after signing his plea bargain than he did before. That is probably true, but I doubt that the deal gave him "a great deal of joy," as he also said.

The implications of the Rushdie capitulation are frightening to freedom of speech throughout the world now that the murderous censors know that they can win through intimidation. Zealots know no stopping point. If they succeeded in censoring Rushdie by putting a price on his head, why not put prices on all who displease them or who doubt their religious dogmas. It is a throwback to the days of the Inquisition, but in an age when the media, and therefore threats of censorship, recognize few national boundaries.

Will we next see Christian fundamentalists threatening to kill the producers of *The Last Temptation of Christ* unless all video rentals are terminated? Will Jewish extremists put a price on the heads of those who deny the Holocaust? Will feminist censors threaten to kill pornographers while right-to-lifers issue contracts on doctors who perform abortions?

The world must not sit idly by while censorship by death threat succeeds. If Rushdie's official publisher refuses to issue his book in paperback or in further translations, then other publishers should take the initiative and issue the paperback and translations without Rushdie's authorization. They should hold his proceeds in escrow, on the ground that his refusal to authorize publication is coerced and thus not legally binding. The purpose of copyright laws is to encourage publication, not censorship by death threat.

Rushdie might formally complain, even file a lawsuit, against the unauthorized publication. But any reasonable court—outside of Iran— would rule that Rushdie's lack of consent was the product of the continuing death threat and not his free will. Though he could not publicly admit it, Salman Rushdie would be greatly appreciative if a brave publisher violated his involuntary wishes and made his book available to all who wanted to read it. But even if Rushdie genuinely disapproved in the last analysis, a published work of literature belongs not to the author alone but also to the reading public.   January 1991

CAN A MINORITY BE RACIST?

There is a debate currently raging over whether blacks and other minority groups and individuals can ever be guilty of "racism." Those who take the negative argue that racism is institutional in nature and thus requires "the institutional power to be oppressors." Since only white males have that power in our society, it follows from this argument that blacks cannot be racist (and that women cannot be sexist). Those who take the affirmative define racism simply as discrimination based on race, without any requirement of institutionalized power. Under that definition, any bigot, regardless of race or gender, can be a racist (or a sexist).

This debate achieved widespread notice when Representative Gus Savage, a black from Illinois, declared that "racism is white. . . . There ain't no black racism." Savage's comment was a bit self-serving, coming as it did after he himself was accused of having made anti-Semitic remarks during his congressional campaign.

Now the issue is in the news again, as several black leaders in Boston are demanding the dismissal of a white doctor who has just been appointed medical director of Boston City Hospital, a facility that serves primarily black patients. State Senator Bill Owens, a black activist, is demanding that Dr. Michael Eliastam must be fired because he is white and he was born in South Africa. Owens deems it irrelevant that Eliastam, while a student in South Africa, was president of a multiracial antiapartheid medical group that built one of South Africa's first neighborhood health centers to serve blacks. He left South Africa twenty-four years ago and is now a U.S. citizen who has devoted much of his career to serving the medical needs of blacks and other minorities.

Notwithstanding Eliastam's *individual* record of support for black causes, Owens made the following statement: "Eliastam, whatever his qualifications are, is a white South African. There is a mentality to people born in South Africa, and even if he doesn't have it, we don't need to be sending this kind of message. . . . Why would I want a white South African deciding medical priorities for a hospital that serves 80 percent blacks and other minorities in this city?"

Whether one characterizes that statement as "racism" or simple "bigotry," it is not only wrong, it may also be illegal if the sentiments contained in it are acted on. The chairman of the Massachusetts Commission Against Discrimination warned Owens that "he was in harm's way" if he persisted in his discriminatory efforts to have Eliastam fired because of his race and national origin. We have laws, both federal and state, prohibiting discrimination on the basis of a person's race and the country in which he was born.

But this did not stop Owens. Borrowing from white bigots throughout history, Owens simply shifted the grounds of his opposition, arguing that Eliastam "is not qualified to do his job," despite his exceptional educational and professional background. Owens's criteria for job qualifications would make the Grand Wizard of the Ku Klux Klan proud.

Another opponent of the Eliastam appointment, Allen Ball, the director of a neighborhood health center in Dorchester, engaged in a double form of bigotry by invoking a highly charged analogy to another ethnic group: "If you were Jewish, it would be like bringing in somebody from Nazi Germany." The analogy might be relevant if the "somebody" from Nazi Germany happened to be an opponent of Nazism who had taken considerable risks to help the Jews! In that case, it would be bigoted to discriminate against him solely on the basis of where he was born.

The essence of bigotry is stereotyping and overgeneralization based on race, national origin, gender, or other factors beyond the control of the individual. Bigotry may be more understandable and less dangerous when it emanates from minorities who lack the power to impose institutional oppression. But it sends an equally pernicious message of hate and discrimination.

The issue transcends any particular community or city. We live in a nation of minorities, where nearly everyone belongs to some group or shares some heritage that has been victimized by discrimination. There is no such dominant group as "white males," as some would have us believe. That overinclusive category represents people of varying ethnic, religious, national origin, and sexual preference backgrounds. The recent history of this country includes episodes of anti-Irish, anti-Italian, anti-French-Canadian, anti-Arab, anti-Jewish, and anti-Scandinavian bigotry. Nor have racial minorities been entirely innocent of all such bigotry. Blacks, Hispanics, Asians, and others have discriminated against each other. There is more than enough prejudice in every corner of American life to allow anyone to feel superior.

Whether Owens's prejudice against white people who were born in South Africa can be called "racism" or merely "bigotry," it has no place in American public or even private life. The kind of prejudgment it reflects cannot help but boomerang. January 1991

"POLITICAL CORRECTNESS" ENDANGERS FREEDOMS

There is now a debate among the pundits over whether the "political correctness" (P.C.) movement on college and university campuses constitutes a real threat to intellectual freedom or merely provides conservatives with a highly publicized opportunity to bash the left for the kind of intolerance of which the right has often been accused.

My own sense, as a civil libertarian whose views lean to the left, is that the P.C. movement is dangerous, and that it is also being exploited by hypocritical right-wingers.

In addition to being intellectually stifling, the P.C. movement is often internally inconsistent. Among its most basic tenets are (1) the demand for greater "diversity" among students and faculty members; and (2) the need for "speech codes," so that racist, sexist, and homophobic ideas, attitudes, and language do not "offend" sensitive students.

Is it really possible that the bright and well-intentioned students (and faculty) who are pressing this "politically correct" agenda do not realize how inherently self-contradictory these two basic tenets really are? Can they be blind to the obvious reality that true diversity of viewpoints is incompatible with speech codes that limit certain diverse expressions and attitudes?

I wonder if most of those who are pressing for diversity really want it. What many on the extreme left seem to want is simply more of their own: more students and faculty who think like they do, vote like they do, and speak like they do. The last thing they want is a truly diverse campus community with views that are broadly reflective of the multiplicity of attitudes in the big, bad world outside of the ivory towers.

How many politically correct students are demanding, in the name of diversity, an increase in the number of Evangelical Christians, National Rifle Association members, and right-to-life advocates? Where is the call for more anti-Communist refugees from the Soviet Union, Afro-Americans who oppose race-specific quotas, and women who are antifeminist?

Let's be honest: The demand for diversity is at least in part a cover for a political power grab by the left. Most of those who are recruited to provide politically correct diversity—Afro-Americans, women, gays—are thought to be supporters of the left. And historically, the left, like the right, has not been a bastion of diversity.

Now the left—certainly the extreme left that has been pushing hardest for political correctness—is behind the demand for speech codes. And if they were to get their way, these codes would not be limited to racist, sexist, or homophobic *epithets*. They would apply as well to politically incorrect *ideas* that are deemed offensive by those who would enforce the codes. Such ideas would include criticism of affirmative-action programs, opposition to rape-shield laws, advocacy of the criminalization of homosexuality, and defense of pornography.

I have heard students argue that the expression of such ideas—both in and out of class, both by students and professors—contributes to an atmosphere of bigotry, harassment, and intolerance, and that it makes it difficult for them to learn.

The same students who insist that they be treated as adults when it comes to their sexuality, drinking, and school work beg to be treated like children when it comes to politics, speech, and controversy. They whine to Big Father or Mother—the president or provost of the university—to "protect" them from offensive speech instead of themselves trying to combat it in the marketplace of ideas.

Does this movement for political correctness, this intolerance of verbal and intellectual diversity, really affect college and university students today? Or is it, as some argue, merely a passing fad, exaggerated by the political right and the media?

It has certainly given the political right, not known for its great tolerance of different ideas, a heyday. Many hypocrites of the right, who would gladly impose their own speech codes if *they* had the power to enforce them *their* way, are selectively wrapping themselves in the same First Amendment they willingly trash when it serves their political interest to do so.

But hypocrisy aside—since there is more than enough on both sides—the media is not exaggerating the problem of political correctness. It is a serious issue on college and university campuses. As a teacher, I can feel a palpable reluctance on the part of many students, particularly those with views in neither extreme and those who are anxious for peer acceptance, to experiment with unorthodox ideas, to make playful comments on serious subjects, to challenge politically correct views, and to disagree with minority, feminist, or gay perspectives.

I feel this problem quite personally, since I happen to agree, as a matter of substance, with most "politically correct" positions. But I am appalled at the intolerance of many who share my substantive views. And I worry about the impact of politically correct intolerance on the generation of leaders we are currently educating.   April 1991

PRESIDENT BUSH DELIVERS POMP, HYPOCRISY

Commencement speeches are often exercises in hypocrisy, as powerful honorary degree recipients preach to graduates about the virtue of honesty, hard work, and other qualities that they themselves generally lack. Several of President Bush's recent commencement speeches are cases in point. At Michigan, our president condemned those who would enforce "political correctness" on university campuses. This is what he said: "Ironically, on the two hundredth anniversary of our Bill of Rights, we find free speech under assault throughout the United States. The notion of 'political correctness' has ignited controversy across the land. What began as a cause for civility has soured into a cause of conflict and even censorship."

Although I agree with the criticism of P.C., it is shocking to hear it from a man who campaigned for president by demanding mandatory flag salutes and pledges of allegiance and by condemning his opponent for having vetoed as unconstitutional a compulsory flag salute statute. The same president who condemns the call for political correctness from the left, calls for "religious correctness" by advocating prayer in the schools and by demanding that federally funded medical clinics recite politically and religiously correct advice about abortion to their indigent patients.

Cartoonist Dan Wasserman of the *Boston Globe* captured President Bush's hypocrisy when he depicted the president complaining about the criminal persecution in Kuwait of a man for wearing a Saddam Hussein T-shirt and questioning, "Are you sure this guy didn't do something else? Like burning the flag?"

President Bush's real complaint about the political correctness movement on campuses today is not that its practitioners are stifling freedom of expression by imposing their views on others. Bush's complaint is that the *content* of the current P.C. is not one with which he agrees. If right-wing students were the ones defining what was politically correct, as they were during the 1950s, you can bet that the president would have made a very different graduation speech at Michigan.

Another recent Bush speech, this one to students at the FBI Academy, was about the virtues of "merit" in hiring and the vices of affirmative action, especially quotas. Again maybe the president is right in preferring merit to quotas, but who is he to preach about the virtues of merit hiring? He is the man who selected Dan Quayle to be his—and our—vice president. If ever there was an example of the failure of the merit system, it is Dan Quayle, who got virtually every job he ever held through family connections, wealth, good looks, and other nonmerit criteria.

And then when there was a recent vacancy in the U.S. Court of Appeals for the Second Circuit, perhaps the most important tribunal below the Supreme Court, Bush skipped over dozens of more qualified judges and picked *his own first cousin* for the job! If "merit" were the real alternative to affirmative action or quotas, there would be a strong case for the Bush position. But many jobs, places in classes, and other benefits of the real world are not allocated on the basis of merit. Jobs are often handed out on the basis of who you know, who your parents are, and what your background is.

In a recent rerun of "All in the Family," Archie Bunker boasted that he didn't need civil rights laws to get his first job—to which Edith responded, "That's right. His *uncle* got it for him." Admission to colleges is often affected by alumni preference, contributions, and other "grandfather" factors. When George Bush went to Yale, it was a bastion of nonmerit exclusion, as were the clubs he belonged to during and after his college days. George Bush's rise to power is not an example of the rewards of merit. It is a story, along with many others, of affirmative action for the rich and powerful. So much then for the virtue of merit, as practiced by President Bush.

At Yale's commencement, President Bush lectured about human rights, and then announced that he would continue to accord China "most favored nation" trade status in the face of its continued suppression of dissidents following the massacre at Tiananmen Square. Bush justified this carrot by pointing to the fact that China voted with us in the Security Council to condemn Iraqi aggression against Kuwait. In other words, China may be hypocritical when it comes to aggression and human rights, but at least they are manifesting their hypocrisy on *our* side. To their credit, several politically incorrect Yale students booed the president's rationalization of rewarding China. I always dread the college commencement season, with its hypocritical speeches, its honorary degrees to often dishonorable recipients, and its meaningless academic pomp. But I guess even education needs its periodic commercial interruptions.   June 1991

MULTICULTURALISM BEATS BIGOTRY

On Thursday, August 15, 1991, Paul Simon and his seventeen-piece multi-national band mesmerized New York City—and much of the rest of the country who watched on TV—with his beautiful blending of African, Brazilian, and American melodies. I was among the enthusiastic 750,000 finger-snapping, swaying, and dancing people of all ages, colors, and nationalities gathering together in Manhattan's Central Park to celebrate musical brotherhood and sisterhood. By our enthusiastic participation and applause, the immense crowd demonstrated our agreement with Simon's principle that the blending of voices, rhythms, and musicians of many cultures improves upon the quality of any one particular genre of song.

At the same time that African-Americans, Jewish-Americans, Italian-Americans, and people of goodwill from every background were joining hands and voices together in Manhattan, a rather different scene was playing itself in the adjoining borough of Brooklyn, where I was raised. At the Bethany Baptist Church in the Bedford-Stuyvesant neighborhood of Brooklyn, hundreds of angry African-Americans joined together—forcibly excluding white reporters at first and then allowing a select number to enter—to celebrate bigotry and to rally in support of an anti-Semitic, anti-Italian, anti-Catholic, and anti-white professor and race-baiter.

The hero of this ugly rally was Professor Leonard Jeffries, the chairman of the African-American studies department at New York's City College. Professor Jeffries teaches his students that blacks (whom he calls "sun people") are racially superior to whites (whom he calls "ice people"). He also lectures about how "the Catholic church initiated the slave trade," how "rich Jews" were instrumental in carrying it out, how "Russian Jewry" and "their partners the Mafia" had put together a system for the destruction of black people, how Hollywood was run by a "conspiracy" consisting of "people named Greenberg and Weisberg and Trigliani," and how no "white boy" can be trusted.

The all-black crowd in the church cheered and yelled "right," "he's telling the truth," and "Jeffries, Jeffries, Jeffries," as they watched a videotape of his bigoted diatribe against Jews, Catholics, Italians, and other whites.

A woman I know, who is a survivor of the Holocaust, said that when she watched a television report of the rally, she was reminded of the early

Nazi rallies in which Aryans cheered as Hitler blamed all of Germany's problems on "the Jews." She worried that a "Holocaust could come here if people like those at the rally ever became a majority in this country."

I assured the anxious woman that only a tiny portion of African-Americans agreed with the bigotry that Jeffries teaches, and that even some at the rally were there more to show solidarity with a brother who was in trouble than to express substantive agreement with Jeffries's ridiculous views. I also told her that there was plenty of bigotry within elements of the white community, as there indeed is within every group. The Holocaust survivor reminded me that in the beginning of Nazism only a tiny portion of the German people agreed with Hitler, and that many people of diverse backgrounds joined the Nazi party for "understandable reasons."

I remain unpersuaded by the woman's understandable fear, because America is different from Germany. Part of the reason for my optimism is what I saw just a few miles north of the Brooklyn rally. Many more blacks were cheering Paul Simon in Central Park than were rallying for Leonard Jeffries in Bedford-Stuyvesant. Many more whites were cheering for the black Africans who played the beautiful music than are joining the skinheads and other racist "white superiority" groups. The vast majority of Americans, whatever their race or nationality, don't need to feel that they are part of a "superior" race, as the Germans did. This pathetic need to feel superior is a pathological symptom of personal inadequacy and failure. People who do not feel like failures do not have the need to scapegoat "others" for their own inadequacies.

Yet there is cause for concern with the rallies—there have now been several—being held for Jeffries. As I document in my book *Chutzpah*, most overt racism within the white community "is concentrated near the bottom of the socioeconomic scale" and tends to abate among more educated whites. In the black community, on the other hand, there seems to be more overt bigotry, especially anti-Semitism, among more educated and wealthier blacks (with many exceptions, of course). This disturbing phenomenon seems in evidence at the Jeffries rallies and in support statements, as many well-educated black lawyers, teachers, and clergymen lend their support to Jeffries's bigotry.

Nor is the problem improving, since Jeffries and his bigoted ilk are teachers and role models for the coming generations of black leaders. Responsible black leaders, such as New York City mayor David Dinkins, who was condemned Jeffries's anti-Semitism, must take a more aggressive leadership role in delegitimating the kind of bigotry that seems to be increasing among some highly educated black role models.

August 1991

POLITICAL CORRECTNESS COPS STRIKE ON CAMPUS

I have written about the dangers to freedom of speech, academic freedom, and diversity posed by the "political-correctness cops" who patrol campuses these days. Now, a personal experience has made it clear how threatening this trend can be, especially to professors without tenure.

In my criminal law class at Harvard, I teach the law of rape as an example of a cutting-edge subject that poses a sharp conflict between the rights of defendants and their accusers. As usual, I take a "devil's advocate" position on politically correct issues. For example, although I oppose capital punishment, I argue in favor of the death penalty and ask the students to come up with better arguments. Unless they can, they will never be able to persuade the 85 percent of Americans, including judges, who favor the death penalty.

Similarly, in the area of rape I argue positions that students are reluctant to defend but which many Americans believe. I point out that according to FBI statistics, rape is both the most underreported and the most overreported crime of violence: For every reported rape there are an estimated ten that are not reported; but at the same time, 8 percent of all reported rapes turn out to be unfounded, and this rate of false reports is higher than for other violent crimes.

Because some rape defendants are innocent, I warn against the dangers of expanding "rape-shield" laws, which exclude some evidence concerning the prior history and actions of the accuser, especially in cases where the defendant claims consent. I argue that women who accuse men of rape should generally be identified in the media, as should the men they accuse.

All in all, my classes on rape tend to be controversial and emotionally charged. The majority of students seem to love the exchanges. Some even change the opinions they brought to class.

But my "devil's advocate" views on rape are "politically incorrect."

Indeed that is precisely why I insist that they be expressed. The education of my students would be incomplete if they heard only the comfortably "correct" views. I tell my students that my job is not to make them feel good about their opinions but rather to challenge every view. That is what the "Socratic method" of law teaching is all about. That is also what the real-life practice of law demands.

Last semester, a small group of students complained about my teaching rape "from a civil liberties perspective." I responded that it was important for the students to hear a variety of perspectives about rape, just as they hear, without objection, about other crimes. I also reminded them that the majority of students who speak in class present the "politically correct" views. I told them that the answer to an offensive argument is not to censor but rather to come up with a better argument.

A few days later, one of the students told me that I should expect to be "savaged" in the evaluations that each teacher receives from the students.

When the evaluations arrived, I realized how dangerous it would be for an untenured professor to incur the wrath of the political-correctness patrol. Most of the students appreciated the diversity of viewpoints ("willingness to broach sensitive subjects and take unpopular viewpoints," "very good at presenting alternative views," "helped me get a less dogmatic view of the law," "open to criticism," "the most engaging class on campus," "the most intellectually honest professor I've had," "eagerness to present views with which he disagrees is a tremendous asset," "as far left as you can get [but] he'll be assailed by the politically correct for challenging their knee-jerk reactions," "fair in presenting sides that usually aren't raised"). But this time, a small group of students used the power of their evaluations in an attempt to exact their political revenge for my politically incorrect teaching. One student said that I do "not deserve to teach at Harvard" because of my "convoluted rape examples." Another argued that women be allowed an "option" not to take my class because I "spent two days talking about false reports of rape." Another demanded that my "teaching privileges" be suspended. One woman purported to speak for others: "Every woman I know in the class including myself found his treatment of rape offensive and disturbing." Another woman felt "oppressed throughout the course."

Although I always try to learn from my evaluations, I will not be bullied into abandoning a teaching style that I believe is best designed to stimulate thinking. It takes no courage for me to exercise my academic freedom, since I have tenure. But if I were an untenured assistant professor, would I have the courage to risk the wrath of the P.C. cops? Are other, less established, teachers being coerced into changing their teaching by the fear of negative evaluations, which can be fatal to tenure? You bet they are, and it poses a real danger to academic freedom and good education.

September 1991

Shortly after I began representing Mike Tyson on his appeal of a rape conviction, a group of Harvard Law Students volunteered their time to the Indiana prosecutor in protest of my handling of the appeal.

THOMAS-HILL SATIRES TEST FREE-SPEECH LIMITS

A Halloween incident at the Harvard Medical School raises classic issues of freedom of speech and ethnic tensions. Two medical students—a man and woman—decided to go to a costume party dressed as Clarence Thomas and Anita Hill, who were then the subject of national coverage. Since the students were white, they wore brown skin makeup. The makeup was not "blackface" or caricature, as it used to be in the old minstrel shows. The students deny that they were trying to make any racial statement. They were simply satirizing two individuals involved in a controversial current event.

A black medical student was not amused. He walked up to "Clarence Thomas" and punched him in the face, causing a gash near his eye that required seventeen stitches. The black assailant was subjected to disciplinary charges, and several black leaders rushed to his support. His lawyer demanded disciplinary actions against the white students for "racial and sexual harassment." Recently, the administration suspended the black student for one year. No action was taken against the white students.

The controversy continues at the medical school, with some people still demanding that the white students be disciplined and the black student be relieved of his suspension.

From a free-speech perspective, the issue is clear. The white students had an absolute right to express any views they wished about the Thomas-Hill matter. They were entitled to wear any costume they chose. The black student should not have responded with violence, no matter how offended he might have been. "Your right to swing your fist," says an old civil-liberties rule, "ends at the tip of my nose." The punch in the face violated that rule.

Up to now, the issue is easy. Most civil libertarians would stop here. But I want to argue that the white students did nothing even remotely wrong in coming to a costume party dressed as Clarence Thomas and Anita Hill and wearing brown skin makeup.

Thomas and Hill became entirely appropriate subjects of mimicry, caricature, and satire when they testified before the Senate Judiciary Committee. Indeed, they were the butt of late-night television comics, editorial cartoons, and person-to-person humor all over the country.

Nor is the right to poke fun at them limited to people who share their skin color. Would it have been preferable for the white costumed student to have left his face untinted? May black students not dress up as Chief Justice Rehnquist or David Duke, and may they not wear white makeup? Recall Eddie Murphy's marvelous burlesque of a Jewish barber in *Coming to America*—and he even indulged a stereotypical Yiddish accent.

There is a historical difference, of course, between blackface and whiteface. Blackface was used in minstrel shows in a manner demeaning to blacks. There is no historical equivalent the other way. But this history should not mean that no white person may ever darken his or her skin on the stage—white actors who play Othello always do—or at a costume party. All it cautions against is the use of blackface in a minstrel-like manner.

I am told that Thomas-Hill costumes were quite the vogue this past Halloween, especially at college and university parties where costumes often mirror current events. (If Halloween were in December, rather than October, many college students would doubtlessly have dressed up as William Kennedy Smith or Patricia Bowman—with a blob covering her face.) Yet Derick Jackson, a black columnist for the *Boston Globe*, calls the Harvard incident a "psychotic act of black-hate" and a "violent assault . . . on the psyche" that demands punishment.

I know another student who went to his party as Justice Thomas dressed in a judicial robe sporting buttons reading, "I'm over the Hill," and "What's Roe vs. Wade?" The student thought about whether to darken his face and decided that as long as he used stage makeup rather than minstrel show "blackface," and so long as he was satirizing a particular individual who happened to be black rather than an entire group, no one could reasonably be offended (except, perhaps, the real Clarence Thomas). He went to a racially mixed party and no one expressed any concern. Several of the black students, who were strongly opposed to Thomas's confirmation, had a hearty laugh and applauded the satire. They did not feel harassed.

The student who slugged "Clarence Thomas" deserved to be disciplined. Perhaps a year's suspension is too great, but certainly a future doctor must learn to control his violence. It would be outrageous to discipline the students who wore the costumes. What they did was not only protected by the Constitution, it was protected by common sense. It may be politically incorrect in some quarters to do or say anything that offends even the most oversensitive black, woman, or gay student, but a society cannot live by such restrictive rules that reflect double standards of humor and discourse.

January 1992

LAW SCHOOL PARODY RAISES FREE-SPEECH ISSUE

Most Americans support freedom of speech, except when it offends them! A case in point is at Harvard Law School, where I teach. Last year, tragedy struck close to home. The wife of one of my colleagues was brutally murdered while on her way to the grocery store. The crime remains unsolved. At the time of her death, the woman, who was also a law professor but at a neighboring law school, was working on an article about feminism in the law.

As a memorial to her, the student editors of the prestigious *Harvard Law Review* decided to publish her unfinished manuscript entitled "A Post-Modern Feminist Legal Manifesto." It was a controversial decision, since the incomplete work was not traditional legal scholarship: It used four-letter words, was more political than legal, and cited Madonna rather than Cardozo.

Every year, around April Fools' Day, editors of the *Harvard Law Review* prepare a spoof of their magazine for an annual banquet. The spoof tends to parody articles that have appeared during the past year. Had the author of the "Manifesto" been alive, her article would have cried out for parodying because its publication was so controversial and its use of words and sources so provocative. But its author was dead, and her husband and children, who are part of our community, were still grieving. The student editors of the spoof should have shown the good sense and good taste to have resisted the temptation to parody the "Manifesto."

But sophomores—even law school sophomores—do sophomoric things. And the editors published a parody in somewhat poor taste. Describing the author of the "Manifesto" as the "Rigor-mortis Professor of Law," the spoof went on to ridicule feminist scholarship in sophomoric fashion. To those of us who knew the murdered woman, it was neither funny nor clever. It was offensive!

When the spoof hit the stands (actually it was leaked), the spit hit the fan. The Harvard Law School community literally went crazy. One professor analogized the student editors to hooded members of the Ku Klux Klan and their parody to rape. Another professor said he intended to notify the bar association and prospective employers that these students were unfit to practice law. Other students put up "wanted posters" with the pictures of the offending students and the names of the judges for whom they are scheduled to clerk. The atmosphere of a McCarthyite witch-hunt was in the air despite profound apologies by the students responsible for the parody.

When several professors got together to discuss the free-speech ramifications of disciplining students for a parody that was protected not only by the First Amendment but also by Harvard's own speech code, one professor said he couldn't care less about freedom of speech: "It's just not my thing," pronounced this legal educator, as he told his colleagues that he would file disciplinary charges despite the fact that there was no violation of any disciplinary rule. Another professor proposed that the dean establish what would amount to an "unHarvard Activities Committee" to monitor politically incorrect offensive speech.

Politically correct offensive speech does not generate comparable emotions, as evidenced by a recent lecture sponsored by Harvard Law School's Saturday School. The lecturer, Abdul Alim Muhammed, whose expenses were officially paid by Harvard, is a Black Moslem who had accused "Jew doctors" of injecting the AIDS virus into black babies. He delivered his predictable anti-Semitic tirade during which he referred to Jews as "Nazis." There was no outcry, no demand for discipline, and no call for committees.

Many students and faculty members argue that the spoof is a symptom of rampant sexism and racism at Harvard Law School. In fact, the opposite is closer to the truth. The overreaction to the spoof is a reflection of the power of women and blacks to define the content of what is politically correct and incorrect on college and law school campuses throughout much of the nation. Whether this power is a function of white male guilt over past patterns of sexism and racism or simply the reality that women and black students are better organized today than white males, the fact remains that there exists a double standard for offensive speech on many of today's university campuses. Women and blacks are entirely free to attack white men (even "dead white men," as they do in describing the current curriculum) in the most offensive of terms. Radical feminists can accuse all men of being rapists, and radical African-Americans can accuse all whites of being racists, without fear of discipline or rebuke. But even an unintentionally offensive parody of a woman or blacks provides the occasion for demanding the resignation of deans, the disciplining of students, and an atmosphere reminiscent of McCarthyism.

There is something very wrong at Harvard Law School, but it is not sexism or racism. Indeed, there are more vigorous affirmative action programs and less of the evils of sexism and racism at Harvard than in the outside world. What is wrong at Harvard is that for too many radical professors and students, freedom of speech for those who disagree with them is "just not [their] thing."   April 1992

The Law School Administrative Board eventually refused to initiate any disciplinary hearings against the authors of the parody.

THE STATE,
THE LAW AND
THE RIGHTS OF
INDIVIDUALS

Part Three

5 // *The Limits of the Law*

DON'T BLAME THE LAW FOR SOCIETY'S ILLS

The great French observer of nineteenth-century America Alexis de Tocqueville wrote that "in our country nearly every great issue eventually finds its way into the courts." As a people, we have always had a love-hate relationship with law, lawyers, and judges. Some of our most enduring literature, film, and theater have featured heroic lawyers and judges. Some of our nastiest jokes feature villainous, corrupt, or greedy lawyers and judges. Whether we love the law and its participants or hate them—and I do both—Americans rely heavily on our legal system not only to vindicate rights but to solve problems.

But the law is a blunt instrument of quite limited utility. It is incapable of solving, or even intelligently addressing, many of society's most pressing problems. That is especially true if we mean by law only the *courts*. "The law," of course, is not so limited. Laws are made by the legislature, enforced by the executive, interpreted by practicing lawyers, and only presented to the courts in a small number of cases. With the growth of "alternative dispute resolution"—nonjudicial methods for resolving disputes by private arbitration, mediation, and other less cumbersome and less expensive mechanisms—courts may become even less significant in the overall landscape of our legal system.

One area in which the law plays a minor role, but for which it takes a great deal of blame and credit, is crime, especially violent crime of the sort that plagues our city streets. Opportunistic politicians campaign on slogans that promise to "get tough" on crime by appointing "law and order" judges who will make the pendulum swing away from the rights of criminals and toward the rights of victims. It's good political rhetoric, but it has no reality. The courts have almost no impact on crime rates. Whether the

"Miranda" or other exclusionary rules are expanded, contracted, or abolished will have no discernible effect on the number of murders, rapes, muggings, or burglaries committed or prosecuted in any given jurisdiction. Even during the heyday of the liberal Warren Court, only a tiny number of "guilty" defendants were actually freed because their convictions had been secured by illegally obtained evidence. Today, the number is infinitesimal. It does not even appear as a blip on the computerized printouts of violent crime.

If the entire right-wing law-and-order agenda were suddenly to be enacted—and with the current Supreme Court that is not an impossibility— there would be no real decrease in violent crime. Neither would there be a discernible increase if suddenly Earl Warren and his liberal court of the 1960s were resurrected and adopted the agenda of the American Civil Liberties Union.

Violent crime is primarily a function of factors beyond the control of the legal system: birth rates a generation ago, familial breakdown, economic conditions. The areas where laws may have some impact on crime—drugs and guns—are so politically controversial that little intelligent thought, research, or experimentation is currently possible.

To be sure, law is important, especially to our liberty, but we should not exaggerate its importance to the many other areas of life in which it plays a role. In a democracy, the attitudes of the citizens are far more significant than the rulings of the courts. Consider, for example, the impact—or lack thereof—of Supreme Court rulings on the availability of pornography. During the period of the Warren Court, the justices became far more permissive about sexually explicit material. In the early 1970s, the new chief justice, Warren Burger, began to shut the door with a series of decisions that narrowed First Amendment protections for such material. In his most important ruling for the high court, he empowered the states and federal government to censor "works which, taken as whole, appeal to the prurient interest in sex, which portray sexual conduct in a patently offensive way, and which, taken as a whole, do not have serious literary, artistic, political, or scientific value." Furthermore, Burger specifically allowed for the censorship of "representations or descriptions of ultimate sexual acts; normal or perverted, real or simulated." *Miller* v. *California*, 413 U.S. 15 (1973). Yet following that decision, we witnessed an enormous proliferation of pornography and sexually explicit material, much of which would not seem to be constitutionally protected under the high court's rulings. The citizens were simply willing to accept fewer restrictions on what they—or others—could read and see.

The same was true of religion in public life. Although the courts outlawed prayer in the public schools and limited displays of Christmas religious symbols on public property, many school boards and cities simply ignored those decisions. The citizens wanted more, not less, public religion.

Judicial decisions do sometimes have long-term effects on the attitudes of citizens and politicians—witness the desegregation decisions of the 1950s and 1960s. But as Justice Learned Hand once observed: "Liberty lies in the hearts of men and women; when it dies there, no constitution, no law, no court can save it; no constitution, no law, no court can even do much to help it. While it lies there it needs no constitution, no law, no court to save it." Learned Hand may have underestimated the role of the courts, at least during transition periods between liberty and tyranny, but he made a crucial point: Do not count on the courts alone to preserve liberty; the citizens must demand it—every day.   June 1992

THE BEST DEFENSE STOLEN MONEY CAN BUY

Should a person who is accused of stealing money be able to use that money, or any part of it, to pay for his legal defense? That is one of those questions that sounds like it has an easy answer—until you start thinking about it and about the Bill of Rights.

The first and most obvious answer is: of course not! The money is stolen. It doesn't belong to the defendant. How can he be allowed to use it to buy anything, even a legal defense?

Then you stop yourself and remember that the defendant is merely accused of stealing the money. He hasn't been convicted of anything. Indeed, under our Constitution, he is presumed innocent. And if he is presumed innocent, shouldn't he be treated as if the money belongs to him?

But if he is allowed to spend the money while he is still presumed innocent, what happens if and when he is convicted of stealing the money? The portion that he has already paid for his legal defense cannot be retrieved—unless, of course, the law can take it back from those who have earned it through their labor. The presumption of innocence thus comes into direct conflict with the reality that most indicted defendants will, in fact, be found guilty.

In addition to the presumption of innocence, our Constitution also guarantees every defendant the right to counsel. Originally, this meant only that the government could not prevent those defendants who could afford to pay for a lawyer from hiring one. In recent decades, this right has been expanded to requiring the state to provide lawyers for indigent defendants.

The broad question posed at the outset has thus been somewhat narrowed: If a defendant can afford to pay a lawyer, but only with money that the prosecutor says was stolen, should he be considered an indigent or should he be deemed capable of paying for his defense?

In either event, he will have a lawyer to defend him. But the difference between a state-provided lawyer and a privately retained one can be considerable. The most important difference is that a defendant with money gets to choose his lawyer—within the limits of his financial ability and the availability of his lawyer of choice. The indigent defendant, on the other hand, has to take what the court or the public defender gives him.

Not all privately retained lawyers are great, and not all state-provided lawyers are bad. But for the most part, the former tend to be more experienced than the latter. Private lawyers also generally have more and better investigative resources and expert assistance available to them. Finally, in an imperfect legal system, where who you know is sometimes as important as what you know, money buys the kind of influence that can help a defendant get a more favorable plea bargain.

Until recently, there was a kind of "gentleman's agreement" within the legal profession under which prosecutors closed their eyes to the sources of legal fees. If a defense lawyer could get money from a defendant, that was well and good. But in 1984, Congress enacted the Comprehensive Forfeiture Act, which authorizes the government to freeze all assets that may have been obtained in the course of drug and racketeering crimes. (Under the law, racketeering is defined very broadly to include many white collar crimes.) If the defendant wins the case, the assets are unfrozen. If he loses, they are confiscated.

This law has created a dilemma for lawyers and clients alike. Lawyers are reluctant to take responsibility for a long and complicated case unless they are paid up front. If the assets are frozen, this cannot be done, and their promised payment will be in the nature of a "contingent fee"—namely, they will be paid only if they win. The problem is that contingent fees are regarded as unethical—and in some states illegal—for criminal cases. (They are permitted in accident, contract, and other commercial cases.) Few lawyers, therefore, are willing to represent clients in cases where the government has frozen the potential legal fee.

Recently, the U.S. Second Circuit Court of Appeals, which includes New York, ruled in a 2–1 decision that legal fees were covered by the Forfeiture Act. In a stinging dissent, Judge James L. Oakes argued that the Forfeiture Act, as interpreted by the majority, "not only intrudes on the individual's right to secure counsel of his choice" but also "shakes the very foundations of our criminal justice system."

Other courts around the country have agreed with Oakes and have permitted defendants to unfreeze enough funds to pay for a defense. The stage is thus set for a confrontation before the U.S. Supreme Court. The high court will almost certainly decide to resolve the conflict over this issue, which is so important to the legal profession and to the criminal justice system. How it will rule is anybody's guess, although recent trends, including the decision authorizing preventive detention of presumably innocent defendants, certainly suggest that defendants will not be allowed to use frozen funds to pay for their own lawyers. January 1988

On June 22, 1989 the Supreme Court ruled that the government can freeze the assets of a criminal defendant before trial without regard to whether the person will have enough money left to hire a lawyer. (See Caplin & Drysdale v. United States).

THE LAST THING WE NEED:
A PLASTIC PISTOL

Why would anyone want to pack a plastic pistol? Metal pistols do the job. They are capable of killing human beings. They are easily concealable. They are light. They are macho. Wyatt Earp would never have been caught dead with a plastic six-shooter.

The only plausible justification for owning a plastic pistol is to be able to circumvent the increasing number of metal detectors that have become a sign of our violent times at airports, courthouses, and other public facilities.

That is why major law enforcement associations are in favor of legislation banning the manufacture and importation of lethal plastic pistols. After all, law enforcement personnel bear the brunt of what is done with those weapons. But the National Rifle Association, which should stick to rifles and get out of the business of lobbying in favor of all manner of handguns, has come out in favor of the manufacture of plastic (or ceramic) pistols that contain only tiny amounts of metal. The theory is that there should be just enough metal to be detected by a machine set to its maximum. This approach is incorporated in a bill sponsored by Senator James A. McClure (R.-Idaho).

Many police organizations oppose the McClure bill because the minimum metal content required of plastic pistols would be too low to facilitate easy detection. Metal detectors would have to be set so high that they would also detect hairpins, zippers, and other everyday items. According to the Police Executive Research Forum, this would create "chaos at airports," because so many more passengers would have to be searched.

But as anyone who flies frequently can attest, the response to plastic pistols with small amounts of metal would not be more thorough searches. It would probably mean more lackadaisical search procedures and more guns getting through security. Airline security is already a fiasco at many airports. Inattentive or lazy security personnel rarely bother to search even when the detector goes off. If the detection level were raised, the attention level would drop correspondingly. The same is true of many courthouses, where more effort is devoted to uncovering concealed tape recorders than concealed weapons. (Judges seem to have greater fear of being taped than attacked.)

Police and law enforcement authorities are disappointed that the nation's chief law enforcement official, Attorney General Edwin Meese, seems to be siding with the National Rifle Association and against the police. Meese originally opposed plastic guns, but the, according to law enforcement officials, apparently capitulated to gun interests by lending his enthusiastic support to the McClure bill.

The Reagan administration's anticrime slogans—"law and order," "victims' rights," "stop handcuffing the police"—are quickly forgotten when a powerful lobby flexes its muscles.

A compromise may now be in the works, and whatever emerges will probably be acceptable to the National Rifle Association. If the compromise is acceptable to that self-serving lobby, it will surely make the detection of concealable weapons more difficult than it currently is. There simply is no excuse for that. Neither the profits of gun manufacturers nor the convenience of gun toters are reasons enough to endanger innocent lives any further.

We already have more than enough handguns of every variety—from Saturday night specials to expensive automatics—in our homes and on our streets. Some parts of our country have become armed camps. Criminals get their guns from the glut of weapons sold originally to law-abiding citizens, and the existing problem will only get much worse if a new genre of killer handguns proliferates. Plastic pistols should be stopped before they start, because it is always difficult to remove weapons from circulation once they have made it to the streets.

It is a scandal that Attorney General Meese, who panders so frequently to law enforcement concerns when he is seeking to curtail the Bill of Rights, is not enthusiastically behind a total ban on plastic pistols. But then again, why expect so much from Meese? He has come down on the wrong side of nearly every important issue of policy, personnel, and ethics.

This is one issue on which the president, who himself was shot by a concealed handgun, should reject his attorney general's advice and stand up to the gun lobby. April 1988

FIRST, LET'S KILL THE LAWYERS

The other day, while on vacation, I was browsing through one of those shops that specializes in cute toys and gimmicks. A small crowd was gathering around one particular set of items. They were called "custom voodoo dolls." The set consisted of the usual objects of derision: mother-in-law, ex-wife, ex-husband, boss, and lawyer.

Naturally, I bought the lawyer, figuring I could have some fun putting a few pins in particularly painful places while fantasizing about several attorneys I have encountered who deserve no less. When I took my lawyer voodoo doll to the checkout counter, the saleswoman laughed and said, "That's all anybody is buying—the lawyers sell like mad."

Everyone seems to want to stick it to lawyers! We are the butt of bad jokes and the object of literary derision.

Here are a few examples of lawyers taking it on the chin in humor.

Ronald Reagan once told this one to Ed Meese: "Do you know why they're now using lawyers instead of white mice for experimentation? First, there are more of them; second, there is no danger that the experimenter will get to like them; and third, there are certain things mice won't do."

Another is the new definition of waste: a busload of lawyers going off a cliff with two empty seats.

Then there is the one about the lawyer, the doctor, and the priest who were shipwrecked near an island. When the doctor and the priest tried to swim to shore, the sharks frightened them back to the wreck. But when the lawyer jumped in the water, the sharks escorted him to the island. The priest asked why the sharks treated the lawyer so well, and the doctor responded, "It must be professional courtesy."

Finally, I was recently told about the holy man who had devoted his life to prayer and the Lord's work. When he got to heaven, he was assigned to a tiny house on a small cloud. One day, he saw a fat, prosperous angel drift by in a mansion on an enormous cloud and he asked the Lord who that man was. The Lord said he was a lawyer. The holy man complained gently about his own comparatively shabby treatment and the Lord responded: "You see, we have many holy men here in heaven, but he's our only lawyer."

We are all familiar with Shakespeare's line, "The first thing we do, let's kill all the lawyers," and with Dickens's characterization of law as "a ass—a idiot." But how many of us know that in Sir Thomas More's *Utopia* "they have no lawyers among them, for they consider them as a sort of people whose profession it is to disguise matters."

Why are lawyers thought of so badly? Why are we found near the bottom of every public opinion ranking of occupations? The answer is simple: Because we deserve it! It is not clear whether lawyers do more good than harm. The vast majority of lawyers' time—especially that of the super-elite lawyers, the ones I help train at Harvard—is devoted to helping the super-rich get even richer and pay less taxes.

This dedication to the rights of the wealthy certainly helps the 1 percent of the population served by these corporate lawyers. But there is a real question whether it helps or hurts the rest of us.

The profession of law is, after all, a monopoly. Only licensed members of the bar can sell legal advice and representation. Generally, when the state gives someone a license to engage in a monopoly, it demands something in return: The monopolist must service *all* of the people, not just a tiny fraction. And this makes sense. If most of those who need legal services are not being served by those who have the exclusive right to practice law, then others—unlicensed paralegals—should be able to compete and provide legal advice and representation to those who are now being excluded.

Something must be done to bring legal services to the people who need them most—working people, welfare mothers, the handicapped, immigrants, the aged. These are people with rights but no realistic remedies.

The Reagan administration has cut back on publicly financed legal aid. Some large law firms, to their belated credit, are helping a bit, but the situation is still critical. It is as if the emergency wards of our hospitals were going unattended while most of our doctors were performing cosmetic surgery.

Cynics may respond that the last thing we need is to have *more* people represented by lawyers. This reminds me of the small town that had no lawyer, and so they invited one to set up practice. He did, but there was no business. As he was about to leave, another lawyer moved into town. Suddenly, there was more than enough business for both.

Lawyers are a contentious lot. Sometimes we create, or at least discover, problems. We operate on the adversary system. We are not supposed to win popularity contests. But in a society full of injustice, we are a necessary evil. It is not enough to poke pins into voodoo doll lawyers, or to make jokes at our expense. Something must be done to bring the benefits of our legal system to all people.   September 1988

TV ADOPTS A LAW
ENFORCEMENT ROLE

It looked like the video version of the old Richard Pryor routine about the way some Long Beach, Calif., police treat blacks. But it was real, at least as real as videotaped stings ever get.

NBC television, at the urging of a black social activist, turned the tables on the cops. Generally it is the police and the prosecutors who set up stings and videotape criminals in the act of committing their crimes. This time NBC and the citizen activist, who happens to be a policeman on leave, videotaped a Long Beach police officer engaging in questionable conduct.

Those who made the tape believed they had reason to suspect that certain members of the Long Beach Police Department have harassed black drivers. The two black citizens, the "bait," dressed themselves in work clothes and drove an old car into the city of Long Beach. Their car, and the one following them, was equipped with video and audio recording devices.

As the target car cruised down Pacific Highway, it was stopped, ironically at Martin Luther King Boulevard. The bait got out of the car and the police officer ordered him to put his hands on top of his head. A somewhat contentious discussion ensued with the bait (who knew he was being taped) asserting his rights in a somewhat contentious manner ("You want to write me a ticket, write me a ticket. Don't mess with me, man."). The policeman (who didn't know he was being taped) responded with expletives and tough-cop language right out of *Dirty Harry*.

Then comes the "smoking gun." The cop grabs the bait, maneuvers him in front of a plate-glass storefront window and slams his head into the window, causing the glass to shatter. He is clearly using excessive force and risking serious physical injury.

The tape fails to support the justification offered by the police for stopping the car in the first place—that it was straddling lanes. Nor does it support the officer's decision to arrest the bait on grounds, among others, of using offensive language and having him spend the night in jail. All in all it seems to provide compelling evidence of police overreaction in at least one case.

This highly publicized incident—it was featured on NBC's "Today Show" and evening news—raises inevitable questions about the role of the media, especially TV, in gathering evidence of misconduct and in creating news. NBC's sting reflected all the virtues and vices of traditional stings. A good sting never *creates* law violators out of law abiders. It simply provides an opportunity for the law violator to "show his stuff" on video.

Here the offending policeman was not confronted with any unusual temptation to deviate from his normal routine. He was presented with a moderately disrespectful citizen questioning his actions and demanding explanations. We are entitled to assume that this is the way the officer generally responds when confronted with this not unusual challenge to his authority.

The vice of even the best sting is that it can cause unanticipated injuries. The bait, knowing he was protected by the presence of the TV cameras and cameraman, may have been a bit more provocative than he would otherwise have dared to be. His subtle body language—all well within his legal rights—may have contributed to the cop's overreaction.

Fortunately, the bait was not injured by the broken glass; the policeman did, in fact, require several stitches.

Another problem with a single sting is that it does not prove any pattern. A viewer simply cannot conclude that the videotape establishes a pattern of racial discrimination. Indeed, it seems to illustrate a more pervasive problem of overreaction by some policemen to "sassy" citizens, regardless of race. Some policemen, unfortunately, seem to regard "contempt of cop"—any response to their authority other than instantaneous subservience and groveling—as the most serious crime on the books.

A pattern of racial discrimination may well exist, and this episode is certainly consistent with such a pattern, but without some controlled experiment involving blacks and whites who are comparably sassy, we cannot prove what many suspect. Surely this videotape, even standing alone, warrants further investigation of police practices in Long Beach.

Of course, one effect of this highly publicized sting is that Long Beach police will probably be on their best behavior for at least the immediate future—if not because they have learned something then certainly out of fear of being the next victim of this new version of high stakes "Candid Camera."

The danger is that in this age of tough movie and TV cops, the offending officer may emerge as something of a hero for "standing up" to the uppity citizen. Already the officer has his defenders as well as his detractors. That, of course, is the way of a democracy.

Television is becoming a growing force in our system of law enforcement. From the "fugitive" shows, to the "spotline team" exposés of corruption, to the "magazine" shows that prove the innocence of inmates, the tube is quickly becoming a creator of news. The NBC sting may be a harbinger of yet a new role for the pro-active video camera.   January 1989

MISUSE OF RICO LAW PUNISHES "PRO-LIFERS"

Whatever else you can call antiabortion zealots who invade abortion clinics in an effort to prevent what they regard as "murder," the one word that does not seem to fit is "racketeer."

Yet under a vaguely worded 1970 federal statute called the Racketeer

ALAN M. DERSHOWITZ

Influenced and Corrupt Organizations Act, or RICO, several courts have ruled that antiabortion protesters who engage in civil disobedience may be declared to be "racketeers" and subjected to the draconian provisions of the RICO law. Now the Supreme Court has given this approach an apparent green light.

When Congress enacted RICO, with its criminal as well as civil provisions, it was plainly targeting "organized crime" committed for profit by "mobsters." Indeed, the major purpose behind the statute's harsh financial penalties, including multiple damages and forfeiture of assets, was to try to take the profit out of organized crime. In 1981, the Supreme Court recognized that the declared purpose of Congress in enacting the RICO statute was "to seek the eradication of organized crime in the United States."

But it is not easy to define "organized crime," "mobster," or "racketeer" with precision, and what the late Justice Potter Stewart once said about pornography is applicable: "Perhaps I could never succeed in [defining it]. But I know it when I see it, and the activity involved in this case is not that."

Congress, unable to define the evil it had in mind, drafted the RICO statute overbroadly to assure that no "racketeers" or "mobsters" escaped its remedies. It used terms such as "enterprise," "pattern of racketeering activity," and "extortion."

Over the years, the terms took on definitions that expanded accordionlike to cover conduct never contemplated by the drafters of the original law. Corporations brought RICO suits against their competitors, including respected and legitimate businesses. Prosecutors used it to prosecute petty criminals, Wall Street traders, and corrupt politicians. By 1985, the Supreme Court acknowledged that RICO was being used primarily against defendants other than the archetypal intimidating mobster, and that it was evolving into something quite different from the original conception of its enactors. But the Court declared itself helpless to remedy the situation, saying that any correction must lie with Congress.

But Congress has not acted, and the problem has gotten out of hand. Several months after the Supreme Court abdicated responsibility for narrowing the scope of RICO, the Northeast Women's Center, a Philadelphia abortion clinic, filed a RICO action against various antiabortion activists who had unlawfully entered the center, strewn medical supplies on the floor, harassed patients, blocked access to rooms, and shoved some employees.

There can be no reasonable dispute that these violent actions were criminal in nature and were appropriately punishable under local trespass and assault statutes. They also caused damages to persons and property that could form the basis for a tort action. The real question, and one that had not been definitively decided by any federal court, was whether these criminal actions could be interpreted as "a pattern of racketeering" under the RICO statute.

Earlier this year, following a jury verdict against the antiabortion activists, a panel of the U.S. Court of Appeals for the Third Circuit ruled that the RICO statute was fully applicable to disruptive conduct that is motivated by political beliefs rather than economic gain. It upheld the $108,000 verdict against the activists despite their claim that "civil disobedience" does not constitute racketeering.

More important than the monetary verdict, the decision invites other victims of politically motivated civil disobedience to unleash the nuclear weapon of RICO against their opponents, so as to bankrupt them and their adherents.

This decision set the stage for a possible confrontation before the Supreme Court. The defendants retained as their lawyer none other than the draftsman of the original RICO law, Professor G. Robert Blakey of Notre Dame Law School. If anyone could know what sort of conduct the law was supposed to cover and *not cover*, surely Blakey would. Blakey argued that under the court of appeals' extension of the law to politically motivated civil disobedience, "Martin Luther King was a racketeer when he trespassed on private property."

He might have added that antiwar protesters of the late 1960s who damaged draft offices and war-related businesses were also racketeers. And most pointedly, if abortion ever becomes illegal—and I fervently hope it won't—those women and men who will inevitably engage in unlawful civil disobedience to protest their lack of choice will see the seed they planted bear a poisonous fruit that will be used against them.

Last week the Supreme Court declined to review the Philadelphia case. It gave no reason, but it is fair to assume that it has once again placed the ball squarely in Congress's court. Congress can no longer remain silent in the face of this dangerous misapplication of a statute intended to address an entirely different sort of criminal conduct.   October 1989

ALAN M. DERSHOWITZ

HOW WILL COURT RULE ON POLICE INTIMIDATION?

It's called "working the bus." A policeman boards a crowded bus, waits for it to start up, and then randomly approaches a young man and asks him where he's heading. After a few minutes of conversation, the policeman points to a piece of luggage near the man, and asks him "Does this belong to you?" It's a trick question, especially if the luggage happens to contain drugs or any other contraband. If the suspect admits that the bag is his, and if a search discloses the contraband, then the suspect has confessed that he possessed the contraband.

If, on the other hand, the suspect denies that the luggage is his, he has, in effect, given the policeman permission to open and inspect the "abandoned" bag without a warrant. Although the question is tricky, there is a correct constitutional answer to it—at least in theory. Politely refuse to answer; do not deny the bag is yours; refuse to consent to any search by the policeman; explain that you will not answer any questions without first conferring with an attorney; ask if you are free to leave; or, if leaving is impossible because you are on a moving bus, ask if you are free to discontinue the conversation; finally, try to get the names and phone numbers of any witnesses to the encounter.

But there is a world of difference between a proper answer in constitutional theory and an acceptable one in real-life practice. The police are trained to be psychologically coercive, to maintain control over the suspect during all encounters. Policemen are taught to regard their requests as offers that can't be refused. An encounter on a crowded bus maximizes the coercive nature of the police questioning, since the suspect is not free to leave the bus or even to walk away from the officer. Getting the suspect to consent to a search of his luggage, or to deny that it is his, is far easier than it would be on a street or even in a bus terminal. That is precisely why the police wait until the suspect boards the bus before beginning their questioning.

The U.S. Supreme Court has a "working the bus" case now before it for decision. In that case, the Florida Supreme Court ruled that it is unconstitutional for the police to question a bus rider without any cause, and get him to "consent" to a search of his luggage. The court acknowledged that the "standard procedure" of "working the buses," like other "random sweeps," is an effective technique for dealing with transient drug couriers.

But a majority of the court used strong language in concluding that the effectiveness of these techniques does not justify their intrusiveness:

"Nazi Germany, Soviet Russia, and Communist Cuba have demonstrated all too tellingly the effectiveness of such methods. Yet we are not a state that subscribes to the notion that ends justify means." If the Florida Supreme Court has declared that Florida is not "a state" that permits the technique of working the bus, why is this case the proper concern of the U.S. Supreme Court? Under our Constitution, every state supreme court has the power to interpret *its own* constitution and policies more protectively than the U.S. Supreme Court interprets the federal Constitution. The U.S. Supreme Court, which claims adherence to "judicial restraint," has no legitimate business second-guessing the Florida Supreme Court's libertarian construction of its own constitution.

Moreover, some of the justices in Washington seem to have no idea what it feels like to be confronted on a crowded bus by a policeman carrying a loaded weapon. Justice Antonin Scalia naively observed during the oral argument that "there is no harm" in a policeman asking questions because "this is a free society," and a bus passenger has "a right to say no, get off the bus, or move three seats away." Chief Justice William Rehnquist mocked the defense attorney's argument that the passenger was intimidated by the policeman's pistol, observing that no reasonable person would expect to be shot "if he didn't consent to the search." These sound like the kinds of arguments made by tyrants throughout history: "If he's really innocent, what does he have to hide and why does he need a lawyer?" These arguments miss the important point that citizens, particularly the young minority citizens who are disproportionately subject to "random" police encounters, do have a reasonable basis for fearing police intimidation.

As the Florida Supreme Court recognized: "Occasionally the price we must pay to make innocent persons secure from unreasonable search and seizure . . . is to let an offender go. Those who suffered harassment from King George III's forces would say that is not a great price to pay. So would residents of the numerous totalitarian and authoritarian states of our day." Let us hope, in the interests of liberty, that the justices in Washington remember what kind of a nation we are supposed to be.　　　March 1991

On June 20, 1991 The United States Supreme Court reversed the Florida Supreme Court ruling and found that the police could, in certain situations, board buses and obtain passenger permission to search luggage. (See Florida v. Bostick).

ALAN M. DERSHOWITZ

LEGAL SYSTEM SHOULD STOP POLICE BRUTALITY

The bad news is that several Los Angeles policemen repeatedly and mercilessly clubbed, kicked, and beat a twenty-five-year-old black man named Rodney G. King. The good news is that an amateur photographer named George Holliday videotaped the assault, and the videotape has been shown all around the world. But the other bad news is that the existence of the tape was made known before the policemen had testified under oath as to their version of what had transpired.

It does not take much imagination to speculate about what the policemen would have said had they been charged with brutality, or had King been accused of resisting arrest, and had they not known that their actions had been videotaped. I have read dozens of transcripts of such boilerplate police testimony; it almost always goes something like this:

"We attempted to place the perpetrator under arrest, sir, but he began to swing wildly at the officers. I tried to place him in handcuffs, sir, but he started to reach into his jacket for what I believed to be a weapon. When I grabbed his hands in order to prevent him from reaching for a weapon, he began to kick in every direction, hitting his legs against the side of the police car and other hard objects. At this point he fell to the ground and started to bang his head and body against the pavement. We attempted to subdue him because we were concerned that he would hurt himself. He was strong and it took us several minutes to subdue him, sir. All of his injuries, and ours as well, were sustained as a result of his resistance and our efforts to subdue him."

The other arresting officers then parrot this testimony, and a knife is produced from the arrested person's pocket or the ground in order to corroborate the tale.

The judge, upon hearing this story for the umpteenth time, generally shakes his head in knowing frustration but accepts the officers' account as credible. As one prominent judge put it several years ago: "There are grounds for believing that 'the guardians of [our] security' sometimes give deliberately false testimony," but when police testimony is not "against the grain of human experience," the judge must believe it. Not surprisingly, many policemen, particularly the bad ones, have become experts at concocting stories that do not appear to be "against the grain of human experience." Yet they are as false as the testimony in the King case would surely have been had the police not been aware of the videotape. Any cops who would commit the crimes of assault and battery against a nonresisting citizen would have little hesitation in later lying about it to protect their own careers.

The Los Angeles videotape had thus alerted the world to only half of a widespread problem. We have seen a few bad cops engaging in vicious vigilante injustice. But the other half of the problem—police perjury to cover up the first half of the problem—is still not sufficiently acknowledged.

Several years ago I had an opportunity to expose an instance of police perjury by using an audiotape of which the policeman was unaware. Unbeknownst to the cop, my client had surreptitiously recorded several attempts by the policeman to turn my client into an informer by making both threats and promises. When I questioned the cop under oath, he denied having made either threats or promises. I then produced the tape, which proved he was lying. Nonetheless, the prosecutors and the trial judge claimed to believe the cop. Eventually, my client's conviction was reversed on appeal.

But this case, and others since, have convinced me that the primary responsibility for the pervasiveness of police perjury lies squarely with those prosecutors who close their eyes to it and with those judges who pretend to believe it. Policemen would not lie so readily if they did not know that they could get away with it so easily. In the case in which my client recorded the policeman's threats and promises, the lying cop was promoted, despite the Court of Appeals' finding that he had lied under oath.

Police misconduct and perjury will continue until and unless the public begins to understand how dangerous it is to every one of us. The police know they can get away with virtually every other form of misconduct, because they can simply lie about what they did. A police badge is neither a license to commit assault nor to commit perjury. The vast majority of honest cops do neither. But the small minority who do both endanger all of our liberties. And the prosecutors and judges who encourage police perjury by their silent acquiescence are the real villains. They, above all, should know better. And they, more than anyone else, can do something about it.

March 1991

All but one of the police officers charged in the beating of Rodney King were acquitted on all counts.

ALAN M. DERSHOWITZ

IS HOMELESS PERSON'S "HOME" HIS CASTLE?

David Mooney used to live under an off-ramp to Interstate 91 in New Haven, Conn. His "home" was a makeshift "room" secluded by shrubbery and relatively isolated from the public way. He slept under the off-ramp and used the area to store his belongings, which consisted of a cardboard box and a duffel bag. Now Mooney lives in a prison cell, though he may not be there much longer, and therein lies a fascinating story of the law and homeless Americans.

One day, when Mooney was away from his "home," the police were led there by his girlfriend. They were looking for evidence of a murder. Without obtaining a warrant, the police opened the box and the duffel and found what they were looking for: blood-stained pants and a belt the same size as the murder victim's waist. On the basis of this evidence, Mooney was convicted of murder and sentenced to fifty years in prison. He appealed on the ground that just as the police need a warrant to search a wealthy man's Gucci briefcase, so, too, do they need a warrant to search a poor man's cardboard box.

The state of Connecticut, which prosecuted Mooney, argued that Mooney was a homeless person who was "trespassing" on "public land" by living under the off-ramp. The box and duffel he left under the ramp were, according to the prosecution, "abandoned property." And under Supreme Court precedents, the police have the power to search abandoned property, such as the garbage we all leave outside for pickup, without a warrant.

In a precedent-shattering opinion, the Connecticut Supreme Court has just ruled in Mooney's favor, concluding that the police violated the homeless person's right to privacy by rummaging through his private box and bag without a warrant. Although the court rejected his principal argument that his place under the ramp was his "home," it agreed with him that his box and bag were sufficiently private to require a warrant as a prerequisite to searching them: "The interior of these two items represented, in effect, the defendant's last shred of privacy from the prying eyes of outsiders, including the police."

The dissenting judges mocked the majority by arguing that its opinion "has allowed the current publicity and concern for the plight of the homeless to create an empathy that in turn has created bad . . . law." The dissent concluded that Mooney "did not have a reasonable expectation of privacy" in his belongings or in his makeshift home. It believed that Mooney had, in fact, "abandoned" them, despite the evidence that Mooney always returned to his place under the ramp each night to sleep and regularly kept his things in the box and bag.

The Mooney decision is a big victory for David Mooney, since it may set him free, if the prosecution is unable to prove its case without the illegally seized evidence. It is a small, though precious, victory for the rights of homeless people in general. It recognized that even people without homes must be accorded some protection against limitless police intrusion into their "last shred of privacy."

The minority's conclusion that homeless people have no reasonable expectation of privacy in their meager belongings is insulting and patronizing. Anyone who has observed a homeless person clinging to their few possessions must surely recognize that their torn boxes, bags, and blankets are as valuable to them as the posh briefcases, overnight bags, and Samsonite are to the wealthy.

The homeless in America are a tragic fact of life. We cannot ignore them *or* their rights. If we do not want the David Mooneys of America to live under our bridges and ramps, then we must do what is necessary to provide them adequate shelter, housing, and privacy. We cannot first deny them the physical means of assuring their privacy and then the legal rights to protect it.

The Connecticut Supreme Court has taken a small, but needed, step toward vindicating the rights of the homeless. In this respect they are a quantum leap ahead of the U.S. Supreme Court, which has cut back on everyone's right to privacy in a series of recent decisions authorizing warrantless searches of garbage pails, warrantless fly-overs of private and corporate property, and warrantless eavesdropping on cordless telephone conversations. Fortunately, for all Americans who care about privacy, each state is permitted to grant its citizens greater protection from the prying eyes, ears, and touch of the police than those granted by the U.S. Supreme Court. The Connecticut Supreme Court has understood better than the justices in Washington—the bitter irony of French novelist Anatole France's famous quip: "The law, in its majestic equality, forbids the rich as well as the poor to sleep under bridges . . ." At least now, under Connecticut law, rich and poor alike have equal rights to the privacy of the possessions they keep under that bridge.　　　　March 1991

ALAN M. DERSHOWITZ

COURT RULING ENCOURAGES
POLICE COERCION

Despite the public outcry over the videotaped beating of Rodney King by members of the Los Angeles Police Department, the U.S. Supreme Court has just issued an opinion that gives a green light to police misconduct, including physically threatening and assaultive behavior. In the case of *Arizona* vs. *Fulminante*, a majority of the high court ruled that some criminal convictions may be affirmed even if the prosecution introduced into evidence a confession that had been unconstitutionally coerced by the police.

In the Fulminante case, the defendant was suspected of murdering his eleven-year-old stepdaughter. A fellow prisoner named Anthony Sarivola was a former police officer who had become an organized crime loansharker and eventually a paid informer for the FBI. Sarivola, who was acting as an agent for the police, told Fulminante that he understood that he was getting some rough treatment from fellow inmates and that Sarivola could protect him but only if he confessed what he had done. Fearing for his life, Fulminante admitted that he had killed his stepdaughter.

The Arizona Supreme Court concluded that "The confession was obtained as a direct result of extreme coercion and was tendered in the belief that the defendant's life was in jeopardy if he did not confess. This is a true coerced confession in every sense of the word." The U.S. Supreme Court agreed that the confession was secured on the basis of a "threat of physical violence" by "a government agent" and was thus "coerced," in violation of the Fifth Amendment. It found that Fulminante's "will was overborne in such a way as to render his confession the product of coercion."

Since the prosecutor had introduced the coerced confession at the defendant's trial, it would normally follow, under previously accepted law, that the conviction would have to be reversed and the defendant granted a retrial at which the confession would be excluded. But the Supreme Court changed the law in the Fulminante case. It ruled for the first time that the admission of a coerced confession, presumably even one beaten out of a defendant by an assaultive cop, could be deemed "harmless error." Harmless error means a mistake made at trial that had no likely impact on the jury's guilty verdict.

How the defendant's own confession, his own verbal acknowledgment of his guilt, can ever be deemed "harmless" is a question many experienced criminal lawyers are asking. It is widely known that once a jury learns that the defendant has confessed, it looks at every other piece of evidence with a heavy presumption of guilt rather than with the constitutionally mandated presumption of innocence. A questionable eyewitness identification will surely be given more weight by a jury that knows the defendant has confessed than by a jury that has heard the defendant proclaim his innocence. The same is true of other kinds of inconclusive evidence. The best test of whether the admission into evidence of a coerced confession was harmless is to hold a retrial without the confession and see if the second jury convicts.

But even putting aside the questionable assumption that the unconstitutional admission into evidence of a coerced confession can be harmless, the really dangerous message of the Supreme Court's decision is the one that will surely be perceived by rogue cops.

They will understand the Fulminante decision as an encouragement to coercing confessions from citizens suspected of crime. Calculating cops will figure that they are better off coercing a confession unlawfully than getting no confession at all. The prosecutors can then decide whether to try to introduce the unlawful confession and take the chance that it will be considered harmless by the appellate court that ultimately reviews the conviction.

There is evidence that some police, encouraged by prior Supreme Court decisions that have riddled the exclusionary rules with exceptions, are thinking exactly that way. In another recent Arizona case, the sheriff of Pima County admitted that his department routinely ignored the Miranda rule, which precludes the police from questioning a suspect after he has requested a lawyer. The sheriff calculated that an unlawful confession is better than no confession at all, because even an unlawful confession can be used to contradict the testimony of a defendant who takes the witness stand. In that case, the defendant, a suspect in a series of rapes, specifically asked for a lawyer, but the police continued to interrogate him for several hours without providing one. In the end, the police acknowledged that they had the wrong man and released him.

The calculating mind-set that gives rise to such abuses is already far too prevalent in many police forces. In addition to the so-called rule of silence that permits bad cops to count on the support of good cops to cover up their bad actions, many police also believe they can count on prosecutors and judges to "believe" their perjurious cover stories.

Now the Supreme Court is also encouraging that mind-set by permitting the selective use of illegally obtained confessions and by not requiring the reversal of all convictions based on such confessions.   April 1991

ALAN M. DERSHOWITZ

STOP IN THE NAME OF THE LAW

When we were kids, we used to play a game called "cops and robbers." The "good guy" would try to find the "bad guy." When he did, he would shout, "Stop in the name of the law!" Upon hearing that command, the robber had to freeze and the game was over.

It is apparent that a majority of the U.S. Supreme Court does not understand the rules of the street where far deadlier games of cops and robbers are played every day for real.

In a recent decision, the high court ruled that when the police chase a suspect and command him to "stop in the name of the law," that show of authority is not a "seizure" under the Fourth Amendment. The Fourth Amendment requires the police to have probable cause or reasonable suspicion before they can seize, frisk, or search anyone.

In the recent case, an Oakland teenager saw a police car approaching him. He began to run, as many teenagers—particularly minority teenagers—are apt to do. The police chased him, demanded that he stop, and eventually tackled him. The police claim that while the teenager was running away, he dropped a package with a small amount of crack. The teenager argued that the evidence must be suppressed because it was the "fruits" of an illegal seizure.

The California appellate courts agreed, ruling that the officers had no constitutional basis to chase the teenager, order him to stop, or tackle him. Since the drugs were dropped in the course of an illegal seizure, the California courts concluded that the evidence had to be suppressed under the "exclusionary rule," which prohibits the introduction into evidence of material obtained in violation of the Fourth Amendment.

As is becoming more and more common, the U.S. Supreme Court reversed the state court decision that had vindicated a constitutional right, ruling instead that there had been no violation of the Fourth Amendment. Justice Antonin Scalia, writing for the 7–2 majority, agreed that the police had absolutely no proper basis for chasing the teenager or tackling him. He also agreed that the tackling did constitute a seizure, and was thus unlawful. But since the drugs were allegedly dropped *before* the tackling took place, the court had to decide whether the chase and the order to stop, without the actual tackling, constituted a seizure. If it did, then the fruits of that seizure would have to be excluded from evidence.

Justice Scalia had no difficulty concluding that the word *seizure* does not even "remotely apply" to a policeman yelling "Stop in the name of the law." Although the cop expects the suspect to stop or be stopped, the constitutional restrictions do not begin to operate until the police have actually laid hands on the suspect.

In the parlance of our youth, the cops have to "tag" the robber before the Fourth Amendment comes into play.

This is an absurd rule for several reasons. First, a police order to stop, backed up by the threat of force, must be governed by the Constitution. As Justice John Paul Stevens asked rhetorically in dissent: "In an airport setting, may a drug enforcement agent now approach a group of passengers with his gun drawn, announce a 'baggage search,' and rely on the passengers' reactions to justify his investigative stops?"

Especially since the notorious videotape of the several Los Angeles policemen beating Rodney King, most Americans understand that being chased by the police is indeed a coercive and intimidating action. The police should not be free to chase, draw guns, and demand a stop without *some* reasonable basis to suspect that the citizen has done something wrong.

The decision also encourages the kind of police perjury that leads to tragic episodes like the Rodney King beating. When the police believe they can get away with lying, they necessarily believe they can get away with *doing* illegal things, such as beating up citizens, because they can then lie about what they have done and be believed.

One of the most common police lies is that the fleeing suspect dropped the drugs. This police version of "the check is in the mail" is so notorious that it has a name: It is called the "dropsy" testimony. The Supreme Court's "chase" decision will encourage even greater resort to "dropsy" testimony in cases where the drugs were actually found in the suspect's pocket *after* he was tackled.

The bottom line is that at a time of increasing awareness of the need to keep the police within constraints of our Bill of Rights, the majority of the Supreme Court continues to invite police to engage in lawless actions and then to fib about it. The high court has become part of the problem of police high-handedness instead of performing its constitutionally mandated role as part of the solution. To the question Who will guard the guardians? must be added Who will guard those who are supposed to guard the guardians?   April 1991

ALAN M. DERSHOWITZ

HIGH COURT PONDERS GANG MEMBERS' RIGHTS

Does a convicted murderer's First Amendment right preclude the prosecution from arguing that his membership in a racist prison gang should be considered in deciding whether to sentence him to death? That was the issue recently presented to the U.S. Supreme Court for review in the case of *Dawson* vs. *Delaware*.

David Dawson, a member of the Aryan Brotherhood, broke out of prison, murdered a woman, and stole her car and money. He was quickly captured and convicted of the crimes. The jury then had to decide whether to sentence him to death or life imprisonment. The prosecution informed the jury that Dawson was a member of the Aryan Brotherhood and that the Brotherhood is a "white racist prison gang." Dawson's lawyer objected on the ground that allowing the jury to consider evidence of membership in an unpopular group would violate his First Amendment rights to freedom of speech and association. The lower courts ruled in favor of the prosecution and affirmed Dawson's death sentence, but in a surprising decision by Chief Justice William Rehnquist, the Supreme Court decided that Dawson was right and remanded his case for reconsideration of the punishment.

The high court ruled that membership in a racist organization might be relevant and admissible in a gang-related or racially motivated murder. But the killing here—of a white woman by a white man—was clearly motivated by Dawson's desire to effectuate his escape. Telling the jury about his membership in the gang was thus gratuitously prejudicial.

What was most surprising about the Supreme Court's decision was that it was written by Chief Justice Rehnquist, who almost always votes to affirm death penalty cases, and that it was joined by seven other justices, including most of the extreme right wing of the court. Indeed, the only dissent was by the court's newest justice, Clarence Thomas, who seems to be positioning himself to the right of even the court's most reactionary justices. Last month, Thomas dissented from a decision declaring that the beatings of prisoners by prison guards was cruel and unusual punishment.

In the Dawson case, Justice Thomas argued that the jurors could reasonably conclude from Dawson's membership in the Brotherhood "that he had engaged in some sort of forbidden activities while in prison." Pretty vague! In an effort to be a bit more concrete, Thomas quoted from a lower-court judge in another case who had observed: "Who do they think they are fooling? What elements of 'membership'—as opposed to 'activity' take place [in the prison]? What are prison gangs for, except to engage in forbidden 'activity'? Surely [they] do not believe that prison gangs meet every month to discuss the Critique of Pure Reason and debate how Stanley Tigerman's buildings differ from those of the Bauhaus school. Gangs affiliate for mutual support, but not the kind contemplated by the National Labor Relations Act."

But even the glib quotation undercuts Justice Thomas's conclusion. In fact, prisoners often join gangs like the Aryan Brotherhood for "mutual support"—that is, to protect themselves from other violent gangs. It is well known by penal authorities that many prisons, especially state prisons, are organized along racial and gang lines. Many, if not most, black inmates belong, some nominally and others enthusiastically, to black gangs. And many, if not most, white inmates affiliate themselves, also some nominally and others enthusiastically, with white gangs. To the extent that such membership, by itself, constitutes a forbidden activity, then, of course, gang membership is tautological proof of "some sort of forbidden activity." But to the extent that Justice Thomas is referring to aggressively violent activity by a particular inmate, it is simply not fair to assume, as he would allow the jury to do, that membership in a "mutual support" group necessarily entails active violence rather than a perceived need to secure protection against threatened violence by others.

It is precisely the vice of generalizing from mere membership in a group that distinctions are not drawn among members on the basis of their particular actions, or the degree of their adherence to the principles of the organization. If the prosecution can prove particular "forbidden activities," let it do so by specific evidence. But if it cannot, then the First Amendment should prohibit punishing any American—murderer or mason—on the basis of membership in any group, no matter how racist or disgusting.

Justice Thomas's dual dissents in the prison guard and prison gang cases both reflect an unwillingness to acknowledge that many prisons are overcrowded and out of control. Prisoners are entitled to protection from physical abuse by guards and by fellow prisoners. The prevalence of prison gangs is a symptom of the inability of many undermanned prison staffs to control the environment within the walls without recourse to violence. The majority decisions in these two cases bring us only one small step closer to civility inside the prison walls, but it is an important step.

March 1992

ALAN M. DERSHOWITZ

CASTRATION PLEA BARGAIN SMACKS OF COERCION

Should a defendant charged with raping a child have the "option" of being castrated rather than imprisoned? This controversial issue was raised recently by a Texas case in which a twenty-eight-year-old man, who had previously been convicted of indecency with a child, was arrested for aggravated assault on yet another child. His lawyer worked out a plea bargain under which the judge, who is a longtime advocate of castration for repeated sexual offenders, agreed to impose a ten-year term of probation if the defendant "voluntarily" underwent castration.

This plea bargain immediately generated a firestorm of criticism from the right, the left, feminists, masculinists, and black activists. The right-wing-lock-'em-up-and-throw-away-the-key types objected on the grounds that castration alone was too lenient. They wanted castration plus the thirty-five years in prison that faced the defendant if he did not submit to the operation. Some feminists agreed, pointing out that rape is a crime of violence rather than one of sexuality, and that violence against women and children can be carried out by castrated men.

Civil libertarians opposed the castration option on other grounds. Characterizing the plea bargain as an offer that could not be refused by a defendant facing thirty-five years in prison, the Civil Liberties Union doubted that the defendant's decision could be "voluntary" in any meaningful sense of the term. Masculinists cried "ouch," arguing against any Frankenstein surgery that would tamper with a man's sexual or reproductive organs. And black activists shouted "racism," characterizing castration of blacks as "social demongrelization."

Only the defendant's lawyer, a woman named Clyde Williams, and the judge, Michael J. McSpadden, seemed to think the castration option was a good one for both the defendant and society. The defendant himself, Steven Butler, at first agreed, then he changed his mind, and then he seemed to agree again. One doctor who examined the defendant raised questions about his mental capacity to understand the full implications of the surgical procedure. The doctor did not, however, comment on Butler's mental capacity to understand the full implications of thirty-five years in prison.

Butler's family has always opposed castration, and recently they held a press conference in which they argued that their relative had been "coerced and brainwashed" by his attorney, who, they claim, told him that the operation was reversible. It is not, but then neither is thirty-five years in prison. The tragic choice faced by Butler was between two irreversible punishments, both of which had very long-term implications.

And therein lies the real objection to the "option" of castration, especially when "offered" by a prosecutor and judge who favor it. In the Butler case, the state had originally offered Butler a deal under which he could plead guilty and be sentenced to twenty years in jail. It was only after the sentence was jacked up to thirty-five years that the defendant "voluntarily" agreed to be castrated. This smacks of coercion. Since there is no "standard" sentence for child rape, it is easy to manipulate the threat of imprisonment so as to make the "option" of castration seem the lesser of the two evils.

The decision to accept castration must be voluntary, since the law does not allow castration to be ordered as a punishment. Mandatory castration is cruel and unusual punishment in violation of the Eighth Amendment. And the courts are generally reticent to accept plea bargains that require defendants to agree to unconstitutional punishments. At the very least, they demand a level of voluntariness greater than that required for other decisions.

Nor is there a scientific consensus over the effect of castration on recidivism. Some Scandinavian research suggests that when used selectively on appropriate offenders—those whose crimes are more sexual than violent—castration can lower the rate of recidivism while at the same time shortening incarceration time. But selecting the appropriate target population is critical, and it cannot be done in the haphazard manner of the plea bargain struck in the Butler case. Moreover, it is unclear whether Scandinavian research on a limited population is transferable to this country, with its very different attitudes toward both sexuality and violence. In any event, a prison sentence of thirty-five years is also an experiment with liberty, which should not be undertaken lightly without evidence of its effectiveness.

As of now, the deal is dead and Butler will face a trial—before a different judge—and likely imprisonment with his organs intact. A test case will have to await a competent and unambivalent defendant who unambiguously chooses freedom with castration over long-term imprisonment with his body intact. When that case arises—as it surely will in these days of increasingly long prison terms—we will have to confront yet another of the law's tragic choices between equally uncomfortable options.

March 1992

Steven Butler is scheduled to stand trial on August 13th, 1992.

OBSCENITY STING MISUSES RESOURCES

Imagine yourself getting a mailing from anticensorship organizations devoted to "counter[ing] right-wing fundamentalists who are determined to curtail our freedoms." They tell you that they got your name off a *Playboy* magazine subscription list. You express interest in their work and ask them to send you more information. Several weeks later, you receive a "sexual attitude questionnaire" asking you to list your sexual preferences and fantasies. They promise to keep your answers confidential, and you respond.

For the next several years, you are bombarded with letters, pamphlets, and solicitations, all from organizations advocating "freedom of choice" including "sexual freedom." One such organization lobbies for change in the current laws governing the definition of obscenity and invites you to buy items from their catalog in order to help fund their activities. The catalog advertises books and magazines that are obviously sexual in nature, but it is unclear whether they cross the line into unlawful obscenity.

Your curiosity is piqued and you send for a magazine. It is delivered to your door and you are arrested. The entire operation was a government sting. There are no such groups. They are the cops pretending to be public-interest advocates. Your government now has a file on your sexual preferences, your fantasies, and your political views. Worse yet, you are facing a long prison sentence for receiving obscenity through the mail. Your government has spent hundreds of law-enforcement man hours and tens of thousands of dollars enticing you into committing a crime you would never have committed on your own.

That, in a nutshell, is what happened to Keith Jacobson, a fifty-six-year-old veteran-turned-farmer who supported his elderly father in Nebraska. His sexual tastes happen to run in the direction of young men and boys, but he had never bought an illegal item of obscenity or committed any other crime. The Postal Service, which is supposed to deliver the mail, not read it, had gotten his name from a mailing list because he once ordered a magazine called *Bare Boys*, which was entirely legal when he ordered it. After thirty-four months of continuous inducements, Jacobson finally ordered a magazine titled *Boys Who Love Boys*. That is the magazine that got him arrested.

Jacobson pleaded entrapment, arguing that he never would have ordered the smut without the government's persistence in its solicitations. The jury convicted Jacobson and he appealed. The Court of Appeals affirmed his conviction, ruling that he was not entrapped, and the Supreme Court decided to take his case.

In a surprising decision, the high court reversed Jacobson's conviction. A five-judge majority, led by Justice Byron White, concluded that Jacobson had been unlawfully entrapped. Quoting from an old case that said "a person's inclinations and fantasies . . . are his own and beyond the reach of government," Justice White found that Jacobson had never previously demonstrated any propensity to break the law.

The court went on to condemn the type of sting imposed against Jacobson:

"[B]y waving the banner of individual rights and disparaging the legitimacy and constitutionality of efforts to restrict the availability of sexually explicit materials, the government not only excited petitioner's interest in sexually explicit materials banned by law but also exerted substantial pressure on petitioner to obtain and read such material as part of a fight against censorship and the infringement of individual rights "

The 5–4 majority surprised many court watchers, because it is rare to get five justices these days to side with criminal defendants in almost any case. The court's newest and most controversial justice, Clarence Thomas, joined Justice White's majority, along with Justices David Souter and the two moderates who occasionally side with criminal defendants, Justices Blackmun and Stevens.

To no one's surprise, Chief Justice Rehnquist and Justices Scalia and Kennedy joined Justice O'Connor's stinging dissent, which argued that no one made Jacobson buy the magazine, and that he was responsible for his own actions. If there were any abuses by the government, she concluded, then the "jury is the traditional defense against arbitrary law enforcement." But a Nebraska jury could hardly be counted on to protect the rights of a man whose tastes and fantasies ran in the direction of young boys. It is precisely the office of the courts—especially the high court—to protect unpopular, even deviant, views from governmental overreaching.

A balance must be struck between the legitimate needs of law enforcement in using stings to ensnare predatory criminals who would commit crimes even without government inducements and the illegitimate manufacturing of crimes by governmental inducements directed against those who would remain law abiding if the government had left them alone. The line is not always easy to draw, but a thirty-four-month sting directed against a fifty-six-year-old fantasizing farmer who had never broken the law falls clearly on the side of governmental overreaching. It was not only unfair to Jacobson, it was also an inexcusable misuse of valuable law enforcement resources, which could have been better directed against habitual offenders who make our streets unsafe.   April 1992

LEONA HELMSLEY: THE TAX SCAPEGOAT OF 1992

Another April 15 has come and gone. Millions of Americans filed their tax returns, most honestly, some dishonestly. Almost every year on "tax day" a prominent American is either indicted or sent to prison to bring home the point that the punishment for tax cheating can be severe.

This year's high-visibility scapegoat was Leona Helmsley, whom I represented on appeal. She began serving her four-year sentence on April 15. Although the judge who scheduled her surrender for that day did not explicitly refer to its significance, it was clear to everyone that he was trying to send a message.

But what kind of message did Leona Helmsley's incarceration really send? To many Americans, it sent the message that if you are an unpopular and highly visible personality—Leona Helmsley was portrayed by the media as "the Queen of Mean"—then the IRS and the government prosecutors can single you out for special punishment.

The case against Leona Helmsley was very questionable. The dispute was over less than 1 percent of the Helmsleys' whopping tax bill. During the years at issue, the Helmsleys paid $57 million in federal taxes alone. Normally, disputes of their kind, where the amount at issue is less than 10 percent of the taxes paid, are resolved by various civil mechanisms.

In this case, moreover, there was a genuine dispute over whether the additionally claimed taxes were actually due. The dispute centered around two rather technical issues: The first was whether the Helmsleys had actually overpaid their taxes because they failed to take certain mandatory depreciation credits on their real estate; and the second was over what percentage of the cost of their elaborate mansion, which was built to entertain business associates, was properly deductible as business entertainment.

Before the IRS even completed all the audits for the years in question, federal and state prosecutors indicted the Helmsleys for tax evasion. Harry Helmsley, who had founded the gigantic real estate empire many years before he married Leona, was found incompetent to stand trial. That left Leona to face the charges alone. She was convicted, largely on the basis of invoices that had been altered to make them appear to be business related instead of personal. But it was clear from the face of the invoices that they had been altered by someone other than Leona Helmsley, since the original invoices—the accurate ones—were signed by Leona, but the altered ones have only a Xerox of her signature. If she had been in on the scheme, she would have signed the phony invoices, but since she was not, the schemers had to use a Xerox of her signature.

Moreover, it was the Helmsley accountants—the ones responsible for deciding whether questionable expenses were business or personal in nature—who made the decision to include the altered invoices as legitimate business expenses for tax purposes. These same accountants decided not to include the altered invoices as business expenses for rent calculations they were responsible for making. Yet the accountants were not prosecuted. Indeed, they testified against Leona Helmsley and denied they knew the invoices were altered. (It was never satisfactorily explained how they could not have known the invoices were altered and still decide not to deduct them from the rent calculations.)

Despite these weaknesses in the prosecution's case, the jury convicted Leona Helmsley. The prosecution's final witness, a maid, put the last nail in Leona's coffin when she testified that Leona once bragged to her that "only the little people pay taxes." It is entirely unlikely that Leona actually said this, since the Helmsleys paid more in taxes than virtually any real estate giants in America. Indeed, another witness to the conversation, a man who hates Leona, recently said that the maid had gotten it wrong, and that what Leona had actually said was that only "Harry Helmsley and the little people pay taxes."

The judge sentenced Leona Helmsley to one of the longest prison terms for a woman her age. Not satisfied, the state also prosecuted her for tax evasion, hoping to add several years to her sentence. We managed to win the appeal in the state case and all state charges against her were dismissed, but we lost the federal appeal by a 2–1 vote despite a strong dissent by the chief judge. And on April 15, 1992, the seventy-one-year-old hotel "queen" began serving her four-year sentence, leaving her eighty-three-year-old husband, who is very sick, to be cared for by his nurses and doctors.

Many New Yorkers wondered whether a sentence of community service, under which the hotel magnate could have used her talents and resources to address the city's homeless problem, might not have satisfied the needs of law enforcement while at the same time improving life for others.

But Leona Helmsley was the April 15 scapegoat of 1992, and scapegoats do not get community service, no matter how much sense such a punishment would make.   April 1992

REVEALING THE SENATE'S TRICKS

As I sat on the floor of the Senate, next to my client Senator Alan Cranston, I felt a bit like a potted plant. The presiding officer reminded me that I could advise my client during the proceedings in which his "reprimand" by the Ethics Committee was reported. But I could not speak in his defense on the floor of the Senate. No lawyer had been allowed to address the Senate since 1807, when Senator John Smith had been expelled.

Cranston had agreed to accept the committee's reprimand for an alleged "linkage" between contributions made by S&L banker Charles Keating to several voter-registration organizations and calls made by Cranston to bank regulators inquiring about the status of various investigations concerning Keating's bank. But Cranston vehemently disagreed with the committee's conclusion that he had "violated established norms of behavior in the Senate."

What were these "norms?" By whom had they been established? And where could a senator find them? The committee had unanimously concluded that Cranston had "violated no law or specific Senate rule," that he had "acted without corrupt intent," and that he "did not receive nor intend to receive personal financial benefit. . . ." The committee had also concluded that there was absolutely "no evidence" that Cranston "ever agreed to help Keating in return for a contribution." It found no "quid pro quo."

What then was there to reprimand Cranston for? The committee concluded that there was too close a linkage in time between the senator having accepted contributions from Mr. Keating for an entirely lawful voter-registration organization and his having made some entirely lawful inquiries concerning the status of certain regulatory matters concerning Mr. Keating. But if there was no quid pro quo and no help "in return for a contribution," how could there be impermissible "linkage?"

In delivering the committee's report, Senator Howell Heflin candidly acknowledged that there were no written rules regulating the proximity between a senator receiving contributions and performing a constituent service for the contributor. He quoted a former senator as suggesting that "a decent interval of time" should be allowed to pass between the contribution and the service. But what is a "decent interval?" And is it designed to assure merely an appearance of property? Heflin described the ethical guidelines as "subjective in nature" and more in the nature of the "rule of man" than the "rule of law." He acknowledged that "men differ when it comes to evaluating ethical conduct," and he could come up with no better formulation than Justice Potter Stewart's quip about pornography: "I may not be able to define it, but I know it when I see it."

The inability or unwillingness of the Senate to articulate a clear, bright-line test indicates a far deeper systemic problem of campaign financing. Senators—indeed all elected politicians—depend on campaign contributions from corporate constituents who expect something in return. These constituents may expect access to the official, help from him, or some other service. The contributions are entirely lawful and proper under current rules. So is the expectation that one's elected representative will perform constituent services. What is not proper is for an elected official to condition such services on contributions or for the constituent to offer the contribution in exchange for services.

And therein lies the rub. Most large-scale corporate contributors, in fact, make contributions in exchange for expected services. Indeed, if they expected nothing in return, they could probably be sued by the stockholders for wasting corporate funds! And most elected officials understand that corporate contributions are not intended merely to promote good government. But both sides of this implicit bargain are expected to pretend that there is no quid pro quo. This game of political charade is, in fact, the well understood "norm of behavior" in the Senate and elsewhere. Cranston violated that norm only in that he did not cover his tracks. He did not allow a "decent interval of time" to pass, so that there would be no "appearance of impropriety." He looked to the reality that there was no quid pro quo.

As I sat on the floor of the Senate listening to the various speeches, I was reminded of another exclusive club. This one is called the "Magic Castle" and it is located in Hollywood. It is a private club for magicians. Several years ago, they reprimanded a fellow magician for showing lay people how the tricks were done. That was Cranston's sin: He showed the public how Congress makes the linkage between corporate contributions and constituent services disappear.

The time has come for Congress to stop dealing with the problem of corporate campaign financing on a case-by-case basis and to understand that it is a question of reality and not mere illusion. So long as elected officials need corporate contributions and so long as corporations need constituent services, there will be linkage in fact. No ethics committee can make that reality disappear. Fundamental reforms in campaign financing are the only long-term solution to a pervasive problem.   November 1991

6 // *The Law and the Rise of the National Security State*

COURT TURNS NORTH ACCUSER INTO DEFENDER

Among a prosecutor's major advantages in a criminal case is the ability to coerce favorable testimony from the defendant's partners in crime. By making a deal with a less culpable partner, the prosecutor can loosen the reluctant witness's tongue and elicit incriminating testimony against the more culpable defendant who is standing trial.

Generally, the deal involves a plea by the less culpable partner to a reduced charge and a recommendation by the prosecutor to the sentencing judge that the partner-turned-government-witness be rewarded for cooperation. This reward takes the form of a lower sentence.

The essential mechanism for effectuating such a deal is that the sentencing must be deferred until after the cooperating partner in crime has completed testifying. This mechanism gives the prosecutor the necessary Sword of Damacles to hold over the head of the cooperating partner so as to assure that he will not back down and do what he would naturally like to do—namely, help his partner by slanting his testimony in favor of the defendant rather than the prosecutor. Under the Sword of Damacles arrangement, if the cooperating partner were to testify favorably to the defendant, the prosecutor would refuse to recommend a lower sentence and would inform the judge that he had refused to cooperate.

This mechanism is so powerful that defense attorneys always argue that the cooperating prosecution witness should be sentenced before he testifies in order to assure that he is not being pressured into slanting his testimony in favor of the prosecution. In my twenty-five years as a lawyer, I have never seen a case in which that defense argument prevailed. The prosecutor invariably insists on maintaining the Sword of Damacles over the head of the reluctant witness, and the courts invariably rule for the prosecution and defer the sentencing until after the witness has completed testimony.

But this rule, like so many others, has been changed for Oliver North. The principal witness against Oliver North is his self-confessed partner in crime Robert C. McFarlane, the former national security adviser who pleaded guilty to reduced charges relating to his misinforming Congress about aid to the contras. Instead of waiting for McFarlane to testify before sentencing him, the judge imposed final sentence—probation and a fine— on McFarlane on the eve of his testimony in the North trial. This denied the prosecutor the necessary leverage to assure that McFarlane would remain a cooperating witness for the prosecution rather than a Trojan Horse witness for the defense.

The result of this special treatment for Oliver North became apparen' last week as McFarlane completed his direct testimony for the prosecution and began his cross-examination at the hands of North's lawyer. Nina Tottenberg of National Public Radio reported that, at times, McFarlane sounded more like a character witness for his former associate than a witness for the prosecution. The *Boston Globe* commented on the prosecutor's "unusual effort to impeach McFarlane's credibility, even though he was called as a prosecution witness."

The reason for this "unusual" turnabout is obvious to any experienced criminal lawyer. By allowing McFarlane to be sentenced before rather than after his testimony, the prosecution gave up virtually all of its leverage over its star witness and allowed him to slant his testimony in favor of his erstwhile associate.

The obvious questions remain: Isn't that the way it should be? Wouldn't it be better if witnesses were free from the kind of government coercion inherent in the Sword of Damacles mechanism of postponing sentencing until after the testimony? Isn't the goal of the system "objective truth" rather than the "prosecution's version of truth"?

The answer to all of these questions is a resounding yes, that is the way it ought to be in all cases. The sad reality, however, is that it does not happen that way in cases other than Oliver North's. In other cases, the prosecution does, in fact, have the power to coerce its version of truth by postponing the sentencing of its cooperating witnesses. And as all experienced lawyers know, there is no such thing as "objective truth" from the mouth of a partner-in-crime witness. Subtle differences in nuance, a willingness to volunteer or withhold certain details, or a change in emphasis—these can all convert a witness for the prosecution into a witness for the defense without any risk of perjury.

There are two important questions raised by the special treatment accorded Oliver North and his defense team. The first is whether the unique rules being applied to him—in the treatment of witnesses, in the special sensitivity toward classified material, in the willingness of the judge to allow him to exercise extraordinary latitude in the defenses, and evidence he is being permitted to introduce—are the right ones. The answer to that question is probably yes. These are the rules that should apply to all criminal defendants.

The second question is why these rules are not applied to other defendants. It is that question of equal justice to which the public is currently receiving no satisfactory answer. March 1989

GOVERNMENT GIVES NORTH TOO MUCH SYMPATHY

As the Oliver North trial proceeds at a snail's pace, the Justice Department maintains that this highly publicized defendant is being treated like any other defendant in a similar situation. Many experienced defense attorneys disagree. Other defendants having similar needs for classified information have *not* been treated as sympathetically as Oliver North. Unlike North, they have been rebuffed by the courts when they sought to subpoena and present classified material as part of their defense.

A recent case in which my brother and I were involved is a mirror image of the North prosecution. In this case, the courts turned a deaf ear to the defendant's compelling claim. Our client was accused of shipping Hawk missile parts to Iran without a license. He admitted the sale, but maintained that he did not need a license because he was part of the covert operation run by Lt. Col. Oliver North and Vice Adm. John Poindexter. Our client was tried and convicted in the federal court in Connecticut, and his conviction has been affirmed. The "principles of law" applied by the Justice Department in his case stand in sharp contrast to those applied in North's prosecution.

The shipments our client was involved with occurred during the same period in which the staff of the National Security Council was coordinating its secret transfer. The list of spare Hawk missile parts he was asked to supply was identical to a list given by Iran to the CIA.

Our client submitted a sworn affidavit prior to his trial attesting to his belief that the people who had approached him to secure the arms were acting for the U.S. government. He had been told that the parts were needed to complete deals that had been concluded between the United States and Iran relating to release of hostages from Tehran. He claimed that at a meeting in London, Oliver North directed him not to leave a paper trail and that President Reagan would authorize the arms shipment to Iran.

The defendant sought to subpoena specific government documents to prove his defense—documents related to CIA involvement in the Iranian arms sale, and documents from the NSC and the State Department confirming that the people who approached him were acting on behalf of the government. The Justice Department opposed the subpoenas, and the court quashed them.

Our client's jury never heard any of this; the trial court's rulings prevented him from presenting the critical facts and documents in his defense. Even the Tower Commission Report, which was released after he submitted his affidavit and which substantiated his claims, was kept out of evidence, at the urging of the government, on grounds that it was "hearsay."

These rulings made it impossible for our client to prove his defense. For example, a critical issue in his case was whether he could confirm that the person he met with in London, and who gave him the orders to send the spare parts without leaving a paper record, was Oliver North. Counsel for North had advised his trial counsel that if called to testify, North would assert his privilege against self-incrimination.

The government sought to show that North was not in London by calling an NSC accounting and budget analyst who testified that he had no travel records showing North was in London during that time. The fact that the NSC also had no financial records of North's now-acknowledged trip to Tehran was considered irrelevant. More importantly, of course, subpoenaed records showing where North *was* on the day our client swore he was in London were never made available to him for use at his trial.

Our client argued on his appeal that precluding his access to relevant classified information was fundamentally unfair. But the court of appeals, lamenting that "we may never know all the details" of the operation run by North and acknowledging that private businessmen were recruited to facilitate the Iran-contra deal, nevertheless upheld his conviction. The fact that he was not allowed to introduce government documents was deemed insufficient to reverse the conviction.

As the court of appeals wrote in its decision, our client was presented with "an interesting dilemma." He was trying to prove that he was working as part of North's Iran-contra operation and was prevented at every turn from securing government documents to prove his claim. Still, the court found his trial to have been "fair."

Based on the government's refusal to provide relevant documents to him, Oliver North has already had the major charges against him dismissed. Some or all of the remaining charges may never reach the jury because of the Justice Department's refusal to disclose classified documents. This is despite the fact that such documents are far less important to North's defense against the narrow charges he now faces than they were to our client's defense.

Our client, who was denied access to government documents that were absolutely central to *his* case, is presently serving a ten-year jail term. Let someone explain to him that Oliver North is being treated just like any other criminal defendant.   March 1989

NORTH HAS MADE PATRIOTIC CRIME PAY

Oliver North will end up making a profit out of the $150,000 fine imposed on him by Judge Gerhard Gesell. Contributions will come pouring in; book contracts will abound; high-paying speeches will be offered. Crime certainly pays, when it is popular crime.

Judge Gesell's sentence is a travesty of justice when judged by any standard. It surely will not deter other overzealous pseudo-patriots from breaking the law in the interest of a perceived higher good. It sets a terrible example for our young. It creates unacceptable inequality for the hundreds of inmates whose crimes were far less severe. It surely will not rehabilitate North himself, who remains a hero to his constituency.

The entire prosecution of Oliver North, from beginning to end, has reflected a double standard of justice: one for popular criminals, the other for unpopular criminals. The prosecution was far too easy on him in dropping some of the most serious charges. The intelligence community was too sympathetic to him in refusing to declassify material that was already in the public domain, thus making prosecution more difficult. The witnesses against him were too willing to forget incriminating facts and remember exculpatory information. Even some of the jurors seemed to be taken in by his boyish facade. Finally, Judge Gesell, who has sentenced many far less culpable defendants to prison, seemed determined to end his long judicial career by imposing a popular sentence.

In the abstract, the sentence against North may appear to be fair, especially to those who are unaware of typical sentences in analogous cases. But for any experienced criminal lawyer—prosecutor or defense attorney— the relatively small fine and community service reflects an inexcusable double standard. Of course, North's organizational skills can be put to good use in the community, but that is true of many talented defendants who are daily sentenced to long prison terms.

The nonprison sentence is especially unfair when compared with sentences imposed on several arms dealers who were simply following North's directives. Some of those who shipped arms to Iran are now serving long prison terms. The courts have rejected their pleas of "official authorization."

Nor are underlings generally spared imprisonment if they were "just following orders." Most judges respond to that kind of plea by pointing out that if underlings are jailed for following orders, it will be harder for the superiors to get people to do their dirty work.

Oliver North was convicted of serious crimes. He was almost certainly guilty of even more serious criminal charges that were dropped. But he successfully wrapped himself in the American flag and conned the justice system into treating him like an overzealous Boy Scout.

He was convicted of shredding incriminating documents. Had he not done so, there might well have been evidence of even more serious crimes. In truth, North was guilty of shredding the Constitution by end-running around the express will of Congress and the law.

Judge Gesell has trivialized North's crimes by imposing this gentle pat on the wrist. He has sent a terrible message about the ends justifying the means. And he has trivialized his own courtroom by having wasted important judicial resources on what will be widely perceived as a charade. Oliver North should have been sent to jail, not for a long time but long enough to mingle with other criminals who also have wonderful excuses for their crimes.

One of the great scandals of the judiciary has long been disparity in sentencing. The same defendant convicted of the same crime before different judges can expect sentences varying between probation and life imprisonment. Many federal judges would have given Oliver North a substantial prison term. Indeed, last year, I conducted a moot court trial of the North case in one of my classes before a sitting federal district court judge. He "sentenced" North to ten years in prison, reasoning that the colonel had abused the high trust placed in him by his powerful office. I disagreed and called for a symbolic sentence—say six months to a year—to demonstrate that North was really being punished but to recognize the complexity of his situation.

Without jail time, the public will perceive the sentence as a victory for North. Only a taste of prison is seen as real punishment, especially when the fine will be paid by others and the community service will involve celebrity cameo appearances. North and his supporters are probably laughing to themselves about the hollow lecture read from the bench by a judge who seems to have little understanding of equal justice.

Oliver North shredded the Constitution's "separation of powers." Gerhard Gesell shredded the Constitution's "equal protection of the laws."

Before long it will probably be a crime, punishable by imprisonment, to shred or burn the American flag. It will be a sad commentary on America when symbolic dissenters look out from behind prison bars at the free Oliver North, who misused the flag to commit crimes and evade justice.

July 1989

A JURY'S PATRIOTISM VS. NORIEGA'S RIGHTS

Now that we have him, can we give him a fair trial? That's the question that lawyers around the country are asking on the heels of Manuel Noriega's dramatic surrender to U.S. authorities. And there are no easy answers, because there really is no precedent for a jury trial of a deposed dictator charged with drug crimes.

Never before in American history has a jury of twelve ordinary Americans been asked to sit in judgment on a major foreign policy goal of a president. Brave soldiers died in order to bring Noriega to justice. Can we really expect jurors to decide that these soldiers died in vain if they conclude that Noriega is probably guilty but there is a reasonable doubt?

ALAN M. DERSHOWITZ

Our presumption of innocence demands that a *probably* guilty defendant be acquitted if there is a reasonable doubt. And it is precisely in this gray zone that a jury is most likely to be influenced by the political and military events surrounding Noriega's capture.

In previous situations where American foreign policy has demanded the conviction of deposed tyrants—for example at the post–World War II war crimes tribunals—the cases were submitted to judges or to courts-martial rather than jurors. The same was true of the trial of the conspirators in President Abraham Lincoln's assassination at the close of the Civil War. It is expecting far too much from ordinary jurors to insist that they maintain a presumption of innocence when the president has put the prestige of our nation behind the claim that Noriega is a common criminal.

It is, of course, always possible to find twelve Americans who have lived in an intellectual coma for the past several years and are simply not aware that our troops invaded Panama to capture Noriega. But such a jury would be incapable of understanding the charges against Noriega and the sophisticated defense his lawyers are planning to raise. Noriega has the option of waiving a jury trial and asking for a judge, but he has the constitutional right to demand a jury trial that is fair.

In addition to this broad issue of a fair jury trial, there are a number of subsidiary problems that will have to be addressed over the coming weeks and months.

First is whether the manner by which we brought Noriega into this country precludes us from trying him here. That one is relatively easy. Under established principles of law, a defendant cannot challenge the methods used to bring him into the country. For example, we recently captured a Palestinian terrorist in the Mediterranean and forcibly brought him here for trial. He has been convicted, over the objections of his lawyers as to the manner of his abduction.

A second issue is likely to be whether Noriega can pay his lawyers with money that our government will claim is derived from illegal activities. His defense lawyers may face grand jury subpoenas to testify as to the sources of their legal fees, and this issue may tie up the case for some time.

Then there is the problem of evidence gathered by our troops in Panama. Soldiers do not follow the legal niceties of the Constitution. The evidence they found after searching Noriega's various offices and residences may be quite incriminating, but its admission at a criminal trial could raise novel and important constitutional questions.

Finally, there is the "Ollie North defense," which was relatively successful for the U.S. Marine hero. North's lawyer managed to get several charges dropped by demanding access to classified material that the government was unwilling to disclose. Of course, in that case, the administration—the president, attorney general, and CIA—were all rooting for North. They erred on the side of withholding classified material, some of which was already in the public domain, precisely in order to help their hero.

In the Noriega case, these same officials will probably err on the side of disclosing classified material in order to thwart any possibility that charges might be dropped. But such classified material might bolster Noriega's claim, if he chooses to make it, that the CIA deliberately closed its eyes to his criminal activity in order to encourage his cooperation with our intelligence needs.

The Noriega case poses a challenging test for the American judicial system. Juries work best in small cases involving obscure defendants. They do not work well in highly publicized cases involving notorious defendants. And they are at their worst when their patriotism is pitted against the rights of the defendant. Federal judges, who are given the protection of life tenure, are supposed to assure the independence of the judiciary and the separation of powers.

The judge who presides over the Noriega case will have more than the fate of Manuel Noriega in his hands. The integrity of the American system of justice will be on trial in that Florida courtroom.   January 1990

Noriega was convicted and his case is now on appeal.

TAPING CALLS VIOLATED NORIEGA'S PRIVACY

The disclosure by the Cable News Network (CNN) of tapes of conversations between Manuel Noriega and members of his legal team raises profound constitutional questions that go well beyond the former Panamanian dictator's case.

The first question is: Why does the government have any power to monitor the conversations of a presumptively innocent inmate who has never been convicted of any crime? It is important to remember that despite the fanfare over Noriega's capture and transfer to this country, he is, in the eyes of U.S. law, a totally innocent man. He should be free on bail to go about any lawful business, even if that business is to regain political power in Panama. The *only* legitimate reason he is confined is to assure that he will, in fact, show up to stand trial. His imprisonment, being preventative, is not intended to punish, since there is nothing to punish him for until and unless he is convicted by a jury. He should, therefore, be free to make unmonitored phone calls, just as the rest of us are free to call our friends and business associates without Big Brother listening.

It is against that constitutional background that we should address the questions of why Noriega's—and his fellow pretrial detainee's—phones are routinely monitored. The only legitimate reason for this otherwise inexcusable violation of his right to privacy is prison security: The need for prison officials to know whether any prison breaks or comparable conduct are being planned. If that is the sole justification for wiretapping the conversations of pretrial detainees, then only conversations related to prison security should be monitored. But because prison authorities cannot know in advance whether a particular conversation will involve prison security, they must be able to monitor and record conversations, but they should disregard and destroy all conversations that do not deal with prison security. They should be prohibited from sharing with prosecutors, the State Department, the media, or anyone else nonsecurity information they overhear.

Conversations with lawyers and legal assistants should be in a different category. In order to assure the absolute confidentiality of such conversations, pretrial detainees should make specific appointments to talk to their lawyers on the phone. These conversations should not be monitored at all, since it is illegal for a lawyer, who is an officer of the court, to participate in planning jail breaks and other breaches of security.

In this case, Noriega's lawyer seems to have been somewhat incautious in allowing his legal assistants to discuss legal tactics with Noriega on a monitored line without first clearly determining that the monitoring had been terminated. It is not enough to *assume* that the prison authorities always understand that a particular conversation is covered by the lawyer-client privilege.

One lesson of this case is that defense lawyers must work out, in advance and with specificity, the ground rules for conversations that are intended to be covered by the lawyer-client privilege. The lawyer or legal assistant should always clearly announce, before beginning a confidential conversation, that he or she is conducting the conversation on the express assumption that it is not being monitored or recorded. If that assumption is incorrect, the monitoring agent should announce that monitoring is being conducted. The lawyer could then go to court and obtain an order assuring confidential communications. If the conversation was inadvertently recorded without having been overheard by a live monitoring agent, then the tape should not be played beyond the point where it is clear that it is a lawyer-client communication.

Then there is the question of whether CNN should be free to broadcast tapes of Noriega's conversations. Critics of CNN cite the conflict between the media's First Amendment right to disclose and the inmate's Sixth Amendment rights to a fair trial and to the effective assistance of counsel. But in an open society, the First Amendment must prevail. The people's right to know is a constant in the democratic process. If the exercise of the First Amendment makes it impossible for a particular defendant to receive a fair trial, then that problem must be dealt with by the criminal justice system: The trial can be moved to a different location; if the defendant is out on bail, the trial can be postponed; the defendant can be given the right to challenge more potential jurors in order to assure an unbiased jury. In extreme cases—and these will be very rare—the prosecution may have to be dropped, but that is the price we pay for freedom of the press.

Noriega's lawyers are, in fact, seeking dismissal of the case against their client on the ground that the taping and disclosure of the prison conversations makes a fair trial impossible. It is unlikely that this drastic remedy will be granted.

Instead, the judge should set clear rules for when and where Noriega and his legal team can discuss his case in absolute privacy. All defendants must have their rights, whether they are free pending trial or in jail.

November 1990

NORIEGA TAPES FUEL DISPUTE OVER FIRST AND SIXTH AMENDMENTS

The U.S. Supreme Court's denial of review in the Noriega tapes case constitutes the first high court decision in modern history authorizing the prior restraint of newsworthy speech. Although denial of review may mean no more than that the justices are not ready to decide whether the courts have the constitutional power to suppress tapes that may include lawyer-client conversations, the court's 7–2 decision bodes ill for the First Amendment. It is particularly disturbing that the censorship in this case seems to be premised on a conflict between the public's First Amendment right to be informed and a criminal defendant's Sixth Amendment right to a fair trial.

Most criminal defense lawyers I know are opposed to prior restraints on the media's right to publish. Although Noriega's lawyers have sought to censor the press in this case—and have received support from some organizations representing defense attorneys—this view does not reflect the consensus of the defense bar.

In the opinion of the defense attorneys I have spoken to, there is no genuine conflict between the First and Sixth amendments. Freedom of the press rarely interferes with the right of a defendant to obtain a fair trial, and in those rare cases where it may, the criminal justice system has adequate means for dealing with the problem without resorting to the radical surgery of censorship and prior restraint. Judges have the power to transfer trials to locations where jurors are less likely to have been exposed to media reports, to postpone the trial until the effects of news reports have been dissipated, and to permit a larger number of juror challenges. Finally, the court has the power, in extreme cases, to dismiss a prosecution or reverse a conviction when the media coverage has absolutely precluded a fair trial. The fact that these drastic remedies are almost never ordered is eloquent testimony to the reality that the so-called conflict is more theoretical than practical.

In those rare cases where prejudicial pretrial publicity may require a dismissal or a new trial, the conflict is not between the First and Sixth amendments but rather between constitutional *rights* under the First and Sixth amendments, on the one hand, and the *power* of the government to convict defendants of crime, on the other hand. If media reporting protected by the First Amendment precludes a fair trial under the Sixth Amendment, the government may lose its power to prosecute a given case, or it may have to prosecute on terms somewhat less favorable to the prosecution.

It is significant that the most persistent calls for governmental restrictions on the press in their coverage of ongoing criminal cases have come not from civil libertarians who support the right of persons charged with crime but rather from constitutional conservatives such as the former chief justice Warren Burger, the current chief justice William Rehnquist, and others who generally side with the prosecution and against the rights of criminal defendants. It is reasonable to wonder whether their alleged concern for the right of the defendant to a fair trial is not sometimes invoked as an excuse for restricting the press.

This concern is reinforced by the FBI's recent seizure of CNN tapes from a hotel in Atlanta. Surely the FBI was not seeking to protect the rights of defendants. Nor was the solicitor general—the government's lawyer—when he advocated suppression of the tapes. It is also reinforced by the fact that the justice most sensitive to the rights of criminal defendants—Thurgood Marshall—dissented from the denial of review in the Noriega case, as would Justice William J. Brennan had he still been on the high court.

It is important to understand that the media does not usually dig up on its own the kind of information that is thought to endanger a fair trial. The information is often deliberately leaked to it by prosecutors, police, and other law-enforcement officials. Yet some of the very jurists who advocate restrictions on the press seem reluctant to impose sanctions on law-enforcement officials who feed the press. In many cases in which I have been involved, the judges have noted that there have been prosecutorial leaks—sometimes hemorrhages—calculated to influence the verdict, but they have stopped short of ordering an investigation into the sources of the leaks, even when an investigation would not require the media to divulge confidential sources.

It would be a constitutional tragedy of considerable magnitude if the U.S. Supreme Court were eventually to decide, in a binding opinion, to carve an exception into the First Amendment in the Noriega tapes case. It would be an act of transparent hypocrisy if *this* Supreme Court, which has shown such disdain for the rights of criminal defendants, were to premise an exception on the false notion that it is necessary to protect the rights of criminal defendants.   November 1990

THE CONSTITUTIONAL POWER
TO BLUFF

Debates over the original intent of the framers of our Constitution tend to be sterile, self-serving, and hypocritical. Like the Bible and Shakespeare, the U.S. Constitution can be quoted to support nearly any desired outcome. Witness the current debate over the relative powers of the president and Congress in the conduct of our military policy.

The Constitution gives Congress the power to *declare* war, but it gives the president, as commander-in-chief, the power to *conduct* war. Those who are against going to war in the Gulf emphasize the former power, while those who are in favor of war point to the latter power. At a slightly more abstract level, those who favor increased congressional power look to the former, while those who favor increased presidential power look to the latter.

As is typical in debates over original intent, the relevant world has changed fundamentally over the past two centuries. Nations simply do not "declare" war the way they used to do. Military options are far more calibrated than they were in the eighteenth century. They include threats, bluffs, development of new weapons, covert operations, massing of troops, small-scale incursions, surgical strikes, full-scale troop movements, and even nuclear attack. Declaring war is also an option, but not a very good one in most situations.

Consider President Kennedy's successful handling of the Cuban Missile Crisis of 1962. The president threatened, readied various weapons systems, blockaded, and, perhaps, bluffed. It worked. The Soviets removed their nuclear weapons without a shot being fired. Had the president been required to obtain a declaration of war before threatening a war or ordering a blockade (which, under international law, is an act of war), a divisive congressional debate would have ensued. Did a majority of Americans really want us to go to war with the Soviet Union over nuclear weapons in Cuba? Did these missiles really pose a qualitatively greater threat to the United States than the thousands of missiles already pointed at us from the Soviet Union and other places?

Fortunately, we never had to answer that question because Khrushchev blinked. President Kennedy, who surely did not want to go to war, was able to convince the Soviets that he might actually do so to keep hostile nuclear missiles off our continent.

Shouldn't President Bush have the same constitutional power to bluff, without his bluff being exposed by a divided Congress? Doesn't our commander-in-chief have the power to lead Saddam Hussein into *believing* that we will attack him if he does not leave Kuwait so that he will leave Kuwait *without* the need for us to attack him? "Of course he should," answer those who demand that Congress declare war before the president commits troops to combat. "But," they ask, "what if this isn't a bluff? What if he does go to war?"

The reality, of course, is that we do not know and *cannot* know whether the president is bluffing. If *we* know, then Saddam Hussein knows. And if Saddam Hussein knows, then it is no longer a bluff. Uncertainty is the essence of every successful bluff.

Nor can Congress be included in a decision to bluff. Even if Congress could keep a collective secret, it would not be right to keep critical information from the public.

Perhaps it is in the nature of democracy that bluffs are impossible. Perhaps that is an inherent advantage that tyrannies have over democracies. Tyrants need not share their powers, and their intentions, with their subjects. Presidents and other democratic leaders must.

But before we abdicate this important tool of military diplomacy—a tool that can often avoid bloodshed—we ought to be certain that our Constitution does not authorize it. I am not so certain that the congressional power to declare war denies the president the power to threaten war—or even to carry through on his threat without a formal congressional declaration of war.

Certainly Congress can *give* the president the power to bluff if it chooses to. And perhaps that is the way out of the current deadlock. President Bush can ask for, and Congress can grant, the power to create a credible threat of military force directed against Saddam Hussein if he does not leave Kuwait by a certain date. If that date arrives and there is no withdrawal, Congress can then give the president the additional authority to use military force at any time that is tactically advantageous to do so.

All this is quite complicated. But we live under a complex system of democratic checks and balances in which the power to wage war is divided between the legislative and executive branches, all subject to public debate and electoral checks. Nobody ever said that democracy was efficient. Nobody ever said the Constitution makes it easy to commit U.S. troops to battle. The "original intent" of the framers provides only the most general outline for how the most important power in the Constitution should be shared. Every generation of Americans has to fill in the blanks.

December 1990

ALAN M. DERSHOWITZ

SHOULD SADDAM HUSSEIN BE BROUGHT TO TRIAL?

The traditional country recipe for rabbit stew begins "First catch the rabbit." Ignoring that bit of old-fashioned advice, the U.S. government is preparing to bring Saddam Hussein to trial for "war crimes" and "crimes against humanity."

Even putting aside the question of whether we will manage to catch this particular rabbit, there are many other barriers—jurisprudential as well as political—to bringing Saddam Hussein to trial.

First, there is no existing mechanism for a Nuremberg-type tribunal. The Nuremberg "court" was established by the victorious allies in World War II. It disbanded after it sentenced the convicted war criminals. Its decisions serve as a substantive precedent but without an enforcement mechanism.

Second, the rules established by the Nuremberg courts have never been applied to any war criminals since the immediate post–World War II period. Nor has that been because of the absence of war crimes and crimes against humanity.

Although we have, thank God, experienced no Hitler since the death of that uniquely horrible man, we have certainly seen other monsters who have committed crimes against humanity. Among the most horrendous have been our own sometimes allies, Joseph Stalin and Hafez Assad. Even Saddam Hussein committed some of his worst crimes against humanity *before* we and our allies provided him military and diplomatic assistance.

Moreover, some of the world's worst human-rights violators—Idi Amin of Uganda and Jean-Bedel Bokassa of the Central African Republic—have been given sanctuary by our own allies in the current coalition against Saddam Hussein. Idi Amin lives comfortably in Saudi Arabia, while Bokassa lives in France. Yasir Arafat, the architect of random terrorism against innocent civilians who has committed countless crimes against humanity, has been given a standing ovation by the United Nations and has been welcomed by the pope.

None of this is to minimize Saddam's current crimes. His actions plainly violate the Nuremberg rules as well as other customary and conventional international laws. His crimes include waging a war of aggression, bombing and murdering innocent civilians, mistreating prisoners of war, supporting terrorism, and creating environmental havoc.

But in light of the world's—and our own—dismal record of ignoring and sometimes even rewarding crimes against humanity during the past forty years, a prosecution against Saddam Hussein would be seen as nothing more than "victor's justice." And victor's justice is an oxymoron. It is not justice at all. It's merely a spoil of winning a war. For there to be real justice in the prosecution of crimes against humanity, "winners," too, would have to be prosecuted by a neutral international court if, in the process of winning, they violated the laws of war.

But to state that proposition is to expose its unreality. Who would appoint such a court and enforce its mandates? Certainly not the United Nations, which has never demonstrated an ability to administer justice fairly. Certainly not the "great powers," which include China and the Soviet Union, who are among the most flagrant violators of human rights.

Alan Ryan, who once headed the Justice Department Office of Special Investigation, which prosecutes Nazi criminals, has proposed that Saddam Hussein be tried by the United States in the District of Columbia Federal Court. That would certainly be the simplest and most effective mechanism. Moreover, there are existing American laws that criminalize much of what Saddam Hussein is accused of having done.

But there are serious problems with this proposal. First, a trial by the United States in a U.S. court would be perceived as victor's justice. Second, there are grave doubts as to whether a tyrant who caused a war with the United States could get a fair trial in this country. Third, if Saddam were to get a fair trial, he would have to be given the right to introduce evidence about the complicity of the United States in the crimes against humanity committed by our once and future allies. He would be given an international platform from which to defend his actions and attack ours. This would be necessary since international law is as much a matter of customs as it is of statutes. Thus, a trial against Saddam Hussein would be turned into a political trial against the United States.

Finally, an independent judge might well rule in favor of Saddam Hussein on important issues of law, thus keeping the case away from the jury and giving him a legal victory that would be widely misunderstood as a justification for his barbarous conduct.

All in all, the rule of law would be disserved by a trial of Saddam Hussein. We must build a stronger, deeper, and more neutral foundation for international law before we selectively invoke it against our defeated enemies.

We will probably not catch the most important ingredient for the legal stew that is being prepared in Washington. If the Iraqis lose decisively, Saddam Hussein will probably be caught and brought to "justice" by his own people. It may be poetic, but it will not be pretty.   February 1991

WILL CIVIL LIBERTY BE A GULF WAR CASUALTY?

If the first casualty of war is truth, then the second casualty has traditionally been civil liberties. During every war we have fought, our government has compromised freedom of speech, due process of law, and the right of privacy. There is every reason to anticipate *new* governmental efforts to curtail our fundamental liberties if the Gulf war continues, particularly if we become bogged down in a long ground war with heavy casualties. The dangers to liberty will become even greater if a draft is instituted, thus increasing the protests and the number of conscientious objectors, as well as the reactions to them.

First, a bit of American history—and a dismal history it has been. During the Civil War, President Lincoln suspended the writ of habeas corpus, thus permitting trial and punishment without judicial review. During World War I, dissenters were thrown in jail for doing little more than opposing American involvement in the war. Shortly after Pearl Harbor brought us into World War II, President Roosevelt authorized the preventive detention of more than 100,000 U.S. citizens of Japanese descent. The Korean War was accompanied by McCarthyism *and* a general attack on civil liberties. The Vietnam War brought us Kent State, an assortment of political prosecutions, and recriminatory drafting of war protesters.

The most dangerous violation of basic freedom produced by the recent wars has been racial, ethnic, and religious scapegoating. During World War I, Italian-Americans, Russian-Americans, and others thought to be sympathetic to "anarchy" were deported and prosecuted in large numbers. During World War II, Japanese-Americans, German-Americans, and Italian-Americans were rounded up (although only the Japanese-Americans were detained en mass).

To his credit, President Bush currently seems sensitive to the rights of dissenters in general and to Arab- and Islamic-Americans in particular. This is a pleasant surprise, considering his self-serving insensitivity to civil liberties during his campaign against Michael Dukakis. A candidate who would make an issue out of the Dukakis veto of an unconstitutional mandatory Pledge of Allegiance law, who would vilify the American Civil Liberties Union, and who would pander to racism with his Willy Horton commercials could not necessarily be expected to go out of his way to defend the rights of unpopular minorities. Yet President Bush has, to his credit, condemned anti-Arab and anti-Islamic bigotry. The president went out of his way to remind us that all Americans, regardless of their ethnic background or religion, have the right to disagree with him and with the majority about the war. So far so good.

But already there are disturbing signs that our liberties may be in danger. Pan American Airlines's decision to ban all Iraqi nationals who do not have permanent residence in this country from their flights seems a bit overgeneral, though not nearly as racist as our government's decision to detain Japanese-Americans during World War II.

In Medford, Mass., the home of Tufts University, city counselors proposed that Congress withdraw federal loan funds and housing privileges from students who protest the Gulf war.

In other parts of the country, there have been similar efforts to show support for our troops by punishing protesters.

Even President Bush's innocent-sounding declaration of a national day of prayer contains within it seeds of divisive religious bigotry. Any presidential declaration about prayer is inconsistent with the separation of church and state mandated by our First Amendment. It makes second-class citizens of those who do not pray. But President Bush's declaration was far worse, since it selected Sunday, the Christian sabbath, as the designated day of national prayer. This suggests that we are a Christian nation—a doctrine long rejected in this most heterogeneous of countries. Although I strongly oppose governmentally endorsed prayer days, it certainly would have been somewhat less insensitive for the president to have declared a period of prayer that covered Friday, Saturday, and Sunday, so that Moslems, Jews, Seventh-Day Adventists, and others whose sabbath does not fall on Sunday would feel included as equal participants.

It is especially important during a time when some Americans blame the Gulf war on Moslems and Jews for the president not to take any actions that appear to marginalize non-Christian Americans. Designating a Sunday as an "official" day of prayer does just that.

Despite these recent problems, we are, thus far, doing considerably better than we have during past wars. But this is only the beginning, and matters appear to be going fairly well in the Gulf. If we experience reversals in our military fortunes abroad, or if terrorism were to become flagrant here at home, the urge to scapegoat and to curtail freedom would increase. The struggle for liberty never stays won, especially during wartime. Our brave troops in the Gulf understand the value of the freedoms for which they are fighting. The best way to support them is to keep those freedoms alive.

February 1991

WHY CASPAR WEINBERGER SHOULD BE INDICTED

If former secretary of defense Caspar Weinberger lied to Congress, as Special Prosecutor Lawrence E. Walsh apparently believes, then it is imperative that he be indicted and prosecuted. According to informed sources, there are direct conflicts between what Weinberger told Congress under oath and what has recently been uncovered from his private papers. The papers suggest that Weinberger was part of a deliberate cover-up of the secret arms sales to Iran—a cover-up aimed at preventing the feared impeachment of President Reagan.

If the special prosecutor is correct in his belief, then the cover-up succeeded by virtue of a deliberate conspiracy to commit perjury by high-ranking government officials. President Nixon was forced out of office and several high officials imprisoned as a result of the unsuccessful Watergate cover-up. Surely government officials who participated in a *successful* cover-up—successful in the sense that President Reagan filled out his term without impeachment or prosecution—should not be exonerated if there is now evidence that they lied under oath as part of that cover-up.

A report in the *New York Times* suggests that Special Prosecutor Walsh is moving with "even greater care" than usual in relation to Weinberger because he feels "a cultural affinity with" people like Weinberger. They are similar in age, background, party affiliation, and social class. It would be unfair in the extreme for Walsh to allow such considerations to enter into his decision-making. If anything, he should lean over backward to be as tough on Weinberger as he was on Oliver North, who has little in common with either Walsh or Weinberger.

Speaking of Oliver North, in a recent interview the former lieutenant colonel inadvertently provided Walsh with additional information on which to evaluate whether Weinberger is a truth-telling person. North confirmed what many people—including me—have been saying for years: that Weinberger lied under oath in the Jonathan Pollard case when he purported to describe the damage done by the former naval intelligence official who pleaded guilty to spying for Israel. Since I was part of Pollard's legal defense team—following his unprecedented sentence of life imprisonment for spying for our ally—I am not free to disclose what Weinberger swore to in his classified affidavit.

But I am free to quote the summary that he provided to the judge as part of the government's sentencing argument. This is what Weinberger said: "It's difficult for me, even in the so-called year of the spy, to conceive a greater harm to national security than that caused by [Pollard]." His reference to the "year of the spy" was intended to compare the damage done by Pollard's giving tactical and regional secrets to Israel with the damage done by the Walker family, Richard Miller, and Ronald Pelton, in providing strategic—including nuclear—and global secrets to our then enemy, the Soviet Union. Weinberger was thus telling the court, under oath, that the damage done by Pollard was greater than that done by the Soviet spies. I have been reliably informed by intelligence officials at the very top of our national security operation that this is a flat-out falsehood. And now, Oliver North has confirmed this by stating that "Weinberger's exaggerated claims of the damage done [by Pollard]" was an important factor in the judge's decision to give Pollard a longer sentence than most of the Soviet spies.

Perjury by high government officials corrupts the democratic processes of government. It instills a sense of cynicism about the equality of the law. If the reports about the evidence are correct, a perjury prosecution against Weinberger seems like an open-and-shut case. His sworn testimony is a matter of indisputable record. His written correspondence and his private papers are also matters of record. All that is required is to compare Exhibit A with Exhibit B. There is no issue of immunity, as there was in the failed North and Poindexter prosecutions. Nor is there any recognized defense for "following orders" or for lying for "national security" purposes. At the very least, the public has the right to *see* the secret documentary evidence that is believed to contradict the public testimony.

It would be a travesty of justice if Weinberger were to escape prosecution without the public seeing all the evidence. We have a right to know whether Lawrence E. Walsh is according equal justice to a fellow elite

Republican because he "feel[s] a cultural affinity" with him. No prosecutor, surely not a special prosecutor appointed to avoid conflicts of interest, has a right to give special privileges to people on the basis of social class and other affinities. Let a jury of ordinary Americans decide whether Weinberger lied when he testified before Congress or when he wrote his contradictory correspondence.

Winston Churchill once said that a nation's commitment to equal justice is best judged by the way it treats its most downtrodden citizens. I'm sure Churchill would agree that it must also be judged by the way it treats its most elevated citizens. May 1992

CASPAR WEINBERGER GETS NO SPECIAL TREATMENT

Even before the ink was dry on the special prosecutor's indictment of Caspar Weinberger, a well-orchestrated political defense was being put forward by Weinberger's supporters. Secretary of State James Baker took to the airwaves to echo the Wall Street Journal's condemnation of the indictment as an attempt to "criminalize policy differences." Senate Minority Leader Robert Dole called it a "witch hunt." And editorials in several newspapers repeated the party line that it was a "political" prosecution.

A close look at the facts, however, demonstrates that the shoe is on the other foot. The indictment of Weinberger is a conventional criminal charge: lying under oath and lying to investigators. Nothing could be more conventional than a responsible prosecutor looking at what a person swore to under oath and comparing it to what he wrote in his own notes. If they do not mesh, then there is the smoking gun of perjury. To ignore that smoking gun just because the suspect held a high government rank and may have lied to protect someone who held an even higher government rank would be to ignore the first principle of the rule of law: namely that no one is above the law, especially the law of perjury.

It is Weinberger's defenders who are trying to turn an ordinary criminal case into a political case by interposing a political defense. They argue that since Weinberger was on the *right* side of the Iran-contra issue—he was against it—it should follow that his perjury must be excused. That is not, however, an argument against "criminalizing differences in policy;" it is an argument in favor of excusing criminal conduct because there is an agreement over policy.

Under the rule of law, we criminalize only criminal acts, not attitudes, opinions or even policies. And we do not excuse criminal acts on the basis of the attitudes, opinions or policies they reflected. It is no irony, therefore, that Weinberger was indicted for trying to cover up, by lying, actions with which he may have disagreed. He was not indicted for failing to blow the whistle on Iran-contra, or even for going along with a policy from which he dissented. He was indicted for deliberately lying about what he knew and when he knew about it. That is a far cry from a political prosecution.

Nor should eyebrows be raised over the fact that Weinberger may have beenoffered a deal under which he would be permitted to escape prosecution or to plead to a lesser offense in exchange for providing evidence against higher-ups. For better or worse, that is the way our system works. Lower- and middle-level operatives are commonly offered plea bargains to inculpate higher-ups. "Mr. Little" is threatened with prosecution unless he turns in "Mr. Middle," who in turn is given an opportunity to turn in "Mr. Big." Mr. Big may be the head of the mob, the CEO of a corporation or—as in this case—the president of the United States. If Weinberger's supporters don't like this approach to law enforcement, let them try to change the entire system. But under the system currently in existence, what happened to Weinberger is no different from what happens to others who are suspected of committing crimes in hierarchical situations.

Indeed, what happened to Caspar Weinberger, in general, is what does—and should—happen to every American citizen caught lying under oath to protect superiors. They should be indicted and put on trial. At their trial, they are entitled to the full panoply of constitutional protections, including the presumption of innocence. What Weinberger's supporters are calling for is special treatment for their friend. Suddenly and hypocritically, law-and-order types who side with the prosecution in ordinary cases and who ridicule civil libertarians as being "soft on crime" are rediscovering the Bill of Rights and are virtually signing up to become card-carrying members of the American Civil Liberties Union. "A conservative is a liberal who's been mugged," goes the old saw. That may be true, but the Weinberger case reminds us of the other side of that saw: A civil libertarian is a conservative whose friend has been indicted.

In the Oliver North case, the courts were extraordinarily solicitous of that popular defendant's constitutional rights. That is fine, so long as the courts are equally solicitous of the rights of obscure and unpopular defendants. Unfortunately, they rarely are. Just as no one is above the law, so too no one is entitled to special treatment under the law. Let the legal chips fall where they may in the Weinberger case. Let us wait and see, after all the evidence is in, whether his legal defense—as distinguished from the political defense that is now being offered—can explain the apparent discrepancies between what th former Secretary of Defense said under oath and what he wrote in his notes.   June 1992

7 // *The "War on Drugs" and the Rights of Individuals*

DROP YOUR PANTS FOR A DRUG-FREE AMERICA

The Reagan administration's approach to the drug problem is best summed up by the cliché made famous by Nancy Reagan: "Just say no to drugs." But to understand the utter bankruptcy of the approach, the emphasis must be placed on the word *just*, since that is about all the current administration seems to be doing.

Of course, there is the usual rhetoric, a few high-profile busts of middle-level dealers, and the recent indictment of Gen. Manuel Noriega. But the drug problem is worse, in many respects, than when President Reagan entered the Oval Office more than seven years ago.

The latest administration gambit is mandatory, widespread drug testing of all manner of workers, ranging from clerical employees to airline pilots. Proponents and opponents of drug testing seem to fall into the usual extreme camps: the Reagan-Meese types who are willing to have everyone drop his pants (or lift her skirt) without regard to the sensitivity of their jobs, the degree of suspicion, or the history of drug use by the person or in the industry, and some uncompromising civil libertarians who are gearing up to fight all mandatory drug testing regardless of the circumstances.

Both extremes are wrong. In a constitutional democracy, the relevant constraints of the Constitution—in this instance the Fourth Amendment—must be the starting point for any resolution of the conflicting claims. That amendment says: "The right of the people to be secure in their persons, houses, papers, and effects, against unreasonable searches and seizures, shall not be violated, and no warrants shall issue, but upon probable cause . . ."

There can be little doubt that a mandatory drug test, designed to determine whether a citizen privately ingested a controlled substance, is a search and seizure. But it cannot be said to be based on "probable cause" if it is demanded of all citizens in a particular occupation without regard to individual proof, or if it is imposed randomly. Thus, no valid search warrant can be issued for this kind of intrusion.

There is only one remaining constitutional basis for such a search: namely, that it is not "unreasonable." The Fourth Amendment has been interpreted by the courts, in a series of hotly disputed decisions, to permit reasonable searches under some circumstances even if there is no individualized probable cause and thus no grounds for a warrant. But the word *reasonable* is the personification of subjectivity: What is a reasonable search to a Reaganite may be an outrageous intrusion to a civil libertarian. I am certain that the British magistrates who authorized the issuance of "general warrants" and who rummaged through the personal effects of our colonial forebears regarded their own actions as "reasonable."

But notwithstanding its subjectivity—and its potential for arbitrariness—the concept of "reasonableness" permeates our legal and constitutional world. It is the standard against which mandatory drug testing has been, and will continue to be, tested in the courts.

The most recent government proposal may well pass that test—if it is applied in a sensible manner. It mandates drug testing for all airline employees in safety-related jobs—more than half a million pilots, navigators, flight attendants, and mechanics. Most Americans, surely most who fly (or take trains or buses) regularly, will agree that testing those in whose hands we place our lives seems eminently reasonable. The fatal Amtrak crash last year, apparently caused by a crew member who had just used drugs, certainly makes a compelling case for testing those who control passenger vehicles.

Whether flight attendants or train conductors, who spend much of their time serving coffee, taking tickets, and attending to the comforts of the passengers, should be included is somewhat more debatable. (Paradoxically, they oppose testing while claiming that they play important safety roles.) Surely ticketing personnel, baggage handlers, and airline executives should not be subjected to mandatory testing, and they are not included in this proposal.

Another difficult issue is whether a positive test result should be admissible in a criminal prosecution, or whether its use should be limited to firing the offending employee or requiring that he enter a drug rehabilitation program. Since the warrantless search is not based on probable cause, excluding its incriminating result would go a long way toward assuring that safety considerations were not being used as a pretense to gather evidence for criminal prosecutions.

The real danger lies in the slippery slope. Once the principle is established that safety-related workers can be randomly tested, there will be those who will push for expanding that category beyond its appropriately narrow confines. The Reagan administration has a penchant for pushing its policies to their illogical—and unreasonable—conclusions. For example, its regulation mandating drug testing for all civilian employees of the military was recently struck down as unconstitutional by a federal district court judge.

Let all Americans who care both about liberty and safety insist that mandatory drug testing be limited to those who have chosen occupations in which steady hands and alert minds are required, and where the use of drugs poses a substantial danger to the lives and limbs of others.

March 1988

TRASHING THE COURT'S GARBAGE RULING

Now that the Supreme Court has ruled that we Americans have no reasonable expectation of privacy for our garbage, the time has come to consider what options we have in disposing trash without exposing all our little secrets.

In its 6–2 decision, the justices reasoned, in one of the classic non sequiturs of all time, that since "plastic garbage bags . . . are readily available to animals, children, scavengers [and] snoops," it is perfectly proper for the local police, the FBI, or the *National Enquirer* to sift through every piece of our trash in an effort to reconstruct our sex lives, reading habits, political or religious beliefs, physical or mental health, and food or drink preferences. The same reasoning would suggest that since Peeping Toms occasionally look through bedroom curtains, the police can videotape our marital privacy.

The dissenting justices pointed out that "members of our society will be shocked to learn" that their closed trash bins are open to all manner of governmental inspection.

Fortunately, one thing seems obvious: We Americans are a hearty and resilient people, able to adapt through ingenuity to changing expectations. As a response to mandatory drug testing of government and corporate employees, for example, an enterprising company began marketing "Bible Belt Urine"—provided by a Bible-study group from Memphis and guaranteed to be absolutely drug free.

With this to inspire, I am confident that we will figure out new ways to keep the probing eye of government out of our trash. Some options:

Follow the example of my old great aunt from Brooklyn, who will have no difficulty adapting to the new decision. She never throws anything out. Her apartment is piled from floor to ceiling with old newspapers, magazines, unopened mail, string, grocery bags, and several items that are so old they can no longer be identified except by collectors of antiquity. There are no food leftovers because she never lets anything go to waste (remember those starving children in India!). I don't think I ever saw a garbage bag in her home. Admittedly, her solution is not attractive to those of us who grew up in the disposable society.

The "Oliver North mechanized response" to this dilemma has a drawback as well. It's limited to the wealthy, the powerful, or those who are prepared to carry their trash to the workplace. Most of us don't have home shredding machines or burn bags. And garbage compactors are no match for modern police-lab technology.

A third option would probably be expensive in the beginning, but its price might decline with mass marketing: Some ingenious American entrepreneur will surely come up with commercially prepared garbage bags whose contents are designed to project the proper image. These bags, fully loaded with the "right" magazines, food and drink containers, etc., would be placed at the front of the house, while your real garbage could be snuck out the back door for discreet disposal.

A variation on this theme for people who wouldn't stoop to commercially prepared ersatz garbage would be dual bins in the home. But instead of dividing the trash into recyclable and nonrecyclable, the categories would be "public" and "private." Under this system, the Dom Perignon bottles and caviar tins would be neatly stacked in the public trash, while the beer cans and beef-jerky wrappers would be consigned to the private garbage.

Yet another possibility is to mingle your garbage with that of friends and neighbors before placing it out on the street. Trash-trading parties, at which bags are exchanged, could replace the Tupperware parties of the sixties. There is no better way to get to know your neighbors or to confuse the local gendarmes than by the mix-and-match method of trash disposal.

If the cops then found a joint in your garbage bag, they would have to put the whole neighborhood on trial.

Finally, there is the rent-a-barge method. But the recent experiences of a New York community that could not find a home for its garbage after loading it on an ocean-bound barge do not bode well for this approach.

Though the implications of the Supreme Court's new decision may have a humorous side, the decision itself raises serious issues. It is yet another step in the erosion of our privacy. In a society as cluttered as ours, everyone has the need to dispose of trash. And trash consists of the remnants of our private and public lives. Our home-disposal bins are daily diaries of some of our most intimate activities. With the development of sophisticated technology, including DNA printing, much can be learned from the most innocent fragment of hair or skin.

Nor are our bathrooms safe from the government snoop. Toilet traps, which divert sewage to governmental receptacles, are already used in extraordinary cases and will now become fair game under the court's decision, since human wastes are simply the body's garbage.

More than half a century ago, the great Justice Louis Brandeis characterized wiretapping as "dirty business." I can only imagine how he would have described governmental rummaging through our garbage pails and toilets.

May 1988

THE CASE FOR MEDICALIZING HEROIN

When *Time* magazine has a cover story on the legalization of drugs, and when Oprah Winfrey devotes an entire show to that "unthinkable" proposition, you can be sure that this is an issue whose time has come—at least for serious discussion.

But it is difficult to get politicians to *have* a serious discussion about alternatives to our currently bankrupt approach to drug abuse. Even thinking out loud about the possibility of decriminalization is seen as being soft on drugs. And no elected official can afford to be viewed as less than ferocious and uncompromising on this issue.

Any doubts about that truism were surely allayed when Vice President Bush openly broke with his president and most important supporter over whether to try to make a deal with Panamanian strongman Manuel Noriega, whom the United States has charged with drug-trafficking.

I was one of the guests on the recent Oprah Winfrey show that debated drug decriminalization. The rhetoric and emotions ran high, as politicians and audience members competed over who could be tougher in the war against drugs.

"Call out the marines," "bomb the poppy fields," "execute the drug dealers"—these are among the "constructive" suggestions being offered to supplement the administration's simpleminded "just say no" slogan.

Proposals to medicalize, regulate, or in another way decriminalize any currently illegal drug—whether it be marijuana, cocaine, or heroin—were greeted by derision and cries of "surrender." Even politicians who *in private* recognize the virtues of decriminalization must continue to oppose it when the cameras are rolling.

That is why it is so important to outline here the politically unpopular case for an alternative approach.

Ironically, the case is easiest for the hardest drug—heroin. There can be no doubt that heroin is a horrible drug: It is highly addictive and debilitating; taken in high, or unregulated, doses, it can kill; when administered by means of shared needles, it spreads AIDS; because of its high price and addictive quality, it makes acquisitive criminals out of desperate addicts. Few would disagree that if we could rid it from the planet through the passage of a law or the invention of a plant-specific herbicide, we should do so.

But since we can neither eliminate heroin nor the demand for it, there is a powerful case for medicalizing as much of the problem as is feasible. Under this proposal, or one of its many variants, the hard-core addict would receive the option of getting his fix in a medical setting, administered by medical personnel.

The setting could be a mobile hospital van or some other facility close to where the addicts live. A doctor would determine the dosage for each addict—a maintenance dosage designed to prevent withdrawal without risking overdose. And the fix would be injected in the medical facility so the addict could not sell or barter the drug or prescription.

This will by no means solve all the problems associated with heroin addiction, but it would ameliorate some of the most serious ones. The maintained heroin addict will not immediately become a model citizen. But much of the desperation that today accounts for the victimization of innocent home-dwellers, store employees, and pedestrians—primarily in urban centers—would be eliminated, and drug-related crime would be significantly reduced.

Today's addict is simply not deterred by the law. He will get his fix by hook or by crook, or by knife or by gun, regardless of the risk. That is what heroin addiction means. Giving the desperate addict a twenty-four-hour medical alternative will save the lives of countless innocent victims of both crime and AIDS.

It will also save the lives of thousands of addicts who now kill themselves in drug shooting galleries by injecting impure street mixtures through AIDS-infected needles.

There will, of course, always be a black market for heroin, even if it were medicalized. Not every addict will accept a medically administered injection, and even some of those who do will supplement their maintenance doses with street drugs. But much of the desperate quality of the constant quest for the fix will be reduced for at least some heroin addicts. And this will have a profound impact on both the quantity and violence of inner-city crime.

Nor would new addicts be created by this medical approach. Only long-term adult addicts would be eligible for the program. And the expenses would be more than offset by the extraordinary savings to our society in reduced crime.

If this program proved successful in the context of heroin addiction, variants could be considered for other illegal drugs such as cocaine and marijuana. There is no assurance that an approach which is successful for one drug will necessarily work for others. Many of the problems are different.

We have already decriminalized two of the most dangerous drugs known to humankind—nicotine and alcohol. Decriminalization of these killers, which destroy more lives than all other drugs combined, has not totally eliminated the problems associated with them.

But we have come to realize that criminalization of nicotine and alcohol causes even more problems than it solves. The time has come to consider whether that is also true of heroin and perhaps of other drugs as well.

June 1988

ALAN M. DERSHOWITZ

U.S. SHIP SEIZURES
VIOLATE LIBERTIES

Israel has been roundly condemned by the United States for its policy of sometimes destroying houses that were used to harbor terrorists on the West Bank and in Gaza. The specter of "collective punishment" has been raised, since the homeowners are not always aware, though often they are, that the person they harbored was, in fact, a terrorist. Complaints are made as well that house destruction can be ordered administratively, without a full judicial trial.

The Israeli authorities have responded to American criticism by pointing out that it is often difficult to prove complicity between homeowners and terrorists, even when they are close relatives. Moreover, they argue that the Israeli policy of swift property destruction is extremely effective as a deterrent: Friends and relatives of terrorists are far more reluctant to "ask no questions" when they realize that ignorance, real or feigned, will not be accepted as an excuse when it is later determined that the person they harbored was a terrorist.

Civil libertarians remain unconvinced by the Israeli reasoning. Individual guilt, proved beyond a reasonable doubt in a court of law, is the only basis for punishment, they insist. The fact that the house destruction is merely an economic penalty—everyone is always removed from the house and surrounding areas before it is destroyed—does not dispose of the principle arguments against collective and nonjudicial punishment.

While this debate continues about the Israeli policy of house destruction, many of the same Americans who are most critical of Israel are calling for and, indeed, carrying out a similar policy right here at home. That policy involves the seizure, confiscation, and sale of large boats, airplanes, and automobiles in which even the tiniest amounts of illegal drugs are found.

This policy, known as "zero tolerance," does not require the Customs Service to prove that the owner of the seized vehicle had any idea that drugs were on board. And, indeed, in recent weeks, several extremely valuable craft were seized under circumstances that made it unlikely that the owners were in complicity. For example, the $80 million research vessel that had been used to explore the *Titanic* was seized after traces of marijuana were found in a crew member's shaving kit. Separately, the pleasure craft *Monkey*

Business—of Gary Hart infamy—was also seized, as were approximately seventeen hundred other conveyances on which drugs were found.

Though some seized property has been returned, much is still in the hands of the government—or auctioneers or purchasers. To illustrate how Draconian the Custom Service believes the law allows it to be, a spokesperson recently warned that if a joint were found on a passenger cruising aboard the *Queen Elizabeth II*, Customs might technically "have the authority to seize it." The agency could also seize homes, places of business, and other "means" used in the sale or possession of drugs without regard to the individual guilt or innocence of the owners.

Nor are such seizures subject to the ordinary rules of criminal punishment. They, like Israeli house destructions, are administrative in nature and require far fewer legal safeguards.

As with the Israeli defenders of house destructions, the Americans who justify vehicle seizure ground their arguments on effectiveness. They say current criminal penalties let too many perpetrators slip through the cracks of the law. Moreover, they contend, vehicle owners who are on notice of the "zero tolerance" policy will be much tougher in making sure that their vehicles are not misused and that they remain drug free. If an occasional innocent has his property confiscated, that is a price worth paying for a drug-free environment.

The arguments in favor of, and against, some degree of collective punishment have been with us since the beginning of time. Even the Bible provides support for both sides. In Deuteronomy, the rule against collective punishment is stated quite dramatically: "The fathers shall not be put to death for the children; neither shall the children be put to death for the fathers. Everyone shall be put to death for his own sins."

But then in Samuel, the Lord seems to violate His own rule when He demands the destruction of the entire nation of Amalek. "Spare no one; put them all to death, men and women and babies in arms, herds and flocks, camels and asses.

The civil liberties position in opposition to all collective punishment is clear and principled. The law-enforcement position favoring collective punishment, at least where there is a high degree of suspicion that the targeted individual may be in a position to do more, is also clear and at least has the virtue of consistency.

But the position of the current U.S. administration smacks of hypocrisy and the double standard. Out of one side of its mouth it condemns an ally who is fighting for its life against the scourge of terrorism. Out of the other side it practices a policy of collective punishment that is just as apt to violate civil liberties and is certainly no more justified by the dangers it seeks to prevent.

When a great nation like ours condemns a far more vulnerable ally, it should at least take a look in the mirror.   June 1988

END THE WITCH HUNT AGAINST POT SMOKERS

Several weeks ago I debated a representative of the Reagan-Bush administration on the issue of drugs. The representative was the U.S. Attorney for the District of Massachusetts—the federal government's chief lawyer and prosecutor for that state.

I favored the medicalization of heroin for mainline addicts, the decriminalization of marijuana use, and further study of our policy toward cocaine and crack. The U.S. attorney, echoing the administration's line, favored tougher law enforcement, capital punishment, and "just say no."

During the course of the debate, I issued the following challenge to the U.S. attorney: "We don't have the stomach to imprison the user, although we hear the rhetoric of full enforcement, because, let me tell you, if you want to put all the users in jail, we'd be criminalizing and felonizing a very substantial percentage of otherwise law-abiding American citizens. And we're not prepared to do that."

The U.S. attorney accepted my challenge forthrightly: "I don't think it is the case that we don't have the stomach. Our office has gone after users. We will continue to go after users. We are now at the point where we have to go after the user, and we are doing that."

Recently, this very U.S. attorney, Frank McNamara, publicly acknowledged in Boston newspapers that he himself had used marijuana within the past four years.

His admission grew out of an episode in which he said he saw his predecessor as U.S. attorney, William Weld, smoking marijuana at a wedding party they had both attended.

Weld denied the charges, and an investigation by the Justice Department completely vindicated Weld's denial. It found "overwhelming evidence" to rebut McNamara's charges. But in the course of the investigation, McNamara was asked how he was so certain that it was marijuana Weld was smoking. McNamara responded that he knew the smell because he himself "had used it in college." The Justice Department report said that "McNamara subsequently told the FBI that he had used marijuana as recently as four years ago, though not while he was U.S. attorney."

If McNamara used the drug in the United States within the past five years (the statute of limitations), he would be subject to criminal prosecution under federal law. And it would disqualify him from working in his own office as an assistant U.S. attorney, since prospective prosecutors are asked about marijuana use and warned that an admission of post-college use will cause their applications to be rejected.

In his debate with me, discussing our national permissiveness toward drug use in the 1970s, McNamara invoked the following biblical metaphor: "We sowed the wind and we are now reaping the whirlwind." He might have been talking about the Reagan-Bush administration's drug policy in general and his own in particular.

Any attempt to prosecute marijuana users will inevitably result in selective enforcement of the law. We cannot and will not prosecute the tens of millions of otherwise law-abiding citizens who partake in the vice of an occasional joint. Prosecutors will have to pick and choose a select few from among the many to indict and bring to trial. In a speech last year, McNamara recommended to other law-enforcement officials that, in exercising their discretion concerning who to prosecute, they should go after "public figures who use drugs." Highly visible federal prosecutors certainly fit that description.

Currently, every user prosecuted—or turned down for a job in the Justice Department or, indeed, elsewhere—can point to the fact that an admitted user holds one of the highest prosecutorial offices in the nation. We cannot tolerate a double standard under which some users prosecute while others are prosecuted.

The tragic case of Frank McNamara is among the best arguments for decriminalizing the occasional use of marijuana. Judge Douglas Ginsburg has already been denied a Supreme Court appointment because he was caught doing what other judges, prosecutors, and lawmakers have also done. Now a U.S. attorney is facing possible dismissal, or worse, for his admitted past use. Countless others are simply not applying for government jobs out of fear that their past peccadillos will be exposed and their careers ruined.

Let us put an end to this witch hunt, lest we limit governmental employment to liars, hypocrites, octogenarians, and the small number of younger people who really never did experiment with drugs—or any other illegal behavior throughout their boring lives.

McNamara's justification for his own drug use is that his "experimentation" had led him to harden his antidrug position. "That's not hypocrisy," he declared.

But it is hypocrisy for society to allow a prosecutor to arrive at his own views on drugs after experimenting with them, while that same prosecutor, and the administration for which he works, continues to prosecute others for engaging in similar experimentation.   November 1988

ANOTHER WAY OF SOLVING THE DRUG PROBLEM

Consider the following "what if" scenario.

What if drug czar William Bennett were to deliver a speech that went like this?

"We have *two* drug problems in the country. The first is that about a million Americans are harming themselves—a few thousand killing themselves—by using drugs. These figures pale by comparison to the number of Americans who kill and disable themselves by drinking alcohol or smoking tobacco. But no one can deny that the first type of drug problem, self-abuse, is a serious one.

"The second drug problem is both more serious and of more appropriate concern to governments. That problem is the violence and corruption associated with the sale of drugs for profit. There is also some violence caused by the ingestion of certain drugs, but such biochemically induced violence is relatively insignificant compared to that generated by the drug-profit motive and the high cost of drugs.

"There is a conflict between efforts at reducing the first and second problems. The more we try to stop people from hurting themselves by using drugs, the more violence and corruption we seem to get. The tougher we make it to get drugs, the more expensive drugs become and the more profit there is for the drug dealers. The more expensive the drugs are, the more robberies and burglaries are committed by drug users desperate to raise enough money to satisfy their cravings. And the higher the profit, the more violence will take place over 'turfs,' and the more bribes will be paid by drug dealers to corruptible law-enforcement officials.

"On the other hand, if we were to legalize drugs, thus lowering the cost of drugs and taking the profit out of drug dealing, it is likely that even more people would harm themselves by trying drugs. That is what happened after the end of prohibition in the 1930s: The violence and corruption associated with prohibition stopped, but more people began to drink and there was an increase in alcoholism.

"This conflict between reducing drug *use* and reducing drug *violence* and *corruption* raises a fundamental issue of the appropriate role of government. Is it not more appropriate for government to try to prevent people from harming *others* than from harming *themselves*? If it is true that our efforts at protecting drug users from themselves are creating increasing dangers to non-drug-using citizens, should we not consider a different approach?

"I have decided to try that different approach for a trial period. During the next five years, all drugs will be legally dispensed at cost—a tiny fraction of their current street price. All the money we now spend on stopping drugs at our borders, law enforcement, and prisons will be used on drug prevention and rehabilitation programs designed to reduce the demand for drugs and to treat drug users and addicts. Special efforts will be directed at pregnant and nursing mothers, since they are harming not only themselves, but their innocent offspring as well. Thank you and God bless you."

If such a speech would frighten you, stop worrying. Neither William Bennett nor any future drug czar will likely propose that kind of approach. No matter how rational it might seem, it is not politically feasible in the current climate of all-out war on drugs. It sounds too much like a surrender.

I'm not even sure that I favor immediate legalization of all drugs. Twenty years ago, when Bill Bennett was a student in my criminal law class at Harvard Law School, I advocated legalization. At that time, our major drug problems grew out of heroin addiction. The case for treating such addiction as a disease rather than as a crime was very compelling. And it still is.

The other problem drugs were marijuana and cocaine, both used widely by college students, yuppies, and others who could afford them. The case for treating those drugs as we treat liquor and cigarettes was compelling. And it still is.

But "crack" has changed the stakes. It is the drug of choice for hundreds of thousands of very young kids, especially from poor and minority backgrounds. If crack were suddenly legalized, its use would likely become even more widespread within these communities. A cynic might argue that crack is already "legal," in the sense that it is widely available there. But certainly some people are deterred by the fear of punishment or the price of the drug. A portion of these might try crack, with its quickly addictive qualities, if it were available cheaply and legally.

The hard question that would be posed by legalizing crack in the context of current use patterns is whether it would be fair to allow the entire burden of our crack problem to fall on the most vulnerable members of our most vulnerable communities. The real mystery is why right-wing Republicans, who have traditionally shown little concern for poor and minority citizens, do not advocate the legalization approach, because it is surely in the best interest of their own constituencies.

I guess it's hard for a right-winger to give up a good war.

September 1989

PUT THAT CORD BACK ON YOUR TELEPHONE

Well, I guess it's back to those telephone cords that I'm always tripping over. No more cordless phones for me, since I have been warned that my privacy is not assured unless my handset is attached with a wire to the base of the telephone. The Supreme Court recently refused to review a lower court decision holding that an Iowa family, the Tylers, had no "justifiable expectation of privacy for their conversations" over a cordless phone.

The Tylers had received their cordless phone as a gift and had used it as any family would. Their neighbors, the Berodts, soon learned that they could overhear the Tylers' conversations by boosting the power switch on their own cordless phone.

At one point, they overheard a conversation that sounded as if it might involve drugs. They called the police, who told them to keep listening. It soon became clear that they had been wrong about the drugs. But the daily monitoring did eventually reveal that one member of the Tyler family may have been involved in improper business dealings.

The decision in the Tyler case, however, was not limited to people who overhear the "bad guys." Unless the law is changed, every busybody in America will be free to eavesdrop on their innocent friends and neighbors who are foolhardy enough to use cordless telephones. And it will only be a matter of time before inexpensive devices will be available in the corner store, allowing snoops and gossips with nothing better to do to listen in as you and your friends exchange confidences. The afternoon soaps may suffer a slump in their ratings as couch potatoes tune in to the real-life gossip of next-door neighbors.

The problem of the nonsecure cordless phone will be particularly acute for professionals such as doctors, psychologists, lawyers, priests, and financial advisers. Anyone who has an ethical obligation of confidentiality should no longer conduct business over cordless phones, unless they warn their confidants that they are risking privacy for convenience.

Other new technologies that are vulnerable to interception include cellular phones, fax machines, and computer modems. You are not even safe if you replace your cordless phone with an old-fashioned model: Should the person with whom you are speaking use a cordless phone, your conversation can be intercepted at *his* end. Nothing is safe from the voracious ear, eye, or recording machine of the snoop who is determined to reach out and tap someone.

I once had a client who was so fearful of being recorded that he conducted all important business meetings in saunas and hot tubs. Since the participants were stark naked, he could easily check them for recording devices. Do we really want to become a society in which everyone must take such precautions to assure privacy?

It is ironic that the U.S. Supreme Court, which guards its own privacy more jealously than any other branch of government, seems so insensitive to the privacy of the rest of us. At a time when Eastern Europeans, and others who have suffered from the totalitarian intrusions of Big Brother, seem determined to establish spheres of privacy, our own guardians of liberty are narrowing our "justifiable expectation of privacy."

The Supreme Court should not be allowed to have the last word in this matter, especially since the justices have spoken through silence. By refusing to review the important issue of cordless phone privacy, the court has warned us that we use this new technology at our own risk. Congress should explicitly declare that the absence of a cord does not change a telephone from a media of private conversation to a public address system.

For more than half a century, Americans have been using the telephone to conduct private business, family matters, flirtations, romances, and other confidential communications. The deep American tradition of privacy regards snooping on one's neighbors as disgusting. It has always been *possible* to eavesdrop, even before the advent of modern technology. But it has always been regarded as wrong. Technology does not change that long-standing moral belief.

Congress should recognize our deep-seated moral tradition against minding other people's business and require that people receive warrants before listening to what Americans are saying over their phones. This is already the law for phones with cords, and it has worked well enough.

Technology alone should not determine constitutional rights. The drafters of the Bill of Rights realized that they could not specifically define every invasion of privacy that might become possible over the lifetime of the Constitution. That is why they wrote the Fourth Amendment in general terms, capable of controlling technological intrusions of all kinds: "The right of the people to be secure in their persons, houses, papers and effects, against unreasonable searches and seizures, shall not be violated . . ."

Many Americans feel less secure today, knowing that cordless phones may be monitored without any reason—beyond the insatiable curiosity of the snoop.   January 1990

WAS MARION BARRY ENTRAPPED?

" 'Will you walk into my parlor?' said the spider to the fly."

The spider in this case was a sultry model named Rasheeda Moore. Her prey was the mayor of the District of Columbia, Marion Barry. Her parlor was a room in the Vista Hotel. The bait was crack cocaine. Once the fly was lured into the web, the FBI sprung the trap by videotaping the mayor smoking the bait in the bathroom. Mayor Barry was stung but good. Against the hypocritical background of his lecturing about the evils of crack, it was surely poetic. But was it justice? Or was Barry illegally entrapped?

Now that Barry has entered a drug rehabilitation program, we may never see the issue of entrapment tried in court. Voluntarily entering such a program is often the first step toward an eventual plea bargain. But even if Barry pleads guilty to some charge down the road, the public is entitled to ask whether the type of trap into which the mayor was lured was a fair and just one.

In the view of many legal experts, there are good stings and bad stings. A good sting is one in which the government simply provides the offender an opportunity to commit a crime he would commit anyway but under circumstances that assure his conviction. For example, a drug pusher who sells crack every day in a particular neighborhood has no real complaint if one of his "customers" turns out to be a plainclothes cop wearing a bug. The cop didn't induce him into doing anything he wasn't already doing. They just got him to do it on tape.

A bad sting is one in which a previously innocent citizen is induced into committing a crime he would not otherwise have committed. For example, in a case several years ago, a woman secretly working for the police invited a controversial newspaper editor to her home. She then proposed that they go to bed together, but only after smoking a joint to relax. After a few puffs, she passed the joint to the editor. As soon as he touched it, the police burst into the room and arrested him for possession of marijuana.

The leading U.S. Supreme Court case on the law of entrapment involved a former drug user who was enticed back to his bad ways. This is what the high court said in throwing out the conviction: "The case at bar illustrates an evil which the defense of entrapment is designed to overcome. The government informer entices someone attempting to avoid narcotics . . . into returning to the habit of use. . . . Thus, the government plays on the weaknesses of an innocent party and beguiles him into committing crimes which he otherwise would not have attempted. Law enforcement does not require methods such as this."

The Barry case has elements of both the good and the bad sting, depending on what one believes about his prior history. The government claims that Barry was a longtime drug user. They have the testimony of an erstwhile Barry associate, himself an admitted drug dealer, to support that claim. But until the bathroom videotape, they had no hard corroborative evidence of the drug dealer's story. And without corroboration, a cautious prosecutor would not risk trying a popular mayor before a jury of his constituents, solely on the basis of the word of a drug dealer whose testimony was purchased in exchange for a light sentence.

It was in order to obtain videotaped corroboration of the drug dealer's testimony that the government conducted its sting. Now, the Justice Department can prosecute Barry not only for the misdemeanor he was caught committing but also for the other crimes that the drug dealer has told prosecutors about. A jury is more likely to believe even a bought witness if his underlying story is corroborated on tape.

The Barry case thus fits uncomfortably between the classic good sting and the classic bad sting. Marion Barry would certainly not have smoked crack *that* night in *that* location had he not been lured there by a beautiful model working for the government. But if the prosecution is to be believed, Barry was no novice to crack smoking. He was not induced to try it for the first time by a government agent. Under the law of entrapment, even if a citizen has been "induced" to commit the crime by the government, he cannot prevail on an entrapment defense if he was already "predisposed" to commit that crime.

But the law is administered by jurors. And it is certainly possible that a District of Columbia jury could react with outrage to the government's tactics in this case, as a California jury reacted to the sting conducted against John DeLorean several years ago.

If Mayor Barry decides to go to trial and defends on the ground that prosecutors used unfair tactics to tempt a weak and sick man back to a habit he was sincerely trying to beat, the jury may yet have the last word on whether Marion Barry was entrapped. January 1990

MARION BARRY'S IGNOBLE DEFENSE STRATEGY

On the eve of his scheduled cocaine trial, District of Columbia mayor Marion Barry has disclosed that he will rely on a strategy that appears to me to be similar to one employed in the 1960s civil rights struggle. But it is not the strategy of Martin Luther King, Jr., that Barry will be using. Instead, he is threatening to copy the approach employed by racist governors, sheriffs, and Klansmen.

During the Mississippi Summer and the other summers that have forever stained the reputation of our nation, bigoted law violators exploited our jury system by appealing to the racist instincts of Southern jurors. They knew that regardless of the facts and the law, all-white Southern juries would simply not convict white civil rights violators. Even when some blacks began to sit on juries, the bigots realized that all it takes is one juror saying "I'm not going to convict, regardless of the evidence."

Now it is Mayor Barry, a veteran of the civil rights struggle, who is seeking to exploit the racial composition of the jury before which he is likely to be tried. Barry was recently quoted in the *Washington Post* as saying: "I think the prosecutors know that in this town all it takes is one juror saying 'I'm not going to convict Marion Barry. I don't care what you say.' "

Barry is already setting the stage for his "jury nullification defense." He announced to the press that the federal government had tried to "kill" him during a sting operation by allowing him to ingest crack cocaine that he had voluntarily sought from his former mistress.

Had the police intervened before Barry had taken the drugs, the mayor would almost certainly now be arguing that there is no proof that he would actually have used the drugs.

No honest juror could possibly believe that the U.S. attorney's office had set out to kill the popular mayor. Had Barry in fact died from the drugs provided by federal agents, it would have been a major embarrassment for the government, and specifically for the ambitious young U.S. attorney who runs the district office.

And no honest juror could possibly believe the arguments offered by the racist governors, sheriffs, and Klansmen in the deep South during the 1960s. Jury nullification does not require jurors to believe the claim actually offered by the defense. It is enough if they, or at least one of them, generally sympathize with the politics of the defendant.

That is precisely what Mayor Barry is aiming at with his preposterous claims that the feds set out to kill him. He is appealing to racial fears, racial hate, and racial pride. He knows that most of his jurors will be black, and he is asking them to vote not on the facts, nor on the law, but on racial solidarity.

In the end, Barry's public posturing may all be a bluff calculated to earn him a better deal if he decides to throw in the towel and plea bargain. By threatening the prosecutor with a hung jury brought about by even a single nullifier on the panel, he may be hoping that the U.S. attorney will let him plea to misdemeanor cocaine possession charges.

To be sure, drug use is not comparable to civil rights violations. As Barry correctly points out: "They can't say we shot anybody [or] robbed anybody." But drug use is a major problem in the city over which Barry presides, and he did campaign vigorously against drugs. The sting that ensnared him was poetic, even if many regard it as unjust.

Jury nullification is a double-edged sword. It is sometimes used, in a nonracist manner, to counter the unfairness of particular laws. It has a long and noble history, dating back in our nation to the jury's refusal to convict John Peter Zenger for publishing defamatory materials about colonial politicians. It was used during the days of slavery to refuse enforcement of the fugitive slave laws. And it has been employed in recent years to protest immoral government policies.

But jury nullification also has an ignoble and racist history. And, unfortunately, Marion Barry has turned to that ignoble and racist tradition in his desperate effort to salvage his political career from the ashes of a drug problem for which he has nobody to blame but himself.

Racism by American jurors around the country continues to hurt blacks disproportionately. All-, or predominantly, white juries are a more frequent phenomenon than all-, or predominantly, black juries.

Indeed, in an effort to offset the impact of anti-black jury racism, the Supreme Court recently ruled that prosecutors may not deliberately employ racial criteria in their selection of jurors. Despite this ruling, white racism in jury selection and in jury deliberation persists. But an appeal to black jury racism is not the answer. June 1990

I eventually consulted on a sentencing issue in Barry's appeal.

LET'S PUT AN END TO THOSE "BOUNTY-HUNTER" DRUG ARRESTS

The Supreme Court has decided to review the power of the Justice Department to hire "bounty hunters" in neighboring countries in order to kidnap foreigners who have violated our laws and bring them into our country for trial. It is an issue with broad international implications, since it is currently Justice Department policy to reach out and grab fugitives, even if the country in which they live has refused to extradite them for trial in the United States. Under that policy, our nation must also recognize the power of foreign countries to hire their own bounty hunters to kidnap American citizens and drag them into foreign countries for whatever form of trial a foreign legal system may provide.

The U.S. Court of Appeals in California ruled such abductions to be lawless and ordered the kidnapped foreigner to be freed. But the Justice Department has appealed that ruling and the Supreme Court agreed to hear the case in March.

The particular facts underlying the case make it clear why the Justice Department feels so strongly about its policy. In 1985, an American drug agent was tortured and murdered in Guadalajara, Mexico. A Mexican gynecologist named Dr. Humberto Alvarez Machain was suspected of complicity in the crime. The U.S. Drug Enforcement Administrator (DEA) paid a group of Mexican bounty hunters $20,000 for bringing Dr. Alvarez into California. The DEA also arranged for several of the bounty hunters and their families to move to the United States.

The Mexican Government was furious over the breach of their sovereignty. They protested to our State Department, demanding the return of their kidnapped citizen. They argued that under the U.S. extradition treaty with Mexico—which has the force of law—Alvarez could not have been extradited. Nor, of course, could he be lawfully kidnapped. The United States refused to return Dr. Alvarez and he was formally charged with complicity in the murder, but the Federal District Court judge in Los Angeles ordered that he must be set free and returned to Mexico. The Justice Department appealed, but the U.S. Court of Appeals agreed with the district court judge. Now, the Supreme Court will have the last word.

In two earlier Supreme Court decisions—dating back to 1886 and 1952—the justices had ruled that if a criminal defendant is physically in the presence of an American court, that court will not inquire as to how he got there. Put another way, the so-called exclusionary rule that excludes evidence obtained in violation of a criminal defendant's rights does not exclude the defendant himself. Even if he was "obtained" unlawfully, he will not be suppressed or returned.

Since those cases were decided, the world has become a much smaller place, and international kidnapping has become quite prevalent. Israel's abduction of the Nazi mass-murderer Adolf Eichmann from Argentina in May 1960 did not create much of an outcry, perhaps because of the scale of Eichmann's crimes and the degree of complicity some countries shared in harboring Nazi criminals. Nor did the world react with horror when the

ALAN M. DERSHOWITZ

U.S. Army invaded Panama and arrested its dictator Manuel Noriega on drug charges.

But if the U.S. Supreme Court explicitly legitimates the current Justice Department's aggressive policy of arrest by kidnapping, we are likely to see a dramatic expansion of international lawlessness. Extradition treaties are designed to introduce a modicum of mutual civility into international criminal law. If each country acts on its "right" to kidnap citizens from their own countries, we can expect a long season of bounty hunting.

Drug crimes respect no national borders. Neither do crimes of political terrorism. Even in the arena of white-collar business crimes, borders are easily crossed by transnational companies and business practices. Organized crime has long connected suppliers and customers in different parts of the world.

Every nation feels that its crime problems are the most serious and that other nations afford too much protection to their own citizens. That is why extradition treaties have always been in the nature of mutual compromises, in which each signatory country gets no more than it gives. Thus, Switzerland, which values bank and business privacy more than we do, refuses to extradite certain white-collar criminals. The United States, which values political and speech freedoms more than most other nations, refuses to extradite certain political criminals. Most Western democracies, which oppose capital punishment, will not extradite a defendant who faces the death penalty in the United States. A delicate balance of mutual values is reflected in our extradition treaties with other nations.

But if the United States takes it upon itself to circumvent these carefully drafted treaties by using bounty hunters, kidnappers, and goon squads, we can be certain that other countries will soon follow suit. The result will be increasing international lawlessness and violence from which few citizens will be safe.   January 1992

The Supreme Court eventually upheld the conviction of Dr. Humberto Alvarez Machain.

THE LAW AND POLITICS OF SEX, LIFE AND DEATH

8 // *Women's Rights, Reproductive Freedom and the Politics of Abortion*

MOTHERS' RIGHTS VS. BABIES' RIGHTS

When a pregnant woman decides to carry a fetus to term, does she give up some of her own legal rights? What if she chooses to engage in behavior that is deleterious to the health of her fetus? What if the offending mother herself is so young that she is an "infant" in the eyes of the law? In extreme cases, should the law be authorized to intervene on behalf of the helpless fetus?

These are old questions that have taken on new urgency with the high number of teenage births and the epidemic of drug addiction and other fetus-destructive behavior by mothers-to-be, especially very young ones.

Nor is the problem limited to drug addicts or young mothers. Some mature mothers reject medical advice that it would be advantageous for the fetus if they were to give birth by cesarean section. They fear the surgery or worry about its disfiguring effects. (A federal appeals court recently agreed to decide whether a pregnant woman dying of cancer could be compelled to undergo a cesarean essential to the survival of the fetus.) Other mothers refuse to stop smoking, drinking, or doing other things that are pleasurable to them but harmful to their babies.

New fuel was added to the debate about legal intervention in such cases by a recent article in the highly influential *Journal of the American Medical Association (JAMA)*. Its authors, both medical researchers, urge doctors not to turn to the courts to protect fetuses from negligent or reckless mothers. They argue that more harm than good results from "making adversaries out of mother and fetus."

But mothers are already in an adversarial relationship with their fetuses if they selfishly refuse to follow elementary precautions necessary to give their babies a fighting chance after birth. And it is a grossly unfair adversarial relationship, since the fetus has no way to fight back and defend itself.

A mother may have a constitutional right to terminate her pregnancy, even though an abortion destroys the fetus's potential life. But it surely does not follow that the mother who has elected to give birth has a constitutional right to engage in conduct that may very well give the baby an irreversible handicap. A mother has no right to deny her newborn infant necessary medical care—even on religious grounds. Similarly, a mother who has assumed the responsibility of bringing a child into the world should be required to undertake certain minimum steps before birth to assure its health.

It is not enough to give the child, after birth, a legal claim against its mother for negligent or reckless maternity, as some have suggested. Something should be done to protect the fetus while it can still make a difference—for instance, compelling expectant mothers to stop taking dangerous drugs or to accept transfusions on behalf of the fetus.

There will, of course, be difficult questions as to where to draw the line. As the authors of the *JAMA* article properly recognize, some doctors and judges, if given the power to protect fetuses in extreme cases, would try to play God. They write: "The extension would be to seek out women for other behaviors. That could be anything from smoking to continuing to work, sexual activity, if contraindicated, or of not following a recommended medical regimen."

But it is the job of the law to establish processes for drawing lines and then to draw them and enforce the rules sensibly. If the difficulty of drawing lines was always to preclude legal intervention, there would be few laws on the books. We do draw lines, even in areas involving the delicate balance between adult autonomy and the protection of children.

There would also be problems of enforcement, of course. As the authors argue: "We recognize that the behavior of women who are abusers of alcohol or drugs poses significant potential for fetal harm. However, there are solid reasons to doubt that a system of legal punishment or intervention would decrease the incidence of this behavior, as it is usually an addiction over which these women have little control."

Enforcement is a matter of degree. Not every fetus will be saved from its mother's abuse. But most people, even some potential drug and alcohol abusers, do obey the law. For example, laws that punish driving under the influence of alcohol or drugs do prevent some tragedies. And in extreme cases of drug addiction, compulsory hospitalization and detoxification of the pregnant mother might be appropriate. Laws in many states already provide for compulsory hospitalization of heroin addicts. Pregnant women should at least be among the priority cases for hospitalization under these laws.

It is never comfortable for society to employ legal compulsion in matters as intimate as pregnancy. There are dangers from several perspectives: Some opponents of abortion will argue that the logical implication of protecting fetuses from ill health is to protect them from death by abortion; and some proponents of compulsory intervention will argue that all maternal activities dangerous to the fetus or newborn must be prohibited by law. The challenge is to come up with a sensible middle ground that affords maximum protection both to the mother's autonomy and the fetus's health.

May 1988

WHEN ABORTION LEADS TO "FEMICIDE"

Does a pregnant woman have the right to know the sex of her baby before it is born? Most reasonable people—certainly most feminists—would argue that a woman's right of reproductive freedom includes learning, if she wishes, the results of an amniocentesis, including whether the baby will be a boy or girl. Does a woman have the right to terminate her pregnancy— to have an abortion—for any reason deemed sufficient to her? Although there is significant disagreement on this issue within the general population, most feminists would probably say yes.

But does a woman have the right to abort a fetus solely on the ground that it is a female? This is a tough one for feminists, and it is an even tougher one for the Indian government, because in some parts of India the issue is not at all hypothetical.

Tens of thousands of Indian women, poor and rich alike, have undergone amniocentesis for the sole purpose of learning whether their fetus is a boy or girl. If it is a girl, they have an abortion; if it is a boy, they don't.

The reason for this strong preference for male babies is both traditional and economic. In many parts of India, boys are perceived as an economic benefit; girls are perceived as an economic burden. Although marriage dowries are technically illegal in India (they are perfectly lawful in the United States), they persist. And the price for marrying off a daughter can run as high as $10,000—the equivalent of a year's salary for a middle-class Indian. Several daughters and no sons can be a prescription for bankruptcy.

It is not surprising, therefore, that private hospitals and clinics promote amniocentesis by the slogan: "Better to spend 500 rupees now than 50,000 rupees later."

The combination of modern technology and traditional values has created a situation in which women, or couples, can and do seek to determine, within limits, the sex of their children. If this is allowed to continue and expand, it could affect the natural balance between males and females.

Throughout history, of course, there have been other factors that have skewed the proportion of males and females: wars, certain sex-linked illnesses, even crime. Generally, however, these factors have *decreased* the number of males. (More males are born, but their lower survival rate tends to even out the proportion during procreative years.) The technique practiced in India threatens to *increase* the number of males, which is a far more ominous development in light of the more bellicose nature of the male of the species.

In addition to upsetting the natural balance, the Indian phenomenon sends a terrible message about the perceived worth of males and females. It is difficult to imagine a more sexist practice. Indeed, it would be fair to characterize it as "femicide"—a sex variant on genocide.

For all of these reasons, it is obviously important to put an end to the process of selectively aborting female fetuses. But the difficult questions relate to the means employed toward this end. Obviously, education would be the preferred means. Prospective parents must be taught that there is no inherent difference in the value of the sexes. And laws should be enforced that reflect this commitment to gender equality.

But if egalitarian education and legislation fail to stem the tide of sex-selected abortions, would it be proper to prohibit pregnant mothers from selectively aborting their female fetuses?

This could be done by making it illegal to disclose to a pregnant woman the sex of her fetus. The government could also prohibit any abortion done for reasons of gender, but such a rule would be all but impossible to enforce if abortion were permitted for a wide variety of other reasons—reasons that could be offered to mask the real basis for the decision.

The Indian state of Maharashtra has opted for a law that bans any prenatal test to determine a fetus's sex. This has driven the testing underground or to other states with no such laws. The economic pressures are simply too great on families with several daughters.

Not surprisingly, Indian feminists are divided over the new law. Some see it as endangering a woman's right to make a fully informed decision about abortion. Others view it as a necessary evil required to counteract the traditional sexism in Indian society.

As one Indian obstetrician asked: "The law has been changed, but what have we done to change social attitudes?"

The tragic situation in India demonstrates both the limits of law in affecting profound social changes and the necessity of using the law to control the most obvious manifestations of sexism. It also demonstrates the conflict between the right of a woman to terminate her pregnancy and the wrong inherent in terminating it on sexist grounds.   August 1988

OVERRULE OF ROE WOULD INJURE POOR WOMEN

The passions on both sides of the abortion debate have generated arguments that do neither side credit. The imminent decision of the U.S. Supreme Court in the Missouri case *Webster* vs. *Reproductive Health Services* has focused public attention on whether the justices will reverse their sixteen-year precedent established in *Roe* vs. *Wade*, which recognizes a woman's constitutional right to choose abortion.

Many of those who want to see *Roe* vs. *Wade* overruled offer the following argument: Life begins at conception; the constitution protects "life"; therefore, no government has the right to permit a woman to abort the "life" of a fetus.

It should follow logically from this argument that it would be constitutionally impermissible for any legislature to enact a statute authorizing abortion.

But many abortion foes do not take their "right-to-life" argument to its logical, but politically unacceptable, conclusion. They demand instead that the Supreme Court leave the issue of abortion to state legislatures, where it was prior to *Roe* vs. *Wade*. Each state could then decide for itself whether to permit or prohibit all or some abortions. If a state legislature chose to permit abortions, then that political resolution of the issue would prevail.

This leave-it-to-the-states argument is simply a ploy for most "right-to-life" advocates. Those who believe in the fetus's right to life will never agree that the mere enactment of a state statute can authorize the killing of fetuses. Yet they persist in their leave-it-to-the-state argument as an initial tactic toward achieving a three-step end to all abortions. The first step is the overruling of *Roe* vs. *Wade*. The second step is the prohibition of abortion by as many state legislatures as possible. And the third step is the enactment of a constitutional "right-to-life" amendment, which would preclude any state from authorizing abortions.

On the other side of the abortion debate, there is the pro-choice argument that goes something like this: A majority of Americans believe in a woman's right to choose abortion; it follows that the issue should not be left to state legislatures, but must instead be decided by the Supreme Court. This bit of illogic was recently addressed to the justices in a full-page advertisement in newspapers across the country, which read as follows:

"Your Honors: Before you vote on *Roe* vs. *Wade*, listen to one final opinion . . . The majority of Americans support *Roe* vs. *Wade*. A Harris poll conducted in January 1989 revealed that this support comes from virtually every demographic and geographic group in America."

The implications of this populist argument completely· undercut the basis of our constitutional system. Constitutional rights should not be decided by public opinion or popularity contests. Indeed, if it were really the case that Americans throughout the nation overwhelmingly support a woman's right to choose abortion, it would not be necessary for the Supreme Court to declare that right as a matter of constitutional law. The majority could simply organize and establish its will through legislation.

Moreover, what would happen to the constitutional right of choice if a majority of Americans became convinced by the "right-to-life" argument. Would the constitutional right to choice suddenly disappear if tomorrow's Harris poll were to reflect a shift in the winds of public opinion?

And what of others' constitutional rights that do not have majority support in this country, such as the expression of unpopular views, the privilege against self-incrimination, or the separation of church and state? Should the Supreme Court also "listen" to "the majority of Americans" on those constitutional issues?

The more politicized the issue of abortion becomes, the greater is the likelihood that the Supreme Court will abdicate responsibility to the political branches of government. For that reason, the pro-choice marches, demonstrations, letter-writing campaigns and advertisements may, in the end, be playing into the hands of those who would see *Roe* vs. *Wade* overruled.

Some of the swing-vote justices may well decide that the pro-choice movement is so politically powerful, well-organized, and influential that it does not need the help of the Supreme Court or the Constitution to accomplish its political agenda.

That would be unfortunate, because if the abortion issue were left to the states, at least some would abolish virtually all abortions. And this would create an unfair situation in which the poorest, least mobile, youngest, and least educated women would be denied the option of legal abortion. The other women would be able to travel to those states—and there would be some in every region of the nation—that authorized abortions.

There is a fundamental constitutional right at stake in the abortion dispute: the equal protection of the law. If *Roe* vs. *Wade* is overruled, some women, the ones with no political or economic power, will once again be forced to resort to the back-alley abortionist, at great risk to their right to life.   April 1989

In June 1992, The Supreme Court upheld a woman's right to choose, while also upholding as constitutional, legislation placing numerous restrictions on this right.

MOTHERS WHO DAMAGE THEIR UNBORN CHILDREN

There is a dangerous implication in some pro-choice arguments that may frighten the Supreme Court into restricting or even overruling *Roe* vs. *Wade*, the 1973 decision that established women's right to abortion.

The implication is that the right to abortion also precludes the state from requiring women to take any degree of prenatal care after they make the decision not to abort. Syndicated columnist Ellen Goodman recently suggested this in criticizing the Bush administration's efforts to overrule *Roe* vs. *Wade*. She wrote: "There are suggestions among those who talk of fetal rights that the government could constrain a pregnant woman's diet and physical activities, stamp out her cigarettes, empty her wineglass . . . or else." Goodman also invoked the specter of mandatory testing and treatment for the fetus.

Now, I am not a "fetal rights" advocate. I favor *Roe* vs. *Wade*. I believe that a pregnant woman should have the right to choose between giving birth or having an abortion. But I *am* a "human rights" advocate, and I also believe that no woman who has chosen to give birth should have the right to neglect or injure that child by abusing *their* collective body during pregnancy.

Once a woman has made the decision to bear a child, the rights of that child should be taken into consideration. What happens to the child in the womb may have significant impact on his or her entire life. One example is the woman who drank a half bottle of liquor a day while pregnant and gave birth to a mentally retarded child. She is now suing a liquor manufacturer for not warning her about the relationship between heavy drinking during pregnancy and birth defects. Anyone who has spoken to an inner-city obstetrician is aware of the near epidemic of birth defects among babies born to heavy drug users.

This is not to argue for intrusive governmental rules on occasional drinking or smoking. But at the extremes, there is a compelling argument in favor of some protection for the future child against maternal excesses that threaten to cause enduring damage. Once a woman decides to give birth, a balance must be struck between her rights during the nine months of pregnancy and the equally real rights of her child during its life span. I believe that the balance should generally be struck in favor of the woman's privacy and against the power of state compulsion. But a balance, nonetheless, must be struck.

My colleague, Professor Laurence Tribe, agrees with Ellen Goodman and argues as follows: "There's no principled way to say that the government can use women's bodies against their will to nurture the unborn without accepting the other serious and totalitarian implications about privacy." With respect, I disagree.

There is a principled distinction between totalitarian intrusions into the way a woman treats her body, and civil libertarian concerns for the way a woman treats the body of the child she has decided to bear. That principled distinction goes back to the philosophy of John Stuart Mill and is reflected in the creed that "your right to swing your fist ends at the tip of my nose." In the context of a pregnant woman's rights and responsibilities in relation to the child she has decided to bear, the expression might be: "Your right to abuse your own body stops at the border of your womb."

To be sure, any recognition that a future child may have rights, even limited ones, in relation to its mother, may be grist for the "right-to-life" mill. Antiabortionists will argue that if a future child has the right not to be *damaged* during pregnancy, then it follows that the fetus has the even more important right not to be *killed*—that is, aborted.

But the second conclusion does not necessarily follow from the first. Under *Roe* vs. *Wade*, a fertilized egg, or even a biologically more advanced fetus, has no right to be born, unless the mother chooses to give birth. But it does not follow, as a matter of constitutionality, principle, or common sense, that a woman has the right to inflict a lifetime of suffering on her future child, simply in order to satisfy a momentary whim for a quick fix.

A principled person can fully support a woman's right to choose between abortion or birth, without supporting the very different view that the state should have no power to protect the health of a future child. The state should begin by making prenatal care available to every pregnant woman. But we need not be frightened by the specter of totalitarianism from considering reasonable regulations designed to reduce the serious long-term problems caused by pregnant women who abuse their future children.

Proponents of a woman's right to abortion should not weaken their powerful argument in favor of a woman's right to control her body.

And in the eyes of many who support choice, they do weaken it when they link it to the far weaker argument denying the state the power to protect babies who are to be born.   May 1989

MAJORITY VIEW ON ABORTION
WILL PREVAIL

No Supreme Court decision, certainly not a splintered decision such as the one just rendered, will finally resolve the abortion dispute in the United States. While upholding the core of *Roe* vs. *Wade*, the ruling on the Webster case undercuts the right of poor women to have access to certain publicly funded abortion services. It also provides states with greater leeway in determining when a fetus becomes viable and subject to governmental protection. Most important, it signals a trend toward greater state legislative power to regulate abortion, particularly when public funding is involved.

The issue of abortion has simply become too divisive for resolution by the courts. It is not subject to the kind of Solomonic compromise acceptable to all sides. And unlike some other divisive issues, such as racial desegregation, there is no one correct moral position that will eventually win the day on the basis of its inherent persuasiveness.

For those who honestly believe that the fetus is a person from the moment of conception, and that all abortion is murder, there can be no moral compromise. One does not compromise about the murder of innocent people.

On the other hand, for those who believe, just as honestly, that the fetus is simply a woman's appendage until the day of birth and that the mother has an absolute right to decide whether to give birth or abort it, there is also little room for compromise.

In its seminal *Roe* vs. *Wade* decision sixteen years ago, the Supreme Court majority did try to compromise by establishing a different balance of rights for each trimester. In defiance of centuries of folk wisdom, it basically said that a woman could be a "little bit pregnant." During the first trimester, she wasn't pregnant enough, according to *Roe* vs. *Wade*, for the fetus to be regarded as a person. During the third trimester, she was too pregnant for the fetus not to be considered almost a person. And during the middle trimester, it was more like a nonperson than a person.

Even many of those who applauded the bottom line of the decision—abortion on demand in most situations—were not persuaded by its logic. It is not surprising that a majority of the current justices seem troubled by its underlying premises. Nor is it surprising that some of the justices who are troubled by Roe's logic are even more troubled by the prospect of directly overruling a sixteen-year-old precedent that has repeatedly been reaffirmed at the core, if weakened at the edges, over the past years.

When Justice Blackmun wrote the high court's *Roe* vs. *Wade* decision back in 1973, the worldwide trend was clearly in the direction of greater abortion rights. Most Western democracies were expanding a woman's right to choose. In other countries, this balance was being struck in favor of choice not by appointed courts but rather by elected legislatures. This trend was also discernible in the United States, as several states enacted laws decriminalizing abortion.

Had the Supreme Court stayed out of the abortion thicket in 1973, many observers believe that most states would have legislated a woman's right to choose abortion under most circumstances. But this legislative recognition of choice slowed considerably after the Supreme Court constitutionalized the issue in *Roe* vs. *Wade*.

Many advocates of choice began to rely on the courts to expand abortion rights and ignored the more cumbersome legislative process. Monday's decision provided a clear signal that exclusive reliance on the courts is now misplaced.

At the same time as advocates of choice were turning to the courts, abortion opponents began to organize popular opposition. By creating a powerful single-issue lobby, they enhanced their power beyond their numbers.

Although the abortion debate has now clearly returned to the political arena, an aura of constitutionality still surrounds it. While the core abortion issue will still be fought in the courts, the state legislatures are quickly becoming a major battleground. Pro-choice groups will have to play catch-up in the lobbies of state capitals, since the right-to-lifers have been well organized there for years.

But as the pro-choicers pointedly advised the Supreme Court in a series of advertisements on the eve of the Webster argument, a majority of Americans seems to favor abortion rights under most circumstances. If this remains true over time, then freedom of choice will prevail, because with an issue as divisive as abortion, the Supreme Court can, in the long run, only play a temporizing role.

The view of the majority of citizens will prevail because, unlike the issue of racial segregation, the right to life versus the right to choice cannot be decided on the basis of one correct principle that all sides will eventually accept. It will have to be decided on the basis of power.

Monday's decision demonstrates that there is no basic consensus even within the Supreme Court. But a trend is discernible: that trend is toward returning to the state legislative process some important practical aspects of the abortion debate. Both sides will now continue gearing up for a series of political battles in key state legislatures around the country.

July 1989

SHOULD PREGNANT WOMEN BE DENIED ALCOHOL?

As the medical evidence mounts that a pregnant woman's use of alcohol, tobacco, and other drugs poses potentially cataclysmic health problems for her fetus, civil libertarians are seeking approaches that balance the privacy interests of the pregnant woman against the medical interests of the future child.

There is no longer any reasonable doubt that a woman who drinks considerable amounts of alcohol during pregnancy creates the real prospect that her baby will be born with Fetal Alcohol Syndrome. An FAS child may suffer curvature of the spine, mental retardation, facial abnormalities, and other untreatable problems.

Even moderate drinking can cause Fetal Alcohol Effect, a less severe manifestation of the syndrome. Dr. Kenneth Lyons Jones, a leading researcher on alcohol and pregnancy, has estimated that one in ten babies born to "moderate drinkers" may have problems related to alcohol. Another researcher has concluded that pregnant women who drink even one or two alcoholic beverages a day during the first two months of pregnancy run the risk of having children with slow reaction time and attention difficulties.

There are similar data for smoking and cocaine ingestion. But attention is being focused on drinking for several reasons. Cocaine is already illegal, and it is widely known, as the mandatory warning declares, that smoking is bad for both the pregnant woman and the fetus.

Drinking is different. Unlike smoking, doctors tell us that one drink a day may actually be good for nonpregnant adults. Many pregnant women simply don't realize that they are putting their babies at risk by continuing their moderate drinking after they become pregnant. Alcohol passes directly into the bloodstream of the fetus, causing the functional equivalent of fetal drunkenness or even alcoholism.

Even some doctors are not aware of the current research and are advising their pregnant patients that a drink or two with dinner is perfectly all right. Others perpetuate the tale that drinking beer is good for mothers who breast-feed. The medical evidence is all to the contrary.

Warnings on liquor bottles are coming. As of November 18, 1989, a warning will appear on alcoholic beverages that "Women should not drink alcoholic beverages during pregnancy because of risk of birth defects." But the warning will take some time to sink in.

Fetal Alcohol Syndrome and other alcohol-related prenatal problems are preventable, but something dramatic must be done to bring the message home to pregnant women.

The concept of "fetal rights" has, unfortunately, become a surrogate battlefield in the war over abortion, but the problem of prenatal alcohol damage is too important to be caught up in the never-ending arguments about "right-to-life" versus "freedom of choice." It is perfectly logical to believe that a woman has a right to decide whether her fetus is to be born, and also to believe that once she has decided to give birth, she is under an obligation—moral, if not legal—to refrain from selfish actions that pose a high likelihood of permanently harming the future child she has chosen to bear.

One does not have to go as far as some Native American reservations, which have been plagued with FAS, have reportedly gone: Locking up pregnant women who will not, or cannot, refrain from heavy drinking.

Warnings should be posted in every bar, liquor store, restaurant, or concession stand that dispenses alcoholic beverages. Doctors should routinely advise pregnant women of the dangers of drinking, and notices should be posted in the waiting rooms of obstetric and gynecological offices. Prenatal education and care should be made widely available, especially to the least educated and poorest segments of our society.

If public education does not do the job, perhaps we should consider taking it a step further. Would it be so terrible to prohibit bartenders, liquor stores, restaurants, and concessions from dispensing alcohol to obviously pregnant women? Such a prohibition would obviously not stop a determined pregnant woman from securing a drink, any more than age restrictions stop determined high school students from getting beer. It might also create embarrassment over the bartender's inability to distinguish a pregnant belly from a beer belly. But it would send a powerful message to all concerned: namely, that it is wrong for a pregnant woman to drink.

Today, it is illegal for a bartender to refuse to serve an obviously pregnant woman several drinks. A good bartender, concerned for the woman's baby, could find himself on the wrong end of a discrimination suit if he did so. At the very least that should be changed.

I will personally not serve a pregnant woman alcohol in my own home, regardless of how insistent she might be or how bad a host she might consider me. I will not participate in creating a risk for her baby, even if she will.

Most pregnant women I know are scrupulously responsible. And those who are not may be the least affected by any government program of education, warnings, or even compulsion. But the problem of FAS is too serious and too preventable to be left to hope, prayer, and inaction.

August 1989

UNUSUAL "CUSTODY DISPUTE" FOCUSES ON EGGS

The media is calling the lawsuit between an estranged couple over seven fertilized eggs a "custody dispute." But it is really more analogous to a putative father's insistence that his estranged wife abort their unborn child. The difference, of course, is that the eggs are not in any person's body.

Mary Sue Davis, whose eggs were extricated from her body and fertilized, wants them implanted back in her body so that she can have a baby. Her estranged husband, Junior Lewis Davis, whose sperm was used to fertilize her eggs, wants them destroyed.

Were this a "custody dispute," the judge could simply give three eggs to each claimant (and hold the last one in reserve for a contingency). But the problem is considerably more complex than dividing up the eggs. It is an issue of life or death.

The genetic father does not want to be forced into fatherhood against his will, although he apparently wanted the eggs fertilized so that his wife could have given birth when the marriage was still intact. His estranged wife is prepared to let him off the financial hook of fatherhood. Her pledge not to seek child support if she were to give birth may not be legally binding, however, since the child would have an independent financial claim against the father. Even if the father could be relieved of all legal liabilities, there is no way, of course, of freeing him completely from the emotional responsibilities of fatherhood.

But destroying potential life is a rather Draconian solution to the problem of paternal responsibility. There is no conflict here, as there is in the abortion context, between the life of the fetus and the unwillingness of the mother to carry it to term. The genetic father has completed his biological job. So has the genetic mother, if the eggs can be implanted in another woman's womb. Neither "donor" should now have a right, comparable to that of the carrying mother in a conventional pregnancy, to terminate the pregnancy if the other parent is prepared to bring the child into the world and raise it.

In the context of a fertilized egg outside the body of the mother, there should be a presumption in favor of creating life, provided that one of the genetic parents is willing and able to provide for the child. If a genetic father wants the eggs to be born—and if he had a willing carrier—then his wishes should prevail over those of a genetic mother who wanted the eggs destroyed. In this case, since the genetic mother favors birth, her wishes should prevail.

Another important factor is the comparative ease with which each party can have a child. There are significant financial and emotional costs attached to in vitro fertilization, especially for the woman whose eggs must be removed.

In this case, Mrs. Davis had five tubal pregnancies and her fallopian tubes are no longer functioning. She should not have to go through the difficult fertilization process again if she already has fertilized eggs that are available for implantation. If the problem of infertility were attributable primarily to the father, then he should get the eggs; the fertile noncustodial person would then be free to have his or her own children with a partner of choice. This, of course, will not resolve the problem of what to do if infertility is a joint problem, as it often is.

Today we have sperm banks and sperm donors. Soon we will have egg banks and egg donors. Surrogate carriers unrelated either to the sperm or egg donors raise complexities of the kind we have already experienced in the Mary Beth Whitehead case. Law, morality, and even religion will have to adapt to the new realities, as they already have to other technological innovations that have helped infertile couples.

We must never forget that "reproductive freedom" is a double-edged sword: It protects the right to use technology without undue state interference both in aid of *having* wanted children, as well as in aid of *not having* unwanted children. We should not fear the unfamiliar, as long as we insist on controlling the technology rather than permitting it to control us.

In resolving the very real dispute between the Davises, the courts should avoid abstractions such as when "life begins," whose "property" the eggs really are, and whether they should be "labeled 'preborn children.' " Instead, the courts should look to the practical consequences of their decisions on the real interests of the parties involved.

In this case, Mrs. Davis's real interest in having a baby and the difficulties she has had, and would continue to have, becoming pregnant by conventional means outweigh Mr. Davis's emotional unwillingness to become a genetic father. He is in a position analogous to that of a sperm donor who has changed his mind, perhaps for good reason.

The donee's interest in producing a child should prevail. The courts should turn the fertilized eggs over to Mrs. Davis so that she can implant them into her body and try to give birth. August 1989

MORE THAN EVER, LAW FOCUSES ON FETUSES

From a legal perspective, 1989 will probably be remembered as the Year of the Fetus. By recent news accounts, there seems to be more litigation over fetuses and "fetal rights" than ever before.

Item: In Missouri, where, according to statute, life begins at conception, a pregnant prisoner named Louetta Ferrar has filed a pair of lawsuits contending that the innocent "person" in her womb should be freed from jail.

In the first suit, she is claiming that the fetus, which is a person under Missouri law, has not been convicted of any crime and is being imprisoned on the basis of guilt by association with its mother. The prisoner argues that no child should suffer for the sins of its mother. Incidentally, of course, the pregnant prisoner points out that the only way the fetus can be released from jail is for her mother to get a free walk. She is claiming innocence by association! If she were to win, there would likely be a spate of pregnancies among convicted women facing long imprisonment.

Many years ago, I represented a woman who was facing the death penalty for allegedly murdering her husband. She became pregnant while in prison in the hope of avoiding the gas chamber. It worked. No woman known to be pregnant has ever, to my knowledge, been put to death in this country—even after her baby was delivered.

Ferrar's second lawsuit, which has a somewhat better chance of succeeding, claims that the fetus is being endangered by the conditions of its mother's imprisonment. According to the complaint, the pregnant mother is not receiving adequate prenatal care, food, and exercise. She is expecting to give birth early this winter, but her term, for forgery, will keep her in prison until 1991. She is seeking special treatment for herself and the approximately twenty-five other pregnant prisoners in the Missouri penal system.

This second suit has created a dilemma for some pro-choice activists. On one hand, they favor increased prenatal care for prisoners and others. On the other hand, they do not want the courts to buy into the "fetal-rights" aspect of the right-to-life movement. As an attorney for the Planned Parenthood Federation of America put it: "The court might agree with some of the contentions that the fetus is entitled to personhood, which could set bad precedent. . . . I hope that if the court awards anything, it is based on the woman's rights rather than the fetal-rights theory."

Item: A sixty-seven-year-old Philadelphia obstetrician faces three and a half years in jail for infanticide after performing an abortion on a thirteen-year-old girl. The prosecution claims that the thirty-two-week-old fetus was born alive and the doctor withheld proper medical treatment, thereby denying the fetus its right to life.

Item: There are several lawsuits in process over what should be done with fertilized human eggs that are now in dispute. In addition to the "custody" fight between the estranged Davis couple in Tennessee, there is also the strange case of the couple who were killed in a plane crash after undergoing in vitro fertilization and leaving several frozen embryos. Since the deceased couple was very wealthy and left their money to their children, the embryos are not only potential children but potentially very rich children. This combination of technology, death, and money has all the ingredients of long litigation.

Then there are the doctors who claim that the fertilized eggs belong to them rather than to the putative parents. The variations are legion, and this is just the beginning of litigations over frozen embryos.

Item: Criminal charges have been brought against a Massachusetts woman who consumed cocaine while pregnant, thus causing injury to the fetus. And in a perverse variation on this theme, an alcoholic mother who gave birth to a child with Fetal Alcohol Syndrome sued the manufacturer of the liquor that she drank to excess. She lost, but soon all liquor will carry a warning label about the dangers of drinking while pregnant.

Each of these complex issues, which grow out of new scientific technologies and medical insights, can and should be addressed in practical terms. Instead, they have become part of the rhetorical war of words over abortion. Right-to-life advocates seize every opportunity to score points for the fetal-rights movement. They argue that if fetuses have any rights in any contexts, then surely these rights may not be entirely extinguished through their "death" by abortion. Pro-choice advocates are afraid to give even an inch in the war over words. *All* rights must belong to the mothers; none to the fetus.

A cease-fire must be declared in this battle over labels. Society's goal must be healthy babies born to loving parents who have chosen to bring them into this difficult world. Each of the above problems should be addressed with a view toward achieving that goal in practical terms, without worrying about its rhetorical implications for the dispute over abortion.

September 1989

CONCEIVING ONE CHILD TO SAVE ANOTHER

Technology is constantly requiring families to confront ethical conundrums that no one could have imagined a few years ago. Now, a middle-aged Los Angeles couple have conceived a baby explicitly in the hope of saving their seventeen-year-old daughter, who is suffering from leukemia.

The teenager, Anissa, needs bone marrow cells from a compatible donor, and a two-year search has failed to produce one. Doctors told the couple that a newborn sibling would have a 25 percent chance of providing compatible cells within six months of birth.

They also told the couple that without the compatible cells, their teenage daughter would almost certainly die, but with them she would have a 70 to 80 percent chance of surviving. Taking cells from the newborn would in no way endanger its health.

Armed with that information, the couple, Abe and Mary Ayala, decided to try to conceive a sibling for Anissa. It was no easy task, since Abe had previously undergone a vasectomy. He managed to have it reversed, and his wife is now expecting a baby.

But while the Ayalas await their doubly joyous event with anticipation, the usual busybody "ethicists" are sniping at them for trying to save their daughter's life by bringing another child into the world.

In news accounts, one ethicist from the Hastings Institute declared, "It's outrageous that people would go to this length." Another from the University of California pontificated that "the ideal reason for having a child is associated with that child's own welfare." He suggested that the Ayalas' decision to conceive one child primarily to save another violated "one of the fundamental precepts of ethics, that each person is an end in himself or herself, and is never to be used as a means to another person's ends without the agreement of the other. . . ."

How dare these "experts" sit in judgment over so excruciatingly personal a family decision! Children are brought into the world for all kinds of "questionable" reasons: to help floundering marriages, to "fulfill the mother's sense of self," to assure continuity of family genes, to achieve a sense of immortality for the parents, to pass on the family business, to carry on the "name," to increase welfare benefits, to provide companionship for another child. Statistically, most children are conceived for no reason at all—simply by accident or lack of planning.

I can imagine few better reasons for parenting a child than to save another child. How rare an opportunity this soon-to-be-born baby has—to come into this world with a lifesaving mission. Understandably, the Ayalas are upset by the judgmental pronouncements of their ethical superiors. "We're going to love our baby," Mary assures them.

The Ayalas owe no assurances to any ethicists who fail to appreciate how noble their decision is. They have a dying seventeen-year-old daughter whose life has a chance of being saved by bringing another life into the world. Any parents who love their daughter as much as the Ayalas do, and are willing to do as much for her as they are willing to do, will be wonderful parents to their new baby.

Moreover, there are precedents for violating the so-called precept that no person should ever be used "solely as a means to another person's end without the agreement of the person. . . ." When Massachusetts General Hospital performed the first kidney transplant many years ago, the donor was a young child, well below the age of consent. His kidney was needed to save the life of his twin brother. Their parents provided the necessary consent.

In that case, the donor child was left with only one kidney. In the Ayala case, the baby will have no missing organs. All it will have is a life it would not have had but for its dying sister's need for a compatible blood cell donor.

The ethical complaints directed against the Ayalas raise profound concerns about the entire enterprise of professional ethicists intruding themselves into the most intimate family issues.

The ethicists who regard the Ayala's decision as "outrageous" or violative of "fundamental precepts of ethics" are, fortunately, without power to enforce their self-righteous views. But more and more hospitals are including ethicists on their staffs and are giving them some power of review.

This is a dangerous development that must be watched carefully. In a democracy, individuals and families should be reluctant to abdicate the most personal life-and-death decisions to a bevy of Platonic guardians who have little hesitation in pronouncing a universal ethic from on high.

Any ethical question about which reasonable people can disagree— and the Ayalas' case surely is one—should be left to the family. If they chose to seek the advice of ethicists, religious counselors, or anyone else, they should, of course, be free to do so. But outsiders must be reticent about lecturing families on how far they may go in trying to save the life of a loved one.   February 1990

Nearly one year after receiving a bone marrow transplant from her younger sister Marissa, Anissa Ayala was married. As a result of the transplant, Anissa is recovering from leukemia.

ALAN M. DERSHOWITZ

ABORTION IS THE WRONG LITMUS TEST

The president, Congress, and the media are all debating whether Judge David Souter should be asked his views on abortion and whether his answer should determine his confirmation. It is the wrong question for several reasons.

One reason is that it is likely to be a time-bound issue. Souter may serve well into the twenty-first century. Yet by the end of this decade, science is likely to overtake law as the arena in which the abortion issue will be resolved.

Pharmacological methods for preventing unwanted births, such as RU-486, will almost certainly replace current-day abortion for many, if not most, women who wish to terminate pregnancy. These pharmacological interventions are more private and less traumatic than physical abortion at a hospital or clinic, and will be seen as more like birth control than abortion. They are unlikely to be as divisive and emotional as the externally induced destruction of a several-month-old fetus.

No one should be nominated, confirmed, or rejected solely on the basis of his views on a single current issue that is unlikely to remain current beyond the next few years.

Even more important, the abortion issue is not a very accurate litmus test of whether the judge will turn out to be a "liberal" or a "conservative," a "strict constructionist" or a "judicial activist," or even a supporter of "individual rights" as against "state power." The abortion issue is simply too complex and multifaceted to be a litmus test for anything.

Some of the nation's most distinguished civil libertarians and liberals are opposed to abortion on demand. Others regard the abortion issue as a difficult one, especially during the latter months of pregnancy. And still others, who personally favor a woman's right to choose, cannot bring themselves to find this particular right in the rather general language of the Constitution.

Put most directly, you can be a good civil libertarian and liberal without believing that the Constitution resolves all abortion-related issues on the side of the pregnant woman. The abortion issue may be a good litmus test as to whether a nominee is a card-carrying *feminist*, but it is an inaccurate test on how the nominee is likely to vote on other more enduring issues, such as freedom of speech, separation of church and state, racial equality, and the rights of criminal defendants.

One of the reasons why some civil libertarians don't regard abortion as a clear constitutional right is that it is an issue with shifting majorities and minorities. Today, it seems as if a majority of Americans probably favor a woman's right to choose abortion under many circumstances. Indeed, that was what some feminist groups were telling the Supreme Court on the eve of the last great test case. They placed ads in newspapers across the country, which read: "Your Honors, Before you vote on *Roe* vs. *Wade*, listen to one final opinion. . . . The majority of Americans support *Roe* vs. *Wade*. A Harris poll . . . revealed that this support comes from virtually every demographic and geographic group in America."

But if that observation is true, it is an argument *against* constitutionalizing the right to abortion. If a majority of Americans in every part of this country favor a woman's right to choose, then this majority should organize its political power and establish its program through elections, lobbying, referenda, and legislation.

The primary role of unelected courts in our system of checks and balances is to vindicate the constitutional rights of unpopular *minorities*— Americans who are incapable of implementing their rights through the popularly elected branches. The true test of a great Supreme Court justice is whether he or she will be bold enough to stand up to temporary majorities and to vindicate the rights of unpopular minorities, such as atheists, aliens, Communists, fascists, the mentally ill, criminal defendants, and the homeless.

This is a litmus test that Souter seems to fail. He has no track record of standing up for the rights of unpopular minorities. To the contrary, as attorney general he defended particularly obnoxious prosecutions directed against Jehovah's Witnesses who refused to comply with New Hampshire's hypocritical law requiring that its motto "live free or die" be displayed on all license plates. As a judge, he has displayed similar insensitivity toward the constitutional rights of criminal defendants, ruling for the prosecution in nearly every case.

The irony is that few of the senators who must confirm Souter have themselves shown sensitivity toward the rights of unpopular minorities, particularly those with little impact on elections. Judicial rulings against the rights of criminal defendants are quite popular with most senators. Robert Bork lost his confirmation battle not because he was insensitive to the rights of unpopular minorities but because he was perceived as being outside "the mainstream" on issues of importance to the majority or to minorities with political clout.

Souter will probably win confirmation, if he can convince the Senate that his constitutional insensitivities are limited to criminals, atheists,

Communists, aliens, and other politically powerless and unpopular minorities.   August 1990

NO-SMOKING CUSTODY: HOW FAR CAN IT GO?

A California Superior Court judge recently conditioned the grant of custody to a mother on the promise that she would not smoke in the presence of her child. This decision, which was rendered before recent published reports that children who grow up with parents who smoke near them double their risk of lung cancer, is sure to be followed by other judges. The hard question is whether the law will next forbid parents who are not in a child-custody dispute from smoking in the presence of their children. Another question is what effect this no-smoking decision could have on pregnant women who breathe smoke into their babies, or on anyone who smokes in the presence of pregnant women.

Custody disputes are commonly the opening wedge into state monitoring of families. In a custody dispute, the judge must decide which parent will be better for the child. All things being equal, a parent who doesn't smoke in the presence of the child is better than one who does. The same would be true of a parent who didn't get drunk or do drugs in the presence of the child.

Under present law, the state has little power to control how parents, who are not seeking a divorce or custody, interact with their children. In the absence of immediate risk to life or health, such as physical or sexual abuse, the state will rarely try to take children out of an intact family home. But in the context of a custody dispute, the courts have enormous power to regulate parental conduct.

Thus, it is extremely unlikely that a court would remove a child from a home in which *both* parents smoked in the presence of a child, despite the heightened risk of lung disease. The same would probably be true if both parents were heavy drinkers or even drug users. But any of these vices could easily disqualify a parent seeking custody in a dispute with an equally qualified parent who engaged in none of these dangerous activities.

Why then does the state tolerate behavior dangerous to children when it is committed by parents who are not seeking divorce or custody? Don't these endangered children, particularly if they are very young and cannot protect themselves, deserve the protection of the state from parents who are abusing their health?

Of course they do. But the price of state intervention into intact families would be very great. In general, our society looks to the family as the first line of protection for the child. The state cannot and should not second-guess every family decision that could have a deleterious impact on children. Certainly, no state agency would prevent parents from spanking a child or even using the cat-o'-nine-tails, so long as no serious physical harm resulted. Nor would the state criticize parents for being too permissive with their kids. Parents are free to overfeed or underfeed their kids, within reasonable limits. They cannot be told which schools to send them to—so long as they meet minimal standards—or whether to bring them up as liberals, conservatives, Communists, or Nazis.

The question is where to draw the line at which family decisions will be overruled by the state. Some guidelines have emerged: In general, parents may not totally neglect their children or abuse them sexually or physically. As medical knowledge increases, the lines may very well change. A generation ago, no court would dream of conditioning custody on a pledge not to smoke in the presence of a child. Tomorrow, it would not be surprising to see states enacting laws prohibiting *all* parents from smoking in the presence of children below a certain age. In the absence of a statute, it is unlikely that any court would now prevent an intact family from smoking near children. Nor is it likely that, absent a statute, any pregnant woman would be prevented from smoking into her fetus, despite the known dangers.

One reason why we are unlikely to see any fetal protection laws enacted is that the issue of fetal protection is seen by many as a surrogate for the abortion issue. The issue of abortion can, of course, be separated from the issue of fetal protection: A woman should have the right to decide whether to have a child, but once she decides to have that child she is obligated to refrain from endangering its future health. But pro-choice activists are so terrified at any recognition of "fetal rights" and so concerned about "fetal cops" monitoring a woman's pregnancy that many have opposed all restrictions on a woman's freedom during pregnancy.

In the end, the responsibility for the health and welfare of children will continue to rest with parents, doctors who counsel them, and the availability of pre- and postnatal care for families in need. Courts, like the custody court in California, will have a limited impact but will be able to

send an important public message about the dangers of smoking and other
activities hazardous to children.   October 1990

DOCTORS SING GOVERNMENT'S RIGHT-TO-LIFE SONG

The Supreme Court recently decided that doctors and other professionals
who work in federally funded clinics must read from a federally drafted
script when asked about the constitutional right to have an abortion.

Regardless of what they believe is best for the particular woman, these
health professionals must recite the following lines: "The project does not
consider abortion an appropriate method of family planning."

The Supreme Court's majority ruled, in effect, that the old saw about
"he who pays the piper calls the tune" is now a doctrine of constitutional
law powerful enough to override the doctor's constitutional rights to free
speech and professional independence, as well as the patient's rights to an
abortion and to independent professional advice.

The implications for indigent women in need of family-planning advice
are staggering. Since few such women can afford private care, most will be
getting their family planning advice from a biased source with a hidden
political and/or religious agenda. Fewer women will exercise their constitutional right to choose an abortion, because they will not be advised that
they have that constitutional right and that medical option.

An individuous distinction will be drawn between those women who
can afford private medical advice and those women who must seek guidance
and care from governmentally subsidized clinics. It will create an understandable suspicion among the poor that the professionals with whom they
are conferring are not on *their* side but rather on the side of a particular
political and/or religious movement that disfavors abortion.

But consider as well the implications of this ruling for other professions.

A great many *legal* service organizations are subsidized, directly or
indirectly, by governmental funds. All litigants, like all pregnant women,
have certain constitutional rights that are not popular with some segments
of society. For example, every criminal defendant, whether innocent or
guilty, has the constitutional right to put the government to its proof by
pleading not guilty. They have the right to trial by jury, to seek the exclusion

of illegally obtained evidence, and to cross-examine witnesses against them. These are all expensive rights that many members of the voting public would rather not pay for, especially on behalf of guilty defendants.

Under the Supreme Court's new decision, can the government that subsidizes legal aid and public defender offices now require "their" lawyers and paralegals to recite a governmentally approved script that conforms to the "law-and-order" political agenda? Will governmentally subsidized defense attorneys now be required to tell defendants that "we do not consider a plea of not guilty an appropriate option for a defendant who is guilty" or "we do not approve of the exclusionary rule in this clinic and will try not to keep the illegally obtained material out of evidence"?

For those who complain that such scripted restrictions will violate the constitutional rights of criminal defendants, the government can give the same answer it has given to pregnant women: You *still* have all your constitutional rights, but you can't ask the government to *pay* for their exercise. Translated to the legal context, this means that only defendants wealthy enough to afford private lawyers will be fully advised of their constitutional rights. A new reality will have been brought to the cynical cartoon that now hangs in many a lawyer's office: It shows a prosperous attorney sitting behind his desk asking his client, "Now just how much justice can you afford?"

More than a quarter of a century ago—in the famous Escobedo and Miranda cases—the Supreme Court ruled that if a citizen possesses a constitutional right he should be informed of that right. As the high court put it in Escobedo: "We have . . . learned the . . . lesson of history that no system of . . . Justice can, or should, survive if it comes to depend for its continued effectiveness on the citizens' abdication through unawareness of their constitutional rights." This important principle of open democracy was violated by the Supreme Court's recent ruling regarding abortion clinics. How far the new principal of subsidized rights will be taken by the high court's majority is anyone's guess.

It is widely believed that Congress will consider, and perhaps overrule, the family-planning decision. After all, a majority of Americans favors a woman's right to have an abortion, at least under some circumstances. And there is a strong pro-choice constituency among the voters and among members of Congress. But there is no voter support for the constitutional rights of criminal defendants. Were the high court to rule that federally funded lawyers had to restrict the professional advice they could give, there could be little congressional relief in sight.

ALAN M. DERSHOWITZ

Thus, even if Congress were to overrule the recent Supreme Court decision in the specific context of abortion counseling, the principle of he who pays the piper calling the tune would still survive. And it is a dangerous and divisive principle for America.   May 1991

CAUTION: YOUR SURGEON MAY HAVE PMS

The trooper stopped the swerving BMW on Thanksgiving night and noticed a strong odor of alcohol on the breath of the woman who was driving her children home from a dinner party. When the trooper asked the driver how much she had to drink, the driver identified herself as "a doctor" and told the trooper that it was none of his "damn business." The trooper then asked her to place her hands on top of her head; instead, she tried to kick him in the groin.

According to the trooper, she then began to yell: "You son of a (expletive); you (expletive) can't do this to me; I'm a doctor. I hope you (expletive) get shot and come into my hospital so I can refuse to treat you, or if any other trooper gets shot, I will also refuse to treat them." After being arrested, the doctor was asked to take a Breathalyzer test, whereupon she kicked the machine. When she finally agreed to take the test, she failed it. She was then charged with drunken driving.

The doctor's defense was that she was afflicted with premenstrual syndrome (PMS). Her lawyer argued that women absorb alcohol more quickly during their premenstrual cycle and that women with PMS become more irritable and hostile than other people. The Virginia judge apparently agreed with this argument and acquitted the woman. It is the first known instance of a PMS acquittal in this country and may serve as a precedent for future cases. The doctor and her lawyer were ecstatic over their victory.

Lest anyone believe that this acquittal was a victory for women, for feminism, or for those women who are affected with PMS, just consider the implications of excusing women with PMS from criminal responsibility. This woman is an orthopedic surgeon who presumably performs delicate surgery all through the month. Does she now have to notify each of her patients that her PMS may make her irresponsible during several days each month? Will she abuse nurses and kick the medical machinery in the midst of a surgical procedure? Should there be special rules limiting the amount of alcohol women with PMS are allowed to drink during their premenstrual part of the cycle? Must women with PMS display a surgeon general's warning during this time alerting all persons who come in contact with them that their PMS may cause irritability, hostility, or drunkenness? May employers now refuse to hire women with PMS for certain jobs? May they require all women to submit to medical tests designed to uncover latent or hidden PMS?

Any defense of criminal irresponsibility is, as Dostoyevski once put it, "a knife that cuts both ways." It may excuse in one case, but it causes suspicion and prejudice in other cases. For example, when we excuse the mentally ill from responsibility for their criminal actions, we stigmatize all mentally ill people as irresponsible and incapable of controlling themselves. Nor is suspicion and prejudice against women who suffer from PMS warranted by the empirical data.

Though *some* women who are irritable and hostile during their premenstrual cycle may well suffer from PMS, the vast majority of women who suffer from PMS do not behave the outrageous way the surgeon in this case did. Her PMS did not *cause* her unlawful and rude behavior. Her actions were caused by her entire background, personality, and circumstances. She is obviously an elitist and deprecating person during the entire month, or else she would not have said what she did to the trooper. PMS alone does not change Dr. Jekyll into Mr. Hyde. She admitted that she had several drinks before she drove that night, and surely her PMS is not responsible for that behavior.

We live in an age when everybody tries to blame someone or something for their failures. Several years ago there was the "Twinkie defense." And then there was the "TV-made-me-do-it" excuse. Now it's raging hormones. This well-educated doctor should have realized that she behaves differently during the premenstrual part of her cycle, and she should have taken precautions against breaking the law. Surely her PMS did not come on suddenly without previous manifestations. Her acquittal sends a doubly dangerous message. First, that our hormones are beyond our control and that we are not responsible for how they manifest themselves. And second, that women with premenstrual problems are somehow less reliable and less predictable than other people. Neither is true.

The PMS defense is a setback to feminism, especially when used in a case like the surgeon's. She ought to take responsibility for her actions. And if her hormones are indeed beyond her control, her patients should be made aware of that dangerous reality. She can't have it both ways.

June 1991

ALAN M. DERSHOWITZ

ARGUMENTS HINT AT NO ABORTION OVERRULE

Millions of Americans probably would have liked to watch the Supreme Court in action during Wednesday's arguments in the case of *Webster* vs. *Reproductive Health Services.* But because television and radio are banned from the Supreme Court chambers, all but the few hundred people allowed into the small courtroom must content themselves with secondhand reports.

Not that you can always tell from an oral argument how the case will be decided, or even how a particular justice will vote. But justices do ask questions, and their questions sometimes reveal the direction of their thinking.

The case involves the state of Missouri's restrictions on abortion, and some fear it could result in an overturn of *Roe* vs. *Wade*, the landmark 1973 case in which the Supreme Court established the right to abortion under the Constitution's Fourteenth Amendment.

Justice Antonin Scalia, who in his short tenure on the high court has already established himself as its most vocal participant, surprised some observers Wednesday by suggesting that the Missouri law, which declares that life begins at conception, may go too far to survive constitutional challenge.

Scalia commented that the American Civil Liberties Union (ACLU) lawyer who argued in favor of upholding *Roe* vs. *Wade* "makes the very good point that it is impossible to distinguish between abortion and contraception when you define abortion as the destruction of the first joinder of the ovum and the sperm."

But he also challenged the ACLU lawyer by stating: "I don't see why a court that can draw [the line between trimesters] can't separate abortion from birth control quite readily."

Justice Sandra Day O'Connor, the court's only woman justice and a potential swing vote, asked questions suggesting that she may favor a constitutional right of procreation. She challenged the position of the lawyer for the United States, who appeared as a friend of the court in favor of overruling *Roe* vs. *Wade*. The lawyer had denied that the Constitution protects the right to procreate (and its corollary right, to *not* procreate).

O'Connor asked: "Do you think that the state has the right to, if, in a future century, we had a serious overpopulation problem, has a right to require women to have abortions after so many children?"

The lawyer for the United States responded: "I surely do not." But he had a difficult time justifying his distinction since he had already argued that there is no constitutional right of procreation.

The newest justice, Anthony Kennedy, who has never voted on an abortion case, seemed concerned that if *Roe* vs. *Wade* were overruled, the right to birth control might also be endangered, since both are grounded in the same right to privacy.

Though justices occasionally change their minds between argument and opinion writing, it is unlikely that any of the current justices came into this argument without a pretty clear view of where they stand on this highly emotional and divisive issue. Most observers believe that this case was all but decided before the arguments even began—indeed, before the briefs were read. Virtually every judge has an opinion on abortion.

Interestingly, however, this case may not be decided on the basis of the justices' personal, or even constitutional, views on the "right to life" versus a woman's freedom of choice. There seems now to be a majority of justices who would not have voted in favor of a woman's right to an abortion if that issue were coming before the court for the first time. But *Roe* vs. *Wade* established that right sixteen years ago. And there seem to be enough justices who believe that precedent should govern even if they would not have joined the original precedent.

The Supreme Court thus appears to be divided into three camps. The first consists of those justices—Harry Blackmun, William Brennan, Thurgood Marshall, and probably John Paul Stevens—who voted (or likely would have voted) in favor of choice in the case of first impression. The second camp—William Rehnquist, Byron White, and perhaps one or two more—do not believe *Roe* vs. *Wade* was correctly decided and would vote to overrule it. The third camp, whose composition is the least certain, consists of justices who would not have voted with the original majority in *Roe* vs. *Wade* but who will not now vote to overrule that sixteen-year-old precedent.

The likely outcome of the Webster argument is that *Roe* vs. *Wade* will not be overruled, because the third camp will join with the first to form a majority on that broad issue.

However, there is a possibility that the third camp may also form a majority with the second on the narrower issue of further restricting public funding and public counseling for abortion—an issue not covered by *Roe* vs. *Wade*. If that happens, the poorest women may well be denied access to safe abortions through public hospitals, while women who can afford private clinics will continue to receive medically supervised abortions.

The justices' questions also left open the possibility that several issues growing out of the Missouri statute may simply not be resolved in the current case.

This outcome is likely to make no one happy. But then again, it's not the justices' job to win popularity contests.   April 1989

. . . BUT IT'S TIME TO OVERRULE ROE VS. WADE

As a pro-choice civil-libertarian, I hope the Supreme Court will overrule *Roe* vs. *Wade* this June. If the high court completes the process of chipping away at a woman's right to choose abortion, the issue will be put squarely in the hands of the American voters.

The abortion issue belongs in the political, rather than the judicial, process because there is no correct constitutional answer, as there was with such divisive issues as desegregation and malproportioned legislatures. For those Americans who honestly believe to the core of their soul that a fetus is a live human being, there is no compelling argument for authorizing abortion. We do not allow parents to "choose" to murder their children, regardless of how "young" they may be.

For most Americans, however, there is a dispositive difference between an unborn fetus and a born infant. For us, the right of a woman to control her own reproductive system requires that she have the right to terminate her pregnancy.

When equally compelling rights clash in this manner, and when the Constitution is silent on the issue, the majority should generally rule. This is especially true when both sides have access to the political process. The right-to-life movement is organized and powerful, as is the right-to-choice movement. If the issue is put to the voters, neither side will win a complete victory, but a woman's right to choose will generally prevail.

Recent public opinion polls show that a substantial majority of Americans—from both parties, both sexes, all ages and most states—favor a woman's basic right to choose an abortion. But beyond that basic right, there is little consensus about other important issues surrounding the abortion controversy, such as government funding for abortions, parental consent for minors, mandatory waiting periods, and required counseling.

Even the American Civil Liberties Union, which has devoted dispro-portionate resources to litigating abortion cases, acknowledges that the issue is largely political. It pushed for the issue to be decided by the Supreme Court before the 1992 presidential election so that if the justices overrule *Roe* vs. *Wade*, the voters can overrule the justices and elect candidates who favor a woman's right to choose. The ACLU is confident that it can win at the polls if it loses in court. The ACLU should not be spending so much of its precious currency litigating in favor of popular causes that are supported by a majority of voters. Its primary mission should be enforcing the constitutional rights of disenfranchised people—such as the homeless, illegal aliens, political and religious dissidents, criminal defendants, racial minorities—who cannot vindicate their rights through the political process. It should leave the issue of abortion to the very capable feminist and reproductive rights organizations, which are issue-oriented rather than civil-liberties-oriented.

The abortion issue is political in another sense as well. It could enhance the election prospects of the Democrats. So long as a woman's fundamental right to choose abortion was protected by the courts, few voters made their decisions on the basis of a candidate's posturing on right-to-life or choice. For example, President Bush received the support of many voters who favor a woman's right to choose, even though he campaigned on an uncompromising right-to-life platform. But his appointment of justices who are believed to be right-to-lifers may come back to haunt his reelection bid. If they form a majority to overrule *Roe* vs. *Wade* four months before the November election, abortion may become a central campaign issue for the first time in our history. That issue, in combination with the recession, could turn women and young voters against Bush in significant numbers.

As a Democrat, I hope that President Bush is defeated in the 1992 election, and I believe that the overruling of *Roe* vs. *Wade* might well contribute to his defeat. But as a right-to-choice advocate, I worry about the short-term implications of overruling *Roe* vs. *Wade*. Until legislation is enacted protecting a woman's right to choose abortion, that option will be more difficult, especially for poor and immobile women in states with rigid right-to-life laws. But the end result will be to place a woman's right to choose on a firmer electoral footing than the ever-shifting votes of nine justices.

The irony is that once the right to choice is firmly established by legislation, the antiabortion forces will take to the courts in an effort to constitutionalize the right-to-life and to strike down choice statutes. Those right-to-lifers who now argue that the issue of abortion should be left to state legislators will be arguing for judicial intervention. And those right-to-choicers who have traditionally sought help from the courts will argue that the issue should be left to the legislators.   January 1992

THE CASEY DECISION

The Supreme Court, in yet another 5 to 4 decision, has reaffirmed an adult woman's fundamental right to procreative freedom, while at the same time placing considerable burdens on her right to freely choose abortion. An adult woman may not be required to notify her husband prior to obtaining an abortion, though she may have to sit through preachy lectures about alternatives to abortion and wait 24 hours. An adolescent female—below the age of 18—may be required to notify her parents before securing an abortion, unless a court decides that she is mature and capable of giving informed consent herself. And a woman is as subject to these burdens in the first trimester of her pregnancy as she is later on.

Ironically, the big winner may be President George Bush, who has called publicly for the overruling of *Roe v. Wade*, but whose political advisers have warned him that such an overruling prior to November could be a disaster to his reelection prospects. Had *Roe v. Wade* been clearly overruled this week, the controversy over a woman's right to abortion would have become a major electoral issue in the current presidential campaign. If President Bush stuck to his rigid opposition position, it would have cost him deeply at the polls, especially among moderates, woman and young voters. Now, following the Court's iddle ground decision, a woman's right to abortion will not assume great importance in this campaign.

The 5–4 decision vindicates those who opposed the nomination of Robert Bork on the ground that he would provide the swing vote in the abortion controversy. The justice who was nominated in his stead, Anthony Kennedy, cast the deciding vote in favor of a woman's right to abortion—not because he favors it but because he, unlike Brok and the other Supreme Court dissenters, believes in the power of precedent.

The Casey decision also vindicates those who were skeptical about Justice Clarence Thomas' claim that he had a completely open mind on the issue of abortion—indeed a virtually empty mind—since he had never even discussed it. It now seems clear that he knew all the time where he stood and how he was going to vote.

The decision itself, muddled as it is, will probably appeal to most mainstream Americans who favor a woman's basic right to choose abortion, but who also favor a parent's right to be notified of an adolescent's decision to have one. The Pennsylvania law clearly places the heavy thumb of the state on *not* having an abortion: it does not, for example require a pregnant adolescent girl to notify her parents of her decision *not* to have an abortion and thus to bear a child; nor does it require counseling about an adult's decision to bear a child. In these respects, the Pennsylvania law—and the High Court's decision—*burdens* a woman's right to choose abortion more than it burdens her right to choose continued pregnancy. Thus, the Court has held that the state need not remainneutral in relation to a woman's right to choose. It may favor her choosing not to have an abortion as Pennsylvania has done.

Looking to the future, the *Planned Parenthood of Southeastern Pennsylvania v. Casey* decision seems to indicate that without a change in personnel, the Supreme Court will continue along its current course of reaffirming a woman's basic right to choose abortion, but also affirming the efforts of some states to make it increasingly difficult for young women, poor women and uneducated women to exercise that right. It is fair to say, therefore, that the High Court's slim majority—really its three-person plurality—regards the right to choose abortion as a right of lesser value than other fundamental rights such as speech, religion and the press. This court would not tolerate the kinds of burdens on those more fundamental rights that it has tolerated on the right to choose an abortion. For some of the plurality justices, the right to choose an abortion seems to ahve an even lower status—it is not a right that they would have recognized at all had they been on the High Court when *Roe v. Wade* was decided back in 1973; it is merely an interest that has assumed the status of a right by virtue of a 19-year old precedent and some other analogous decisions.

This week's decision in *Planned Parenthood of Southeastern Pennsylvania v. Casey* is a political wake-up call to advocates of a woman's right to choose abortion. They cannot rely exclusively on the Supreme Court. They should continue their political campaign in favor of legislative parachutes and their judicial campaign in favor of state constitutional safety nets in the event the High Court changes its collective mind or its individual membership.   July 1992

ALAN M. DERSHOWITZ

IS THERE A RIGHT TO NONPATERNITY?

King Solomon had it relatively easy compared to the case recently decided by the Supreme Court of Tennessee in which a divorced man was given the right to prevent his former wife from using frozen embryos made with his sperm and her egg. Justice Martha Craig Daughtrey had before her several embryos that had not yet been implanted to a "host mother" for development and ultimate birth. The genetic "father," or sperm donor, did not want "his" potential progeny to be born. The genetic "mother," the egg donor, wanted "her" potential progeny to be born. To complicate matters even further, the *genetic* mother did not want to carry the progeny herself; she intended to "donate" the frozen embryos to a *biological* mother who would carry the progeny to term and give birth to it. If that biological mother had a husband, he would become the *legal* father to the child.

Because there were no donees designated to "harvest" the embryos, Justice Daughtrey did not have to consider the rights of the potential parents to give birth to the embryo. But in a future case, where donees have been designated, the legal issues may be even more complex.

Even among the genetic contributors to the frozen embryos, the issues—legal, moral, and psychological—are difficult. To begin with, it is far more painful, intrusive, and traumatic to contribute an egg than to contribute some sperm. Eggs, moreover, are in far shorter supply than sperm for several reasons: Women have only one egg per cycle and stop producing them in their forties; men produce millions of sperm well into old age.

Consider, therefore, the situation of a woman in her forties who is no longer capable of producing eggs but who did contribute eggs that were fertilized by her former husband. She desperately wants to bear a child that has her own genetic material. Accordingly, she formally absolves her erstwhile husband of all responsibility for the child and insists on having the embryo implanted into her. The man objects, insisting that his genetic material not be used to produce a child. Should his right to nonpaternity prevail over her right to maternity?

What if a slightly different, but more common, procedure were employed whereby the egg was fertilized in the laboratory and immediately implanted into the egg donor? Within days, the man divorces the woman and demands that the pregnancy be terminated. Surely in that case no court would insist that the woman undergo an involuntary abortion, even if that could be done without any pain, risk, or inconvenience. The man's demand that he not become a father would be subordinated to the woman's desire to bear the child, just as it would in a case of conventional impregnation after which the man changed his mind.

The only difference between the case of the frozen embryo stored in the lab and the embryo immediately implanted into the woman is the trauma to the woman. The man's "right" not to have a child born of his genetic material is identical, regardless of the "location" of his contribution at any particular time. Another practical difference is that if the embryo is frozen in a lab, there is time to litigate the issue, as the Tennessee case was litigated. Once the embryo has been implanted, the clock is ticking and the embryo is developing into a fetus.

The issues raised by the Tennessee case and its variations pose a dilemma both for pro-choice and anti-abortion absolutists. Many pro-choice absolutists would argue that a man does have the right to prevent the implanting of a frozen embryo but not the right to remove an implanted embryo. But they would be uncomfortable justifying that distinction on the ground that once the embryo had been implanted and begins to develop, its status has changed. Surely they would not argue that it had become a "life" deserving of constitutional protection. They would instead have to argue that once the embryo had been implanted into a woman, that *woman* has the right to determine its future without interference either by the sperm donor or by the state. But why should everything turn on whether there had been implantation, especially if termination were to become a matter of taking a pill? Doesn't any such distinction give too much credence to right-to-life arguments about developing fetuses?

For anti-abortion absolutists, the Tennessee case also poses a dilemma. To be consistent, they must take the unpopular position of opposing the eminently sensible decision of the Tennessee court to destroy "life," even when "life" is merely a frozen embryo. If there is a right to nonpaternity, there surely must be a right to nonmaternity as well.

The Tennessee court's decision was clearly right on its specific facts: The right of a woman who is still capable of bearing children to "donate" the embryos to an undesignated couple does not outweigh the right of the man to prevent that donation. But it should not be interpreted to recognize a general right to "nonpaternity" in other situations.   June 1992

9 // *Capital Punishment*

DEFENSE OF RETARDED MAN FAILED HIM

The other day I went to the U.S. Supreme Court to observe the oral argument in one of the most important cases of the decade. The issue was whether it would be cruel and unusual punishment for the state of Texas to execute a mentally retarded man who had been convicted of a rape-murder. He was thirty-two years old, but the man had the intelligence of a six-year-old, the emotional maturity of a nine-year-old, an IQ of 53, and a long history of abuse and institutionalization.

At stake was not just the life of John Paul Penry, whose case made headlines because his victim was the beautiful sister of football kicking star Mark Mosely. For as many as three hundred other mentally retarded inmates on death row, the Penry decision may well mean the difference between institutionalization and death by electrocution or injection.

Watching a Supreme Court argument is usually a grand experience. The courtroom is majestic, the justices ask probing questions, and the lawyers are generally well prepared. I anticipated witnessing the high art of life-or-death advocacy—until the advocate for John Paul Penry strode up to the podium.

To say the least, his presentation was a disaster. The attorney spoke haltingly and his words were difficult to understand. He seemed not to understand some of the justices' questions. When he did, he frequently gave the wrong answers. He couldn't find needed references. He became so bogged down in technical detail that Justice O'Connor had to remind him, with only three minutes left in his argument time, that he had not addressed the main issue—whether it was constitutional to execute a mentally retarded prisoner.

How poorly the interests—the lives!—of retarded death-row inmates were being represented! This well-intentioned, good-hearted lawyer was simply not up to the job of arguing a complex case in the Supreme Court.

As I watched him, I felt compassion for this lawyer who was so clearly out of his league. According to the *Fort Worth* (Tex.) *Star-Telegram*, he had "retired comfortably from years of public service and joined a special legal assistance project that the Texas Department of Corrections had established to aid death-row inmates with appeals."

Indeed, the fault did not lie with him—he was doing the best he could. Instead, the fault lay squarely with the justice system, which had to rely on retired do-gooders to do the difficult work of trying to save lives. There simply weren't enough active and experienced lawyers willing to do the job.

Although it is a temptation to remain silent for the sake of a fellow lawyer, I cannot do so after what I observed in the Supreme Court. The lives of hundreds of mentally retarded inmates, unable to defend themselves or even to understand that they are not being well represented, lie in balance.

For too long, professionals, whether they be lawyers, doctors, or airline pilots, have been unwilling to blow the whistle on their colleagues. Underqualified doctors have been permitted to perform delicate surgery because their peers were unwilling to say what they saw in the operating rooms. Lawyers have been equally malfeasant.

Of course, no corporation faced with a $50,000 lawsuit would have allowed so bumbling a defense of its position before the high court. No intelligent criminal, facing even a year in prison, would have allowed a lawyer so obviously out of his depth to argue for his freedom before the justices. But John Paul Penry is mentally retarded. He can't tell the difference between a good lawyer and a poor one. He must depend on the judgment of others.

It would be a double travesty of justice for the Supreme Court, when it makes its decision in several months, to permit the execution of a mentally retarded "child" who could neither exercise good judgment in the commission of his crimes nor in the selection of his attorney.

Something must be done to assure the competence of the legal representation of death-row inmates. While lawyers help the rich get richer, those most in need of excellent legal representation—the mentally retarded, the poor, the homeless, the stateless—have to rely on well-motivated volunteers, retired lawyers, and underpaid public defenders.

If John Paul Penry is "put to sleep," as one old friend of Penry's put it, it will not be because of his crimes alone—only eleven people were executed in the United States in all of 1988. It will be because he picked the wrong person to kill, he was born to the wrong parents, and the wrong lawyer represented him.   January 1989

In June, 1989 the Supreme Court ruled that mentally retarded defendants may be executed, but that the jury must be advised of their condition. Penry remains on death-row.

EXECUTIONS EMBOLDEN FAME-SEEKING KILLERS

If the highly publicized electrocution of Ted Bundy has any effect on mass murderers, it is likely to encourage rather than deter them.

Mass murderers, whether they be Bundy or Patrick Purdy, the sicko who killed five school children in Stockton, Calif., seem to thrive on media attention. And there is no surer way of achieving instantaneous infamy than to become the object of a "death watch." The eyes and video cameras of the world focus on the doomed denizen of death row as the countdown to execution ticks away toward its deadly conclusion.

The media hangs on every last word of the celebrity killer as his lawyers go through last-minute efforts to stay the executioner's hand. Suddenly, a man who was never believed before becomes the paragon of truth as he confesses to new crimes in a desperate attempt to enhance the value of his life, even for a few additional days. Those who disbelieved his previous excuses now rush to publicize his final pathetic ploy—that "pornography" made him do it.

Pretty clever! Bundy was smart enough to know that his final interviewer, a religious psychiatrist who led the campaign against smut on the Meese pornography commission, would welcome his pointing the finger at the "devil porn." But even that didn't work.

No one can seriously believe that his victims would be alive today if he hadn't read the latest soft-core drugstore magazine, an activity innocently enjoyed by millions of law-abiding citizens. Even the Meese commission concluded that violence is more likely than erotica to cause crime. The violence of state-administered execution may well contribute far more than the occasional skin flick to the deadly atmosphere of bloodshed.

Not only were each of Bundy's warped ideas reported in the media, but his execution became the subject of songs, ditties, jokes, chants, and even T-shirts. The announcement of his death was greeted by cheers and shouts. Witnesses to his final moments became sought-after interview subjects. His final words were quoted repeatedly on the evening news. On at least one network, the story of his electrocution led the evening news, relegating President Bush to second place.

It is easy to imagine how the warped mind of a potential mass killer might react to the unseemly attention paid to every last detail of Ted Bundy's final moments on earth. Some of the sickest psychopaths crave attention, and it doesn't much matter whether the attention is positive or negative. Nor does it matter, at least to some, whether the attention is precipitated by their own imminent death.

The frequent phenomenon of suicide following mass killings, most recently by the Stockton killer of the schoolchildren, demonstrates that the prospect of death does not always deter those who are determined to even out some imagined score with society by murdering its most vulnerable citizens.

Indeed, the most immediate effect of the highly publicized Stockton murders and suicide was the dramatic increase in purchases of the deadly semi-automatic assault rifle the AK-47, used by the killer. Gun-control opponents may sloganize that "guns don't kill, people do." But no reasonable person can dispute the obvious fact that people armed with semi-automatic weapons are a lot more likely to kill a lot more victims than if they were unarmed.

I would not be at all surprised to see an increase in mass killings following the combined impacts of the highly publicized Bundy death watch and the Stockton killings. The frenzied crowd outside the Bundy execution site was calling for blood. One woman, interviewed on national television, demanded that those who were protesting the death penalty "fry along with Bundy."

We live in a violent society, with the highest homicide rate in the civilized world. Those states that execute the most people have among the highest murder rates in the country. I claim no direct causal relationship. But neither can advocates of capital punishment claim any support in this relationship for their unproven hypothesis that death deters more certainly than long imprisonment.

One of the most perceptive observations about the death penalty was made several years ago by Judge Gerhard Gesell (now presiding over the Oliver North case) as he imposed sentence on the killer of two young FBI agents:

"The court has concluded that it would not serve the ends of effective justice to allow the defendant the luxury of all the special attention a capital penalty would generate. His mistaken views of his own importance would be fed by the continued controversy and supplications surrounding the current legal controversy on the matter of capital punishment. Mr. Bryant, you will die in jail, but at such time as God appoints."

If more judges and juries would follow the sensible approach suggested by Judge Gesell, mass killers would receive exactly what they deserve—a lifetime of confinement and obscurity—and the public would be better protected against those who kill for publicity.　　　　　January 1989

SEEKING: A HANGMAN, EXPERIENCE PREFERRED

The state of Washington has finally managed to fill a grisly job that had been vacant since 1965. The job is that of official hangman. No American has been hanged since Richard Eugene Hickock and Perry Edward Smith, the central figures in Truman Capote's *In Cold Blood*, were sent to the gallows back in 1965. Only four states still provide for hanging as a means of execution; three of them—Montana, Delaware, and New Hampshire—have not executed anyone for more than forty years, and no hangings are imminent.

Washington State, which currently has seven death-row inmates, gives each condemned person the right to choose lethal injection. But condemned killer Charles Rodman Campbell has refused to exercise that "right." Under Washington law, therefore, he must be hanged by the neck until he is dead. And the person who hangs Campbell must be, under the law, a "qualified" hangman. But since hanging has all but disappeared from the civilized world, it is difficult for would-be practitioners of this trade to gain the necessary experience to become "qualified."

After a long and difficult search, the Washington Department of Corrections claims to have found a qualified hangman who is willing to put the noose around Campbell's neck for $1,500. I have no idea how many aspiring hangmen applied for the profitable post. Nor do I know what kind of employment agencies—"headhunters"?—handle hangmen's applications. I can hardly imagine what the résumés and letters of recommendation would look like.

The American Civil Liberties Union, ever vigilant to protect the quality of death as well as life, has some doubts about this new employee. Since Washington refuses to disclose the identify of its hangperson designate—we should not assume that the anonymous executioner is male, though I bet he is—the ACLU is protesting that it cannot check up on his qualifications for the job. They are demanding access to public records in order to determine whether the hangman meets the criteria for being "qualified" under the law.

This, of course, raises the obvious question: What makes someone qualified to serve as an official hangman? Obviously, there are the minimal technical skills necessary to assure that he doesn't botch the job, as Captain Kidd's hangman did in 1701. The definitive history of English criminal law recounts how "the rope broke and [Kidd] had to be raised from the ground and hanged again." Such "accidents were of frequent occurrence" in the old days, even when Englishmen were strung up with regularity by experienced hangmen.

Execution accidents have occurred in this country as well, even after the "modern" electric chair replaced the primitive gallows as the primary means of inflicting capital punishment. In 1946, a seventeen-year-old black youth— he was fifteen at the time of the crime—had an "insufficient" shock of electricity sent through his body by a defective electric chair. He was reexecuted a year later, after an unsuccessful claim before the Supreme Court that a second try would place him "twice in jeopardy of his life." In 1953, Ethel Rosenberg had to receive a second jolt of electricity after the first rendered her unconscious but not dead. Thus, a qualified hangman must know how to kill efficiently and with a minimum of suffering to the hangee.

Efficient hangmen will be harder to find now than they were when hanging was prevalent and practice made perfect. There are no experienced executioners in Western Europe, because capital punishment has not been practiced there for a generation. American executioners now specialize in the lethal injection, which is quickly becoming the capital punishment of choice in many states.

But despite the fact that we have had no hangings in this country for a quarter century, the Washington authorities assure us that the winning applicant for the job of Washington State Hangman comes from the United States. This means that the hangman must either be a real old-timer, a novice, or an amateur who may have learned his craft by participating in extra-legal lynchings.

Charles Campbell's last sigh will certainly be one of relief, secure in the knowledge that the hand placing the noose around his neck is that of a civilized American and not a barbaric foreigner.

ALAN M. DERSHOWITZ

I wonder how an executioner feels after he has completed a job. In the case of Charles Rodman Campbell, it may be difficult to shed too many tears. He was convicted of murdering a woman who had testified against him after he assaulted her. If there are any appropriate candidates for capital punishment—and that question has divided civilized people for centuries—Campbell would seem to be one of them.

But what about Randall Adams, who was just minutes away from execution when the courts spared and eventually freed him, after another man confessed to the murder? Or W. Thomas Zeigler, who was the subject of a recent public television debate, after which nearly two-thirds of the viewers who called in believed he was not guilty? Or the dozens of other death-row inmates who may well be innocent?

The anonymous hangman hired by the state of Washington may be qualified to assure that Charles Rodman Campbell is efficiently hanged by the neck until he is dead. But what really qualifies a human being to take another human being's life?   March 1989

DEATH-ROW INMATES DESERVE A LAWYER'S AID

Chief Justice William Rehnquist's trigger finger is becoming itchy once again. Every few months he takes to the soapbox urging the legal system to speed up the process of executing people.

Citing the recent execution of serial murderer Ted Bundy, who was not killed until nine years after his death sentence was imposed, Rehnquist argues that the death penalty appellate process is often "chaotic and drawn out unnecessarily."

Rehnquist is correct in pointing to the "chaotic" nature of the process, but he fails to note that he himself is primary villain in this drama of death. In 1974, Rehnquist wrote an opinion declaring that a defendant, even on death row, has no right to an appointed lawyer after the first appeal.

Since a defendant is entitled to a federal review of constitutional claims—indeed, 40 percent of all death sentences are reversed by federal courts—the Rehnquist ruling means that many death-row inmates do not have a lawyer during the most critical phases of their case.

Even if the defendant seeks review by the U.S. Supreme Court, that court will not appoint a lawyer for him on his petition for review (called "certiorari").

I remember a particularly poignant example of this refusal in a case involving two young boys who were on Arizona's death row because they were held legally responsible for murders committed by their father after they helped him escape from prison.

They wrote a letter to the Supreme Court asking it to appoint an attorney for them "at this critical state in our appeals." The letter said "neither Ricky nor I finished high school and we do not have the education it would take to carry our appeals to this court, so we beg of you honors to please appoint a lawyer."

They did not understand "why anybody charged with a minor crime can have a lawyer appointed, but why we, who are facing execution for murders we had nothing to do with, cannot have a lawyer appointed."

The Supreme Court clerk's office responded, telling the boys that the Supreme Court does not appoint lawyers "to assist litigants in the preparation of petitions for writs of certiorari in any case." All defendants get lawyers appointed at trial and on the first appeal but not thereafter. The clerk suggested that the boys write to the National Association for the Advancement of Colored People or the American Civil Liberties Union.

Eventually I took their case to the Supreme Court and certiorari was granted. The case is still in litigation—more than ten years after the sentencing—not because of any delays on the part of the lawyers but because the issues are complex and the courts have had them under consideration for all of that time.

The major reasons for unnecessary delays do not result from the *presence* of lawyers but rather from the *absence* of lawyers in a good many death cases. As many as one-third of the approximately two thousand people currently on death row do not have lawyers actively litigating their cases. Lawyers begin to become active on the eve of execution. And then they often have to make up for years of inaction.

Lawyers help the court sort through the issues, separating the wheat from the chaff. Without the help of lawyers, the desperate death-row inmates simply throw darts in the dark, raising some issues that are worthless and failing to raise others that are meritorious. This complicates and delays the process unnecessarily.

The best way to avoid unnecessary delays in capital cases is to provide for competent counsel from the day of arrest to the day of execution. No death-row inmate should ever be without a lawyer. Death row is the emergency ward of our legal system, and it is a continuing scandal that there are not enough lawyers—in the most overlawyered society in the history of the world—to attend to those who most need legal help.

Chief Justice Rehnquist finally seems to be recognizing that lawyers may be a help rather than a hindrance to his game plan of speeding up executions. He is now proposing some broadening of the right to counsel for death-row inmates.

In the end, the reason why it takes so long to execute a condemned criminal is because of the awesome finality of execution. We must be certain that every doubt has been laid to rest along with the inmate's remains. There is no second chance to undo an injustice.

In assessing the time between conviction and execution, it must be recalled that the condemned person is not at liberty. He remains in prison—on death row. His punishment does not begin with the execution. It ends with it. Indeed, a sentence of death, by its very nature, is a sentence of lengthy imprisonment followed by execution.

Chief Justice Rehnquist should not be inciting courts into taking shortcuts to execution. His job is to defend the Constitution, not to lead the mob demanding quick death. February 1989

In 1992, the Tison brothers were finally spared the death penalty.

TECHNICALITY MAY MEAN DEATH FOR INMATE

Why should a guilty criminal go free just because "the constable blundered"? That is a question many decent Americans ask when an obviously guilty killer, rapist, or robber has their conviction reversed on the basis of a so-called legal technicality. Politicians love to score points by attacking the "exclusionary" rule—the court-created doctrine that keeps evidence out of court if it was obtained in violation of the Constitution. Former president Ronald Reagan used to regale his audiences with stories of mass murderers set free to kill again because the police officers who arrested them had accidentally checked the wrong box on the search warrants.

Of course, no such case has ever occurred, but it makes for crowd-pleasing rhetoric. It is true that occasionally, according to a recent government report, *very* occasionally, a guilty person is freed solely because the arresting officer obtained an invalid warrant. In one case, the police waited until after their search warrant had expired and conducted the search without asking the judge to renew it. There was an immediate outcry from politicians and law-enforcement officials, complaining that substantive rights should not turn on whether the police were a few days late.

Now the Supreme Court has agreed to review a case in which the shoe is on the other foot. In *Coleman* vs. *Smith*, it was the defense attorney who was late—one day late. Roger Keith Coleman is on Virginia's death row after having been convicted of killing his sister-in-law. He claims that he received an unfair trial and is not guilty of capital murder. But the federal courts have refused to consider his claims, valid though they be, because his lawyer filed an appeal thirty-one days after the lower court had rejected his petition. The rule required that the appeal be filed within thirty days. Coleman, who was locked up on death row when his lawyer bungled, was in no way responsible for his lawyer's tardiness. Yet Coleman may die because, unbeknownst to him, his lawyer messed up.

Whenever I hear about a defendant suffering because of his lawyer's mistake, I'm reminded of the story of the lawyer who just completed his argument to the Supreme Court. His client, who was out on bail, asked the lawyer: "If we lose, where do we go from here?" To which the lawyer replied: "What do you mean *we*? You go to jail, and I go back to my office."

It is impossible to know how many inmates are now in prison—or on death row—because of their lawyers' incompetence. Just as doctors bury their mistakes, lawyers' mistakes are often locked out of view behind the bars of our penitentiaries.

It would be a particular tragedy if Roger Keith Coleman were to be executed as a result of his lawyer's blunder, because Coleman has become more than just a model prisoner. While on death row, Coleman began a highly praised program directed at youngsters called "The Choice Is Yours." It involves letters, ideas, and meetings with students designed to persuade young people from high-crime areas to stay out of trouble. The Catholic Diocese of Richmond, Va., was so impressed with Coleman's efforts that it made a film about the program showing the consequences of making wrong choices through the eyes of a man on death row.

It will be interesting to see how the politicians and police officers, who complain so vociferously about cases turning on technicalities and blunders, react to the Coleman case. Somehow, I don't expect to hear many politicians making emotional speeches about how a death-row defendant's case should not turn on his lawyer's mistake in filing an appeal one day late.

Even more interesting to watch will be the reaction of the reactionary wing of the Supreme Court—the justices who claim to be searching for truths rather than technicalities. I predict that we will be treated to a considerable amount of selective amnesia by the Rehnquist crowd, some of whom will conveniently forget their prior opinions in which they inveighed against technical rules that punish citizens for the mistakes of the police. I doubt that those justices who argue that if the constable blunders, he and he alone should be punished, will take that argument to its rational conclusion and rule that when a lawyer, especially a state-appointed lawyer, blunders, that lawyer *and only that lawyer* should be punished.

The Coleman case is a testing ground for how much of the rhetoric surrounding "law and order" reflects a genuine interest in justice for all concerned, and how much of it is result-oriented hypocrisy calculated to assure that the cops always win.

Roger Keith Coleman should be given his day in federal court. If he was denied a fair trial, his conviction should be reversed. We cannot, as a civilized people, allow a man, who might otherwise be saved, to go to his death because his lawyer was one day late.   November 1990

On May 20, 1992 Roger Keith Coleman was executed. (See Demjanjuk and Coleman *on page 31).*

DON'T PULL PLUG ON
TELEVISED EXECUTIONS

So now they want to televise executions. "Snuff films"—movies of actual killings, long rumored to be part of the underground "pornography" industry—may soon become mainstream, as a California public television station demands that its cameras be allowed to transmit the proceeding from the gas chamber. Videotapes of executions, from lethal injections to electrocutions to firing squads to hangings, will become available for rental at the corner video shop. Certain favorites may become cult classics.

Already the political lines are being drawn. Some victims' rights advocates argue against televising executions on the grounds that it will engender sympathy for the condemned. Instead of televising the agony of the criminal, they insist, the agony of the victim should be shown in living color—the wounds, the suffering, the humiliation.

Some defendants' rights advocates would be willing to permit televised executions, but only if the condemned person consented—as some have already done—to their last moments being telecast to millions of viewers. Opponents of the death penalty are split, depending on whether they believe that televised execution will be so traumatic as to generate revulsion, or so crowd-pleasing as to create new fans for a lethal public spectacle. If the long history of public executions is any guide to present attitudes, opponents of the death penalty should not be encouraged to believe that the public will be repelled by the spectacle of a condemned man being shown suffocating to death during a televised execution.

First Amendment activists, many of whom are opposed to the death penalty, are also torn, especially those who believe that public executions will increase the demand for more extensive use of the death penalty. First Amendment opponents of televised executions point out that, under our First Amendment, there is a difference between the government denying the media *access* to an event—such as an execution, a cabinet meeting, or a military encounter—and directly *prohibiting* the media from publishing material they have obtained on their own. (The Pentagon Papers case is a useful example of that distinction: The press had no right to secure copies of those classified documents, but once the *New York Times* obtained copies on its own, the government could not prevent its publication.)

But an execution is a quintessential public event in the sense that it involves the controversial use of ultimate governmental force to achieve a deterrent goal. Moreover, the media is generally allowed to cover and report on executions, subject, of course, to security considerations. Although the California legal authorities have raised the claim that television cameras may compromise security, that is obviously a make weight, since it would be a simple matter to arrange a secure way for a single pool camera to transmit the execution.

Nor is there any real concern that the information itself would pose security problems, as would the precise location of a military battle. Thus, the argument that justifies controlling the access of the media to military encounters, cabinet meetings, or classified information doesn't really work when it comes to televising executions. First Amendment supporters, regardless of their beliefs on capital punishment and the likely impact of televised executions or the future of the death penalty, should favor the right of the media to televise executions and the right of adult citizens to view these spectacles if they choose to. Obviously, discretion would dictate that the telecast be at night when children are unlikely to be watching, and that advanced warnings be provided so that only willing adult viewers are exposed.

No First Amendment advocate should be influenced by what he or she believes will be the *effect* of televising executions on the controversial policy and constitutional debates over the death penalty. It is the essence of the First Amendment that decisions about freedom of speech must be content-neutral and must not depend on whether the likely impact of the speech on the open marketplace of ideas is favorable or unfavorable to one's politics. Thus, although I personally suspect that televising executions may well generate a demand for more executions and although I oppose the death penalty, I favor the right of the California public television station to televise executions.

If executions are televised, I, for one, will exercise my First Amendment right to turn the channel and watch something else. I might also try to persuade the television station not to exercise its right to televise executions, once that right was recognized by the state. But I would not stand between willing telecasters and willing viewers, even if I disapproved of the reason why the viewers were tuning in, or were afraid of the likely impact of their viewing on the debate over capital punishment.

That is what freedom of speech is all about: the right of those with whom you disagree to mount the most effective argument—rational, symbolic, or visual—against your position. My fellow opponents of the death penalty are just going to have to come up with more powerful arguments, if we are to prevail in the highly competitive marketplace of ideas and images.

May 1991

IS THE DEATH PENALTY RIGGED BY RACISM?

Two recent executions—one in Georgia, the other in South Carolina—reveal a terrible truth about how capital punishment really works in our nation. On September 25, 1991, Warren McCleskey was executed for killing a policeman during the course of a robbery. McCleskey was black, and the policeman was white. Had McCleskey been white and the policeman black, there is virtually no chance that he would have received the ultimate penalty. The U.S. Supreme Court heard evidence that in Georgia it is ten times more likely that a black man who kills a white will be sentenced to death than it is for a white man who kills a black.

Indeed, between 1944 and September 6, 1991—a period of forty-seven years—no white person had been executed in the entire United States for killing a black person. During that same period, more than a thousand people have been executed, including hundreds of blacks who had been convicted of killing whites. In fact, a recent study of the nearly sixteen thousand executions recorded in this country since colonial times found that only thirty whites were executed for murdering blacks, and this includes the killing of slaves, which was regarded as an economic crime against their white masters. The study also showed that in those few cases where a white was executed for killing a black, the killer invariably had a long record, often including the prior killing of whites.

This brings us to the other recent execution, this one in South Carolina on September 6, 1991. In that case, Donald (Pee Wee) Gaskins, a white man, was put to death for the contract killing of a black fellow inmate. He was the first white man in nearly half a century to die for killing a black. But Gaskins was no ordinary killer. He has previously been convicted—and this may sound hard to believe—of nine earlier murders! All of his prior victims were white. In one sense, therefore, it may not be fair to categorize Gaskin's execution as one resulting from the murder of a black; he was sentenced to death, at least in part, for his prior record of killing whites. But even if Gaskins's execution is categorized as resulting from the killing of a black, the rarity—indeed, the singularity—of such an execution during the past forty-six years underlines the racism inherent in the process by which our legal system determines who shall live and who shall die.

The late Justice Potter Stewart, an Eisenhower appointee and certainly no liberal, once described the death penalty process as analogous to "being struck by lightning." But being hit by lightning is truly random: A bolt of lightning does not pick its victims by race. The death penalty "lottery," on the other hand, is rigged. It decides matters of life and death by the race of the defendant, the race of the victim, and other invidious factors such as wealth, physical appearance, and the quality of counsel.

Nor can the vast disparity between the number and percentage of executions based on the race of the defendant and victim be explained by the fact that more blacks kill whites than whites kill blacks or that black killers have longer records than white killers. Even taking these and other possible legitimate variables into consideration does not account for the historical or current disparity. The only explanation for the phenomenal disparity is simply that the American legal system and its participants—prosecutors, judges, jurors, pardon boards—place a greater value on white life than on black life. A process must be judged by its results. Our process obviously regards the killing of a white victim as a more serious crime, deserving of a more serious punishment, than the killing of a black victim. It also regards white killers as more deserving of sympathy than black killers.

This disparity is unacceptable in a society premised on the equality of all citizens. I challenge any criminologist, lawyer, or statistician to offer a nonracist explanation for the kind of disparity shown by the execution figures quoted above. These figures shift the burden of persuasion to thos who would argue that our death penalty process is fair. It is a burden that cannot be met.

The crowning injustice of Warren McCleskey's execution is that Georgia may well have executed the wrong person. McCleskey has admitted participating, with three others, in the robbery, but he has always denied being the one who shot the police officer. The other robbers were not sentenced to death. McCleskey was convicted of the shooting on the basis of the uncorroborated testimony of a cellmate who swore that McCleskey had confessed to him. But unbeknownst to the jury, this cellmate had a strong motive to lie; he had been promised a reduction in his own sentence if he produced incriminating evidence against McCleskey. Two of the jurors who voted to convict McCleskey said they would have voted differently if they had known of the promise. September 1991

COURT DISTORTS JUSTICE IN DEATH-ROW CASE

In a recent case, the U.S. Supreme Court, unlike the wise King Solomon, decided that they should cut the human body in half. The justices ruled that Leonel Herrera's claim that he was innocent of the murder for which he was sentenced to death, was sufficiently compelling that review by the entire Supreme Court was warranted. But they also ruled that Herrera should be executed *before* the Supreme Court decided his case. Talk about a split decision!

I can imagine Herrera's lawyer delivering the message: "The good news is that the Supreme Court is going to hear your case and might declare you innocent. The bad news is that you won't be around to learn their decision."

How did this perversion of Solomonic justice come about? It came about as a result of the Supreme Court's unusual rules for how many votes are required to decide certain procedural issues.

In order to decide that a case is important enough to hear, only four justices need vote to grant the writ of certiorari. This rule, known as "the rule of four," makes good sense, since if any significant number of justices want to hear a case, that should be enough to place it on the Court's docket. In the Herrera case, four justices voted to hear the argument.

But in order to grant a stay of execution, it takes five votes. The same four justices who voted to hear the case also voted to stay the execution. But the five justices who did not want to hear the case also voted to put Herrera to death immediately. Talk about sore losers and gamesmanship! Not a single one of the justices who voted against hearing the case was willing to defer to his brethren and sister (Justice O'Connor was among those who wanted to hear the case), even on the issue of granting a temporary stay of execution.

Consider what this says about the open-mindedness of the five justices. They are plainly announcing that no argument, by their fellow justices or by the lawyers, could possibly persuade even one of them to change his vote. Their collective minds are firmly made up even before the case has been briefed and argued. So much for the Supreme Court as a deliberative body! This action demonstrates that the current majority of the high court—Justices Rehnquist, Scalia, White, Kennedy, and Thomas—are rigid, dogmatic ideologues, uninterested in legal arguments or evidence, even when it comes to matters of life and death. They have the votes and the minority be damned—and ignored.

Obviously the "rule of four" contemplates that if a death penalty case is going to be heard by the Supreme Court, then the defendant will be kept alive pending the decision. Indeed, the high court has another rule that if a death-row inmate dies—even of natural causes—before his appeal is decided, the case will be dismissed as moot and not decided at all. There are no posthumous victories in the Supreme Court. Thus, the decision of the five to let Herrera be executed was a transparent attempt to circumvent the rule of four. It is precisely the kind of gamesmanship about which these same justices complain when lawyers engage in it.

And it came perilously close to working. Leonel Herrera was minutes away from execution when two Texas state court justices granted a last-minute stay. Had it been up to the Supreme Court alone, Herrera would now be dead, despite its decision to hear his case.

This is simply intolerable behavior by five justices who are sworn to uphold the rule of law. It makes a travesty of the Supreme Court. If asked to defend their outrageous conduct—and being a justice means that you never have to defend your conduct, no matter how questionable—the five justices would argue that since a majority voted against the stay, it is inevitable that Herrera will eventually lose his case by a 5–4 vote. "Might as well kill him now rather than later," they would argue. And they are probably right, because the five seem totally close-minded when it comes to capital punishment. When the Herrera case is argued before them, they will sit on the bench a bit like the three monkeys, with hands over their eyes and ears, but not their mouths—they will talk plenty during the argument, but they will not be listening.

The most shocking aspect of this case is that Leonel Herrera may well be innocent and another man may be guilty. There is compelling new evidence that his brother Raul committed the murder. But unless Leonel Herrera is kept alive while the high court considers this new evidence, we will never know whether another innocent man has been executed. A majority of the Supreme Court now seems to regard capital crimes as so heinous that even innocence should not be a defense!   February 1992

10 // *The Right to Die*

TRAGIC MERCY KILLING CASE DIDN'T BELONG IN COURT

The dean of the law school I attended teaches a course aptly entitled "Tragic Choices." It presents the young law students with moral dilemmas that have no "good" outcomes. The choices tend to be among "worse," "worser," and "worsest." For example, how should the law decide who, among several medically eligible potential organ recipients, will receive—or be deprived of—a scarce liver or heart? Or, if only one Siamese twin can be saved by surgery, which one shall it be?

Several months ago, I received a call from a doctor who had faced a tragic choice in his personal life. His wife was dying of a fast-spreading form of cancer. She was in excruciating pain and her doctors told her it would just get worse. Death was inevitable—within days or weeks.

The woman, who had two teenage children, decided that she did not want to die alone, suddenly and in pain. She determined to die with dignity, surrounded by her loving family. After preparing for the end, she selected the time and the means of her death. She even appeared on television and discussed her situation, hoping to provide solace and courage to others faced with similar tragedies. She wrote letters and gave small gifts to her friends.

On the day of her scheduled death, her stepfather and half-brothers were summoned from out of town. Her family sat down to a farewell dinner. She then went to the bedroom with her husband. They drank a glass of wine, kissed, and embraced. She then asked her husband to give her pills that she had selected for a painless death. The children were given mild sedatives and put to bed, expecting to awaken only after it was all over. She swallowed the pills and drifted off, expecting to die in her sleep.

But something went wrong. She did not die immediately. In fact, her coma began to lighten, and her husband could see she was in pain. He said that he then administered some painkiller to her, but still she did not die. Finally, the terminally ill woman's stepfather placed his fingers over her nose and mouth, thus cutting off her breathing. She died within minutes.

The call I received from the dead woman's husband came from jail. He was asking me to help him save his life. Nearly a year after he made his tragic choice, he went on television to explain and justify it. Shortly thereafter he was arrested and charged with murder, a crime carrying the death penalty. (The woman's stepfather was given immunity, before he told the prosecutors that it was he who administered the coup de grace, in exchange for testifying against his son-in-law.)

Although the state of Florida, where this took place, has a statute punishing anyone who assists another in committing suicide, the local authorities decided to treat the husband as if he were an organized-crime hit man.

The authorities were not alone in considering his act of love to be the equivalent of the worst forms of sadistic murder. On a nationally televised talk show, the director of the International Antieuthanasia Task Force characterized this act of family devotion as akin to a "serialized gang murder."

What happened during that tragic night in Florida was neither murder nor euthanasia. It was dignified suicide. The woman died as a result of cancer. Were it not for that ravaging disease, she would be alive today. She did not choose *to die*. The cancer made that decision for her. What *she* chose was the timing and circumstances of her death. Euthanasia—mercy killing—occurs when *another* person makes the decision to take a life for humane purposes. Here, the decision was made rationally by the woman herself. It was a mercy suicide, which is no longer considered a crime in any civilized nation.

Should this terminally ill and suffering woman not have had the right to avoid a few more days of painful—and, in her view, undignified—life? Could a devoted husband reject her last wish—to die in his loving arms, surrounded by family to whom she had said her farewells?

Individuals have very different views on these tragic choices. Religions provide different answers to these unanswerable questions. There is no absolute right or wrong when it comes to coping with the final days of a grievously suffering loved one's life.

But generally the government should stay far away from the deathbed of a grieving family. This prosecution, and the attitudes of some of those who were pushing it, are the best proof of the inability of most prosecutors to deal sensitively with personal tragedies of the kind experienced by this family.

Anyone who does not understand the difference between a "serialized gang murder"—indeed, any murder—and the tragic choice confronting that aggrieved family in Florida should not be in the business of telling others how to live—and how to die.

The jury in this case acquitted the doctor, but he never should have been put on trial in the first place. He did the right thing in helping his wife. The prosecutors are the guilty parties—guilty of politicizing a personal tragedy.   December 1988

HIGH COURT NOW ASKS: WHEN DOES LIFE END?

The U.S. Supreme Court is once again entering the right-to-life controversy, but this time the question is not when life begins but rather when it ends.

On the same day that the high court upheld most of the contested provisions in the Missouri antiabortion statute, it also agreed to hear another Missouri case in which that state's highest court had refused to allow a thirty-one-year-old woman who was in a persistent vegetative state to have her feeding tube removed at her parents' request.

The woman, Nancy Beth Cruzan, had suffered devastating brain damage six years earlier in an automobile accident. According to her doctors, she had no cognitive function, no awareness of her surroundings, and no chance of recovering. However, her breathing was normal and so, with the aid of a feeding tube, she could be kept "alive" indefinitely.

Her parents had petitioned the courts to allow the feeding tube to be removed so that their daughter could die. Although Nancy Beth had not left a "living will"—a formal document authorized in many states, including Missouri—she had apparently told friends, before her accident, that she would not want to be kept alive with serious injuries unless she could live "halfway normally."

A Missouri probate judge had granted the petition brought by Nancy Beth's parents and had ruled that under the tragic circumstances Nancy Beth had a constitutional right to die. The Missouri Supreme Court overruled the probate judge, holding that Missouri had an "unqualified interest in life" and a legislative policy "strongly favoring life."

Under that policy, Nancy Beth would not be permitted to die, because the medical treatment she was receiving to keep her alive was not "oppressively burdensome," and there was no clear evidence that she wished to end her life.

Interestingly, the Missouri legislature had not specifically enacted legislation expressing any policy in favor of keeping vegetative patients alive over their parents' well-grounded objections. The court derived the state policy on which it relied from the Missouri antiabortion statute, which declares that life begins at conception.

It ruled that "at the beginning of life, Missouri adopts a strong predisposition in favor of preserving life . . . at the end of life, this state maintains its policy strongly favoring life."

Thus, the Missouri Supreme Court has expressly relied on an analogy between "life" in the womb and "life" in a persistently vegetative state. As the former president of the Missouri Citizens for Life, an antiabortion group active in opposing "right-to-die" petitions, put it: "Our view is that the state must protect human beings from conception until natural death."

Ironically, Missouri, like other right-to-life states, does have the death penalty. And it also has one of the highest death-row inmate populations (seventy-three people as of July 1) in the country.

There are some superficial analogies between "life" in the womb and "life" in a persistently vegetative state. In both situations, outside assistance is required to maintain the nutriments of life. In both situations, there are important signs of life, such as cardiac and neurological activity. In both situations, medical technology has a major but not always decisive influence on policy decisions. In both situations, according to some religious beliefs, there is a soul. And in both situations, there are claims of privacy and autonomy that conflict with the state's interest in preserving life.

But there are many differences as well. The fetus has a potential for living a full life after birth, whereas the persistently vegetative patient has no such potential. The fetus has had no opportunity to express a preference for life or death, whereas many vegetative patients have, in fact, expressed preferences prior to entering into their terminal situation. In order for the fetus to be kept alive, at least during the first and second trimester, it must remain in the mother's womb, whereas the vegetative patient can be maintained in a hospital, without parental involvement.

The important point is that despite some superficial analogies between "right-to-life" and "right-to-die" issues, they are, in fact, very different. The Supreme Court, in considering the Missouri "right-to-die" case next term, would be wise to write on a clean slate. It would be a serious mistake to try to build a "right-to-die" doctrine on the crumbling foundations of the abortion decisions.

The medical profession is crying out for guidance as to when it is lawful to withhold treatment from terminal patients. Many doctors today make their own decisions, sometimes after consulting family members, sometimes without the benefit of much consultation. The American Medical Association has adopted guidelines that would permit removal of the feeding tube in a situation like the Cruzan family's, but their guidelines are not binding on the courts and do not provide protection for doctors who act on them.

Numerous groups, ranging from medical associations, to right-to-die organizations, to antiabortion lobbies, to organized religions, will be inundating the Supreme Court with "friend-of-the-court" briefs in an effort to influence its decision. The high court's first decision in this controversial and highly emotional case is likely to be narrow. But it will portend the direction in which the courts will be moving over the coming decades.

Just as all eyes were on the court last term for its decision on the "right to life," all eyes will be focused next term on the "right to die."

July 1989

On June 25, 1990 the Supreme Court ruled that Nancy Cruzan's parents had not shown "by clear and convincing evidence" that she would have wanted her life sustaining treatment stopped. Therefore the court ruled that the state of Missouri could continue to sustain Nancy Cruzan's life against the objection of her family. The court did however find that a person, who has made his or her wishes clear, has a right to the discontinuance of life sustaining treatment. On December 14, 1990 A Missouri judge allowed the Cruzan family to remove the feeding tube from Nancy Beth. On December 26, 1990 Nancy Cruzan died.

DR. KEVORKIAN AND HIS SUICIDE MACHINE

Most doctors spend their days trying to save lives. But Dr. Jack Kevorkian seems determined to achieve his fifteen minutes of fame by helping "terminal" patients take their own lives.

Kevorkian admitted that on June 4 he connected fifty-four-year-old

\\ 265

Janet Adkins, who was suffering from Alzheimer's disease, to a suicide machine he had devised, and told her how to press the button that would bring her death.

His active role in the suicide raises profound legal and ethical issues. The U.S. Supreme Court, which has the right-to-die case of Nancy Cruzan before it this term, will undoubtedly be addressing some of these concerns.

The Kevorkian-Adkins case is an extreme one for several reasons. First, there is some question as to the meaning of "terminal" in the context of a fifty-four-year-old, otherwise healthy woman who apparently had early symptoms of Alzheimer's disease.

Alzheimer's is a difficult disease to diagnose. An article in the *Journal of the American Medical Association* reports that between 20 and 30 percent of diagnoses are mistaken. As one leading researcher recently put it, "These people have other kinds of dementia that often are treatable." Even when it's diagnosed correctly, its prognosis is not always identical in degree and time frame. In some instances, it takes several years for the symptoms to become debilitating.

Moreover, Alzheimer's is a disease that, even in its earliest manifestations, may impair certain cognitive capacities. This, too, is a matter of degree. But absent a full mental status examination, doubts remain as to whether Janet Adkins was fully competent to make the irreversible decision she made when she pressed the button of death.

This is a particularly troubling issue when the doctor is the only witness to the suicide. It becomes even more troubling when the doctor is as much of an advocate as Kevorkian obviously is. He is a zealot on the issue of assisted suicide. This is what Kevorkian said after Adkins's death: "My ultimate aim is to make euthanasia a positive experience. I'm trying to knock the medical profession into accepting its responsibilities, and those responsibilities include assisting their patients with death."

A doctor who has "ultimate aim(s)" beyond those of doing what's best for a particular patient should not be the one advising that patient whether to terminate her life, and deciding whether her decision is competent and unequivocal. As one medical ethicist said, "I would like to have had a videotape of all the conversations he had with her and her family. I would want evidence."

In this case, Kevorkian not only had an "ultimate aim" beyond the welfare of a particular patient, but it was his death machine that was being tested. Moreover, he had tried to advertise his machine in a medical journal last year, but he was turned down by the medical society. Janet Adkins's death became his front-page advertisement around the world.

This is not to suggest that Kevorkian has any financial or other crass motivations for his actions. But he is not an unbiased, neutral healer seeking only to help a patient. He had a stake in Adkins's decision to commit suicide. He provided the machine, the transportation, and the location.

I think it's fair to suggest that he would have been disappointed after all that planning, investment, and hard work, if Adkins had shown some hesitancy in going through with the grand plan. On an even more subtle level, Kevorkian might not have picked up on signs of ambivalence that a more objective witness would have noticed.

Despite all these problems, it doesn't necessarily follow that the doctor should be criminally prosecuted for assisting suicide, or for other crimes growing out of his actions. He carefully selected Michigan as the state in which to conduct his medical-moral-legal experiment. Unlike most other states, Michigan law is unclear on whether someone who assists another in committing suicide is guilty of criminal conduct.

Before anyone is criminally prosecuted, the law must be crystal clear that his actions constitute a crime. If Michigan now wants to clarify its law, it must do so prospectively and not by applying ambiguous language and precedents to past conduct.

But regardless of whether or not the Michigan prosecutors decide to invoke criminal law, Kevorkian's actions demonstrate the need for careful, balanced Supreme Court consideration of the complex issues surrounding the debate over whether there is a "right to die."

If there is such a right, it must be circumscribed with procedures adequate to assure that the decision to end life is being made by competent and fully informed persons whose only interest is the welfare of the patient.

June 1990

IS ASSISTED SUICIDE FIRST-DEGREE MURDER?

The first-degree murder charge leveled against Dr. Jack Kevorkian has rekindled the debate over whether doctors should be legally free to assist terminally ill patients in ending their lives. But regardless of how that broad issue is ultimately resolved, it is absolutely clear that Kevorkian should not be convicted of the highest level of murder—a crime that carries a mandatory term of life imprisonment with no possibility of parole.

When we think of first-degree murder, we imagine a gangland execution, a terrorist assassination, or a deliberate killing to collect insurance. In each of those cases, the victim did not want to die. An innocent life was taken against the unambiguous will of the victim. Kevorkian's "victims," on the other hand, actively sought out his assistance. They wanted him to help them die. Surely, there is a world of difference between these "crimes."

I am not a supporter of Kevorkian or his death machine. Kevorkian is a zealot, an advocate of an extreme view of the role of doctor as a facilitator of dignified and painless death. Zealous advocates make poor judges, especially when they purport to sit in judgment over decisions in which they have a stake. Moreover, the woman whom Kevorkian helped to die was not a typical "terminal" case.

She was apparently suffering from the very beginning stage of Alzheimer's disease, a relatively slow and physically painless illness that is difficult to diagnose at its inception. According to her own doctor: "Mrs. Adkins could expect several more years during which she would be able to maintain self-care and enjoy the types of experiences (spending time with her grandchildren, outdoor activities, etc.) she was currently enjoying. Mrs. Adkins was in good spirits and did not appear to be suffering." Her doctor "strongly urged" Kevorkian "not to perform this procedure."

I share the concerns of those medical ethicists who worry whether Kevorkian was "in any position to judge her competency" on the basis of a relatively hasty examination. And I join those who argue that "a person who promotes euthanasia and the right to die is not someone you want advising people on whether they should take their life."

But I cannot "applaud," as some medical ethicists have, the murder charges against Kevorkian. If the state of Michigan, or any other state, wants to ban what Kevorkian did, let the legislators debate this issue of medically assisted suicide and then enact a new statute specifically directed at the problem. The first-degree murder statute is far too general to do the job. The murder statute does not, for example, distinguish between what Kevorkian did in the Adkins case and what a family doctor might do in a case involving a patient with an extremely advanced and extremely painful cancer. It does not distinguish between cases based on the degree of competency or consent of the patient. And it does not differentiate between the active and passive involvement of the doctor. It leaves everything up to the discretion of the prosecutors. And the attitude of the Kevorkian prosecutor in this case leaves much to be desired. His goal, like Kevorkian's, is to "send a clear message." The prosecutor's message is designed to avoid Michigan becoming "a magnet for this kind of murder."

It is in the nature of criminal law that it must always play "catch up." It can almost never anticipate new problems, such as the one posed by Kevorkian's death machine, which allows the patient to trigger her own death by pressing the lethal button on the device. Since the criminal law must always punish *prospectively*—that is, it must first define the crime with specificity and only then punish *future* violators of the law—there will always be some who "get away" with "crime" in the beginning. The conduct of the first "credit-card criminals" and the first "computer thieves" was not covered by existing statutes. The laws were quickly changed to encompass these new crimes and subsequent criminals were punished under the new laws.

That is what should be done with assisted suicide. Kevorkian's questionable actions should be used as a stimulus to changing the law. New statutes, with appropriate exception, procedures, and punishments, should be considered by legislators around the country. These new laws should not, in my view, give individual doctors carte blanche to decide whether a patient has really thought through the life-and-death decision. But nor should prosecutors be permitted to roam at large through the thick volumes of existing crimes looking for the closest analogy. That is especially so where the prosecutor selects a crime punishable by life imprisonment with no possibility of parole. Whatever else he may be, Kevorkian is not a first-degree murderer, and he should not be treated like a gangland hit man.

December 1990

In July, 1992 murder charges against Kevorkian were dismissed.

IS IT MURDER IF LIFE SUPPORT EXTENDS LIFE?

As Nancy Cruzan drifted toward death, her precedent-setting case on the right to die suggests yet another legal issue that is currently being litigated. That issue is whether a person whose criminal actions cause a victim to become vegetatively comatose can be charged with murder when the victim finally dies years later.

ALAN M. DERSHOWITZ

The Cruzan case graphically illustrates how long a "brain dead" person can be kept alive. In her case, she has been in a coma for seven years. Sunny von Bülow, whose husband Claus was first convicted and then acquitted of attempting to murder her, remains in a vegetative coma ten years after she was hospitalized. It is now possible to keep a body functioning for decades though the brain is barely working.

Traditionally, the law permitted a murder prosecution only if the victim died within a year and a day of the criminal act. This so-called year-and-a-day rule originated more than eight centuries ago as part of the English common law. It reflected an age when medical science could not easily trace a distant death to an earlier blow, when victims died quickly of relatively minor wounds, and when artificial means to extend life were unknown. The year-and-a-day rule set an arbitrary cutoff period beyond which a murder prosecution could not lie. The opposite side of this defendant-protecting rule was that any criminal injury that contributed to death within that period could be punished as murder even if the blow was "not in itself so mortal" and even if it could have been cured "with good care."

The American states originally adopted this rule as part of the common law, but many have not abandoned it as medical science has made it easier both to keep wounded victims "alive" for protracted periods of time and to determine the causal link between the criminal act and the eventual death.

The real question is not *whether* the year-and-a-day rule should be abolished, but *how* this inevitable change should be brought about. There are three possibilities.

The most obvious is for the state legislature to enact a new murder statute that permits prosecution for deaths caused by criminal conduct that occurs at any time or during an enlarged period of time. California, for example, has legislatively extended the year-and-a-day rule to three years and a day. Other state legislatures have eliminated all such barriers, so long as direct causation can be shown.

In some states, where the legislatures have failed to act, the courts have changed the rule. But some judges have ruled that courts are empowered to make the change only prospectively—that is, for *future* cases. The ex post facto clause of the U.S. Constitution has been interpreted to deny courts the power to expand the scope of the criminal law and apply the newly expanded law to an incident that has already occurred. Generally, this salutary rule has forbidden courts to make criminal what was not criminal at the time it was done. In the case of the year-and-a-day rule, the original act was already criminal when it was done, but it was not *murder* unless the person died within the specified period.

There is now a case pending in Georgia in which the prosecution is asking the courts to abolish the year-and-a-day rule *and* to apply its change to the past conduct of the defendant. The case involves a man named David Cross, who stands accused of shaking his three-month-old daughter so hard that she suffered fatal injuries from which she died a year and a half later. The defendant denied that he intended to injure the child, claiming that he was trying to dislodge a blockage in her throat.

The Cross case is complicated by the fact that the baby was kept alive by a respirator for more than a year, and the prosecutors have argued that the defendant may have participated in the decision to use "artificial life-maintaining apparatus" for the specific reason of delaying her death beyond the year-and-a-day period. As the prosecution put it, "appreciating his unique position as a father as well as a slayer, the defendant was able to avoid the pronouncement of his victim's death for more than one year and a day."

Even if this were true—and the defendant denies it—that is not a sufficient reason for applying a change in the law retroactively. It is a good reason for changing the law in all future cases. There is no longer any good reason for preserving an ancient rule that has lost its scientific underpinnings. Now that medicine can maintain some semblance of life in a vegetative victim for indeterminate periods of time, the law must adapt to this new reality. As Oliver Wendell Holmes once put it: "It is revolting to have no better reason for a rule of law than that it was laid down in the time of Henry IV."   December 1990

WHO REALLY KILLED THIS STABBING VICTIM?

A tragic right-to-die case in Maine is raising perplexing questions about the law of homicide. Several years ago, a man named Noel Pagan stabbed a man named Mark Weaver following a chance encounter and an exchange of words. The victim was hospitalized in a coma and the assailant was charged with attempted murder. Eventually, lawyers reached a plea bargain under which the attempted murder charge was dropped and the defendant, who claims he acted in self-defense, pleaded no contest to assault charges. The defendant served his three-year sentence and went back home to Massachusetts, believing the entire matter was behind him.

Then he received a phone call informing him that the victim's mother was seeking to terminate the life support systems that were keeping Mark Weaver alive. If Weaver dies, Pagan was warned, he could face murder charges for killing him.

Pagan was understandably confused and frightened. I'm not the one who's going to be killing him, he must have thought; Weaver's own mother, assisted by the court, is "pulling the plug." Pagan certainly did not want Weaver to die. But what right did he have to interfere with the decision of Weaver's mother?

The assailant's court-appointed lawyer called the state attorney general and asked him for an assurance that if Weaver were permitted to die, Pagan would not be charged with murder or manslaughter. The attorney general refused to give any such assurance, even though Weaver's mother reportedly prefers that there be no further prosecution of Pagan.

As a result of the attorney general's refusal to preclude homicide charges, Pagan's lawyer has been placed in the uncomfortable position of having to oppose the termination of life support for Weaver. So long as Weaver remains alive, Pagan cannot be charged with murder or manslaughter, since an element of these crimes is that the victim must be dead. As soon as the victim dies, that element will have been satisfied, and the attorney general might well commence a homicide prosecution.

To reduce the legal risks to his client, Pagan's lawyer thus reluctantly intervened in the right-to-die case. He sought to prevent the removal of the life support systems. The courts have rejected his attempt to intervene, and it now appears that Weaver will be allowed to die. But Pagan's lawyer has made his point and preserved his legal argument.

If Pagan is eventually prosecuted for homicide, he will have an intriguing defense available to him. Technically that defense is called "intervening cause," which simply means that the actions of someone else actually caused the death. In this case, it would be the actions of the mother, authorized by the courts, to remove Weaver's feeding tube. The medical cause of death will be dehydration and starvation.

The prosecution will argue that the legal and moral cause of death was the stabbing. But for the stabbing nearly four years earlier, Weaver would not have been in a coma and his mother would not have been faced with so tragic a choice.

Both sides will be right. If not for the stabbing, Weaver would have remained alive. But if not for the removal of the feeding tube, Weaver would also have remained alive, at least in the legal sense of that word if not in any other meaningful sense. It will be up to the courts to decide whether the state may prosecute someone for a death that it helped, through its courts, to bring about.

This is not the first case raising questions of this kind. Several years ago, a shooting victim who was brain dead had organs removed for transplantation to another person. The defendant claimed that the immediate cause of death was the removal of the organs, not the bullet wounds. In another case, an assault victim was being driven to the hospital in an ambulance that crashed and killed him. The variations are endless, and the outcomes of these cases are as varied as the facts.

Until recently, nearly every state had a year-and-a-day rule under which the victim had to die within that time frame for the assailant to be charged with murder. If the victim died after this period, even if the death was directly attributable to the assault and there were no intervening acts by others, there could be no murder charge.

In states that still have such a rule, and some do, a decision to terminate life support within a year of the assault could make an enormous difference in the outcome of a case, especially if the victim would have survived for more than a year on life support. It could literally mean the difference between life and death not only for the victim but also for the assailant.

It is not clear whether Maine retains its old year-and-a-day rule. If it does, then Pagan cannot possibly be convicted of murder, since the assault occurred nearly four years ago. If Maine no longer has the rule and if the prosecutors decide to charge Pagan with homicide, this case may become one of the most perplexing prosecutions in modern history.   April 1989

On April 7, 1989 Mark Weaver died after his mother won the right to terminate life support. On January 25, 1990 the Maine Attorney General's office announced that they would not charge Noel Pagan with murdering Mark Weaver.

11 // Sex Crimes, Child Abuse and the Rights of the Accused

THE TYSON CASE: PRACTICING LAW IN AN EMOTIONAL MAELSTROM

There is a wonderful story in the Talmud that reminds me of my years at the Yeshiva—the Jewish parochial school I attended through the twelfth grade:

> If a fledgling bird is found within fifty cubits [about seventy-five feet] . . . [of a man's property], it belongs to the owner of the property. If it is found outside the limits of fifty cubits, it belongs to the person who finds it.
>
> Rabbi Jeremiah asked the question: "If one foot of the fledgling bird is within the limit of fifty cubits, and one foot is outside it, what is the law?"
>
> It was for this question that Rabbi Jeremiah was thrown out of the house of study.

I, too, used to get thrown out of my Yeshiva class for asking questions like that.

But hair-splitting questions about line drawing lie at the heart of every legal system. And virtually every line drawn by the law is arbitrary, whether the lines are based on age (for voting, emancipation, consent to sex, drinking, driving, etc.), quantity (drugs, money, participation in a conspiracy or a mob, number of prior offenses, etc.), or less objective factors such as sanity, consent, or knowledge.

It used to be thought that there were some lines that were crystal clear. Remember the old quip about not being a "little bit pregnant" or a "little bit dead"? But today it may matter greatly whether a woman is a little bit pregnant or a lot pregnant. The right to have an abortion may turn on the trimester of the pregnancy. Even the issue of what constitutes "death," that absolute of absolutes, may now be hotly disputed in close cases.

Polemicists and absolutists on all sides of these and other gray-area issues refuse to recognize matters of degree. To an absolute right-to-lifer, life begins at the moment of conception and is as sacred then as it is at the moment before birth. To an absolute pro-choicer, a woman's right to terminate pregnancy is as compelling in the last trimester as in the first. Some radical feminists regard acquaintance rape in which the man honestly but mistakenly believes his friend has consented as indistinguishable from a stranger rape at knife point. A recent letter to the editor critical of one of my columns on date rape made the point as follows:

> Dershowitz further endears himself by explaining that date rape and acquaintance rape is an area in which differing perceptions may produce inadvertently false testimony about actions that fall into a gray area. Let me explain something: No means no. There is no gray area.

Nor is there a paucity of hypocrisy on both of these issues. Religious zealots who believe that all life is sacred are more apt to be seen trying to block an abortion clinic than an execution. Although the Catholic church is adamantly opposed—at least in theory—to the death penalty, its opposition is generally more polite and less confrontational when it comes to executions, even of possibly innocent defendants, than when it comes to abortions. Many radical feminists who claim to believe in "the right to choose" would limit that right to women facing the choice between abortion or birth. They would deny a man the right to choose to gratify himself sexually by the use of pornography and would deny women the right to choose a career in sexually explicit films or photography.

It should not be surprising that consistency is often absent when it comes to such emotionally charged issues as life, death, and sex. Of all the controversial defendants I have represented, none has caused more raised eyebrows and clenched fists among my friends and family as Mike Tyson. I have received countless letters, phone calls, and personal arguments denouncing me for agreeing to represent Tyson on his appeal for the rape conviction growing out of his late-night date with Desiree Washington. Here are some excerpts from the letters:

> It's too bad that a punk like Tyson can afford to pay for the top legal representation . . . but since you had the right to refuse to represent him, I fault you!

It saddens me that you yourself continue to worship at the altar of the great god of violence and fear of women.

I don't care what the law says, you did not have to take the case. He [Mike Tyson] is an animal and you know it. . . . You are tarnished, baby, you are tarnished.

Mr. Tyson is a convicted rapist with obvious psychological problems who needs a psychiatrist not an attorney who will argue excuses for his behavior! If, through your efforts, Mike Tyson is not held accountable for his behavior, then you do a disservice to all women and we become victims of a pandemic legal system gone awry!

Mike Tyson? He doesn't deserve the best—it's a *shanda*!!

When you choose to represent someone like Mike Tyson, you attach the Jewish community to your action. . . . I now find it hard to understand how you can mount a passionate defense for a convicted rapist.

Shame on you, Alan Dershowitz, if you handle this appeal.

I hope my correspondents and my readers will withhold judgment until all the facts are known and all the legal issues resolved. You may be surprised when you learn what a miscarriage of justice has occurred.

July 1992

On June 25, 1992, the Rhode Island Supreme Court ordered Desiree Washington's erstwhile lawyer to disclose documents to the Indiana Supreme Court which might well show that Washington had committed perjury by denying that she had a contingency fee agreement concerning a possible civil suit against Tyson. The case is far from over.

CHILD ABUSE CASE DEFIES COMMON SOLUTIONS

You think it's so easy to be a judge? OK, you decide the appropriate punishment in the Debra Ann Forster case!

Forster, an eighteen-year-old mother of three children, was recently convicted, on a guilty plea, of two counts of attempted felony child abuse. She had left her two baby boys, then six months and eighteen months old, in a sweltering Arizona apartment for two days last summer. If her estranged husband had not found the babies, they almost certainly would have died. They were, in fact, hospitalized in serious condition for malnutrition, dehydration, and skin lesions.

Forster admitted abandoning the babies, claiming she was unable to deal with the pressure of taking care of them. She also admitted taking drugs and attempting suicide. Several months after this near-disaster, while in jail, Forster gave birth to yet another baby, this time a daughter. There is no evidence that her emotional state has improved. What is a judge to do under these circumstances?

It is always easier to decide what a judge should not do. In this case, Judge Lindsay Ellis Budzyn handed down a sentence that is sure to offend civil libertarians, religious fundamentalists, feminists, and nearly every other "ist" or "ian." The judge sentenced the defendant to use and remain on birth control for the rest of her childbearing life. In addition, Forster may never again see her children, who have been put up for adoption, and she cannot baby-sit for others.

This sentence of legally mandated childlessness will be enforceable through the mechanism of lifetime probation. Unless the defendant can provide "written proof"—whatever that means in this context!—that she is using birth control, she will be sent back to prison.

Understandably, the Civil Liberties Union of Arizona is objecting to this "stunning violation of a person's rights," as is Forster's public defender. Religious conservatives who oppose birth control will complain, along with feminists who believe in a woman's right to reproductive freedom. Many others, with no particular political or religious affiliation, will also be uncomfortable with governmentally imposed birth control—a concept associated more with totalitarian regimes than with democracies.

Nor are the constitutional issues mooted by the fact that Forster has the option of going to jail rather than complying with the judge's birth-control order: When a court gives a defendant a choice of punishments, all the options must be constitutional.

For example, a judge should not be able to give a defendant the choice between attending church services or going to prison, since no government official is empowered to mandate religious observance.

But the question remains: What is to be done to a woman who is biologically capable of giving birth but emotionally incapable of bringing up babies? Enforced sterilization has been used, even in the United States during this century, against persons believed to be mentally retarded. But this may be the first case in which mandatory birth control has been imposed as a punishment for crime.

To be sure, long sentences of imprisonment have occasionally been used as an indirect form of birth control. But the facts of this case, and others, seem to prove that women can give birth and even conceive while behind bars.

Among the most offensive aspects of Judge Budzyn's sentence is its duration. Forster has been condemned to a lifetime of childlessness, regardless of how she may mature or change over time. As Judge Budzyn recognized, Debra Ann Forster is "a child, bearing children." But one hopes Forster will not always be a child. Children do grow up (at least if given the chance that Forster nearly denied her babies). In a few years, it is possible that Forster will be emotionally capable of caring for children.

I suspect that Judge Budzyn was engaging in a bit of muscle flexing, as well as media hype, in imposing the life sentence. If Forster were to come back to court in a few years with some reliable expert assessment of her capacity to raise children, it is unthinkable that a court would actually say: "This was a punishment of lifelong childlessness, and I'm sticking to it." But Forster—even an older, more mature Forster—will have a heavy burden to overcome if she seeks to get off the court-imposed pill (or whatever form of birth control the court wants her to prove she is using).

What Judge Budzyn did was wrong. But I ask you to consider what would have been the *right* punishment, or other response, for an eighteen-year-old child who insists on bringing into the world children who deserve far more than she is able to give them. (In another recent case, a judge sentenced a welfare mother to stop smoking, since she was too poor to both support her children and her several-pack-a-day habit.)

"To let the punishment fit the crime" may have been the "object all sublime" of the fictional Mikado, but real-life judges have few options available other than the traditional punishments of imprisonment and fine.

And in cases like Forster's, these black-and-white options seem inadequate in coping with the real-life tragedies of life and death confronting the sentencing judge in the Forster case.   June 1988

SHOULD RAPE VICTIMS' NAMES BE PUBLISHED?

The Supreme Court recently agreed to review a case that threatens to divide some feminists from civil libertarians. It involves the gut-wrenching issue of whether a newspaper may print the name of a woman who claims to have been raped. (I say "claims," because under our constitutional presumption of innocence, the accused rapist should not be presumed guilty until he is convicted.)

Many newspapers and other media throughout the country have a self-imposed policy of not printing the names of rape victims (or juveniles) involved in the criminal justice system. Florida has a mandatory statute prohibiting publication of the names of sex-crime victims. In the case of *Florida Star* vs. *B.V.F.* (the victim's initials), a small weekly newspaper in Jacksonville, which has a voluntary policy of nonpublication, inadvertently included B.V.F.'s full name in a listing of "police reports." The police report had been made available to a reporter-in-training by the sheriff's office.

The newspaper was not criminally prosecuted by the state, perhaps because the publication of the name was inadvertent, but B.V.F. sued the paper and was awarded $100,000 in damages by a jury. (She had also sued the sheriff, but that case was settled for $2,500.) The Florida appellate courts upheld the jury's verdict and the Supreme Court agreed to review the case, thus setting the stage for a major clash between the alleged victim's right of privacy and the newspaper's First Amendment right to publish a truthful account of a police report.

The arguments on both sides are compelling. Many rape victims would prefer not to have their identity disclosed to the public. Tragically, in some social milieus it is still regarded as a stigma to be the victim of a rape. Some sexists still believe that women who are raped are somehow responsible for their victimization. Others adhere to the misogynistic notion that rape victims are "damaged goods." Despite the absurdity—indeed perversity—

of these anachronistic views, they help to explain why some rape victims feel so strongly in favor of rules prohibiting publication of their identities.

Because of these strong feelings, it is assumed that unless rape victims are assured that their names will not be published, fewer of them will come forward and report rapes. Since rape is already one of the most underreported of violent crimes, this is a serious problem.

On the other side of the ledger is the defendant's presumption of innocence. When a woman reports a rape, indeed when anybody reports any crime, the law must presume that the accused person is innocent. It follows, therefore, that the law cannot assume that the alleged victim's story is necessarily true—even in those cases where the evidence seems overwhelming.

This constitutional presumption of innocence, which underlies our entire system of criminal justice, applies only to our courts; the media are not obliged to respect it. Newspapers are free (subject only to libel laws) to declare the accused person guilty even before trial, but generally they refer to the defendant as the "alleged" rapist. Some opponents of the Florida-type law—prohibiting the publication of identities of rape victims—argue that the spirit of the presumption of innocence is undercut when the newspaper prints the name of the alleged rapists but does not print the name of the alleged victim. It leads the reader to conclude that the *alleged* victim was indeed a *true* victim and that the alleged rapist is indeed guilty.

Related to this somewhat theoretical argument is the very practical reality that if the name of the alleged rape victim is published, there is a greater likelihood that members of the general public might come forward with information useful to the defendant. Consider, for example, a case involving an alleged rape victim who had falsely accused others of rape in the past, or who had boasted to friends that she would falsely accuse the defendant of rape. Publication of her name would provide the information necessary for those witnesses to come forward.

Though these are surely farfetched examples, it must always be remembered that some accusations of rape, like some accusations of other crimes, are false (the Tawana Brawley case is a recent reminder of this possibility). If all accusations were true, there would be no need for a trial and we could adopt the Alice in Wonderland approach of "sentence first, trial later."

In the end, the Supreme Court's decision, whichever way it turns out, will not have a profound impact on the way the media report on rape accusations. Even if the Florida law is struck down as unconstitutional, most newspapers will continue to treat alleged rape victims differently from alleged victims of other crimes, whose names are routinely published.

So long as sexists persist in their anachronistic views about rape victims, so long as some Americans continue to attach a stigma to being raped, the press will be reticent about publishing their names. Only when we come to realize that rape is a crime of violence, an aggravated assault, will we be able to treat it like other crimes of violence—both in court and in the media. October 1988

REASONS TO PUBLISH RAPE VICTIMS' NAMES

A recent event in the news highlights the correctness of the Supreme Court's ruling that a newspaper cannot be held liable for reporting the name of an alleged rape victim.

In the case of the *Florida Star* vs. *B.V.F.*, the high court reversed a damage award against a Jacksonville weekly newspaper that had published a "police report" about a rape. Generally, the police do not reveal the names of rape complainants, but, in this instance, the alleged victim's full name was inadvertently included in the public records of the police department, and the newspaper published it. The woman sued and won, but the Supreme Court, in a 6–3 decision, reversed the decision.

To place this ruling in context, it is important to go back to our basic constitutional presumption of innocence. A man is not guilty of rape just because someone accuses him of that terrible crime. There has to be a trial and a conviction before the "alleged" rapist becomes the "convicted" rapist. Despite the presumption of innocence that protects everyone accused of any crime, newspapers routinely report the names of those arrested on charges of rape.

Nor would we want to have it any other way in a nation committed to open trials and public accountability. In some countries—China, for example—the names of those arrested are not published unless and until the authorities decide it is in the government's interest to do so. Not so in this country. We do not tolerate secret arrests, secret trials, or secret executions.

It is important to publish the names of alleged rapists for other reasons as well. Citizens reading the name may come forward with additional information proving the defendant's guilt—prior rapes, evidence that the suspect was seen in the vicinity of the crime, statements he might have made about the complainant. Publishing the defendant's name may also generate evidence of his innocence in the form of an alibi or character witness.

Similar benefits may flow from publishing the name of the alleged rape victim, despite its painful consequences for some victims. Witnesses may come forward to support her story. But—and this is a crucial constitutional "but"—witnesses may also come forward to undercut her story! We cannot assume that every accused rapist is guilty.

Here is where the current event in the news comes into play. A few weeks after the highly publicized gang rape and near killing of a woman jogger in New York's Central Park, another woman reported to the police that she, too, had been raped at gunpoint in Central Park shortly after she arrived in New York from North Carolina. There was no reason to doubt her story or her identification of the alleged rapist.

The man was arrested and confined in jail, and his name published in the newspapers for all to read. The alleged rape victim's name was not published. But fortunately for the defendant, the woman had a prior conviction that was a matter of public record: She had been convicted of filing *eleven false rape complaints* in California. She had also filed false rape complaints elsewhere.

The alleged rapist has now been freed, and the alleged rape victim has been arrested for filing a false rape complaint. The original story of the "rape" was given far more prominent coverage than the subsequent story of the defendant's exoneration.

Had the false accuser never been convicted of other false accusations, the only way the innocent defendant would have learned of her prior acts would have been for a previous victim of her false accusations to have read her name in the newspaper and communicated with the defendant.

Feminists who urge the system to treat rape as it treats other crimes are right. There should be no special "corroboration" requirements or distrust of the word of the alleged rape victim. But, as with all other crimes, there are occasional false accusations and erroneous identifications. As with other crimes, "it is better for ten guilty to go free than for one innocent to be wrongly convicted." And as with other crimes, there should be no law absolutely prohibiting the publication of the names of alleged rape victims under all circumstances.

There are cases, particularly cases where crucial elements of the crime are disputed, in which publication of the name is necessary. Such publication may, of course, be painful to the alleged victim. But that is true with other crimes as well. Rape is an aggravated assault. There should be no stigma attached to a victim of rape; however, among some people, there is such a stigma.

The publisher of one newspaper that does publish the names of alleged rape victims has said that the general policy of not publishing such names exacerbates the stigma and is rooted in male chauvinism. And the editor of the *Des Moines Register* argues that it is comparable to withholding information that a death was caused by AIDS. In both cases, she says, the stigma is reinforced by treating the information as devastatingly damaging.

But the most important reason for leaving it to the media, rather than the law, to decide whether to disclose the name of the alleged rape victim, is to assure that innocent people are not wrongly convicted of this heinous crime. July 1989

THE RAPE THAT NEVER HAPPENED

Remember Gary Dotson and Cathleen Crowell Webb? Back in 1977, Cathleen charged Gary with raping her. Gary claimed complete innocence, saying that he had never had sex with her. It was her word against his, and hers was believed. Gary was convicted and sentenced to twenty-five to fifty years in prison.

After Gary served six years, Cathleen suddenly came forward and recanted her testimony. She said that she had made up the entire rape story because she was afraid that she had been impregnated by her boyfriend. Now it was *her* word against *her* word. She had given two conflicting stories under oath. She attributed her born-again honesty to a religious conversion.

Many people, including the judge, rejected her recantation, reasoning that since she was obviously a liar, her new account should not be believed. Others argued that since she was a liar, *neither* account could be believed.

Finally, the Illinois governor broke the logjam and commuted Gary's sentence to six years imprisonment, the time he had already served. This was not the finding of innocence that Gary was seeking, but it did free him from prison.

The six years in jail had, however, taken its toll on Gary. He began to drink heavily and found himself back behind bars on an assortment of relatively minor charges. He has been living in an alcohol treatment center as part of his parole.

In the meantime, his lawyers were keeping busy trying to corroborate Cathleen's recantation. Finally they hit paydirt as the result of a new forensic technology that had not been developed at the time of Gary's original trial.

The technology, known as DNA testing, is a sophisticated method for comparing blood, semen, and other bodily tissues. Three scientists compared the semen found in a stain on Cathleen's underwear on the day she cried rape with Gary's semen and the semen of her then boyfriend. Lo and behold, the test results completely corroborated her retraction. The semen on her underpants was not consistent with Gary's semen but entirely consistent with that of her boyfriend.

Although the prosecutors still claim that the tests are inconclusive—they seem to be waiting for a heavenly voice to proclaim Gary's innocence—the judge granted Gary's motion for a new trial and dismissed all charges. The judge would still not utter the dreaded "I" word—"innocence"—and admit that the system had failed Gary. But the judge's actions constitute an indirect acknowledgment that Gary had served six years in prison and six more under a cloud of guilt for a "crime" that never took place.

Although this is an isolated instance of injustice, there are lessons to be learned from the sad tale: There *are* some false charges of rape, just as there are false charges of other crimes. It is neither heretical nor sexist to believe in the presumption of innocence in rape cases.

It would be sexist to single out rape complainants for special skepticism, as our law used to do. But a dose of skepticism about all single-witness cases is a healthy antidote to the "lock-'em-up-and-throw-away-the-key" mentality that seems pervasive today. The presumption of innocence is not a "legal technicality." It does free some guilty people. But that is as it must be if we are to remain faithful to the principle that it is better for ten guilty defendants to go free than for one innocent to be convicted.

Gary Dotson was an innocent defendant. And he is not the only one. Ronald S. Monroe was to be executed in Louisiana on August 30 for a murder he probably did not commit. The facts are strikingly similar to those in the Dotson case.

The likely killer, the estranged husband of the victim, made remarks that a cellmate took to be a confession to the murder. That confession is corroborated by the fact that the husband has been convicted of killing one former wife and accused of attempting to kill another. Also, a neighbor filed an affidavit saying that the husband abused and intimidated one of the victim's children. The children were the sole witnesses against Monroe at his trial.

There is one major difference between the Dotson and Monroe cases. Dotson's innocence was established after twelve years, and Dotson is alive to enjoy his vindication. In the long run, Monroe's innocence also probably will be established. But if his execution had been permitted to go forward, he would not be alive for his exoneration.

The courts should recognize that a convict has a constitutional right not to be executed if the real likelihood of innocence exists. Even if no specific legal errors can be pinpointed—and there are numerous errors in the Monroe case—our constitutional prohibition against cruel and unusual punishment cannot tolerate the execution of a man who may not have committed the crime. The Dotson case demonstrates that our criminal justice system is not foolproof.

Just two weeks before Monroe's scheduled execution, Louisiana governor Buddy Roemer said he would commute the death sentence to life without possibility of parole. The governor said that he was still convinced of Monroe's guilt, but that enough doubts had been raised to warrant commutation of the death sentence. Now Monroe will await his vindication in prison.

August 1989

PROTECTING THE RAPE VICTIM— AND SUSPECT

Imagine the added agony of being raped by a stranger in our age of AIDS. If the horror of a rape ever ended with the cessation of the sexual violence itself—and I doubt that it ever did—it certainly doesn't these days. A woman (or a man) who "survives" a rape without immediate injury or death is still not out of danger. If she was infected with the AIDS virus by the rapist, she may die from the rape in a year or two or five or ten. She cannot even be tested accurately for several months after the rape, since the AIDS virus can avoid detection, even if present, during the initial stage.

In addition to the obvious reasons that every rape victim would want to know whether she has been exposed to the virus, there are especially compelling cases. For example, a pregnant woman might choose to have an abortion if she knew she could transmit the AIDS virus to her child. A woman trying to become pregnant might stop trying and would want to urge her mate to use a condom. But special cases aside, every rape victim surely has the right to know whether she has been placed at risk of infection, so that she can plan her life and her medical treatment.

But defendants also have rights, one of which is the presumption of innocence until proven guilty. The inevitable delays between arrest and trial generally amount to several months. Although the presumption of innocence does not preclude all interference with the defendant's privacy—he can be searched, held on bond, questioned, and so on—there are limits to what the government may compel him to do between the time he is arrested and the time he is convicted (if he is convicted). It is precisely that period which may be the crucial time. It is during these first few months that the victim herself cannot be accurately tested for the presence of the AIDS virus.

This conflict of rights is generating heated controversy among groups that are generally allied with each other: feminists, gay rights activists, civil libertarians, and public health officials.

Many feminists, who are understandably sympathetic to the plight of the rape victim, are calling for testing of rape suspects upon demand by the victim. They are joined by "victim's rights" advocates, who generally downplay the rights of all defendants. Civil libertarians, who are worried about compromising the presumption of innocence, are resisting this call, especially if it would result in near automatic testing of all rape defendants. Some gay rights advocates are concerned about any movement toward more widespread compulsory testing. And some public health officials fear a panic reaction from mandatory testing of all rape suspects, pointing to the relatively low risk of contracting AIDS from a single sexual episode, even a violent one.

While it is true that very few rape victims will, in fact, contract AIDS from a rape, the risk is still there—a risk not chosen by the rape victim.

My proposal is that any woman who has been raped should be able to apply to a judge—not the same one that will preside at the rape trial—for an order requiring her alleged rapist to be tested. If she makes a sufficiently compelling case that the suspect is probably her rapist and that the sexual act posed a significant risk of transmission (not all rapes involve transfer of fluids), the judge should order the suspect to be tested. The suspect would, however, have the right *not* to be notified of the results of the test, if he—foolishly, in my view—chose to remain in the dark. But the victim would be told the results, conditioned on a promise that she would not disclose them beyond what is necessary for her legitimate needs. Nor could a positive result be used against the defendant at a trial—unless, of course, the government could independently prove that the defendant knew he had the AIDS virus when he committed the rape.

Under this proposal, which is obviously not perfect, a balance would be struck between conflicting rights. The victim would learn an important fact about her risk level. The suspect would have to submit to a blood test (which the courts have already ruled, in other contexts, does not violate his privilege against self-incrimination). But he would not have to be confronted with a reality that he prefers to avoid.

The real problem for the suspect is that if he does test positive and the victim is told of that result, there is no realistic way to ensure that the victim will comply with the gag order.

This merely goes to show that there are no perfect solutions to difficult problems in our imperfect world. Nor are contemporary problems capable of solution simply by reference to the ambiguous text of a two-hundred-year-old Constitution. We must apply the spirit of that living document to issues not contemplated by its framers. My solution plainly errs in favor of the victim and against the suspect. But it tries to do so with a sensitivity to the suspect's rights.   September 1989

CHILD IS MISSING, BUT ADULTS HAVE RIGHTS

Whenever the constitutional rights of adults conflict with the government's need to protect abused children, we are likely to see some compromise of the adults' rights.

A dramatic case raising such a conflict was recently argued in the U.S. Supreme Court. And the high court's ruling, expected within the next few months, is likely to have considerable impact both on the meaning of the Fifth Amendment's privilege against self-incrimination and the power of states to protect children.

The case involves a missing three-year-old boy who had been abused by his mother in the past. When he was just a few months old, the infant was hospitalized for a broken leg and other injuries. Hospital workers saw his twenty-year-old mother, Jacqueline Bouknight, throw or drop her child.

He was taken from her and placed in a foster home. But six months later, after the mother promised to seek reform and training, the child was returned to her.

Within a year, however, the mother was refusing to cooperate with social workers. She was on drugs, and the baby's father had been shot to death. Then the baby dropped from sight. After he was missing for a month, the Baltimore Department of Social Services began to suspect foul play. It sought a court order compelling the mother to either produce her child or tell the authorities where he was.

At the same time, state police authorities had been—and still are—pursuing a criminal investigation against the mother on possible charges of murdering her son. And therein lies the conflict between her rights and his safety.

As a potential criminal defendant, Bouknight is legally entitled to refuse to answer any question that might tend to incriminate her—that is, expose her to possible criminal prosecution. At the moment, the state has no solid proof that she harmed the child, since its own extensive investigation failed to locate him. But if she were to respond to the court's order by producing the child or leading authorities to his whereabouts, she might be incriminating herself. She would be admitting that she knows where her child is.

The Supreme Court has repeatedly ruled that the Fifth Amendment's privilege against self-incrimination was designed to protect the guilty as well as the innocent against "the cruel trilemma of self-accusation, perjury, or contempt." Bouknight is arguing that the court order in this case confronts her directly with that trilemma: If she produces her son, she will be accusing herself of whatever she may have done to him; if she lies about his whereabouts, she invites a perjury prosecution; and if she defies the court order, she remains in jail under contempt of court charges.

The Maryland Court of Appeals agreed with Bouknight's self-incrimination argument and ordered her freed from her contempt-of-court imprisonment. But Chief Justice Rehnquist, obviously anticipating that the Supreme Court would overrule the Maryland high court, ordered her to remain in jail until the court could decide her case.

Most observers believe that the justices will find some way to compel her to produce her child. But there is wide disagreement about what rubric the court will use to reach that politically popular result. The attorney general of Maryland has argued that the demand made of Bouknight does not come within the protection of the Fifth Amendment, because producing the child is not *testimonial*: It is an *action* and not a *statement*. He compares it to providing a blood or hair sample. But the analogy fails. The act of producing the missing child is different from the act of producing blood or hair. The former entails an admission of knowledge. The latter does not.

There is a way out of this quandary. The state can give Bouknight immunity against any use, in a criminal trial, of the fact that it was she who produced the child. If she were given that kind of immunity, known as "production immunity," she could no longer legally invoke the Fifth Amendment, and she would have to produce her child. But if the child turned out to have been killed, no jury could ever learn that it was his mother who led the authorities to the child's body. The state would have to prove its criminal case by evidence independent of the fact that she produced the child.

Such is the constitutional compromise struck by our Fifth Amendment and the Supreme Court cases interpreting it. Some argue that the Fifth Amendment exacts too great a price from law enforcement to protect the guilty. The lawyer for the child argues that even if the Fifth Amendment does apply to this case, society's interest in protecting children should outweigh the Constitution.

Therein lies the road to tyranny. Once we allow constitutional rights to be "outweighed" by pressing needs, even those of victimized children, we open the door to an inexorable process of erosion of our most fundamental rights.   November 1989

In February, 1990 The Supreme Court ruled that Bouknight could not invoke the Fifth Amendment because she had a special relationship with the state resulting from her agreement to accept state supervision if her child were returned to her.

THE LAW STRUGGLES WITH SEX ABUSE CASES

Three centuries ago, the lord chief justice of England, Matthew Hale, declared that accusations of sexual misconduct are "easily to be made and hard to be proved, and harder to be defended by the party accused, tho' never so innocent."

He was wrong about sexual misconduct charges being "easy to be

made." Victims, especially children, are sometimes terrified of the consequences of accusing a parent or teacher of sexual misconduct. But the
lord chief justice was probably correct in observing that charges of sexual
misconduct are difficult to defend against, even by those who may have
been falsely accused.

Two current cases illustrate the difficulty that persons accused of
sexual misconduct may have in proving their innocence.

After the longest criminal trial in American history, a Los Angeles
jury rendered its verdict in the McMartin Preschool case, acquitting Peggy
McMartin Buckey on all counts, and acquitting Raymond Buckey on most
counts. The jury was unable to reach a unanimous verdict on thirteen counts
involving Raymond, though there was apparently a majority for acquittal
on each of them. Now the district attorney of Los Angeles has decided to
retry Raymond on the deadlocked counts. He pointed to the fact that several
of the jurors had indicated that they believed that some of the children may
have been molested, but that there was insufficient proof that Raymond was
guilty beyond a reasonable doubt.

It will again be his uncorroborated word against the uncorroborated
accusations of the children. How a second jury is to be expected to render
"better" justice than the first jury was never explained by the district attorney.

In New York City, the Reverend Bruce Ritter, founder and director
of Covenant House, a home for runaway and sexually exploited children,
has been directed by his Franciscan superiors to take a leave of absence
pending further investigation of charges that he engaged in sexual improprieties with young men who were in his program. After being notified of his
suspension, Father Ritter, who has been a vigorous campaigner against
pornography and child abuse, issued the following statement: "I have no
way of proving my innocence. My accusers cannot establish my guilt."

The Buckey and Ritter cases are different. Buckey stands charged
with serious felonies that carry long prison terms. Ritter faces embarrassment and destruction of his life's work. But they share one important
characteristic: Both have been accused of sexual improprieties by youngsters with whom they had admittedly been in contact. There is no hard
evidence capable of proving the charges, nor is there any hard evidence
capable of disproving them. No Perry Mason will trick either the accuser
or the accused into admitting that his story is false. In the end, there will
always be some doubt, some uncertainty, some possibility that whatever
conclusion is reached may be wrong.

How then should the legal and political system deal with such inevitable uncertainty in so emotionally charged a setting? In the context of a criminal prosecution, such as that faced by Raymond Buckey, we have a rule that requires us to err on the side of innocence. Even if the defendant is most probably guilty, he must be acquitted if there is a reasonable doubt. We glory in our presumption of innocence, pursuant to which "it is better for ten guilty defendants to go free than for even one innocent defendant to be wrongly convicted." If we mean what we say, then we must insist that doubtful cases be resolved in favor of the person accused.

That is precisely what the jury did in the first McMartin trial: It did not declare Raymond Buckey innocent; it issued him no certificate of good character; it merely found that there was a reasonable doubt concerning his guilt. That should end the matter so far as it relates to criminal charges. But it does not mean that he should necessarily be allowed to reenter the preschool business. A different standard should govern the granting of permits to operate a preschool; perhaps the person seeking such a permit should have the burden of establishing his or her good character.

Father Ritter does not currently face any criminal charges. The standard of proof beyond a reasonable doubt does not, therefore, apply to him. But he faces the loss of his life's work if his accusers are believed. Contributors to Covenant House are entitled to apply any standard of proof they regard as fair. But before any institutional sanction may properly be applied—before Father Ritter is permanently suspended—the body passing judgment should be convinced that his accusers are not lying.

We must be more sensitive to the victims of alleged sexual misconduct than was the lord chief justice. We must understand how horrible it is to be a victim of sexual abuse. But we must also remember how horrible it is to face a false accusation of so heinous a crime and not be able to disprove it.   February 1990

WHICH PARENT ABUSED
HILARY FORETICH?

It seems likely that someone is guilty of child abuse in the tragic case of Hilary Foretich. The seven-year-old girl recently turned up following a thirty-month sojourn that took her from this country to Plymouth, England, and then on to her present "home" in Christchurch, New Zealand.

Hilary's mother, Dr. Elizabeth Morgan, claims that her former husband, Dr. Eric Foretich, sexually abused their daughter since the time she was two and a half years old. Foretich, Hilary's father, categorically denies these charges and claims that Morgan is mentally ill. Now there are also allegations that Hilary may have been abused by her mother's father. She has been living in hiding with her maternal grandparents since her mother disobeyed a 1987 court order authorizing Foretich to visit her without supervision.

That order was issued by a District of Columbia judge who, after hearing evidence on both sides, rejected Morgan's claims that her former husband had sexually abused Hilary. Rather than comply with the order to allow Hilary to visit with her father, Morgan simply defied it and sent her daughter into hiding.

Morgan spent twenty-five months in jail for refusing to disclose the whereabouts of her missing daughter. She was finally released after Congress passed special legislation limiting incarceration to twelve months in District of Columbia child custody cases.

If Morgan is correct in charging her husband with sex abuse, then her actions are understandable, if not legally justifiable in light of the court's order. But if she is lying, if she is falsely charging her former husband with this terrible crime to get even with him or to obtain some tactical advantage in divorce-related litigation, then it is *she* who might be guilty of child abuse. This would be especially true if she turned her daughter over to a grandfather who was sexually abusing the child.

Whatever the true facts are, Morgan and her parents have obviously persuaded young Hilary that her father is a frightening and abusive man. She has become terrified of him. It is not difficult for those who have total control over the flow of information to a seven-year-old to turn that child against a father she has not seen for several years.

This tragic reality places the New Zealand judge, who now has the case, in a terrible situation. If he considers only Hilary's present wishes and short-term best interest, he would probably have to rule in favor of the status quo. If he looks beyond her current fears, he will have to consider the implications of allowing Morgan and her parents to take the law—and Hilary's life—into their own hands.

And if he decides to take into account the interests of children in general, he will surely not want to reward kidnappers who defy lawful court orders that are usually in the best interest of the child.

Everyone understands the horrors of sexual abuse of children. But falsely charging a parent with that crime and using the child as a pawn in a vengeful struggle between former spouses may be as abusive as sexual molestation. Sexual abuse of children is horrible not primarily for the physical damage it causes but for the psychological scars it leaves.

The realization by a child that a parent would exploit his or her trust is the primary harm produced by parental sex crimes. That harm is produced just as surely when one parent falsely convinces a child that she has been sexually abused by her other parent.

It will be difficult for any court to ever learn the full truth of what happened—or did not happen—to Hilary several years ago. Nor can any of us do more than guess at who is telling the truth on the basis of the available information. Each side has its champions in the media and among ordinary men and women who are watching this unfolding drama. But the most we can do is believe, more on faith than facts, that one side or the other is probably right.

That is why significant weight must be accorded to the prior judicial determination made back in 1987, before Hilary was sent into hiding and before she was completely brainwashed by her mother's parents.

The child should be returned to the United States, and Foretich should be allowed to gradually reestablish a healthy parental relationship with her. Under U.S. law, as well as New Zealand law, no person may be labeled a child molester simply because his former spouse claims he is.

The evidence does not support Morgan's charges against her former husband. But the evidence does establish that Morgan and her parents have defied the orders of the court.

If Morgan is rewarded for her unlawful complicity in shuttling her daughter halfway around the world, the message will be clear to all spouses who are dissatisfied with court orders: Take the law into your own hands.

March 1990

In November 1990 a New Zealand Family Court awarded sole custody of Hilary to Dr. Elizabeth Morgan.

ALAN M. DERSHOWITZ

SACRIFICING CHILDREN TO RELIGION

The Church of Christ, Scientist, is fighting back. In a series of full-page ads and other statements, the church, founded by Mary Baker Eddy in 1879, is complaining about what it calls "selective prosecution of Christian Scientists." The focus of its complaint is the prosecution of a young Christian Science couple in Boston whose two-year-old son died after the couple chose to treat him with prayers rather than medicine.

The state contends that if the child, who was suffering from an obstructed bowel, had been treated by traditional medical means, he would almost certainly have survived. The church, in its statement, does not dispute that conclusion. It argues instead that members of the Christian Science faith have a constitutional right to seek to heal physical disease "by spiritual means alone."

The courts tend to agree that competent adults do have a First Amendment right to risk *their own lives* in the exercise of their religious freedoms, but they do not have the right to place *others* at risk in the name of their own religion. Thus, the Supreme Court has held that no one has the right to opt out of a program of universal inoculation against a contagious disease on religious grounds. Since contagious diseases know no religious differences, all must be inoculated to curtail their spread.

The issue presented by the Boston prosecution does not involve a contagious disease, but nor does it involve a competent adult risking his or her own life. It raises the question of whether competent adult parents, who truly believe in the superior healing powers of prayer over medicine, may impose their religious beliefs on a legally incompetent infant. That question assumes grave proportions when the infant is suffering from a disease that is curable when treated medically but fatal when "treated" by prayer alone.

The Christian Science church denies that if parents were permitted to choose prayer instead of medicine, "children would be sacrificed to religion." But whatever the benevolent intentions of the parents, the malevolent result is precisely that an otherwise curable child is allowed to die because, in the words of the church, "medical and spiritual means are incompatible." That *is* sacrificing children to religion.

In biblical times, the sacrifice of a child was the true test of an adherent's faith. Abraham was ready to sacrifice Isaac, and Jephthah did sacrifice his daughter. In a secular democracy like our own, Abraham would be indicted for attempted murder and Jephthah for murder. Perhaps they were rewarded in heaven for following the dictates of their God, but here in America, adults are not permitted to sacrifice their children to religion.

The Christian Scientists argue that their method of prayer has achieved an "exceptionally good" record of success in curing illness. They argue that loving parents should surely be permitted to choose a potential course of treatment for their child's illness which is, in their view, superior to conventional medicine.

And they may be right—in circumstances where the empirical evidence is questionable or close. For example, where a child is affected with an inoperable brain tumor and conventional medicine gives that child virtually no hope for survival, parents should be allowed to substitute prayer for an invasive procedure that may only postpone the inevitable. Or where a psychosomatic illness has not been treated successfully by drugs, parents should be able to opt for prayer over some approved psychotherapeutic regime.

But where the issue is beyond real scientific dispute—as, for example, with an operable malignant tumor, a case of acute appendicitis, or a treatable condition like juvenile diabetes—the state must have the power to compel parents to treat their children medically until they become adults.

Once the children have become adults, they will have an entire lifetime to practice their chosen religion. But children don't always follow their parents' religious practices into adulthood. Children, too, have the right to make an eventual choice as to their religious and secular destiny. But if their parents' choices are imposed on them in life-and-death situations, the children of Christian Scientists may never get the opportunity to make their own religious decisions as adults.

Christian Science is a wealthy and powerful institution, which claims two thousand churches throughout the world. It has managed to get statutes enacted in numerous states that give its adherents "the right to rely on Christian Science treatment." Some of these statutes are limited to adults, others are silent as to children in life-threatening situations. Efforts are under way in a number of states expressly to allow parents to forgo medical treatment for their children if they sincerely believe that prayer is more effective. These efforts are being opposed by medical and child-care experts.

The right to prefer prayer over medicine should continue to be recognized as it applies to competent adults with noncontagious diseases. But it should not be extended to children, especially infants, who are too young even to realize that the decision being made by their parents may deny them the right to life itself. April 1990

The Boston couple were eventually convicted of manslaughter in the death of their son and were given a 10 year suspended sentence. An appeal of their conviction is pending.

PUNISHING FALSE ACCUSATIONS OF RAPE

The crime of rape is so horrendous that it used to be punished by death in many states. Some who believe in the death penalty still argue that rape deserves the ultimate punishment.

It is precisely because rape is so serious a crime that falsely accusing someone of rape should be regarded as an extremely serious crime as well. Imagine yourself or a "loved one" being falsely accused of raping a woman! Think of what it would do to your life, your children's lives, your marriage, your job, your friendships.

If you have difficulty imagining, then consider what actually happened to Gary Nitsch, a forty-three-year-old married man and father of two. The alfalfa-mill worker was accused by Elizabeth Richardson, a married twenty-four-year-old meat-packing worker, of raping her.

As a result of the charge, Nitsch was arrested while shopping and taken to jail until his brother could post a $30,000 bond. He lost his job. His children were greeted in school with shouts of "Your dad's a rapist." Neighbors bought guns to protect their frightened wives from him. His wife could not go shopping or show her face in public.

Richardson testified under oath that Nitsch had raped her. But soon thereafter she admitted that she had made up the entire story. Her lawyer explained that her then husband, a long-distance truck driver, had bragged to her of his extramarital affairs, and that she made up the rape charge because "she was trying to get her husband's attention." She thought that if she claimed she had been raped, her husband would be more inclined to stay home.

Richardson was charged with perjury and pleaded no contest. On June

8, Judge John Murphy imposed sentence on her. Although the maximum sentence for perjury in Nebraska is twenty years, and although Nitsch could have received fifty years if he had been convicted of rape, the judge gave Richardson a slap on the wrist. He sentenced her to serve six months in jail. He also ordered her to apologize to Nitsch in a half-page advertisement in four newspapers and in ten spot announcements on two radio stations. The total cost of these public apologies is about $1,000.

The American Civil Liberties Union (ACLU) is up in arms about the sentence, complaining that the public apology constitutes cruel and unusual punishment in violation of the Eighth Amendment. They also claim that it violates her right of free speech and her guarantee of due process.

I, too, am outraged by the sentence. It is far too lenient, in light of the enormous harm it did to Nitsch and the potential harm it could have caused both to Nitsch and to the entire legal system. There are already too many people all too eager to disbelieve actual victims of rape. Every time a woman falsely accuses a man of rape, that false accusation, like the classic tale of the boy who cried wolf, strengthens the hands of sexists who would go back to the bad old days when accusations of rape required external corroboration—when a woman's word was not enough.

Ironically, the overly lenient sentence for a false accusation of rape trivializes the seriousness of the crime of rape itself. It fails to take into account the serious consequences that do—and should—flow from a conviction for rape.

The ACLU has a point about the First Amendment, but it's not a very persuasive one in light of the fact that Murphy has allowed Richardson to put her apology in her own words. Richardson, by pleading no contest, has already publicly acknowledged that she falsely accused Nitsch of rape. Her false accusation was carried in the newspapers and on the radio. Her admission that the accusation was indeed false should also be carried—at her expense—in the same media, so that the public will know that Nitsch was an innocent victim of her perjury.

As Murphy put it, "I told her the reason. The rape charges were all over the papers, but when he was exonerated nobody hears about it. I told her the only way to get it out was to have her do it." To avoid all possible First Amendment problems, perhaps the judge should simply have ordered Richardson to pay for an ad that reprinted the admission of guilt she had already made in open court.

If ever there is a crime that warrants public apology it is the crime of falsely accusing another of something as awful as rape. Elizabeth Richardson, who is appealing her sentence, should willingly place the ads in the newspapers and on the radio, and she should thank her lucky stars that she wasn't sentenced for her crime in France. Under French law, a person who falsely accuses another of a crime receives the same punishment the falsely accused person could have gotten.   July 1990

In September 1990, Elizabeth Richardson began running radio and newspaper ads apologizing for fabricating rape charges against Gary Nitsch. (For additional information, see The Washington Post *article* Unfounded Reports of Rape Confound Area Police Investigators—*June 27, 1992.)*

SHOULD THE MEDIA IDENTIFY RAPE VICTIMS?

Everyone in the United States who reads the press or watches television knows that William Kennedy Smith has been accused of sexual assault by a twenty-nine-year-old Palm Beach County woman who met him at a bar and accompanied him to the Kennedy compound. Although Smith is presumed innocent—indeed, he has not been charged with anything—no newspaper or TV station has had any hesitation in printing his name and delving into his personal and family life. His accuser, whose account may be true, false, or somewhere in between, has been spared the publicity of having her identity disclosed by the media.

The reason why Smith's accuser has not been identified is because there is a conspiracy of silence among the media when it comes to victims of rape. Although there is no law precluding the media from naming Smith's accuser, nearly every newspaper and TV station has a policy of never disclosing the identification of alleged rape victims.

Is this fair? Is it good journalism? Does it serve the interests of rape victims in particular or women in general? Is it consistent with the policies underlying the presumption of innocence and the constitutional right to confront one's accuser? These are questions that more and more journalists, lawyers, rape counselors, and ordinary citizens are now asking.

It is not as if the media is generally solicitous of the feelings of crime victims. Newspapers routinely print the names of murder, robbery, burglary, assault, and extortion victims despite the fact that many such victims and their families would strongly prefer anonymity. For example, when a crime victim is attacked while involved in an embarrassing activity—for example, buying drugs, soliciting a prostitute, engaging in extramarital sex, or submitting to extortion—the media will not, as a matter of policy, withhold the victim's name simply because publication will cause pain. Indeed, the only other genre of names not published by the media is that of juveniles. But when it comes to juveniles, neither the names of victims nor the names of *suspects* is published.

Why then are adult women who are alleged victims of rape treated by the media as if they were juveniles? The reasons offered by those who would justify the nearly uniform policy of not reporting the names of rape victims are mostly throwbacks to the bad old days when rape victims were believed—in the sexist language of a bygone age—to be "damaged goods," or to have "asked for it."

But feminists have properly educated us to the reality that rape is an aggravated assault and that the victim is no more responsible for her victimization than is a murder or mayhem victim. Nor would any reasonable person today regard a rape victim as less valued because of her ordeal.

Indeed, the policy of singling out rape victims for special treatment by the media helps foster precisely the old sexist stereotypes that were responsible for the anachronistic rules of evidence that singled out the testimony of alleged rape victims for special scrutiny and required that it alone had to be "corroborated" by "real" evidence before it could be believed.

If rape is just like other aggravated assaults and is a crime of violence rather than an act of sexuality, then the media should begin to treat rape like it treats other crimes and rape victims like it treats other victims.

Beyond the sexist origins of the no-name policy when it comes to alleged rape victims, there is also the unfairness to the person accused. The no-name policy presumes that the alleged victim's story is true—that she is indeed a rape victim and that the person she has accused is in fact guilty. Moreover, it denies the accused person an important safeguard: If the public does not know the name of the accuser, it cannot provide information to the defense about that accuser.

For example, several years ago in New York City, a woman accused a man of having raped her at gunpoint in Central Park. The man was arrested, imprisoned, and his name publicized. Shortly thereafter it was learned—quite fortuitously—that the alleged victim had previously been convicted of filing eleven false rape complaints in another part of the country. In that case, the discovery was made by law-enforcement officials, but if that had not happened, the suppression of her name would have denied the falsely accused defendant the help of newspaper readers who might have been aware of his accuser's highly relevant past history.

I am not necessarily proposing a blanket policy of always printing the name of every alleged rape victim. But certainly in cases where the accuser's name and background may be relevant—as it surely seems to be in the Smith case, where there are allegations of possible theft by the accuser—the media should use its discretion and name the accuser along with the accused.   April 1991

ACCUSER'S IDENTITY SHOULD BE REPORTED

As the investigating phase of the rape accusation made against William Kennedy Smith draws to a close, many questions about the law of rape and the practices of the media remain unresolved.

The controversiality of these issues was reflected most acutely in the pages of the *New York Times*. On April 17, 1991, the *New York Times* published both the name of Smith's accuser and a detailed biographical account that included a quote from an unidentified high school friend to the effect that she "had a little wild streak." It also noted that she had given birth to a child out of wedlock and frequented bars in Palm Beach.

The reaction to the *Times* story was largely critical. *Newsweek* reported that "virtually everyone in journalism now agrees that the nation's most highly regarded newspaper has egg on its face." Following a contentious staff meeting and petition, the newspaper printed an unprecedented apology in the form of an editor's note, in which it said that "the article should have explicitly asserted that nothing in the woman's known background could resolve the disputed testimony [sic] about the encounter with Mr. Smith." But was the *Times* right in apologizing? "All the News That's Fit to Print" is not limited to information that could *resolve* disputed contentions. (There has been no "testimony" yet from either party.) It is generally enough that information be *relevant* to a dispute.

If a man says that a woman consented to having sex on their first date and the woman has a ten-year pattern of *never* agreeing to sex until after a long courtship, surely that pattern would be relevant to showing that she did *not* consent. This pattern of monogamy would not, by itself, resolve the dispute, but it would provide useful information in helping to decide who was telling the truth. Similarly, if a woman has a ten-year pattern of consenting to sex on a first date, that pattern, too, would be relevant, though it would certainly not "resolve" the dispute over whether she consented on that particular occasion.

Obviously, the conduct described in the *Times* article is not as relevant as either of these patterns, but it does provide background information useful in assessing the conflicting stories, as would a comparable story about the accused.

The law recognizes the relevance of such background evidence, even when it excludes it under the so-called rape shield or bad-act exclusionary rules. The reason it excludes this kind of relevant evidence is because it has made a legal policy judgment that information about the prior sexual history of the complaining witness might unduly prejudice the jury or might discourage rape victims from testifying. Newspapers are not generally in the business of making or implementing these kinds of legal policy judgments.

For example, when the courts exclude from evidence a coerced confession or the fruits of an illegal search, the media generally discloses the contents of the excluded evidence, as well it should. The public has a right to know what is being *excluded* from a trial as well as what is being admitted. Legal rules of admissibility apply to juries, not to citizens or the press.

One interesting suggestion that has been made is that every rape complainant be given the choice as to whether her complaint will be kept private or made public. If she opts for a private complaint, then neither her name *nor the name of the person she is accusing* would be disclosed by the police until the trial. But if she opts for a public complaint, then both names would be disclosed. Although that would be fair to the accused—who is, after all, presumed innocent—it would deny the public the right to know all the relevant facts about an ongoing criminal case.

The current debate over press reporting of rape accusations has also disclosed a dangerous practice by some police departments of not disclosing rapes in their cities or towns. It was recently revealed that since February of 1990, eleven rapes of young females between the ages of nine and sixteen were committed in a section of Buffalo, N.Y. Neither the fact of the alleged rapes nor the modus operandi of the alleged perpetrator were made public. A similar policy of nondisclosure was recently uncovered in Somerville, Mass. Authorities said it was part of an effort to protect the privacy of rape victims. But the consequences of this cover-up policy may well be to deny potential rape victims information necessary to protect themselves from serial rapists.

In the end, we must recognize that we live under a democratic system of criminal justice, open to public scrutiny by the press and the citizenry. Any compromise with that openness, even when done in the name of privacy or other important values, is a compromise with one of the most important safeguards of liberty: that no person shall be tried for a serious crime by an anonymous accuser who is unwilling to be confronted both in a court of law and in the court of public opinion.   May 1991

DECIDE RAPE CHARGE WITH TRIAL NOT POLITICS

In the days following the Palm Beach prosecutor's decision to charge William Kennedy Smith with rape, various "women's rights leaders" have already taken sides on whether the charge is true or false.

The president of the Massachusetts chapter of the National Organization for Women (NOW) declared that "feminists" are "obviously pleased" with the prosecutor's decision to charge Smith with rape. The national vice president of NOW echoed these statements, which were replete with references to what the "victim" has been "through." Their only concerns seem to be about "how long it took for the investigation to get off the ground" and whether "*she* can get a fair trial. . . ."

Perhaps these feminist leaders have access to a videotape of what happened on the beach that night, but the rest of us have no idea who is telling the truth. The complainant has provided an account that the defendant has called an "outrageous lie." The reason we have jury trials is to determine whether the defendant, who is presumed innocent until a verdict is reached, is guilty or not guilty.

Some feminist leaders seem to believe that the feminist movement has a political stake in Smith being found guilty. That view is a perversion of both feminism and civil liberties. All fair-minded people have a stake in Smith being found guilty only if he is guilty. They have an equal stake in his being found innocent if he is innocent, or if there is reasonable doubt about whether he raped the complainant.

Thoughtful and fair-minded feminists recognize that some men are falsely accused of rape and that falsely accusing someone of so serious a crime is itself a horrible crime.

Just last week the *Boston Globe* reported that a twenty-year-old University of Rhode Island student had raped his ex-girlfriend at gunpoint. The victim "confided the incident to her two roommates, who helped her to the campus infirmary," where an examination confirmed the presence of semen. The name of the alleged rapist was provided by the police and published by the *Globe*. The next day's *Providence Journal* reported that the alleged rapist was in Chicago at the time of the reported attack and that the woman "admitted that she made the whole thing up." She was arrested on misdemeanor charges of filing a false report. The *Boston Herald*'s story of the false report did not include the woman's name, even though she was arrested. It did include the name of her victim.

Numerous other incidents of deliberately false reports of rape have been documented, the most notorious of which was Tawana Brawley's false accusation against an assistant district attorney. Others have included a gunpoint Central Park rape reported shortly after the horrible assault on a jogger in Central Park. The alleged rape victim turned out to have made eleven false rape reports in the recent past. Then there was Elizabeth Richardson who pleaded no contest to perjury after admitting that she falsely charged a neighbor with raping her in order to get her "husband's attention."

Remember also the case of Gary Dotson, who was falsely accused of raping Cathleen Crowell Webb and spent six years in prison before Webb recanted and DNA tests corroborated her retraction. And recently a unanimous Massachusetts Supreme Judicial Court reversed the "date rape" conviction of a Brandeis student, finding the alleged victim's account in many ways "contradictory" and "inconsistent with an allegation of rape."

This is not to say that most, or even a large percentage of, rape reports are false. It is to say that a considerable number, especially in cases where the complainant and the defendant know each other, are exaggerated or false. It is also true that a great many rapes are not reported. But that tragic reality does not change, or in any way mitigate, the equally tragic reality that a considerable number of reported rapes turn out to be false.

The latest FBI uniform crime data show that 8.4 percent of reported forceable rapes turn out to be "unfounded," according to police investigations. This means that of the approximately 100,000 reported rapes each year, about 8,000 may be false. According to Kristine Waskiewicz of the

FBI, this percentage is more than twice as high as for any other index crime.

William Kennedy Smith claims that the accusation against him is one of these false reports. We all have a stake in learning the truth, not in hoping that the verdict confirms some preexisting political perspective on rape.

A former president of the Massachusetts Civil Liberties Union once complained that "some radical feminists regard rape as so heinous a crime that even innocence should not be a defense." That may be a burlesque of their views, but statements made by some "feminist leaders" make it sound as if they are more interested in the perceived political benefits of a conviction in the Smith case than in the truth—whatever it may be—emerging after a fair and neutral trial.   May 1991

HIGH COURT RULES ON RAPE SHIELD LAW

Against the background of the highly publicized rape prosecution of William Kennedy Smith, the U.S. Supreme Court has just ruled—for the first time— on the constitutionality of a so-called rape shield law. The Michigan law in question, which is typical of laws in several other states, prohibited a rape suspect from telling the jury that he and the alleged victim had engaged in a prior consensual sexual relationship unless the suspect's lawyer notified the prosecution of his intent to do so ten days in advance of the trial.

In the case before the high court, the alleged rape victim acknowledged that she had a "torrid" affair with the defendant over the previous two months, but she claimed that he had forced her to have sex with him on the day at issue. Her story was that he had grabbed her, held a knife to her throat, and raped her; his story was that they had consensual sex and that she cried rape only because he wanted to end the relationship.

The jury had to resolve this evidentiary dispute by deciding who was telling the truth and who was lying. Yet the jury never learned of the admitted preexisting sexual relation between the couple. For all the jury knew, the defendant and the complainant were strangers in the night at the time of the alleged rape.

The reason why the jury never learned about this crucial fact was because the defendant's lawyer had failed to file the required written notice ten days prior to the trial. As a result of the technical violation by the lawyer, the defendant was denied his constitutional right to confront his accuser with admittedly relevant evidence that could easily have affected the jury's verdict.

Evidence of a prior consensual relation between a defendant and complainant is, of course, not conclusive proof of his innocence: A man can certainly rape a woman with whom he has engaged in consensual sex, and the prior sexual conduct does not justify, or even minimize, the crime. Even a husband who forces his wife to have sex against her will is guilty of rape in most states. And in this case, the woman did allege, quite persuasively as evidenced by the jury's guilty verdict, that she was raped on the day in question.

But surely the prior relationship is relevant evidence for the jury to consider as to whether the sexual encounter at issue was a continuation of the consensual relationship or a felonious rape. To require the jury to decide the case as if it were a dispute between two strangers is to deny the fact finder the context from which to judge who is lying and who is telling the truth.

It is particularly ironic that the conservative majority of the high court approved this highly technical exclusionary rule at a time when it is chipping away at the exclusionary rules of the Fourth and Fifth amendments. These constitutionally based rules require the exclusion of evidence secured against citizens by government officials without proper warrant or other legal basis.

Some of the same justices who bemoan the exclusion of relevant evidence when it is the prosecutor who is seeking to introduce evidence against the defendant, seem entirely comfortable with excluding relevant evidence that is offered by the defendant against the prosecutor. These judges argue that citizens should not suffer because the "constable bungled" in gathering the evidence. Why then should the defendant—and, indeed, the truth—suffer because the defendant's lawyer may have bungled? The high court majority did not explain this inconsistency, concluding instead that the lawyer's bungle could indeed "justify even the severe sanction" of excluding otherwise relevant defense evidence.

Justice Sandra Day O'Connor, writing for the majority, concluded that "rape victims deserve heightened protection against surprise. . . ." But that begs the critical question: Was the complainant indeed a "rape victim" as she contended, or was the defendant the victim of a false accusation, as

ALAN M. DERSHOWITZ

he contended? Under our constitutional presumption of innocence, the legal system cannot *assume* the former in justifying a rule of evidence that denies the defendant the right to prove the latter. Since the complainant in this case acknowledged that she and the defendant had a consensual sexual relationship, how could she be "surprised" by the truth emerging at trial?

Justices John Paul Stevens and Thurgood Marshall dissented, arguing that the Sixth Amendment's right to confront one's accuser gives all defendants, even those accused of rape, the right to present all "potentially relevant evidence."

That is how the issue should be framed under the rape shield laws. Evidence that is irrelevant and highly prejudicial, such as the complainant's prior sexual history with other men at other times, should generally not be permitted to divert the jury's attention from the issue of whether this man raped this woman at this time. But technical rules, such as requiring ten days prior notice by the lawyer, should not be permitted to undercut the search for truth. In this case, truth suffered and the defendant was denied a fair trial—for no good reason.   May 1991

EXPLAINING PEE-WEE'S ARREST TO YOUR KIDS

An Associated Press story, following the arrest of Pee-wee Herman for indecent exposure in an adult movie theater, gave the following advice to parents to tell their inquiring children: "He was doing things that were inappropriate. He went to a place that Pee-wee Herman shouldn't have gone to, and he did something wrong."

Thanks for the expert advice, but that is most certainly not what I would tell my child. If a child is old enough to ask what happened to Pee-wee, that child is old enough to be given an important lesson in Americanism and basic liberties.

I would tell my child that in the United States, adults are allowed to do what they want in private as long as it doesn't hurt someone else. The police are not supposed to peek into anyone's bedroom window to see what they are doing in bed. That is what we call privacy. Nor should the police be sneaking into adult movie theaters in order to spy on people and see what they are doing to themselves in the dark.

306 //

I would emphasize to my child that the police often make mistakes and that in this case Pee-wee's friends made the following statement: "According to Paul [Pee-wee's real name], the facts as stated by the vice squad were totally untrue, and he never exposed himself or engaged in any other improper behavior."

I would tell my child that under U.S. law we should believe that Pee-wee is telling the truth unless the police can prove he is lying.

If my child asked me why she can't see Pee-wee on TV anymore, I would tell her that the people who decide what to show on TV don't seem to understand that in the United States we don't conclude that someone is guilty just because the police say he is.

It's never too early to begin educating a child in values. And values include far more than the misguided values of the Sarasota, Fla., vice squad. From what I can gather by reading the news accounts, Pee-wee did nothing wrong—even if the police story is true. Any adult has the right to frequent an adult movie theater. If the police believe that the films shown in the theater are obscene, they have the power to prosecute the theater owner and stop the films from being shown. But the adult theatergoer has done nothing wrong by watching an adult movie.

Nor has he done anything wrong by being sexually aroused by the movie. Indeed, that is a major purpose of these kinds of movies. If you don't think that's true, ask yourself why "triple X-rated" videos are so popular for home rentals.

Will the next step be for police to monitor the home uses to which X-rated films are put? Will TV networks now require their stars to sign pledges concerning their movie tastes and their sex lives?

But Pee-wee was not watching the films in the privacy of his bedroom. He was in a movie theater, which is open to the public. Doesn't that change everything? Certainly not morally! If what Pee-wee was alleged to be doing in the darkness of a movie theater is morally wrong, then it is equally wrong to be doing the same thing in the privacy of one's bedroom. The only real difference is that the "moral offender" is more likely to be caught in the theater than in his home. And surely the moral quality of an act is not measured by whether one is or is not caught.

Indeed, Pee-wee's real sin is that he was caught. In a hypocritical society in which many common practices are criminalized, the real vice is being caught. There is no allegation that Pee-wee hurt, or even offended, anyone. Plainclothes cops, who regularly patrol these theaters in search of masturbators, say they caught him engaging in a "victimless crime."

The only reason he was probably in that theater in the first place is that he was too embarrassed to rent an X-rated movie and bring it home. In that respect the movie theater affords the viewer more privacy than the home rental from a video store that keeps records on who rented what kind of film.

We are moving ever closer to a "Brave New World" kind of society, where there is no zone of privacy in which an individual adult can satisfy his emotional, intellectual, or sexual needs without some record being kept by big government, big business, or big busybody groups. The Pee-wee Herman case is just the tip of a very dangerous iceberg. Let us not teach our children to become accustomed to Big Brother and Big Sister accusing us of "doing things" that they deem inappropriate. Let us instead use the Pee-wee Herman case to educate our children about the right of privacy, the limitations of government, and the presumption of innocence.

August 1991

FACING THE ACCUSER: IS THE SMITH TRIAL FAIR?

As the complaining witness in the William Kennedy Smith rape trial was examined by the prosecutor and cross-examined by the defense attorney, the six jurors were looking at her face for clues to her credibility. If and when Smith takes the witness stand, the jurors will be examining his face for similar clues. Yet the rest of us—the millions of citizens who are watching part or all of the proceedings on television—are being denied the opportunity to observe the face of the complaining witness as she testifies.

While watching her direct testimony on television, I very much wanted to see her facial gestures as she cried, as she accused Smith of raping her, and as she said she did not recall important events leading up to the encounter. I could not begin to decide for myself whether I believed all or part of her story, whether her crying was genuine or rehearsed, and whether she honestly did not remember or was making a calculated effort to minimize the damage from her failure to include some details in her prior police statements.

I was relegated to reading newspaper accounts describing how "the woman looked directly at the prosecutor," how "occasionally she looked at the jury," and how "once" she looked "directly at Mr. Smith, as if to fortify herself for what she had to say." These secondhand descriptions are a poor substitute for firsthand observations.

I understand the accuser's desire for anonymity, but that understandable personal desire is outweighed by the public's right to assess her credibility. Ironically, everyone in Palm Beach knows who she is. Her name has appeared in local newspapers, in the *New York Times*, and on NBC national news. Everyone who enters the courtroom—and any citizen is entitled to attend the public trial, subject of course to space limitations—can see her face and hear her name. I believe that anyone who accuses another person of a serious crime loses their anonymity in an open democratic society. The identity of the accuser is extremely relevant information in assessing his or her credibility. So is the identity of the accused. This is especially so where, as in this case, the accuser's family has allegedly had a long-term grudge against the accused's family.

But even if I am wrong about disclosing the name of the accuser, the argument for allowing the television-watching public to see her face during direct and cross-examinations is even more compelling. There is something markedly unfair about the television camera masking the face of the accuser as she testifies while focusing on the face of the accused as he reacts to her testimony.

William Kennedy Smith is on trial before two juries. One is in the courtroom itself. The other is in the courtroom of public opinion. Both are important to the defendant as well as to his accuser. As Smith commented before the trial began, whatever the jury's verdict, half of the American public will probably believe that he is a rapist. In our country, the citizens are allowed to form their own opinions about guilt or innocence. We are not bound by jury verdicts or even appellate decisions.

Consider, for example, the Thomas-Hill dispute. The Senate decided in favor of Justice Thomas. Yet a significant number of Americans believe that Professor Hill was telling the truth. In that dispute, we were able to watch both witnesses as they testified to diametrically opposite stories. Would our ability to decide for ourselves have been as great if Professor Hill's face had been blocked by an electronic ball?

The most bizarre news report was on NBC news the night of the accuser's direct testimony. The commentator mentioned the accuser's name a half dozen times. Yet the visual picture showed her face blocked by the ball. Even if NBC decided to show the accuser's facial gestures during her testimony, they could not do so. The reason is that the court ruled that television cameras in the courtroom may not show the accuser's face.

This is government censorship, not an exercise of discretion by the private media.

To be sure, governments do have the power—at least for now—to exclude all television cameras from courtrooms. Does it follow from that power that courts may also restrict the content of what television cameras may transmit? I don't think so. The power to require selective editing of a trial is the power to influence public opinion selectively. It is a dangerous power to give to government and to courts. At the very least, the court should have to find a compelling need for its selective censorship ruling. No such finding was made in the Smith case.

The courtrooms of America are open to the public. The American public has the right to judge for itself who is telling the truth in a highly publicized case. We should be able to see the accuser's face as she testifies against the person she has accused. December 1991

DOES THE SMITH VERDICT MEAN HE'S INNOCENT?

What are we—the legal system, the media, and the general public—to make of the jury's ninety-minute acquittal of William Kennedy Smith after a ten-day trial and forty-five witnesses? The easy answer would be for us to say that the jury merely found that there was a reasonable doubt. But that won't do. This jury seems to have concluded that Smith was innocent and that his accuser's story was false, at least in material respects. Does that mean that Smith should now be regarded as the victim, and his accuser as the perpetrator of a wrong? Or does it reflect the inherent difficulty of successfully prosecuting a date-rape case?

One point seems abundantly clear. There really are some false accusations of date-rape. Although we are all familiar with the important verity that rape, especially date-rape, is the most underreported of serious crimes, we are not as familiar with the equally important reality that rape is also the most overreported of serious crimes. FBI statistics demonstrate that the rate of "unfounded" rape charges is 8.4 percent as compared to unfounded rates of 2 to 3 percent for other violent crimes. That translates to more than eight thousand false rape accusations each year. This should not be surprising in light of the politicization of rape as well as the lack of clarity in the law. Many women today define date-rape differently than many men do, and the law has not resolved this conflict definitively.

For example, in the Smith case, it is certainly possible that the complaining witness believed she was raped but concluded that if she told the whole truth about the circumstances, the jury would have disbelieved her. She may therefore have "improved" the real story—consciously or unconsciously—in order to make it more salable to a jury. I suspect that many actual rape victims feel it necessary to improve their stories because they fear that the jury may refuse to convict if the victim acknowledges that she consented to sexual foreplay, even if they also believe that she said "no" prior to intercourse. That is rape as a matter of law, but many jurors might not so regard it, especially in the absence of "staircasing" of rape charges into more and less aggravated degrees of criminality.

I suspect that the jury in this case found so many holes in the accuser's account that they didn't even focus on the ultimate issue of whether she consented to unprotected intercourse. An accuser cannot win a one-on-one credibility contest if the jury believes she lied about critical elements of her story.

It is interesting to speculate how this case might have come out in the absence of exclusionary rules. The prosecution was denied the right to introduce evidence of alleged prior sexual misconduct by the defendant. And the defense was denied the right to introduce evidence about the complaining witness's prior sexual history. Both sides were shielded from prejudicial information being heard by the jury. Both sides complained that relevant facts were improperly excluded. But the law is correct in narrowly limiting the evidence. The alternative would be a diffuse trial of the backgrounds and characters of the protagonists, rather than a trial focused narrowly on what happened on the night at issue.

We must remember that this was only one jury verdict in one case, though it was the most highly publicized rape case in history. Many people are concerned that the verdict in this case, combined with the Senate confirmation of Clarence Thomas, will send an unfortunate message to victims of rape and sexual harassment. They have a point. Some feminists put too high a stake on these two cases. They were rooting too overtly for the alleged victims to be vindicated. In fact, Anita Hill was vindicated in the court of public opinion (at least by most objective and informed viewers).

The accuser in the Smith case has not been vindicated. One reason for this difference may be that we were able to see Anita Hill's facial expressions during her testimony, while the face of Smith's accuser was hidden behind an electronic ball.

The verdict also raises the question of whether the media was correct in censoring important information—the name and face of the accuser—from the public. It also raises the question of whether the media should continue to protect the identity of a defendant who may well have falsely accused an innocent person of a serious crime.

In the end, the big winner in the Smith case, besides Smith himself, was the American legal system. The public saw a trial judge who was unusually sensitive to the rights of criminal defendants. We also saw a jury that paid close attention to the evidence and rendered a correct judgment on the facts of this case.   December 1991

HOW *NOT* TO TELEVISE TRIALS

For the past twenty years I have been advocating the televising of courtroom proceedings for educational purposes. What I, and many others who share my view, had in mind was a not-for-profit educational production company under the supervision of bar associations and law schools. Such a company would work together with court administrators to assure that court proceedings—trials, appeals, hearings—would be presented in a dignified manner conducive to educating rather than titillating.

Instead we have Court TV, a commercial enterprise run by Steven Brill, who had made a specialty of commercializing the law. His magazine, *The American Lawyer*, has succeeded, almost single-handedly, in turning the practice of law into a crass, bottom-line business. Before the "Brillization" of the law, as it has come to be called, lawyers claimed to be part of a learned profession. We did not always live up to that claim, but at least it was an aspiration. *The American Lawyer* changed all that. Now law firms are ranked not primarily by their professionalism, their ethics, or even their litigation successes. They are ranked by their bottom-line profits.

This kind of crass commercialism is already in evidence from Court TV. In anticipation of the William Kennedy Smith case this past August,

Court TV claimed that it had "exclusive rights" to the trial. It used this misleading claim to solicit subscribers and advertisers at a time when it acknowledged that it was "struggling to get advertising."

Court TV's claim of "exclusive rights" was misleading because the only "right" Court TV had was to be the "pool camera" in the courtroom. Even that limited right has been abused for commercial advantage. In its "raw feed agreement" with local television stations, Court TV demands a per diem payment for "each day of Court TV's coverage of the trial" and requires that the station "will not protest this arrangement . . ." Since Court TV is the sole pool camera, this is an offer that can't be easily refused.

Court TV's goal is to monopolize the television transmission of trials at enormous profit to itself. It brags that it already has exclusive camera rights in more than 80 percent of televised trials, and Brill is trying to parlay these rights into big bucks. As a recent story in the *Boston Herald* concluded: "Brill now says he has received inquiries from cable operators interested in picking up the service. That agreement, however, does not come without a price. The contract between Court TV and a cable operator runs for ten years."

Brill's attempt to monopolize the televising of trials also carries with it significant dangers of censorship. Local stations, even networks, that use the Court TV transmission cannot decide for themselves whether to show the faces or disclose the names of the accusing witnesses in cases like Smith's. The contract in the Smith case required every station to block the face and withhold the name. In a television interview, Steven Brill said it was his decision to censor the name and face of the accuser. Whether this information should or should not be disclosed is a hotly debated issue. But it seems abundantly clear that the decision should be made by each network or station for itself. The decision should not be dictated by Brill as a self-appointed censor for the entire nation. (To be sure, any local station that chose to send its own people to Palm Beach could have picked up the feed directly from the courthouse media center and sent it back home uncensored, but the economic realities make that impossible for most stations, and indeed none, to my knowledge, did it.)

Another great danger of the commercialization of Court TV is that few lawyers are prepared to criticize it publicly. Their reluctance comes from two sources. Brill has a reputation for punishing his critics in the pages of his magazine. He also has a reputation for rewarding those who praise him. I have experienced both the stick and the carrot. Most recently, when I first criticized Court TV for its commercialism, I received two frantic phone calls and a letter inviting me to become one of the Court TV commentators. Since I regarded this invitation as an obvious attempt to "buy off" my criticism, I turned it down.

But now the issue is beyond mere criticisms by lawyers. Several lawsuits are currently before the courts challenging Court TV's commercial exploitation of litigants to sell advertising time. I wonder if Court TV will cover those cases.

The day after the verdict in the Smith case, Steven Brill called me to say that if I continue to criticize Court TV, I will be undercutting my own long-term efforts to bring television cameras into the courtrooms of America. I responded that Brill's warning had confirmed my worst fears, namely that his way of televising trials—selecting the most salacious and atypical ones for maximum commercial exploitation—will be seen as the only way to televise trials. We must come up with a nonprofit educational format for the televising of American legal proceedings.   December 1991

WHEN WOMEN DON'T TELL THE TRUTH

A recent conference about sexual harassment and rape, at which Anita Hill spoke, was entitled "Women Tell the Truth." Of course, most women tell the truth, just as most men do. But some women lie, just as some men do. That is why our legal system demands that all accusations of crime be subjected to the truth-testing mechanisms of confrontation, cross-examination, and proof beyond a reasonable doubt. Our legal system, unlike some others, prefers that ten guilty go free rather than one innocent be wrongly convicted.

When it comes to the serious crime of rape, it appears that both men and women lie, exaggerate, or misremember more often than with other, less emotionally charged, crimes. According to FBI statistics, in 1990, 8.6 percent of all reported forcible rapes were "unfounded" as compared to a figure of 2.3 percent "unfounded" for all violent crime. The data for 1989 was similar. Of course, "unfounded" doesn't necessarily mean fabricated, though a significant number of recent rape accusations have turned out to be made up.

Earlier this month, a Dedham, Massachusetts, woman accused four men of rape. Several days later the charges were dropped because the accuser recanted when approached by the district attorney with inconsistent forensic evidence along with information that she had falsely accused other men. The names of the falsely accused men were published in the press, but the false accuser's name has been withheld.

Last November, St. Paul, Minnesota, police determined that within one week, two reported rapes were false. In the first case, a woman reported being abducted and raped by a man who hid in her car as she gave a talk to a chemical dependency treatment group at a local high school. When police checked the story, they found that the treatment group had never heard of her and that she didn't own a car. In the second case, a sixteen-year-old girl claimed to have been abducted at a downtown bus stop, imprisoned in a closet, and sexually assaulted by a man and his son over a thirty-three-hour period. In reality, the woman had been seen with her boyfriend several times over that thirty-three-hour period and had apparently been bruised by him. In both cases the women gave police detailed descriptions of their attackers and in both cases the alleged assailants were black.

Last year, a seventeen-year-old girl from Washington State accused three twenty-year-old men of holding her down and raping her. Several days after the men were arrested, the woman recanted saying she had made the whole thing up out of spite. In a statement to police, the woman admitted, "When I was leaving, [he] called me a whore and a slut . . . and I became very angry and decided over the weekend that I would get back."

In Rhode Island, a college student reported that her former boyfriend raped her at gun point. She admitted that she made up the entire story after learning that the man she accused was 1,500 miles away at the time.

In New York, a woman who claimed she was raped at gun point was arrested after it was discovered that she had filed eleven false reports of rape.

In Nebraska, a woman was required to broadcast an apology to a man she had falsely accused of raping her in order to "get the attention of her husband."

In Great Britain, a number of highly publicized rape accusations turned out to be false. A nineteen-year-old woman from Lincolnshire accused her former boyfriend of raping her after she spent the night with a different man. A jilted nurse falsely accused her former lover of beating her and also falsely accused his best friend of raping her. After analyzing several such cases, Angela Lambert, a British journalist, concluded that there are "plenty of reasons why a woman might falsely accuse a man of rape." She went on to argue that "The belief that all women are truthful and all men are rapists does not prove us good feminists; quite the contrary. It reveals us as prejudiced, narrow-minded, and as bigoted as any racist."

The tragic reality that rape is the most underreported of crimes must not blind us to the equally important reality that rape is also the most falsely reported of crimes. Moreover, "acquaintance" or "date" rape is an area in which differing perceptions may produce inadvertently false testimony about actions that may well fall into the gray area between aggressive seduction and criminal sexual assault. When it comes to sexual encounters, both men and women often "remember" differently from what a videotape would show. The truth-testing mechanisms of our criminal justice system must not be compromised in the service of some "politically correct" nonsense that when it comes to rape only women always tell the truth.   May 1992

For additional information see The Washington Post *article*, Unfounded Reports of Rape Confound Area Police Investigators—*June 27, 1992*.

OBSERVATIONS OF AN AMERICAN JEW

Part Five

12 // European Anti-Semitism

EUROPE'S ENDURING ANTI-SEMITISM

Among the questions I am asked most frequently is, "How can you explain the persistence of anti-Semitism, even after the Holocaust?" My reluctant answer is, "I can't." Nor do I believe that a single explanation is possible. Like other persistent forms of hate, anti-Semitism is largely irrational. But there are clearly some factors that encourage and legitimate this most persistent of bigotries. Primary among these is the refusal of many important leaders and role models to condemn anti-Semitism forthrightly, consistently, and credibly. Indeed, many leaders have themselves said and done things that, whether deliberately or inadvertently, have led their followers to believe that they are legitimating anti-Semitic attitudes and failings. A few cases in point.

During a recent electoral campaign in Poland, Lech Walesa stated that he was "100 percent Polish," while at the same time appealing to Jews in public positions to "reveal themselves," and while his supporters spread rumors that his chief rival, Tadeusz Mazowiecki, was a "secret Jew." After being told that he had invoked an old Polish stereotype—that "secret" Jews wielded disproportionate power—Walesa apologized. But the damage had been done. Several months earlier, the Primate of Poland, Joseph Cardinal Glemp, had publicly accused Jews of "plying [Polish] peasants with alcohol" and of "spreading communism." In so doing, Glemp echoed similar accusations made by his predecessors, Cardinals Wyszinski and Hlond.

In Germany, Helmut Kohl accused Jewish leaders of trying to derail the reunification of Germany, thus invoking the canard of undue Jewish power and dual loyalty.

Yassir Arafat, the influential head of the Palestinian Liberation Organization, described *Jews*—not Israelis—as "filthy," "dogs," and "dirt."

Even here in the United States, President George Bush attacked Jewish-Americans who had lobbied their elected representatives in support of loan guarantees for Israel. The president complained that he was "up against powerful forces" and that "there were something like a thousand lobbyists on the Hill working the other side of the question. We got one little lonely guy down here doing it." Bush, like Walesa, ultimately apologized after realizing that he had invoked a dangerous stereotype. But again, the damage had been done, and it is difficult to put the genie of bigotry back in the bottle once it has been let out.

I cannot explain the underlying causes of anti-Semitism because they are varied and because they often reflect deep-rooted psychological pathology. (That is why I prefer the term *Judeopathy* to *anti-Semitism*.) But I think I know the one step that could contribute, perhaps more than any other, to its delegitimization: unequivocal and repeated condemnation by all important national and international leaders. That is why the strong statements made by recent popes, as contrasted with earlier popes, have been so important. That is why I and others tried so hard to persuade Mikhail Gorbachev to denounce anti-Semitism while he was the ruler of the Soviet Union (see page 329). And that is why all people of goodwill—Jews and non-Jews alike—must continue to persuade our leaders that being "soft" on anti-Semitism is both wrong and dangerous.   July 1992

OLD ANTI-SEMITISM TAINTS "NEW" POLAND

It is a historical irony that Poland's first act of independence from communism, the selection of a Solidarity prime minister, reflected old-fashioned Eastern European anti-Semitism.

The obvious choice for prime minister was Solidarity's chief parliamentarian Bronislaw Geremek. Indeed, initial reports were that he had, in fact, been selected. But then quite suddenly, his name disappeared and another emerged: that of the relatively unknown Tadeusz Mazowiecki, who was not even a member of Parliament.

Geremek, it is said, was vetoed at least in part because he was born Jewish. Joseph Cardinal Glemp, the Polish primate and lifelong supporter of Endicja, a virulently anti-Semitic Polish nationalist party, had pushed for Mazowiecki's selection on the ground that Mazowiecki would be more subject to the influence of the church. Cardinal Glemp has more than once denounced Solidarity for being infiltrated with Jews and people "devoid of Christian ethics."

It is a sad reality that a candidate's Jewish background is still a disqualification in the new Poland, which continues to suffer from one of the oldest forms of bigotry. As *Newsweek* put it, even a rumor of one's Jewish roots constitutes "a handicap in a nation where anti-Semitism still runs deep."

Moreover, much of the anti-Semitism emanates from elements within the Polish Catholic church itself. For example, when forty-two Jewish survivors of the Holocaust were murdered in the town of Kielce in 1946, more than a year after the Germans had left, Stefan Wyszynski, then bishop of Lublin and soon to be primate of the Polish church, refused to condemn the killings. He instead proclaimed that the Jews themselves had "quite understandably" turned the people against them. He also declared that it was still "undetermined" whether Jews engaged in "ritual murder" of Christians.

Then in the 1950s and 1960s, the church stood by silently as the small Jewish remnants of the Holocaust were pressured into leaving Poland. More recently, Father Jozef Tischner, the acknowledged spiritual leader of Solidarity, has told his flock that "the Israelite" will "one day be placed in the dock" for "the crime of deicide."

Solidarity is an uncomfortable amalgam of diverse strands within Poland. It unites intellectuals who truly crave freedom, clerics who prefer the authoritarianism of the church to the totalitarianism of the Communist party, workers who seek better wages, and nationalists who desire independence from Soviet hegemony.

The victory of Solidarity over communism is a welcome development for all freedom-loving people. But there are still battles to be fought *within* Solidarity. Tragically, the first such battle—for the office of prime minister—seems to have been won by the forces of bigotry.

Similar internal battles are taking place in the Baltic states and within Russia itself. Estonia, Latvia, and Lithuania have long traditions of fascism dating from before the Second World War. Many Baltic nationalists welcomed the German occupation of Estonia, Latvia, and Lithuania and worked closely with the SS in carrying out the Nazis' "final solution." Some of the most notorious of these collaborators came to the United States after the war and established nationalist emigre groups, which maintain contact with nationalist groups within the Baltic states.

The World Jewish Congress, after a year-long investigation, has concluded that various Baltic emigre groups have been conducting a campaign "tinged with anti-Semitism" to suppress "the historical fact that Hitler's annihilation of 6 million Jews was carried out not by the Germans alone, but rather with large-scale assistance from Lithuanians, Latvians . . . Estonians, and other Europeans." Though the current nationalist leadership within the Baltics appears to be welcoming some Jews into the movement, it is important to monitor developments in order to assure that there is no revival of the kind of fascist ultranationalism that led to the atrocities of World War II.

In Russia itself, one of the first manifestations of glasnost was the emergence of anti-Semitic organizations such as Pamyat. Indeed, the first public mass protest rally permitted in Moscow, under the new freedom, was held by Pamyat on May 6, 1987, in front of Moscow City Hall. One of the Soviet "officials" who received the Pamyat delegation was Boris Yeltsin, the popular Moscow reform leader. Although Yeltsin later said he was "appalled" at the group's anti-Semitism, he proposed that it be accorded legal status.

Natan Scharansky, who served nine years as a Soviet political prisoner, has recognized the "dilemma of freedom" in the Soviet Union: "As soon as glasnost . . . provided an opportunity for more freedom of expression, we could witness the rapid growth of Pamyat and similar ultranationalistic, reactionary, and anti-Semitic mass organizations."

That is the paradox of the new freedom in parts of the world where old prejudices persist. Freedom of expression includes the right to express bigoted views. Freedom of the ballot includes the right to vote one's prejudices.

There is a dark side to the good news from Eastern Europe. It is important to recognize and monitor that dark side, in order to assure that one form of tyranny does not replace another in a part of the world with no real history of tolerance and liberty.   August 1989

AUSCHWITZ DISPUTE SPARKS SLANDER LAWSUIT

Can an American rabbi sue a Polish cardinal for defaming him during a religious homily? That is the intriguing question raised by a sermon Joseph Cardinal Glemp recently delivered in Czestochowa, Poland. During the course of his remarks to 150,000 Polish Catholics, Cardinal Glemp accused Rabbi Avraham Weiss and several other "Jews from New York" of seeking to kill Catholic nuns in a convent at Auschwitz.

The background of this grave accusation grows out of a long-standing dispute over the location of the convent, established in 1984. It is situated in the building that had stored the poison gas used to murder millions of Jewish men, women, and children during the Holocaust. Fund-raising literature for the convent suggested that the Auschwitz nuns were praying for the "conversion" of the Jews. This enraged many Jewish leaders, who claimed that the placement of a Catholic convent at the site of the greatest tragedy in Jewish history was insensitive to the unique suffering experienced by Jews solely because they were Jews. Jewish leaders also pointed to a 1972 United Nations Convention that includes Auschwitz among historical sites that must not be disturbed.

In 1987, a formal agreement was reached between Jewish leaders and several Catholic cardinals. The agreement provided for the erection of a Jewish-Christian dialogue center outside the gates of Auschwitz and the relocation of the convent to that center by February 1989.

When that deadline passed, several Jewish leaders protested. Among them was Rabbi Avraham Weiss of Riverdale, N.Y. Along with six students, he engaged in a peaceful "pray-in" at the convent: After being refused admission, the group climbed the fence, put on their prayer shawls, and began to pray. They were attacked by bystanders, beaten, sprayed with water, and carried away, amid anti-Semitic shouts of "Heil Hitler" and "Rip off their skullcaps!"

It was this incident that formed the basis for the following statement made by Cardinal Glemp: "Recently a squad of seven Jews from New York launched attacks on the convent at Auschwitz. In fact, it did not happen that the sisters were killed or the convent destroyed, because they were apprehended."

As *Newsweek* magazine reported, Glemp's statement was "against all the evidence." But it was widely believed by an audience all too eager to place the blame on "aggressive Jews." Glemp also accused the Jews of fomenting anti-Semitism and of being an aloof people who control the international news media. The speech was all too reminiscent of the kind of primitive bigotry that had caused violence against Jews throughout Polish history.

Rabbi Weiss was outraged by the cardinal's false accusation. It was not his intention to harm the nuns or damage the convent, but rather to conduct Jewish prayers on what he regarded as a sacred Jewish burial ground.

Whether he was right or wrong in trespassing on the grounds of a convent is beside the point. He clearly would not have "killed" anyone if he had not been "apprehended."

Falsely accusing someone of intending murder is defamation both under Polish and American law. Clerics—even cardinals—are not above the law. Accordingly, Rabbi Weiss has decided to sue Cardinal Glemp for defamation, both in Poland and in the United States. He has asked me to serve as his lawyer, and I am in the process of researching the relevant law.

As it turns out, Cardinal Glemp is scheduled to be in the United States during the last half of September. This makes it far easier to sue him here. If he can be served with a complaint while in an American state, he can be sued there, provided that his defamatory comments were foreseeably published in that state. Since Cardinal Glemp had to know that so provocative a charge would make front-page international news, he can be sued virtually anywhere he can be found.

Rabbi Weiss will probably be deemed a "public figure," and so he will have to prove that Cardinal Glemp knew, or should have known, that his statements were false when he made them. This will not be difficult to prove, considering the fact that virtually all the media in Poland had reported that Rabbi Weiss had engaged in a peaceful "pray-in."

Cardinal Glemp chose to level his accusation "against all the evidence." That constitutes "malice" under American law.

This is not a lawsuit by "the Jews" against "the Catholics" or "the Polish people." It is a suit by one individual against another. Indeed, virtually every Catholic church leader who has spoken about Cardinal Glemp's statement has condemned it. To emphasize this point, we have obtained the legal assistance of several Polish Catholic lawyers in our lawsuit.

In the end, suits alone cannot resolve historic conflicts such as those surrounding the convent at Auschwitz or the broader issues of Polish-Jewish relationships. But a rabbi who has been defamed by a cardinal has legal rights under the law. Rabbi Weiss's decision to invoke these rights may break new ground in the law of defamation.   September 1989

AUSCHWITZ NUN REVEALS ANTI-SEMITIC VIEWS

Amid the continuing furor over the Carmelite convent at Auschwitz, there is one group that, up until now, has not been heard from.

The nuns themselves, who pray for the souls of those murdered at Auschwitz, have been portrayed as helpless pawns in the struggle between Catholic and Jewish leaders. They were not consulted when the Catholic and Jewish leaders agreed, back in 1987, to move the convent into an interfaith center outside the gates of the Auschwitz death camp.

They were not consulted when the Vatican reaffirmed that agreement recently. They were victimized when a New York rabbi and six students conducted a pray-in at the convent. They were again victimized when the Polish Primate Joseph Cardinal Glemp used them as an excuse for leveling his baseless anti-Semitic accusation that the rabbi had come to Poland intending to murder the nuns.

Now for the first time, the Mother Superior of Carmelite Sisters of Auschwitz, Sister Teresa, has given an interview to a friendly reporter. And what she told him is certain to ignite yet another firestorm of controversy between Jewish Holocaust survivors and those Polish Catholics who insist that the nuns should remain at Auschwitz.

Sister Teresa's interviewer was Col. Francis A. Winiarz, a retired psychologist with the U.S. Air Force and now active in Polish-American affairs. His interview was published in a Polish-American weekly called *The Post Eagle*, which editorializes in favor of the nuns remaining at Auschwitz.

Among other things, Sister Teresa is quoted as asking, "Why do the Jews want special laws and treatment in Auschwitz only for themselves? Why don't they realize that the best arrangement for everyone would be if each religion built its own temple of prayer? Do they still consider themselves the chosen people?"

She accuses "the Jews" of "creating such a disturbance for us." She denies that there was any Polish anti-Semitism before World War II, pointing to the "fact" that "the Jews were an insignificant minority group in Poland with a majority of privileges." She accuses Israel of anti-Semitism for "mistreating the Arabs." As she put it, "Greater anti-Semites are hard to find" than the Israelis.

Sister Teresa then proceeds to place virtually the entire blame for communism and for the failure of the Polish economy on the Jews. According to the interviewer, she believes that after World War II "the entire Polish government consisted of 75 percent Polish Communist Jews, appointed by Joseph Stalin, with the specific intention to introduce atheism into Poland."

She goes on to list all "the Jews" who had run Poland after World War II. The story says, "According to Sister Teresa, following World War II, the fate of the Polish economy was in the hands of Henry Minc, a Jew. Military affairs minister was Jacob Bermann, another Jew. . . . The minister of defense was Marian Spyhalski, a Jew. . . . Another Jew was the president of Poland prior to Wojciech Jaruzelski. His name? Heinric Grunbaum, changed to Henryk Jankowski."

It turns out that the first two were in fact born Jewish, though neither practiced that faith. The second two were not Jewish in any sense of that term, except perhaps under Nazi racial laws, which traced a person's "blood" back several generations. The entire enterprise of listing the Jews who were "prototype Bolsheviks" goes back to Adolf Hitler's days.

In fact, the tiny Jewish population of Poland, the remnant of the Holocaust, suffered terribly under Stalin—a reality not mentioned by Sister Teresa in her interview.

Tragically, Sister Teresa's bill of particulars against "the Jews" is not all that unusual among elements of the Polish clergy. While some Polish priests—most particularly Cardinal Macharski of Krakow and his predecessor in that role, the pope himself—have been trying to diffuse tensions between the Catholic and Jewish religions, these bridge-builders have been sabotaged at every turn by some local Polish clerics who insist on repeating old anti-Semitic canards.

Sister Teresa ended her interview with the following message of defiance: "You can tell the Americans that we are not moving a single inch." And she also said: "Let the Jews understand that the prayers of the Carmelite nuns are also offered for the souls of those victims who were also of the Jewish persuasion."

But many Jews will not understand and accept the prayers of an unreconstructed anti-Semite like Sister Teresa. Her ignorant bigotry about the Jewish role in Communist domination of Poland, her gratuitous accusation that it is harder to find "greater anti-Semites" than the Israelis, and her insulting reference to the "chosen people" are all the hallmarks of traditional anti-Semites.

I hope that Sister Teresa does not speak for the other good sisters of the Auschwitz convent, but as the mother superior, her views cannot be ignored. Those who murdered the Jews at Auschwitz were yesterday's anti-Semites. We do not need—or want—one of today's anti-Semites to pray "for the souls of those victims who were also of the Jewish persuasion."

Let Sister Teresa pray for her own bigoted soul. God knows she needs it.   November 1989

ANTI-SEMITISM RISES IN EASTERN EUROPE

WARSAW, Poland—I was in Auschwitz, nearing the end of a recent visit to several Eastern European nations, when I learned of the barbaric desecration of the bodies and graves of Jews in France. I was not surprised, after what I had learned during my trip about the resurgence of anti-Semitism in Europe.

I began my journey in Leningrad on the Saturday that Pamyat, an anti-Semitic organization, had scheduled a pogrom against Leningrad's Jews. I went to the synagogue and discovered a group of terrified Jews. One of Pamyat's leaders had just called for another "final solution" to the Jewish Problem and had prophesied "Russia would be the one to eliminate" the evil of world Jewry. Nor does Pamyat accept emigration as a possible solution. They demand that Jews remain in Russia to be punished for "their crimes."

There was no pogrom that Saturday, but the Jews of Leningrad remain frightened for their future as Pamyat seems to be striking a responsive chord not only among the Soviet riffraff but also among Russian intellectuals.

From Leningrad I flew to Bucharest, Romania, where my hotel room overlooked the student demonstrations in University Square. There are hardly any Jews left in Romania, but there, too, a Jewish issue has emerged.

ALAN M. DERSHOWITZ

I met with one of the leaders of the National Salvation Front, Professor Silviu Brucan. Brucan had stood up to Nicolae Ceausescu and had been arrested by the dictator. Following Ceausescu's execution, he was running for the legislature. One of his opponents, the vice president of the National Christian Peasants Party, had been a member of the Nazi Iron Guard during World War II. His party "exposed" Brucan's Jewish ancestry, by plastering posters with Stars of David superimposed on his quoted words.

Brucan eventually had to resign from his position as a member of his party's Executive in order to avoid hurting the party in the election. The former Nazi proudly retains his post as vice president of his party. In post-Ceausescu Romania, it is apparently better politics to have a Nazi background than a Jewish one.

From Bucharest I flew to Prague, where President Vaclav Havel has repeatedly condemned anti-Semitism. There is virtually no trace of anti-Semitism in the Czech portion of his country, but it is rampant in Slovakia, where nationalistic parties praise Hitler for having established an "independent" Slovakian government during the Nazi occupation.

I then drove on to Poland, the unmarked gravesite of more than 4 million Jewish men, women, and children who were gassed and burned in Auschwitz, Treblinka and Sobibor. The Primate of Poland, Cardinal Joseph Glemp, last year accused the Jewish survivors of the Holocaust of introducing communism into Poland. He also accused the "Jews" of introducing vodka. When the Solidarity newspaper gently criticized Glemp for his choice of words, there was an outcry against the paper for "supporting the Jews." A Polish Catholic reporter for the Solidarity newspaper told me, sadly, that "Cardinal Glemp speaks for the majority of Polish Catholics on the Jewish issue."

I learned that a prominent right-wing professor had recently expressed concern that "presently Jews are beginning to dominate in the Polish political establishment and in the editorial staffs of many newspapers," despite the reality that there are probably only a few hundred Jews under the age of 70 left in all of Poland. Another right-winger raised the specter of the Auschwitz crematoriums when he said that "each of us would happily roast one Michnik on a grill." Adam Michnik, an assimilated Jew, is a former dissident who went to prison for his courageous opposition to Communist Party chief Wojciech Jaruselski and had been a longtime adviser to Lech Walesa. Now even Walesa has begun to attack Michnik and another adviser with a Jewish background as "pluralists and intellectuals"—code words in Poland for Jews.

One of the most striking aspects of the visit to the new Eastern Europe is how much the people seem to be preoccupied with Jews. Considering the fact that in Poland, Czechoslovakia, and Romania there remain fewer than 25,000 Jews—out of a prewar population of nearly 5 million—it is remarkable that so much attention is paid to them. As one commentator recently observed, there is "only one issue: Are you pro- or anti-Jew?"

It is remarkable that nearly a half-century after the Holocaust, this obsession with the Jews persists, especially in parts of the world where they were murdered to the point of near extinction.

Anti-Semitism also exists in the West, as evidenced by the desecration in France. The difference is that President François Mitterand immediately condemned the desecrations. In Poland, Cardinal Glemp and Lech Walesa have remained sinfully silent as have the leaders in Romania. Even President Gorbachev has limited his criticism to one vague comment against anti-Semitism "and all other 'isms.' " Only in Czechoslovakia has President Havel done the right thing.

The United States has extended Most Favored Nation status to Czechoslovakia, but has withheld it from Romania, Poland, and the Soviet Union. We should continue to withhold trade benefits from any country whose leaders have not forcefully condemned recent and primitive manifestations of the world's most persistent bigotry.   May 1990

COME TO THE SYNAGOGUE, PRESIDENT GORBACHEV

On September 19, 1990, President Mikhail Gorbachev will convene the first Moscow Conference on Law and Bilateral Economic Relations in the Kremlin Palace. More than two thousand American and Soviet lawyers, judges, and government officials will be meeting to discuss a range of legal and economic issues of mutual concern to both of our nations.

I have been asked to speak on the pressing issue of "how freedom of speech can be reconciled with the need to protect ethnic and national minorities against those who would use freedom of speech to stir up repression." Here in the United States, we have worked long and hard on trying to achieve a delicate balance between our First Amendment's guarantee of freedom of speech and our Fourteenth Amendment's guarantee of equal protection of the laws. In general, we have opted for a rather fulsome protection of expression, even when it is offensive to racial, religious, ethnic, and other minorities. But the issue is far from resolved, as evidenced by the recent flurry of restrictions on racist and sexist campus speech.

The problem in the Soviet Union is far more acute and profound. Until recently, there was no freedom of speech. There was also governmental-sponsored bigotry, especially—though not exclusively—anti-Semitism. In 1983, a distinguished international panel of experts concluded, after an extensive review of Soviet publications, that "a wave of anti-Semitism is inspired officially by the Soviet Union, which employs to this end books and all possible media facilities. . . ."

Now we are seeing the beginning of freedom of expression and the cessation of governmental-sponsored anti-Semitism in the Soviet Union. But suddenly putting an end to sanctioned anti-Semitism cannot and has not immediately changed attitudes that were officially instilled in Soviet citizens—and earlier in czarist subjects—for many generations. Anti-Semitism remains rampant throughout Soviet society. It is common in certain intellectual circles, as well as among the masses. *Pravda* itself recently acknowledged that anti-Semitism is growing rapidly, and "it affects the whole of Soviet society and its efforts at political, economic, and social reform."

It should not be surprising, therefore, that when freedom of expression began to emerge in the Soviet Union several years ago, one of the first public demonstrations in Moscow was conducted by Pamyat, an ultranationalistic, anti-Semitic organization whose program calls for an all-out attack on the "dirty Jews, who have infiltrated our society."

I was in Leningrad on May 5, 1990, the day that Pamyat had pledged to conduct a pogrom against the "Yids" who are "plotting the takeover of Russia." Fortunately, no violence took place. But that day in the Leningrad synagogue, I saw many frightened Jews who were frustrated at the freedom being given to Pamyat and other anti-Semitic groups. "Why doesn't the KGB arrest them for what they are saying?" I was repeatedly asked. "There must be limits to freedom of speech," a young Jewish intellectual insisted. I urged the frightened Jews of Leningrad, who I met that day, *not* to call for censorship of Pamyat, but instead to insist that respected government officials—such as President Gorbachev and the Russian Republic president Boris Yeltsin—use their bully pulpits to condemn anti-Semitism publicly and forcefully.

Although President Gorbachev has promised President Bush that he will speak out against anti-Semitism, thus far he has not done so in a manner calculated to have any real impact on Soviet citizens. He has limited himself to vague criticisms, such as his general condemnation of "anti-Semitism and all other 'isms.' " But he has done nothing dramatic to bring the message home.

That is why, when I speak in Moscow during the Conference on Law and Bilateral Economic Relations, I will extend an invitation to President Gorbachev to join me at the Moscow synagogue during the Rosh Hashanah services that week. I will urge him to ascend the pulpit of that venerable old house of worship and use the occasion to condemn anti-Semitism in the most unequivocal of terms. Just as Pope Paul went to the Rome synagogue to declare that he "deplores the hatred, persecutions, and displays of anti-Semitism directed against the Jews at any time and by anyone," President Gorbachev should announce that anti-Semitism has no place in Soviet politics or Soviet life.

The correct answer to bad speech has never been censorship. It has always been *more speech.* In our country, presidents and other high officials have used their bully pulpits effectively to combat bigotry. I hope President Gorbachev, who seems eager to borrow American success stories, will be willing to learn from our long experience in trying to preserve free speech, while at the same time condemning those who use their freedom to threaten vulnerable minorities. Come to the synagogue, President Gorbachev, and condemn anti-Semitism, thereby demonstrating to your people that Soviet Jews are first-class Soviet citizens in the new world of perestroika.

September 1990

WILL GORBACHEV DENOUNCE ANTI-SEMITISM?

While attending a conference in Moscow on law and economics, I had the opportunity to spend several minutes conversing with President Mikhail Gorbachev. The circumstances leading up to this encounter tell as much about the man as does the substance of our conversation.

At the closing dinner of the conference—attended by two thousand delegates—President Gorbachev made an unscheduled appearance. He came directly from an emotional meeting of the Supreme Soviet at which he sought emergency powers to confront the economic crisis. Gorbachev spoke to us for about twenty minutes on the importance of economic cooperation between the United States and the Soviet Union.

The day before this event, I had met with Jewish activists in Moscow who were terrified over the increasing anti-Semitism in Russia. Organizations like Pamyat have threatened violence against the "dirty Jews, who have infiltrated our society." (Jews have lived in Russia for more than a thousand years.) Even some so-called intellectuals have joined the chorus of hate directed against the Soviet Union's most vulnerable minority. The Jewish activists told me that the one dramatic deed that could delegitimate anti-Semitism in the Soviet Union would be a strong public statement by President Gorbachev.

Following my talk with the Jewish activists, I tried to get the conference organizers to vote a resolution urging President Gorbachev to issue a public condemnation of anti-Jewish bigotry. The organizers were reluctant to get involved in this issue despite the fact that several Soviet lawyers had agreed to sign a letter to President Gorbachev about the problem of anti-Semitism.

It was against this background that I saw President Gorbachev beginning his meal at the conference dinner, after finishing his speech. No one was talking to him, so I simply walked up to the dais and asked whether I might have a word with him. I expected to be stopped by security guards, but there were none. President Gorbachev extended his hand and said he would be delighted to talk to me. I introduced myself and told him that he could, by making one statement, do a great deal of good for human rights and for the cause of economic cooperation between our two countries. He asked me what that statement would be, and I told him that he should issue a strong public condemnation of anti-Semitism and of organizations like Pamyat that preach it. He told me that he thought that would be a good idea and asked me what occasion would be most appropriate for such an announcement. As I was beginning to answer, he interjected, "I have an idea. In a few days, I will be meeting with Israeli diplomats. I will use that occasion to make the statements you want."

Gorbachev then added that there were problems of ethnic tensions between many of the ethnic groups that comprise the Soviet Union. I told him that I understood this, but that the problem of anti-Semitism is different because it has been governmental-sponsored for so many years—from the czars, to Stalin, and up to the present time. I told Mr. Gorbachev, on a personal note, that if not for czarist anti-Semitism many of the American lawyers attending the conference might today be Soviet lawyers, had their grandparents not emigrated to America because of Russian anti-Semitism.

Gorbachev smiled and asked whether some of those lawyers would consider coming back and helping rebuild the Soviet Union. I responded that it would be too late for him to get us back, but that he should not make the same mistake with the current generations of Jewish doctors, scientists, lawyers, and other productive Soviet citizens who wish to remain in the Soviet Union and live lives of equality with Russians.

I said that I hoped it would be possible to end the tensions between the Soviet government and the American Jewish community by finally bringing down the curtain on anti-Semitism in the Soviet Union. Gorbachev agreed that this would be a good thing. He asked for my card. I gave it to him and thanked him again.

Now it remains to be seen how strongly and how publicly President Gorbachev condemns the oldest form of bigotry. It will not be easy, because anti-Semitism is good populist politics in the Soviet Union, and Gorbachev needs all the support he can get from the widest array of groups. If he does what he told me he would do, such a statement would go a long way toward ending an evil that threatens both Soviet society and the full cooperation between our countries. If he does not, the tensions will continue. Bridges of cooperation cannot be built securely over the troubled waters of persistent bigotry.

President George Bush recently used his bully pulpit to condemn anti-Arab attitudes among some Americans generated by the Iraqi aggression. I hope that President Gorbachev will follow our president's lead and condemn anti-Jewish attitudes and actions in the Soviet Union.

September 1990

Since my brief meeting with President Gorbachev, he has publicly denounced anti-Semitism saying "The democratic Russian public denounces anti-Semitism and will do everything in its power to uproot the phenomenon from our society." In June 1992, Mikhail Gorbachev visited the State of Israel and was honored for his contributions to Israel, Russian Jewry and the fight against anti-Semitism.

ALAN M. DERSHOWITZ

BE WARY OF INVESTING DOLLARS IN POLAND

Poland's Lech Walesa has been touring the United States urging American businesses to invest in his country. His pitch is not political or emotional. It is economic: Potential investors should send their money to Poland because that would be a sound business decision. "Come to Poland and make money," he urges investors.

But is it now prudent to invest in a country whose *legal* system—whose system of assuring that foreign investors will be protected by the law and treated equally under the law—is in a state of shambles?

Let me relate a recent experience that I had with the Polish legal system. It should give pause to any American business executive considering investing his or her shareholders' money in the Polish economy.

The story begins August 18, 1989, when the Primate of Poland, Joseph Cardinal Glemp, delivered a viciously anti-Semitic attack to a large audience in the Polish city of Czestochowa. In it, he accused "the Jews" of introducing both vodka and communism into Poland, of controlling the international media, and of causing anti-Semitism. He then specifically accused a New York rabbi, who had come to Auschwitz with six of his students to engage in a peaceful sit-in protesting a Catholic convent on the grounds of the death camp, of intending to "kill" the nuns and "destroy" the convent.

The international press featured the story of Cardinal Glemp's speech on its front pages. Every journalist reported that the cardinal's reference to the "squad of Jews from New York" was intended to describe Rabbi Avraham Weiss of Riverdale, N.Y., and his six students. Every journalist, including several who covered the Auschwitz sit-in, also reported that Cardinal Glemp's accusation was entirely false. *Newsweek*, for example, described it as "against all the evidence," and Albert Cardinal De Courtray of Lyon, France, characterized his fellow cardinal's accusation as "pure nonsense."

Rabbi Weiss decided to sue Cardinal Glemp for defamation in Poland. He asked me to be his lawyer. With the assistance of a Polish Catholic lawyer now living in the United States, I filed a lawsuit in the Czestochowa district court, seeking a retraction of Cardinal Glemp's false and defamatory statements. My Polish-American friend and I also tried to get local counsel in Poland. We were prepared to pay American legal fees, which far exceed Polish legal fees.

Several lawyers expressed an interest, and we initially retained a prominent lawyer (who has since become a leading member of the Solidarity government). He told us that the case was a clear one, and that "under the law you must win," since Cardinal Glemp's statement was so obviously false. Several days later this lawyer and his wife called us trembling with fear and weeping. They had been threatened with severe recriminations if he continued to serve as our lawyer. "Our professional and personal lives would be destroyed," he apologized. We asked him to recommend another Polish lawyer, but he assured us that after what he had been threatened with, no Polish lawyer would be willing to help us. His prediction was correct. Our requests to the Polish Bar Association, the courts, and individual attorneys all fell on deaf ears.

Without a local Polish lawyer, the courts gave us a run-around, reminiscent of the way Northern civil rights lawyers were treated in the South during the 1950s and 1960s. Eventually, the district court rendered a decision dismissing our lawsuit without a trial on the ground that there was no proof that Cardinal Glemp was referring to Rabbi Weiss and his six students when he levied his false accusations against the "squad of seven Jews from New York." There had, of course, been no other "squad" of Jews from New York other than Rabbi Weiss's, and every journalist had reported that Glemp was, of course, referring specifically to Rabbi Weiss. Our Polish-American lawyer was embarrassed by the decision, which he characterized as the product of "pressure from outside" rather than a correct application of Polish law.

That, in a nutshell, is the current state of Polish justice when it comes to outsiders suing insiders. There is no reason to be confident that the attitude would be much different in a commercial dispute, pitting Americans against locals. If outside pressure can successfully be brought to bear on the courts in one kind of case against an influential insider, it can be brought to protect local interests in other kinds of cases as well.

In his recent round of pitches for investment, Lech Walesa said he will ask all visiting Americans: "Did you do any business here? And if they say no, they will be asked, why not?"

If American businesses are asked, "Why not?" they should point to the sad state of the Polish judiciary and ask in return what assurances they can be given that they won't be treated the way their fellow American, Rabbi Weiss, was. Unless there is a persuasive answer to that question, American businesses should be very wary of investing American dollars in Poland.   March 1991

ALAN M. DERSHOWITZ

A CARDINAL COPS A PLEA

For the first time in recent history, a cardinal of the Catholic church has retracted and apologized for an anti-Semitic statement he made. The statement was made by Joseph Cardinal Glemp, primate of the Polish Catholic church, in a homily he delivered to a crowd of 150,000 Catholics in the Polish city of Czestochowa on August 26, 1989.

In that homily, Cardinal Glemp accused "the Jews" of "spreading Communism," of "plying [Polish] peasants with alcohol," of "collaborating" with the Nazis, and of controlling the world's "mass-media." He accused the Jews of deliberately "provoking" anti-Semitism in Poland, and claimed that without such provocation "there would also not be any anti-Semitism" in Poland.

The cardinal, who has a long history of anti-Semitic utterances, then accused a Jewish rabbi from Riverdale, N.Y., of coming to Poland to murder nuns and destroy a convent. In fact, Rabbi Avraham Weiss and six of his students had engaged in a peaceful pray-in at a Catholic convent that had recently been established on the grounds of the Auschwitz death camp, where a million and a half Jews and 75,000 Polish Catholics were killed. Rabbi Weiss was protesting the establishment of a Catholic convent on what he considered a place of Jewish martyrdom. Whether one agrees or disagrees with the protest, there is no doubt that it was peaceful. Yet this is how Cardinal Glemp described it in his homily: "Recently a squad of seven Jews from New York launched attacks on the convent at Auschwitz. In fact, it did not happen that the sisters were killed or the convent destroyed, because they were apprehended."

Newsweek reported that Glemp's statement was "against all the evidence." And Albert Cardinal Decourtray of Lyon, France, denounced it as "pure nonsense," as did several other church leaders. But it was widely believed by an audience all too eager to place the blame on "Jews from New York," and to accept the fantasy that a rabbi would kill helpless nuns.

As soon as Cardinal Glemp's defamatory comments were published on the front page of the *New York Times*, Rabbi Weiss called me and asked me to represent him in a defamation action against the cardinal. "He slandered me, as well as the entire Jewish people—and he cannot be allowed to get away with doing that," the rabbi said with a mixture of sadness and anger. "The Polish people have to be told that the cardinal's statements are untrue. Accusing me and the students of wanting to kill the nuns is a modern-day version of the blood libel."

Working together with a Polish Catholic lawyer, we filed a lawsuit in Poland against Cardinal Glemp charging him with defaming Rabbi Weiss. We did not seek monetary or punitive damages but rather a retraction and an apology.

At about the same time that we were filing our lawsuit in Poland, Cardinal Glemp announced that he would be making his first trip to the United States. I wrote the cardinal a letter, telling him that unless he retracted his false statement, we would sue him in an American court for libel, since his defamation against Rabbi Weiss was published in American newspapers. Cardinal Glemp immediately postponed his trip to America. Now he is planning to visit this country in late September. We again demanded a retraction. This time it was forthcoming.

Cardinal Glemp issued a statement in which he admitted that he now "understands that seven members of the Jewish community who disturbed the peace of the Carmelite sisters . . . did not intend to kill the sisters or to destroy the convent." He then said, "I am not anti-Semitic." But he failed to retract the other bigoted statements he had made about "the Jews."

The cardinal's limited retraction was clearly in the nature of a plea bargain. It was designed to be the minimum necessary to get us to drop our lawsuit, but it certainly did not reflect repentance on the part of a sinner who was admitting his sin with a repentant heart.

We have not yet decided whether to drop the lawsuit or continue with it. That will depend on whether Cardinal Glemp's retraction is published in Polish and throughout Poland. It is important that the Polish people learn that their primate has admitted that he misled them when he accused the rabbi of coming to Poland to kill the nuns.

Even if we do decide to drop the lawsuit, that will not make Cardinal Glemp welcome in our country. He has still not retracted, nor apologized for, his bigoted statements about "the Jews" being responsible for communism, alcoholism, and even anti-Semitism. It would be a tragedy if good and great Catholic leaders, who have done so much to build bridges between American Jews and Catholics, were to welcome Cardinal Glemp without first demanding that he retract all of his anti-Semitic statements, not just those upon which the lawsuit is based.   August 1991

Soon after Cardinal Glemp's public admission regarding the protest at the convent at Auschwitz, he repeated to a reporter his belief that Jews were responsible for "plying [Polish] peasants with alcohol" and "spreading Communism." Cardinal Glemp explained that these accusations were supported by history and sociology: "go ahead and research it." In part as a result of these statements we proceeded with our lawsuit and served the Cardinal with a Summons and Complaint during his visit to the United States in the Fall of 1991. The lawsuit was eventually dismissed when a Federal Judge found that the Cardinal had not been properly served. Rabbi Weiss intends to serve him again on his next visit to the United States.

FAIR PUNISHMENT FOR LITHUANIANS' CRIMES

The recent decision of the newly independent Lithuanian government to "rehabilitate" defendants who were convicted by Soviet Communist courts of having committed Nazi atrocities during World War II poses a terrible conflict for all people who care about justice and civil liberties. It is a conflict between the unmitigated evil of Communist injustice and the unparalleled evil of massive Lithuanian complicity in Hitler's genocide.

No reasonable person can dispute either of the following historical facts: (1) the Communist system of "justice" imposed by Stalin on Lithuania following the end of Hitler's occupation of the Baltics was anything but just; (2) that large numbers of Lithuanian citizens eagerly participated in—and often instigated—brutal mass murders of Jewish babies, grandparents, and ordinary Jews who had been living peacefully in Lithuania for hundreds of years.

After the war ended, thousands of Lithuanians were convicted of complicity in Hitler's murders. Thousands of others who were guilty of atrocities escaped—many to the United States. Many of the killers have confessed their guilt. A few were tried by American courts or by tribunals whose fairness is not open to serious question. But the vast majority were tried by Stalin's "courts of terror," as Telford Taylor, America's chief prosecutor at Nuremberg, has denominated them.

What is Lithuania now to do with the thousands of mass murderers whose guilt was determined by an unjust legal system? To complicate matters further, some of these convicted killers are now regarded as Lithuanian heroes because they fought against the Communists—no matter that they sided with the Nazis and murdered innocent Jewish civilians in the process! Thus, the decision of the new Lithuanian government to pardon and rehabilitate these killers has generally been greeted favorably in Lithuania. But much of the rest of the world has reacted with horror to the blanket rehabilitation program.

There is a middle ground that should satisfy all sides, at least in theory. The judgment of each convicted Nazi collaborator should be reviewed again. All the available evidence should be placed before a fair tribunal, which would then decide whether the totality of the evidence warrants relief. The relief could take several forms. Those defendants who now seem to have been victims of mistaken identification or false testimony should be rehabilitated. Those defendants who may well be guilty but whose guilt is now difficult to establish because of the passage of time should be given a document that attests to the lack of sufficient evidence, but not one that declares them innocent. And those defendants whose guilt is clear should be declared guilty anew by the current tribunal.

Consider, for example, the case of Jusozas Krasiskas who was recently rehabilitated. A Jewish woman named Riva Bogomalnaya has provided the new Lithuanian government with extensive documentary evidence that Krasiskas was in charge of the mass killings in her village of Egirdonys, during which many of her relatives were murdered. Ms. Bogomalnaya claims that the Lithuanian authorities did not seem interested in her evidence: "No one calls," she was quoted as saying. "They laugh at us. . . . In another five years, it may be impossible to have a trial for a man like this. . . . The truth is easy enough to find, but people here don't want to find it."

I had an experience that corroborated the new government's apparent lack of interest in finding out the truth. I was visited recently by Mr. Vidmantas Povilionis, a deputy of the Lithuanian Parliament. He was in the United States meeting with human rights advocates. During our discussion, he told me that he was planning to meet with various Lithuanian-American groups in various cities throughout the United States. I cautioned him to be careful of certain individuals in some of these groups who are known to be Nazi sympathizers and supporters of Nazi war criminals. His response was that his government had decided to "forgive" all former Nazis. When I asked why, he said that it was part of an evenhanded decision also to forgive the Jews who had collaborated with the Communists. I was struck by his singling out of the tiny number of Jews who had survived the Holocaust and the even smaller number who had collaborated with the

Communists. Why did he not mention the vastly larger number of non-Jews who had collaborated with Stalin? And how could he equate the admitted evils of postwar communism with the genocide of 200,000 Lithuanian Jews?

It seemed to me then—and it seems to me now—that there is insufficient passion among many in the new Lithuanian government for the fair prosecution of Nazi criminals.

Public pressure from the world now seems to be driving the Landsbergis government toward a more selective use of rehabilitation. It has now agreed to work with the Israeli and the U.S. governments to make individualized determination of guilt or innocence. The memories of the victims of the Holocaust and the dictates of due process demand no less.

September 1991

Since May 2, 1990 when the Landsbergis government began rehabilitating those convicted of resisting "the occupying regime," almost 23,000 convicts have been rehabilitated. However, more than 600 appeals for rehabilitation have been rejected because evidence was found linking these convicts to war crimes committed during World War II. Many survivors are still critical of the softness of the Lithuanian government on Nazi crimes.

13 // *Embattled Israel*

THE CASE FOR EMBATTLED ISRAEL

I am constantly amazed when I hear "hawkish" American conservatives—whether they be President Bush, Patrick Buchanan, or James Baker—condemning Israel for doing exactly what they urge the United States to do in relation to perceived enemies, both foreign and comestic. Israel is a truly embattled democracy surrounded by real enemies sworn to its destruction. The United States, on the other hand, is the strongest nation on earth, yet we waged preemptive war on Grenada, Panama, and Kuwait—to focus only on very recent events. We *always* resolve doubts and ambiguities in favor of our own protection, broadly defined. We *always* err on the side of protecting the lives of our own soldiers, regardless of the risks to enemy soldiers or innocent civilians, and I am not criticizing these policies. All nations, even the most compassionate, act in this manner.

But when embattled Israel employs the same criteria and resolves doubts in the same way, the world, including those who most vigorously advocate such self-protective policies when we engage in them, is quick to single out Israel for criticism. This double standard should be evident to anyone who observes with an objective eye. Yet it persists.

Israel is far from perfect when it comes to civil liberties during times of threat. It acts just about the same way other Western democracies have acted during comparable, or even lesser, threats. Consider the American response to Japanese-Americans during World War II; to draft opponents during both world wars, Korea, and Vietnam; to student protests, such as Kent State, during Vietnam. Consider the Canadian, British, and French reactions to the crises over the Front de liberation du Quebec, over Northern Ireland, and over Algeria. None of these democracies distinguished themselves in terms of civil liberties, especially toward alleged terrorists. They all received B-minus grades, which are about as good as democracies ever get. Israel, too, deserves a B-minus grade for its response to the deadly Intifata and the lethal terrorism that its civilian population endures on a daily basis. Yet in terms of international and even domestic American evaluations of Israel's actions, one would think that Israel deserves an F minus.

There is something quite dangerous about this double standard. It is dangerous to any objective assessment of civil liberties and human rights. It is dangerous in terms of promoting anti-Zionism and anti-Semitism. And it is dangerous to Israel's survival.

Many of Israel's most strident critics deny that they are anti-Zionist. They claim to oppose only the policies of *conservative* Israeli governments. This is particularly unconvincing coming, as it often does, from American conservatives and reactionaries.

The hypercritical attitude of the Bush administration toward Israel is particularly difficult to explain in light of the hard line of the former Israeli government. It may be more understandable if we look at the personalities and backgrounds of the major players. Neither President Bush nor Secretary of State Baker has any historical commitment to or appreciation of Israel. Nor did former White House chief of staff John Sununu. The former prime minister of Israel is no matinee idol to the American public. He is a rough-and-tumble Israeli who would not fit comfortably into the waspy world of Bush and Baker. Yitzhak Shamir's persona made it easier for Bush and Baker to rationalize their negative attitudes and actions as anti-Shamir rather than anti-Israel. It remains to be seen whether their attitudes and actions will change now that Shamir has been replaced by Rabin following his victory in the June 1992 elections. Especially because Rabin's victory in June 1992 seems to have been less of an affirmative vote for Labor's policy regarding peace talks or settlements, and more of a vote of disapproval regarding Israel's economic situation. However, regardless of the recent change in government, Americans must never be allowed to forget that Israel is the only country in the Middle East that has an *electorate* and an *elected* government. It is the only nation with an independent judiciary—more independent these days than our own. It is the only place in the region where freedom of speech and press is allowed and where universities are free even in the occupied territories, where basic freedoms are restricted by military authorities. Arabs in Israel have more freedom than in virtually any Arab country.

It is important to keep these realities in mind as we assess how Israel confronts its external and internal enemies. And it is imperative to hold

Israel to no higher a standard than we have held ourselves and our other allies when facing comparable dangers.   July 1992

ISRAEL IS STILL A TRUE DEMOCRACY

When even Woody Allen—a longtime supporter of Israel—feels moved to wonder whether he is "reading the papers correctly," it is clear that Israel is having a serious problem. In a recent op-ed column in the *New York Times*, Allen makes it plain that he has "no sympathy" for the way the Arabs have treated the Israelis, and that he is still "rooting for Israel to continue to exist and prosper."

Then he gets to the real point: "Indeed, sometimes you get the feeling you want to belt them [the Arabs]—but only certain ones and for very specific acts." Allen's criticism of recent Israeli actions—a criticism widely shared by many supporters of Israel, both in the United States and in Israel itself—is that innocent Arab bystanders, along with rock-and-bomb-throwing Arab provocateurs, are being beaten, deported, and even shot.

There is certainly some truth to that perception. Some young Israeli soldiers have undoubtedly overreacted to the violent provocations of the rock-and-bomb throwers. But it is important to understand how easy it is to provoke democratic nations into overreaction. Recall the English overreactions to violent provocations of the Irish Republican Army, or the Canadian overreaction to the Front de liberation du Quebec, or the American overreaction at Kent State.

The true test of a democracy is not its immediate reaction to provocation. Few democracies have ever passed such a test. The real test is how its judiciary ultimately responds: whether, after careful reflection, the courts legitimate the overreaction or condemn it. The great U.S Supreme Court Justice Robert Jackson put it well when he dissented from the court's affirmation of the detention of more than 100,000 Americans of Japanese descent after the attack on Pearl Harbor: "A military commander may overstep the bounds of constitutionality, and it is an incident. But if we review and approve, that passing incident becomes the doctrine of the Constitution."

Israel's supreme court has responded magnificently to the occasional overreactions of the Israeli army and security officials. That court, which is among the best in the world, has repeatedly ruled in favor of Arab claimants who have been treated unfairly. Indeed, many Israeli Arabs, both from the West Bank and from Israel proper, have decided not to seek relief from the court precisely because they know they will win; and when they win in the supreme court, they will lose in the court of public opinion.

And it is to the court of public opinion that Arab demonstrators are directing their demonstrations. They are deliberately trying to provoke overreaction from Israeli soldiers in order to get the media to portray Israel as a repressive occupier. They are succeeding beyond their wildest dreams. The picture of the young Arab Davids with slingshots resisting the heavily armed Israeli Goliaths is too ironic to resist. The fact that some of the Arabs are also throwing Molotov cocktails merely complicates the simple story that works so well in the thirty seconds allotted to it during the evening news.

Israel is a vibrant democracy fully capable of keeping its house in order. Its press is among the most free in the world. Despite occasional overzealousness by military censors, the most free Arab press in the Middle East is published in Israel. There is more open debate and dissent, both among Jews and Arabs in Israel, than anywhere else in the area.

Any Arab who dislikes life in Israel is, of course, entirely free to leave and move to the many Arab states in the region. (Contrast that to the Syrian policy of preventing emigration of Syrian Jews.) Some Arabs have done so. Many have not. Part of the reason so many of the demonstrators—violent or otherwise—have chosen to stay is the demonstrable truth that life is far better for Arabs in Israel than in the neighboring Arab states.

It is important to keep these realities, as well as the reality of constant Arab aggression against Israel in 1948, 1967, and 1973, in mind when criticizing Israel for its current overreactions. The State Department, in its recent report on human rights around the world, correctly characterized the current Israeli response to Arab violence as "spontaneous." It is plainly a blemish, but it is not a cancer.

The reason why it is not more invasive to Israel's body politic is that the Israeli political "immune system" is working quite well. Its press remains free; its judiciary remains responsive to legitimate Arab complaints; and most of its citizens remain sensitive to human rights and civil liberties—even as they realize that their security is endangered by sworn enemies.

Woody Allen's question was the correct one: "Am I reading the papers correctly?" The answer is that he is reading correctly what the papers have chosen to print. But the papers, and the rest of the media, have not told the complete story.   February 1988

DEMJANJUK'S LAST HOPE

The defense offered by John Demjanjuk's legal team was doomed to failure. It was a classic example of a losing litigation strategy. In order to accept it, the fact-finder had to believe far too many implausible scenarios. Among them were the following:

• The Trawniki ID card was a forgery, and the best proof of its KGB origin was that it was so perfect that even experts could find no flaws.

• Demjanjuk had spent the war years innocently as a POW in Chelm and had never been in an extermination camp.

• Despite the fact that according to Demjanjuk's account, he had nothing to hide or to be ashamed of, his repeated lies to American authorities concerning his whereabouts during the war can be explained away.

• Likewise, his qualified admissions of some complicity in bad acts can also be explained away, as can the scar from the removed tattoo in the spot where the SS tattooed its unit members.

• All the eyewitnesses who placed him at Treblinka must be mistaken or lying.

• Ivan the Terrible was, in fact, killed during an uprising at Treblinka.

This kind of defense—sometimes called "multiple choice" but more aptly "all or nothing"—rarely succeeds before judges or juries. The reason for its poor track record is that it requires the fact-finder to find too much bad faith on the part of too many people.

The worst example of this defense is one that simultaneously challenges different genres of evidence. That is precisely what the Demjanjuk defense tried to do with its attacks on the authenticity of documents, the memory of eyewitnesses, and the relevance of Demjanjuk's obvious lies.

The kind of defense that has a far better chance of success is the single-focus attack on one type of evidence. In the context of this case, the defense would have had to acknowledge the authenticity of the ID card (which placed him at Trawniki and Sobibor but not at Treblinka) and to admit that he had been part of the SS killing machine at Sobibor. Then he could have focused his attack exclusively on the eyewitness testimony.

If he had been at Sobibor and *not* at Treblinka, then nearly all the remaining evidence against him—with the exception of the eyewitness testimony—could be admitted and logically explained. His pattern of lies to the Americans is as consistent with his having been a guard at Sobibor as with having been Ivan the Terrible at Treblinka.

The same is true of his tattoo scar, as well as his alleged "admissions" (except for the highly speculative inference concerning his statement about his interrogators trying to move him toward Treblinka).

Had he acknowledged the authenticity of the card and his presence at Sobibor, then the only issue would have been whether he was part of the killing apparatus at Sobibor or Treblinka. Instead, the issue became whether he was an innocent POW at Chelm or Ivan the Terrible at Treblinka.

Since his Chelm story was preposterous on the face of it and contradicted by documentary, eyewitness, false-alibi and admission evidence, it was easy—and proper—for the court to disbelieve it in its entirety. The court, which was scrupulous in its professionalism, would have had a much more difficult time finding beyond a reasonable doubt (or as it put it, beyond any doubt) that he was at Treblinka rather than Sobibor.

In order to so conclude, the court would have had to rely *solely* on one type of evidence: the forty-five-year-old memories of eyewitnesses. And the defense could have focused its attack solely on this genre of evidence.

Although uncorroborated eyewitness testimony is acceptable by courts throughout the civilized world, it leaves open the possibility of well-intentioned errors.

Certainly, if the issue is whether he is Ivan the Terrible of Treblinka or Ivan the Innocent of Chelm—if these are the *only* alternatives, as his lawyers framed the issue—then no reasonable person could opt for the latter. But if the issue is whether he was Ivan the Terrible of Treblinka or Ivan the Very Bad of Sobibor, then it becomes a somewhat closer question.

There is, of course, the possibility—a possibility considered by the court even though it was not raised by the defense—that Demjanjuk had been at Sobibor *as well as* at Treblinka. But if he was at Sobibor for any length of time, that would reduce the likelihood that he was Ivan the Terrible, who was responsible for the months of sustained barbarism at Treblinka.

It may well be too late for Demjanjuk to change his story once again—

even if it is true that he was at Sobibor but not at Treblinka. An admission that the ID card is authentic and that he was at Sobibor would be an admission that he was involved in the murder of thousands of Jews.

But he stands condemned on a different charge: that he was Ivan the Terrible of Treblinka. If that charge is not true, then John Demjanjuk has only one hope. He must come forward and admit—indeed prove—the only other plausible alternative: that he was part of the killing machine at Sobibor.   April 1988

SENTENCING IVAN THE TERRIBLE

From his smiling lips, the man in the dock blew a kiss in the direction of the audience. It was hard to tell whether it was a gesture of contempt directed at the victims and survivors who were sitting in the first row, or a message of love to his son in the second row. The bald, large-headed man who blew the kiss had been convicted a week earlier of being Ivan the Terrible—the Butcher of Treblinka, who savagely tortured and murdered thousands of Jewish babies, mothers, and fathers during the Holocaust. Though there was some dispute about whether his particular killing field had been located at Treblinka or Sobibor—both Nazi extermination camps in Poland—there could be little doubt that John Demjanjuk was a Nazi murderer with barrels of blood on his meaty hands.

This was to be his day of reckoning. After decades of freedom during which he, along with other Nazi mass murderers, lived the good life surrounded by friends and family, Ivan the Terrible was to be sentenced. The options were death or imprisonment. Until April 25, the only person who had ever been sentenced to death by an Israeli court had been Adolf Eichmann, the bureaucratic manager of the Holocaust.

The sentencing argument began on a technical note, and Demjanjuk looked bored, alternating wide yawns with inappropriate smiles. Whenever the prosecutor referred to the facts of the case—to the unspeakable crimes such as cutting off women's breasts, bashing in heads of babies, and torturing trembling women on their way to the gas chambers—Demjanjuk shook his head muttering the words, "Not me," and making the sign of the cross with bold, defiant strokes.

Though I was interested in the legal arguments, I couldn't keep my eyes off the defendant. I have been in the presence of many murderers, even some convicted mass murderers, but I have never been so close to so cruel and brutal a human being. Those who say you can see evil in a person's face or eyes have never been in the presence of John Demjanjuk. There was nothing special about his appearance. His evil was not in his persona but rather in his deeds.

I kept looking at Demjanjuk for another reason. I imagined him as *my* killer. At the time he was murdering babies, I was five years old. My family came from a part of Poland that was within the jurisdiction of his extermination camps. But for the grace of God, and the foresight of my grandparents who had left Poland well before the Holocaust, I could have been one of the thousands of nameless and faceless babies he grabbed out of the hands of screaming mothers and shoved into gas chambers. I imagined him laughing with sadistic joy as he killed entire families, ending their seed forever, after taunting and torturing them gratuitously.

I sat there wondering why I hoped his life would be spared. Certainly if any human being deserved the death penalty it was Demjanjuk. In many ways he was worse than the bureaucrat Eichmann who himself had neither killed nor ordered the deaths of those whose shipment to the camps he managed. Demjanjuk personally tortured—beyond the call of duty or superior orders.

Nor did Demjanjuk's own speech to the court provide much sympathy: "I am innocent, innocent, innocent," he protested. "My witness is God," he exclaimed, pointing to heaven with an outstretched hand. He acknowledged the horrors of the Holocaust and expressed his belief that there was an Ivan the Terrible who had brutalized Jewish people. "I hope they have all reached heaven," but "my heart is pure."

As we waited for the court's judgment, I reflected on why I felt so strongly about sparing Demjanjuk's life. I believe he received a fair trial and that he was a mass killer. But I knew that if the court were to order Demjanjuk's execution that fact would entirely change the dynamics of the case. Abolitionists from around the world would turn their energies to saving this miserable man's life. A sentence of life imprisonment would relegate Demjanjuk to the obscurity of his cell. Only the organized Ukrainian community—most of which has no record of long-standing concern for civil liberties—would persist in defending him out of parochial interests and in an ineffective manner. The vice president of a committee to raise funds for Demjanjuk—Peter Jacyk, a leader of the Toronto Ukrainian community—warned, according to press reports, that "Jews would pay for the conviction of Demjanjuk as they have paid for the crucifixion of Jesus." With these kinds of friends Demjanjuk needs no prosecutors. He does not deserve the kind of widespread attention and broad support the death penalty will give him and his cause.

Nor is it clear to me that a country of victims can fairly administer the death penalty in a case involving the death of so many of its own. Every society values the lives of its own people more highly than the lives of its perceived enemies. Finally, there is the lingering possibility that the defendant may be innocent. The moral force of this argument is somewhat muted in Demjanjuk's case because even if he was not Ivan the Terrible of Treblinka, he was certainly Ivan the mass killer of Sobibor.

The audience of survivors and survivors' children waited for the court to return its verdict. The mood was tense as the judge began to speak. He announced that the sentence was to be death, noting that there was no mitigating the awful crimes of Ivan the Terrible.

As soon as the verdict was announced there were screams of relief from the audience. One woman simply started to read off the names of her family members murdered at Treblinka. Others sang religious songs. Demjanjuk's son, John, Jr., spoke to the press. "This verdict will shame Israel, the United States, and the 6 million murdered Jews," he said with no shame. "I would characterize the three judges to be the criminals," he added, unable to recognize the difference between doers of justice and undoers of justice. There was no emotion in his voice. He hoped the appellate judges would review the trial dispassionately.

I left the courtroom saddened by the sentence. The death of one man, even one as terrible as Ivan, will not soothe the memory of the murders of the millions.   April 1988

PATRICK BUCHANAN'S "VICTIM"
IS NO HERO

Why does Patrick Buchanan regard John Demjanjuk, the convicted Nazi death camp guard, as something of a hero? Buchanan has called him "the victim of an American Dreyfus case," an inept comparison since Colonel Dreyfus was entirely innocent of any crime; he was deliberately framed for the explicit purpose of generating anti-Semitism.

John Demjanjuk is indisputably guilty of numerous crimes. He was denationalized by an American court for committing perjury in his application for immigration, intended to cover the fact that he had been trained as a Nazi death camp guard at the notorious Trawinki camp. The evidence is also overwhelming that Demjanjuk served as a guard at the Sobibor death camp, where thousands of Jews were murdered.

These crimes are proved by documentary evidence that has been authenticated by some of the world's leading experts. The evidence includes an identification card bearing Demjanjuk's photograph, his name (Ivan Demjanjuk), and his description. Although Buchanan at first claimed that the card was a "forgery," he now seems to acknowledge that it is authentic and, in fact, cites it in support of his current claim that Demjanjuk is not the man who was known as Ivan the Terrible of Treblinka.

In support of this defense, Buchanan points to evidence that another man, named Ivan Marchenko, was called "Ivan the Terrible" by Treblinka inmates. Back in 1987, after attending several sessions of the Demjanjuk trial in Jerusalem, I publicly stated that I would not be surprised if there were several Ivan the Terribles at Treblinka. Most of the guards at Treblinka were Ukrainians, and Ivan—Ukrainian for John—is the most common Ukrainian name. Any brutal guard named Ivan would be called Ivan the Terrible. The fact that there was a guard named Ivan Marchenko who was called Ivan the Terrible certainly does not prove that Ivan Demjanjuk was not also known as Ivan the Terrible. Indeed, in what Demjanjuk supporters claim is a remarkable coincidence, Demjanjuk actually used the name Marchenko in his American visa application. He falsely gave it as his mother's name. Demjanjuk now claims that he "forgot" his mother's actual maiden name—the name of his own grandfather!—and picked the name Marchenko because it is a common Ukrainian name.

This story is as unbelievable as the other cock-and-bull stories that Demjanjuk has given. Demjanjuk has been caught in so many lies about where he spent the war years, that the Supreme Court of Israel rightly considered his pattern of perjury as evidence that nothing he said could be believed.

Yet Buchanan not only believes Demjanjuk's shifting stories, he serves as a character reference for this "family man."

But even if it turns out that Demjanjuk was not Ivan the Terrible of Treblinka, he was certainly Ivan the Bloody of Sobibor. Indeed, Buchanan himself seemed to have acknowledged as much in a column in which he wrote "Authoritative Soviet sources insisted he served at Sobibor . . . where he was known as Ivan the Bloody." Now that is one heck of a defense: "No your honor, I wasn't Ivan the Terrible. I was Ivan the Bloody!"

That defense, unsympathetic as it is, may well save Demjanjuk from the death sentence. If there is a reasonable doubt about whether Demjanjuk was Ivan the Terrible of Treblinka, he should be given a new trial.

In 1987, I wrote an article for the *Jerusalem Post* in which I argued that it was a close question as to whether Demjanjuk "was Ivan the Terrible of Treblinka, or Ivan the Very Bad of Sobibor." Because of the closeness of the question, I argued against the imposition of the death penalty.

Demjanjuk's current claim is now before the Supreme Court of Israel. Even his erstwhile American lawyer declared that the Israeli trial had been fair. If a mistake has been made, I am confident it will be corrected on appeal.

John Demjanjuk may turn out to be the subject of an honest mistake. He may be Ivan the Bloody of Sobibor rather than Ivan the Terrible of Treblinka. But he is surely not "the victim of an American Dreyfus case." At the very least, he is a Nazi death camp killer and a flagrant perjurer. I can understand why civil libertarians would be concerned about the Demjanjuk case. But Patrick Buchanan deplores soft-on-crime civil libertarians. Indeed he once called upon the United States to "suspend civil liberties" as part of our war against crime. He prides himself on being a "law-and-order" type who sides with the prosecution. Except, it seems, when it comes to Nazi war criminals. This led Alan Ryan, the former head of the Justice Department's Office of Special Investigators, to observe that "great numbers of people are asking themselves: Why is Pat Buchanan so in love with Nazi war criminals?" As a presidential candidate, Buchanan must answer that question.   December 1991

INDICT YASIR ARAFAT FOR MURDER

The U.S. decision to deny Yasir Arafat a diplomatic visa to address the United Nations has less to do with freedom of speech than it does with diplomatic immunity from criminal prosecution.

Denying Arafat a prosecution-free entry into our country does not deprive him or any potential American audience of substantive free speech rights. Arafat has complete access to the American media. He has appeared frequently with Ted Koppel on "Nightline." His speeches and statements are widely reported. He can get an American audience at any time by simply arranging a satellite remote interview. If anything, the American decision to deny him a visa—and the attendant publicity—has enhanced Arafat's ability to get his message to the American public.

What is at issue is diplomatic immunity. Whatever else Yasir Arafat is, he is also a criminal. Our government has wiretap evidence that Arafat personally gave the signal to murder the American deputy chief of mission in the Sudan back in 1973. That makes him an actual murderer, not merely an accessory.

And there is compelling evidence that he was behind other, more recent terrorist killings of American civilians. The notches in his gun represent hundreds of dead men, women, and children. Were Arafat to come to the United States without diplomatic immunity, he would immediately be served with an assortment of legal summonses and subpoenas.

As chairman of both the Palestine Liberation Organization (PLO) and its component group Fatah, he could be sued by relatives of those Americans murdered by his organizations. Under the legal principle of *respondeat superior*—the responsibility of a superior for the injuries caused by his subordinates—he would be accountable for all PLO and Fatah injuries.

He would also be subpoenaed to appear before grand juries to give testimony concerning the organizational structure and history of his criminal organization. In law, he would be treated like the boss of an organized crime family or of a Colombian drug cartel.

The fact that Arafat is also the head of a political organization should make no more difference than it does in the case of Gen. Manuel Noriega, who is both a head of state and a criminal.

If the United Nations were to invite General Noriega to address the General Assembly, would the United States grant him a diplomatic visa— with its accompanying immunity—to enter and leave the United States without answering for his crimes? If the answer to that question is yes, then Arafat, too, should be given a visa. But if the answer would be no for Noriega, then it should be no for Arafat.

Every country has, and exercises, an inherent right to deny diplomatic visas to criminals it regards as persona non grata. Whether that right extends to criminals invited to address the United Nations is a more complex issue. But the U.S. decision, even if wrong under the U.N. Headquarters Agreement, does not deny the Palestinians, or even the PLO, the right to be heard in person at the United Nations. The PLO already has an observer-representative there. If it wishes to send another speaker to present its position, it is free to do so, so long as he or she is not a criminal.

Nor does it matter that Arafat is not yet under indictment. That is only a matter of prosecutorial discretion. He could easily be indicted on the basis of his own taped words and those of his immediate subordinates. And, indeed, he should be.

Beyond the issue of diplomatic immunity is the message that would be sent by legitimating Arafat and his terrorist methods. There are numerous stateless groups throughout the world seeking self-determination. Many have far more compelling claims than the Palestinians. The Kurds, for example, are facing genocidal gas warfare at the hands of Iraqis. The Bahai are similarly endangered by the Iranians. The Estonians, like the Palestinians, have declared themselves an independent state. The list goes on and on, but the world seems to care *only* about the Palestinians.

This is so for three apparent reasons. The first is that the PLO has murdered more innocent civilians and received more publicity for its terrorism than any other stateless group. The second is that it has oil-rich and strategically powerful friends. And the third is that its perceived oppressors are the Israelis, who make an easy scapegoat in a world still too eager to blame Jews.

Were the United States to exempt Yasir Arafat and his gang of terrorists from criminal liability for their murderous acts, the lesson it would teach other stateless people would be devastating to world peace, justice, and safety: The more innocent civilians you murder, the more fear you instill in international travelers, the more media attention you garner—the more recognition and legitimacy you can expect. Many countries, as well as the United Nations, are already sending that bellicose message by lionizing Arafat.

The United States would send a far better message by indicting terrorist capo Arafat as it indicted drug capo Noriega. Let Arafat then come to the United States and try to make his case before an American jury.

December 1988

ALAN M. DERSHOWITZ

THE WORLD SHOULD NOT HONOR TERRORISTS

The message behind the medium of random terrorism, including the blowing up of civilian aircraft, is an inherently immoral one: that the end justifies even the most inexcusable means.

The terrorist's message rejects all civilized rules of proportion. It arrogates to every aggrieved group—indeed, every individual—the sole right to judge whether a given act of terrorism is justified. Terrorism is not a moral appeal to the conscience of the world; it is an extortionate demand for its attention.

Dramatic acts of violence have sometimes been used to force the world to acknowledge little-known moral claims. But these acts have usually been aimed at guilty targets or have been suicidal, such as self-immolation or starvation. The perpetrators took care to avoid the immorality of harming innocent bystanders.

However, when random violence is directed against the softest and most innocent of targets—families traveling together—there can be no substantive message from the terrorists other than "We accept no limits on what we will do until our demands are met."

If the demands are met, the response given to terrorists is that the immorality of the means they employed has a greater impact than the morality of its ends. This encourages groups with the weakest claims on the conscience of the world to commit the most vicious acts of terrorism.

It is no historical accident that those with the highest claims on the conscience of the world have not generally resorted to random terrorism, and that those who have resorted to it have not had particularly high moral claims.

For example, the Jews of Hitler's Holocaust did not randomly kill civilians; the Cambodians of Pol Pot's genocide did not try to blow up airplanes; the Armenians who suffered Turkish atrocities did not murder babies.

Nor was it weakness alone that caused these and other moral sufferers to forbear random violence. It was a refusal to lower themselves to the immoral means used by their oppressors.

In contrast, those who have resorted to random terrorism have not been subject to genocide or even physical danger. Palestinian terrorism began before the Israeli occupation of the West Bank and Gaza Strip. The grievance of the pre-1967 Arab terrorists was primarily over disputed land. Even after the occupation, the grievance was over statehood, not life or liberty. Any Palestinian could live in any one of a dozen Arab nations.

This is not to denigrate the claim of Palestinians—or that of stateless people such as the Kurds, Estonians, Tatars, and numerous others—to political nationhood. It is to demonstrate that on a scale of moral claims, that of the Palestinians ranks comparatively low. As measured by support from the United Nations and individual countries, disproportionate world attention has been paid to them.

Palestinian groups, beginning with Yasir Arafat's Palestine Liberation Organization, have resorted to the most vicious forms of terrorism. They invented, then perfected, attacks on civilian air travelers. They have murdered old people at prayer, young people at play, and infants in their mothers' arms.

The world may have to deal with terrorists in order to save lives. Indeed, it should welcome information from terrorist informers, just as it welcomes information from organized-crime informers. But the moral scandal is that in addition to simply dealing with terrorists, much of the world has honored them. The standing ovation accorded Yasir Arafat, the architect of international terrorism, by many U.N. representatives in Geneva will live in infamy. The willingness of world statesmen, including the pope and other moral leaders, to treat Arafat as a person deserving of tribute is beyond moral comprehension.

In response, it is often argued that Israeli prime ministers Menachem Begin and Yitzhak Shamir had also been terrorists. That is a false analogy for several reasons.

First, the nature of the Begin-Shamir terrorism—unjustified as it was, in my view—was very different from Arafat's. It was not random; it was directed primarily at British and Arab military targets, not at families traveling on civilian airliners. Second, neither Begin nor Shamir were rewarded for their terrorism; indeed, they paid a heavy price, first being imprisoned and then being relegated to minority status within the Israeli political system for decades. It was only after nearly thirty years that they became leaders within their own countries.

Finally, they have never, to this day, received the kind of honor and tribute bestowed on Arafat. And these rewards have come while Palestinian terrorism persists and not long after Arafat had been taking responsibility for it.

The price we pay for honoring terrorists is to encourage terrorism. The most recent probable victims of this pernicious policy were the passengers on Pan Am Flight 103. But we are all potential victims.

Every group with a perceived grievance will learn the Arafat lesson: that "moderate terrorists," those who used to pick their innocent targets randomly and now pick them somewhat more selectively, can expect to be honored by the world community.   January 1989

INVASION ALTERS
ISRAEL'S OCCUPATION

As a liberal and a supporter of Israel, I have long believed that Israel should end its occupation of the West Bank. Though the legal and historical case for holding on to territory captured during an ongoing defensive war is compelling, I was convinced that the moral cost of a continuing occupation was simply too high. The Intifada made it plain how high this cost was, not only for those subject to the occupation but for the occupiers as well.

But Saddam Hussein's unprovoked invasion of Kuwait and his chemical sword rattling against Israel have made me reconsider my position.

All that now stands between Iraq's million-man army and Israel's population centers are Jordan and the West Bank. King Hussein of Jordan is well known for his lack of courage in standing up to powerful Arab dictators. He cannot be counted on to stand up to Iraq's superior army if it decided to cross over from Iraq to Israel. Indeed, there is evidence that Iraqi military officers are currently engaged in joint "training" operations with the Jordanian army and air force. If the West Bank were today under the control of a Palestinian government, Israel's enemies could place troops and chemical weapons within a few miles of Jerusalem and Tel Aviv.

Israel, of course, could not accept such a risk to its tiny population. It would have to take preemptive action against any concentration of forces or weapons on or near its vulnerable borders. Thus, the security borders of Israel would remain essentially what they are today, despite where the political borders may be. The only difference—and a major difference it is—would be that if Israel were to return the West Bank, it would have to invade an Arab buffer area to maintain its security in the face of Iraqi aggression. Now it can simply send its troops and its surveillance planes into the territory it already occupies.

I continue to believe that Israel should not control the day-to-day political life of Arabs in the occupied territories. It should agree to some form of autonomy as proposed at Camp David. Nor should Israel annex the West Bank, or in any way make its occupation permanent. It should announce in unequivocal terms that it is prepared to give up most of the West Bank (subject only to minor territorial modifications based on security needs) as part of an overall settlement of the ongoing Arab-Israeli state of war.

As soon as the rest of the Arab nations recognize Israel's right to exist and make real peace with the Jewish State, Israel will relinquish control over the critical military buffer it continues to occupy for security reasons. This, of course, is precisely what it did with the Sinai, after Egypt signed a peace treaty. Israel should make it clear that it maintains control over the West Bank buffer solely for protective military purposes and not for religious or nationalistic reasons, but that it would be suicidal to return this launching pad to enemy control while the threat of a holy war of annihilation by Arab armies persists. No nation in history has ever returned strategically crucial territory captured in a defensive war without real assurances that it would not be used to launch additional attacks.

Such an announcement by Israel—and a declaration of support for that entirely reasonable position by the United States—would make it clear to those who seek statehood for the Palestinians, that they have a stake in trying to get the Arab states to make peace with Israel. Since much of the belligerence directed against Israel by the Arab nations is done in the name of Palestinian statehood, let the PLO tell these Arab nations that belligerency toward Israel is counterproductive.

If the world becomes convinced that Israel will, and should, give up the West Bank only as part of an overall Arab-Israeli peace, then there will be an incentive for those who truly desire Palestinian statehood to end the Arab belligerency toward Israel.

With Saddam Hussein's troops in Kuwait and his chemical weapons threatening Israel, there will be no movement toward ending, or even ameliorating, the occupation of the West Bank. In that respect, the PLO is already among the big losers in the Iraq invasion of Kuwait. Despite Yasir Arafat's public embrace of Hussein following his naked aggressions against an Arab neighbor, Arafat must understand—or must be made to understand—that every time Israeli security is threatened by Arab belligerence, his dream of Palestinian statehood becomes more distant. This important message must be brought home to the Palestinians: In addition to negotiating with Israel over the future of the occupied territories, the PLO must begin to pressure the Arab states to make peace with Israel. Such an overall peace is the surest and perhaps the only road toward Palestinian statehood.

August 1990

SADDAM HUSSEIN'S ISRAEL PLOY

Saddam Hussein's latest "peace" proposal would require Israel to leave the territory it occupied after the 1967 war as a condition for Iraq leaving Kuwait. The United States has rejected this condition, but various Arab-American organizations are claiming a parallel between Israel's occupation of the West Bank, the Gaza Strip, and the Golan Heights, on the one hand, and Iraq's occupation of Kuwait, on the other hand.

There is no parallel, either as a matter of law or morality. In the first place, Israel captured the territory it now occupies in a *defensive* war, whereas there was absolutely nothing defensive about Iraq's oil and land grab. It is instructive to recall how the 1967 war began. President Gamal Abdel Nasser of Egypt had threatened—without provocation—to "drive the Jews into the sea." He denied Israel access to the Gulf of Aqaba by closing the Straits of Tirān, and he declared that he would pick the time for his military attack against Israel. Israel responded to this casus belli by destroying the Egyptian air force, as it had every right to do under international law. As an analogy, had the United States learned of Japan's plan to bomb Pearl Harbor in 1941, we surely would have been entitled to launch a preemptive strike against the Japanese air force.

After the war between Israel and Egypt was under way, Israel did not attack Jordan, despite the existence of a military treaty between Egypt and Jordan. To the contrary, it sent a clear message to Jordan that Israel would not cross into Jordanian territory if Jordan stayed out of the war. Jordan ignored this offer and continued its attacks on Israel. After considerable loss of life, Israel captured the West Bank, which was then under Jordanian control. It also captured the Golan Heights, from which Syria had been shelling Israeli settlements for more than twenty years. And it took the Gaza Strip and the Sinai from Egypt, the initial aggressor in the war.

Every Israeli government since the Six-Day War has indicated that it would comply with U.N. Resolution 242, which calls for Israel to return territories it captured during the war as part of an overall regional peace in which Israel's security is assured.

When Egypt recognized Israel and made peace with it, Israel returned the Sinai, along with its oil wells. None of the other Arab countries recognizes Israel's right to exist. They all continue in a formal state of war with the Jewish state. No country in history has ever returned land captured in a defensive war to enemies who refuse to make peace with it. Jordan has now given up all legal claims to the West Bank, insisting that it be made part of a Palestinian state under PLO control.

The PLO is Saddam Hussein's sole Arab ally. They support his take-over and continued occupation of Kuwait, and components of the PLO have volunteered to engage in terrorist acts against the United States on behalf of their hero. The PLO charter still calls for the total destruction of Israel, and regards all of Israel as "occupied Arab land."

Israel retains control over its occupied territories—wisely or unwisely—as a matter of self-defense against sworn enemies who are constantly threatening holy war. Saddam Hussein's version of holy war includes chemical and nerve gas directed at Israeli population centers.

The bottom line is that Iraq's unprovoked grab for Kuwait oil has absolutely nothing in common with Israel's retention of territories it captured in a defensive war. Indeed, Israel itself has nothing to do with the current crisis in the Gulf, although Iraq is trying every which way to bring the Jewish state into an Arab conflict of Iraq's own making.

If Iraq can manage somehow to draw Israel into the conflict, it would unite the Arab world around a conflict with its common enemy. To its credit, Israel is maintaining a low profile, despite its understandable fear that Saddam Hussein may try to carry out his threat to "destroy half of Israel" with chemicals and gas. To date, Israel's role has been to help the United States with its intelligence-gathering operations.

The world community should not allow Saddam Hussein to draw Israel into his conflict. Were pressure to be placed on Israel *now* to withdraw from its occupied territories as a condition for Iraqi withdrawal, Saddam Hussein's naked aggression would be rewarded. He would be seen as the Arab Savior who got Israel to do what no other Arab had gotten it to do. And he would have accomplished this goal by naked aggression. Rewarding aggression only invites its repetition, as the world learned so clearly in the 1930s.

Saddam Hussein must be made to withdraw from Kuwait without

conditions and certainly without any benefits. When criminals rob banks, they must not only return the money, but they must also be punished. If Saddam Hussein were to be rewarded for returning the land and oil he stole, it would only encourage further aggression by like-minded tyrants—and by Saddam Hussein himself. August 1990

WHY IS THE PLO STILL SO POPULAR?

Now that the latest Gulf war is over, the Palestine Liberation Organization and its supporters are escalating their demands for the creation of a Palestinian state on lands now occupied by Israel. It is a strange time for these demands to be escalated, since the PLO was on the losing side and its leadership behaved abominably.

The PLO, which purports to be the "sole representative" of the Palestinian people, supported Saddam Hussein, militarily and diplomatically. Its members cheered as Scud missiles rained down on American soldiers and Israeli civilians. They would certainly have cheered even more loudly if chemical and biological weapons had been used against civilians. Indeed, it was the PLO that invented the strategy of mass terrorism against innocent civilian targets.

As a result of its immoral support for the war-criminals of Iraq, the PLO, which has also been guilty of war crimes against civilians, has lost the support of many of its oil-rich benefactors in the Gulf. Its current leadership has also lost the support of many Palestinian intellectuals and people of goodwill.

Why then, it should be asked, is the PLO still so popular in many parts of Europe, on some American college campuses, and with a considerable number of media pundits? The answer, I am told, is that the claim for Palestinian statehood is so morally compelling that it justifies the bad acts and awful alliances of the PLO.

But just how compelling is the Palestinian claim for statehood? How does it compare, for example, with the far more modest demands of Kurdish people who also live in the Mideast and who also seek some degree of political control over their own people?

The Kurds are a non-Arab people who have been seeking some degree of autonomy and independence for many years. Approximately 15 million Kurds—more than four times the population of the Palestinians—live in mountainous terrain in remote areas of Iraq, Iran, and Turkey. They are far more distinct, in culture and in language, from their Arab neighbors than the Palestinians are from theirs. There is no other Kurdish state to which they can move, whereas there are twenty other Arab states in which many Palestinians already live.

The Kurdish people have been subjected to near-genocidal violence by the Iraqis over the past fifty years. An estimated 350,000 Kurds have been murdered and seventy villages razed by Saddam Hussein alone. Poison gas has been used against children, women, and the old. The Kurdish language has been banned in Turkey.

The establishment of a Kurdish homeland would not endanger or even compromise the security of any nation. The territory over which the Kurds seek autonomy has been theirs for centuries, and it consists primarily of mountainous regions with little military or strategic value. The West Bank, on the other hand, is among the most strategically significant buffer-zones in the world. One reason why the Iraqi Scuds directed at Tel Aviv could not be armed with chemical or biological warheads was because of the long distances they had to travel. Had the Scud launchers been located in a PLO-controlled West Bank state, the civilian casualties could have been astronomical. Moreover, the West Bank serves as a buffer against a ground attack from Jordan or Iraq.

The Palestinians have been as lucky in their choice of enemies as the Kurds have been unlucky. The Jewish state of Israel is a perfect enemy to have at the United Nations and in many parts of the Third World. The oil-rich Arab states have been perfect friends. (Whether the Gulf states will continue to be friends of the Palestinians remains to be seen.) The Kurdish people, on the other hand, have picked oil-rich states—particularly Iraq and Iran—as their enemies and have no real friends. But their moral case is considerably stronger than that of the Palestinians.

Not surprisingly, the PLO does not support a Kurdish homeland or Kurdish autonomy. Indeed, it has supported Iraqi repression against the Kurds just as it supported the Chinese massacre of student protesters at Tiananmen Square.

If the Palestinian issue is to be addressed by the world community, so must the Kurdish claims. To consider only the Palestinian claim is to reward terrorism, war crimes, and complicity with aggressors such as Saddam Hussein.

In the end, both the Kurdish people and the Palestinian people should be autonomous and not under the control of others. Palestinian autonomy should follow a peace treaty between the Arab states and Israel, and any Palestinian homeland would have to remain a demilitarized buffer zone. Kurdish autonomy should also be achieved as part of the "new order." It has been promised to the Kurdish people since the Treaty of Sèvres at the end of the First World War—well before the Palestinians even recognized themselves as a separate Arab people. March 1991

ISRAEL DEPORTS WHILE ARABS KILL

As the United Nations Security Council unanimously condemns Israel for ordering the deportation of twelve West Bank Arabs, few Americans have any idea why Israel has had to resort to deportation in its efforts to prevent increasingly violent terrorism against its civilian men, women, and children.

In Arab countries, deportation is not needed to prevent threats of violence. Anyone perceived as a threat—violent or otherwise—is simply rounded up, locked away, or shot. There is no semblance of due process in any Arab country today. Even in Egypt and Jordan, which perhaps come closest to complying with at least some forms of due process, political and religious dissidents are routinely detained. For example, just recently a special Egyptian "state security court" sentenced author Alaa Hamed to eight years in prison on charges of blasphemy against Islam. His "crime" was writing a novel about Moses that allegedly "incited impiety." President Hosni Mubarak refused to reverse the court's decision, asserting that "you cannot come and harm religions and then say never mind." There is no appeal to any court. So much for due process. (At least a contract was not put out on the life of Alaa Hamed, as it was on the life of Salman Rushdie by the Islamic government of Iran.)

The Palestine Liberation Organization, which is objecting most loudly to the Israeli deportations, also has its way of dealing with dissent. It invokes what George Bernard Shaw once referred to as "the ultimate form of censorship"—namely "assassination." During the last two years of the

Intifada, 386 Palestinian Arabs were killed by other Palestinian Arabs. (During the same period, 179 Palestinians died at the hands of the Israeli Defense Force.) When the Arab mayor of Bethlehem proposed a cease fire in the Intifada in exchange for peace talks, Arafat threatened: "Whoever thinks of stopping the Intifada before it achieves its goals, I will give him ten bullets in his chest." There is no appeal from an Arafat-ordered political execution.

Throughout the Arab world, suspects are simply rounded up and never heard from again. "Trials," when they occur at all, are conducted by military tribunals, special security courts, religious organizations, or political "cells." Nor is the governmental-controlled media generally allowed to report on these kangaroo proceedings.

Israel, on the other hand, has a Western-style legal system, with due process, rigid rules of evidence, and appellate review. At the pinnacle of this legal system is the Supreme Court of Israel, which is widely regarded as one of the most independent and professional high courts in the world. This court has overruled the Israeli government and military authorities on numerous occasions, on issues ranging from the expropriation of Arab land for Jewish settlements to the blowing up of Arab houses that were used as bases for terrorism.

Indeed, it is precisely because the Israeli supreme court is so demanding that the military authorities have insisted on using the extraordinary remedy of deportation against Palestinian Arabs suspected of fomenting terrorist violence against civilians. In any other Mideastern country, these suspects would simply be tried and convicted of terrorism on the basis of hearsay and rumors. In Israel, a high level of admissible evidence is required for any criminal conviction—even for security crimes.

For deportation, on the other hand, heresay evidence—if it is sufficiently compelling to the military authorities—will suffice. Thus, for example, if a reliable undercover agent reports on a terrorist plot, the Israeli military can prevent the plot without disclosing the identity of the secret agent. There is appellate review of military deportation orders, but it is not nearly as rigorous as for criminal cases. Nor should it be, since deportation is far less punitive than long-term incarceration.

New Republic columnist Leon Weiseltier has echoed many Arab critics of Israel by comparing Israeli deportations and transfers of Palestinians, on the one hand, to Nazi deportations and transfers of Jews during the Holocaust, on the other. The comparison is obscene: Palestinians are deported to freedom in other countries; Jews were deported to death camps. Every Jew in Germany or Poland during the Holocaust would have given anything to be deported or transferred anywhere out of the clutches of the Nazis.

This is not to diminish the impact of deportation on the person deported or on his family. Nor is it to justify what Israel is doing. But Israeli deportations, which have been relatively few in number over the past few years, must be placed in a comparative context. In that context, it is abundantly clear how hypocritical the Security Council is being when it applies a different standard to Israel than to those who are terrorizing its civilian population.

In a world in which political executions, kidnappings, and kangaroo justice are still so prevalent, it is scandalous that Israel, a democratic nation trying to cope with terrorism within the rule of law, is the only country singled out for strong condemnation by other countries, many of which would do well to comply with Israel's imperfect standard of civil liberties.   January 1992

14 // American Anti-Semitism and Anti-Zionism: From the Right

IT CAN HAPPEN HERE: AMERICAN RIGHT-WING ANTI-SEMITISM

Throughout history, anti-Semitism has been primarily a right-wing phenomenon. The very term *anti-Semitism* originated with right-wing political parties in Western Europe. It was a term used with pride. The boast "I am an anti-Semite" would assure politicians a significant following during the late nineteenth century. Even in the United States, where political anti-Semitism never had the kind of following it claimed in Europe, social and economic anti-Semitism was practiced openly until the 1960s. Henry Ford gave it respectability through the publication of his Jew-hating diatribes in the *Dearborn Independent*. Father Charles E. Coughlin gave it a degree of religious respectability by virtue of his Jew-hating radio sermons, listened to by millions of Christians during the 1930s. And Charles Lindbergh gave it a modicum of popular acceptability by his know-nothing mouthings in the period just before our nation's entry into World War II.

The public reaction to Hitler's genocide of 6 million Jews brought with it a decline in anti-Semitism immediately following VE Day in 1945. But the beginning of the cold war and the red-baiting antics of Joseph McCarthy brought with them a revival of anti-Semitism in the guise of anticommunism. Although only a tiny percentage of Jews had ever been Communists, and only a small percentage of Communists were Jewish, even that tiny percentage virtually disappeared following the Hitler-Stalin pact (German-Soviet nonaggression pact) of 1939—some of the most visible Communists had Jewish names. Headlines about Julius and Ethel Rosenberg, David Greenglass, Morton Sobell, and Judith Coplin provided right-wing anti-Semites a propaganda field day.

The establishment of Israel by socialist kibbutznicks and labor Zionists and its immediate recognition by the Soviet Union and other Communist regimes reaffirmed the suspicions of the reactionary right. Nor did Stalin's murder of the Jewish intelligentsia and political leadership undercut the right wing's perception that Jews were on the vanguard of international communism.

The highly visible alliance between Jews and blacks during the civil rights demonstrations of the 1950s and 1960s made Jews the target of renewed hatred by many right-wing racists. But in the end, the civil rights period brought with it an end to much of the social and economic discrimination suffered by the Jews.

Even when most discrimination against Jews ended, there was always a persistent undercurrent of anti-Semitism from the extreme right. Organizations such as the Liberty Lobby, with its widely read newspaper *The Spotlight*, continued to spread the message of bigotry and hate. Swastikas continue to be painted on synagogue walls and the Anti-Defamation League continues to keep score of anti-Semitic incidents that were largely generated by the extreme right.

But for more than a quarter of a century—from the early 1960s till the late 1980s—there was little *mainstream* anti-Semitism in the United States. No politician with national or even statewide aspirations would dream of making statements that could be construed as anti-Jewish. And those few who did—Jesse Jackson and Congressman Paul Findley, for example—paid a high political price.

And then, in the beginning of the 1990s, something seemed to change. The stalking horse for change was David Duke, a "former" Nazi and Klan leader who took off his swastika and hood and ran for statewide office in Louisiana on a platform that used code words rather than overt bigotry. It nearly worked. Duke received a majority of the white votes in Louisiana when he ran for the U.S. Senate. Only a coalition of blacks, Christian moderates, and Jews narrowly defeated him. But Jews were very much the silent partners in this coalition. Jewish leaders feared that overt Jewish opposition to Duke might actually help him win votes among undecided whites.

Then came the announcement that Patrick Buchanan would make a run for the Republican presidential nomination. I had predicted that he would in my columns and in my book *Chutzpah*. I had also exposed his anti-Semitism in a series of columns dating back to October 1989—well before Abe Rosenthal wrote his famous *New York Times* column of September 14, 1990.

The most surprising reaction to Buchanan's candidacy came from his old friend and mentor, William F. Buckley. After analyzing Buchanan's record in detail, Buckley came to the following conclusion: "I find it impossible to defend Pat Buchanan against the charge of anti-Semitism . . . [Buchanan has] said things about Jews that could not reasonably be interpreted as other than anti-Semitic in tone and substance." He also placed the issue of Buchanan's anti-Semitism into a broader historical perspective: Buckley concluded that Buchanan would not have survived politically ten years ago, but that he does today because of "a creeping cultural-political insensitivity to anti-Semitism that is both [morally] wrong and alarming." But then, in a shocking turnabout, Buckley said that if he were a New Hampshire resident, he would vote for Buchanan in the then upcoming Republican primary. To be sure, Buckley made it clear that his vote for Buchanan would merely be a protest against President Bush's policies, but it clearly would also strengthen Buchanan's power base and legitimatize his anti-Semitism.

The Buchanan phenomenon also casts an interesting light on the relationship between right-wing anti-Semitism and right-wing anti-Zionism. Many conservatives in the United States are strongly pro-Israel, and for understandable reasons. Conservatives generally favor Western democrats over Third World tyrannies; they generally despise Communist-inspired terrorism; they generally support U.S. allies and oppose our enemies; and they generally favor the Judeo-Christian tradition over other religious traditions. For these, and perhaps other reasons, Patrick Buchanan used to be a knee-jerk supporter of Israel, while at the same time expressing negative attitudes toward Jews. When accusations concerning his anti-Semitism began to surface, Buchanan engaged in a dramatic aboutface in his attitude toward Israel. Suddenly, the plight of "the Palestinians"—an unlikely people for Buchanan to care about—became a major cause for him. A supporter of right-wing repression throughout the world, from Franco's fascism to South Africa's apartheid to South and Central America's death squads, suddenly Buchanan caught a dose of human rights sensitivity when it came to Israel's response to terrorism. It was all quite transparent to anyone who bothered to think about it. Buchanan decided to deflect legitimate charges that he was an anti-Semite by quickly becoming an anti-Zionist. He could then claim, as he loudly did, that he was being called an anti-Semite *because* he was an anti-Zionist. And since it is entirely respectable to be an anti-Zionist but not an anti-Semite, Buchanan had a ready-made defense. The flaw in his reasoning is, however, quite obvious. He was an anti-Semite well *before* he became an anti-Zionist, and thus he cannot blame the accusations against his anti-Semitism on his Johnny-come-lately anti-Zionism. He has, however, offered no plausible explanation of his sudden shift away from support for Israel or, for that matter, of his statements that have been characterized—by his friends and foes alike—as anti-Semitic.

The problem of right-wing anti-Semitism still plagues this country and the world. The sad reality that it has been supplemented by increasing left-wing anti-Semitism does not diminish the threat from the right. It makes it all the more necessary not to tolerate any bigotry from whatever direction it may originate.   July 1992

BUSH'S CAMPAIGN AIDE SUPPORTS ARAB CAUSE

Governor John Sununu of New Hampshire is co-chairman of George Bush's presidential campaign, Bush's principal surrogate, and his spokesman on the Republican Platform Committee. He has also been mentioned as a possible vice presidential candidate.

But because he is governor of a state that borders Governor Michael Dukakis's Massachusetts, Sununu has been assigned the equally important task of leading the negative campaign against Dukakis. A recent newspaper headline asked: "Sununu Dogs Dukakis: Is He Bush's 'Pit Bull'?"

If Sununu's job is to attack Dukakis's credibility, then it is important to provide some information about Sununu himself, so that voters will be able to assess the attacker's own credibility and biases.

First, as a politician, Sununu has always operated in Dukakis's shadow. While Massachusetts was experiencing its economic "miracle," New Hampshire residents crossed the border in droves to partake of its southern neighbor's prosperity by working in Massachusetts jobs. To be sure, a few Massachusetts residents have moved to New Hampshire, which has virtually no state taxes and few services, while continuing to work in Massachusetts. But the Massachusetts economy is the dominant force in the region.

A recent report concluded that New Hampshire owed its relative prosperity to the fortuity of "being in the right place at the right time"—namely, near "the robust Boston metropolitan area." And New Hampshire residents seem to realize this, as evidenced by Dukakis's popularity in Sununu's home state. Indeed, in a 1986 poll, New Hampshire voters were asked who they would vote for if Dukakis were running against Sununu, and Dukakis won by 10 percent.

Sununu is not seeking reelection as New Hampshire's governor, and pundits predict that he would be offered a post in Washington by a Bush administration. This has many people worried because of some of Sununu's bizarre views, both on domestic and foreign policy issues.

On domestic issues, Sununu does not seem to understand that all of America is not rural New Hampshire. He has a simpleminded view of the role of government in the economy—a view that has not worked well for New Hampshire and would be a disaster for the more complex America.

On foreign policy issues, he is even less in the mainstream. When the U.N. General Assembly voted in 1975 for a resolution stating that Zionism was a form of racism, nearly every American—and certainly every responsible American political figure—saw that bigoted condemnation of Israel, our democratic ally, as an indirect attack on the United States. It was universally condemned throughout the civilized world. But Sununu has stood out as the only governor unwilling to condemn the resolution.

His excuse was that as "one of the highest elected Arab-Americans in the country," he would hurt his credibility in the peace process. His other excuse—completely contradictory to the first—is that he does not involve himself in foreign policy. This lame excuse is also contradicted by the facts: As governor, Sununu has signed several foreign policy declarations involving Afghanistan, Lithuania, and other places far from the Granite State.

His real reason is that he supports the Arab position in the Middle East, a position backed by neither major party in this country.

Bush has urged Sununu to condemn the U.N. resolution, but Sununu has refused. Bush was then asked to repudiate his campaign co-chairman, but he declined, on the ground that he does not "demand unanimity of opinion from everyone who works with him."

Some New Hampshire residents who have met with Sununu worry that his desire to maintain credibility with some questionable elements within the Arab world also motivated his decision to refuse invitations to attend Holocaust memorial services and other nonpolitical events that might be perceived as too pro-Jewish. Although Sununu did eventually sign a bland proclamation remembering the Holocaust, even the Manchester, N.H., *Union Leader*—a bastion of conservative Republicanism—condemned his hypocrisy in not acknowledging that "the kind of thinking" underlying the Zionism-equals-racism resolution was precisely what led to the Holocaust.

The time has come for Sununu to choose sides: Does he want to retain his credibility with those mainstream voters whom he is asking to support Vice President Bush? Or does he insist on maintaining credibility with extremists and anti-Semites who believe that support for the democratic state of Israel constitutes racism?

Unless Sununu chooses the former and is prepared to renounce the notorious U.N. resolution equating Zionism with racism, Bush should dismiss him as his campaign co-chairman.

Bush cannot have it both ways. If he believes, as he obviously does, that the Zionism-equals-racism resolution is an obnoxious form of anti-Semitism and anti-Americanism, he cannot allow his campaign co-chairman to remain in bed with those who support the resolution.

Candidates for office are properly judged by those whom they have chosen for important posts in their campaigns. This is especially true if the campaign aide is a potential appointee in the event of victory.

There is no room in a presidential campaign or in a presidential administration for a governor who refuses to condemn international bigotry.

July 1988

PAT BUCHANAN, THE JEWS, AND THE NAZIS

Unbeknownst to most decent Americans, there exists in this country a genre of racist newspapers that specializes in promoting anti-black, anti-Catholic, anti-Jewish, and anti-foreign-born bigotry. Bearing such titles as *Thunderbolt*, *S.O.S.*, *National Socialist Bulletin*, *Race and Nation*, and *White Power*, they preach separatism and superiority, whipping their paranoid followers into a frenzy of fear and hatred of outsiders.

These racist rags are the price we pay for our freedom of the press— the flotsam and jetsam of our Constitution. Fortunately, no mainstream American columnist would legitimize any of these fringe newspapers by writing for them.

It is against this background that a recent column by Patrick Buchanan, who appears in one hundred newspapers and is seen on national television, must be viewed with some alarm. In his recent column about the tragic dispute over the Carmelite convent at Auschwitz, Buchanan foments religious warfare between Catholics and Jews. At a time when responsible leaders of both religions are seeking to build bridges, Buchanan is planting dynamite under these very bridges.

In his column Buchanan invokes "Catholic rage" against the Jews. Instead of urging his readers to understand the pain that some Jewish survivors of Auschwitz must feel at Polish efforts to "de-Judaize" Hitler's final solution, Buchanan invites his fellow Catholics to mock Jewish sensitivities. He declares that "to orthodox Catholics, the demand that we be more 'sensitive' to Jewish concerns is becoming a joke." He deliberately misquotes an anti-*Polish* comment by Israeli prime minister Yitzhak Shamir to make it appear as if it were an anti-*Catholic* slur, and he converts an everyday military incident on the West Bank into an anti-Catholic provocation. Then, in a tone reminiscent of an incitement to a nineteenth-century religious pogrom, he prophecies that "the slumbering giant of Catholicism may be about to awaken." Lest there be any doubt about the target of this giant's wrath, Buchanan points to "those who so evidently despise our Church"—namely "the Jews."

Buchanan goes on to warn the Jews not to count on the bridge-building efforts of American cardinals, such as John Cardinal O'Connor and Bernard Cardinal Law. He regards their conciliatory statements, obviously blessed by the Vatican, as "the clucking appeasement of the Catholic cardinalate." He warns these princes of reconciliation to "step aside" and make room for "bishops and priests ready to assume the role of defender of the faith."

Buchanan probably has in mind for this role excommunicated Archbishop Marcel Lefebvre and other right-wing French priests who helped to hide unrepentant Nazi war criminal Paul Touvier in various monasteries until he was recently arrested to face trial for mass murder.

Buchanan himself has come to the defense of other fugitive Nazi war criminals, including such genocidal killers as Klaus Barbie, John Demjanjuk, Karl Linnas, and the SS murderers buried at Bitburg. Buchanan's support for Nazi war criminals and for the abolition of the government office that investigates them led former Justice Department official Alan Ryan to comment, "Great numbers of people are asking themselves: Why is Pat Buchanan so in love with Nazi war criminals?"

Buchanan's lovefest with Nazi criminals certainly cannot be explained by any sustained commitment to the rights of accused defendants. In almost every other context he supports the rights of victims and rails against defense attorneys. Buchanan's rationalization—"I see these people as un-defended"—rings hollow in light of his history of ignoring others who cannot count on the support of various Eastern European ethnic groups and defense funds.

Buchanan's other rationalization—Nazi cases rely on Soviet evi-dence—is simply not true. Most of the evidence has come from eyewitness testimony. In some cases, most prominently the prosecution of Klaus Bar-bie, *none* of the evidence comes from Soviet sources. Yet Buchanan has snidely characterized the French prosecution of the Butcher of Lyon as "all this wallowing in the atrocities of a dead regime."

The most plausible answer to the question of why Buchanan seems to be more sensitive to Nazi killers than to Jewish victims was provided by Buchanan himself when he acknowledged to the *New York Times* that he had, to quote the *Times* story, "frequently been accused of anti-Semitism." Well the shoe fits. Patrick Buchanan just loves to sock it to the Jews.

Buchanan is, of course, not the only writer in America to express anti-Jewish views. But he is the most widely read and listened to since Father Coughlin in the 1930s. He is also the only overtly anti-Jewish figure to serve in high federal office—as director of communications in the Reagan White House.

The anti-Jewish views expressed by Patrick Buchanan are not reflec-tive of mainstream America. They belong in the hate-mongering media, not in a nationally syndicated column and not on national television. His column about Auschwitz would be right at home in one of the lunatic fringe newspapers that few Americans would use even to wrap their garbage.

October 1989

SENATORS ADVERTISING IN A RACIST JOURNAL

In twenty-five years of writing about the First Amendment, I have never criticized a court decision that has favored freedom of the press. But this time, a federal judge in Miami may have gone too far.

Judge James W. Kehoe ruled recently that a Broward County sheriff violated the First Amendment when he withdrew his legal advertisements from a newspaper that had run a series of articles criticizing him. The court ruled that by taking his business to more friendly newspapers, the sheriff was punishing the unfriendly journal for its criticism. Since the sheriff is a government official, such financial retaliation constituted government censorship, according to the judge.

Though this decision seems protective of free speech, its implications are frightening. Consider a newspaper that has become a racist propagator of hate. Must the government continue to support it financially through its advertising? Isn't it enough, under the First Amendment, for the government to permit it to disseminate its racist propaganda without also supporting it with public money? Wouldn't black citizens who are vilified by the newspaper's editorials have a legitimate right to see their tax dollars *not* used to finance their own degradation?

Lest this seem hypothetical, let me assure you that there are such newspapers in this country. Consider, for example, a weekly rag published in Clifton, N.J., called *The Post Eagle*. Although it purports to be the voice of the Polish-American community, its bigoted message has been denounced by Polish-American leaders.

Its pages are filled with racist and anti-Semitic diatribes. In its 1988 Christmas issue, the *Post Eagle* ran an ad "from the Slavic members of the Ku Klux Klan" wishing "all Polonia a merry White Christmas." That racist wish was illustrated by a drawing of Santa Claus wearing a Klan hood. Its editorials refer to Jews as "vermin," "cretins," and "animals," and it warns that "we Christians should never forget and forgive them for deciding to kill our God." It accuses the "rabbis and Jews" of lying about the Holocaust, and it features ads for crude anti-Semitic and racist publications.

Over the years, the *Post Eagle* has become a bible of bigotry for haters throughout the country. It is promoted by other racist rags such as the Georgia-based *Truth at Last*, which preaches the racial inferiority of blacks. The *Post Eagle*'s subscribers and advertisers include Nazis, Klansmen, and other professional race-baiters.

Several weeks ago, I received a printed "Christmas card" bearing a large swastika and conveying "best national socialist wishes" from E. J. Toner, Jr., who proudly identified himself as a "*Post Eagle* subscriber" and a retired lieutenant commander of the U.S. Navy. (I checked and this Nazi really was in our navy.)

No wonder the *Bergen Record*—Northern New Jersey's most respected newspaper—characterized the *Post Eagle* as a journal of "hate," specializing in "vitriolic anti-Semitic diatribes."

Because the *Post Eagle* claims to have sixteen thousand readers, prominent New Jersey politicians have submitted paid advertisements each year to a special Christmas edition. Legal ads have also been placed in its racist pages. Following the publication of the Ku Klux Klan ad, the *Hudson Dispatch*, another New Jersey paper, asked whether elected officials should continue to support the *Post Eagle* by submitting paid personal and legal ads. I raised the same question in a letter I sent to advertisers, urging them to "please send your advertising dollars to another Polish or Catholic newspaper of your choice, one that reflects the greatness of Polish and Catholic traditions."

The response has been gratifying. Several officials withdrew their ads, and it seems that the *Post Eagle* is not getting any legal advertising now. Nothing in our Constitution requires a public official to pay for an ad that will appear side by side with a greeting from the Klan or a Hitler-like editorial dehumanizing Jews. This year there was also an ad from E. J. Toner, the navy veteran.

Let Nazis and other bigots continue to support the *Post Eagle*, but no decent person need feel ashamed for refusing to advertise in a journal of hate.

Indeed, the only officials who should be ashamed are those who continue to advertise in racist publications. For the information of all decent voters, here is this year's dishonor roll of officials whose ads were published in the most recent Christmas issue of the *Post Eagle*: U.S. representatives Bernard J. Dwyer, Matthew J. Rinaldo, and Frank J. Guarini; New Jersey state senators Raymond J. Lesniak, Joseph Bubba, and Thomas F. Cowan; New Jersey assemblymen Louis J. Gill and Thomas J. Duch; Bayonne, N.J., mayor Dennis P. Collins; Secaucus, N.J., mayor Paul Amico and Kearny, N.J., mayor Daniel Sansone; and Sheriff Edward J. Webster, Hudson County, N.J.

Contacted by my office, these public officials said now that they are aware of the bigotry of the *Post Eagle*, they will no longer advertise in its pages. That is in the highest tradition of our First Amendment.

January 1990

Despite my 1989 letter-writing campaign, The Post Eagle *has persisted in its anti-Semitic editorial policy and recently in its 1992 Easter edition editorial it revived the myth of Jewish responsibility for the death of Jesus. Once again I sent letters to the advertisers of* The Post Eagle *asking them not to support the paper's bigoted message while also clarifying the Vatican's statement that "the Jews" bear no responsibility for the death of Christ. Nonetheless, The*

Post Eagle continues to publish anti-Semitic diatribes and the paper has recently taken to suggesting that its readers write Harvard University, urging that I be fired because of my letters to the paper's advertisers.

A CARDINAL TEACHES BY EXAMPLE

A small gesture by a great church leader deserves to be praised and contrasted with the actions and inactions of other "leaders." Last Sunday, at a large antiabortion rally in Boston, Bernard Cardinal Law rose to address the large crowd. He looked out at the cheering audience—many holding antiabortion signs—and he paused. Amid the signs he noticed one in particular. It blamed abortion on "the Jews."

Before beginning his speech, the cardinal demanded that this anti-Semitic sign be removed. "I want you to put down that sign," he repeated three times. Finally, the sign holder, a well-known anti-Semitic agitator named Joseph Mlot-Mroz, who leads an organization of "Polish Freedom Fighters in the United States," obeyed his cardinal and removed the sign. Only then did Cardinal Law begin his speech.

In his address, Cardinal Law added the following spontaneous response to the anti-Semitic sign: "No people in history have suffered as much from hatred and violence than our Jewish brothers and sisters. We can never forget that."

Cardinal Law's emphatic denunciation of anti-Semitism was especially welcome in the context in which it occurred. I doubt that there were many Jews in the antiabortion audience to which he spoke. Although Orthodox Judaism prohibits abortion in most circumstances, most American Jews favor a woman's right to choose. Cardinal Law, unlike Pat Robertson and some other religious leaders, did not condition his criticism of anti-Semitism on agreeing with his church's political agenda. He recognized anti-Semitism for what it is: an unmitigated evil and an unqualified sin. Pat Robertson, on the other hand, refused to condemn anti-Semitic protests against the movie *The Last Temptation of Christ*, which was neither written nor directed by Jews, unless the Anti-Defamation League also condemned the film and demanded its withdrawal from circulation. Jews should not have to negotiate condemnations of anti-Semitism from people who claim to be our friends.

Contrast Cardinal Law's brave act with the cowardly silence of many African-American leaders during the recent Crown Heights riots in Brooklyn, during which a Jew was murdered and others injured following the accidental death of a black youngster. Speaker after speaker at black rallies said nothing as anti-Semitic signs, some praising Hitler and demanding that the genocidal job he began be completed, were proudly held high. Many of these same leaders have refused to condemn the anti-Semitism, but too many others said and did nothing.

And contrast Cardinal Law's forthright condemnation of anti-Jewish hatred with the vacillations of Joseph Cardinal Glemp, the primate of Poland. Cardinal Glemp declared that he was not an anti-Semite, but then in the same breath he told his Polish followers that historians and sociologists would prove that he was right in blaming "the Jews" for many of Poland's problems, ranging from alcoholism to communism. Indeed, his statement denying that he was anti-Semitic while continuing to scapegoat the Jews made it sound like one could maintain these bigoted accusations without being labeled an anti-Semite. Even after his visit to the United States and his meetings with several Jewish "leaders," Cardinal Glemp could not bring himself to make a clean break with Poland's anti-Semitic past and with his own bigoted statements. Maybe he will someday, but as of now, his efforts at clarifying his previous anti-Semitic positions have, if anything, made matters worse.

Perhaps Cardinal Glemp will follow President Mikhail Gorbachev's lead. After years of vacillation, Gorbachev has finally denounced anti-Semitism in the Soviet Union and recognized its continuing impact there. After several years of pussyfooting around the issue, Gorbachev finally acknowledged that "social expressions of anti-Semitism have not been surmounted, and certain reactionary articles are exploiting this fact."

Last year I had the opportunity to meet with President Gorbachev in the Kremlin where I asked him to condemn anti-Semitism. He promised me—as he had promised others—that he would, on the right occasion. That occasion was the ceremony marking the fiftieth anniversary of the slaughter of thirty thousand Jews at Babi Yar, outside of Kiev.

Neither the spontaneous denunciation of anti-Semitism by Cardinal Law nor the belated acknowledgment of its existence in the Soviet Union by President Gorbachev will bring an end to this most persistent of bigotries. But the failure of other "leaders" to condemn this evil, unconditionally and promptly, contributes to its persistence.

People of all faiths who deplore bigotry of all kinds must join together in praise of Cardinal Law's small gesture of solidarity, as we praised the pope's gesture of speaking at the synagogue in Rome several years ago. Out of such gestures are bridges of brotherhood and sisterhood built.

October 1991

IS ANTI-SEMITISM ON THE RISE?

The Anti-Defamation League (ADL) of the B'nai Brith has just released a two-month audit of anti-Semitic incidents in New York City. It noted an increase in the number of swastikas painted on synagogue walls, the number of racist attacks on Jews, and other gross acts of obvious bigotry.

The ADL's undertaking tells an important *part* of the story of anti-Semitism in our nation. But it only tells *one part*—and the most obvious and visible part at that. Nor is it necessarily the most important part. For example, during the years when anti-Semitism in the marketplace was dramatically abating, when Jews were no longer systematically excluded from law, banking, and insurance firms, the number of swastika incidents may well have risen. That would not necessarily mean that anti-Semitism, as a whole, was increasing. It would only mean that while anti-Semitism in the workplace was declining, other manifestations of anti-Jewish bigotry in certain neighborhoods were increasing. The total picture may have been one of decreasing anti-Semitism, but the focus on the increasing number of swastika incidents would distort that big picture.

Why then does the ADL focus exclusively on swastika-type incidents? I think I know. There is rarely any ambiguity about the anti-Semitic nature of a swastika incident. The ADL does not want to be accused of crying anti-Semitism in questionable cases, lest it lose credibility.

Yet this cautious attitude creates a dilemma not only for the ADL but for others who care deeply about anti-Semitism in the United States. The dilemma is this: Some of the most important manifestations of antiSemitism—important in the sense of being mainstream rather than lunatic fringe—are also among the most subtle. The more mainstream a manifestation of anti-Semitism is, the less likely it will be as crude or obvious as a swastika.

It may take the form of a Patrick Buchanan column, in which the widely read and watched commentator voices doubts about the Holocaust, tells "Orthodox Catholics" that the "demand that we be 'sensitive' to Jewish concerns is becoming a joke," and calls upon the "slumbering giant of Catholicism . . . to awaken" against "those who so evidently despise our Church"—namely the Jews. Or anti-Semitism may take the form of an effort by White House Chief of Staff John Sununu to blame his problem of excessive use of government airplanes on Jews who don't like Sununu's "position on Israel." It may take the form of what Oliver North, in his new book, characterizes as "an ingrained streak of anti-Semitism in our government." Or it may take the even subtler form of President Bush complaining that in trying to postpone a vote on loan guarantees, he was "up against powerful forces" and that "there were something like a thousand lobbyists on the hill working the other side of the question. We got one little lonely guy down here doing it."

President Bush, to his credit, realized that he had—perhaps inadvertently—invoked anti-Jewish stereotypes of "dual loyalty" and "undue influence," when he began to receive praise for his remarks from neo-Nazis and other obvious anti-Semites.

In recent weeks, I have been criticized for pointing out anti-Jewish stereotypes in two best-selling books. The first was a novel by Michael Thomas called *Hanover Place*. The character in this novel talks about how the "damn Hebes are going to ruin this country" and how the Jews "rub their money in our faces." When questioned about the views of his characters, the author reiterated his bigotry in the *Washington Post*—this time in his own voice:

"If I point out that nine out of ten people involved in street crimes are black, that's an interesting sociological observation. If I point out that nine out of ten people involved in securities indictments are Jewish, that is an anti-Semitic slur.

"The Steinbergs, Kravises, etc. shove their faces in ours . . ."

The second book is titled *Den of Thieves*—a reference to Jesus chasing the Jewish money changers out of the temple—and is about a group of Wall Street bankers who were convicted of various crimes. All of them (including my client Michael Milken) happen to be Jewish. The author, James Stewart, goes out of his way to refer to their religious backgrounds, although he never shows how these backgrounds are relevant to what they did. The positive characters he chooses to write about are almost all non-Jewish, and he goes out of his way to make that point: "a non-Jew from Cincinnati," "a Tough Irishman," "a Methodist." The non-Jews are described as "scrupulously honest," "urbane," "soft-spoken," and having "unshakable integrity," in sharp contrast with the Jews who have "loose mores," "ugly, nakedly aggressive tactics," and are "sinister" and "wheeler-dealers."

A reader would come away from this book erroneously believing that there were no gentile criminals on Wall Street, and that all prosecutors are non-Jews!

It is important to call attention to these more subtle, indeed some even debatable, manifestations of anti-Jewish stereotyping precisely because they are mainstream.   November 1991

SHOULD NEWSPAPERS PROMOTE "CRACKPOT IDEAS" OF JEW HATRED?

A crackpot named Bradley Smith claims that the Holocaust never happened, that there was no Nazi "policy to exterminate the Jewish people," and that the gas chambers were "lifesaving . . . fumigation" rooms.

Every legitimate historian knows that millions of Jews—infants, grandmothers, men, and women—were ingathered from throughout Nazi controlled Europe and systematically murdered as part of Hitler's genocidal final solution. Entire Jewish communities and villages were exterminated by machine-gun squads, mobile gas vans, and large gas chambers. Many members of my own family were slaughtered in Poland. When I visited Auschwitz-Birkenau, I saw the names of my relatives on the list of those gassed and cremated. I know survivors, like Nobel Prize winner Elie Wiesel, who experienced the death camps firsthand. I have spoken to American soldiers who liberated death camps at the end of the war.

Despite the incontrovertible evidence of the Holocaust—the Nazis themselves documented many of the killings—there are cruel bigots who are trying to convince naive people that the Holocaust is a "myth" perpetuated by Jews "promulgating anti-German hate propaganda." By the use of this "double-speak"—accusing the victims of employing hate propaganda—Bradley Smith and his ilk have been trying to turn an incontestable historical fact into a "debatable issue."

The Holocaust deniers realize that they cannot win the debate during this century. They envision a two-step process; the first step is to make the truth of the Holocaust a debatable issue; the second is to win the debate in the next century, when the victims and perpetrators of the Holocaust will all be dead.

As part of this process, Smith has tried to buy full-page advertisements in college newspapers. These ads call for "open debate" on whether the Holocaust occurred. Invoking currently voguish language about "campus thought police" and "political correctness," Smith says that students should be "encouraged to investigate the Holocaust story the same way they are encouraged to investigate every other historical event."

I agree with that formulation. The Holocaust should be studied in the same way that "every other historical event" is studied. American slavery is studied, but no one "debates" whether there were slaves, because that is not a debatable issue. The detention of Japanese-Americans during World War II is studied, but there is no debate about whether this historical event occurred, because it is not debatable. Who killed President Kennedy is debatable, but not whether Kennedy is still alive, as some tabloids have occasionally claimed. The occurrence or nonoccurrence of a universally accepted historical event does not become a legitimate issue for academic debate just because some crackpot says it is debatable. An initial burden of persuasions must be satisfied before a ludicrous "idea" is given the imprimatur of reasonable debatability. Holocaust denial has not come close to meeting the preliminary burden.

In addition to its demonstrable falsehood, Holocaust denial is cruelly hurtful to survivors. Just imagine how a man like Elie Wiesel must feel when he hears a call for "open debate" about whether his family was murdered by the Nazis.

For these reasons, many college newspapers turned down Smith's dirty money and refused to run his nasty ad. In doing so, they followed their policy of being selective in the advertising they will accept. Many refuse ads for phone sex, quack medical cures, or racist, sexist, or homophobic views.

Some college newspapers ran the ad, as I would have done. The most questionable decision was made by the Rutgers *Targum*, which turned down the ad but then ran it as an "opinion" column—for free! It also ran contrary opinions. The *New York Times* praised this approach, arguing that the "editors thus transformed revulsion into education."

I wonder whether the *Times* considered the implications for other crackpot ideas that seek to become debatable. Will the *New York Times* now run ads that are rejected for their dishonesty and offensiveness as op-ed articles? If so, it can expect an influx of ad applications from advocates of racist, sexist, homophobic, and anti-Semitic views that are the common fare of such bigoted rags as the *Spotlight* and *Race and Truth*, but that are not regarded as worthy of editorial coverage by the mainstream press.

Private newspapers have a First Amendment right to publish or decline anything. Only the government may not censor because of the content of expression. Our government has never tried to censor Smith's garbage, nor should it.

Recently, Smith invited me to debate whether the Holocaust occurred. He knows he cannot win, but he would like to be able to say that Alan Dershowitz regarded the issue as worthy of debate. I have written him that I will debate the Holocaust, but only as part of a series on the following subjects: (1) that slavery did not exist in America; (2) that Elvis Presley is still alive; and (3) that the earth is flat. That is the company of crackpot "ideas" into which Holocaust denial comfortably fits.   February 1992

BUCHANAN MUST BE TAKEN SERIOUSLY

The vote for Patrick Buchanan in New Hampshire demands that the media and the voters begin to scrutinize Buchanan's background and record as if he were a real candidate for president. Until New Hampshire, no one took Buchanan seriously. This is not surprising in light of the fact that Buchanan has never held elected office or a job that has prepared him for the presidency. He has been what serious journalists refer to as a "media personality"—someone seen frequently in the media but not regarded as a real journalist. His only stints in government have been in the area of partisan political propaganda.

Many pundits still do not take Buchanan seriously, pointing out that most of those who voted for him in New Hampshire have little positive feeling for him. According to an exit poll, more than half of the Buchanan voters said they would vote for the Democratic candidate if President Bush won the Republican nomination.

Treating Buchanan merely as a protest candidate misses the point for several reasons. First, Buchanan's 37 percent to 53 percent "victory" in New Hampshire positions him as the only current contender. If President Bush were to become too ill to run, Buchanan rather than Vice President

Dan Quayle would likely get the Republican nomination. Even if President Bush is reelected and serves out his entire term, Buchanan is now in a good position to beat out Quayle, Baker, Robert Dole, or other potential contenders for the 1996 Republican nomination. In other words, Buchanan now has a serious chance of becoming our president at some point in the future.

That prospect is frightening. Here is a man who has expressed admiration for fascist dictators Francisco Franco and Adolf Hitler. He has defended so many Nazi war criminals—even admitted hands-on participants in the Holocaust—that Assistant Attorney General Alan Ryan of the Justice Department's Office of Special Investigations said: "Great numbers of people are asking themselves: Why is Pat Buchanan so in love with Nazi war criminals?"

Nor can Buchanan's defense of Nazis be justified on civil liberties grounds, since Buchanan despises civil libertarians who defend the rights of people charged with crimes. When I was a frequent guest on "Crossfire," he always berated me for being "soft" on crime. (By the way, Buchanan has issued a directive that I can no longer be a guest on "Crossfire," ever since I began to expose his record of bigotry.) Buchanan always sides with the prosecution and with the victims. Except when it comes to Nazis! Suddenly, Buchanan begins to complain about the fairness of our Justice Department in dealing with convicted killers of babies and the aged. Suddenly, Buchanan's sympathy for victims seems to diminish when he writes of victims of the Holocaust. He says that these victims suffer from "Holocaust Survivor Syndrome," which he claims involves "group fantasies of martyrdom and heroics." In writing about the controversy over a Catholic convent at the Auschwitz-Birkenau death camp, where millions of Jews were gassed, Buchanan said: "To orthodox Catholics, the demand that we be more 'sensitive' to Jewish concerns is becoming a joke." He also expressed doubts that any Jews had actually been gassed by exhaust fumes at Treblinka.

No wonder Elie Wiesel, the soft-spoken winner of the Nobel Peace Prize, recently concluded: "I rarely use the word *anti-Semite*, but he comes very close to one."

No wonder Buchanan's old friend and mentor, William F. Buckley, also concluded that Buchanan "has said things about Jews that could not reasonably be interpreted as other than anti-Semitic in tone and substance."

In addition to the prospect that this equal-opportunity bigot—he has made insensitive comments about African-Americans, women, and gays— may someday become our president, there is another widely ignored aspect of his current campaign that demands attention. Buchanan has attracted to his campaign some of the worst elements of our society. My paralegal Daniel Eisenstadt went to New Hampshire in the last days of the primary campaign and attended several Buchanan campaign rallies. This is what he reported:

"At a rally in Manchester, crowd members urged staff to remove a rabbi engaged in a peaceful protest of Buchanan's candidacy. Several individuals shouted the following slurs: 'If you want me to take care of the Jews, I'll do it right now,' 'Go back to Israel, you damn bastards,' 'They should have finished you all at the camps.' Outside of the rally, the rabbi was surrounded by Buchanan's followers shouting: 'You should be baptized immediately, rabbi,' and 'We are not going to stand for this, from you Jews, anymore!' Staff member Amy O'Neill explained that 'Jews would always be persecuted because, as God's chosen people, the devil would always want to take little shots at them.' The staff member commented that she had discussed this view with Mr. Buchanan, and he had agreed!"

Distinguished Americans of all backgrounds and party affiliations must unite against this dangerous bigotry.   February 1992

THE MORAL CASE AGAINST BUCHANAN

It is immoral for any decent American to support Patrick Buchanan for president, even if one agrees with his political program. Buchanan has disqualified himself from receiving the support of decent people by his bigotry and anti-Semitism. His racism includes the denigration of black life and suggestions that blacks are intellectually inferior. His anti-Semitic utterances range from his admiration for Hitler and Franco, to his support for the SS and assorted Nazi war criminals, to his mockery of the suffering of Holocaust survivors and his revisionist suggestions that Jews were not gassed at Treblinka. It is too late in history for any moral person to say, "I agree that Buchanan is a bigot and anti-Semite, and I disagree with him on those issues, but he is entitled to my vote on the basis of his positions on other issues."

That is how Adolf Hitler was elected in Germany, it is how David Duke won election to the Louisiana legislature, and how Louis Farrakhan maintains his base of support among so many African-Americans.

The majority of people who voted for Hitler in the 1932 election were not anti-Semites; they voted for Hitler because they agreed with his economic policies. They did not disqualify him, as they should have, because of his anti-Semitism. Many Duke voters do not share his support for the Klan or Nazi party. They agree with his views on affirmative action and other issues. They are willing to vote for him despite his bigotry. The same is true of most blacks who support Farrakhan: They do not support him because of his anti-Semitism, but rather because of his black self-help programs. They simply refuse to disqualify him because of his anti-Semitism. I hear many of Buchanan's supporters making a similar argument.

A variation on that theme was sounded recently by William F. Buckley, whose intellect I respect. He wrote a long essay on anti-Semitism for the *National Review* in which he assessed Buchanan's statements about Jews. This is what Buckley said about his old friend and fellow conservative:

"I find it impossible to defend Pat Buchanan against the charge that what he did and said during the [recent] period under examination amounted to anti-Semitism. . . . [Buchanan has] said things about Jews that could not reasonably be interpreted as other than anti-Semitic in tone and substance."

Buckley ended his essay by asking why Buchanan has "survived" these legitimate charges of anti-Semitism—charges that have been documented by conservative *New York Times* columnists William Safire and A. M. Rosenthal as well as by several respected journals. Buckley concludes that Buchanan would not have survived ten years ago, but that he does today because of "a creeping cultural-political insensitivity to anti-Semitism that is both [morally] wrong and alarming."

Two cheers for William F. Buckley. But hold the third. Shortly after publishing his comments about Buchanan, Buckley was asked the following question by talk-show host Charlie Rose:

"If you were a citizen of the great state of New Hampshire and you had an opportunity as a Republican to vote in the primary, would you vote for Pat Buchanan?"

Buckley said that he would! Then he explained why: "On the grounds that I, as a conservative, have found out a way to finally register my disappointment with George Bush. . . ."

Think of what that means. William F. Buckley is willing to vote for a man whom he has found guilty of anti-Semitism. To be sure, it is only a protest vote. But a protest vote, in combination with other votes, could help elect Buchanan as president. Even if that seems unrealistic, every vote for Buchanan helps to legitimate his anti-Semitism.

Buckley, himself, is thus contributing to the "creeping cultural/political insensitivity to anti-Semitism" that he finds morally "wrong and alarming." I hope he will reconsider and declare that he would not, under any circumstances, cast his ballot for a man whom he cannot defend against legitimate charges of anti-Semitism.

Nor can there be any doubt that many bigots are supporting Buchanan precisely because of his bigotry. They see in Buchanan a champion who is willing to say in print what they whisper among themselves in barrooms and on street corners. Several racist and anti-Semitic newspapers—such as the *Spotlight*, for which Buchanan once wrote, and the *Post Eagle*—favor his candidacy. My current mail includes anti-Semitic letters promising that Buchanan will finish what Hitler began.

Recently, a group of independent New Hampshire voters—mostly white Christians—have established a Committee Against Bigotry, which is urging voters who wish to protest to do so without casting a ballot for bigotry. The moral campaign against Buchanan seems to be catching on. As one pollster put it: "It is not only Jews and blacks who are concerned. [W]hite Christians don't want to elect anti-Semites and racists . . . either." Now that's a moral application of the Golden Rule that deserves three cheers.

February 1992

15 // *American Anti-Semitism and Anti-Zionism: From the Left*

THE SOCIALISM OF FOOLS: LEFT-WING ANTI-SEMITISM

While anti-Semitism and anti-Zionism from the extreme right has been a problem throughout history, anti-Semitism and anti-Zionism from the extreme left is a relatively recent phenomenon, especially in the United States. I mark its beginning with the highly publicized statements made by Father Daniel Berrigan, a left-wing "peace" activist, shortly after the Six-Day War. Berrigan characterized Israel as a "racist" state and "a criminal Jewish community" that "manufactures human waste." He accused American Jews, who were more active in anti-Vietnam protests than any other group, as ignoring the "Asian holocaust" in "favor of economic and military aid" to Israel. Berrigan's Der Stürmer–style characterizations were quickly echoed by other knee-jerk leftists such as William Kunstler and Angela Davis.

The National Lawyers' Guild, the legal arm of the extreme left, took up the campaign against Israel as well. Soon anti-Zionism, tinged with anti-Semitism, became legitimatized among elements of the extreme left, especially the Third World–oriented left. Jesse Jackson's notorious statements characterizing Zionism as "Judaism's poison well" and New York as "Hymietown" contributed to the legitimization of anti-Zionism and anti-Semitism among some leftists and African-Americans. To his credit, Jackson has apologized and avoided a repetition of this kind of bigoted rhetoric. But to his discredit as a black leader, he has refused to condemn similar, and worse, utterances from some of his supporters, such as Reverend Louis Farrakhan, and from other black leaders, such as Professor Leonard Jeffries.

The good news is that some overt anti-Semites such as former congressman Gus Savage have been defeated for reelection and that other Jew-baiters such as Reverend Al Sharpton have no significant political base.

The bad news is that the atmosphere in some communities is such that anti-Semitic rhetoric and violence can be triggered even by a noncriminal automobile death like that which triggered the murder of an innocent Hasidic Jew in Crown Heights in the summer of 1991 and rallies that included Jew-baiting slogans and signs.

The greatest dangers are not, however, from the extreme left or the extreme right, though the manifestations of anti-Semitism and anti-Zionism are most visible from those quarters. The greatest dangers lurk in the insidious and often invisible process by which the bigotry of the extremes creeps gradually into the mainstream. I am seeing that happening today on many university campuses, where the thoughtless rhetoric of the extreme left is helping to define what is "politically correct" and "incorrect." Leftist gurus such as Professor Noam Chomsky of MIT are becoming the arbiters of political correctness not only within the extreme left but also within elements of the moderate left. (The "moderate left" in many American university campuses would be the extreme left in most parts of the real world.)

Chomsky's rabid anti-Zionism has made it respectable for many students to support the terrorism of the PLO and to apply hypercritical standards to Israel's actions. Chomsky's support of those who deny the existence of the Holocaust and his ridiculous statements that there are "no anti-Semitic implications in denial of . . . the Holocaust" have even made it respectable in some academic quarters to question the indisputable evidence that millions of Jews were murdered in Nazi gas chambers.

The challenge is to keep the anti-Semitism and anti-Zionism of the extreme left as marginal as possible. If it remains the exclusive province of noncreditable extremists such as Berrigan, Kunstler, Farrakhan, Jeffries, and Chomsky, then anti-Semitism will remain, as August Bebel once characterized it, the "socialism of fools." But if it were to become mainstream, as I fear it is becoming, then it could pose a serious and divisive problem for every decent citizen of the world.   May 1992

ALAN M. DERSHOWITZ

THE PAPER ALICE WALKER SHOULDN'T HAVE SIGNED

What is Alice Walker, author of *The Color Purple* and other sensitive works about suffering, doing calling for the destruction of Israel? Recently, Walker joined a group of radicals, terrorists, and other Israel-haters (and America-haters) in signing a manifesto demanding the "dismantling" of Israel and its replacement with "a democratic, secular Palestine."

This formulation has long been a code phrase for substituting a radical Palestinian state, which would become allied with the Soviet Union, for America's only democratic ally in the Mideast. The formulation itself hides the truth. Israel is already the most democratic and secular state in the region. Arabs, both Moslem and Christian, sit side by side with Jews in Israel's Knesset. The deputy speaker is an Arab, as are others in high positions.

There are, of course, no democracies and no secular governments among the Arab and Moslem states. No Jews sit in their parliaments; in fact, no opponents of the regimes in power play any role in government. And the most undemocratic—indeed antidemocratic—organization in the world today is the Palestine Liberation Organization (PLO), the "government in exile" that would immediately take control of any Palestinian state. The PLO's definition of democracy is a state in which the only right a dissident has is the right to a bullet in the back of the head after a "people's" trial. The PLO has given fresh meaning to George Bernard Shaw's aphorism that "assassination is the ultimate form of censorship."

The pro-PLO manifesto does not even pretend, as radical opponents of Israel's existence used to pretend, that it is calling for a "bi-national" state on the model of Lebanon. The disastrous fratricide in Lebanon between Christian and Moslem Arabs has put an end to that pretense. Now the radicals openly call for the dismantling of Israel and the substitution of an entirely different state—a state that would, in practice, be just like the existing "secular democracies" of Iraq, Syria, and Libya.

The other signatories of this manifesto are a strange and motley collection of knee-jerk radicals, supporters of terrorism, and general do-badders. Gore Vidal is among them. He has a long history of rabid hatred for Israel. In a 1986 article, he characterized Israeli Jews as "predatory people" with an "alien theocracy," and American Jews as a "fifth column," whose loyalty to Israel will always outweigh their loyalty to America. And he predicts—

one senses with a touch of glee—that "as Armageddon draws near," the moral majority will "either convert all the Jews . . . or kill them."

I am not surprised that on the fiftieth anniversary of the Nazi occupation of Austria, which marked the beginning of the end for European Jewry, an insensitive bigot like Gore Vidal would call for the dismantling of Israel, a country whose people he hates with a passion. But I am amazed that others with somewhat more credibility, such as Nobel Prize winner and vitamin C-pusher Linus Pauling and writer Jessica Mitford, would lend their good names to so ignoble a cause.

One name that stands out among the signatories will be unfamiliar to most Americans but is familiar to me. It is Fouzi El-Asmar, who served time in an Israeli detention center as a suspected terrorist organizer after a captured Jordanian terrorist fingered him as "very active in the field of sabotage and terrorism."

Another of the signatories is attorney William Kunstler, with whom I have worked on many cases and causes. Kunstler is candid in acknowledging that he applies a double standard: He will never criticize a "socialist" country for its abuses of human rights, no matter how extreme; but he will always savage Western democracies at the jerk of a knee.

Many of the other signatories are old-fashioned anti-Semites like Stokely Carmichael and William Randolph of the All African People's Revolutionary Party, whose literature proclaims that "Jewish capitalists" control America and have a "stranglehold over the economic, social, and cultural life of the African community," and that "the Zionist movement" is responsible for the "wholesale murder and exploitation of billions of people all over the world."

I don't know whether Alice Walker and other decent people whose names appear on the PLO manifesto were aware of who their co-signers were or for what they stood. By now they must be presumed to know. Ignorance may be an excuse once, but it is rarely persuasive a second time.

Fortunately, the vast majority of Americans, of every political persuasion, race, religion, region, and ethnicity, support the right of Israel to exist. There is, of course, room to criticize particular Israeli policies, as many Israeli and American Jews do. But calling for its dismantling is both immoral and against the best interests of the United States. It is what radical Arab governments like Libya, Iraq, and Syria truly desire. And it is the acknowledged goal of the PLO.

Every so often, it is important to be reminded that Israel's enemies threaten it with total destruction, not just the loss of territories captured

during a defensive war. The pro-PLO manifesto signed by Alice Walker
and others is just such a reminder.   March 1988

HALF-TRUTHS ABOUT ISRAEL
PERVADE MEDIA

JERUSALEM—During four weeks of intensive interviewing and research
in Israel, it has become clear to me that the gap between American media
reporting and reality is cavernous.

An American who follows the news of the Middle East, particularly
during recent months, must come away with the impression that the Palestinians are seeking to establish a democratic state that would constitute no
threat to Israel, while the Israelis are brutally repressing political demonstrations by uncontrolled and disproportionate force.

The reality is very different, indeed, as illustrated by a comparison of
some items Americans read in the press and the actual facts:

• In a widely read op-ed article, Americans were assured by a member
of the Palestine National Council that a Palestinian state "surely will be
democratic and secular," and that the Palestine National Council "is the
equivalent of the U.S. Congress [and] the most representative political
assembly in the Arab region."

We are not told what the West Bank Arabs themselves say they want.
The results of a poll conducted by Bir Zeit University, a Palestinian school,
paint a far different picture of the nature of a possible Palestinian state.
Sixty-six percent of those polled rejected the idea of a "democratic and
secular" state, opting either for an Islamic fundamentalist state or an Eastern European Marxist state. Only 34 percent preferred "some form of
democracy."

Moreover, the notion that any part of the Palestine Liberation Organization, including the Palestine National Council, its political branch, is
"representative" like the U.S. Congress is an obscene comparison. The
PLO tolerates no public dissent, as evidenced by its recurring threats to,
and murders of, Palestinians who disagree with its one-party line.

Nor would most Palestinians be content with a Palestinian state limited
to the West Bank and Gaza. The vast majority favor an Islamic state in all
of "Palestine," which of course would mean the end of Israel.

This is not to say that Israel might not be better off taking the enormous risks that would be entailed in surrendering most of the territories in exchange for a promise of peace. The alternative—continuing to control an increasingly hostile population under occupation—may be even riskier and more deleterious to Israeli democracy. But the issues are not nearly as simple as the American press often makes them out to be.

• Americans are told by distinguished journalists that the Israeli military response to the Arab rock and bomb throwing is utterly lawless. For example, Anthony Lewis of the *New York Times* reported that, following the tragic shootings in the Arab village of Beita, the Israeli army deported six Arabs without any due process: "As always in these cases, there were no charges, no trial, just a quick dumping of the men into Lebanon." Other newspapers carried similar reports.

These accounts are simply inaccurate.

In fact, there was an appeal of the deportation order. The six men were represented by excellent lawyers, including members of the Association for Civil Rights in Israel. The hearing was going extremely well for the accused, and it looked as if they were going to win. At that point, the accused all decided to withdraw their appeals. Their lawyers advised them that they had a good chance of winning, but the accused apparently did not want to blunt the political impact of their deportations by having them rescinded by the Israeli authorities. It was only after the withdrawal of the appeal that they were flown into Lebanon.

The difference between the American press accounts and what really happened is no less than the difference between lawlessness and a good-faith attempt to adapt the rule of law to the exigencies of a violent uprising.

The point is not that Israel is handling the uprising well. Many Israelis are critical of deportations, detentions, deadly force, and house destructions. But, again, the issues are far more nuanced than they appear in the American press.

• The American press reports on the Israeli government's attempt to deport Mubarak Awad, an American citizen of Palestinian origin, characterize him as an "advocate of nonviolence." His own words on the subject of violence are not reported.

Here are some of them as reported in the Israeli press and by an Israeli freelance journalist: "There are those who use guns, and we are not against them"; "Today we throw stones; tomorrow we might think that stones are not enough, and we'll have to jump on an Israeli soldier and take his gun"; "If [my people] think they can achieve things in guns, that is up to them";

"I do [believe in a coalition with the people who are doing violent actions because] to me a Palestinian who carries a gun and a Palestinian who believes in nonviolence are both reaching to one aim."

This is not to say that the Israeli authorities should deport Awad. That issue is currently before the Israeli courts. But American readers should not be misled into believing that this double-talking supporter of Palestinian violence is a follower of Mahatma Gandhi or Martin Luther King.

Perhaps I should say I object not to what the American press reports about Israel but, rather, to what the press omits. As a result of my month-long investigation, I must report that the concerned American who relies on the media for information about Israel is not getting a complete or representative picture.   May 1988

JACKSON'S SILENCE FUELS ANTI-SEMITISM

Jesse Jackson may win high marks for oratory, but he flunks the required course in courage. He apparently lacks the guts to criticize black leaders who are racist, no matter how bigoted their words and deeds.

Jackson, who speaks up on virtually every important domestic and international issue and who claims the mantle of conscience of the nation on civil rights, has remained ineloquently silent on the recent rash of racist rhetoric by some black leaders. Those include friends and former associates of his in his home town of Chicago.

What is going on in Chicago is downright disgusting. Steve Cokely, an assistant to acting mayor Eugene Sawyer, publicly declared that "the AIDS epidemic is a result of doctors, especially Jewish ones, who inject AIDS into blacks." He warned that there was a Jewish conspiracy "to rule the world." Following some breaking of windows at Jewish-owned stores on the anniversary of the Nazi Kristallnacht, Cokely accused Jewish merchants of breaking their own windows to gain sympathy.

When the Anti-Defamation League of B'nai Brith and others asked for Cokely's dismissal, several black leaders expressed solidarity with the black racist and his paranoid ranting. The Reverend Herbert Norton, executive director of the Chicago Council of Human Relations, solemnly declared that Cokely's comments had a "ring of truth," and that "sometimes the truth is rather inflammatory."

A black state representative, William Shaw, threatened that if Jews "target Reverend [Norton], I will call for a boycott on everything dealing with the Jewish community." Black alderman Alan Streeter accused "a Jewish artist" of painting a controversial portrait of the late mayor Harold Washington. The artist was not Jewish, but no black leader corrected Streeter's apparently welcome mistake.

The situation has become so poisonous that the Reverend Andrew Greeley, a Catholic priest and Chicago writer, remarked that "If I were Jewish, I would be terrified."

Finally, after much inaction and not a public word from Jesse Jackson, Mayor Sawyer reluctantly dismissed Steve Cokely as his assistant. Cokely was immediately offered a job by Louis Farrakhan, who placed tapes of Cokely's anti-Semitic speeches on sale at his mosques. Alderman Streeter has tried to rehabilitate Cokely by inviting him to appear before the City Council's Health Committee to share his wisdom.

Jackson's response to overt racism in his own city has been a profile in cowardice. He has remained silent when a critical voice was called for, and when he did speak, his words were even worse than his silence. He recently speculated that anti-Semitism among blacks had been exaggerated, thus implicitly joining the attack against Jews and others who were guilty of the exaggeration.

He refused to condemn Cokely by name, satisfying himself with the vague retort: It is "time to consider the source and move on." Then he invoked a false analogy sure to score points for him in certain quarters: "I don't see anyone holding press conferences condemning Koch," a reference to New York's Jewish mayor Ed Koch. Koch, who had attacked Jackson during the New York primary for his views on the Middle East, was, in fact, widely criticized by Jewish leaders for his polarizing political attacks on Jackson.

Nor is Jackson's selective silence a new phenomenon. For the past four years, he has repeatedly refused to condemn the notorious racist Farrakhan, who provided security for the Jackson campaign in 1984. As recently as this past November, Jackson publicly embraced Farrakhan at Harold Washington's funeral.

It is not enough that Jesse Jackson has refrained from repeating his own anti-Jewish comments of several years ago. His inaction in the face of blatant anti-Semitism, coupled with his ambiguous comments and his embrace of Farrakhan, sends a subtle message of acceptability—at least to those who want to read it that way.

There are several possible explanations for Jackson's actions and inactions. Either he is so anxious not to lose the support of the small number of racist blacks who would be offended if he were to criticize the anti-Semitism of some black leaders, or he believes that there is a "ring of truth" to what some racist black leaders are saying. Some Jackson apologists have tried to persuade me that Jackson is so deeply involved in national and international issues that he cannot take the time to comment on every local injustice.

But it seems clear that if white politicians in one of America's great cities made anti-black statements comparable to the anti-Jewish statements made in Chicago, Jackson would not remain silent. As Martin Luther King recognized: "Injustice anywhere is a threat to justice everywhere."

Even if Jackson were belatedly to speak out now, in response to criticism of his long silence, he would deserve no prizes for courage. Abraham Lincoln's words fit Jesse Jackson's silence: "To sin by silence, when they should protest, makes cowards of men."   August 1988

In July, 1992 Jackson condemned anti-Semitism, but again refused to focus specifically on the troubling phenomenon of increasing African-American anti-Semitism.

HOW CAN A QADDAFI PRIZE HONOR ANYONE?

Yes, it's true. A Socialist Swiss deputy has announced the establishment of a $250,000-"prize" named in honor of that great practitioner of international and domestic human rights, Col. Muammar Qaddafi.

Obviously rejecting such unworthy names as Dr. Martin Luther King, Mother Teresa, and Elie Weisel, the committee of African and European "intellectuals" who decided the honoree must have had a tough choice— Qaddafi, Ayatollah Khomeini, Abu Nidal, Idi Amin, or Meir Kahane?

The same committee of intellectuals will administer the $10 million fund and select its annual recipient. I imagine Qaddafi himself will personally present the prize, if he's not too busy training terrorists or manufacturing chemical weapons to kill civilians in the name of human rights.

As a law professor, I am one of those eligible to propose nominees for the Nobel Peace Prize, but I doubt that I will be asked to suggest recipients for the Qaddafi prize. Even so, here is my list of dishonorees:

The Qaddafi prize for putting profits before courage goes to those European publishers who decided to break ranks with other publishers from the Free World and sell their wares at the Iran Book Fair in Tehran. The technical books, all approved in advance by the Khomeini Koran Committee, do not offend anybody and sell for big bucks. Two American publishers who originally joined the Europeans canceled their participation under pressure from American authors. Salman Rushdie's novel *Satanic Verses* will not be exhibited, but his photograph will—on a reward poster.

The chutzpah prize goes to the ayatollah himself for filing a lawsuit—he really did—in a Yugoslavian court against three journalists who "criticized" him for demanding Rushdie's death. Perhaps next year the committee of "intellectuals" will come up with a prize named in honor of Khomeini as the person who best exemplifies freedom of speech.

The human rights award for sensitivity to women goes to Mike Saenz, who designed an interactive computer program which he calls "MacPlaymate" but which critics aptly characterize as "MacRape." The program begins with a fully clothed woman who invites the computer hacker to "take off my clothes." The program then proceeds to instruct the "player" to shackle and gag the victim and then to "explore her orifices with tools" from a "toy box."

The clear prize-winner for sensitivity to Jews goes to linguistics professor Noam Chomsky who is currently in a squabble with Moravian College. He was supposed to get some kind of an award from Moravian, until several professors learned that he was a political supporter of notorious French anti-Semite Robert Faurisson. Faurisson denies that millions of Jews died in Hitler's gas chambers and declares the Holocaust is a "historic lie" and "hoax" perpetuated by the Jewish people.

Chomsky is still campaigning for the Moravian award, but his own written words are likely to disqualify him. This is what Chomsky has written: "I see no anti-Semitic implications in denial of the existence of gas chambers, or even denial of the Holocaust. Nor would there be anti-Semitic implications, per se, in the claim that the Holocaust (whether one believes it took place or not) is being exploited, viciously so, by apologists for Israeli repression and violence. I see no hint of anti-Semitic implications in Faurisson's work."

I hope that Chomsky will use his Qaddafi prize money to take a first-year course in linguistics himself, so he can learn the meaning of anti-Semitism. Maybe then he will understand, especially during this month of remembrance for victims of the Holocaust, that it *is* anti-Semitic to accuse the Jewish people of a lie and hoax about the murder of 6 million of them.

The Qaddafi environmental award should go to White House Chief of Staff John Sununu, who criticized the press for reporting on how much oil was *spilled* from the *Exxon Valdez* rather than how much was contained in its shattered hull. I'm sure Sununu will want to share his prize with the Exxon Corp., which seems to be devoting more energy and money to restoring its image than to restoring the damaged environment, while collecting higher prices at the service stations for its gas.

The Qaddafi double-standard award is shared by King Hussein of Jordan and Mikhail Gorbachev of the Soviet Union. Hussein had his nation cast a vote to condemn Israel for limiting access to the Al-Aqsa mosque after some Moslems who had attended prayers there threw rocks at Jews worshipping at the Western Wall. The following week Hussein himself limited access to mosques in his own country after riots over food prices. Gorbachev criticized Israel for putting down riots with tear gas, while authorities in Soviet Georgia used poison gas in suppressing disturbances. Twenty were killed.

Finally, Muammar Qaddafi himself must be given some recognition for uniting the entire civilized world, which excludes the so-called intellectuals who are administering his anti-human rights prize, in regarding him as an international outlaw. No self-respecting human rights activist should accept a prize named after Qaddafi, regardless of how much money comes with it.   May 1989

YOM KIPPUR EXAM REEKS OF ANTI-SEMITISM

Imagine a white professor in a state university announcing to his class that he intended to grade "by a stricter standard" all black students who attended a memorial service for Martin Luther King. There would be an immediate and justified outcry from civil rights advocates throughout the country. Leading the chorus of criticism would be Dr. Harry Edwards, the Berkeley sociologist who has become the symbol for the demand for sensitivity toward, and equality for, black athletes.

Yet, as reported in the *New York Times*, Professor Edwards has been accused of displaying incredible insensitivity toward Jewish students by scheduling the midterm in his sociology class on Yom Kippur, the holiest Jewish holiday of the year. Virtually all Jews, whether orthodox, conservative, reform, or even secular, regard Yom Kippur as the one day on which they will not participate in work- or school-related activities. For observant Jews, it is absolutely forbidden to write or attend classes on Yom Kippur. They spend the entire day in synagogue, praying and fasting. But even for nonobservant Jews, there is something special about this Day of Atonement.

Professor Edwards must have known all this when he scheduled his midterm exam on October 9—well before the middle of the term. He must have known because a memorandum is circulated to the faculty each year specifying the date on which Yom Kippur falls and setting out the official Berkeley policy of avoiding conflicts between "the academic calendar and religious holy days." He also must have known that in a class of five hundred students, there would be a considerable number of Jewish students who observe Yom Kippur. One student told the *New York Times* that she had always attended synagogue and fasted on the holiday but felt compelled to violate her religious principles: "I felt I would be at a disadvantage by not taking the midterm, but it put me in a situation where I felt that I was backing out of my own religion."

When numerous students, Jews and non-Jews alike, complained about this insensitivity, Edwards reportedly gave an excuse that would have made a white Mississippi voting registrar proud during the 1950s: "It was the best time for an exam." Then, according to the *Times*, he added the following: "As long as we have separation of church and state, that is how I'm going to operate. If the students don't like it, they can drop the class." The report said Edwards spent an hour of class time defending his action in a talk characterized by freshman Chris Fogliani as "pretty weird." Fogliani was quoted as saying that Professor Edwards, "didn't seem very sympathetic toward the Jewish students' feelings."

To aggravate matters, the *Times* reported, Edwards refused to schedule a makeup exam, a simple matter that is routinely done by college teachers. Instead, he decided to punish the students who had gone to synagogue by requiring them to write a makeup research paper that he announced would be graded by a *stricter standard* than used for the midterm. No wonder some Jewish students felt compelled to violate their religious observance. The ones who attended religious services were threatened with stricter standards, which translates into lower grades for comparable performance.

This is unequal treatment based on religion. In addition to being insensitive and anti-Semitic, it is also an unconstitutional abridgement of the students' free exercise of religion, as well as a violation of California law. Berkeley is a state university, and a decision to discriminate against Jewish students who observe their holiest religious day of worship constitutes "state action."

The U.S. Supreme Court has said that the constitutional guarantee to free exercise of religion means that a state cannot put "substantial pressure on an adherent to modify his behavior and to violate his beliefs," absent a compelling government interest. A state employee like Professor Edwards cannot deny someone an "important benefit" because he or she refuses to violate a religious requirement. But Edwards conditioned the Jewish students' receipt of fair grades, an important benefit to which students are entitled, on a violation of the Jewish religion.

A California statute also forbids such conduct. It states that any student at the University of California must be allowed to take all tests "*without penalty*, at a time when that activity would not violate the student's religious creed." The only time the university can escape this requirement is when accommodating the student creates an "undue hardship."

The university has the burden of proving that it could not "reasonably" have accommodated the students' religious needs. Here Professor Edwards easily could have scheduled the exam on another day, or provided for a makeup examination to be graded by the same standards as the regularly scheduled test.

In America, the law guarantees rights to all citizens and must be applied equally. Professor Edwards should be proud of himself for sensitively struggling to protect the rights of black athletes. He should be ashamed of himself for insensitively violating the rights of his Jewish students.   October 1989

Paul Torday was born in 1946 and read English Literature at Pembroke College, Oxford. He spent thirty years working in engineering and in industry, before fulfilling his long-harboured ambition – to write.

His love for the countryside, people and wildlife around his home near the River North Tyne was often reflected in his novels, but can be seen most clearly in his debut, *Salmon Fishing in the Yemen*, which became an immediate international bestseller when it was published in 2007. It has since been translated into twenty-eight languages and was made into a film starring Ewan McGregor and Emily Blunt. Paul published a further six novels and two novellas, all to great critical acclaim, including *The Irresistible Inheritance of Wilberforce* and *The Girl on the Landing*.

The Death of an Owl is Paul's last book, which he was working on right up until his death in December 2013. Knowing how much he wanted to finish and publish the book, his eldest son, Piers, an award-winning author in his own right, undertook to complete it. Happily, he succeeded and the result is a wonderful final chapter in what has been a glittering career.

www.paultorday.com

Also by Paul Torday

Salmon Fishing in the Yemen

The Irresistible Inheritance of Wilberforce

The Girl on the Landing

The Hopeless Life of Charlie Summers

More Than You Can Say

Two Eerie Tales of Suspense

The Legacy of Hartlepool Hall

Light Shining in the Forest

Praise for Paul Torday

Salmon Fishing in the Yemen

'Paul Torday's debut novel is about an impossibility . . . And the remarkable thing is that a book about so deeply serious a matter can make you laugh, all the way to a last twist that's as sudden and shocking as a barbed hook . . . As with all good comedy, there's a tragic underside . . . And there is satire . . . To write a novel lampooning the looking-glass world of Blairite government must have given Torday as much gruesome fun as he gives his readers . . . *Salmon Fishing* is extraordinary indeed, and a triumph' *Guardian*

'[A] tender hearted book . . . [and a] thoroughly enjoyable debut' *Sunday Times*

'Captivates the grumpiest reader within moments . . . if you imagine *The Office* crossed with *Yes, Minister*, you may get some inkling of how very funny it is . . . the intelligence, inventiveness and humanity of this novel in comparison to the usual run of literary fiction is as wild salmon to the farmed' *Daily Telegraph*

'This is a book of considerable charm, an echo-chamber of a dozen different voices adroitly ventriloquized . . . [it's] a moral tale about the importance of believing in something and the comparative importance of everything else' *Independent*

'His prose remains anything but safe. It is supple, skilful and literary . . . this is a fabulously good yarn' *Observer*

'It seems Paul Torday can do no wrong. *The Girl on the Landing* is his third book and destined to do as well as the other two' *Daily Express*

More Than You Can Say

'The certainties of the imperial world in which Buchan's heroes operated have long gone, but Torday shows that today's more ambivalent realities can also be pressed into service to produce intelligent and readable adventure stories'
Sunday Times

'A Buchan-like set-up that pitches Gaunt into thriller territory . . . It's a brave stylistic gamble' *Daily Mail*

'There are good reasons why Torday has found success, as this novel shows. There's real substance to the characterisation . . . a keenness to incorporate the dark and the serious . . . and to engage with contemporary politics and issues. Above all, there's his desire to entertain and to keep his readers turning those pages' *Guardian*

'Torday's prose whips along in this involving, enjoyable novel' *Vogue*

The Hopeless Life of Charlie Summers

'Charlie is a wonderful creation, at once sad and heroic, whose search for redemption attains real pathos at the end of this affecting, skilfully crafted novel' *Financial Times*

'Brilliantly and sympathetically drawn . . . this wonderfully written, clever book does not miss a single trick' *Daily Mail*

'Shades of both Greene and Ambler here, both in the crispness of the exposition and the marrying of humour with something close to tragedy' *Spectator*

The Legacy of Hartlepool Hall

'More intriguing is the skein of darkness that, in common with much of Torday's fiction, runs discretely through the story – one sequence is sufficiently macabre as to recall the work of a young McEwan' *Literary Review*

'This is a novel about decay and destruction, but bracingly unsentimental and surprisingly moving' *Guardian*

'A gloriously enjoyable wallow of a read' *Daily Mail*

'It's a novel that should enhance his reputation for excellent, ingenious writing' *Metro*

Light Shining in the Forest

'A well-crafted novel . . . there is momentum, and there is excitement' *Spectator*

'[Torday] has blended some excellent social satire and even a dollop of the supernatural . . . this is an excellent mash-up, well-written, well-crafted and constantly gripping' *Daily Mail*

'Tautly written, the tone acid and angry' *Evening Standard*

'Paul Torday switches water for woodlands in *Light Shining in the Forest*, a tale of missing minors' *Vogue*

'[A] grippingly dark thriller . . . Great writing from a master storyteller' *Red Magazine*

Piers Torday was born in Northumberland and is the eldest son of Paul Torday. He has worked in theatre, comedy and TV and is the bestselling author of three children's books: *The Last Wild*, which was shortlisted for the Waterstones Children's Book Award and nominated for the CILIP Carnegie Medal; *The Dark Wild*, which won the *Guardian* Children's Fiction Prize 2014; and *The Wild Beyond*. He lives in London.

www.pierstorday.co.uk

Praise for *The Last Wild* trilogy

'A wonderfully strange and strangely wonderful book' *FT*

'Written in a vivid, urgent style, it may be as critical to the new generation as *Tarka the Otter*' *The Times*

'An action-packed, eco-thriller with memorable characters, both animal and human, and a powerful message about the interdependence of man and nature. A promising debut'
Daily Mail

'Highly recommended' *Sunday Times*

'*The Wild Beyond* is a triumphant finale to an anarchic trilogy'
Guardian

The Death of an Owl

PAUL TORDAY

with

PIERS TORDAY

WEIDENFELD & NICOLSON

First published in Great Britain in 2016
by Weidenfeld & Nicolson
an imprint of the Orion Publishing Group Ltd
Carmelite House, 50 Victoria Embankment,
London EC4Y 0DZ
An Hachette UK Company

A CIP catalogue record for this book is available
from the British Library

978 0 297 86750 0 (cased)

Typeset by Input Data Services Ltd, Bridgwater, Somerset

Printed in Great Britain by Clays Ltd, St Ives plc

The Orion Publishing Group's policy is to use papers
that are natural, renewable and recyclable

One Author's Note

I grew up thinking my father ran an engineering business. Naturally, I rebelled by harbouring dreams of becoming an actor or writer. This modified into becoming a producer, first in theatre then in television. I made other people's stories. But after about a decade, I'd had enough. I wanted something else. Which was when Dad dropped the bombshell . . . He had been writing a book all along. Not just any book either, but the publishing and film sensation that was *Salmon Fishing in the Yemen*.

I was immensely proud, and this gave me the confidence to undertake a creative writing course. It took a while, but four years later, I had published a book too – *The Last Wild* – the first in a trilogy about a boy trying to keep the last animals in the world alive.

Sadly, during that time, Dad had more dramatic but less cheering news – a diagnosis of stage-three kidney cancer. Miraculous drugs gave him another six years, and eight more wonderful books.

In the last year of his life – not that he knew that – he began writing his ninth book, called *The Death of an Owl*. It was, he told me, about a man who couldn't help but tell the truth, and how that played out when he gets involved in a scandal involving a politician who runs over an owl by mistake . . .

He really wanted to finish the novel. I know it was a lifeline for him when things got bad. But by the final weeks, it became clear he was not going to. Even so, he was still making notes until a few days before he died. We never talked much about what would happen to the book. There were more important things to discuss.

A few months after Dad's death, I began the process of going through his papers. I found the manuscript. Everyone – family, his agent, his editor – of course wanted to know what it was like. I knew he had been anxious that the painkilling drugs had addled his mind and that this would be evident in the story. I was relieved and delighted to find the opposite – a book that combined the political wit and perception of *Salmon Fishing* with the unsettling gothic tone he had made his own in *Girl on the Landing*.

I was gripped.

But it wasn't finished. It stopped mid-sentence at a key point.

I dearly wanted to find out what was going to happen next. But Dad was no longer around to tell me. There was only one thing for it. I was going to have to make it up myself . . .

Piers Torday
London, 2016

The Death of an Owl

I

OXFORD AND AFTER

I

Autumn, 1981

As we bent our heads in prayer I glanced down and saw that beads of dew, left by the wet grass at the side of the churchyard path, where I had strayed for a moment to look at an old tombstone, glistened on my polished black shoes. The shoes were new; as was the dark grey suit I now wore, purchased in anticipation of my going up to Oxford in a few months' time. The decision to buy the suit had been brought forward a little due to the importance of the occasion: the memorial service for my Uncle Roland.

Roland Fryerne was my father's older brother. From this day on, my father would become head of our rather eccentric and dispersed family. If he chose to, he would be entitled to call himself 'Charles Fryerne of Fryerne Court': a feudal title dating back to the fifteenth century to which the family – if nobody else – attached great importance. Roland, genealogist and historian, had been cremated earlier in the day. The urn containing his ashes, no doubt still warm, nestled on a table garlanded with lilies, whose heavy scent filled the church. I felt no particular grief at my uncle's death. I had hardly known him, as we had lived abroad for many years. My uncle had visited us once in New York, when I was all too young to remember, and half a dozen times in Lausanne, where we had lived for most of my life so far. He had not been at ease with children; or perhaps I had not been at ease with uncles.

Now my father's employers had transferred him to a position in Head Office in west London. 'Putting me out to grass,' my father told my mother. At the time I had no idea what the phrase meant, but I was captivated by the idea of my father standing in a paddock and kneeling down now and then to munch the fresh pasture. I could see his grey head and his broad pinstriped back directly in front of me now. My elderly mother stood beside him, wearing a formal high-necked dress of midnight blue. If you met my parents for the first time you would judge them as elegant if somewhat chilly, and I am not sure that further acquaintance would have modified this impression. They were very private. They had none of the bonhomie that some expatriates displayed on returning home to England – a form of insecurity as the new-comers struggled to rediscover their place in the social order, unconscious of the fact that 'society' was changing so fast they might as well have just stepped out of a time machine.

My father always took a perverse pride in describing his line as late developers, of which I was a prime example, not having been born until both my parents were well into their forties. They had been slow to marry, late to parenthood and now it seemed doubtful whether they would make anything of their retirement. But they were Fryernes and therefore had long ago chosen obscurity over insecurity as their distinguishing feature.

In Lausanne we had lived quietly, but all my parents' friends were comfortably off and so, I assumed, were we. Their social circle consisted of bankers, diplomats, or senior employees of organisations such as the United Nations and the Red Cross. Not merely a late child but an only one, the much older children of these professionals were my few friends; their mothers were my mother's friends. Cocktail parties and dinners were infrequent and discreet. Dances were occasionally arranged for the younger generation – evenings of extreme dullness and great propriety.

Amongst the three of us, though, we had fun whenever my father had some time off. Long walks in the hills above Evian in the early summer, amongst the alpine flowers and the remainder of that year's snow; sailing on Lake Geneva where we kept a small boat in one of the marinas; weeks spent in a rented villa in Menton, on the Côte d'Azur; and of course, skiing once the snow came.

I was already missing the shores of Lake Geneva. What I had seen of England so far did not encourage me to think life in west London would be much of a substitute for the life I had left behind. The prospect of going to university and mingling with a host of people who had all been at school together did not appeal either. I could speak three languages already, and the International Lycée I had attended had given me as good an education as you could wish for, but nobody I knew was going to Oxford. Those of my friends and contemporaries who had felt the need for further education had obtained places at Harvard, Princeton, the Sorbonne, Padua, Tübingen – even Cambridge. Already they resembled embryos of the successful Eurocrats or bankers they would no doubt one day become. If I was an embryo of anything, I didn't have any idea what it might be. I didn't really know what I believed in and I faced the future with a certain sense of dread.

The memorial service drew to a close. We shuffled out of our pews and processed behind the vicar out into the fresh air. I was standing beside my mother and, unaccountably, took her hand. 'Don't cling,' she said, but not unkindly. I let go. The congregation had broken up into small groups who were chatting and enjoying the autumn sunshine after the chilly gloom of the church interior. I turned and studied the view around me. A suburban road separated two very different worlds. Behind me was the ancient church of St Mary's-Without, a building of Norman origin, set in its own island of green and bounded by a copse of trees. A different landscape lay on the opposite side. I had seen the sign on our arrival: the road was called Fryerne Way. Behind me I heard my father say, 'And that is Fryerne Court Estate.'

I turned and recognised Bradford Fryerne, a distant American cousin who appeared able to drop everything and cross the Atlantic at a moment's notice in order to attend family gatherings of this kind. He had been a near neighbour in New York.

'Wow,' he said.

I gazed at the rows of detached houses, each with its own pocket-handkerchief-size front garden, off-road parking and garage. The few cars that were parked there at this time of day all seemed new or nearly new: Rovers, Jaguars and the occasional sports car. I could see nothing that warranted a 'wow'.

'No trace of the old family home, then?' asked Bradford.

'No,' said my father with relish. 'Not a brick. Not a chimney pot. There was no nonsense about listed buildings in those days. They got a wrecking ball in and flattened the lot.'

For a while longer we studied the housing estate. I had always imagined that the original Fryerne Court might at least have survived in the curve of an ivy-covered archway, or perhaps the remains of a kitchen garden or hothouse; a weed-shrouded knot garden. I had no excuse for such

6

fantasies; my father had always assured me that nothing remained of the old house. It seemed as if Bradford had cherished a similar dream, for he stared at the row of houses as if at any moment he expected a veil to be pulled aside and the ghost of Fryerne Court to emerge like Camelot from the shining mist.

Once the memorial service was over the plan was for us all to make our way to the Fryerne Arms a mile or so away. We had passed this pub, draped in banners advertising 'All You Can Eat Carvery!', on our way to the church. It had been selected for the sentimental associations of its name rather than for any practical consideration. The fake-Tudor, half-timbered exterior and the fibreglass reproduction of our family crest attached to a pole in front of the pub were not inviting. The noise of car doors slamming stirred my father from his thoughts: reminiscences of Uncle Roland for his after-lunch speech; worries about his new job, or his new house.

'Lunch,' he said with a shudder. We moved off to join my mother.

My Uncle Roland's work as an historian had produced various short essays, published in architectural journals, of interest mainly to specialists in the design of church roofs. Later in life he took it upon himself to write *A History of the Fryernes of Fryerne Court*, which began with the events of Bosworth Field in 1485. The Charles Fryerne of the day had distinguished himself during the course of the battle – it was not clear how – and had earned the gratitude of Henry Tudor. In an untypical and unhistorical way, Roland had allowed himself to speculate as to what those services might have been. Rescuing the colours? Diverting an axeman from attacking the future king? No firm conclusion was reached, but it was a fact that the services had led to a grant of land on the edge of the South Downs. A few decades later the accumulated rents were sufficient to finance the building of a house, which became known as Fryerne Court. At first it was a simple, graceful structure with leaded roofs and mullioned windows and high chimney stacks. As the original Tudor building was added to by successive generations of Fryernes, it lost its purity of conception and form, and its domestic scale, and became a large and uncomfortable-looking house with a surfeit of tack rooms, stable yards and grooms' cottages. It also became too expensive to run on the income from farm rents, which had supported it quite comfortably for the first two hundred years of its existence.

Twenty-five years before he embarked on the project, someone had tipped off Uncle Roland that an oil painting of the original Tudor house was coming up for auction at Christie's. He bought it. A colour plate of this picture was reproduced on the dust jacket of his book. He also possessed a black and white photograph taken in 1920 of the much-enlarged building that was pulled down soon afterwards. This was reproduced as the frontispiece. My father believed that it was the oil painting that had originally inspired Roland to undertake his final, and greatest, project. The resulting self-published tome was the crowning achievement of my uncle's life.

The history of my ancestors, as related by Uncle Roland, was one of many small deeds and no great ones. The narrative sections of the work were brief, but undoubtedly dull out of all proportion to their length. The book was garnished with numerous genealogical tables, with headings such as 'The Fryernes of New South Wales'. Bibliographies, indices and extensive footnotes filled the rest of its pages.

Indeed the Fryernes had achieved a kind of obscurity so comprehensive as to be rather unusual in its way: not a single politician nor bishop nor general nor nabob graced our ranks. For the most part we lived out our lives quietly, most of us within our means, troubling nobody. The last Fryerne to live in the house itself was another Roland, my uncle's grandfather. This Roland was less dull and more ambitious than his forebears and it struck him that the family had played too modest a role in the country's affairs. He wanted a seat in Parliament and a larger house. The seat eluded him, but he went ahead with his designs to build a residence suitable for a county magnate and a man of standing. In order to finance the ambitious extensions to the original building he decided to invest in South American railway stocks, which promised spectacular results. The results were indeed spectacular, but not in the way investors had hoped. That earlier Roland clung on as long as he could in the financial wreckage that followed the South American Railway Crash, which also brought down the great banking house of Overend & Gurney and a host of other speculators, but a few years later, Fryerne Court had to be sold. My ancestor went off to die in a boarding house in Hove, ending his life racked with guilt for losing the house on his watch.

Fryerne Court was not long enjoyed by the new owners. It did duty during the First World War as a temporary nursing home and by the time it was handed back by the Army the house was in a bit of a state. There was talk about trying to convert it for use as a school, but in the end the least risky solution was simply to pull it down. After all, the new owners had hardly lived there. They had performed no heroics at Bosworth Field. The site had development potential, but it was not until the 1950s that some developers obtained planning permission for residential housing. Then the ruins, parks, and stands of trees, so carefully landscaped over the last four hundred years, were felled, flattened, ploughed up and built over to bring into existence the desirable executive housing that was the Fryerne Court Residential Estate.

I thought about this as I sat at a narrow and overcrowded trestle table in the dining room of the Fryerne Arms, squeezed in between my mother on my left and a very large lady who said she was my cousin on my right. It was difficult to move my elbows. My father had foregone the option of the carvery and had chosen the menu for all of us. The starter was a prawn cocktail, which required only a spoon and wasn't that tricky to eat. The second course was accompanied by bowls of steamed vegetables and mounds of mashed potato, placed at random around the table. On our plates were rubbery-looking chicken breasts. I managed to get the point of my knife into mine, and a thin stream of hot, garlicky butter shot across the table and splashed on to the plate of a girl sitting opposite me. I had noticed her in church: one of the few people close to my own age, although she was probably four or five years older than me.

'Hey!'

'Sorry. I didn't expect it to do that,' I said.

'That's the trouble with chicken Kiev. Don't worry, it didn't quite make my dress.' She dabbed some of the butter from the table with her napkin.

'Is that what this is? Chicken Kiev?'

'That's what it says on the menu. Now, which one are you?'

'I'm Charles Fryerne. Uncle Roland was my father's older brother.' I gestured to where my father sat by waving rather inelegantly with my fork.

'So now your father is the Fryerne of Fryerne Court?'

I had been listening to her voice. It was rather deep and melodious and had a familiar twang.

'He is now, I suppose. You're from New York, aren't you?'

'That's smart of you. Yes, I am.'

'We lived in New York when I was little. A block away from Brad Fryerne on the Upper East Side.'

'Oh, but Brad's my uncle! I'm Caroline Woodchester.'

I looked along the table at Brad. I could see no likeness. He was tall, pear-shaped, with thinning brown hair and a big moon-like face that had once been square-jawed but whose outlines were now beginning to blur. Caroline was about my height and solidly built, with dark hair and a lively, attractive face: not by any means beautiful, but a face you looked at and didn't forget. She watched me making comparisons and added:

'His niece by marriage, of course.'

As Brad had worked his way through several wives, this connection was difficult to challenge, but I found myself wondering whether she wasn't really his mistress. My expression must have been easy to read, because a look of annoyance crossed her face.

'So what do you think of all this nonsense?' she said, somewhat abruptly.

'Nonsense?'

'The gathering of the clans. Talking about a house that was pulled down sixty years ago. Inheriting a title that doesn't entitle you to anything. Except maybe being teased?'

I didn't like the idea that anyone should mock my father.

Still less did I believe that anyone would dare. I bent my head over my plate and struggled for a moment with my chicken Kiev. Brad's niece was nettled by my silence.

'I certainly won't be tricked into coming to one of these shows again. I'm only over here to see about getting on a course for a year or two and to escape from home for a while.'

'Your uncle seems to like coming to family gatherings,' I replied.

'Too much money and not enough to do.'

Looking up the table I saw my father hunting through his pockets, probably trying to find the notes for his speech. I turned back to Caroline.

'Well, to each his own, I suppose,' I said rather grandly, hoping to bring our prickly conversation to an end.

After a few moment's silence she said, 'Boy, was that a pompous remark.'

'I didn't mean to be pompous,' I apologised. Nor had I. I didn't want to quarrel with anyone, least of all this girl who would probably have been good fun if I had met her on a less trying occasion.

A look came into her eyes, an expression of pure mischief. She leaned forward a little so that only I could hear her words.

'Let's find a room upstairs before the speeches begin. There will be speeches, won't there? There always are when you English get together.'

'A room? What do we need a room for?'

I was mystified, but only for a moment. She mouthed, rather than spoke, the next words, but her meaning was unmistakable.

'Sex, of course.'

'What?'

I could feel the blood rising in my cheeks and my mouth fell open. I saw that Caroline was trying not to laugh, delighted with the effect her words had produced.

'It might be fun,' she added. 'God knows anything would be better than sitting here a moment longer.'

She rose from her chair and, not knowing what else to do, I began to struggle upright as well. This caught the attention of my mother who, until then, had been deep in conversation with her neighbour on her left.

'Where are you going?' she asked me, tugging at my sleeve.

'We thought we'd go and get some fresh air, Mrs Fryerne, and maybe Charles could keep me company while I smoke a cigarette. I'm dying for one but I don't want to light up while people are still eating.'

'Well, Charles can't go,' said my mother. 'It would be most inconsiderate of him to leave just as his father is about to make a speech. His father is head of the family now, you know.' These last few words were spoken with emphasis, as if she expected to exert her influence over Caroline as well as me.

'Thanks, Mrs F,' replied Caroline in a breezy manner. 'All the same, I think I'll sit this one out.' She turned and headed for the door, threading her way between the tables.

At the precise moment she left, someone tinged a glass with a knife and my father stood up. Clutching a sheaf of notes, he studied them intently for a few long moments until his audience began to fidget and worry that he had the wrong piece of paper in his hands: a laundry list, for example. Then he began, his speech slow and measured.

'I cannot say how much comfort it gives me to see how many of you have made the effort to come here on this day.

Some of you have travelled great distances to be here: from New York, from Aberdeen, from the Solomon Islands . . .'

'What a very ill-mannered young lady,' my mother hissed in my ear. I did not react.

'From Santiago in Chile, from Saint Helier in Jersey, from Loughborough in the Midlands . . .' said my father, continuing his eclectic selection from the points of origin of the guests.

But I was further away than the Solomon Islands. In my imagination I was outside the dining room. I was walking up the narrow flight of stairs to the first floor of the pub, a few moments behind Caroline so that we would not be seen ascending the steps together. Then we arrived on a landing. I took hold of her hand. In my imagination it was cool and firm and not trembling as mine was. Together we tried the door-handles of several rooms until we found one that was unlocked. We peered cautiously in. There was nobody inside. The single bed was neatly made and had an eiderdown on top. Caroline pulled off the eiderdown and sat down, pulling me beside her on to the edge of the bed.

'Now then, Charles, here's what we do.'

At the head of the table, my father was just beginning to get into his stride.

2

A few weeks before I went up to university, my father handed me the Chapman & Hall edition of *Brideshead Revisited* by Evelyn Waugh.

'It's all very well you choosing to study Politics and Philosophy or whatever it is, but don't neglect your inner life,' he warned me, without apparent irony. 'Now, this is mostly sentimental rubbish, but there are some passages about being an undergraduate in the twenties that might amuse you.'

His words, and the book, were forgotten in the flurry of activity required to send a young man away from home for about eight weeks. My mother supervised the packing of my trunk.

'You'll need a cricket bat, of course, and a tennis racquet.'

'But, Mummy, we didn't play cricket in Switzerland. I really would have no idea what to do.'

After much argument the bat came out and the racquet stayed in. Similar discussions arose over clothing. My mother's view was that I needed armfuls of tweed. I managed to sneak in a pair of jeans as well.

Then there were the books. Most of the volumes of history or philosophical tracts on my reading list could be purchased second-hand at Blackwell's, but like my father, my mother insisted on a few novels being packed, so that 'people can see you are not entirely illiterate'. I didn't rediscover and, finally, read the Evelyn Waugh until well into my second term.

I think they had both hoped that, like my father, I would read English, and perhaps develop a sense of belonging in our new home through an understanding of its literature. To be more precise, I think they hoped I would develop an affection for a particular type of novel that affectionately portrayed a certain class at a certain time. They so longed for me to discover the Britain they had once understood, but which, as far as I could tell, no longer existed in any meaningful way.

I had grown up in the long shadow of the UN, and mixed with the children of diplomats, lobbyists and politicians at international schools. Half awake as I was then, even I could see that the world was changing. Margaret Thatcher and now Ronald Reagan, both in power. Not only the Cold War but the whole post-war consensus, on everything from workers' rights to free trade, was beginning to disintegrate before our eyes. As the great powers began to shift and realign, a large part of me was curious to understand why. Studying novels and poems had only led my father to a dead-end desk job for a pharmaceutical company, and I felt no desire to follow in his footsteps. In the UK and America, a chorus of voices proclaimed a brand-new world. My sheltered upbringing with my parents had put me on the fringes of all this excitement. Now, on the cusp of adulthood, I had a craving to be – for the first time in decades – a Fryerne on the inside looking out, rather than the other way round.

I find it hard, however, to recall the Oxford I actually experienced. The university in the early 1980s felt very far from the world of Brideshead. Also my recollections are overlaid by images from TV programmes and films. A conflation of these produces a town forever bathed in afternoon sunlight gleaming on the domes of the Sheldonian and the Radcliffe Camera, and on the spires of St. Mary the Virgin and Tom Tower. In my memory the mediaeval city still dominates amongst the office blocks and some of the newer and more experimental college buildings. The reality in my own day was that one didn't look at the skyline too often because one's gaze was lowered to avoid the lash of incessant rain. You needed to keep your eyes focused and your wits sharp in order to avoid being mown down by marching columns of tourists following their guides, poking out the eyes of the unwary with the spokes of their umbrellas.

What it is like today, I don't know. Maldwyn Christie sometimes goes back to alumni dinners and will doubtless end his days as Master of some grand institution there.

I never go back.

My college was one of the smaller ones. It was – in those days – relatively undeveloped, with only one new dormitory block at the end of a row of converted houses where most of the first year had rooms. There were two quadrangles where we sometimes sat and picnicked on mossy, slightly damp green lawns. The dining hall was an imposing Victorian addition, no doubt a trade-off for the college when Fellows of the day accepted some particularly unsuitable undergraduate on to the books in exchange for a new building. The chapel was a jewel. Taken as a whole, it was a pretty, tranquil place in which to spend one's time.

Slowly I began to make a few acquaintances: firstly, other undergraduates with rooms on the same staircase as mine, then the people I shared tutorials with. It was all much easier and friendlier than I had expected.

However, perhaps due to the influence of my parents, or

the dog-eared volumes they had stuffed in my trunk, at first
I was nonplussed, disappointed even, at the characters I met.
In my head everyone was going to be dazzlingly clever, full
of political zeal in one direction or another, or at least possessed with some form of wit. In reality, many of the early,
stumbling encounters I had in common rooms or local pubs
made my parents' desultory cocktail parties seem like something out of *The Great Gatsby*.

Of course, we all subjected each other to long, earnest
monologues on the unions, the Falklands, Ireland – or whatever the topic of the day was. There was never any shortage
of opinion in the college bar. But what I thirsted for was different. An outsider to the country – and somewhat dazed – I
didn't at first naturally align myself with either left or right.
In fact, many of the noisily voiced orthodoxies I encountered
seemed to me as delusional as the system they claimed to be
reforming. In retrospect, I see that I was searching for someone who could explain the world to me, not as they wished it
to be, nor as it lay sighted through one particular telescope,
but as it actually stood, regardless of how uncomfortable
that viewing might be.

Gradually I became aware of another class of human being
in the college, who took great care to absent themselves from
all this wrangling and political debate. These were members
of a dining club called Merlin's. Sometimes one saw them
gathering in the quad to take cocktails in the spring evening
sunshine before one of their dinners, resplendent in black tie
and their distinctive primrose waistcoat and forget-me-not
cummerbund. The club was supposed to have been going
for over two hundred years. For most of these it had existed
in suspension only, banned by the authorities for various
manifestations of over-exuberance. But five years ago, like a

dragon's egg, it had unexpectedly hatched out again and so far had not been shut down. Perhaps these periods of suspended animation, followed by violent activity, had inspired the choice of name, I thought – the enchanted wizard roused from his sleep and riding out to reclaim England for King Arthur. I learned later that Merlin had in fact been the name of the club's first wine steward, who tore up various IOUs for the privilege of lending his name (and his credit) to the club. Membership was exclusive and considered to be the height of privilege in the college.

One day towards the end of the spring term, a printed notice arrived in my pigeonhole in the porter's lodge. It informed me that my name had come up as a suitable candidate for election to Merlin's, and would I have any objection? Any objection? A few minutes earlier membership of Merlin's seemed as remote a possibility as being asked to become a Knight of the Garter. Now I was being asked to join. I couldn't understand it, but I didn't feel able to sidle up to one of the members and ask why my name had been put forward. It would be too embarrassing; especially if it hadn't been. The whole thing was probably an elaborate practical joke, the point of which I hadn't yet grasped. I returned the form, signing where asked, and addressing it to The Secretary.

Almost by return I received another printed letter, saying that I had been duly elected, and inviting me to send quite a large cheque to the Secretary for my subscription (breakages and fines not included), for the summer term. This was either a genuine bill, or a complicated fraud. In either case I couldn't afford it.

I rang up my father.

'My dear boy,' he said. 'Of course you must join. It's not the Bullingdon, you know, more Middle England than the

House of Lords. But you will probably meet some good chaps.'

'Good chaps' was one of the greatest expressions of approval my father was capable of. His support was unexpected but welcome.

'But I can't afford it.'

'I'll stand you the cost for next term and then we'll see how it goes.'

Becoming a member of Merlin's was expensive. The dinners were not very cheap, the wine bills eye-watering, and the principle of collective responsibility was applied to any fines that followed a Merlin event. These might be simply a question of covering the cost of broken crockery, or a smashed window or two. However, on one legendary occasion they included rebuilding an entire Indian restaurant, which the club had hired for dinner. The guests had rendered themselves entirely insensible with strong drink, and then began shooting poppadoms as if they were clay pigeons – inside.

My election to Merlin's took place just before the Easter holidays. When I went home I discovered my father, too, had been a member, although the Second World War had rather interrupted the club's activities and he had only managed to attend one dinner. His enthusiasm for my membership was explained: it was a way of obtaining some vicarious pleasure from all the dinners I would enjoy and that he had missed. It also resolved the mystery of why I had been invited to join: the sons of previous members were automatically put forward for membership and, unless they were especially obnoxious, all were elected. My father studied the membership list that had been sent to me, with little grunts of recognition.

'Ackroyd-Smith. His father was there in my day. Not a man to be trusted. I believe they locked him up for embezzlement in the end. Illingworth Maxwell. Good family. Very well-off. Stockbrokers often are. Their clients less so.'

I also noticed that from the day of my election to Merlin's my father began to address me as an adult, no longer a child.

The first Merlin's dinner I attended was held on a sunny evening only a few days after the beginning of the summer term. It was a tradition of the club that new members should be led in by an existing member, so that they could be introduced and generally have the ice broken for them. I was in my room getting ready and had just finished tying my bow tie when there was a knock on the door. I opened it to see a tall, fair-haired man I had noticed about the college but had never spoken to.

'Good evening,' he said. 'I'm David Illingworth Maxwell. I've come to walk you into dinner.'

We shook hands, rather formally.

The rooms Merlin's usually hired were in the main college, near the Dining Hall. The club had its own chef and wine cellar, facilities of which the Senior Common Room was said to be very jealous. When David and I arrived small groups of people were standing about, almost as if they had been posed by a passing artist. Everyone was very well turned out, hair gleaming, bespoke dinner suits freshly pressed. They looked to me as if they were almost too grand to speak. Then a servant came in with a tray of the famous Merlin's cocktails. I can't remember the recipe for this toxic drink but it included champagne, and a lot of Cointreau. Within minutes the party had livened up and the noise level increased tenfold.

Dinner was simple but very good. The wines were excellent, including a Rioja, which was the latest new fad. David

Illingworth Maxwell sat next to me and subjected me to a gentle interrogation: what was it like being at school in Switzerland, what did my parents do, and so forth. With my tongue loosened by the cocktail and the wine, I may have given him more information than he expected.

'That sounds very interesting,' he said, doubtfully, as I was explaining the attitudes to tertiary education in different Swiss cantons. I saw that we had better change the subject.

'Have you thought what you might do when you leave this place?' I asked.

'Oh, it's already written in stone. I will join the family firm in the City.'

'Won't that be rather hard work?'

David called for a steward to pour us both another glass of wine.

'I don't know,' he said, after a moment's reflection. 'I don't think you have to be in much before ten, and you get a jolly good lunch in the partners' dining room. Of course I won't be a partner to start with, but as my pa is senior partner I don't suppose anyone will object if I turn up for the occasional session of browsing and sluicing.'

'And do you have to take any more exams?'

'I haven't looked into that,' said David. Instead he looked at his gold enamelled plate and slowly congealing slab of beef Wellington. I shuffled in my seat uncomfortably. If this was the charmed world over which my father had reminisced so fondly, in which he hoped I would make my way, he might well be disappointed. To me, this network in the making seemed to have even less to say for itself than the armchair politicians in the bar. I studied my wine glass, thinking hard of something clever or funny to move the conversation along, but instead I found myself saying 'Well that sounds like a colossal shame to me.'

'I don't follow you.'

'I mean, you're presumably bright, otherwise you wouldn't be here. It seems a waste of that natural intelligence to put it solely to use suffering through long lunches in the partners' boardroom when you could be helping to solve some of the world's considerable problems?'

It wasn't just the wine. It simply didn't occur to me *not* to say it, because it seemed to be the truth. It would also be the first such slip of many. As if I had glanced in a mirror and noticed a change in my reflection, I suddenly had a sense of the person I might become. Or at least, a sense of who I definitely wasn't.

David Illingworth Maxwell's pale, taut and unsmiling face did not appear inclined to answer. He turned to his neighbour, in search of an escape, but found none.

Then, because he was very polite, he asked:

'So how about you? Have you thought about the noble path you might follow when you go down? Or perhaps you are so fortunate and enlightened you won't have to work for a living?'

'Oh, I'll have to work all right,' I said. It is a curious fact that until that evening I hadn't given a moment's thought as to how I would actually earn my living. I had no interest in the drug company that employed my father, and I am sure he would have been shocked if I had asked him to help me get a job there. I had felt free to challenge my neighbour on his inherited ambition without having a clear life plan of my own. Perhaps I was more naturally an observer than a participant in any of these worlds. There might even be some virtue in watching from the sidelines. I am making it sound more thought-through than it was, more of a conscious decision, but at that point a notion did creep into my mind. No doubt the idea had been gestating over the last few weeks, the realisation slowly dawning that no prophet was going to simply reveal to me the truth about the world. And certainly not David Illingworth Maxwell.

I was going to have to discover it for myself.

'I might try and get a job as a journalist.'

He raised a doubtful eyebrow at me. 'Indeed. Covering what, exactly?'

'I'm not sure. Politics, perhaps.'

And there it was. Once the notion had materialised, it felt perfectly right. From that moment on, I was clear about what I wanted to do with my life. It was an exciting thought.

Looking back, I still don't fully understand why I continued to attend Merlin's. In part it was to prove to myself that I was not, as I had feared, an outsider, but an insider, a member of an elite. I did not then realise that a display of privilege is not always a sign of power. It is often no more than a reminder of where power once lay. They may have made a show of protecting their confidences from putative hacks such as myself, but in reality the other members of Merlin's were not powerful, either in the context of Oxford or, when they left, in the context of the wider world. When I left, in the mid-80s, it wasn't even something you dared put on your CV.

Of course, what happened with Andrew and the owl would change that perception for good. But I'm jumping ahead.

In any case, I continued to eagerly attend the club's gatherings throughout my first year. Through a chance meeting with a third-year student at one such drinks, I managed to secure my first piece of journalistic experience – writing some restaurant reviews for *Cherwell*, the university paper.

Admittedly, it was not quite the political essay slot I had in mind, but my years in Lausanne and New York, trailing after my parents on the international circuit, had given me a broader experience of restaurant dining than many of my contemporaries. Few of them had eaten out anywhere other than a hotel, and that was often limited to melon balls in a stainless steel coupe followed by duck à l'orange. There was not a hugely more imaginative range of food on offer at Oxford, but for a term or two my forthright and often unfavourable 500 word summaries of everywhere from the long-established Elizabeth to the local kebab van seemed to strike a chord.

Merlin's had very strict rules about revealing any conversation which had taken place at one of its events, so partly in search of that lead which might give me a break at the *Cherwell* beyond writing up curry houses, I took every opportunity to socialise with its members outside the formal dinners. This even extended to my accepting an invitation to join David and his family for a golfing week in Scotland over the long summer holiday. He derived great amusement by introducing me to everyone as 'Charlie, who wants to write about politics and change the world', which had the net effect of scaring them off, including his attractive elder sister. It rained for much of the week, and I spent the time mainly in my room, reading the early journalism of Winston Churchill.

That there might be people for whom membership of Merlin's was of no account, struck me as unlikely. Even the politicians at the common-room bar seemed to view it with slightly covetous eyes. But gradually I became aware that in my own small college there were individuals whose influence was of a different order, whose networks were wider than the college or even Oxford itself.

One such man whose star burned more brightly outside the university than within it was Maldwyn Christie. He was in my year and also reading PPE. He was either never asked to join Merlin's, or rejected their invitation. Regardless, he seemed far removed from the often petty and juvenile pre-occupations of that association. He was small, plump and quick of speech, whereas so many of my dining companions affected a languid drawl. I first met him at one of his break-fast levées, and remembered him mostly because of the thick tweed suit he wore whatever the weather. Maldwyn was often quick-witted and rather amusing, his eyes twinkling behind thick spectacles as he teased me about Merlin's. His banter was of a different order to what one heard at the club. It was more intellectual, more outrageous, and often referred to people who had the temerity to exist outside Oxford, who came from political or artistic circles in London and elsewhere.

It was not a huge surprise the following term to hear that Maldwyn had been elected President of the Oxford Union. I felt irresistibly drawn to write a profile of him, for the *Cherwell*. To my surprise, it was not only accepted and published, but created a brief sensation for its uncompromising and occasionally unflattering description of my friend. I found most student profiles in university rags reverential and naive to the point of fawning. There was a further stir when a staffer at Conservative Central Office came across the piece and invited Maldwyn to make a speech at the forthcoming party conference. He was barely twenty-one.

This feeling that the real world lay beyond the circumference of Merlin's grew on me as my time at Oxford rolled by until, halfway though my second year, I almost began to regret having spent so much of my time with fellow members of what was, after all, only a dining club. I increasingly thought of the conversations we had not as the height of elegant discourse, but as shallow and uninteresting. That judgement might appear harsh, but it was strengthened when I met someone who was a member of Merlin's but had never bothered to turn up to a single dinner or cocktail party. The idea that you could be eligible to join the club, rich enough to pay its dues, and yet never bother to share in its social life, was a hard one for me to grasp.

The name of this unusual individual was Andrew Landford.

3

1983

I first met Andrew Landford by chance. It was a dour, muggy afternoon in the early autumn of my final year, and I had nothing to do. That is to say, I had two essays to write for a tutorial later in the week, a lecture to attend, and a week's reading to catch up on. As I felt all these tasks could wait a little longer, I had arranged to wander up to the university rifle range and have a look around. The Oxford Rifle Club was on a recruiting drive. I had been promised that one of their star members, a third year with plenty of experience, would meet me at the range and show me how it worked.

The man who met me was taller than me, over six foot, with curly black hair framing a pale face, a strong mouth and nose and greenish eyes.

We introduced ourselves. He regarded me for a moment, as if weighing up a potential opponent. 'I know. You're the chap who wrote that profile of the mighty Maldwyn. Most unexpected.' It wasn't clear whether this referred to my ability to produce an article or Maldwyn's sudden elevation. He frowned, then broke into a friendly smile. 'Well, come and see how it all works.'

He showed me the gun cupboard where the rifles were kept. Most belonged to the club, but Andrew had his own weapon, a Rigby which he took out and let me handle.

'It's beautiful,' I said. The polished stock and the dull metal barrel were the work of a master craftsman. I gave the gun back to him but instead of locking it away, he signed it out in the book and carried the rifle and a box of shells down to the range itself. There he showed me how to lie in the firing position, and how to squeeze off the shot, using a blank. He had an ease with the gun that was extraordinary to watch, cocking it open, loading, taking aim and ejecting the spent cartridge almost in a single movement, as if the rifle were merely an extension of his arm. I tried to copy him, in a ham-fisted way. He watched without comment for a few minutes.

Then he said, 'Right. How about some live firing?'

'Are you sure? I don't want to kill anyone.'

'I won't let you kill anyone,' said Andrew. 'Get yourself comfortable and put the ear defenders on, while I set up the target.'

Twenty minutes later, my ears still ringing despite the defenders I'd worn, we left the range. I felt rather shaky, but elated at the same time. I had hit the target several times, including one shot that clipped the edge of the bull.

'You did well,' said Andrew.

'Hardly.'

I'd just watched Andrew fire three quick shots into the bull. My face was flushed and my fingers were trembling with the focus and effort but Andrew remained pale and cool, as if we had just been sitting around reading books, rather than pumping rounds of live ammunition into paper cut-outs of enemy soldiers. His control and mastery gave me a strange thrill, but at the same time I felt uneasy. There was something about his white-knuckled grip on the gun, his determination to hit the bull every time, that I found unattractive, even alarming.

'I'll never make it to your level,' I managed to say.

'You can't know that,' he replied, adding, 'I taught myself. It's just a matter of practice. Most things in life are.'

I thanked him again and went back to my flat.

By that time I was living in rented rooms outside college, sharing a small flat with a law student called Mark Davidson. He was making tea and toast when I arrived. He handed me a slice and a cup and put some more toast under the grill for himself. I described my experience at the range to him.

'Oh, you met the College Swan, did you? You are honoured.'

'The College Swan?'

'That's what they call Andrew Landford. He likes to make it look as if everything he does is effortless, but underneath the water he's paddling away furiously. Did he tell you he's got a blue, or half-blue, or whatever they give you if you shoot for the university?'

'No, he didn't mention it.'

'He wouldn't. He cultivates an air of extreme modesty, but he is the most fiercely competitive man I've ever met. He's a bit much for most people.'

'Why do you think he never comes to Merlin's?' I asked. 'I know he's a member. I saw his name on the list.'

'Most people think it's because he's too grand. I don't agree. He's just bored by other undergraduates. He's too grown up for most of us. Did he mention that he was captain of the university ski team as well?'

'No.'

'You see? He never talks about himself. He knows we all

do it anyway. He doesn't need to be a self-publicist when everyone else is gossiping about him.'

'Anything else I should know about this paragon?' I asked. I was already beginning to feel I disliked Andrew Landford, although he had done nothing to deserve such a reaction.

Mark took a contemplative gulp of tea and frowned.

'Why, are you planning a piece on him?' I shook my head. 'Still, I'd watch yourself with that. There is one thing . . . I don't know if it's true or not. But I heard this story in the college bar one night. Something about him poking someone's eye out with a punt pole.'

'That sounds improbable.'

'It does, rather. But apparently he was trying to impress some girl or other with his prowess on the water, and these tourists – who were drunk – kept getting in the way, bumping their boat, giggling and splashing them. The tourists followed them halfway up the Cherwell. Landford brushed it off at first, until one of them leaned over and said something to the girl in Spanish.'

'What?'

'I have no idea, but the story goes that Andrew's reply was in the language that needs no translation. He flipped his pole out of the water and sent the man head over heels into the drink.'

I laughed, but Mark didn't.

'It could have been much worse. As it was the poor chap clipped his eye on the corner of the boat and had to go to the Radcliffe. They say the surgeons couldn't save it, but I have no idea if that's really true.'

'Did he press charges?'

'If he did, I never heard about it. It's quite possible Landford paid him off. He's very rich, of course. Parents own a gold mine or a tea plantation or something. He doesn't have to work when he leaves here.'

'But you said he was competitive. Doesn't that mean he is ambitious as well?'

Mark wiped a drop of melted butter from his chin and grinned at me.

'Oh, he only wants to be the youngest prime minister since Pitt.'

A couple of days later I was in college for a tutorial. When it was over, I walked across the quad, heading for the library. As I passed the chapel I noticed that one of the doors was slightly open, and from within I could hear the sounds of the organ being played. Whoever had written the piece, it was faultlessly executed by the organist. He contrived to make the single instrument reproduce the sound of an entire orchestra. The beauty of the music was mesmerising. I stepped inside the chapel in order to listen. As I stood there, I realised it wasn't the college organist playing but a bigger, younger man. When he finished, I clapped and he turned on his seat to see who had been listening. It was Andrew.

'That was wonderful,' I told him.

'Oh, hello, Charles. I'm sure it was the most frightful racket. I still haven't quite got the hang of it.'

He stood up, switched off the lights and walked down the aisle towards me.

'Don't let me interrupt you,' I said.

'I'm finished anyway. I've got to get up to London this afternoon – dinner at the Carlton Club tonight.'

We walked out into the quad.

'The Carlton Club?' I asked. 'Isn't that a sort of unofficial headquarters for the Conservative Party?'

'Yes, it is,' replied Andrew. He looked annoyed with himself, as if he had committed an indiscretion.

'Are you after a seat in Parliament?'

He flushed, which made me feel my question, though frivolous, was close to the mark.

'Look, I'm sorry, I must rush. I've quite a lot to do before I catch my train. We must have lunch some time.'

Without saying anything further, he turned and strode across the quad. I wouldn't speak to him again for years.

The halcyon undergraduate days rolled past and became weeks in the blink of an eye. The weeks became months. Then the months became terms, and before I knew it, my final days as a student had pulled into the station.

I had sometimes tried to make time stand still, by telling myself, 'You'll never be this free or this happy again. Live for the moment.'

And I had lived for the moment a lot of the time. There were endless parties. There were picnics on the river. There were cricket and polo matches, and I played tennis for the college. Occasionally I would remember to attend a lecture. I managed to get to most of my tutorials although even I had to admit that my work was getting scrappier. In part, my studies were fighting a losing battle with the various romances I found myself embroiled in. They were initially, without exception, tempestuous and short-lived. But towards the start of my third year, I had begun a more satisfactory relationship with a girl I had met from one of the women's colleges.

Or so I thought.

Now finals were approaching and everyone was becoming more aware of the great divide between the fairyland we were living in and the obligations and opportunities of the 'outside' world. Everything changed when we both attended the wedding of some mutual friends who had decided to get married before they graduated. The occasion was riotous and even romantic, but at the back of all our minds questions were forming: where will they live? What will they live on? The couple concerned had only just turned twenty, and were good-looking and popular figures at Oxford. But how would they survive the cold glare of real life? Even then, some of us were showing signs of a survival instinct; others seemed happy enough to contemplate a penniless existence on some hippy farm in the Welsh Marches, with babies crawling around in the mud.

'That could have been us,' said my girlfriend, as we lay in one another's arms in the post-alcoholic haze that followed this occasion.

'No, it couldn't have been, not really. We're a little bit too realistic about life.'

'Why couldn't you have pretended just for a moment? You always want everything to be so literal.'

A tear ran down the side of her nose, sooty with mascara. I smudged it away and we comforted each other, but we both knew the end of one part of our lives was approaching, and that we would not go on together.

My exams took place during the first hot week of the summer and for five days I endured the torment of sitting in the Examination Schools, wringing out of myself whatever drops of knowledge I had absorbed in the last three years. The windows were wide open to try to keep some air circulating. The invigilators sat and nodded and then jerked awake again while the candidates scribbled away. Outside some thoughtless person was playing the latest hit from Frankie Goes to Hollywood, and the music drifted into the hall. Instead of concentrating on the question in front of me my thoughts strayed to images of grass lawns, cool drinks and girls. That in itself does not explain why I got a 2:2 instead of the 2:1 I had been aiming for. The truth is I hadn't done enough work, and maybe I wasn't as clever as I thought I was. The summer heat was just an excuse. For all I know that might be an invented memory. More than likely it was a typical English day in June: rain sheeting down.

A few days later I found myself in a punt in an alcoholic haze once more and, nearly for the last time, being poled along by a rather beautiful girl I had picked up at a drinks party. She was a good deal more competent at steering our craft than I had been; I was glad she had offered to take over after I became entangled in a curtain of overhanging dog rose, which had nearly pulled me into the water. As I watched her effortlessly guiding us back towards the place where we had hired the punt, I had one of those moments when one thinks the meaning of everything is becoming clear at last. I lay with my head on a cushion gazing at the evening sky. I could hear the water lapping and gurgling a few inches from my head. I felt like Mole, in *The Wind in the Willows*. Here I was, another soon-to-be graduate churned out by the university. I had learned nothing of any great value. I would of course keep in touch with the close friends I had made, like Maldwyn, but might well never see many of my more casual acquaintances again. What on earth had the last three years been about? What would I take away with me, except for a few confused and mostly happy memories? What mattered now was what the next three years would bring. Where would I be in three years time? I might not even settle in this country – the demand for political journalists seemed to be scant, and I couldn't think of anything else I wanted to do. I might even be married by then.

I came out of my trance and looked at the girl standing in front of me. Her movements were elegant and economical as she steered us back towards the jetty. I realised that I was deeply in love with her and always had been, ever since I had first set eyes on her at five o'clock that afternoon. The air was warm. The river was still except for the ripples that flowed backwards from our craft. My life at Oxford was over, and what a perfect evening on which to end this period of my life and start the beginning of the next.

'Mary,' I said. 'Will you marry me?'

'No,' said the girl, with great decision. Then she added, 'You might at least get my name right. It's not Mary. I'm Sophie.'

Somewhere in the soft folds of the trees on the bank, an owl hooted.

Such an innocent sound.

4

1984

My notion of becoming a political journalist had only grown and deepened since I first found myself declaring it at a Merlin's dinner. Other than my unexceptional degree, a modest portfolio of reviews, columns and articles was about the only substantial product of my university years. The brief attention I had attracted over the Maldwyn profile in the small and incestuous world of student journalism had given me an inflated sense of my own talents – which was perhaps essential to making any kind of start at all.

Upon leaving I made grand applications to *The Times* and the *Daily Telegraph*; then, when they turned me down, the other broadsheets. After that I tried some of the weeklies, such as the *Spectator*. They seemed to be overrun with applications not just from people like me, but also those with first-class degrees or masters' from Harvard or Johns Hopkins. Other applicants had already made something of their lives: they had walked across Afghanistan; they had been ice-climbing in the Andes; they had studied the lost tribes of the Amazon basin. The newspapers had lots of bright, confident people to choose from. I had done nothing apart from reviewing a kebab van and interviewing one of many student politicians. I had left university, found a rented flat in Muswell Hill, and had little else to offer except what, if anything, was between my ears.

'Have you ever thought of using your language skills?' asked one interviewer, more kindly than the rest. 'People are beginning to discover that not all foreigners speak English. Your Italian or your German might come in handy?'

But I didn't want to consider giving up on my chosen career before I had even started.

At last I was offered the position of junior reporter on *Mayhem*. You may remember it: it ran a series of dispatches from the front line during the Miners' Strike. These were full of descriptions of police brutality and the starving families of the strikers. At one point the magazine achieved a circulation of five thousand a month.

It was a strange world to find myself in, after the candlelit Merlin's dinners and afternoons spent on punts, but I think I wanted a change. By the end, I had found the gilded atmosphere of Oxford stultifying and I needed some fresh air. Perhaps, looking at my background and the friends I had made at university, it seems purely a matter of course that my politics would be traditionally conservative. But the truth was that, emerging blinking into the daylight of real life, I had no defining passion for either end of the spectrum. What did fascinate me was the way those who were driven by passionate ideologies attempted to communicate their beliefs to an often indifferent electorate. Then there was the gap between what politicians thought voters wanted to hear, and what they actually believed was the right direction for the country. I felt that gap was growing, and deserved closer scrutiny. If I was ideologically enthused at all, it was for those politicians who dressed up their message the least, rather than those who modified it according to the audience.

At least, that was what I said in the job interview, earnestly pressing my fingers to my lips, talking too quickly.

Mayhem operated out of the basement of a house in a Georgian square in Islington. The house was owned by one of our backers. The three rooms we occupied were cramped and were never cleaned until it became impossible to fight one's way into a room past the mounds of crumpled paper and piles of empty coffee cups. Then we would have a housekeeping day, and for the next few days the offices looked almost normal, before disorder took over again.

I joined at the end of September 1984, not long after the Battle of Orgreave, when NUM pickets clashed violently with the police. The tide – meaning the national press – was beginning to turn in favour of the government and *Mayhem*'s backing of the NUM was already beginning to look a bit futile. It had become important for the magazine to find a new cause to fight for.

My first assignment was to write an editorial on the aftermath of the Brighton hotel bombing by the IRA, in which five people, including a Tory MP, had been killed. After a week of furious writing and rewriting and endless telephone calls, I handed in the article. I wasn't optimistic about its reception but even so I was unprepared for the swiftness with which my editor handed it back to me.

'On the one hand; on the other hand . . .' he sneered. 'Your job is to get readers stirred up, not write a history essay. This is of no use to me.' He held up the two pages of typescript I had offered him. 'Thatcher had it coming. That's what our readers want to see.'

'But she seems to have come out of it more popular than

ever,' I argued. It was the self-evident truth of the matter, whatever one's personal politics, and it seemed delusional to refute that.

Mike McFarlane wasn't an unpleasant man, on the whole. But he role-played the hard-bitten editor to perfection. He wore braces; he chewed on unlit cigars. Dark crescents of sweat dampened his shirt beneath the arms even on cold days. 'Who are you to judge who's popular or not? Leave that to me. Your job is to write articles that sell papers. My job is to tell you what sells papers, and what doesn't. I don't want journalists like spaniels. I want Rottweilers.'

And so, cold call by cold call, doorstep by doorstep, I set about transforming myself, if not exactly from spaniel into Rottweiler, at least into a reasonably interrogative terrier. I could no more replicate Mike's carefully crafted bark than I could share his taste for cigars, but over time, my tenacity began to complement his more pugnacious approach. Hanging around at endless protest marches, party meetings and in the press lobby of the Commons, I began to build up relationships with the more approachable members of the various factions. At first, these were minor and of little consequence, but they provided an entry link into the chain of communication, and gradually I began to haul myself up.

Almost despite myself, I turned out to be much better at my job than I had ever expected. I overheard a rumour in Annie's Bar one night that a top civil servant in the Foreign Office had some classified documents regarding the Falklands that he felt the public should know about. Perhaps he was naive, as very senior people of his position and generation could be, or perhaps he thought a minor magazine such as *Mayhem* would be a less risky bet for him than the national press.

Either way, I was astonished that after various approaches through an intermediary, he agreed not only to speak to me, but also to give us access to the documents.

'I've read some of your work,' he said to me at our first cloak and dagger assignation on a park bench. 'You don't dress stuff up much, do you?'

It was not through conscious effort on my part, but my refusal to take sides in my writing was gaining me trust, even amongst those who potentially stood to lose from such unbiased coverage.

In this case, the result was sensational. It was not so much the documents themselves – their contents only confirmed aspects of the war planning that had long been suspected – but the whistleblower was suspended and charged under the Official Secrets Act. He was eventually acquitted, but the trial provided one of the news highlights of an otherwise dull summer. *Mayhem*'s circulation exploded, and for a brief while the bigger beasts of the media jungle began to treat us more seriously.

I was promoted to Political Editor. My colleagues, who had only thinly disguised contempt for my non-committal position on many of the issues they cared so deeply about, did not exactly celebrate. Nevertheless, we managed to pull off a small scoop over an internal attempt to 'purge' the Labour Party of 'militants', and my coverage of the Westland affair was enthusiastically lapped up by our readers. When obvious incompetence or hypocrisy were involved rather than ideological judgement, I found it easier to twist the knife in the way my editor and colleagues demanded.

One day in the warm and thundery summer of 1989, as we were attempting to put our latest issue to bed, Mike and I nearly came to blows over the editorial line on a piece commemorating the closure of the last coal pit in Kent. I thought it might be a good idea to let him cool off for a while, and stepped outside to get some air. As I emerged on to the street, I literally ran straight into Maldwyn Christie. He spread his hands and goggled at me, the very parody of a man experiencing extreme surprise.

'Maldwyn!' I exclaimed. 'What's a hard-right Tory doing in a den of Bolshevism like this?'

'Has old Mike been giving you a bollocking?' he replied, ever adept at not answering a question directly. 'I can see that he has. Let's have a cup of coffee when I've finished with him.' Then, in response to an impatient roar from inside the office, 'I'm coming, dear! Keep your hair on.'

I had been back at my desk for about ten minutes when Maldwyn reappeared. 'Come on. There's a pub in Upper Street you ought to be introduced to.'

'I thought you said coffee?'

'You can have the coffee if you really want. I wouldn't recommend it.'

A few minutes later we were sitting at a table in Maldwyn's pub of the month – he had a passion for such places and then went off them, or else they went off him. He could be quite a disruptive force, in his way. Once we were sipping at our pints of Guinness, Maldwyn said, 'I saw the College Swan at a drinks party the other day.'

'Do you mean Andrew Landford?'

'Who else?'

'Where was this?' I asked. I had forgotten all about Andrew. We had been acquaintances at Oxford, not friends. All the same, the mention of his name aroused my curiosity.

'He's bought a house in Notting Hill. One of those up and

coming streets where the gentry are moving in and the locals are moving out. Actually, it's rather nice. I like rooms with high ceilings . . .'

'What was the drinks party in aid of?'

'Andrew is financing something called a think tank.'

'A what tank?'

'It's a group of people who are supposed to dream up new policy ideas. There were some left of centre politicians, and some of Labour's young rising stars too. A whole lot of intellectuals. A Rothschild or two. And, of course, me.'

'Why of course you?'

Maldwyn wriggled his shoulders in a display of false modesty.

'I'm hurt you haven't followed my own career more closely.'

'I have. That's why I was surprised to see you at our office today.'

Maldwyn already had a reputation as one of the brighter newly elected Members of Parliament. He had a remarkable ability to get himself noticed by the media and was being spoken of as a man to watch, someone who might be on the fast track to the Cabinet when Mrs Thatcher went – whenever that might be.

'The art of success is to know what your enemy is planning.'

'Ancient Chinese saying?'

'No, modern Maldwyn saying. I've been asked to do an article on "Life after Thatcher".'

'She hasn't gone yet,' I remarked.

'No, but it can't be long, can it? Anyway, are you yourself enjoying working for Mike's rag?'

We talked about the personalities at *Mayhem* for a while. Maldwyn claimed to have read and enjoyed my work, mentioning the classified documents, then praising my 'perceptive' take on some of the Conservative Party's more toxic scandals. It was a gift he had, making whoever he was talking to seem like the centre of his world. Maldwyn was unprepossessing to look at when he wasn't speaking, but when he spoke, which was most of the time, one found oneself caught up in his charm and his encyclopaedic knowledge of whatever subject was under discussion. There was no doubt about his intellectual powers, or his debating skills, and I could quite easily imagine him as a Cabinet minister one day. I couldn't quite imagine him going all the way to the top, but you never knew.

Suddenly Maldwyn looked at his watch, shook his head and said, 'I'm late for a meeting. I must go. Let's keep in touch, now we have met again. You can always get hold of me through my constituency office.'

He handed me a card.

I didn't get much work done that day. It wasn't the Guinness. Drinking at lunchtime was not so unusual back then and the habit of clutching a bottle of water to one's bosom as if it were a comfort blanket was not widespread. Large glasses of white wine or a pint or two at lunch were a common-place. So it wasn't the alcohol that had disturbed me: it was this sudden glimpse, through the person of Maldwyn, into a world other than my own, where people were beginning to do things with their lives. Maldwyn was surging forward in the political world. Andrew Landford must be doing in-credibly well, even to think of funding a think tank. Perhaps he had inherited his parents' gold mine. David Illingworth Maxwell I still kept in touch with. He had been made a part-ner in his family stockbroking firm. I had read the other day that it had been bought lock stock and barrel for hundreds of millions of pounds by a French bank. Some of the proceeds had to be heading in David's direction.

All this was clear evidence, if evidence were needed, that my own career had become somewhat becalmed.

When I tried to examine myself in these rare moods of introspection, I came up a blank. I was happy enough at *Mayhem*, but the magazine lived on the edge of a financial cliff and might fold from one week to the other, if any of its backers pulled out. Rumours that we were a second front for the Socialist Workers Party persisted, although if there were hidden puppet masters, I was unaware of them.

Whatever way you looked at it, it was a precarious venture and I had no idea what I would do if the magazine fired me or else closed its doors. I had a reasonable social life. There were a couple of girls I saw from time to time; the relationships were cheerful and uncommitted on either side. I had a small allowance from my parents, which meant I should never be quite destitute. I saw little of them. My father was fast approaching retirement and was inclined to be grumpy at the prospect. My mother was falling under the spell of what we later realised was dementia. Long silences and disconnected sentences made one aware that all was not well.

But I realised I wasn't really going anywhere. Around me my former friends surged onwards like migrating salmon, their presence revealed by the occasional flash of silver. I, who had no idea what to do with myself next, no strong feelings for or against any political party, no relationships that might drag me out of my self-absorption – I just swam around in circles flicking up mud with my tail.

I see things quite differently now, of course. I see them for what they actually were.

5

1989

My flat in north London was near enough to Hampstead Heath, so that I could go running there every Saturday morning. I had persuaded myself that whatever was happening, or not happening, in my working life, I would at least keep fit – although perhaps my leisurely pace made it more of an amble than a run. I was jogging – gently – from the Heath towards Hampstead tube station on a calm, misty morning in early autumn, when I became aware of another runner overtaking me. As he moved past I saw a tall figure, moving easily and with longer strides than my own. He wore a blue tracksuit with a towel draped over his shoulders. His black hair curled over the nape of his neck, worn quite long. The profile was familiar.

I stopped, caught my breath and said, 'Andrew? Andrew Landford?'

It was indeed him, and he recognised me straight away.

'Charles. I was just thinking about you. I met Maldwyn the other day and he said you'd had a catch up.'

We stopped speaking, catching our breath, our hands on our hips. I was starting to drip with perspiration, not an entirely pleasant sensation, as my body cooled down.

'Look,' said Andrew. 'What are you doing now?'

'Doing now? I'm going to go home, take a shower and

have a beer. Not necessarily in that order.'

As if by magic a large black Mercedes with a driver pulled up alongside the kerb next to Andrew.

'My car,' said Andrew, without any attempt at false modesty. It was an unexpected accessory in someone who could not be more than twenty-seven.

'Come home with me. You can take a shower in the guest bedroom. It's all en-suite. I can lend you jeans and a shirt; we're about the same size, bar an inch or two. It would be lovely if you stayed for lunch. I know that if you don't come now, we probably won't see each other again for years. Maybe never!'

Andrew looked so melodramatic as he said this that we both burst out laughing. Then he said, 'Phone, Bertie.'

Bertie the driver opened the window and handed out a phone on the end of a flexible lead, while Andrew gave instructions to someone concerning lunch and wine. Then we climbed into the car. Inside it was large and spacious. There were papers strewn across the back seat. Andrew stuffed them into a folder to make room for me and we moved off.

'This is the life,' I said. 'Is it mandatory for all former members of Merlin's? I never got the memo if so.'

'I don't know what Merlin's has to do with it,' Andrew said, perhaps sounding more defensive than he meant to. 'I mean, I make a lot of money and I spend a good deal too. You probably think it's a bit flash,' he added.

I wondered if he was already beginning to regret his sudden decision to invite me back, so I reminded him of our last meeting outside the college chapel. 'You said we must have lunch sometime. And here we are, on our way to lunch. Only six years later.'

Andrew screwed up his face. 'I don't remember that . . .

no, I do remember,' he said pensively. 'I was practising for a charity concert. It was a disaster. I kept turning over two pages at once.'

In an extraordinary way it was as if we were suddenly old friends, whereas in truth we scarcely knew each other. But the common ground of Oxford, and even in an odd way Merlin's, gave our meeting more significance than perhaps it might otherwise have had. What else would I have done that day? Gone home, had a shower, a couple of beers; grazed from the fridge; fallen asleep on the sofa; gone to see a film in Hampstead with some friends later on: a routine, aimless afternoon had awaited me and I was not sorry to be doing something entirely different.

Andrew's house was just what one might have expected. I could well imagine 'the occasional Rothschild' lingering in these high-ceilinged rooms. The place had an air of money, power and knowledge that came from being at the centre of things. Magazines and books lay in artless piles here and there, suggesting either the hand of a diligent interior decorator or, more likely, that Andrew really did read the *TLS* and the *New York Review of Books* and volumes on ballet and Tuscan architecture, international finance and modern geopolitics. He arrived downstairs and found me handling a weighty tome on the future of the Soviet Union.

'This fellow takes a gloomy view,' I said, putting the book down.

'In the short term. It's going to be a bit like the Wild West there before too long. Very little law, lots of oil and wheat and gold. It'll be a question of who gets the key to the larder.'

Andrew poured me a cool glass of Pils and another for himself.

'I've read some of your stuff in *Mayhem*,' he said in a neutral tone of voice.

'Like it? Hate it? Bored to death by it?'

'Oh, I like the way you write. No question.' A *But . . .* lingered unspoken in the air. I didn't pick him up on it. Instead I asked, 'And you?'

'I'm an investment banker. With a small New York firm. We've been going since the 1920s but there are only about a dozen partners. Slow and steady is our motto. I'm supposed to be helping grow our business in London and Eastern Europe. We've decided that a little bit of risk from time to time might be a good thing after all.'

Even I had heard of Andrew's firm. It was old New York money; never known to put a foot wrong. If you were chosen as a partner there you were made for life: you would become not just rich, but phenomenally rich.

'Including the Soviet Union?'

'Including that, or whatever that becomes.'

There was a silence while we sipped our beer. It was delicious and I felt I could quite easily sit here all afternoon. But at the same time there was tension in the air. It was Andrew: it was as if he felt a compulsion to analyse, to probe, to question. You could feel the lightest pressure of his will, like a percussion note too deep to be heard but which throbbed in the air.

'Maldwyn said you were backing a think tank of some sort.'

'Typical Maldwyn. He's not very discreet, is he? But one knew that. No – it's not a secret, really, and if you take someone like Maldwyn on board, you know his type, one has to expect that sort of thing. Don't worry. You haven't dropped him in it.'

I didn't quite know what to make of the reference to Maldwyn. What did Andrew mean by his type? I didn't feel like asking. I said, 'So tell me about this think tank?'

'Oh, it's an idea I've had for some time. We discuss factors likely to change the way we lead our lives. For instance, are we really going to have another ten years of Tory rule, or misrule, as some would say? What's going to happen to the bankrupt Soviet Union? Why don't we know more about what's going on in China and India, two of the most sizeable marketplaces on the planet?'

The room we were sitting in had long green velvet curtains and a pale green wallpaper with some sort of floral motif. In fact there was very little furniture apart from a large grand piano in the corner. I wondered if it was ever played now, recalling Andrew's musical skill from our university days. Overall the space had the curious feel of an aquarium, in which we swam around, our mouths opening and shutting to let out bubbles of air.

'What's in it for you?' I asked Andrew, regretting the crassness of the question as soon as I had spoken. There was something in his demeanour, as he sat ensconced in his enormous sofa, that made me want to nip at his heels. But he seemed untroubled by my question.

'One of the things we do in my business is wealth management. We look for unconventional investment opportunities for very high net worth individuals. We run what the Americans call a hedge fund. The think tank occasionally sheds light on some of the situations we are looking into, especially in Russia. So a think tank aligns with both my personal and my business interests.'

At that moment a maid in a black dress and white apron appeared in the doorway.

'Lunch is ready, Mr Landford.'

This was so beyond the realities of my world that it made me want to laugh. I composed myself as Andrew stood up and led me through to the kitchen. A contemporary of mine already endowed with a cook/housekeeper, a chauffeur, and heaven knew who or what else: it was just a little bit too much.

The kitchen was another large room with a table, made from some pale wood, laid with place settings for two and bowls of salad, plates of smoked salmon and saucers of quail's eggs. There seemed to be enough for six people, let alone two.

'Thank you, Marcia,' said Andrew. 'We won't need you to stay.'

Marcia disappeared like a genie back into her lamp. Andrew gestured to me to help myself while he poured me a glass of red wine.

The wine and the food were very good and we chatted away like the old friends we weren't until Andrew said, 'Why don't you join the think tank? A journalist with your background might be just the thing we need.'

'Me?' I asked incredulously. 'But I'm just a hack. I fear I'd be a bit underpowered compared with all the heavyweights you've got lined up.'

'We haven't really got anyone lined up as such. We want to approach George Soros – he's another of these hedge fund Americans, although really he's a Hungarian. Then Maldwyn's a possibility. He's very bright, and a darling of the left wing of the Conservative Party. I hope he'll join and I hope you will too. You'd bring all sorts of insight and information that others wouldn't.'

'When you said the think tank aligned with your personal

interests,' I asked, 'what are those, exactly?'

'Oh, I intend to go into politics. I've always planned on doing that. But my observation is that you can either do it through a mixture of wit and charm – what they call "charisma", I believe – or else by making lots of money first. I am quite devoid of wit. Set me alongside Maldwyn and you'll see the difference straight away. But the House of Commons is stuffed with barristers, solicitors, teachers and social workers. A candidate with lots of money, a good, old-fashioned, self-made man, will always find his place if he shows he can be useful. Therefore the think tank, which will cost me a lot of money but which will, I hope, gain me access to senior people in the party . . .'

'. . . who will all want to know what you can give them.'

'Exactly.'

Andrew munched his way through a lettuce leaf. The thing about Andrew was that he appeared to deal in reality. I knew few people who did this: people who decided to act in the morning and by night had so acted, moved the world on a bit, changed something. I didn't deal in reality. I wrote speculative pieces that, as far as I knew, changed nothing. Maybe they influenced opinion, although I rather doubted it.

There was so much about Andrew that one could have made fun of. The trappings of considerable affluence, which would have appeared ridiculous if displayed by most of my other contemporaries, fitted Andrew like a glove. It would be pointless to mock: he just was who he was.

'Come along one evening,' said Andrew. 'Next Wednesday about six, if you can, and meet some of the others, see if you think you would enjoy it. If nothing else, you'll meet some unusual people. It's worth an hour or two of your time, I should have thought. The ground rules are very simple and, as you are a journalist, I should mention them. Whatever is said on one of those evenings is spoken in confidence. People need to know that their innermost thoughts won't appear as front-page news the next morning. Chatham House rules and all that.'

'I wouldn't dream of it,' I said, a little nettled.

'I wasn't thinking particularly of you. There are other journalists who might join us.'

At this point a door banged and a cheerful voice shouted out, 'Hello? Anybody home?'

The voice held a familiar twang, but before I could even wonder where I had heard it before, a girl stood in the doorway. 'I'm back early,' she announced. 'Teacher was unwell.'

She was tall, about my height, which is five foot ten. She had dark hair curling over her shoulders and a plump, smiley face with bright hazel eyes. Andrew stood up and put his arm around her shoulder and kissed her on the cheek. Then he turned towards me, intending to introduce the new arrival, but I beat him to it.

'Caroline!' I said in surprise. I don't know how I recognised her but I did. At the age of seventeen she had been my nocturnal companion, invading my dreams as she sat beside me on the bed saying, 'Now then, Charles, here's what we do.'

Those last four words had formed the basis of many imagined embraces. Their memory may even have brought colour to my cheek as Caroline put her arms around me and said,

'It's my long-lost third cousin twice removed! Charlie! Charles Fryerne of Fryerne Court!'

All this required so much explanation between the three

53

of us that it was some minutes before we all sat down again and resumed our lunch. Caroline Woodchester was just as I remembered her: maybe a shade heavier, but also more adult – a woman, in fact, not a girl. She and Andrew had met through a mutual friend from Cambridge, where she had been doing a course in Art History. This had all occurred three or four years after Caroline and I had first met.

'What are you doing now?' I asked Caroline.

'I sculpt. Or at least, I'm learning how to. You're in luck. An hour ago I was covered in lumps of clay.'

'How extraordinary that the two of you should know each other,' I said.

'Not extraordinary at all. As a matter of fact we met in New York, not Cambridge. I mean properly met.'

She glanced at Andrew, who glanced back at her with a look that was more proprietorial than fond.

I can't remember much more of the lunch. I think it broke up not long after Caroline arrived. The moment of intimacy, or faux-intimacy, that had existed between Andrew and me dissolved into something more general. But when I left in a taxi, it was agreed I should drop in on the next 'think tank'. When I arrived home I found that the car was pre-paid for. Some ungracious instinct forced me to make the driver wait, while I paid the bill myself.

Nevertheless, I did go to one of Andrew's think tank evenings. It was rather a let down if one was a celebrity hunter: no George Soros, no Rothschilds. The people in the room – apart from myself – were undoubtedly high-powered, but there was nobody who was obviously famous. At the same time, it was an enjoyable evening and I found, which would not have been the case if there had been somebody famous in the room, that I was able to talk quite freely. There was no agenda; nobody took any notes. From time to time Andrew threw in a prompt but otherwise it could have been any other gathering of men and women enjoying a glass of wine and chatting together.

Out of this mist some order emerged: there was to be a monthly newsletter starting in three months' time, and an (unpaid) editorial board was nominated. To my alarm I found myself amongst its members. Jeremy Cutler, who worked for a firm of parliamentary lobbyists, was another. We had met before, whenever he was trying to push a line to get coverage or comment in *Mayhem*. We agreed on some themes for the newsletter and some avenues for the think tank to explore. Sir Anthony Meyer had just mounted a leadership challenge to Thatcher. It was clear he wasn't going to succeed, but it was equally clear that his attempt would not be the end of the story. Change was in the air. It was a great time to launch.

That was about as far as it ever got. A few weeks later, Andrew Landford announced, via a round-robin letter and without any sign of embarrassment, that he had been asked to move to Moscow for a couple of years and that the think tank 'was on ice for a while'. But of course his departure was its death knell, before it had even got off the ground. I felt a curiously sharp sense of disappointment when I read his message. I had been more flattered than I realised by Andrew's seductive proposals. Even without the attendance of the famous names that had been promised, it sounded like an unparalleled opportunity to witness the machinations of real power at first hand, rather than picking up the leftovers from backbench MPs or party activists in tea rooms and bars. If I was to be an observer rather than a player, I wanted the best viewing spot I could find.

Andrew asked me to dinner with Caroline just before he left. I almost didn't accept. What would be the point? It was unlikely our paths would cross again once he left London. But in the end I went. I still felt an odd magnetic attraction to Andrew that was powerful enough to make me rouse myself and take the tube to Notting Hill.

'Are you selling the house?' I asked, as he handed me a glass of wine.

'No. Caroline's going to move in and look after the place for me. I'm only away for two years. It seems like a long time now, but it isn't really. Is it, darling?'

He reached across and attempted to squeeze her hand. She withdrew it and said with some asperity:

'It may not seem like a long time to you, buddy, with your busy and interesting life, but it is for me. I can't guarantee I'll want to stay here, rent-free or not.'

'Why wouldn't you?' asked Andrew. 'Many people would give their eye teeth to live in a house in this part of London. You'll love it. You practically live here now anyway.'

I could see the evening degenerating into a kind of low-intensity guerrilla war between the two of them, whilst I sat in silence watching them score points off each other. I was determined not to let that happen.

'So do you really hope to revive the think tank when you return?' I asked. 'It seems a hell of a long shot to me. We're heading towards a period of rapid change and you're going to be out of the country. You might even return to a Labour government. You might find yourself on the outside of everything looking in.'

'Andrew will never be an outsider,' replied Caroline. She was still angry. 'I expect in two months he'll have a dacha outside Moscow, a permit to drive in the Zil lanes, and a Russian hooker on his arm, with all those old Commies foaming at the mouth for an invite to one of his cocktail parties.'

Andrew and I both laughed a little nervously. I realised, as I had suspected before, that Caroline was an unusually direct person. She spoke her mind, which was not always the best course of action. At any rate, she was not dull. Andrew brushed her remarks away with a flick of the hand.

'Don't let's worry about old Commies. Let's have some dinner. We've got grouse tonight. I don't expect I'll see that on a menu for a while.'

Despite my best efforts, the evening was not a success and I rather wished I hadn't come.

'Look me up,' suggested Caroline as I left at about eleven. 'You know where I am, at least for now. I'll probably get sick of this joint in a few months, but keep an eye on your poor abandoned third cousin.'

'Yes, keep an eye on her,' agreed Andrew with a faint smile. '*Dasvidanya*, and all that.' He gave me a firm handshake. 'We'll meet again, Charles, and I look forward to it.'

6

1990

Another, less predictable result of Andrew's abortive attempt at setting up a think tank was a mysterious phone call some months later from the lobbyist Jeremy Cutler.

'Can we talk?' he asked, when I picked up the call one morning in the office.

'Well, we're talking now,' I pointed out.

'No. Not on the phone. I need about half an hour with you.'

'What do you want to talk about?'

'Trust me, it will be worth the effort. Why not now? How busy are you? Could you slip out and meet me in Upper Street?'

I looked around me. It was, even by our standards, a quiet day in the office. Mike was out to lunch at *Private Eye* and unlikely to reappear that afternoon. My own desk was relatively clear. I was working up a piece about the decision to join the European Exchange Rate Mechanism, a proposition of the first importance and at the same time so staggeringly dull that I doubted my ability to write anything at all on the subject, let alone be entertaining about it. I agreed to meet Jeremy in an hour's time.

As I walked along Upper Street I wondered what this was

58

about. I really knew very little about Jeremy. We had chatted for a few minutes at Andrew's think tank evening and I couldn't remember what we had talked about. I wasn't even sure that I would recognise Jeremy when I saw him. An impression of a man with a doughy, smiling face and sleek brown hair formed itself in my mind but that was all. So why was I now preparing to listen to whatever Jeremy might have to say? Perhaps he wanted to talk about a reincarnation of Andrew's think tank, without Andrew, in which case I wasn't interested. No, the thing that was pushing me along Upper Street, not pulling me, lay at my point of origin.

It was *Mayhem*. I was beginning to wonder what I was doing there, and where, if anywhere, it was leading. Before I could explore this thought more fully, I arrived at the coffee shop. In a street full of bright designer boutiques, jazzy kebab joints, noisy pubs with live music coming out on to the street even at that hour of the day, Jeremy had managed to choose an austere-looking café that looked something akin to a monks' refectory.

I had no problem identifying my host. A man in a suit with an open-necked white shirt sat at one of the tables. Other than him, the place was empty.

'Hi,' I said, sitting down opposite.

'Thanks for coming,' he said. 'Coffee?'

We ordered and Jeremy pushed a card across the table. It read 'CCC – Cutler Corporate Communications'. The design and font were elegant and understated, suggestive of large amounts of money somewhere in the immediate background.

'That's me,' said Jeremy, unnecessarily.

'As of when? I thought you worked for a parliamentary lobbying firm?'

I wasn't quite sure what that meant. I knew there was a

dark side and a brighter side to the lobbying business. The dark side showed itself in murky attempts to influence policy through cheap holidays for MPs, gifts or even bribes. This was fairly unusual. The day-to-day business of lobbying was fairly transparent and probably a good thing as it allowed the occasional leakage of common sense, and even expertise, into the drafting of bills coming before the House of Commons. Jeremy was definitely one of the straight guys. More than that, I didn't know.

'I did. Then one of our corporate sponsors offered to back me if I set up a business in corporate communications. Same job, but a different audience: institutional investors, pension funds, people making big financial decisions who want to know more about what they are buying into. It's a bigger opportunity and while the ethical dimension is still there, you don't have to be quite so super-sensitive as you do when you are lobbying MPs.'

'And?'

Our coffee arrived.

'And now I have an office and a bag of gold, but no partner. I'm not allowed to take anyone from my old office with me, so I have to look elsewhere. You're it.'

'Me? I know nothing about the City. Nothing about PR. And I know nothing about you and you know nothing about me.'

Jeremy laughed.

'Well, that's fairly blunt. Which is why I want you to join me. You will join me, anyway, once I tell you the terms. OK, so why you? Because I've read your articles and I've noticed a rather odd thing. You can't avoid telling the truth. You spoke your mind at that meeting Andrew organised. Some of your pieces for *Mayhem* have been terrific, you must know that.

They've really cut through to the heart of the matter and people are beginning to sit up and take notice. The trouble is, *Mayhem*'s last accounts didn't look too clever. Have you seen them?'

I admitted I hadn't. As long as my monthly salary cheque didn't bounce I didn't care. I thought that someone as financially illiterate as myself had no business writing stuff for a financial PR company, and said so.

Jeremy dismissed these concerns.

'That's not why we want you. Your truthfulness is why I want you. It will sometimes hurt us but mostly it will help. Trust is everything in this game. If people trust that you are giving them a true picture of what you are writing about, that will buy us more credit than any slick journalese.'

As we talked our coffee was left untouched and grew cold. Jeremy ordered some more 'to pay the rent'.

When he told me what the pay would be, I was hooked. It was a multiple of what I earned at *Mayhem*, and I could double that if I earned a bonus. We shook hands and then at last sipped our coffee. It was bitter and cold, but, at that moment, it tasted like champagne to me.

I walked on air back to the office. Mike was still out, so I sat at my desk, refused to take calls, and tried to think straight. I didn't fully understand this 'truthfulness' business. Other people had accused me of being too literal; of never giving them any slack; of being the most boring man on the planet, because I was constitutionally unable to buy into other people's fantasies about themselves. Mike still complained that I would never write to an agenda: i.e., *his* agenda. If he wanted a hatchet job done, I was not the man to do it. I would always find good alongside the bad, or vice versa.

For some reason, and I thought I glimpsed why, Jeremy wanted this quality, and was prepared to pay for it.

There were no strings attaching me to *Mayhem*. The working conditions were cramped and sometimes, on warm spring days such as this one, they were intolerable. The pay was wretched. I didn't know anybody of my age and education who was paid as little as I was, and if it weren't for an allowance from my parents I wouldn't have survived. My father was recently retired and I felt sure I ought not to be taking any more money from him. Mike was an amusing character to work for but his fuse was growing increasingly short, and I wasn't sure how many more of his intemperate outbursts I could take. The rest of my colleagues were friendly enough but the gap in our political beliefs meant that we rarely mixed out of work beyond the odd drink in the pub.

Churning out pieces for *Mayhem* month after month had acquainted me with some of the shadier recesses of our political world; it had taught me to sniff out the stories lurking there and how to write these, but that wasn't enough. I was learning that to forge a career as a successful political journalist you also needed either to believe in something, or to know what you stood against. In truth, I could lay claim to neither position. Instead, the closer I found myself to the wheels of power, observing political operators at close quarters, the less I believed in any of their promises.

The decision to join Jeremy Cutler's business was perhaps as much a leap into the dark as any of my career decisions thus far.

But the money was good. In two months I would earn what it would take me six months to earn at the magazine. I was tired of always being a few pounds away from breaching my overdraft limit with the bank. And it might be more fun. It could hardly be less so.

Without a great deal more thought than that, I made a decision that would change my life. I composed a brief letter of resignation, which I left in an envelope on Mike's desk. I had no idea whether he would cheer when he read it, or whether he would try and persuade me to stay.

He certainly wasn't happy.

'Cur,' he said. 'Capitalist hyena.'

We both laughed, but not very easily.

'Why the hell are you doing this? You might have become quite good at this job if you'd had a bit more patience. You don't learn a trade like ours in five minutes.'

'It's been a bit longer than that, Mike,' I reminded him. 'The job's not going anywhere. And I can't afford to live on what you pay me.'

Mike gave a deep sigh. 'I can't afford to live on what I pay myself,' he said. 'I admit the pay is crap and the working conditions are dreadful. What happened to idealism?'

'I don't know,' I told him. 'I never caught any of that.'

There wasn't much more to be said. Mike couldn't begin to make a counter-offer even though I hadn't told him what my new salary was going to be.

'Your timing might be quite good,' he said. 'I don't know how much longer we can keep going. The circulation is flat-lining and we're being kept afloat by bank guarantees as it is.'

I didn't want to hear any more. I was beginning to feel guilty about my decision, although nowhere near guilty enough to change my mind and give up my new salary. We shook hands, and Mike told me to leave that afternoon.

'Bad for morale to have you dicking around if you've really decided to bugger off. I'll get Sheila to send you a P45 and a cheque at the end of the month.'

There weren't many other goodbyes to make. A handful of my colleagues accepted an invitation to a nearby wine bar, and we bought each other a few rounds, making cordial but non-committal promises to stay in touch. Nobody stayed long and I was back at my flat before nine.

Had I really made such little impression on this place? I wasn't one of their own, that was all. Nobody, least of all myself, knew what my true politics were, in a mazagine that was conspicuously on the far left wing of the Labour movement.

As I walked off down the street, I realised I hadn't thought about what working for Jeremy Cutler would actually be like, or fully considered what my job might involve. But I knew I was bored. Even the most strident editorials *Mayhem* produced were no longer tapping into the same undercurrent of popular rage they once had. The political centre was shifting, and Mike's uncompromising socialist views – which were not exactly cutting edge to begin with – now looked positively antediluvian. Yet I had learned the beginnings of my craft from him, and for that I would forever be grateful. But the world was moving on, and I was anxious not to be left behind.

7

It came as no surprise to hear that *Mayhem* had closed its doors a few months later, in the autumn. Somebody had pulled the plug. I heard Mike got a job at the *Guardian*. After that *Mayhem* was just a footnote to the political miscellanea of the Eighties.

Jeremy Cutler was entirely different to Mike. He was an operator, and he got the new business up and running within three months. We had a smart office in Bloomsbury; a glamorous receptionist and a small but growing team of account executives and writers. Our first few clients were already on board, including our original investors, and I had produced my maiden project for the business: a campaign to explain why banks had been buying stockbroking firms, wealth-management outfits, mortgage lenders and insurers, and why this was a good thing. More than a decade later, when we sold the company, we were still writing about banks, although by then we were trying to explain why they had managed to destroy value on such a momentous scale.

When we started, our main assets were a presentation suite with a glass boardroom table and an overhead projector which only Jeremy knew how to operate. By the time I left we had teams in London, Hong Kong and New York. We dealt in mergers and acquisitions; reputational turnarounds (as in, explaining why one CEO had left very quickly and why the new one was so much better); brand building for our clients; pitching in on one side or the other in a hostile takeover bid; using the new social media to reach an exponentially increasing audience online. It was all very different, and in the end rather alien to me. But I am jumping ahead.

For some weeks after leaving the magazine, I was utterly submerged in my new job. Jeremy's rather languid appearance concealed an enormous appetite for work. His network of contacts reached back beyond his days in parliamentary lobbying to a spell at the *Financial Times*. His address book was phenomenal. There was practically nobody he did not know, or had difficulty in gaining access to. The business grew very fast as a result.

We began at seven in the morning and it was unusual to leave the office before seven in the evening. Even then, our discussions sometimes spilled out on to the doorstep of the office and then continued for an hour in the pub before, our brains scrambled by everything that had happened during the day, we finally went home.

In my last few days at *Mayhem* the dowdy office seemed permanently clouded not just with cigar smoke, but with a draining inertia as piece after piece failed to land a single blow on its intended targets. By contrast, there was an energy at Cutler that was hard to resist. Multiple clients and accounts, all with differing demands. I had to summon every last reserve of energy I possessed to deal with the endless phone calls and faxes, piles of documents delivered by courier, meetings and presentations. At *Mayhem*, we had held small editorial conferences at the start of each week, then set about following our appointed leads with a steady diligence.

There was focus and clarity, but also yawning longueurs, while one waited for calls to be returned and contacts to be exchanged. There was no such luxury in my new office. Half the time one forgot mid-phone call who the client was, and once I even sent a client's draft presentation to their rival.

But it didn't matter. Communication skills were becoming indispensable in every area of corporate life. The simple media-management techniques I had picked up while hanging around politicians for five years (diversion, distraction, going on the offensive) were lapped up hungrily. Even if our clients weren't always telling the truth, what I told them about the science of communication most definitely was. It commanded every ounce of my being, but in return, I was finally in a job where I felt I was actually doing something useful.

In the midst of this chaos I managed to carve out a couple of weekends in which I moved from my rented rooms in Muswell Hill to a ground-floor flat in Holland Park of which I, or at least I and the bank, were the owners. But weeks went by and I failed to make any progress in furnishing it. There was a double mattress in one room with a couple of sheets and a bedspread and a phone and a lamp on the floor beside it. There was a table and two chairs in the kitchen, some glasses and a few plates from Ikea in a glass cupboard. Not to mention an entirely empty fridge. And that was it.

'Jesus,' said Caroline Woodchester as I opened the bedroom door and then quickly shut it again. I hadn't remembered to pull the sheets back in place before leaving for work that morning. 'What the hell is this? Conceptual art?'

'No, I just haven't got a cleaner yet,' I told her. 'I'm not sure I can afford one. Anyway, now you've seen the place you can understand why I'm not offering to entertain you at home.'

We went out into the drizzly November night. I wasn't feeling as wealthy as I had hoped after trebling my salary. My vast mortgage ate up almost every pound I earned, leaving me with not much more spare cash than I had ended the month with at *Mayhem*. But it was all in a good cause. I was an owner, not a renter, and one day house prices would rise again.

All the same I could not afford to take Caroline anywhere smart, and I didn't see why I should. I had received a call out of the blue from Andrew Landford in Moscow. We hadn't spoken since the previous year, and now here he was, sounding concerned that Caroline was lonely, asking me to ring her up and take her out. 'She's feeling a bit low at the moment. You know where she lives, so give her a bell and cheer her up. Can I ask you that favour? Congratulations on your new business venture, by the way. Most unexpected of you, but I am sure you will do very well . . .'

So here we were, facing each other across a rather low, uncomfortable table in a restaurant that couldn't decide whether it was a bistro or a pub. A television sat in one corner with the sound turned down. There weren't many people about. We ordered wine and steak and chips.

'So how are you?' I asked Caroline.

'Exactly as you would expect, I guess. Boyfriend in Siberia, missing presumed in the office – I mean, I literally haven't seen him for nearly a year now. And sculpting turns out to be hard work. I know, who knew, right? Plus staying in Andrew's mansion feels like squatting in a five star hotel . . . I feel totally guilty about not paying any rent, but he says I'm helping him out, housesitting . . . and right now I'm not picking a fight on that one.'

'It's quite a place for someone of our age.'

'Andrew isn't just "someone of our age", though,' said Caroline, laughing. 'I've met some of the guys he works with. They all have two endgame scenarios. One, they burnout on the job and leave in a bodybag. Or two, they stick it out and become billionaires. Not millionaires, *billionaires*. I don't see Andrew doing either, funnily enough. He'll get rich, for sure, but then he wants to go into politics, before he looks too old and grey for the cameras. He has it all planned out. Believe me, you'll be telling your grandkids that you used to know that Landford guy, and they'll be mighty impressed.'

Our food arrived. I waved a fork around with a rubbery chip on the end of it.

'Do you really think he'll make it as a politician?'

'I reckon. He said he wants to be prime minister by the time he's in his forties. He probably won't get that far, but you never know. I can't figure out if he's capable of becoming a crowd pleaser. There's serious steel in Andrew, and that could put off people who prefer their leaders a little more homespun. But if wanting something bad enough can get you anywhere, then don't go betting against Andrew.'

I enjoyed talking to Caroline. My few encounters with her in the past had made me feel that she, too, could be steely. Or rather, that she had a hard, down-to-earth manner that didn't entirely appeal to me. But tonight, perhaps tempered by Andrew's long absence, she was more relaxed and easier to talk to.

'Well, if Andrew's that good at planning, I hope he told you that Mrs Thatcher was going to resign this morning,' I said.

'Of course! He forecast it months ago: the event that is,

not the date. He even put a hundred pounds on John Major as successor. He got terrific odds, you won't be surprised to hear.'

On the television, as if in tune with our words, they began rolling the tape – for the umpteenth time that day – of a tearful Mrs Thatcher leaving Downing Street for the last time and getting into her car for the drive to the Palace.

'Poor dear,' said Caroline.

'Not everyone would agree with you,' I remarked.

'I'm a Yank, I don't take sides over here. I can say "Poor dear", though. Imagine. All that power and glory gone in a flash. It started when they blew up that hotel. She never got over it, if you ask me. But what a fall from grace.'

The phrase resonated with me: what a fall from grace. I began to revise my opinion of Caroline and found myself studying her across the table. She was an attractive girl, a little shapely and – if one was a purist – rather inclined to cover herself in bits of clay. But that suggested an intensity about her attitude to her art. I wondered if she was any good. She caught my gaze and our eyes met for a second. Then she broke off the eye contact, pushed her steak away and said, 'Do you mind if I light up? I can't eat any more of this.'

'It's tough, isn't it? Bad choice of restaurant. I'll try to do better next time.'

'Next time?'

I didn't say anything. There was a quizzical look on her face as she wreathed us both in cigarette smoke so that my eyes watered. I gave up trying to eat.

'I didn't mean to be presumptuous,' I said apologetically.

'You weren't. It's sweet of you to oblige an old pal like this.' She raised an eyebrow. 'I mean Andrew, of course.'

'Andrew's not really an old "pal". We were barely aware

of each other's existence at Oxford. We're new friends, if anything.'

'And I am your third cousin twice removed.'

I was getting tired of that joke.

'That is the furthest thought from my mind,' I said. 'The Fryerne clan gatherings mostly proceed happily without my attendance at them.'

I ordered coffee. We had successfully established that there was almost no possible connection between us and the conversation seemed to be running out of steam. After a moment I put my hand over the saucer containing the bill.

'Well, I'll just deal with this . . .'

As we stood up she said in a serious voice, without the teasing tone that sometimes crept into it, 'That was so nice of you. Thanks.'

'The steak . . .'

'Forget about the steak. I'm not normally Miss Picky with my food. Call me again sometime, if you don't believe me . . . and next time, it's my treat.'

I stood up and took the bill to the bar to settle it. When I turned around again, she had disappeared. I waited for a moment in case she had simply gone to the loo, but when she didn't reappear I went outside to see if she was waiting for me there. She wasn't.

She'd simply gone.

Even allowing for differences in culture, upbringing, views about social conventions, this seemed a bit abrupt. Of course she'd gone. She'd eaten her food, or rather some of it. She'd thanked me. She'd left. What was I looking for? A medal? I'd taken the poor girl out for a rather second-rate dinner in one of the few really unattractive restaurants in this part of London. I'd been my usual boring self, had failed to cheer her up and indeed I hadn't even really tried. Half my mind had been on her and half on a piece I would have to write as soon as I got into the office in a few hours time. I was tired. She was tired. We'd gone our separate ways.

Still, saying goodbye costs nothing and most people find the time to do it.

I decided I'd fulfilled any obligation I had to Andrew and I would leave it at that. This strange American art-student quasi-relative could get through life without further assistance from me.

The invitation to the viewing arrived at the CCC office address. I picked it up and studied it:

Caroline Woodchester
Has pleasure in inviting you to
A Private Viewing of her work at
6:30 p.m. on 10 December 1990
The Wylman Gallery, Clifford Street

I remembered Caroline saying she was struggling with her work, but that hadn't prevented her from putting on a show. I looked in vain for any personal message on the card. There was none. I was about to flip the invitation into the bin when Jeremy twitched it out of my fingers and studied it for a second.

'If you're not going, may I use the invitation? I'd be quite interested to see what she's been up to. We might see something to buy for the office, show people we aren't just soulless money men.'

I hesitated for a second and then said, 'Let's both go.'

And so it was that, despite my decision not to bother

myself any further with Caroline, I found myself walking down Clifford Street one frosty December evening. On the office television that night when Jeremy and I had tuned in to the evening news, there had been pictures of the country shrouded in a blanket of snow. Here in central London we were free of that, but not from the plunge in temperature. When we arrived at the gallery, we found there were already a dozen guests there, stamping their feet and blowing on their fingertips. Then they began fingering the catalogues and peering at the sculptures. These were not sculptures of the sort I had been expecting. As a matter of fact I didn't know what I had been expecting. In my mind's eye I had speculated on large formless shapes of stoneware or bronze, challenging and unsatisfactory. Caroline's work ranged from full-blown sculptures to simpler studio ceramics: porcelain bowls and pots with striking designs and deep glazes reminiscent of amphorae; vases; bowls that looked as if they belonged in a tea-ceremony. The pieces looked timeless and graceful, mostly not more than a foot or two in height. A few larger figures which, with a bit more self-confidence I might have labelled Rodinesque, lurked in corners and doorways as if unsure of their final destination.

Caroline came up to us, followed by a waiter carrying a tray of drinks.

'How sweet of you to come,' she said. 'So long since we last met.' Jeremy smiled and nodded. Turning to me she added, 'You too, Charles. Come find me before you go if you can. I'd love a moment of your time.'

'Yes, of course,' I said, for some unaccountable reason cross with myself and with her. More visitors were arriving and Caroline went off to welcome them. Jeremy and I studied the work. I was then much more ignorant of sculpture and ceramics than I am now, but even I could tell this work was rather good. The shapes and forms of the pots and the occasional figurine were elegant and subtle. The glazes were deep brown or blue, overlaying designs that looked as if they represented thousands of peacock eyes, or else an infinity of small wavelets breaking on a beach. Jeremy decided to buy one of the larger pieces, not a pot but a ceramic stone figure reclining on a black plinth.

'That would look rather good in the reception area,' said Jeremy. Without waiting for an answer he went off to find the gallery owner and start haggling over the price. The last thing I wanted was to have Caroline find me trying to shave a few pounds off her already no doubt slender profit – I knew a gallery in this part of London would take an enormous cut – so I left him to it. The outcome must have been successful, for a few minutes later a red spot had appeared on the plinth.

'Right. I've dealt,' said Jeremy, reappearing at my elbow. 'It's getting rather hot and noisy in here. I think I'll push on. What about you?'

I said I'd stay a little while longer and Jeremy left, to be replaced by Maldwyn Christie who had just arrived.

'Did you see any of the coverage of my speech in the House last night?' he asked, not bothering with a more formal greeting. I was quite surprised to see him there, but then remembered that Maldwyn had also been picked as a possible member of Andrew's think tank.

'No.'

'You are always, by a very long chalk, the least rewarding member of my fan club. I talked about how ridiculous it was that a few inches of snow should bring the whole country to a standstill. I was rather funny about it. Even Neil Kinnock cracked a smile.'

'I don't doubt you had them rolling in the aisles.'

'Anyway, it's rather pointless talking to you because now you aren't at *Mayhem* you don't hear any decent gossip. Not that they ever let you in on any of their real secrets. They always had you down as a potential mole.'

'Really?'

'Mike did. He was just waiting for you to reveal yourself.'

'Poor Mike. I must have been such a disappointment to him.'

I disliked being reminded of what an outsider I had been, but it was true.

'What's it like, working with the extremely tough Mr Cutler?'

'Good. We get on. Why do you call him tough?'

'I've seen him operate,' said Maldwyn. 'He brought down more than one aspiring politico when he was at the *FT*. Fortunately he never had me in his sights.'

'Perhaps you weren't important enough?'

Maldwyn took off his spectacles and rubbed them with his tie.

'God, it's noisy in here,' he complained, placing his glasses back on his nose. 'For a moment there I thought I heard you say I wasn't important enough. I must have been mistaken because nowadays, Mr Fryerne, I am very, very important. There's even talk – although being you, you either haven't heard or don't care – of me becoming a junior minister one of these days. So, watch out. Now, enough about me. We won't talk about you, because you are far too reticent and shy. Instead, let's have a look at your dear cousin's work.

75

From where I am standing, it looks a good deal better than I imagined.'

We started to circulate around the room once more. I followed in Maldwyn's slipstream as he chattered away. 'She is really quite good. I don't know what I was expecting – an installation; video clips; papier mâché images of Morecambe and Wise. Not many people doing really good work in porcelain these days . . . so unfashionable and yet so nice . . .'

Maldwyn didn't appear to need any comment or response. As I trailed behind him, I was again struck by the levels of proficiency Caroline had attained. Those glazes would be difficult to reproduce. I wondered how much she had had to throw away when the firings didn't work. Caroline was with us again now.

'Darling,' said Maldwyn, 'Mwah! Mwah!' He kissed her in noisy self-parody on each cheek.

'Do you think everyone will decide it's time to go soon?' she asked me with a touch of pathos in her voice. 'I can't wait to leave.'

'Tell them to stop serving drinks,' I suggested. 'That usually does the trick.'

'A bit brutal,' said Maldwyn, 'but it will work. You've sold quite a few pieces tonight anyway. I should have a word with the owner – he's really the man picking up the tab tonight, although in the end, dear Caroline, it will come out of your pocket. And therefore,' he said, snatching a flute from a nearby waiter. 'I shall have one more glass of this rather disgusting champagne and then go.'

Caroline went across to talk to the owner, a small bearded man with the sleek features of an otter.

Maldwyn had used the opportunity of the fresh drink to abandon me and intrude upon another small group, amongst whom I recognised the face of a well-known member of the Shadow Cabinet. I decided to leave him to his networking and re-examine Caroline's ceramics. It was odd. The fragile formality of the small porcelain bowls, the subtlety of the colours, the intricacy of the wavy designs: all these had come from within her and therefore were, in some way, the essence of her. I had yet to grasp how art can distance itself from its creator: how someone like F. Scott Fitzgerald, absolutely broke and drinking hard, could produce a work as lyrical as *Tender is the Night*, writing to stay alive and to pay for his wife's sanatorium expenses. These things I learned, in time. Just now I marvelled only that I had not foreseen Caroline's art in Caroline.

Her work invited me to re-evaluate her, to forget the awkwardness of her social manners. But then, it was just as likely that any awkwardness in our relationship was because of me. I knew that I was ignorant of much of what passes for social graces in ordinary life; I was tactless and distracted, living in my head too much, stepping from one cloud to another but overlooking the demands of life outside my work. I was working for probably the one person in London and in the one job where this detachment was acceptable, even valued. No, I reasoned, if there was anything gauche or untoward in Caroline's behaviour then it was a reflection of mine towards her. At this moment she returned.

'Hi,' she said brightly. 'All done. We'll close up in ten. Do you want to come out afterwards with Josh' – she indicated the owner – 'and me? I'm not sure where yet, maybe a few drinks, something to eat.' She glanced at the hangers-on still drifting round the gallery. 'It looks like there's going to be quite a crowd of us.'

The invitation was sufficiently uninviting. We all know

that kind of evening. You begin by arguing for about twenty minutes about which restaurant to go to and when you get there it is full. You find somewhere else. It takes about twenty minutes for two of the party to catch up because they couldn't get a taxi. By now, nobody is in the least bit hungry and all anyone wants is a drink, followed by bed, with luck on one's own. But then the business of choosing food nobody wants takes another half an hour and by the time it finally arrives you have begun to wish you were dead.

I said no.

'Suit yourself,' she said, taking out a cigarette in defiance of the no smoking signs everywhere. 'Just thought I'd ask.'

'It was nice of you. You said earlier you wanted a word?'

'Did I?' she said vaguely, exhaling smoke all around me. 'I can't remember now. It will come to me later, but then you won't be there and I'll forget again. Sure you won't come?'

'Quite sure. Caroline . . .'

'What?' she asked as my sentence trailed away. She sounded fierce, as if I had offered her a present and then taken it away.

'I like your art . . . I like what you're doing. I am the last person in the world to judge, but I think it is really good.'

She looked at me in surprise.

'Why, thank you, Charles. I'll take that as a compliment.'

'Take it as the truth,' I said.

Then I left.

8

Visits to my parents had changed in character. Once I had considered them as a sailor might view a return to a much loved and well-remembered harbour. Now my parents had taken on the aspect of remote islands in a distant sea.

The journey to Uxbridge was not so daunting in itself. Their house stood at the corner of two identical-looking avenues of villas.

On the outside it presented a mixture of sooty brick and dark red paintwork. Some of the windows had been done in coloured glass: roundels set with figurines, perhaps saints. Inside, the house appeared to be larger than it had looked from the outside. Entering through the front door, one arrived in a cavernous hall, with a staircase leading up into gloomy silence.

Usually I was intercepted by my father before I could penetrate any further. He would appear in the doorway of his day room. He was always carefully dressed, in a cardigan, brown corduroys, shirt and tie. His other accessory was a rumpled copy of the *Daily Telegraph*, which he clutched, as if fearful that someone would remove it if he let go for longer than a second. He pretended to look enormously surprised at my appearance, as if either the day or the appointed hour of my arrival had been omitted from his diary. His first words were – nearly always – 'Good Heavens! Is it that time already?' before he beckoned me testily inwards, as if further delays or reluctance on my part would ruin the entire day. Then I would seat myself opposite him, and we would strive to obtain information from each other with very limited success.

Communication with my father had become difficult; with my mother it was all but impossible. She was relatively young, not yet seventy, but now sat shrouded in silence. Her very features seemed to melt as Alzheimer's took hold. Her firm mouth had become slack, with snail tracks of saliva glistening down one side. Her eyes were cloudy, not because of cataracts but because an habitual lack of focus made it impossible to know at whom or what she was looking.

There were carers to help, and my father angrily rebuffed suggestions that he could not cope. As a result most of my visits were spent in painful denial: denial by my father that his wife would not 'get better'; denial by me that I was fast losing any sense of connection with my own parents.

It hurt a bit. I remembered too well the happy summers we had spent sailing on, or walking above, Lake Geneva. Everything up to the point where we finally left Lausanne for the delights of west Uxbridge was clear and sharp in my memory. After that, it had all gone downhill. In the end my father had well and truly been 'put out to grass', as he had feared. He was given almost nothing to do and after a year or two he had finally taken voluntary redundancy, which I suppose had been his employer's plan all along. I believe he had once been considered as rather good at his job. Then suddenly he had found himself transplanted from a busy and useful existence in Switzerland, from the sunny shores of a Swiss lake, from Swiss coffee and French cooking, to this: a house that crushed the spirit even on a sunny day. The place stank of over-cooked food and unwashed clothes and a general airlessness I found increasingly difficult to tolerate.

At the beginning of 1991 my mother died, quite unexpectedly. There was no crisis: only dissolution. The carers went, my father having been assessed as physically and mentally fit enough to live on his own. At first I made an effort to be with him nearly every weekend. I don't think he appreciated my company, however. It became obvious to me, if not to him, that he was discarding any ties that bound him to life. At first I just went home anyway. But with each fresh visit I noticed further signs of deterioration in the house, and in my father, as if they were competing to see who could collapse first. Doors warped and got stuck; lights blew out all over the house and I had to keep replacing the bulbs. Supplies of coal and wood ran out because my father forgot to re-order them. I used to bring carrier bags of food with me to keep his fridge stocked; but as I threw out an almost identical quantity of spoiled or wasted food, I realised there was little I could do to make him actually eat anything when I wasn't with him. When my mother went, some vital component inside my father broke, and now the whole circuit was shutting down.

From June that year I became increasingly immersed in the new business. It became harder and harder to find time for anything or anyone else, to the point that I scarcely saw my friends, never mind went down to Uxbridge. So I told myself, and it was probably true. The awful and greater truth was that my father didn't really want to see me: he just wanted to curl up and die, without interruption or distraction. It is only

of lessons and readings, we were both exhausted. The wine was all but gone: I poured out just enough to wet the bottom of our glasses and then raised my own:

'To a good job well done – I couldn't possibly have done it without your help. I feel enormously relieved.'

'My pleasure. I never imagined I'd become quite so involved in your crazy old family rituals, but now it's done.

'You'll come, of course?'

'Yes, I'll come.'

Without thinking, I picked up her hand and then squeezed it.

'Thank you.'

For a moment her hand lay in mine: a good, strong hand with blunt fingers and short fingernails. A practical hand; an artist's hand. Then she withdrew it, not abruptly but with decision, as if a voice were whispering, 'This hand is reserved for Andrew, so this is where I draw the line.'

The moment of awkwardness, if it had been there at all, passed. A few minutes later Caroline left, and I didn't see her again until the day of the service.

9

Caroline went back to New York for Christmas. I spent a gloomy morning escorting my father through the due processes of the Kensal Green Crematorium, returning home with the ashes which, unaccountably, I put in the cupboard under the stairs – thus causing a huge panic when the day of the memorial came around and I couldn't remember where I had left them.

I had a low-key Christmas, most of the friends I'd managed to keep up with fleeing the city for family homes in the country or house parties with friends abroad. I saw Maldwyn for a drink. Jeremy invited me to a family lunch on Christmas Day, which I refused. It was enormously kind of him, because he saw me all day every day at the office and I think he was quite relieved when I said I just wanted to spend a couple of days with my feet up.

And that was what I did. I sat and watched endless old films sipping from a glass of white wine and occasionally heating up some ready-made mince pies and other assorted snacks. As a matter of fact I felt so tired I could hardly speak or move. The last few months had been more strenuous than I had realised, both mentally and physically, and it was wonderful to do nothing, to sit with an empty mind gazing at the flickering screen.

Not entirely empty, however. From time to time I found myself thinking about Caroline. Andrew had been away in Moscow making his billions for well over a year now. He hadn't even come back to see her for Christmas. I began to wonder exactly what it was that she saw in him.

As far as Andrew was concerned I received the occasional call with odd bits of news. He rang me from Moscow on Boxing Day to say he'd just heard about my father from Caroline and sent his condolences. After quickly disposing of that subject he went on to give me some of his own news: cautiously phrased, I thought, Andrew clearly presuming his phone calls might be overheard by a wider audience than the pair of us. He seemed to be enjoying himself in what sounded like a dangerous place for a Westerner to be living at the time, although the expatriate community was growing fast in anticipation of the implosion of the Soviet Union, and the possibility that someone might leave the keys in the door to the sweet shop. Not only the keys to the sweet shop, but the oil and gas and aluminium and nickel shop. There was much debate about 'shock therapy' being administered to the Russian economy, the need for a rapid transition to a Western model: in other words a free-for-all. It didn't take much imagination to hear the sound of gunfire once that all kicked off. I admired Andrew for hanging on in such a fraught environment. I wouldn't want to be there myself. I wondered what his communications with Caroline were like, and how she was surviving on a fairly minimal diet of affection and shared moments.

Was I interested in her myself? I supposed I must have been, because otherwise why did I keep thinking about her – despite the fact I told myself she was not my type. But what was my type? Was there such a thing as 'type' and did the idea have any meaning? After all, I was just as much a 'type' as anyone else. I was often tactless, introspective: the patina of Englishness achieved at university overlaying a rather more complex upbringing as an expat child in New York and Lausanne. Whose type was I? I wondered. Either I liked Caroline (and she liked me) or I didn't. The fact I even had to ask myself the question was revealing. I just wasn't sure. There were times when I thought she loathed me; others when she adopted that quizzical look, as if she saw before her, not me, but a lump of clay that could be kneaded into a more acceptable form.

And did I like her? There was not the slightest tickle of sexual attraction between us – as far as I could tell. But I was usually rather slow when it came to that side of relationships. Indeed the few girls I had slept with had all been surprises – I was surprised that they would contemplate such an act with me and then even more surprised when it turned out they had been waiting for me to make a move. Apart from that one serious relationship at university, my liaisons had never lasted, and I hadn't even managed a fling since joining Cutler.

In many ways, I simply hadn't woken up. Some people remain in a form of sleepy trance for their entire lives. A few awaken, or are awakened by events outside their control. A small number – perhaps Andrew Landford was one – are awake from early on and realise that, in the kingdom of the half-asleep, the truly conscious person can carve himself an empire.

I told myself that, in any case, Caroline was Andrew's long-term partner. It was only a matter of time before he proposed, surely. The offer of a rent-free home while he was away in Moscow was a honey trap: difficult to refuse at the time, it would bind Caroline to Andrew long enough to allow him to recommence his wooing on his return. I didn't want to do anything that smacked of taking advantage of Andrew's absence, either. I thought that would make me look rather cheap, and I didn't want to put myself in that position.

January went on in the same manner as December had ended. A grey wind howled out of the north. My blood ran thick and slow. Everything seemed an effort. Even going to the office, which before had been as addictive as a drug, failed to excite me now.

The day of the memorial came at last. It was another bitter day, with half-formed flakes of snow swirling in the wind then settling for a moment on coats and umbrellas or dissolving into pinpricks of icy water on one's hands and face. Caroline and I took a taxi from the station to St Mary's-Without and went inside to greet the vicar. An attempt had been made to heat the church with two small blow-heaters reinforcing the ancient-looking central heating pipes that ran the length of the church. It was still too cold to take one's coat off, and our discussions were brief and businesslike. Perhaps because of the discouraging weather, the turnout was not especially good. There seemed to be far fewer people than at Roland's send-off, and the mood was more sombre. My father, I realised, had cut himself off from more than just me. To many of those attending it must have seemed as if he had been dead for years.

The vicar trotted through the service as fast as he decently could and the congregation dispersed. The idea was to have a buffet lunch at the Fryerne Arms, and for me to make a brief speech. Where were those notes? I patted my pockets but couldn't immediately locate them. By then we had arrived at the pub. A row of fairy lights draped across the entrance was blinking nervously. Only a few cars had turned up. I suspected that some of the family felt they had done all they needed to by turning up at the church and had chosen to pass on the cold buffet I had thoughtfully organised for a sub-zero afternoon. Brad had given Caroline and me a lift from the church. When we got into the car, which had a driver, Brad had levered himself around in the passenger seat and extended a huge hand to me. I grasped it and then found he wouldn't let go.

'Your father was one helluva guy, Charles. I miss him. We all miss him.'

'Thank you,' I said faintly. The circulation was beginning to go in my right hand but still he clung on.

'It's been an honour to act as marshal to the American side of the family. We value our history, Charles. We surely do. This is one special relationship that will remain intact, as it has done over many, many years.'

Inside the pub a fake gas fire with imitation logs burned merrily in the hearth, giving out no heat whatsoever. A dispirited looking waitress began handing out drinks. Nearly everyone went for the orange juice rather than anything alcoholic. When she had done this she returned with a gilt silver tray on which sat a few sandwiches surrounded by wilted lettuce and crisps. It wasn't what I'd arranged but as there were at best a dozen of us in the room, ordering yet more food seemed pointless. Brad introduced me to an elderly gentleman called Alan Fryerne-Smith. His was a face distantly recalled from earlier gatherings. I couldn't remember whether I had last seen him at Roland's memorial. He was tall and thin and of military bearing; a solicitor from a country town in Dorset.

'I was just saying to Charles here,' said Brad, 'that his father was a damned fine fellow.'

'Oh yes, very much so. You won't find many like your father on the average London bus, Charles. He was a different kettle of fish altogether. A very special sort of chap. I forget what it was that he did. Was he in the dry-cleaning business?'

I explained that my father had worked for a global pharmaceuticals company.

'Exactly,' replied Alan Fryerne-Smith. 'I knew it was something of the sort. A very fine chap. We'll miss him.'

Brad, who had looked somewhat winded when his friend suggested my father had been a dry-cleaning executive, now broke in and said:

'But the person who'll miss him most will be you, of course.'

'Yes, I do miss him,' I agreed.

'You must miss him very, very much.'

'Exactly,' said Alan Fryerne-Smith. 'Very, very much.'

At this moment Caroline elbowed me sharply in the ribs and said to Brad sweetly, 'Do you mind if I borrow Charles for a moment?'

'Of course. I'm not sure he's ours to lend, but you may borrow him.' Brad laughed explosively and we withdrew to a table a few feet away.

'If you don't make your speech in the next thirty seconds I shall kill myself,' she said in a low voice. 'I'm not sure I can take any more of this.'

'What? Me? Now?'

'Yes, goddammit.'

Without waiting for a reply she picked up a knife and dinged an empty wine glass. What little conversation there was faded into mutterings and then stopped.

I had rehearsed my speech briefly and consigned it to a few cards on which I had written out the main bullet points, e.g.:

- Long history of family reaching back into the late Mediaeval period
- Astonishing loyalty and cohesiveness of the Fryerne family over hundreds of years
- No house, but the tradition of Fryerne Court preserved, which is the thing of greatest value . . . and no tax to pay on tradition yet, thank God (wait for laughter)
- Now honoured to become the Fryerne of Fryerne Court and hope I can bring what credit I can to the title and tradition etc. etc.

But in the panic that morning when I was looking for my father's ashes – which were to sit at the foot of the altar during the memorial service – I had left the notes on the kitchen table. Perhaps it was just as well. By now the dozen or so people in the room were looking at me expectantly. I began to speak without the least idea of what I would say next.

'I feel far too young to have become the bearer of the title that my father held. Today we are honouring the man who held the title as much as the title itself. My father was a good hard-working man whose job was taken away from him. Personally I think that's what finished him off at such a relatively young age – he was only 71 this year – that, and the premature death of his beloved wife, and my mother, Emily. So, he has left us too soon and I for one regret that I never really had the time to get to know him properly in his retirement. I feel somehow that he and I have been robbed

of each other's company – that we might reasonably have expected to have another ten or fifteen years to enjoy together.
But that was not to be. So now we must recall why we are
here: I would like to propose a toast to my father, and to
all of you who have taken so much trouble to be here. To
my father Charles Fryerne and to all of us, the Fryernes of
Fryerne Court!'

All this gushed from me as effortlessly as if I had written
it down. Where it came from, I do not know. But after all, I
am in the communications business and I must have learned
something over the years.

'When did you make that up? asked Caroline a few minutes later.

'I don't know. I forgot the notes I had prepared. I think it
helped that you pushed me in at the deep end.'

'You really are full of surprises, Charlie boy. I nearly wept
when you talked about your dad. Brad was gushing tears.
Gushing.'

One by one the guests finished their orange juice and
crisps and took their leave. I felt slightly ashamed that I
hadn't been more generous but perhaps on a day such as
this, it didn't really matter. Thin pickings after the feast at
my Uncle Roland's memorial, though. Brad left issuing many,
many invitations 'to come visit with him' in New York. Then
barely forty minutes after we had arrived, the dining room
was empty of all but Caroline and myself.

'What you and I need,' I said to her, 'is a proper drink.'

I called the waitress over and ordered a bottle of the nicest
looking Bordeaux on the list, which wasn't saying much.

'This is where we first met, isn't it?' I said to Caroline,
handing her a glass.

'Was it? I don't recall. Oh yes, I do though . . .'

I was not at all sure she did not blush and I couldn't resist reminding her.

'You offered to take me upstairs to have sex, right in front of my mother. I mean you spoke to me in front of my mother. The other event was to be a shade more discreet.'

'I didn't, did I?'

Now there was no doubt that she was blushing, all the way to the roots of her hair. We caught each other's eye and then looked away again. I wished I hadn't raised the subject. At the same moment I became aware for the first time since that long ago day, of a surge of desire for her. I remembered all the dreams I'd had in the months immediately following that first meeting, when I dreamed that we had in fact gone upstairs together in that pub; that we had in fact found an unlocked bedroom, where she had sat on the bed and patted the space beside her. I still remembered the words she had spoken, only ever in my dreams and never in real life:

'Now then, Charles. Here's what we do . . .'

The dream had always ended there and had faded over time.

I didn't dare look at Caroline or touch her for fear of giving myself away. Still blushing, she managed to say:

'That was wicked of me, Charles. What a tease I was. I take it you've forgiven me?'

'There was nothing to forgive. You made me feel rather wonderful for a moment, I do remember. I couldn't believe someone like you would take any interest in a prissy, pompous youth like me.'

'You sure were pompous. I remember that, all right. That's probably why I behaved the way I did. But still. What happened next?'

'You went outside to smoke a cigarette, and my father

made his speech. It was much better than the one I just made. Certainly longer. And you left, or at any rate I didn't see you again until you turned up that day in Andrew's house.' I looked very hard at my wine, trying not to give anything away. 'You must miss him.'

Caroline's shoulders sank. 'You could say that. He's been away so long I don't really know what I'm missing. We speak once a week, or at least we try to, his schedule permitting . . . And then all he can talk about is his precious job. Double-crossing Russians, lawyers on the make, caviar and lobster filled banquets in old haunts once reserved for the KGB . . . I try to sound interested.' She took a large gulp of her drink. 'Don't get me wrong, he's sweet enough. He sent me some sensational jewellery on my birthday, and he's always telling me how he's going to set me up with an art dealer in Moscow . . . apparently the art market is really taking off there now as well, but . . . well, when push comes to shove, the guy's just never around. And that's hard.'

I didn't know what to say, and we sat there in stunned silence for a moment. In a determined effort to heave the conversation on to a fresh track, Caroline asked me, 'Anyhow. That guy, Alan Fryerne-Whatever, he was something else, wasn't he?'

'The weirder fringe of the Fryerne clan . . . Caroline, why do you think all these people come here every time someone dies or gets married or christened? The same people don't always show up, but at all the gatherings I have been to there have been at least forty or fifty people. Some of them are from just down the road in Petersfield or Alton. But some of them rock up from South Island in New Zealand, or the Upper West Side in New York. They spend thousands getting here. It's like a herd of elephants gathering from all over the plains at the ancestral burial grounds. What makes us all do it?'

She was silent for a moment, thinking.

'I honestly have no idea. Maybe it's like a chain letter. People feel they have to pass it on and keep the chain unbroken, or there will be seven years bad luck.'

'No . . . that doesn't explain it to me,' I replied after a moment.

We sat in the quiet dining room. The waitress had disappeared without bothering to tidy up and we sat amongst a litter of plates bearing half-eaten sandwiches, unfinished glasses of orange juice and club soda. The reason for the continued existence of a pub as dreary as this was as much a mystery as the rituals of the Fryerne family. And yet, in that strange place, I saw for the first time the beginnings of intimacy between Caroline and me. Until now there had always been a barrier between us: a combination of her defensiveness and my own diffidence. That had disappeared now. I felt more at my ease talking to her than I had done with anyone for a very long time.

'My own theory,' I said after a moment, 'is that we are a group of very ordinary people. Not a group in the sense that we have something in common, as if we were all members of the same religious sect or political party. But we do have one thing in common: we all believe we are the dispossessed. The American Fryernes and the New Zealand Fryernes use our name as a link to the old country because for whatever reason they have not rooted well where they are. The English Fryernes cling to a title that was invented by themselves, for themselves, as a way of creating an identity – they received land from Henry Tudor but no other form of recognition, so they've had to invent one. They were on the cusp of glorious things, but whatever our ancestor did, it was only quite good and not good enough. But why we have kept going since the house was sold and pulled down, I don't know.'

'I kinda like that,' said Caroline. 'The dispossessed . . . I'm not sure that we ever owned very much we could be dispossessed of, but hey, that'll do for me.'

I poured some more wine for us both.

'Maybe nobody dares to break the chain. That part might be right. There aren't many younger people coming to these things, I've noticed. I don't go often myself. Maybe it will just peter out.'

'I won't weep too many tears if it does. But, you now – you're the official head of the family. It's up to you to give us our battle plan, restore our global dominance.'

She was mocking me again, but not unkindly. We sat for a while longer, until the wine was gone, and then summoned a taxi to take us to the station.

On the train we sat side by side at a table opposite an old lady, who gently removed herself at the next stop. The dark grey afternoon was turning to evening, enfolding itself around us while occasional sleet showers rattled against the windows. The temptation to close my eyes was overwhelming. Caroline fell asleep first, her head reclined on my shoulder. Shifting to get comfortable I put my arm around her and the two of us dozed until the bright lights of London and the robotic cries of 'Mind the Doors' awoke us. I was the first to fully awaken and disengaged myself so as not to embarrass her, but an eye opened and she smiled sleepily.

'That wine certainly did the trick. I'm sorry. Does your shoulder have any feeling left in it?'

'I've been asleep until this very minute.'

She nodded and, yawning, stretched herself like a cat.

'Will I see you soon?' I asked her.

'I guess so. If you want to, that is.'

'Oh, I want to. I'll call you.'

We said our goodbyes at Waterloo. That night, for the first time in many years, I had the dream again: I was following a girl up the staircase that led from the dining room at the Fryerne Arms to an upper landing. There we found a bedroom door unlocked. The room was clean, the bed made up. Caroline sat down on the bed and then looked up at me with bright, teasing eyes.

'Sit down beside me, Charles, and I'll show you what we do.'

The words were somehow different but even in my sleep I was aware that the gates of dreamland had opened again and welcomed me into the land beyond.

10

The first I heard about it was a call from Caroline, cancelling an arrangement we had made to go and see a film together.

'I can't make it,' she explained. Over the phone her voice, normally cool and collected, sounded a little breathless. 'Andrew is coming back from Moscow today.'

'Today!'

I don't know why I should have been so surprised. I struggled to keep the disappointment from my voice, but Caroline picked it up.

'He just comes and goes as he pleases,' she said. 'I'm going to have to spend the next few hours getting his palace in perfect condition. He lands at Heathrow tonight.'

'You'll be very pleased to see him again,' I said. I intended no sarcasm or bitterness: why should I? But again she picked up a note in my voice I hadn't even heard myself.

'Don't be difficult,' she said. 'Think what it's like for me.'

We hung up, making no alternative plan. From now on, or for however long Andrew planned to be in London, I would only see Caroline if it suited Andrew.

The next few days were surprisingly painful. Caroline was not my lover, or my girlfriend. She was barely even my friend. And yet now that I couldn't see her – at least not without

Andrew, because anything else was unthinkable – I somehow felt a little denuded and empty. I found I actively missed the warm sound of her voice; the quick, interrogative flash of her eyes as she picked me up on some remark I had made. I realised I missed her. And yet she and Andrew were living together only a few streets away. I could go around tonight, now, and it wouldn't cause any consternation. But for some reason, I just didn't want to see them together. I presumed they would also have gone back to sharing a bed and suddenly the thought of that upset me more than it ought. The whole thing was ridiculous.

I did my best to forget about them and for a few weeks was able to immerse myself in work. But even there I was challenged one morning by the arrival of the sculpture we had bought before Christmas at Caroline's exhibition: a reclining figure in ceramic stone, which sat upon a polished granite plinth.

'It fits the space well, doesn't it?' said Jeremy, who had come into reception behind me.

'Yes. Good choice.'

'She's a talented girl, your friend.

This felt like dangerous ground, and I was keen to steer us away from it as quickly as possible. 'She's been helping out with a lot of family stuff since my father died.'

'Well, you'll be seeing less of her now, I would have thought. Andrew's back,' said Jeremy. 'But you probably knew that anyway. I spoke to him on the phone. He sounds pretty pleased with life.'

A couple of days later Andrew phoned me to invite me to dinner. He sounded exactly as Jeremy had suggested, very satisfied with his lot.

'How are you?' I asked, with as much enthusiasm as I could muster.

'Never better. Things are a bit hairy in Moscow, though. Lots of tanks and soldiers all over the place. There's been talk of a coup against Yeltsin by the old guard. He's rushing through his economic programme at some speed and not everybody is quite as keen as he is.'

'How long are you over here for? Or is it a permanent move?'

'Come to dinner on Saturday night and I'll tell you all about it. We've a few friends coming. Jeremy and his wife will be there, so that's two familiar faces.'

I couldn't really refuse.

Saturday night came and I made my way to Andrew's house. The curtains were open and I could see people in the drawing room, picking at canapés laid out on top of the grand piano. The maid, who had disappeared during Andrew's absence abroad, was now re-established as part of the household and met me at the door to take my coat.

Andrew seemed unchanged: tall, good-looking in a cold sort of way, and quite uninterested in small talk. He handed me a glass of champagne without asking me what I wanted and said, 'By the way, before it goes out of my mind, thank you for keeping an eye on Caroline while I've been away. She appreciated it. As did I.'

'It was a pleasure,' I mumbled.

'Sorry about your dad.'

'Caroline was a great help with all of that.'

Perhaps there was a flicker in my eyes, or some unwanted colour in my cheek, but Andrew changed the subject abruptly.

'Of course the great thing about Yeltsin is that he's completely uninhibited. He's going to change Russia, and he doesn't care who or what gets in his way. He'll just steamroller right over them. Things might get a bit messy.'

'Is that why you've come back?'

'Partly. The threat level has gone up slightly and my partners wanted a briefing. I'll probably be here for around six weeks and then see if it's OK to go back.'

He handed me on to somebody and went to greet his next guest. I looked for Caroline but she wasn't in the room. Then, suddenly, she was, wearing a dark blue evening dress, much smarter than the rest of us who were all decked out in the usual miscellany that is known, for some mysterious reason, as 'smart casual'. For this reason, if no other, she now looked like an attractive interloper, an unknown but intriguing addition to the party. She went around the room saying hello to people. When she came to me she gave me a cool smile, the smile she used to give me when we first met. It was as if the growing intimacy of our last few meetings had never existed. Perhaps it had all been my own imagination? How could this stranger be the same Caroline whose head had rested on my shoulder as we sat in the train to London? We were standing in a space of our own, for a moment, as members of the party began to collect around Andrew who was telling some anecdote about Moscow. Without the least forethought I said to Caroline, 'I miss you. I don't like seeing you back with Andrew.'

She went white, then red. Her eyes began to brim.

'How could you?' she whispered fiercely. 'You bastard. At my own dinner party?'

Then she was gone, flicking away a tear with an unobtrusive gesture that I think only I noticed. I felt as if I had been in a car crash. My legs were so wobbly I had to pull up a chair and sit down for a second.

I really don't remember much about the rest of that party. We moved into the dining room and I must have been hell to sit next to. I doubt I spoke a coherent sentence all night. I left as early as I could, pleading some excuse about a headache. Andrew came to the door with me.

'We've hardly said a word all evening,' he complained. 'We must have a proper chat sometime.'

'I'm sorry I was in such bad form,' I apologised. 'I think a couple of aspirin will sort me out, but yes, let's speak soon.'

Caroline didn't say goodbye.

I was to see Andrew again much sooner than I had expected, in our own boardroom. Jeremy had buzzed to ask me to come through without offering any further explanation.

'Andrew!' I said, in surprise. For a moment I wondered if guilt was written in every line of my face, but it couldn't have been because he shook my hand warmly.

'I hope you're feeling better.'

'Absolutely.'

Jeremy handed coffee around.

'Andrew might want us to do some background stuff on the new Russia, to try and explain what his bank is doing there.'

'It's certainly not there for the fun of it,' said Andrew. Now that we were in daylight I could see what I had not noticed before: lines of strain around his eyes and mouth, a dusting of grey along the edges of his neatly trimmed black hair.

'How bad is it?' I asked.

'Oh, it's perfectly OK ninety per cent of the time. Then

you hear of someone working for a law firm or another bank who's had a run in with the FSB. Tossed out of the country at five minutes' notice. Some of the locals have been beaten – nobody who works for us, I might add. It makes you wonder just how long it can go on without some kind of catastrophe. Yeltsin is parcelling up the economy and handing out chunks of it to crony investors and it's not a popular policy if you're not on the inside track.'

'So how can we help?' asked Jeremy.

'We want to explain why our bank is there and why we believe that in the long term – in the very long term – whatever replaces the current set-up will work. Huge mineral resources, a well-educated population, vast internal markets, an emerging middle class . . .'

We talked for some time and Andrew agreed to commission some work from us, which I would write.

'We tell it like it is,' I warned him. 'That's our house style.'

'Is there any other way?' asked Andrew. 'I'm planning to go back to Moscow in about a fortnight. Can you deliver me a first draft before then? We want to present it in the form of a client newsletter. I'll fax you a sample.'

We parted, and I agreed to get in touch as soon as I had something on paper.

I did my research and over the following days prepared a draft article for Andrew. I went through it with Jeremy and then, my pulse raised, I rang Andrew's number. He answered almost instantly.

'Oh, it's you,' he said, sounding disappointed.

'Were you expecting a call? I can ring back later. I was calling about the newsletter you commissioned.'

'Of course. No, fire away.'

'You did say you wanted a look at this before you went back,' I reminded him.

'Can you bring it round?'

I hesitated a moment, then agreed.

'OK. See you in a few minutes,' he said.

I hadn't quite meant that I would drop everything that second but Andrew was the client. I took a taxi to Notting Hill and Andrew met me at the door.

'Come in,' he said. 'Everything's a bit of a shambles – I'm in the middle of packing.'

Apart from a couple of suitcases in the hall the place looked as tidy as ever.

'Is Caroline out?' I asked. I had been mentally preparing myself to face her on the way over. I don't know what I had been thinking at the party. Perhaps I had drunk too much champagne on an empty stomach. My words had been reckless and I cringed every time I remembered her furious reaction . . . And yet, at the same time, what I had said had the ring of truth. There were no two ways about it. I really was beginning to feel something for her. But who knew how she might react the next time we met?

'Caroline's out, all right. She's walked out on me.'

I couldn't have been more surprised and it must have shown in my face.

'What do you mean? Have you had a row?'

Andrew looked irritated but then composed himself.

'We'll look at your article in a minute. I've some coffee on the go – do you want a cup?'

We sat at the kitchen table with our cups of coffee. Andrew ran a hand through his hair. He looked exasperated but did not have the air of a man who had lost control. For him, having his girlfriend abandon him instead of welcoming him back from his self-imposed exile was a glitch; nothing more.

'What do you mean, Caroline's walked out?' I repeated.

'After that dinner party you came to. The next morning. She was sleeping in one of the spare bedrooms – we haven't shared a room since I got back, she says I'm taking her for granted – and by the time I awoke she had packed and was on her way out. If I hadn't caught her she mightn't even have said goodbye.'

My mind was in such turmoil I could hardly speak, but somehow I managed to squeak, 'How odd.'

'Yes. Very odd. The truth is, Charles, I'd planned to ask her to marry me on this trip home. I thought it was only fair to give her a reason to stay with me while I still have this commitment to be in Moscow for at least another year.'

'Perhaps you should have come back earlier.'

'Did she mention she was finding it difficult? I know you saw her a couple of times while I was away.'

I felt myself going red.

'She didn't really confide in me.'

'Sorry. Unfair of me to ask, but I just wondered. I can't understand why she should walk out on me though. I'm aware she's a very special girl, talented, and I'm proud of what she's done. You went to the exhibition, didn't you? I saw that piece Jeremy bought.'

I nodded.

'But I'm going to be very well-off if I stick it out in Moscow. The bank will make me a partner, and when that happens, it's a very big step up in terms of salary and bonuses. A massive step up. Why would she turn her back on all that, or put me under pressure to do the same?'

'I don't know. She never mentioned anything to me.'

Andrew seemed reluctant to believe that Caroline and I

hadn't spent all our time talking about him. It simply didn't seem possible that he wasn't the main topic of any conversations we'd had.

'Well,' he said after a while. 'I don't see how I can propose now. I'll try and see her before I go, of course, although I have a lot to do and not much time to do it in. I still keep in touch with the political world over here. I'm not sure that Major can win an election. There are some interesting people on the Labour benches and I want to meet them.'

I didn't see how he could sit there talking about politics, when his whole world should have been crashing around his feet. But that was Andrew: steely, self-absorbed, allowing nothing to deflect him from his life's goals, even the – no doubt temporary – absence in his life of the woman he had decided to marry.

'Look,' I said. 'If there's anything I can do to help, let me know. But can we look at this article now?'

Andrew smiled.

It was the kind of smile I imagined he must have given over many boardroom tables, to partners, colleagues and competitors alike. The kind of smile that closed down a conversation, sealed a deal, won an argument or even threw down the gauntlet. I felt unnerved. There was nothing dangerous in his tone and his expression seemed sincere. Yet there was something in his eyes, a splinter of pure ice, that made me feel uncomfortable.

'Quite right, Charles. We must deal with the matter in hand. I apologise for dragging you into my personal affairs.'

We spoke several times on the phone after that but didn't meet again before he returned to Moscow. On our last call, a verbal sign-off on the work we had been doing for him, he surprised me by saying, 'I don't suppose there's any particular reason for you and Caroline to be in touch but do me a favour, please? Look her up and let me know how she is. I'm particularly interested in her state of mind with reference to myself. Anything you can report along those lines would be hugely appreciated. I'm sure you know that I am determined to marry Caroline, and if you can assist me in understanding why she's being so difficult at present, that would help me enormously.'

Andrew wasn't given to using words like 'hugely' and 'enormously', which I imagined were designed to make me feel important, otherwise his request would have sounded like an instruction to one of his staff. I gave a vague reply and rang off. I was rather fed up with Andrew, and as for Caroline, I no longer knew what I felt for her. I wondered if she would simply go back to New York, although on reflection that would have been a perverse decision, since her career was just beginning to take off in London. I didn't know who Caroline's friends were and whether she would be staying with one of them, or whether she had found a room in a hotel or a furnished flat.

Andrew went back to Moscow and we exchanged letters and faxes as we continued our work for his bank. Caroline stayed hidden from sight.

All this changed when Caroline rang me one evening to ask if she could come and see me.

'Of course,' I said, with a feeling in the pit of my stomach that was either excitement or dread. 'When?'

'I'm in some pub up the road. I've been waiting for you to get back. I can see the lights in your apartment right from where I'm sitting.'

This sounded so forlorn that I told her to come around immediately.

'Charlie, now don't freak out or anything, but I've got my bag. I swear I'm not coming to stay, I'm just on my way to a girlfriend's for the night.'

A minute or two later she was with me. We embraced at the door. She felt tense and stiff, yet yielding at the same time.

'Come in. Have a drink. You look shattered.'

'Thanks, buddy. You always did know how to make a girl feel good.'

Caroline came into the kitchen and looked about awkwardly, as if unwilling to commit herself to the act of sitting in one chair rather than another. I put a glass of wine on the table and then took her by the shoulders and guided her down on to the nearest seat.

She did look shattered: tired, haunted, mixed-up, all those things.

'So I guess Andrew told you about us?'

I explained I'd seen him but she cut me off.

'That accounts for this week's look. The shattered look. Recommended for all women who have brutally dumped their long-term lover when he has been nothing but kind, generous and supportive.'

'Kind, generous and self-centred, more like it, not to mention controlling. He's not interested in you, Caroline. He wants a wife to go with the millionaire toy kit he is building himself: dream job, dream house, dream wife.'

I didn't know where this had come from. Still, it was true.

Caroline looked at me with interest.

'So you *do* have a bitchy streak in you after all. And I'm nobody's dream wife, I can tell you.'

'You might be,' I told her. 'And I'm not bitchy. I'm just saying what I believe.'

There was a long, long pause.

'Does that apply to what you said at our dinner party?'

'Look, I'm sorry. That was hugely out of line, I don't know what I was thinking. Perhaps it was the booze. I don't even know what I was trying to say.'

Sometimes honesty is not the best policy.

'You don't even know what you were trying to say? Jesus, Charlie, you're really charming the pants off me tonight.'

I flannelled, buying time while I tried to get my jumbled thoughts in some sort of order. 'I suppose what I was trying to say was . . . it upsets me, the way Andrew treats you. As if he has abandoned you. I can't understand why he would do that . . . and why you would let him.'

Caroline drummed her fingers on the table.

'Mind if I smoke?'

'No – I'll get an ashtray.'

She lit up and inhaled, then blew a long stream of smoke towards me. It calmed her and made my eyes water.

'You know, he's never even told me that he loves me,' said Caroline. She sipped some wine. The tension had gone out of her face and she looked less haggard. 'Andrew used to say "what a great couple we'll make". As if he was my brand manager and I was some kind of product he was going to promote. He also liked saying that when he was a partner he would find sponsorship for my sculpting shows, as if that was the only way I could ever possibly make it. Like a little girl's game, pretending to be an artist, propped up by some stockbroker's cash.'

'Why are you telling me all this?' I asked, without conviction.

'Because you once told me, Charlie boy, and for this I will always be grateful, that you thought my work was good. You then ruined it by qualifying yourself as incapable of judging good art or bad, but all the same, it gave me one helluva boost when I needed it.'

She stood up with a yawn, and then stretched, as if she was about to go. The evening was drawing to a close quicker than I had hoped.

'Where were you going with that suitcase?' I asked her rather too quickly.

'Where I am going with that suitcase is to stay with a girl-friend until I can find a new place to live.'

'Andrew's been gone for weeks. Have you been living in friends' flats ever since?'

'You don't make much money sculpting, believe it or not, and my father cut my allowance when I broke loose from the law firm. So it's going to take a while to find somewhere within my budget.'

I asked her how much that was and she told me to mind my own business. I thought for a moment and then told her:

'Top of the stairs on the right is my spare bedroom. That's yours for as long as you want it. No strings. It's not good for you to keep moving around and it can't possibly be good for your work.'

Of course the answer was no, at first, but as we sat talking companionably I knew in the end that it would be yes. It was not complacency that made me think that: far from it. It was the sense of inevitability that had surrounded us ever since we met at Andrew's house; or perhaps even further back, to our meeting at the Fryerne Arms and her light-hearted teasing of me then. Maybe that was stretching it, but before an hour had passed she had phoned her friend to explain and gone upstairs to unpack. She reappeared at the head of the stairs in her pyjamas.

'I won't come down again,' she said. 'I'm too tired to talk any more. I'll see you in the morning.'

'I leave early,' I said. 'I won't wake you. I'll leave a note and some spare keys on the kitchen table.'

It felt strange, going to bed in my flat knowing that Caroline was sleeping only a few yards away. I thought I could hear faint snores coming from that direction and I smiled. I wasn't quite sure what I had just done or where it would lead, but I felt more contented and at peace that night than I had done for a long, long time.

There are watershed moments in life and that was one. Before me stretched the endless prairies of time that you think you own when you are in your thirties. Decisions can always be postponed; life will go on and your youthful energy will never dissipate. But those prairies can be lonely, pointless places to wander on your own.

Caroline never did go to her girlfriend's flat. She moved in, and stayed for good. Over the following months, we grew closer, until she was no longer sleeping in the spare room. By the following year, there was no more confusion or ambiguity in our feelings for each other. It seemed as plain as day that we should spend the rest of our lives together.

And so I proposed, a second watershed moment.

Others would follow. The betrayal of a family name. Careers destroyed and lives ruined.

Later, many years later, as I lay beside Caroline in bed one night, her small snores reminded me for a second so vividly of the very first time she had slept under my roof all those years ago. That flash of recall triggered thoughts in me, taking my mind away from the book I was trying to read. My light was still on, and I was attempting, without much success, to stay awake long enough to finish a chapter.

The sound of her snores, the noise of a small, contented animal, might have been a vignette of marital contentment. A well-off, middle-aged, slightly overweight husband nestles up to his beloved wife of many years. Outside, the orange glare of sodium street lighting penetrates through the curtains as they move in the draughts that flow and eddy everywhere in this ageing, restless house. The house sits in a leafy suburb of Newcastle, a city I came to when I accepted a job in the newly formed Department of Strategic Communications at the university.

I like this house. It has big rooms, high ceilings. A merchant's town house, once upon a time.

Once upon a time.

Once upon a time a professor of Strategic Communications, his wife the sculptor Caroline Woodchester, the deputy leader (and some would have said future Leader of the Opposition) Andrew Landford, and Andrew's beautiful, sexy, intelligent wife Helen, all went for a journey in a car together. Not a car really: it was a three-tonne package of gleaming metal and glass. What happened next was not the fault of the car. That much, at least, is clear. The rest isn't.

I had always prided myself on my ability to discern the truth. It was my one marketable asset. But on the one occasion in my life when it really, really mattered, truth became the victim of circumstance; and other things, too.

I close my book and put it on my bedside table. Outside an owl hoots. I switch off the bedside light.

Click.

2

GILCASTER HEAD

I

2010

Clunk-click.

'Are we all strapped in?' said Andrew cheerfully, as he pulled shut the door of his car. 'Otherwise this wretched vehicle whines at you until you give in.'

Just like old times: Andrew taking control of things again, or in this case, his car. It was the newest of the new Range Rovers: enormous, luxurious, an emblem of success and power. I sat in the front beside Andrew while Helen and Caroline sat in the back, making bright, awkward conversation as we drove out of Newcastle Airport. Considering that Caroline had once nearly become Andrew's wife rather than mine, I didn't think they were doing too badly. But then Helen had charm, lots of it. I'm not saying that Caroline didn't, but she didn't have all those little upper-class English tricks designed to make the other person in the conversation feel flattered, needed and inferior. As for Andrew, having the girl he might have married and the girl he did marry in the back seat of his car must have made him feel good about life. I could almost write the subtext for him:

'Pity Caroline's let herself go – she always used to be so careful about her weight. She ought to ask Helen where she gets her hair done. Helen has a man in Mayfair who does her hair. Looks a million dollars. Costs it too.'

But that was my subtext, really, as Andrew would never bother himself about where people got their hair done. I was the one worrying that my wife looked rather ordinary sitting next to Helen.

A worry that in itself was indicative of how we now felt about each other, I suspected. As marriages go, ours had been happy to start with. There had been holidays, and explorations, adventures across golden sands and frozen seas. I had discovered a taste and modest ability for cooking Caroline's favourite Far Eastern dishes to her satisfaction, even daring to experiment and create new ones of my own. We shared memories of countless private views, gallery openings, warm speeches, even warmer glasses of wine, the high-frequency and highly forgettable chatter of a successful night trailing off into the dusk. The occasional Fryerne clan gathering. Walks in the hills, sitting alone together in a deserted cinema on a Monday night, lying in bed while the smells of breakfast drifted in from next door. That, at least, had not changed.

Yet much also had.

Caroline had struggled to get her work recognised in the way it deserved. This was not for want of trying, she never seemed to be out of her studio, and exhibited on a regular – some might say too regular – basis. She had her buyers and admirers, but they were rather too select a group to propel her to the stellar career we had both envisaged. I found much to be proud of – her inclusion in a new EU-funded sculpture garden for Durham, several appearances in the Royal Academy Summer Show and winning a commission to create a permanent exhibition for the new languages centre at Newcastle University. But for some reason these seemed to deflate Caroline rather than inspire her. She took criticism personally, and dwelt upon it. What the critics often said I secretly agreed with; she had so much innate talent and imagination, yet even her best work often felt constrained, self-edited, as if some invisible barrier was holding her back.

None of this was helped, of course, by my relative success in my chosen field. To my slight embarrassment, I was now regarded as something of an industry guru. Jeremy and I had sold our business to a global media agency a couple of years back. Jeremy stayed on, but I had been offered an academic position at Newcastle University as Professor of Strategic Communication Studies. It wouldn't be going too far to say they practically created the department around me.

The change of location did more for me than it did for our marriage or Caroline's career. We found an old Georgian house in one of the city's leafy suburbs, in which we rattled about well enough, but she kept on her studio and our old flat in London, which is where she bolted when she needed to work. These days, that seemed to be nearly all the time.

I can't remember when things started to go wrong. Perhaps it was the question of children. In our early years, focused on our careers, we had both agreed that starting a family wasn't a priority. Occasionally the odd Fryerne at a memorial service or landmark birthday party would remind me of my supposed duty to the clan, with questions that were as sharp as they were teasingly phrased. So much so that when, in more recent years, Caroline broached the subject again, I was more receptive to the idea. Alas, in some never fully diagnosed way, our bodies were not. We tried and tried, every treatment, every old wives' tale. We never formally admitted defeat; we just stopped talking about it.

The new Mrs Landford, of course, had already provided

our host with a son and heir, a child that had been packed off to boarding school as soon as he was of age. That was about the sum total of my knowledge about Helen. She could have been a model. Maybe she had been. I think in fact she had been a successful corporate lawyer until she met Andrew. Then, by degrees, she had abandoned her career and became a lady of leisure. I suspect it would have been difficult for Andrew to deal with two high achievers in the same marriage. Somehow he had managed to persuade Helen that she could be more of a help to him in his career just by being glamorous and intelligent, and making middle-aged bankers and politicians feel good about themselves. She seemed to have accepted her new role. Physically she was a perfect specimen: long legs, good hair, made up to perfection so that she really did convey the impression of someone who had just jumped off the front cover of Vogue – and certainly not someone who'd had a child.

Beside her, Caroline did not look exactly frumpy, but she was . . . just Caroline: a little thickset these days, but still with a good figure. Hair not Mayfair, but still plenty of it. Clothes bought mostly online. The difference was probably in her face: Caroline wore a look of determination, experience and humour, which more than made up for any other inadequacies as far as I was concerned.

I don't suppose physical comparisons worked in my favour either. Andrew was one of those people who liked to tell you he could still get into the clothes he wore at university. Tonight he wore a beautifully tailored charcoal grey suit with a peacock blue silk lining. I wore what one wore in my job: a blazer and rumpled chinos, nothing too smart. Smart suits and big cars were not the way to ingratiate oneself in the academic world, or at least my corner of it.

Making a low hum like a spacecraft the Range Rover pulled out on to the motorway.

'Good luck you two girls being on the same flight from London,' said Andrew, cheerfully. I had taken the Metro from Newcastle and Caroline had come straight from her studio in London, where she had been working all week.

'Yes, wasn't it?' said Helen. 'We could have made a plan to sit together if I'd known.'

Caroline's reply contained the bare minimum of enthusiasm and regret. She wasn't sure about this whole weekend. Neither of us had seen much of Andrew over the fifteen years or so that had passed since the rather awkward letter I wrote to him announcing my engagement to Caroline. Neither of us had met Helen before. And other than that very uncomfortable conversation in his house after the day Caroline left, he and I had never discussed the matter.

Regardless, Andrew had remained a client of our firm; he wasn't going to let a little thing like the break-up of his relationship affect a business arrangement. But Jeremy had tactfully put someone else on as account handler, so Andrew and I had only met on his occasional visits to the office, with a quick handshake in the corridor or the occasional cup of coffee.

Maybe his self-esteem was wounded by what had happened; maybe it wasn't. Andrew was very good at rationalising and I imagined he would have taught himself to believe that being abandoned by Caroline wasn't a setback, but an opportunity. And so it had proved. He had gone out and found himself a new wife who fitted the job description perfectly. If he became leader and Helen was allowed her share of the limelight, the press photographers would love her.

We were now heading towards Gilcaster Head. At Oxford,

people had spoken of Andrew's parents as being rich expats who had owned, variously, either a gold mine or a tea plantation. How these rumours had got about, I don't know. I can only imagine that Andrew had started them himself out of some warped sense of mischief. The reality was more prosaic: his parents owned several manufacturing businesses, amongst them a factory that made the edible wrapper that contains our morning sausage. On retirement, they had sold out and bought a small farm at Gilcaster Head, not far from Hadrian's Wall where it crosses from Northumberland into Cumbria. Their choice of location was hard to fathom: perhaps it represented some kind of rural idyll. They grassed over their few acres and settled down, dying one soon after the other only a few years ago. Now Andrew had taken over Gilcaster Head. It was an odd decision. The farm was in a most inconvenient place and with few neighbours. But he liked the idea of 'a place in the country', and spent a good deal of money doing it up.

The weekend was not planned as a reunion between the four of us, although in one sense that was what it was. Andrew had gone part-time at his bank a few years ago and had become an MP. This was something I believed he had been manoeuvring towards ever since his university days. At any rate, he now had a safe Conservative seat in a constituency in the North West of England. Time spent migrating between London and Gilcaster Head must have put a strain even on someone as resourceful as Andrew. But it hadn't interfered with his rapid rise through party ranks to a position on the front benches. At that time this was the Opposition front bench, after a tight general election, but Andrew was hopeful all that would change in the next year or two. Political parties were as noted for what they disagreed about amongst themselves as for the policies they claimed to be fighting for.

Andrew told me all this when we met one night in London. He wanted me to join his Praetorian Guard: a group of 'special advisers', the energetic bright men and women who would protect him and write his speeches and think his thoughts for him and generally help him in his plan to become party leader. Just now all was going well for him. The current incumbent had been weakened by a poor general election result. But Andrew wasn't the only person dreaming of running the party. Maldwyn Christie was interested too, and the public warmed to him rather more than they did to Andrew. This was what we were going to talk about that weekend, I supposed.

My role could only be guessed at, but I was interested, and I must admit, flattered as well. I was also intrigued to see a bit more of Andrew. Had he changed over the years? How was his master plan (become a millionaire, take charge of the Tories, then become prime minister) progressing? So far it sounded as if it was running like clockwork. In addition, I was lured by the idea that I could have a part to play on the periphery of power, however brief and minor it might be. It could be an interesting experience for a few months, just observing political life on the inside track, rather than from the outside. It was exactly the sort of project the university would encourage me to become involved in, as long as I was discreet about it.

All in all I was looking forward to our weekend. I didn't expect it to be comfortable – in the sense of easygoing – but it had to be better than some of the long silences that Caroline and I endured in each other's company, especially over recent months. I hoped this weekend would cheer her up, or at least lift her out of what seemed to be a long-lasting depression; anything that might buoy her in some way. There were too many retreats and silences in our relationship, too much entrenchment. We had backed ourselves into a series of dead ends, and any change in scenery that might offer a way out was to be welcomed.

The light was fading fast as we drove past the escarpment along which the wall stood. To the south, a red-rimmed sky cast its autumnal light over the empty landscape, which was broken up only by a few hill farms (mostly now trading as bed and breakfasts) and scattered blocks of conifers. To the north of the road stood the wall. Few of its mile castles still remained, but in the gathering gloom one could easily imagine what it must have been like once: the edge of the known world. It hadn't ever really been the last outpost, even in its hey-day – Roman castles and earthworks ran up through the borders and right into the Scottish Lowlands. But on a quiet evening like this, one could fancy oneself on the brink of nowhere. We passed a larger set of ruins where the outline of a fort and troop-houses could be seen.

'That's Housesteads,' said Helen to Caroline. 'We can come and look over it tomorrow if you like, while the men are talking business?'

'Really?' said Caroline. 'I hope the men aren't going to be talking too much business.' She sounded as if she was on the verge of an outburst of bad temper.

'Not at all,' said Andrew from the front. He could read Caroline's mind as well as I could, for what that was worth. 'We will try not to be dull. Never let it be said that I bore my guests.'

'You're about the only man I know who could get away

with a remark like that,' said Caroline, and everybody laughed. The shadow of hostility lifted and then our attention was diverted as we turned off the main road on to a single track with passing places. 'God help us if we meet another car on this road,' said Helen nervously.

'Do you come up here much?' I ventured.

'Not as much as Andrew would like me to. Of course I've got to show up in the constituency from time to time and wave the flag. There's been a lot of flag-waving recently, hasn't there, darling?'

Andrew grimaced but did not answer.

We passed a crossroads. The scenery around us had become wilder: low hills and rocky outcrops clad with gorse and pine. There were few other houses – the odd farmhouse with a gleam of light in the kitchen window, and the glow of a village over to our right. Wind swirled fistfuls of leaves across the road, and in the distance there was the rumble of a late summer storm.

'Not far now,' said Andrew. 'I feel a gin and tonic coming on.'

He turned his head and smiled at Caroline. As he did so, something appeared in the dusk, just beyond the windscreen – a flurry of beating wings and burning eyes staring in at us.

'Andrew!' I called out, but it was too late.

There was a thud against the windscreen; a crescendo of white wings. A screech, as the car swerved then stopped without going off the road.

'Oh Christ!' shouted Andrew. He sounded rattled. 'Is everybody all right?'

'You hit an owl,' I told him.

'I never had a chance. It just flew straight at the car.'

'It's the owl you should be worrying about.'

'Hang on,' said Andrew. He opened the door and jumped out. I could see the owl in the light from the headlamps. It was still conscious and was hopping around in circles, dragging a wing.

'Oh God,' said Andrew. 'What should I do?' He sounded in a panic, quite unlike his usual self. He hopped around the owl and the owl hopped away from him. Eventually he picked it up by a leg and then let go with a yelp as the bird pecked him viciously.

'You little bastard!'

'It's not the poor owl's fault, darling,' said Helen. 'Oh, somebody please do something. Andrew's so useless at things like this. Can't you help, Charles?'

'I'm not useless,' shouted Andrew, with alarming fury. 'I didn't ask the sodding thing to fly into my brand new car.' He made another grab at the creature. There was a brief tussle of man and bird and then Andrew, seizing both its legs this time, lifted the owl up and slammed its head against the top of a dry stone wall. There was another screech and a frantic flapping of wings. Then they began to tremble.

'There! That'll shut the fucker up!' He slammed the owl again and again against the wall until the bent and crushed upper parts of the bird and its twisted head indicated that the unequal battle was over. 'Little fucker!' Andrew repeated again, bending down and wiping his hands on the grass. We all stared at him in mute horror. As he straightened up he caught our look and said, 'Well, what was I supposed to do?'

'Take it to a vet and get its wing pinned?' I suggested.

'What a carry on that would have been. I've no idea where the nearest vet is. And can you imagine Helen and

Caroline holding on to that vicious bird while we looked for one?'

I looked at Caroline. Her expression was one of revulsion. 'That was so horrible,' she said, almost inaudibly.

Andrew ignored her, speaking to me, 'And then, can you imagine the vet phoning the local paper – Andrew Landford runs over protected species?'

In a tone unlike any she had used before, Helen Landford said, 'Andrew, will you stop buggering about. Get rid of that poor bird, drive us home, and pour us a drink.'

Andrew held the bird up. 'What should I do with this?'

'Take it home?' I suggested.

'I'm not having that in the car,' said Helen. Andrew tossed the corpse into a field.

'Someone will see that,' I told him.

'So what? It's like dead badgers. Everyone thinks they're roadkill but half of them have been shot by keepers or farmers and then been reversed over.'

He climbed back into the car. Nobody said a word until we arrived at Gilcaster Head a few minutes later. We got out of the car in silence and then Helen, with an effort, remembered her role as hostess and directed us to our room.

'Come on down in five minutes when you've had a chance to freshen up, and we'll have a drink. I'm sure we all need one after that.'

The house had been turned around at some point in its history so that we arrived at what must once have been the back door. I had an impression of a jumble of low, sloping slate roofs, gable ends and high chimney stacks. Inside any notion that one was entering a rural farmhouse was dispelled immediately by the fact that the house was not only warm, but hot. A wood-burning stove glowed in the small entrance hall and the central heating was on even though it was still only mid-September.

When we got to our bedroom I managed to open a window and let in some fresh air. Caroline looked around the room and said, 'God, everything's so London.'

It was true. The six pillows on our bed, the overstuffed duvets, the luxurious wallpaper, the swagged curtains all indicated the fairly recent presence of an expensive interior decorator who had been assigned the task of making the occupant of the room feel that while it might be Cumbria outside, inside it was Knightsbridge.

'Are you all right?' I asked Caroline.

'Yes. I'd clean forgotten about Andrew's charming psycho side, that's all.'

I looked at her across the bed. She had never described him like that before. Controlling, perhaps. I had seen him use a rifle as if his brain was wired directly to the trigger, and noticed his brusque manner with those who worked for him, but I had never witnessed him behaving as savagely as he had with that bird.

Caroline turned away to get dressed and a few minutes later we went downstairs into the drawing room.

Another fire blazed here, and the sofas and armchairs had all been upholstered in a golden yellow damask with blue piping. We found Andrew opening a bottle of wine.

'What'll it be?' he asked. 'Wine or something stronger?'

'Gin for me,' said Caroline.

'Whisky.'

Helen appeared with a flute of champagne. Her hair was perfect once more, and she had fully recovered any composure she had misplaced in the car.

'Well, our trips here aren't always quite so dramatic,' she remarked.

'I'm sorry you had to see that,' said Andrew to Caroline. 'There really was nothing else I could do. I couldn't leave the poor thing to die of its injuries.'

'No. Quite right,' said Caroline, with a completely straight face. At first I couldn't tell whether she was being ironic. 'One dead owl. Problem solved.'

'The funny thing is,' said Andrew, 'I'm on the parliamentary Committee which just toughened up the Wildlife and Countryside Act.' He paused, thinking about it. 'I say, I wonder if I've put myself in a rather awkward position?'

'Least said, soonest mended,' I told him.

'Is that your strategic advice?' asked Andrew, laughing without much enthusiasm.

'I'm off duty tonight.'

'Yes,' said Helen. 'Let's not talk about death and owls tonight.'

Dinner was cooked and served by a couple who lived in a flat over the stables, Gurkhas from Nepal. They were known as John and Mary, although I doubted those were their actual names.

'Frightfully loyal and hard working, and so keen to please,' murmured Helen between courses. It was obvious she didn't have to do a hand's turn to keep Gilcaster Head going. She simply arrived, told them when to run her bath and when dinner was to be served, and that was more or less that. 'We couldn't possibly cope without them,' Helen told me, and I believed her. At any rate their presence left her free to look after her guests and after the very unpromising start to the evening, things showed signs of being back on an even keel.

I felt myself mellowing under the influence of all this luxury and Andrew too had lost some of the tension I had sensed in the air even before the accident. After dinner we went back into the drawing room. Helen and Caroline sat on the floor in front of the fire. Our host and I sat in two armchairs opposite them, on the other side of the room.

'You know,' said Andrew softly, as he handed me a whisky and water nightcap, 'it's a pity that we allowed your marriage to Caroline to come between us. We should have been more grown-up about it. I blame myself.'

He had a unique gift of making an admission sound like a veiled threat. I shifted in my seat.

'If anyone is to blame that would have been me. But let's agree to forget all that now.'

'I'll drink to that,' said Andrew, smiling.

That night, as Caroline and I undressed for bed, I said, 'You know, I quite enjoyed seeing Andrew again. How did you get on with Helen?'

'Oh, Helen. She's sweet, really. I don't know what she does with herself all day.'

'Organises Andrew's life for him, I expect. Anyway, I'm glad we've all got together again.'

'Mmm.'

'You don't sound convinced. Andrew's not such a bad chap, you know.'

'Unless you're an owl.'

2

We were woken next morning by the smell of bacon cooking, one of the surest ways to tempt me out of bed. After a good cooked breakfast, Andrew and I decided to go for a walk and chew over the implications of the previous night's events.

Daylight revealed the full extent of Gilcaster Head. The back of the house was made up of an array of old farm buildings that had been merged into one over the years and converted into living space. The rest of the house had a handsome Georgian exterior, and a back door with three steps leading down from it into the garden.

The garden was rather scruffy in comparison with the immaculate interior of the house. Gardening was either not an enthusiasm of Andrew and Helen's, or it simply was not practical here, but the bare minimum of work had been done. The mostly unkempt lawn was bordered by a ha-ha, more like a ditch, and protected from marauding sheep by a few strands of barbed wire. Beyond that, fields of rough pasture heavy with dew and dotted by clumps of thistles led up towards a long plantation of conifers. They were not trees I had ever liked. Planted in blocks I found them more like black holes than forests, sucking the light out of everything around them. But these spruces were different to the huge swathes of neat commercial forestry a bit further up the valley. There was something ragged about them, their branches twisted with age. I wondered if they were the oldest thing about Gilcaster Head, although of course, their longevity would still be nothing compared to the remains of the Roman Wall a mile or two away.

Andrew pointed out the extent of his grazing, a hundred or so acres that he let to a local farmer, and then we set off down the lane for a walk. As we strolled along I became aware that another walker was approaching us from the opposite direction.

'That's a neighbour,' said Andrew. 'He's called Tom. I've forgotten what his surname is. He's one of those townies who've gone native: grows his own vegetables, drives a hybrid car – extremely impractical decision living somewhere like this – anti-fracking, pro-badgers, you name it. He's even got a bee in his bonnet about the remains of some ancient Roman temple near us that hasn't been properly excavated. As if this part of the world needs any more Roman ruins . . . He's not a bad chap, just a bit over-enthusiastic, like a born again missionary.'

We stopped and greeted each other.

'This is Professor Charles Fryerne,' said Andrew, introducing me.

'Tom,' said the newcomer. 'Tom Gazelee. Are you staying the weekend?'

'Yes, we all got up last night. We're just getting some good Cumbrian air into our lungs.'

'Ah, I've been doing that for a few years now. You should try and spend more time here, Andrew. God's own country.'

Tom Gazelee wore a woollen cap on his head and a Carlisle United scarf over an ancient Barbour, jeans and walking boots. He was like a hundred others you might meet on a country lane.

'Did you notice anybody about when you came home last night?' Tom asked Andrew.

'How do you mean?'

'I'm not really sure. Poachers, maybe. It's just that on my way to get the papers this morning I spotted a dead owl just inside a gateway off this road. About a mile further along, near the crossroads.'

'A dead owl?' said Andrew, his smile frozen on his face. I, too, felt awkward.

'Yes. Poor thing. It was a barn owl. Someone had battered its head in. Amazing how savage people can be.'

'Where is it now?' asked Andrew.

'I took it to the police station in Brampton and reported it. It's a crime to kill an owl, as I'm sure you know. You're on that parliamentary Committee.'

'How on earth did you know that?' said Andrew. He was struggling to remain calm.

'Oh, I Google you from time to time to see what my famous neighbour is getting up to. We're proud to have such a leading politician spend some of his time in a remote spot like this.'

Tom appeared to be perfectly sincere in his praise.

'But to go back to the owl – you must have come that way last night. Did you see anything unusual on your travels?'

There was a pause, and then Andrew said in a dry voice, 'No, I can't say that we did.'

'Oh well,' said Tom. 'Of course they will get away with it, whoever they were. All I can do is to tell people to keep their eyes open. There are some evil bastards walking the earth, aren't there?'

'Yes indeed, Tom.'

We parted and walked on slowly in silence. After we had gone a hundred yards or so Andrew said, 'Model citizen.'

He laughed humourlessly. I waited for him to speak again.

'Calling in a crime even though it's only a dead bird, even though the police will no doubt have to go about interviewing people and chasing around after non-existent poachers and filling in reports. Do you know how big a problem drug abuse is in country schools, Charles? It's massive. The police don't have the resources to deal with something as serious as that and yet here's good old Tom diverting them to find the killer of a poor bird that was more than halfway dead already.'

We strolled on and Andrew said, 'You're not giving me any advice, I notice.'

'It's a bit difficult to know what to say.'

'You're telling me. What to say or what not to say.'

We faced each other. Andrew didn't look angry, or tired, or anxious, just preoccupied. There was a problem to be solved, and he was going to solve it. And I was expected to help him.

The trouble was, Andrew's version of events was factual yet also omitted to tell the full story.

'In a way,' said Andrew, 'I've missed the boat. I suppose I should have told Tom Gazelee all about it. But I really couldn't. I mean, can you imagine me saying, "Oh, by the way, yes, it was me who smashed that bird's head to bits on a stone wall, I'll just hurry along home now and ring the police."'

'A difficult line,' I agreed. 'But what you could do is go to the police station now, with me, and say that the owl flew into your windscreen and that it was virtually dead when you picked it up. You put it out of its misery. I can corroborate all of that.'

'What, go right now?'

'There's no time like the present. Get it over with. It was an accident.'

There was a long pause. Then Andrew said, 'No. There's too much downside and not enough upside. I've already told Tom I saw nothing. I didn't quite mean it but that's how it will have sounded to him.'

That's how it had sounded to me as well, but I said nothing.

'It will all blow over, anyway. One dead bird, for God's sake. I know it's an owl. I know barn owls have protected status under the Wildlife and Countryside Act because I'm on the damned Committee. It's very unfortunate that the bird should have flown into my car but that is hardly my fault and I don't see why I should deliberately put my head on the block and let them chop it off because of one unfortunate bird. No, I'll take your original advice after all, I think.'

'What advice?' I asked in alarm. I didn't remember advising him about anything.

'Last night you said: least said, soonest mended. That's the line I'm going to follow.'

'That was in a slightly different context,' I reminded him.

'Nevertheless,' said Andrew firmly.

I was an adviser; I had advised him; he had taken the advice. That was the end of the matter. We walked back to the house in silence. In my mind were his words: too much downside and not enough upside. He was thinking in terms of risks and benefits, not in terms of truth or lies.

After lunch Helen went off to 'do her household accounts', which I suspect meant a snooze in a back sitting room somewhere. Caroline decided to go out for a walk, leaving Andrew and I alone together in the drawing room.

'I've been following your career with great interest,' Andrew began. 'And Jeremy's too. CCC was a tremendous success and I gather Jeremy is quite happy working in a bigger firm now you've sold it.'

'Seems to be,' I agreed.

'But your move was interesting. Did they create that Chair especially for you?'

'Not exactly, but the timing was right: I was free and they were looking to build up the department.'

'And you do what?'

'Provide the training and groundwork for people who want to do what Jeremy and I did, or who want to go into lobbying, or brand management.'

Andrew stretched his legs out in front of him and steepled his fingers on his stomach. We chatted for a while before he got to the point.

'Making me into an acceptable candidate for party leader is what's on my mind. Do you think you can do it?'

'Do you think *you* can do it?' I asked him. Andrew laughed.

'Answer a question with another question? That's the guru technique, right there.'

'I'm not the one who is going to have to sell himself to the party at the conference. You are. If you don't believe it, let's stop now.'

Andrew frowned.

'Of course I believe it. That's a given. But it's what's in the speech that counts. That's where you come in.'

'You've got a speechwriter for that, haven't you?'

There was a silence, during which we heard a car drive up. As Andrew rose to his feet, the doorbell rang. Andrew went into the hall and I heard him talking to someone. Whoever it was wasn't invited in. Then the door was shut and, after a moment, the car drove off. Andrew came back into the drawing room and sat down. He seemed a little paler than before.

'I'm sorry for the interruption. What were we saying just now?'

But he had lost his composure and when I said, 'Who was that?' with a strong feeling that I knew the answer, he answered irritably:

'Well, if you must know, it was the police. Can you believe it? Two of them in a patrol car on a Saturday afternoon, when there's a football match on in Carlisle. How can they spare the men to go on a wild goose chase like that?'

I waited. When Andrew could see I wasn't going to comment, he said, 'Maybe it's better if you don't know any more about this.'

'Well, I already know that they've driven away without taking any notes or photographs of your car.'

'One of them was examining a chip on the windscreen,' said Andrew, 'nosy bastard. They'll be looking for owl DNA next, for God's sake.'

'So I know that, whatever they asked, you answered in the negative.'

'Oh, don't be so evasive, Professor Fryerne,' said Andrew. 'They asked if I knew anything about a dead owl. I said yes, someone had told me about it. They asked if I had seen anything on the drive home last night. I said that I had seen no other cars or any unusual activity that might suggest poachers or anyone else was prowling about. Then one of them said to me, "You want to get that chip on your windscreen ground out, sir. It might shatter while you are driving." I said

I would call the glass people, and then they left.'

Andrew's answers were not outright untruths. They were literal and, as far as they went, accurate. It was just that he hadn't told them what he knew. I began to wish I hadn't got myself involved in all this. I had become part of a lie: someone else's lie, but a lie nevertheless. It was all very complicated.

'Look, Andrew,' I told him. 'You're asking me what I can do to help you communicate with your voters. All my professional life I have found that there is a distrust of professional communicators such as myself and a huge distrust of those who use their services. Senior politicians are contaminated by this lack of trust, this feeling the public have that they are being spun to.'

'Which they are,' said Andrew.

'Which they are. My response, and my guiding principle through my career, has always been to tell the truth. By that I mean, giving the public the unedited truth rather than presenting them with a menu of items that might be truthful but don't really give you a proper or complete idea of who the candidate is. The hard part is to avoid boring the audience while giving them both the bad news and the good news. If you can achieve that, you have a winning formula.'

Andrew yawned. For a moment it was as if the mask had slipped. Instead of the youngish, energetic politician of a moment ago I saw lines of fatigue, a face portraying utter exhaustion.

'Sorry, that police visit has scrambled my brains a bit,' he said. 'Did I mention we've got Matt Dilcombe joining us for dinner?'

'Matt Dilcombe!'

Matt Dilcombe was one of a new breed of adviser, a kind of gun for hire who was tasked with mapping out tactics during a political campaign. He had achieved fame, or maybe notoriety, by turning around an electoral campaign in New Zealand and snatching victory from the jaws of defeat – or whatever cliché the newspapers had reached for at the time. He certainly had an impressive record.

'I didn't realise he was on your team,' I said to Andrew.

'He isn't yet. He might be. I wanted the two of you to meet. You would do the big-picture stuff and he would be responsible for execution. He's coming up by train and John's picking him up at Carlisle in about an hour.'

'It's a long way to come for dinner,' I said flippantly.

'Matt Dilcombe would go to Timbuktu for dinner if he thought it would give him an edge. He's a very driven man. If I can get him – and you – in harness, then my campaign to become party leader stands a very good chance of succeeding. Now, I need to catch up with the newspapers, so let's pick up again over a drink when Matt arrives.'

I was – politely but firmly – dismissed and left to my own resources for a while.

For Andrew, reading the papers was not, as it was for others, a pleasant interlude; it was a religion. I had already spotted all the Saturday papers laid out on a coffee table, including the *Financial Times* and the *Wall Street Journal*, together with the *Spectator* and *Prospect*. Andrew would go through these with scissors and yellow highlighters, cutting articles out or highlighting things that interested him. He made an unholy mess, which John and Mary had to tidy up afterwards, although I never heard them complain. Then he would sit at his laptop and scroll through the news sites and political blogs.

I admired his application even though I thought it was a complete waste of time. He claimed it kept him 'in the loop'.

That was another thing I was going to have to get Andrew to unlearn. He believed that all information had value, no matter how tiny, and you couldn't afford to miss that last scrap of gold dust. I believed that most of what you read in the papers was rubbish, and that other people's opinions were a distraction. You had to sort out what you believed first.

I met Caroline in the hall.

'Christ, this is a boring weekend,' she said, as she struggled out of her wellington boots. I hushed her – she either didn't know she could be overheard or didn't care – and followed her up to our room. She sat on the bed, and continued her complaint.

'Helen can't really be doing "household accounts" this afternoon, can she? That's what people like Helen employ accountants to do. Either she's sleeping or' – a thought struck her – 'maybe she's a secret drinker and she's sitting in her little room boozing. That would certainly make life more interesting!'

'Surely not?'

'Well, what else are you expected to do here? Either you have to go for a walk in this tedious bit of country, or else you might as well go to sleep yourself.'

'It's no more boring than being at home,' I said, before I could stop myself.

Caroline stared at me for a moment. Then she said, 'Thanks, buddy. Thanks very much for that. That certainly makes me feel a whole lot better.'

She burst into tears. I came and sat beside her, and put an arm around her. She shrugged me off and lay flat on the bed with her face in the pillows. I couldn't tell whether she was still sobbing, but reached a hand out towards her, across the crumpled sea of the bed cover. 'I'm sorry. You know I didn't mean that, darling. I'm just as bored as you are and it's put me in a bad mood. That was an unforgivable thing to say.'

Caroline ignored me. Eventually she sat up and said, in a peremptory manner, 'I have a very bad feeling about that owl. I think Andrew has done something terrible, and doesn't realise it. You have no idea what he is capable of.'

'But it was just an accident. What's one dead bird to anyone?'

She took my hand, looking at me mournfully.

'Sometimes I really wonder whether you understand anything about how the world works at all.'

Then she turned away from me, curling up on the other side of the bed. In the unflattering grey light of late afternoon, we lay on the bed waiting for an angel to come and rescue our marriage.

3

Matt Dilcombe arrived at about six. Half an hour later we joined him on the garden terrace. It was a mild evening for the time of year and the garden door had been flung open. John had brought out a table and chairs so we sat outside with our drinks. Matt was a small man, with tight dark curls covering his head, and sharp brown eyes. He crackled with energy, and had a direct gaze that could make the recipient uncomfortable.

He took my hand when we were introduced, as would someone who has been offered a dead fish to hold, and dropped it immediately. I told myself it was just his manner. He gave me an interrogative stare when Andrew told him what I did.

'I Googled you,' he told me. 'Strategic Communications, huh? We could use some of that around here.'

That sounded like a criticism, and I was about to say something when Andrew handed us our drinks.

'You can see the Roman Wall from here,' said Andrew. 'Beyond Minniver Wood.'

'Minniver Wood?' I asked.

He pointed up at the long planting of spruce that bordered the pasture beyond the garden. An evening breeze stirred the tops of the trees, and for a moment they seemed to bend apart, as if the forest were opening up. I stared at them, but could see only shadow beyond.

At that moment there was a distant screech and as we watched a large white bird detached itself from the trees and began skimming and quartering the ground. An owl, hunting for shrews and voles. Helen flinched as the bird came closer. Then with another cry it turned away and flew back into the wood.

No one said a word. Caroline took a large gulp of her drink, and brushed a loose strand of hair away from her forehead.

'Let's go inside,' said Andrew abruptly, standing up. 'I'm being bitten. Aren't you, Matt?'

'Can't say I am, but we'll go inside if you like.' He glanced round the table at us all, frozen like statues, and chuckled. 'You lot look like you've seen a ghost.'

At dinner our visitor was scathing about the present state of party politics.

'Nobody is in charge in a coalition,' he said, 'certainly not in this new one. All the headline policies are about rubbish collection, carbon trading, a tax on goodness knows what. Nobody has anything to say about what our policies are on defence, on energy, on Europe – they're too frightened of being held hostage by the other side. It's pathetic. The first person who can answer the really hard questions is the one who deserves to win the confidence of the party and the electorate.'

'Charles always says that telling the unvarnished truth is the only option when faced with a cynical electorate,' Andrew told him.

'Then we shall get on,' said Matt firmly. 'That's exactly what is needed.'

'What about Maldwyn?' asked Andrew. 'How much should I worry about him?'

'Maldwyn is a dead duck. He just doesn't know it.'

I was fascinated.

'Why is Maldwyn a dead duck?'

'Yes, why?' asked Caroline. 'I know he's your rival, Andrew, but all the same I'm fond of Maldwyn, and they say he has heaps of friends on the back benches.'

'I'm fond of him too,' agreed Andrew. 'We were at college together and he's one of the few, apart from Charles here, that I've kept up with.'

'Maldwyn's got some good ideas,' said Matt, 'and we can use them when he withdraws from the leadership contest. I like his ideas on asymmetrical demobilisation.'

'What on earth's that?' I asked.

'Hang on a minute,' said Andrew. 'What on earth makes you think that Maldwyn will withdraw from the leadership contest?'

There was a pause while Matt glanced around the table, trying to gauge the impact his words might have. Then he continued, 'Because in about a fortnight's time one of the weekend nationals will do an op-ed piece on the fact that Maldwyn is gay. The headline will be along the lines of "Can you remember the last time a gay man led the party?"'

There was a silence and then an explosion of indignation from Caroline and Helen.

'You can't do that to Maldwyn, that would be vile,' said Caroline. Helen's face had the lustrous glow of someone who has had too much to drink. She hadn't overdone it at dinner, as far as I could see. Maybe Caroline was right and she was a secret drinker.

Helen said, 'Yes, poor cuddly Maldwyn. We all love him.'

'All the women do,' said Matt. 'The story has been out there for a while but nobody has picked it up yet. But they will. If we take charge of the way it comes out then at least it will be done sensitively. We'll praise him as a man and as a politician. But we'll ask the question: will the grassroots members vote for a gay man to become party leader? Will the voters choose him as the next prime minister? And the answer we will get is no. Sorry, everybody, but the country isn't ready for that yet.'

Maldwyn had never made a particular secret of his sexuality, but we had rarely discussed it together, and I found it hard to gauge how he would react to such a public outing.

'Who will stick the dagger in?' I asked.

Matt named a well-known columnist.

'He likes Maldwyn. He really wants to save him from the scurrilous reporting that the tabloids will put him through – if they don't get to the story first.'

I felt blank. I couldn't be part of this, could I? The political assassination of an old friend was a depth to which I had not thought to sink. Maldwyn might never speak to me again. But Matt talked as if the whole process was inexorable: a few hundred words of newsprint that would effectively destroy Maldwyn's political career before it had really taken off. It would either be written by someone well-disposed to Maldwyn, or by someone hostile who would write something poisonous. I shook my head. Where was the choice? There was none.

'Aren't you going to say something, Charles?' asked Caroline in indignation. But Matt held up his hand.

'Listen. Back home I've run more than one successful election campaign using what I call the flat possum strategy.'

Caroline nearly spat out her drink. 'A flat possum?' said Andrew, frowning.

'Very common roadkill where I come from, I'm afraid. They dash out from the bush and pick a fight with a truck or trailer that they're never going to win. But I'm talking about winning arguments here. Maldwyn is a strong candidate with a loyal following. The more he shores up his base, the less good the picture looks for you. So I recommend you slap him in the face with a flat possum, so to speak.'

We all looked at each other. Did Matt know something about the previous night's events? No one had said a word to him, as far as I knew. 'What I mean is that if you really slapped Maldwyn in the face with a flat possum, everyone would be appalled and shocked. What a disgusting thing to do to someone. So what? They would be so busy moaning and wailing about the squashed possum, they would no longer be talking about his strengths as a candidate. And while your main opponent and the commentariat are distracted with debates about his sexuality, even the rights and wrongs of revealing it, you will have a window to present your alternative vision as leader.'

There was a long silence while John poured out more wine. I took a very long draught. I had no idea this weekend was going to be so packed with flattened animals.

Andrew was the first to speak.

'We have to do this. Matt, can I assume you are happy to work for my campaign, together with Charles?'

'Assuming the terms are the same as we discussed last week, then yes.' He extended his hand across the table and I took the proffered handshake. 'And I'm happy to work with Charles.'

This time his grip was firm.

'Charles?' asked Andrew.

'I'm in, but I don't want there to be any briefing against Maldwyn by any of our team.'

'Good God, no,' said Matt. 'That would kill us. Our line will be distress that this subject should be taboo for so many people in the second decade of the twenty-first century, and our hope that we shall see Maldwyn on the front bench soon despite the prejudice of some sections of society.'

And so we agreed, if not comfortably, to what amounted to the psychological murder of one of our friends and colleagues who just happened to be a rival.

Matt and I arranged to meet in London the following week.

It was over coffee that the next difficult conversation occurred. Matt heaped three spoonfuls of sugar into his cup and stirred the resulting syrup with vigour. Confident he had our attention he said, 'And now, it's skeleton time.'

'It's what?' asked Helen, in an amused voice, as if Matt had just proposed a game of charades. But Matt was not joking.

'Skeleton time is when we 'fess up to our own dark secrets. Has anyone been convicted of anything that I don't know about? Has anyone borrowed a large sum of money they're unable to repay? Has anyone sold any shares in a public company of which they are a director, and if so, how much did they earn and when?'

'Oh dear,' said Helen. 'That doesn't sound much fun at all. Can't we discuss this tomorrow morning?'

'I've got to leave around 6:30 so that John can get me to the station on time.'

'Well, let's get on with it,' said Andrew. 'Do the girls have to sit in on this?'

'They're your wives. They are part of it. Let's start right there. Was there any acrimony when you and Caroline split up, Andrew?'

For a moment, a look flickered across Andrew's face, then he assumed a politician's fixed grin once more, as we all re-assured Matt there had been no serious tension. Our words sounded brittle and unconvincing, but the truth was there had been no explicit falling out, more of a falling away. In fact, as we recounted the events of the past fifteen years, it became tedious to see what blameless lives we had been lead-ing. We talked about tax; driving offences; we didn't quite get round to disclosing overdue books at the local library. I wondered if Andrew was going to mention that story I had once heard about him and a punting pole at Oxford, but either it was just a rumour or he considered the episode suffi-ciently buried not to merit a mention. I was relieved, because the stream of mundane confession was exhausting enough and it must have been close to midnight when Matt gave up writing notes.

'Is that all?' he said.

I looked at Andrew, and he caught my glance and nodded hesitantly. He knew that if he didn't bring the subject up, I would.

'There is one thing. It's a silly thing, really,' he said with visible reluctance.

'Tell me,' said Matt.

So then the whole story came out: the owl flying into the windscreen; its impromptu killing; the meeting with the neighbour and the visit from the police.

'Sounds like they're on to you,' said Matt. 'That wasn't

just a random visit. How many cars go up and down this lane every day? Not many. And you said there was a chip in your windscreen?'

'That could have been a stone hitting it.'

'Mmm,' said Matt. 'Maybe. You seem to have dug yourself into a bit of a hole. Leave it to Charles and me and we'll try to come up with something if the police decide to interview you again.'

'Let's go to bed,' said Helen, yawning. We all stood up and Andrew stretched himself.

'I thought we might spend some of this evening talking about what we might do for the country if we win the leadership. How we might take the party into the next general election. Instead, we've ended up discussing owls.'

'Thanks to your Committee's recommendations, it is now a notifiable offence to kill one, even if by accident.' Matt reminded him.

There was a strange taste in my mouth, and I felt a sense of creeping unease. We shouldn't have been discussing owls at all. Andrew was a potential future prime minister. And yet here we were.

John suddenly appeared in the doorway behind us, as if by magic, and cleared away the coffee things while we went to bed.

4

When I drew the curtains the morning was dour and grey. Caroline awoke as the daylight touched her face and stretched.

'Let's get out of here,' she said, 'straight after breakfast.'

'We're supposed to stay for lunch,' I reminded her.

'They'll be as glad to be rid of us as we will be to go.'

This proved to be the case. Andrew accepted my weak excuse of needing to clear my desk before I took on his work with the merest formality of a protest.

'Mary will be so disappointed – she loves to show off her English roast, it's really very good,' said Helen. 'But of course you must go. Only try to make it a longer stay next time?'

They waved us off from the doorstep: Andrew in bright yellow corduroys and a blue sleeveless cardigan, Helen in a tweed skirt and cashmere top – the very image of the perfect English couple dressed for the countryside.

As John drove us away in the Range Rover Caroline said, 'What a weekend that was! Never again.'

I pointed to John and to my ears to indicate the need for discretion, but Caroline pressed on regardless.

'She's a soak, by the way.'

'What do you want to do about lunch now we're not

getting any at Gilcaster Head?' I said by way of distraction.

'I could smell it on her breath before dinner. She was fried even before we sat down.'

John had gone very quiet in the front. He had an unnerving habit of constantly glancing at his phone while he was driving. I thought he would have learned the way to the station by now. Caroline was oblivious.

'And that weird little guy, Matt Dilcombe! Actually, I kinda liked him.'

I leaned forward and said to our driver, 'Since my wife is determined to talk me through our whole weekend, would you mind turning on your radio so you can't overhear everything?'

John smiled, and with a slight shrug of his shoulders, put away his iPhone and turned on the radio. Caroline glanced at me angrily and subsided.

When we got back to Newcastle she started again, banging around the kitchen with pots and pans in an effort to produce something for lunch.

'What did you think of Helen?' she asked, 'Apart from the eye-candy aspect.'

'I think she could be very tough if she didn't get her way. Andrew had better deliver the goods.'

'Mmm. Yes. I don't think Gilcaster Head will survive. She'll be on at him to sell up and get a place in the Home Counties where all the smart people live.'

Some kind of lunch emerged from the Aga and I poured us both a gin and tonic. We both felt like children who had been let out of school early.

'That was a bizarre weekend,' said Caroline.

'Do you think Andrew has changed much?' I asked. We

had rarely talked about the period when Caroline had been Andrew's girlfriend. She glanced at me.

'Hard to say.'

'What did you mean when you said something about his "psychopath side"?'

'Oh, that,' said Caroline. 'He didn't beat me, or yell at me, if that's what you're thinking. But he was super-intense. He hated not being in control of whatever was going on. Sometimes it came out in small things, like deliberately not tipping a waiter who had pissed him off.'

'That just sounds mean, not psycho.'

'Mean is a good word. He had a mean side to him.'

'He wasn't just mean to that owl. He battered it to death. We could have saved that bird. As far as I could tell, it had only broken its wing.'

'Then you should have said so.'

'I know,' I admitted. 'It all happened too quickly.'

We finished our drinks and ate lunch, a dish which included a lot of pasta and not much else. Caroline was not a good cook, which had surprised me when I first found out. She said that taking pots in and out of ovens all day at the studio was enough for her and she didn't much care for doing it in the evenings as well.

'Andrew was very intense,' Caroline continued, 'and very self-absorbed. He was generous with gifts but I always felt that when he gave me one of those little blue boxes with something wonderful inside, he was really telling me that he had the money to do what he liked. There was nothing the least bit romantic about it. You would be amazed at how much jewellery I acquired during the three years we were together. I sent it all back, of course, when I left him.'

'But you never saw him in a rage before?'

'Oh yes,' said Caroline. 'He would go very quiet and then completely pale. He wouldn't speak to me – or anybody – until he had sorted the problem out. It was usually something to do with his work.'

'He never got angry with you?'

'Of course he did, sometimes.'

Caroline reflected for a moment.

'It was chilling. He would sit me down and say something like, "You need to understand my red lines, Caroline. If you cross them, our relationship is something we will have to review together." I mean he talked to me as if I were some subordinate at his bank.'

I laughed.

'You must have found that hard to take?'

'Very. I told him not to talk such crap. He would just give a little laugh and say, "Don't ever make the mistake of thinking I don't mean what I say." That usually shut me up.'

'And what were his red lines?' I asked.

'Andrew objected to people who didn't take him seriously. He would fly into a rage and I really believe that when he was like that he could have killed somebody, maybe even me. But it's all history now, anyway. We're talking about over a decade ago.'

I saw no point in pursuing the matter. Andrew Landford was an unusual, possibly great, man. Everything he had set out to do – playing the piano, rifle shooting, doing deals with the first generation of Russian oligarchs – he had done not well, but extremely well. Somebody I knew who had heard Andrew giving a private recital said that he could have been a concert pianist if he had chosen to.

My own views about Andrew were mixed. I had to admit his talents. His other qualities were less clear. Did he have the warmth to bond with his party? Could he enthuse the backbenchers and the grassroots party activists enough to support him?

The policies he was going to promote at the forthcoming party conference were, of course, set in stone long ago. As was the agenda. There would be no actual leadership challenge. There would be no real debate apart from the possibility of hecklers from the extreme right of the party. But the conference would be alert to a possible challenge sometime in the near future. The incumbent was a dead man walking – his failure to win an outright majority in the recent general election had seen to that. But no clear challenger had emerged. Nor would they at this conference. There might be mutterings off-stage. Glances would be cast towards Maldwyn and Andrew. Maybe a journo or two would try their luck with an off-the-cuff question: 'Will you be putting yourself forward for election, Mr Christie?' And they would receive the standard reply: 'There is no leadership contest that I know of. I'm just getting on with my job.' In 1990 the challenge hadn't come until November, well after the end of the conference season, when Mrs Thatcher had withdrawn after failing to get enough votes. She had lost not only because of splits over Europe; there were real questions about her ability to govern. People doubted her ability to work with her own Cabinet.

I wondered if that was the issue with Andrew. Would people think that he was too aloof, too self-assured? He was a talented only child who – so far – had never been given any convincing reason to believe he could ever be wrong about anything. He'd made his millions and didn't need to work. This feeling that I had whenever I met Andrew, that he was intellectually my superior, would affect other people in different ways. I tolerated it: but why? Because I had known him a long time, because I knew he had meant to be kind when he first asked me to 'look after Caroline' while he was away in Moscow, because he had not kicked up a fuss when I ended up taking Caroline away from him and marrying her. Other people would not be aware of Andrew's more human side, as I was. How would they react to him?

In the middle of the night, something strange happened. At first I thought I was having a nightmare, but I wasn't. I was awake, Caroline clutching at my arm. Her hand felt cold.

'Listen,' was all she said.

Trying to clear my head, I heard a violent noise coming from the windows. A storm rattling the frames, banging a branch against the glass. There was a yew branch overshadowing one wall of the house. It must have grown more than I had imagined this summer. I had earmarked it for cutting back next year but the job might have to be done sooner than I had thought. I started to get up to see what it was, but Caroline grabbed my arm again, pulling me closer.

'Just listen!'

For a brief moment, it sounded as if some monstrous creature was trying to get in, so violently was it scratching the window. I tried to rationalise the sound away. A branch from a tree had snapped off in the storm, and perhaps become trapped against the window. Or was it just a neighbourhood cat, clamouring to get in? I had just woken up and the room was pitch-black. In such moments quite innocuous noises can seem distorted and louder than they really are.

We lay there, saying nothing, just willing the noise to go away. Then, all of a sudden, the wind dropped, and the scratching subsided. In the long silence that followed, some distance away, I heard a solitary hoot, echoing through the empty streets.

'You see darling,' I whispered, 'it was just an owl. We've got owls on the brain, that's all it is.' I put my arm around her and pulled her against me. After a while she stopped shaking. We both slept, wrapped tight around each other, the first time we had done so in a long while. By the time morning arrived, any memory of alarm had faded with the night. The innocent yew branch that I thought had woken me was far too short to reach the windows. We went around the house closing all the windows that hadn't already been rendered unusable by the last lot of careless painters. But subsequent events would recall this as the moment when it all began.

5

I decided I needed to see Andrew with his supporters. I needed to see him work a crowd. That was one of the main topics over lunch when I met Matt Dilcombe in London the following week. We met in a small Italian restaurant on one of those anonymous streets north of the British Museum. The taxi driver had some trouble finding it and I arrived a few minutes late. There was only one table occupied in the gloomy little room. With Matt was a woman I did not recognise.

'Hello, Charles. This is Jane Everett. She has kindly agreed to be Andrew's campaign manager, if we get a shot at the top job.'

'I'm sorry I'm late,' I said, as we shook hands. 'Had some difficulty finding the place.'

We sat down.

'It has the advantage of being quiet, so you are unlikely to be overheard, or meet anyone you know. I didn't choose it for the food, as you'll discover,' said Matt. A depressed-looking waiter arrived and took orders for drinks and handed out menus.

Jane Everett was an MP for a Home Counties constituency. She was, I guessed, in her forties and was bright with an easy charm.

'At this stage I'm here to listen and I can't stay too long as I need to get up to Birmingham this afternoon. Conference starts this weekend but I have to be up a day or two early. I want to hear what people are saying about our leader, and what they're saying about Andrew and Maldwyn.'

'Are there any other names in the frame that you know of?' asked Matt.

'Not so far.'

The waiter arrived with drinks and we studied the menu. Once we'd ordered, Matt said, 'You know about the story that's going to break on Sunday, don't you?'

Jane said, with visible distaste, 'Yes. I wish it didn't have to happen this way. You do realise it could backfire on our candidate.'

'I don't see why,' said Matt. 'We didn't leak the story. It's been out there for ages and a journalist – someone who likes Maldwyn, by the way – has decided to do an op-ed. After all, he's only asking the question: is the party ready for a gay leader? For all I know, the answer might be a resounding yes.'

'It won't be, though, will it?' I asked.

'Of course not. But the story will do three things. It will imply very clearly that there *will* be a leadership challenge, and soon. It will beg the question of whether Maldwyn is a suitable candidate. And for those who don't think Maldwyn is the right person, it will get them thinking about who is right. That's where you come in, Jane.'

'Yes, I understand. You want me to work the conference, and some of the fringe meetings, to take soundings for Andrew. When Parliament is recalled, you want me to work the tea rooms, and start having one to ones with some of the key people.'

'Including the chairman of the 1922 Committee.'

'Yes. Him. He might be difficult.'

'It's all difficult,' said Matt. 'But we want Andrew to win. We need a no-confidence letter with fifty signatures or thereabouts to get the ball rolling. Andrew mustn't start promoting himself at this conference. And it's better that you don't attend, Charles. We don't want our campaign team to be visible just yet.'

'I haven't been invited, as it happens,' I admitted. As an adviser for hire, I tried to keep my private beliefs and my professional life separate, even when they intersected, and had never been a paid-up member of any political party.

'What do you think about our timing?' asked Jane.

'I'm thinking mid-November. Later than that and we'll struggle to get press coverage coming into the Christmas period. If we try sooner, it doesn't give us enough time. Later than Christmas and we'll risk losing momentum and the whole thing will have to be pushed back. And that might allow too much time for another candidate to emerge.'

'Or another story,' said Jane. 'I mean, I like and respect Andrew but I don't feel I really know him. I take it there will be no surprises on his side. No skeletons in the cupboard?'

'No skeletons,' said Matt. The food arrived, providing a useful distraction. Matt had committed us. The owl incident would remain hidden. 'But if you don't feel you know Andrew, it's time you did. He's at conference and I'll arrange for you two to meet again, as long as it's discreet.'

'Oh, I know him well enough to feel he's the best possible candidate right now. And I know we can't go on with the present leader. But I don't have a sense of Andrew as a person. That's what's missing.'

When Jane had left to catch her train, Matt said, 'So how are you going to portray Andrew?'

'To whom?'

'I'll take care of that. We just need a storyboard to work with. A profile of Andrew that we can place somewhere high-profile or give to a journalist to make their own. About two thousand words ought to do it. What's your take going to be?'

I tried to collect my thoughts. 'Well, we tell it like it is. Only child, a loner, a self-made, driven man. Doesn't have to be in politics but wants to be, has a strong sense of civic duty – all the old-fashioned virtues. Passionate about whatever he does, a happily married man with one child, so understands about family issues.'

Matt grimaced.

'You make him sound like some rich banker who has time to kill and has gone into politics to stop himself dying from boredom.'

I laughed.

'Could be. But if you don't put the basic facts about Andrew out there, people will unearth them and reconstruct them in different and possibly less favourable ways.'

'It could be tough to get people to like him,' said Matt.

'Maybe people don't want someone they like. Maybe we don't want matey-down-the-road to be our next prime minister. I think we're telling people that our man is supremely competent at whatever he does. He'll get the job done. He's worked in places like Moscow where they play hardball, and he's come out on top. He's survived and prospered in the real world. He's someone you'd want on your side in any argument. Think of Mrs Thatcher. Not everybody liked her, but a lot of people respected her because they knew she worked harder than most, was master of her brief, and unafraid to be unpopular as long as she was right.'

Matt was thoughtful.

'That's a good analogy,' he said after a while. 'I can see where you're going. We'll tell it like it is.'

'It's the only way,' I told him.

Conference came and went. I watched some of the coverage at home, making notes for the profile of Andrew I was writing for Matt. What I saw was boring, as it was bound to be after such a disappointing election. Everyone spoke as if they were attending the memorial service of a not particularly well-beloved colleague. In a way, they were. The triumphant music playing over the loudspeakers as the present leader took his seat jarred. Maybe the PR company that had organised the staging had overlooked the fact that they had just lost an election, not won it. The leader seemed physically diminished: he sat, a tired grey man in a grey suit that suddenly seemed too large for him, presiding over what even he must have realised were the declining days of his power. The other Cabinet ministers seemed equally deflated and uncertain of their message. A year ago they had been towering and victorious, more than mortal men; now they were shrunken, almost invisible. Unelectable, one might even say.

All that changed when Andrew came on to the podium as the warm-up for the leader's main speech. I had to admit he looked good: almost presidential. He was taller than the leader and better dressed. His command of his brief – which was really only to act as cheerleader – was nevertheless absolute. In the two or three minutes when he had the conference's attention he appeared – and sounded – to be everything we could have asked for in a candidate. He said not one single word he shouldn't have. By neither gesture nor omission did he detract from the praise he had heaped on the leader. But at the end of his short slot I doubted there was anyone at conference who, if they hadn't already been wondering about Andrew Landford's potential to go further, wasn't thinking about it now. It was impressive.

Conference ended on a Wednesday. The phone call came the following day. I was in my office in Newcastle and Caroline was working in her studio in London (I had tried and so far failed to persuade her to move her kilns and gases and other equipment north). It was from Andrew.

'Are you free this afternoon?' he asked abruptly.

'No, I'm not free,' I said rather testily. 'I do have other work to do here.' The article on Andrew was taking up more time than I had allowed, and my Head of School was beginning to grumble about my repeated absences.

'You need to come to the police station in Carlisle.'

For a moment everything disconnected. Then I said, 'Not that owl thing?'

'Yes, that "owl thing",' replied Andrew flatly.

'What do they want?'

'They've had information lodged with them that claims I was responsible for the death of that stupid owl. They want to interview me under caution. In fact they want to interview all four of us, but I explained that the girls were in London and couldn't get up until the weekend.'

I felt a little out of breath.

'Hang on,' I said. 'Information lodged with them. Do you mean your neighbour?'

'They aren't saying. But I wouldn't be surprised if it was him. Tom's just the type. He's never quite forgiven me for

'Bloody hell,' I said, not very helpfully.

'What are we going to do, Charles? What shall I tell them?'

'The truth. What else? We don't know what they know and what they don't know.'

'And how will I explain the fact,' asked Andrew, 'that this story will be different from the last one I told them?' Andrew sounded rather acerbic, as if it were my fault he'd been caught out telling a lie.

'Say you were in the middle of an important meeting and you just wanted the police, and the problem, to go away.'

'So if the press ever get hold of this, we will just have to hope they decide the matter is as trivial as you're making out,' said Andrew. 'I'm on the Wildlife and Countryside Committee. We've just updated the legislation protecting threatened species. These fucking barn owls are a threatened species. What will the press say when they hear about that? They'll think it's Christmas and Easter come together. They'll dance upon my grave.'

'Andrew, I don't know what the press will do. The first thing is the police. Let me give you some thoughts.'

Andrew began to calm down, and the slightly hysteric note that had crept into his voice disappeared. We ag

allies.

we were going to need to find him some more vocal

mind, regardless of the consequences. But at this

ual leader; someone who wasn't afraid to

s, of course, it was an essential

pt Andrew was at acquir-

all.'

d for me.

'What do we do?'

'Call me after the interview and meanwhile I'll see if I can catch any whispers of this out in the jungle.'

Andrew picked me up from the station car park in Brampton and we drove into Carlisle, to the regional police headquarters. We sat in a waiting room until a large officer came to meet us. He didn't mean to be intimidating, but he was. Andrew glanced at me nervously as we followed the officer down to the check-in desk where we gave our personal details. To our great surprise, Andrew was then arrested and fingerprinted and read his rights. By this stage Andrew was in shock. Nobody had told him what to expect, and he obviously hadn't known.

'I'm a Member of Parliament,' he kept saying.

'Yes sir, we're well aware of who you are.'

not letting him dig up my land to poke...
...dates
...disaster
wants to be leader. He'll have t[o]
a potential leadership challenge – a[nd]
are damaged. It will be a complete an[d]
for the party if there isn't a credible contes[t]

'The whole thing. It's all...
reaction, or the whole th...
'When you say, "no...
time, before she be...
'In fairness, yo...
I did vote for the latest round of cuts, afte...
temple or other. Or maybe the local police have it...
I hadn't noticed before how ade...
ing enemies. In many wa...
speak the...
quality in a pote...

'Does she h...
'Mmm. I...
between...
tene[d]...
B[ut]...

'They can't do this to me,' he kept saying to me until I told him to be quiet.

'They can, and they are, and they will,' I told him. 'Meanwhile, least said, soonest mended.'

My mind was racing as I tried to think of a way out of this mess. And the selfish part of my brain was thinking 'if I get a criminal record through my association with Andrew, how will that affect my job?'

Andrew was taken into an interview suite, a small windowless room with twin tape decks set into the wall, beside which was a table surrounded by four chairs. Then the officer from the Wildlife Crimes Unit, the intimidating man who had greeted us at the entrance, closed the door behind him. As he did, he scowled at me.

When he opened the door again, just twenty minutes later, his voice was mild. 'Thank you, Mr Landford,' he said. 'You are free to go now.'

'Is that it?' asked Andrew as he walked out, as if he had been expecting to be chained up and thrown into a dungeon.

'I will pass this report on to my superiors who will decide whether we wish to take any further action following your statement. I will be in touch in due course. Please make sure you are available and don't leave the country until you have heard from us again.'

'How long might that be?' I asked.

'I can't say. It could be days, or months, depending on the case load.'

'And until then the information will remain confidential?' I asked. The interviewing officer almost growled.

'That goes without saying, sir.'

I had the sense to keep my mouth shut until we were back in the car.

'I thought that went OK,' said Andrew as we drove away. He sounded as if he had just emerged from a successful job interview.

'It was a very short interrogation. What did you tell them?'

He glanced at me.

'Exactly what we agreed. That over a month ago, I was driving my Range Rover when an owl flew into the windscreen.'

'Did they ask about the chip in the glass?'

'Yes. I fudged that, saying it was dark, and could have been caused by anything.'

Andrew relayed the rest of the conversation, which seemed reassuringly perfunctory. He had described to them very briefly how he had 'tried to put the owl out of its misery' and then the interview was over.

'You did the right thing by telling the truth. Unfortunately, you had no choice as somebody else out there has been in touch with the police.'

Andrew said, 'Well, we're all going to have to wait and see what the police decide to do.'

I looked at him in surprise.

'They'll send the file to the Crown Prosecution Service, of course. The CPS will decide whether they have enough evidence to prosecute. Did you hit the bird? Yes. Did you pick it up and kill it? Yes. It sounds rather like you've admitted to both those charges.'

'True, but in my defence I can say that I clearly didn't intend to hit it. After that, killing it was the right thing to do.'

I winced. 'The right thing to do' was one of my least favourite political clichés.

'The most humane thing to do, perhaps?'

'That's it. "Humane", that's a good word.'

I couldn't understand Andrew's mood. It was almost euphoric. Perhaps now that he had finally told the truth, he felt as if a burden had been lifted from his shoulders.

'Andrew, you do realise the trouble we're in, don't you?'

'Oh, I expect a few silly headlines will emerge at some point. And I'm going to have to explain my actions to the Committee.'

'What will you say?'

'Oh, I think we were all agreed that the owl had to be put out of its misery. That's what I'll say. And I'll apologise for not telling them before I was called in by the police. That should mend any broken fences, I think.'

Maybe that's the quality all successful politicians need to possess. To come up with some version of the truth that suits them, oblivious of how it might appear to other people. That's what Andrew was doing. He had his story. It wasn't the truth. The truth was that he hadn't told the truth until the police cornered him.

I had to try to get his feet on the ground.

'Do you want to go on with the leadership campaign?' I asked.

Andrew looked at me as if I were mad.

'Of course. I shall be talking about political crises to come: the debt mountain, and how to solve it without endless decades of austerity. You're talking about a trivial incident with a dead owl. Who on earth is going to worry about me knocking a wounded bird on the head? It's a diary piece, not an editorial. A bit of amusing gossip that I shall have to endure and which you will help me to play down. We're talking about the leadership of the party, and then probably the leadership of the country. In two or three years' time I expect to be prime minister, Charles.'

I shook my head and muttered, 'Men, not measures.'

'What's that?'

'Oh, just something that a Victorian novelist once wrote: that in the end people vote for the man, not the policy.'

'I'm afraid I don't have the time to read novels these days, and if I did, I don't think I'd bother with one that was over a hundred years out of date.'

We drove on in silence until we approached Brampton.

'I'll tell you what I think privately.'

'What do you privately think, Andrew?'

'The police and the CPS will sit on this. They know I'm an ally of the Wildlife Crimes Unit. They know I've been fighting for their corner and campaigning for more resources to help police wildlife crime. The last thing they will want to do is weaken my position.'

'You think so?'

'I do think so.'

I didn't reply. If Andrew wanted to delude himself then there was nothing I could do to stop him. Maybe he would come to his senses in a while. Or maybe he was right?

Maybe commitment was more important than the truth?

'There's another thing,' said Andrew. 'Are the police and the CPS going to consider the political impact of prosecuting me? I mean, even the Director of Public Prosecutions might have to weigh up the fact that I might be the next prime minister.'

'Andrew, this isn't Moscow. They don't bend the rules here. They don't do favours.'

He looked hurt, and gave me a wounded expression as he dropped me off at my car.

'You'll see,' was all he said.

6

I drove back alongside the Roman Wall as the sun dropped behind the horizon, looking at all the backpackers hurrying to finish their day's march before the light went. There was very little cloud, and the evening sky felt electric. The stars above this dark stretch of land would be spectacular to-night. I envied the hikers, especially the solitary ones, often having huge stretches of countryside to themselves at a time. It was quite safe, of course, and there were plenty of hostels and pubs one could turn to for shelter if the weather took an unexpected turn for the worse. There had been a time, of course, when any lone wanderer might have encountered a marauding reiver on their horse or, even further back, a Roman patrol armed with spears and shields.

Quite without warning a large shadow passed across my windscreen, blocking my view for a moment, and I had to brake sharply, only just avoiding a young family who were crossing the road to reach a car park on the other side. The car behind me honked loudly. I looked at myself in the mirror. I had gone quite pale.

What was I doing, daydreaming about reivers and Romans? I had to focus on the matter in hand. I had to ring Matt. What could I tell him? That Andrew thought the incident wasn't a problem any more? That he had said he reckoned the whole thing would just blow over, with no more impact on his leadership campaign than a fieldful of thistledown.

And maybe Andrew was right. Maybe the concoction of half-truths he had come up with would suffice. The great British public might buy into the 'humane killing' argument. Which of us has not killed a sparrow or run over a hedgehog whilst driving our car? Perhaps the story would even work in Andrew's favour: to err is human.

I rang Matt.

'I don't see what else he could have done or said,' he remarked when I'd gone through the gist of Andrew's conversation with the police.

'Do you think he will get away with it?'

'It depends what you mean by that. If you mean, do I think the whole thing will remain buried, the answer is no. But if you're asking me how much it matters when the story – a story – leaks out, the answer is less obvious. I think Andrew may have muddied the water so much that it won't matter. It won't be a fatal blow to the leadership campaign, although it won't help.'

I drove on in a state of some confusion. It seemed that, after all, I lived in a world where telling the truth wasn't that important. Telling half-truths, changing the truth until the distinction between truth and lies became less important: that was the way to prosper in today's world.

I was in a grim mood when I arrived back home.

On Friday afternoon when Caroline came up from London, we immediately had a disagreement about something. We didn't have the energy to have a full-blown row. We were both tired and inclined to be grumpy. Caroline had a show on in London, which I hadn't been to see yet because spending the day with Andrew had meant postponing my trip to London. It wasn't selling very well and had not been favoured with many reviews. The reviews she did get were relatively kind: 'Woodchester has recaptured some of her earlier visionary talent' was the sort of line they were taking, as if suggesting the best was now in the past. Maybe it was?

I was in a bad mood because I was beginning to regret my whole involvement with Andrew Landford. Why had I agreed to support him? Did I really think that, from behind the walls of academia, I could reach out into the real world without fear of corruption, and guide a man as hungry for power as he was towards some greater good? I was astonished to discover that despite years of experience, of witnessing first-hand evidence to the contrary, some of my beliefs were as naive and as unchanged as when I had first arrived at Oxford. In my head I had never stopped being an outsider observing the British system of power, with its incestuous oligarchies and slavish adherence to the status quo. And yet here I was, acting as an establishment insider. I had fantasised about being able to exert some form of benign, restraining hand on power, from behind the throne, but I had not restrained Andrew Landford. At worst, I had merely accommodated him, in order to satisfy my own desires. The whole business was a terrible mess and Andrew was retreating from reality at great speed.

It was a cold and unfriendly weekend. Grey and windy skies overhead. Inside the house, draughts made doors slam unexpectedly and window casings rattle, so that it seemed as if an army of unseen people was walking about the house. Caroline was sitting in the kitchen, watching television and drinking coffee when I walked in to see what she was doing.

She switched off the TV and immediately began to tell me that splitting her time between London and Newcastle was damaging her concentration and her work. The quality of her glazes, her instinct for form, had all declined since she had begun commuting. Maybe it would be better if she just lived in the London flat and came north for the occasional weekend. This sounded like the precursor to a more dramatic decision, and I fought back, arguing she should spend all of her time in the north. Caroline countered by saying that all her customers were in the south.

'Then find new buyers up here,' I suggested. 'There's a growing market for ceramics in Newcastle.' This was true, but she wouldn't accept it. She was already working on a new show, but for the first time in our marriage, she wouldn't tell me anything about it. Laptops were slammed shut as I came into the room, drawings shoved hurriedly out of sight under piles of catalogues and periodicals, enquiries left hanging in the air. All I knew was that her work was taking her away from me more and more, and I wondered if the reveal would be worth the secrecy.

We went to bed early on Saturday night, conversation at a stalemate, spirits low.

One week later, everything changed. The following Sunday morning I got up and went straight over to the newsagent on the corner, to buy a copy of every paper he stocked. I went into the kitchen and covered the kitchen table with them. I soon found the piece on Maldwyn. The article began by speculating about a forthcoming leadership election:

For the first time in his party's history, Maldwyn Christie looks set to be a candidate in what everyone now believes to be inevitable: a leadership contest sometime this autumn. So far nobody has put his hat in the ring and the official line is that the leader is just 'getting on with his job'. But we are reliably informed that a letter of no confidence, with the requisite number of signatures, will soon be produced and may even already be in circulation. In this case, Maldwyn Christie would put his name forward as candidate, and maybe others too, including Andrew Landford.

Having set the scene, with a few more rounded phrases, the writer moved on to the question of how suitable a candidate Maldwyn might be.

Maldwyn Christie is an engaging, highly articulate individual who has certainly captured the loyalty and often enthusiastic support of wide sections of the party. He scores high on recognition amongst the grassroots activists so treasured by pollsters and other commentators. But are they in possession of all of the facts? It is perhaps not widely known outside his intimate circle that Mr Christie will be the first gay politician, if he prevails, to lead the party and therefore be a candidate to become our next prime minister. Mr Christie has not made any secret of his sexual preferences, but neither has he openly proclaimed himself as gay.

The question we now face, after all the divisions within the party, and the country, over gay marriage is: are we ready for a gay leader? And are we confident that voters will accept Mr Christie for what he is; namely a fine, instinctive politician who commands wide respect? Will that respect survive the inevitable debate about his sexuality? Will the party grandees support what must inevitably be seen as a risky candidacy? Above all, will voters be open-minded enough to accept that in the twenty-first century, such issues should no longer be relevant in judging a person's suitability to run for the top job.

What the party needs right now is a candidate who can bring the party, whose loyalties have been sorely tested, back together again. Unfortunately Mr Christie's campaign promises to be divisive. Had he chosen to bring this issue before the public himself at an earlier stage, maybe we would not have had the uncomfortable duty of bringing it to the public's attention at this juncture, before the formal processes of a leadership challenge have begun . . .

And so on, and so on.

The story was reproduced in different form in a couple of other broadsheets. One tabloid had got in on the act, somehow snatching the story out of the air. The headline ran:

PINK OR BLUE? WHAT'S YOUR FANCY?

I couldn't read the rest of the article. My head spinning with the complexity of the web we now found ourselves tangled up in, I pushed aside the rest of the papers. I summoned enough focus to boil a half-decent egg and butter some toast. Caroline came downstairs in her dressing gown and made herself a mug of tea.

The phone rang.

I could have ignored it but I knew it would just go on ringing, so I picked up.

It was Maldwyn.

'Did you know about this piece?' he asked me, without saying hello.

I didn't know how much he knew about my involvement with Andrew.

'I had heard some rumours on the grapevine . . . but you have to believe me, Maldwyn, it was a totally independent article. I really don't think there was anything we could have done to stop it.'

Maldwyn gave a weary sigh.

'Even if you'd wanted to, which I suspect you didn't. You could have given me a heads-up on this, Charlie. I mean, we have known each other for twenty years or so.'

'You know as well as I do that that could have backfired, and done you more harm than good. I really think it will blow over by tomorrow.'

'Oh well, what are friends for,' said Maldwyn, 'if not to dump on you from a great height. I'll do the same for you, Charlie, when your turn comes.'

He rang off. Strike one old friend from my Christmas card list.

'Who was that?' asked Caroline. I handed her the newspaper folded open at the article about Maldwyn. She read it carefully.

'Well, it could have been a lot worse.'

'I suppose that's true,' I said, somewhat surprised. 'The publicity generated by the conference will all be consumed by this, rather than by our failure to win a majority.'

'I meant,' said Caroline, 'that it wasn't too mean to Maldwyn. Now everyone who has a gay friend or relative will be asking themselves the question: should you be condemned to stay out of civic life? Would you vote for a gay prime minister? I think it's a thoughtful piece. It's a pity they didn't ask you to write it. Why didn't they?'

'Somebody else had the story and was determined to write it. It's lucky for us that he chose a neutral stance.'

The phone rang again.

I picked it up as if it were a snake about to bite me. It was Matt.

'I thought the tone was about right, didn't you?' he asked. Without waiting for my reply he went on, 'Nobody can accuse our team of hitting below the belt.'

'I've never asked you, Matt, but who actually leaked that story?'

'You don't want to know,' he told me.

I couldn't bring myself to reply. Matt smoothed his way on, quite unruffled.

'Charlie, politics is not a clean game. Not always. I know your pitch is that you always tell the truth, but truth is a strange commodity. It's one thing to me and another thing to you. It's never an absolute. It's sometimes a point of view. Do bear that in mind, because otherwise you might start to feel very uncomfortable. Meanwhile, if the press call you – I think it's unlikely, your connection to Andrew is not widely known – then you are to keep schtum. Don't know, never heard of him, and so on.'

'Point noted,' I said. Matt hung up.

The phone rang.

'Jesus,' said Caroline, 'is this going to go on all day?'

'Probably.'

It was Andrew. I put the phone on to speaker.

'Caroline's in the room,' I said.

The two exchanged a cautious good-morning.

'Well, that wasn't too bad after all,' he said cheerfully.

'I suppose not.'

'Quite funny, really.'

'That's not the word I would have chosen,' I said. If Andrew was going to start gloating, I would hang up on him. I was surprised at his choice of words.

'Well, when you consider what the coverage might have been. I was bracing myself for something a lot more savage than what we got.'

An awful doubt was beginning to emerge in my mind.

'Andrew, what are we talking about here?'

'The owl thing, of course.'

'I thought you were talking about the article on Maldwyn?'

'Oh, that,' he said.

'Oh, that?'

My incredulity finally reached Andrew.

'Yes, I'm very pleased that the article wasn't too personal. But that's not what I'm ringing you about. Diary on page thirteen of the *Daily Mail*.'

'Hang on a moment,' I said, struggling with the heaps of newsprint in front of me. 'Got it.'

The piece was written in typical style.

A BIT OF AN 'OWLER?

We hear that Andrew Landford ran over an owl the other night. Couldn't have happened to a nicer guy, as they say, except – hang on, isn't he on the parliamentary Committee that amended the new Wildlife and Countryside Act? Doesn't it say something in there about running over owls? What a hoot, as they say.

'What do you think?' said Andrew, rather as if he had just handed in an essay and was expecting praise.

'You think that's the end of the owl thing?'

'Well, no, they might run a follow-up, but I don't expect that to be too troublesome.'

I wondered if I was becoming paranoid.

'Let's hope you're right.'

We returned back to the question of the Maldwyn Christie piece. Andrew sounded bored by the topic.

'Kid-glove stuff,' he said.

'Would you mind if it was you?'

'If you can't stand the heat, as a famous predecessor at Number 10 said, get out of the kitchen.'

His arrogance staggered me. I wanted to shout at him. But all I said was, 'You think your campaign is in the bag, then?'

'You can never say that. To quote the Lady again, never say never. Was she the one who first said that?'

'I think it was Julius Caesar.'

Caroline had been half-listening to this. When I had finished, the phone mercifully remained silent for a while.

'Why do you work for that guy?' she asked.

It was fast becoming an increasingly difficult question to answer.

'I wish I knew. I said I'd do it, though. So now I'm stuck with a candidate who I think is dead in the water. In his own mind, he's already won.'

'You can pull out. I would,' said Caroline.

'I can't. I still believe I can make a difference here. I'm committed.'

'Is that what you say to yourself when you think about our marriage?'

I rocked on my heels as if I'd taken a punch. In a way, it was true. I pushed the papers away from me, then put out my hand to take hers but coolly she withdrew it.

'Come on, Charlie, you're a grown up. This is no time

for sentiment. We're talking about our marriage, not a love affair. How are we going to get by? Are we going to get by?'

She stood up. She had no make-up on yet, and in the morning light her skin looked grey. Had I done this to her, I wondered? What had happened to the girl from the Fryerne Arms all those years ago? Or to me, for that matter. It was hard to tell whether it was the years of marriage that had changed us, or whether we had been changed by external forces beyond our control, pulled in different directions, only appearing now as distorted reflections of the people we had once fallen in love with. I would have done anything to return us to some semblance of our former selves, but I had no idea how.

'I'm going to take a bath and get dressed,' she said, stretching. 'And then, because I never got around to any shopping, you're going to take me somewhere nice to have Sunday lunch. And I don't mean soggy Yorkshire pudding and floury roast potatoes, either. Let's get a bit of glamour back into our lives, buster.'

As she closed the bathroom door the phone rang again. It was Matt.

'They've shoe-horned Maldwyn into the *Sunday Politics* show.'

'Today? This morning? Who's his media guy? That's very quick work.'

'I think it's smart of Maldwyn to get on it. He'll have national attention by tonight. How did your conversation with Andrew go?'

'Like talking to someone in outer space.'

Matt sounded amused.

'Andrew's been asked to appear on a Radio 4 documentary about politics and the environment. It's a set-up, of course.

He's been asked to talk about the effects of pollution on UK wildlife. Halfway through owls will get to the top of the agenda. I've told him not to accept. He wants to do it but it's all risk and not much reward. We have a grid and I want him to stick to it. When's your own piece coming out and what are you going to say?'

'I'll have it by Tuesday. I don't know what I'm going to say yet. I'll send you a draft on Monday night.'

7

I found a restaurant with a view of the Tyne and an elaborate menu. We sat and gazed at the river below, with its many bridges, and the spire of St Nicholas's Cathedral. There was a flood tide and the river was full, the flow upstream meeting a headwind so that white caps broke the surface of the water. For a while we were both absorbed in the view, our silence punctuated by the padding of waiters' feet; the leather-bound menus and wine list were handed round so reverently they could have been illuminated fourteenth-century missals.

When the necessary business of ordering food and drink was complete, I asked Caroline, 'So what did you mean when you asked me this morning, "are we going to get by?"'

Caroline gave me a tired smile. Weary as it was, it recaptured for me many of the reasons why we were still together. She still fascinated me. Her intelligence was livelier than mine; her ability to cut to the chase, no matter what the circumstances. There was a dimple beside the curve of her mouth that had always entranced me.

'Well, we're just going through the motions, aren't we? You don't even make love to me. Even our arguments aren't any fun.'

'Fun?'

'Well, you know what I mean.'

I did know. In the old days we had enjoyed some fiery

rows, which Caroline seemed to relish more than I. My response was, inevitably, to retreat into silence, fleeing the slamming doors for a solitary walk along the river. It was true though that whilst I found these micro-dramas intensely discomfiting, they were also cathartic, and our relationship often felt on a more even keel afterwards.

'I know what you mean.'

Some indescribable mixture in a shot glass with a tiny spoon was placed in front of us.

'What the hell is this?' asked Caroline. Without flinching, the waiter gave us a brief description.

When he had gone I asked, 'But are you telling me you want us to separate?'

'We are already separate,' said Caroline. 'We lead separate lives and most of the time we live in separate places. You don't even pretend to be excited by my work and as for yours – I am still trying to get my head around what it is that you actually do.'

'Oh, come on. We've just spent most of a weekend doing it.'

'You used to tell me that "truth speaks to power". But in the last few weeks your version of the truth has become elastic. The closer you've got to real power – meaning Andrew and Matt – the more you've changed. Andrew's been covering his tracks on the owl story as fast as he can. Don't think I haven't noticed. "We decided to put the owl out of its misery", not "I decided". He's made you – and me – an accessory to whatever breaches of the law that entails. Doesn't that bother you? Apparently not. Then there's the story that was leaked about Maldwyn. I heard you tell Maldwyn, when you were on the phone to him this morning, that you knew something was in the wind. That was double-talk, buddy. And don't give me that innocent look. You knew all about it.'

The food arrived at that moment, and the wine, and four waiters to lift the silver covers from our plates. A candle was lit and the sommelier looked thoughtfully at the colour of the rather indifferent wine I had ordered, and pronounced it fit for consumption. At last we were able to speak again.

'Are you saying I'm telling lies?'

'No. But you're close.'

'What's this got to do with us?'

'All I know is you're a different person to the one I married.'

The food looked delicious, and for a while we were caught up in that religious peace that settles over a room where people are gathered for a really good lunch.

'Mmm. This is delicious,' said Caroline.

'I was thinking about our wedding earlier,' I said.

'Oh yeah. We had that colossal row about whether we should ask any of your so-called family.'

'But we had to ask Uncle Brad, and that rather let the cat out of the bag.'

Caroline smiled at the memory.

'Andrew sent flowers, didn't he?' I asked.

'A sinister-looking bunch of lilies,' agreed Caroline.

I remembered that bunch of lilies, like a cold finger laid upon my hand; a reminder: she was mine before she was yours. The gesture was typical of Andrew. He needed to exert his will over us even when there was no longer any point. For in those days Caroline was mine. Whatever relationship she had with Andrew had disintegrated.

'Must we separate?' I asked Caroline. 'Is there no hope for us?'

'You're hurting me,' she replied, and I realised I was clutching her hand.

'I'm sorry, I didn't mean to.'

She didn't speak for a moment, just softly massaged her fingers where I had gripped her.

'It will just happen, Charlie, won't it? I'm not seeing anybody else and I haven't the strength to even think about what life would be like without you. But we're drifting apart. There's no commitment any more. And I'm not sure I can spend much more time in that house, not after dark.'

'The house? What do you mean?'

She didn't reply. She didn't need to. I knew perfectly well what she was referring to. The scratching at the glass that now woke us most nights. The faint solitary hoot that had now become a chorus of hoots, haunting our dreams. I didn't want to talk about it. I couldn't. It felt irrational and absurd even to acknowledge it. I had to focus on Andrew's campaign.

Down below the wind had dropped, or else the tide had turned, and the surface of the river was like glass, dark and implacable.

Checking my phone afterwards I found a stack of calls waiting for me on my voicemail. There were two press calls, which was worrying. Nobody was supposed to know of my connection with Andrew. I ignored them. There was also another call from Andrew himself, so I returned that first.

'Very funny,' he said.

'What was?'

'Maldwyn's interview on the *Sunday Politics* show.'

'I don't understand . . .'

'Oh, you know what he's like,' said Andrew. 'Instead of moaning on about smear tactics and character assassination he was actually quite funny about it. It's no good me trying to imitate him, you must watch it on iPlayer or something. Can you do that?'

'I think so,' I told him.

'Watch it and tell me what you think.'

I turned on the TV and scrolled forward until I saw Maldwyn appear on the screen.

'What are we to make of these disclosures in the newspapers today?' asked the presenter.

'The disclosure that I might be seeking to run against the leader of my party for his job is embarrassing but inevitable after an election like the one we've just had. We all have to shrug our shoulders and just get on with our day job. We'd like to talk about our policies; the media want to talk about personalities.'

'In your case there is an allegation about your private life as well.'

Maldwyn smiled. He seemed quite at ease.

'I don't know where that story came from – I assume you are referring to the question about whether I am gay or not – but I do know why it was published, which was as a distraction from the real issues: the need to bring down our borrowing, to reduce the cost of the state and to create more space for the private sector to grow . . .'

'Are you gay?' asked the interviewer.

'Anybody who knows me knows that yes, of course I am. It's not a secret. I'm gay, middle-aged, white and I support Chelsea. That's all there is to know about me, really.'

'Do you think these revelations will harm your candidacy?'

'I'm not a candidate for anything, but if I were, I imagine I might have alienated a few Arsenal or Man U supporters. I hope not.'

The presenter laughed. That was Maldwyn's secret. He put you at ease. He made you laugh despite yourself. The interviewer began again, 'But . . .'

'I'm not avoiding the question,' said Maldwyn. 'You want to know whether, if I were to become a candidate – which I repeat, is not my present position – voters would desert me because I am gay. The answer is, I don't know. I'd like to think that my constituents and any other supporters I may have would be rather offended if you asked them that question. I think they'd ask you to go away and come back with a question about my political preferences, not my sexual orientation. Haven't we all got past that stage of the debate?'

As Maldwyn spoke the camera moved to focus in on him. He was wearing an old tweed jacket over rather grubby corduroy trousers, a checked shirt and a paisley tie knotted somewhere under his left ear. His horn-rimmed spectacles lent him a perpetual air of mild surprise. He was the despair of every PR man in the business who had ever tried to tidy him up. Now he ran his hand through receding, curly hair and waited for a reply.

As I watched the discussion I saw an extraordinary thing: the BBC, or more correctly the mainstream voice of middle England that the presenter was speaking for, went on the defensive. It was as if the interviewer had intruded not only on Maldwyn's private life, but on all our private lives, on our right to be who we were without fear of censure. I heard myself say out loud, 'Well done, Maldwyn!' It was almost a cheer. When the interview concluded a few minutes later I felt a sense of elation that was quite at odds with my job. My job was to ensure Andrew ran as the main candidate and won. The last ten minutes or so had changed everything. I didn't think it had much altered people's view of Maldwyn's suitability as a future prime minister; but it had altered the terms of the debate.

We weren't talking any more about Maldwyn as a gay MP.

We were talking about Maldwyn as a human being, someone you could imagine sitting at your kitchen table and discussing politics or football with you. Whether I could position Andrew against him as a 'man who got things done' and whether that would be enough to counter Andrew's lack of warmth, that was the challenge now.

Later that week I happened to be in London for a conference, still trying to juggle my academic day job with the increasing demands of Andrew's campaign. I agreed to meet Matt for a drink afterwards. Yet again he chose an unassuming venue, a Victorian pub just off Tottenham Court Road, packed with builders still in their work clothes and local shop workers. We sat in a gloomy wooden corner, his eyes darting nervously around the crowd. He wanted to know what I thought of Maldwyn's TV appearance.

'If I'm honest, Matt, I'm worried that we might come out of it looking rather grubby.'

'We weren't the ones who started this. The article was going to be written whatever we did. I must admit I did think it might shut Maldwyn's campaign down. Now it's not so obvious. Our line, by the way, is that "we respect Maldwyn's right to a private life and we don't think it has any bearing on his eligibility as a leadership candidate or any other position he might be interested in."'

I nodded, but it was a fraught conversation, and I was relieved when Matt didn't accept my offer of a second round, allowing me to catch an earlier train back to Newcastle.

On the way back I tried to call Andrew but his line was busy so I left a message. It was probably for the best – I was rather fed up with the whole business. When I got home, the door was on the latch but the house was unlit. Surprisingly

185

– given the previous weekend's conversation – Caroline had come up from London earlier than usual. I found her lying on the bed in the spare room. It was a small room with only one high window which faced a wall. She wasn't asleep, but lay with her eyes wide open, staring at the ceiling.

'I might sleep in here tonight,' she said. 'Do you mind?'

I couldn't see that anything would be gained by insisting otherwise.

'Of course,' I said. 'Is there anything I can get you?'

She looked at me in surprise.

'Yes. You could get rid of them. I don't care what you do, or how you do it, just make them leave us alone.'

I glanced up at the window. There was nothing there, apart from a single long scratch down the middle of the pane, which I couldn't recall having seen there before.

That night I decided to write my piece on Andrew, which would be shaped and no doubt reshaped by Matt and our other media advisers. I hoped that what emerged in the newspapers and elsewhere would bear some resemblance to my original document.

It was a hard piece to write, made more difficult by Andrew's current mood which seemed to me to be curiously detached from what should have been one of the most important weeks of his life. He believed he had dealt with the twin challenges of Maldwyn and the owl incident, which I felt was still out there but which Andrew had decided was nothing more than a joke for the diary columns. And hovering like a warning over every phrase I wrote were Caroline's words. She was right. I had always prided myself on telling the truth – to those in power, to the public, to whoever cared to hear it. It was the basis for my whole career. But what did

I really know about Andrew, other than a few spare facts? Moscow, or Westminster, or a toxic combination of the two experiences had altered him, and his true self remained a mystery to me, wrapped in smoke. I believed in his ability to lead, to be decisive, but I struggled to expand that obvious gift into anything approaching a philosophy. Once or twice I picked up the phone half-inclined to talk to the man himself, but I couldn't bring myself to do it.

It was late when I finished the article but I reread it before I went to bed. I had downloaded a photo of Andrew from a press library. It had been taken when he was still with his bank in Moscow and showed a gaunt-looking figure, his face thinner than it was now, with intense, brooding eyes. Behind him was a brick wall unrelieved by door or window. Snow lay on the ground. My text started from that point:

Andrew Landford is a driven man. He learned his trade in Moscow in the 1990s (see picture above) which was not a place or a time for the faint-hearted. Nevertheless, great things were achieved, and fortunes were made and lost. Much that was accomplished in those chaotic days has been overlaid and replaced as successive governments came and went, and the era of Putin began. Whatever one's views about Putin, there is now a desire to invest in Russia and some of the battles that had to be fought to assist the progress of democracy and the rule of law were fought by Andrew.

It is that same drive to succeed, that same stubborn intensity that makes Andrew Landford the most eligible person to emerge so far in the race for a future party leader. At home, he is a different person. His wife, Helen, is a former corporate lawyer. She well knows the world that Andrew once worked in and is equally at home in political circles . . .

I read through this and more of the same, before starting the weary process of editing. Eventually I had had enough and closed up my laptop for the night. When I went upstairs I looked around the door of the spare room. Caroline appeared to be fast asleep, but her face was flushed. She murmured something into her pillow as I stood there. I waited a moment and then gently pushed the door to.

I went to bed alone, which I was used to, but never before when Caroline had actually been at home with me. It felt odd: a little alien. The windows rattled, as they always did on windy nights. As I fell asleep I heard a familiar noise, like the whistle of a passing train. But that was long ago, I told myself sleepily, they don't make trains like that any more. The next second, it seemed, I was woken by a drumming of rain on the windows; or was it the scraping of twigs? The noise was slow, deliberate and insistent.

I sat up in bed, feeling Caroline's absence immediately.

'Hello?' I said, stupidly.

The drumming turned into a hammering, which turned into such a thunder of force against the glass that I thought it would smash. I wanted to get out of bed and snatch the curtain away, so that I could see it was nothing but a stupid trick of the mind. I couldn't. An unknowable fear pinned me where I sat.

The hammering became a cacophony of wing and claw, accompanied by harsh shrieks.

This time there was no mistaking it.

The owls were trying to get in.

8

The following week, the war began.

It started, as all wars do, with hints of mobilisation underway, of divisions being manoeuvred into position. In the lobbies and in the bars and tea rooms the talk was all about Maldwyn and Andrew. Jane and Matt, who seemed to have access to everyone and everything, kept me up to date. My piece on Andrew was handed in, quarrelled over and edited. Various forms of it began to appear in the broadsheets. The *Daily Telegraph* gave it a page. The gaunt black and white picture of Andrew was shown alongside a picture of Maldwyn looking no less tousled than usual in a pinstriped suit that didn't quite fit him.

The comment in the left-of-centre dailies and weeklies was more or less hostile. They portrayed Andrew as a banker on the make, but through the sometimes contemptuous commentary, one sensed fear. They thought Andrew might win the leadership election, and they feared his hard-nosed approach might do real damage in a general election. He wouldn't pull his punches.

The interviews began, and more in-depth pieces appeared featuring both candidates. In all of these, Andrew scored highly. He spoke of Maldwyn, if he spoke of him at all, as 'a really nice guy – someone I knew at university but sadly

lost touch with while I was working in Russia'. The implication, never spoken but left hanging in the air, was that
while Andrew had been working his guts out, Maldwyn had
been playing around. 'Lightweight' was the adjective Andrew
was indirectly trying to attach to Maldwyn, although it was
probably Matt's idea.

Nobody said anything, or asked anything, about owls.

The decision came as no surprise when it arrived. Under
Tory Party rules, the leadership could be changed only if the
current leader resigned or a letter of no confidence collected
a sufficient number of signatures. In the event, the leader decided to pre-empt the no-confidence process. It was clear he
no longer had the backing of his party so he decided to move
on before he was pushed. Still carrying himself like a wounded man, he popped up on television to repeat his willingness
to do his duty for his party and his country, but asked the
chairman of the 1922 Committee to accept his resignation.
This was duly written and accepted. To the leader's credit he
did not hang around and let uncertainty damage his party
any further than the current level of speculation already had.
On the other hand, the casual way in which his party – and
even his friends – had turned their backs on him was quite
something to behold.

In the second week after the appearance of the letter, the
first round of voting began. Andrew now openly lobbied his
cause in the tea rooms and bars. It did me good to see this:
he was not too proud to work his cause. He and Maldwyn
met one night in the Strangers' Bar. I was with Andrew that
evening, watching him at work and trying to get a feel of
how the debate was running. With us was a Yorkshire MP
and his wife. The man from Yorkshire had piggy eyes and

was as hard as nails. He was pro-Andrew, pro-anybody who would speak out for Good Honest Party Principles, as he saw them. Maldwyn had just come into the bar with another MP and was buying drinks.

'Hello, Andrew,' he said – we were only a few feet apart – 'I'd offer to buy you a drink but I expect that would count as bribery. How are you?'

'I'm very well, Maldwyn. And I couldn't drink another thing. I've had enough cups of tea to sink a battleship.'

'It's hard work, this electioneering business. So, you think you are going to win?'

There was some laughter from around us.

'Go, Maldwyn!' somebody said.

'Who can say?' Andrew replied. 'It's in the lap of the gods.'

'Or in the hands of the bookmakers,' said Maldwyn. 'Or even a certain wise goddess.' He turned away with a laugh as if he'd just made a joke. If he had, it was a very obscure one and left his companion looking as baffled as everyone else.

Andrew turned quite white for a second. 'What did he mean by that?' he said quietly to me. 'I'm going to ask him.' I looked across to where Maldwyn was now standing at the centre of a group of people, exerting his customary charm. I put a restraining hand on Andrew's elbow.

'Don't even think about it,' I said.

A certain wise goddess. The only one who immediately sprang to mind was Minerva, the goddess of wisdom, and by long association . . . owls. But to imagine that Maldwyn was making a deliberate allusion to the bird incident was surely ridiculous. To me the exchange had an almost random quality to it, as if Maldwyn had scarcely known what he was saying. The whole thing was odd; very odd.

On a normal day it would have been something to follow up on but this was not a normal day. When the votes were counted at the end of the first ballot several names that one expected to see on the list appeared with predictable results. However, most of the attention was focused on Andrew and Maldwyn. The surprise was that there was no outright winner. Andrew had a lead, but it was not decisive. Under party rules, the candidate with the lowest number of votes dropped out, but as several MPs had put their names forward, the ballots would continue until there were only two candidates left, at which point the contest would be thrown open to the whole party via a postal vote.

The following week I was in London again to see Caroline's current exhibition, having missed the private view, thanks to Andrew and his police interview. It was the least I could do. She greeted my arrival at the flat with her face half-averted so that a kiss aimed at her lips was deflected to her cheek. I told myself it was not an outright rejection.

'Shall we go out to dinner after the show?' I asked.

'I suppose so. Let's see who's there.'

Ignoring the implication that my company wasn't enough, I spruced up after my train journey and we took a taxi to the gallery.

'It's not my most exciting work ever. Do say if you can't stand it and we'll leave,' said Caroline anxiously. In fact the work was better than I had expected from her remarks. There were a decent number of red spots. There was a ceramic toad prince that I rather liked and would have bought if somebody hadn't got there first.

'I love this,' I told her.

'It's just a lightweight thing. A joke.'

We wandered along the rows of sculptures. Straightening up after bending to look at a white Ophelia in a pool of ceramic lilies with a graphite glaze I bumped into someone.

'I'm sorry,' I said, without looking round.

'And so you should be,' said Maldwyn sharply. 'I cut you off like a dead hand and now I gather you never even noticed. I clearly need to work on my technique.'

'I wasn't sure you wanted to speak to me,' I said. 'The article doesn't seem to have done you any harm. You've been extremely good at turning the situation around.'

'Now you listen to me, young feller me lad,' said Maldwyn. 'If you think I went into politics for a pile of sloppily written pieces chuntering on about how many nice gay friends people have, and what a good cook and conversationalist I must be . . .'

'Don't be so cynical Maldwyn,' said Caroline, trying to leaven the mood. 'It doesn't suit you.'

He punched her lightly on the arm. 'Oh don't you worry. I'll let you know when I'm being cynical. There's no fun in it otherwise.' He paused, then said, 'Look here, what are you two ne'er-do-wells doing later on?'

'Having supper, I suppose.'

'I rather fancy we all need a proper chinwag, don't you, Mr Fryerne?' He eyeballed me in that Maldwyn way which suggested there was only one answer to the question. I shrugged. 'It'll be just like old times, only we'll be talking about grown-up things, like who should run the country. There's a rather nice little place round the corner. I wouldn't touch the food if were you but the cellar's not bad . . .'

My face must have given me away.

'Don't worry, old fruit, I'm not asking you to betray

Andrew. Much as it pains me to admit it, I might actually have an olive branch stuffed up my sleeve.'

'Why don't you talk to Andrew himself?'

'And end up all over the front pages of tomorrow's newspapers, thanks to that Kiwi terrier who's always scuttling along behind him? I'm rather over negotiation via the press, if you don't mind. Forgive me for being terribly old-fashioned, but I like the expression "smoke-filled backroom deal" and that's exactly what I intend to do.'

I left the two of them and went and looked out of the window. This felt like a set-up of some sort. But was there more to it than that?

There was only one way to find out.

'OK,' I said, turning back. 'No photos, no tape recordings, no leaks of this meeting at all. Is that understood?'

'Yes, yes, I'll stand MI5 down,' said Maldwyn, and stepped outside to make a call.

'Well done, darling,' said Caroline.

'Were you in on this?' I asked her.

'Well, he did ring me about an hour before you arrived,' she said. 'I thought it was time you two sorted things out.'

We hung around the gallery for a while in case anyone important came in, then shut up shop and went outside. We walked down Kensington Church Street. The three of us were dressed in drab grey coats and looked like a bunch of conspirators heading for a putsch. Perhaps we were. It was still quite early but the street lamps were on, haloed in a soft drizzle. Maldwyn dived down a side street until we came to the dimly lit entrance to a restaurant. We let ourselves in and found a dark, comfortable area with cane chairs and glass-topped tables, which I suppose was the bar. A waiter came and took our coats and our drinks order. Maldwyn said nothing until his whisky and water arrived.

'Well, how does my fine friend think he's doing?' he asked abruptly, before taking a large swig.

'He's content,' I said.

'Content . . . an interesting choice of word.'

'What did you want to talk about, Maldwyn?'

'Oh, I rather fancied a bit of a heart to heart with you. Maybe even do a deal. But let's order first. I'm so much more relaxed once I'm certain of proper browsing and sluicing.'

So the waiter was summoned and we ordered and then Maldwyn leaned back in his chair until it creaked dangerously and said, 'I'm at a turning point. I've had all the nice little "the only gay in the village" pieces I'm going to get. It's becoming rather thin gruel. Next week the wheel will turn, and out will come the backlashers, as they always do, dragging their chains behind them. Is a man like me going to be strong enough in times of crisis? Are Mr and Mrs Middle England sitting in their conservatory in Nuneaton ready for such a revolution? And will it be fair to the other person in my life who will no doubt be named and whose whole past will be given a forensic going-over, as if he were a common criminal.' Quite unexpectedly for Maldwyn, he flushed, and there was a crack to his voice.'I can see all the ghastliness coming and I just don't think I can face it.'

'The tide went out and now it's coming back in,' I nodded sympathetically.

'Maybe so, King Canute,' said Maldwyn. 'Meanwhile, I'm busy in my Exchequer counting up the votes I think I can guarantee for the final round. I might have picked up a few riders from fallen horses, but equally a few of my own have tumbled into the ditch. When I tot it all up what it comes down to is this – I don't think I can win.'

We'd already thought about this and were coming to the same conclusions: a dull, attritional campaign, which was the last thing any political party needed and might even tempt the interim leader to put himself forward as a compromise candidate. That would be the worst sort of intervention.

Caroline looked at me. Maldwyn looked at me. Did I get it? Had I understood the meaning of this plot?

Our dinner arrived and with it my light-bulb moment.

'You want to offer yourself as deputy leader and Andrew as leader. Then everybody's happy. We march on in step and win the next election.'

'By jove, I think he's finally twigged,' murmured Maldwyn, dry as a nut.

Between Andrew and Maldwyn they could command enough votes to shut out any rival candidates. It was a 'dream ticket': Andrew's hard-edged style would appeal to some in the party; others would look to Maldwyn to be a softening and more humanising influence, likely to smooth the ragged edges in Andrew's persona and make him more electable when the day for the real election came: the one that counted. The next general election.

I could see everything that was to be gained by saying yes. I couldn't – I didn't see – what reasons there might be for saying no. I didn't see what was out there.

I realised everyone was waiting for me to say something.

'I'll take it to Matt and Andrew.'

'And?' asked Maldwyn and Caroline simultaneously.

'I'll say I think we should go for it. Matt might be a little disconcerted he wasn't consulted first.'

'Let me get on the blower to my own people first before

you send the cavalry dashing in with Andrew,' said Maldwyn. 'Best we pitch it as my genius invention, roping you in as a go-between for old times' sake. Don't you think?'

After that the evening became just another dinner. It was like the good old Oxford days, sitting around a table with Maldwyn, who in his usual unassuming way was the centre of our conversation. They were his jokes we laughed at; his gossip that was the freshest and the most revealing. Before we left, I had the chance to ask him a question unobserved while Caroline was collecting her coat.

'Maldwyn, the other day when you met Andrew, do you remember that you asked him if he thought he would win?'

'Vaguely.'

'You did. And he answered that it was in the lap of the gods.'

'Fair enough,' replied Maldwyn.

'But you then said: or in the lap of a certain goddess. What did you mean by that?'

'Did I? I really can't remember, my dear,' answered Maldwyn. 'Does it matter? It's precisely the sort of inane remark one makes on such occasions, the kind I pray any considerate biographer will strike from the record.'

And that was how the matter was left that evening.

9

The following morning I rang Andrew and told him we needed to talk about a proposition from Maldwyn. We agreed we should meet, and I went to his office in St Stephen's Buildings. He summoned me into his inner sanctum with a nod and shoved a cup of black coffee across the table without asking me what I wanted. He was drinking a glass of water and looked tired. There was a rawness to his features I had not seen before. He must have seen me staring, and batted away my unasked question. 'I've not been sleeping well. It's . . . nothing.' He drummed his fingers on the table. The nails were bitten to shreds. 'So, you've been having secret meetings with the competition, have you?'

He was in a sour mood, which I tried to temper.

'It's not quite how it looks. I only agreed to the meeting because I thought we should hear what he had to say.'

'You could have called me first. Or maybe it might have been nice to invite Matt. At a stretch you could even have asked your boss – that's me, by the way – whether contact of this sort was appropriate at this stage of the campaign.'

I decided I could be equally bad-tempered.

'Andrew, that's just not the way it happened. One minute Maldwyn arrived in the gallery, and fifteen minutes later we were sitting down with him. After all, he is an old friend.

He said he wanted to talk and then told me his idea. I felt there was a deal to be done – subject to your approval – and that deal was either going to be done now or we could just continue on with the current process and go into yet more rounds of voting. You know what I think about the risks of that.'

'What you think doesn't matter. Matt is in charge of tactics.'

We both went silent. Then Andrew caved in.

'Tell me what the fucking deal is then.'

I told him.

The problem for Andrew was that the deal was irresistible. It gave him a lock on the leadership and an almost guaranteed run for prime minister at the next general election. Even Andrew had to concede that Maldwyn's presence as deputy would be a terrific plus. It would demonstrate as clearly as possible that the party rejected any prejudice and indeed it embraced the strengths that Maldwyn could bring as leader. Andrew thought about it for a long time while I sat opposite him, drinking his bitter coffee. In the end he tried to look stern, failed and allowed a thin smile.

'Well, you rat,' he said. 'I guess you think you've got it all sewn up, don't you?'

'The decision rests with you, Andrew. You need to tell him yes or no. That's how I left it. When you've spoken to Maldwyn, he'll call Matt and apologise for not bringing him into the loop before now.'

'I need to know what Maldwyn's view of a deputy leader's duties are before I can sign up to this.'

'Quite right. You need to ask him that.'

We talked for a while longer and then Andrew stood up. 'I'll speak to Matt and then Maldwyn. Your role in this business is over now. Please don't have any more contact with Maldwyn until it is all put to bed. I don't want any crossed lines.'

'But you're going to say yes?'

'I'm going to say yes.'

At that moment everything appeared to be within our power. The doubts and anxieties that had been clouding the horizon over the past weeks suddenly lifted, and I felt the bright, dazzling surge of light one always receives from a new Jerusalem. My mind was already bent on our campaign for the next general election.

I got up to go, but Andrew stayed me with a hand on my arm. 'Oh, by the way, Charles, I should probably mention the police at Carlisle have asked to speak to me again about this wretched owl business. This evening. They assure me it's still routine, but I'm going to take my lawyer with me this time. Just to be sure.'

I nodded.

'How tiresome. Will you let me know what they say?'

'Of course.'

He beamed and we grasped each other's hands in a sort of valedictory handshake.

When I left Andrew's office it was with the self-conscious step of an operator, someone who got things done, who made kings out of princes. I felt so buoyed up that I only just noticed the flap of broad wings, soaring overhead from one rooftop to another, as I strode off down the street,

That weekend the media awoke to the possibility of a Land-ford/Christie ticket sweeping away all before them. I hadn't been asked to do any press releases or articles so I assumed that Matt had organised all that. If so, he had done it very well. There wasn't a single negative comment in the press at all; nothing but praise for 'a carefully crafted deal that none of us could see was staring us in the face until Landford and Christie had the courage to shake hands on it'.

Other headlines followed:

LANDFORD AND CHRISTIE:
COULD THIS BE THE WINNING TEAM?

read one.

STRONG DOUBLE TICKET THREATENS TO
SHORTEN ODDS AT GENERAL ELECTION

read another.

The ballots had now reduced the field to Maldwyn and Andrew. So when Maldwyn formally withdrew from the contest that week, Andrew became the new leader of the Conservative Party and the postal vote was no longer necessary. The flurry of commentary and analysis after the announcement came to the conclusion that the double ticket deal had indeed given Andrew the deciding edge. Maldwyn may have been honest and humorous about his outing, but in the final analysis he paled as a weaker figure alongside his square-jawed rival. This perception was nothing, commentators were at pains to underline, to do with his sexuality, but rather it was the downside of his mild and self-effacing public demeanour. He would therefore, all agreed, make an outstanding deputy.

Standing in front of Conservative Central Office, the short victory speech the new leader gave, which was covered live online and across all the news channels, was Andrew

Landford at his most unforgettable. I watched from hundreds of miles away, on Caroline's ancient, juddering kitchen TV, and still felt the hairs rise on the back of my neck. The backdrop of weathered pillars and a cluster of bright young men and women, stern-faced with their hands clasped, set the mood. Helen swayed gently in front of them, flushed with colour, a distant look in her eyes. Maldwyn stood to the side, shrewd and pensive. Someone had helpfully erected a lectern for Andrew, a prominent Union Jack emblazoned on the front, with the name of the party in smaller letters underneath. The general election to come almost seemed an irrelevant detail, as Andrew strode out, looked the cameras in the eye, and began to speak.

'It is a very great honour and privilege to have been given the opportunity to lead your party at this difficult time for the country. Let me say now, I will do it with every fibre of my being, and I will not rest until the job is done. Nothing will distract me from the task in hand.'

Perhaps it was my imagination, but he seemed to glance up at the sky when he said this. He went on to thank Maldwyn and the other candidates and to commend their campaigns as decent and well fought, praising Maldwyn for his honesty, 'which has set an example to us all. No longer can a person's sexuality be a barrier to public service, even at the very highest levels.'

Andrew looked forward to 'gathering the many and diverse talents of the party under one roof. Then together, we will fix that roof and make it a stronger one for all of Britain. A roof to last in all weathers, in the good times and the bad.'

Then he stopped looking down at his notes and relaxed his shoulders, giving a half-smile.

'I have to say, whoever you voted for, I am sure you are all glad that I have been elected leader of the Conservative Party, and not President of the RAC. Suffice to say, I will, from now on, be making full use of the driver that comes with the job.'

There was a ripple of polite laughter, although Maldwyn frowned. As the scrolling subtitles below the picture hurried to try and explain the reference, Andrew knitted his brows, and returned to his serious tone.

'I shall use that time in the back of the car, as I shall be using all my time now, to think deeply about the problems that face us as a nation. How we can learn to pay our way in the world. How we can continue to be valued partners to our allies, yet always defend our own interests. How we can once more make this country a place we want our children to grow up in.'

He went on to list his now familiar policy shopping list: achieving sustainable economic growth, public service reform, eradicating the Westminster bubble, promoting renewable energy and, of course, protecting the wildlife that helps make this country great.

The words began not just to scroll along the bottom of the screen, but to drift into my head and dissolve into a blur of 'trust . . . values . . . responsibility . . . principle . . . challenge and change'.

Some changes are easier and quicker to make than others. I was at first surprised, then hurt, to find that my post-victory phone calls, texts and emails to Andrew went unanswered. As the wall of silence built, with no communication from even Matt or Jane, it became clear I had been shut out from the inner circle.

Too much initiative was a dangerous thing to have, it

appeared. I had played a part in the deal with Maldwyn that had unlocked power for Andrew, but now Andrew had to protect that power. His main rival was now his deputy; a threat contained but also given a potentially dangerous advantage. I suspected that Andrew thought if he removed intermediaries such as myself, Maldwyn would be further isolated from the real seat of power.

This suspicion was confirmed when two days later there was finally a text:

'Please accept this note as termination of your contract of employment with Andrew Landford. An email confirmation will follow, on which your signature will be required.'

It came as Caroline and I were sitting down to supper together in our house in Newcastle. We seemed to have arrived at something of an uneasy truce. She had spent, as ever, the week in London working on her mysterious new show, but had returned home without comment. I wondered if it was a temporary reprieve, and whether this news might help the situation. I handed her my mobile so that she could read the text.

'Bastards,' she said. 'I wonder what Maldwyn will think about that?'

The answer came the following week.

IO

The casual observer might have passed over it at first – only a paragraph or two in a satirical magazine. The piece ran:

Andrew Landford likes to have his cake and eat it. First of all he cuddled up to Maldwyn Christie to ensure his leadership election chances rose from something less than 50% to something close to 100%. Now he's trying to bury the affair of the dead owl to ensure that doesn't get in the way of his general election chances.

The affair of the dead owl began a couple of months ago when a car containing Andrew Landford, his profiler Charles Fryerne and his wife, and Helen Landford, collided with an owl. The owl, according to an independent source, sustained only a broken wing. What killed it were multiple injuries to its head. Landford claims this was done on the advice of his passengers. In one version it was his passenger Charles Fryerne who killed the bird. These are murky waters.

What is not murky is that the owl was found by a passer-by and handed in to the police. In their efforts to trace witnesses, police interviewed Landford informally and he denied any knowledge of the incident. Then when interviewed under caution on a later occasion he accepted he *had* been present when the owl was killed. We don't seem to be able to get a straight answer as to why or how the owl was killed, or why Landford simply didn't call the incident in when it happened. Could it be he was embarrassed by serving on the parliamentary Committee which recently amended the Wildlife and Countryside Act to give further protection to certain endangered species, including barn owls?

I didn't know for sure, but I would have put money on the fact that Maldwyn had spied this growing scandal from afar as he sat making his plans. I felt a flush of shame, recalling his description of his treatment in the press, his fear of what might yet come of it. He wasn't a natural at revenge, but this little jab in the ribs had his mischievous touch all over it. The casual remark in the House of Commons bar, and now this. Perhaps he and his advisers had realised that you can't kick a man's feet from underneath him when they are floating two feet above the ground. But you can start to bring him down to earth.

I just wished that they hadn't chosen this particular story to take the shine off Andrew's halo. A minor accident months ago was now in danger of being blown out of all proportion. The Tory Party had always been an unofficial coalition of those on the right, centre and left of Conservative political thought. It was natural that having settled for deputy, Maldwyn would want to consolidate his position and prevent Andrew from becoming an unassailable fixture. But he was playing around with some very explosive material. I was tempted to tell him so, except that would have meant accusing him of the leak to the magazine, which he would have furiously denied.

The article prompted me to cast my mind back over the owl incident. What had made Andrew completely lose himself like that? It would surely have been possible for him to cradle the bird, to handle it gently until we could find a vet. But he had grabbed at it and then, when it had understandably pecked him back, he had smashed the poor bird's skull to bits. Was it because he thought it might have damaged his new car? Or was it because he hated not being in control?

The following days were bad ones for me. Not only had I been kicked out of Andrew's team for no good reason – in fact for helping Andrew get what he wanted – but I could see a danger that this random encounter on a northern road could mutate into a much bigger story. One that risked engulfing us all.

My fears proved to be quite right when the following Monday it was my turn to be summoned by the police in Carlisle for a little chat. 'Just to gather further evidence after our conversations with Mr Landford, sir,' said the voice on the phone. They gave me next to no notice, and despite repeated attempts to contact Andrew so we could coordinate our stories, that line of communication appeared to be permanently down.

The same interviewing officer as before ushered me into the tiny interview room, along with another policeman, the one who had come to the door at Gilcaster Head. There was a brief preamble, while they set the tapes going, before he launched in with – 'Mr Fryerne, did you see or hear anything on the Friday night in question that could help us identify how this owl died and who was responsible for its death?'

The tone threw me, and the hairs prickled on the back of

my neck in warning. They knew who had killed the owl. I'd been with Andrew when he came to this very station and confessed. But something had changed, and I didn't know what. I began to babble.

'Andrew had no chance at all, officer,' I said. 'The owl flew out of nowhere. It must have been dazzled by the headlights—'

'I'm not talking about what Mr Landford did or saw, sir,' the officer broke in. 'I'm talking about you. What you did and said. Or rather, didn't say.'

I took a deep breath and tried to tell the story of the evening in my own words, as calmly and truthfully as I could. Yes, we were driving slowly because we were on a narrow single-track road. No, there had been no time at all to avoid the bird. It was flying fast and had come straight at us. I added that I had advised we look for a vet to get the bird's broken wing pinned. I accepted this might have been impractical given the bird's demeanour but I also noted that Andrew had picked up the bird and killed it before any discussion could take place. Then I said, 'The bird was badly injured, you see. Mr Landford couldn't bear to see it suffer so he killed it as efficiently as possible.'

'Mr Landford certainly used plenty of force,' said the other policeman. 'He crushed the bird's skull.'

I winced. 'We didn't want there to be any possibility of the bird dying a lingering death. We couldn't think of what else to do.'

'*We* couldn't think of what else to do? So you're saying he killed the bird under your instruction?'

This I furiously denied, but the police just scratched their heads and kept asking me if I was sure, that I was being interviewed under caution, and so on. One of them even asked if I had been driving the car. 'Mr Landford cannot recall whether you were in fact driving at the time.'

'Of course I wasn't,' I replied sharply. 'I hope his memory has improved because I cannot agree with his statement that I advised him to kill the owl.'

'But the fact remains that both of you decided not to report the incident.'

'No,' I said firmly. 'We were just anxious to get home. I suppose we thought it was something we could worry about in the morning, as the bird was obviously dead.'

'And did you?' asked the interviewing officer.

I stared at him blankly.

'Did we what?'

'Worry about it in the morning?'

'Yes. We went for a walk but before we got to the place where the incident had taken place we met a neighbour who said he'd found the bird and had handed it in at the police station in Brampton.'

'So did you tell him you were responsible for the owl's death?'

'No, I did not,' I said indignantly. 'Because I wasn't.'

'Did you contact the police at Brampton to notify them that a protected species had been killed, accidentally or not?'

'No, I didn't. It was just an accident. I wasn't even driving the car!'

I felt events unravelling between my fingers.

'Just trying to find out if there is any evidence of criminality,' said my interviewer. 'As you know, your former employer, Mr Landford, was on the parliamentary Committee which recently made an amendment to the Wildlife and Countryside Act, so you both must have been aware of your obligation under the new Act to report the death of a protected species as soon as possible. He is doing fine work there, if I may say so, sir. It encourages me and my colleagues to see Parliament giving some time to conservation issues.'

I looked at him in complete astonishment.

'And you were working for him in the capacity of a . . .' The man looked down at his notes. '. . . Communications Adviser?'

'Yes, but—'

'So you would have been familiar with his work as an MP? In order to promote and communicate the value of that work to his constituents?'

'Up to a point, of course.'

'In which case he would surely have explained to you that the death of an owl in such circumstances is a notifiable event.'

'Perhaps he did, but I'm not sure how—'

'So you should have, in compliance with the strict letter of the law, notified us, Mr Fryerne.'

I slammed my hands down on the desk. 'I don't know why you're asking me these questions! I wasn't driving the car. I didn't run the bloody bird over. It wasn't my idea to wring its neck.'

The officer raised his eyebrows, and slid a sheaf of typed pages across to me. They were the transcript of a conversation: Andrew's last interview with the police.

'That's not what Mr Landford says, sir.'

In due course I was allowed to go. Somebody at Carlisle must have been swift to get hold of the new twist and call Andrew about it because the next thing I heard was an interview on the radio the following morning.

'Andrew Landford, you're the newly elected leader of the

Opposition. You could one day be our prime minister. So why did you lie about butchering an innocent owl?' demanded the presenter, jumping in with both feet, as usual.

Andrew tried to laugh it off. 'I didn't butcher anything . . . it was the most awful and unfortunate accident, and the immediate advice I was given was to do the humane thing, which was to put the wretched creature out of its misery. As I've said before, this whole story is a huge distraction from the real issues—'

'You say "immediate advice" . . . Did you decide to kill the owl, or were you told to by one of your advisers? There are stories in the papers this morning which say that your communications manager, Charles Fryerne, who was travelling with you has now been interviewed under caution as well?'

'Look, you'll have to ask Charles about that—'

'It sounds like you're saying you killed the owl on his advice, which he's denying – is one of you not telling the truth?'

'The difficulty I have,' said Andrew, 'is that Charlie is by trade a professional storyteller. He has been a very valued colleague but at the same time he has made his living – and a very good one too – by writing articles that are invariably spun in one direction or another. But let me be clear about one thing. The time has come for politicians to stand alone, and speak for themselves. The public is tired of spin. They want to hear the truth, direct from our own mouths, and that's something I'm determined to do. Not just about personal matters such as this, but on the issues that really matter to real people. I will speak out loud and clear, for myself, about Europe, the NHS, the economy . . .'

I turned off the radio. It had obviously been a last-minute piece, a phone call to Andrew based on the piece in the magazine and that morning's papers. I didn't like being called a storyteller, especially when criminal charges might be involved. But what I liked least of all was what was happening to Andrew. It was as if a familiar but relatively harmless beast was sloughing off its skin to reveal something more sinister beneath. He sounded almost mad to me. His behaviour ever since the owl incident had been unbalanced and now it seemed that what he believed had supplanted the facts he actually knew.

It was Caroline, who had unexpectedly decided to stay up in Newcastle for the week, who brought me the next instalment in the saga. She had gone downstairs to make a mug of tea and came back with the newspaper folded open at a particular page.

'News for you, lover boy,' she said in a laconic voice.

It was news.

The gist of the article was that the Crown Prosecution Service was considering filing charges against Andrew Landford for obstructing the course of justice. The matter in question was his failure to report the death of an owl, as required by the newly updated Wildlife and Countryside Act. There was a bit more about Andrew's membership of the Committee reviewing penalties under the Act. Clearly, despite his attempt to fling as much mud at me as he could scoop up, none of it had stuck. The police had not been convinced by his story, and nothing I said had given them reason to change that opinion.

I took the paper off to the bathroom, whistling.

At breakfast, Caroline asked me why I was so cheerful.

'Because, don't you see—'

Then I stopped. Part of me felt vindicated after the way

he'd treated me. Yet there was also a part that felt sad because despite his obvious flaws, and our differences, I had once truly believed he would make a good leader for the country.

'I see that it's a mess all right,' said Caroline. 'I could see him getting ready to fire you a mile off. You crossed one of his precious red lines, and that's never a smart move. Now he's trying to pass the buck over for that poor bird too.'

This was followed by the long silence that now fell upon us whenever the owl was mentioned.

My life with Caroline seemed to be hovering on the edge of a precipice as she spent increasing amounts of time browsing through property websites. She could afford to buy, and passed hours every day comparing places, but as far as I knew, she rarely viewed anywhere. Perhaps she thought the birds would follow her wherever she went.

She also seemed to be waiting for something to change in me; but I didn't know what it was, what part of my moral landscape needed to be changed or abolished. I didn't like to ask. We continued to sleep in separate rooms and now I had begun to ache with the absence of her at nights: the drowsy press of warm flesh, her scent.

My inability to ask her a simple question or two that might have resolved the whole matter was partly due to the fear that the question itself would dynamite what was left of our relationship. It was also partly because of what I would call the Fryerne tradition. The Fryerne of Fryerne Court was supposed to remain true to an imagined Englishness: to the stiff upper lip, a communal wall of silence erected by a disjointed and perhaps dysfunctional family whose only common ground was a legend. We could not even be sure if this legend had any basis in reality. Perhaps if I gave up some of my time to researching our mythology, I could liberate my own life. A search for the truth. I didn't know what I'd do with it when I'd got it.

But life doesn't often proceed according to plan. The next thing to happen was an article in one of the tabloids entitled 'The Owls Have It'.

New Tory leader Andrew Landford is blaming the press for exaggerating the scandal that is threatening to derail his political career.

The former member of the Wildlife and Countryside Committee is facing more and more questions about the incident that took place on a road near his luxury country mansion two months ago, when he ran over a protected barn owl in his state-of-the-art Range Rover.

In a bold attempt to deflect attention, he accused the newspapers and media of focusing on a 'minor car accident, when they should be focusing on the real issues which matter to party members – Europe, the NHS and the economy'.

Despite the slightly frivolous title the piece didn't pull any punches. When the tabloids started to sharpen their knives for a new Tory leader, the outlook was not good. My heart sank further when I read the next line.

'Landford appeared to suggest that his advisers were as much at fault as he was, for suggesting that he kill a wounded bird rather than take it to a vet.'

What had begun as a shadowy insinuation was taking on the lurid hue of a full-blown lie.

There was also a full-page leader in one of the broadsheets.

This contained nothing new but recited the facts of the owl affair in an orderly and senatorial way that could not be ignored. Indeed it was a delight to read, with sonorous phrases such as 'had Mr Landford had more regard for his new role as Her Majesty's Leader of the Opposition – a position he now seems unlikely to occupy for long – his cavalier treatment of the truth would not seem so reprehensible'.

The point being made was that Andrew had – allegedly – obstructed the course of justice by repeatedly changing his evidence. He had also used his position as a member of the relevant Committee to blow smoke over the story. He was in trouble and it looked like he wanted to try and drag us all, or more specifically me, down with him.

Caroline and I had a conference over the breakfast table, the newspaper sitting between us.

'It says that Andrew could face criminal charges,' she said.

'Don't worry, darling,' I said.

'But I do,' she said. Unexpectedly, she leaned over the table and took my hand. 'Your whole life has been built on people placing trust in you. Whatever else may have gone wrong between us, you've always been the straight guy, Mr Plain Talker, the person who tells the truth. That's what I first liked about you. From the moment we met, and you wouldn't come upstairs with me. You stayed put to hear your dad's speech. Now you're the head of the family, and you seem to come out in hives just thinking about it. Maybe this whole Fryerne thing is one big private joke between you and me, but I bet the others take it more seriously, and deep inside, you do too. If you're hurt, they are. If your reputation suffers, they suffer too.'

'You don't really believe that, do you?'

I felt appalled by what she had said yet at the same time I knew it was true. Being able to claim kinship to Charles Fryerne of Fryerne Court was the reason some of them got out of bed in the morning. If the present incumbent threw away his reputation, and their trust in him, what was left for them? Of course it might just mean they could ignore all future family gatherings, possibly with some relief. But I suspected not.

'With what's been going on here, I could believe anything,' Caroline said. Her face was pale, and she looked exhausted. I felt the same. She didn't need to explain what she meant. We both heard the sounds at night, the tapping, the gentle but persistent scratching, as if something was trying to get in. I had thought of contacting the council, but the thought of being ridiculed as well as slandered was too much.

A tiny brush with a single bird on a deserted country road was quickly transforming into a full-scale political scandal. Above and beyond all of that, I cared about Caroline and what this was doing to her. To us. Whether we were imagining the owls that haunted our house at night or not, she was suffering as much as I was. She had expected Andrew to behave in the way he had. But now my failure to stand up to him had placed our marriage at risk.

One man had started this, and only he could end it. He might be Leader of the Opposition, protected by powerful gatekeepers, but it didn't matter.

I had to see Andrew, before he destroyed everything.

3
MINNIVER WOOD

I

Eventually, after numerous phone calls to assistants and badgering emails, I tracked Andrew down. He seemed curiously subdued. 'I'm still not sleeping at all well,' he admitted. It was heartening to hear that Caroline and I were not the only ones.

I suppose, given all that had occurred since my last visit to Gilcaster Head, I should have been more surprised that after I put my case, he warily agreed to meet me at Gilcaster Head that Friday night. Perhaps I was meant to feel flattered. In fact I felt anything but as I took the train to Carlisle on a blustery winter evening, gazing out of the window at black branches twisting in the wind. I felt restless, unable to concentrate on a book or even a newspaper.

On previous visits, Andrew had been content to let me take a taxi from the station or send John in his car. But now I found him pacing up and down the platform, a dark tweed coat wrapped around him, like the villain of some Victorian melodrama. When he saw me he did not smile, but reached out both arms to grasp my hands. 'So good to see you,' he said, moving from the darkness into the light.

I stepped back in shock. His eyes were red from exhaustion, and there were scratches on his face that looked inflamed.

'You've got some explaining to do,' I said.

'Some,' he said. 'Let's go.' He picked up my case, a gesture of hospitality he had never made before, and we left.

He said nothing on the journey back. His profile in the dying light looked gaunt, and hard, like it had all those years ago when he arrived back from Moscow. The sky was almost black as we turned up the lane that led to Gilcaster Head. Beyond the house loomed a dark cloud that might have been Minniver Wood. The security lights snapped on and then we were inside. My case and coat were taken and a whisky and water handed to me by the ever-efficient John, then I was seated in an armchair. The damask was grubbier than I remembered, and some of the blue piping had been ripped away from the sides, as if a cat had got its claws into it.

For a while we talked of this and that, like old friends who hadn't seen each other in some time. This with a man who had just sacked me, then gone on the radio to drag me further into the mess he had created. With anyone else, you could hardly warrant it, but Andrew had this ability – as he had when I began my relationship with Caroline – to effortlessly march on from the past as if it had never occurred. Perhaps that was what he was trying to do with the owl as well.

Stiffly at first, but with growing ease, we raked over the economy, and what the big new ideas were from various think tanks and central banks. None of them seemed that big or that new on closer inspection, but Andrew had a forensic grasp of detail which meant he was able to dissect the science of each one with a ruthless precision, getting straight to the heart of the matter while I was left grappling with the broader implications.

John slid silently in and topped up our drinks, as we

moved on to the various members of the government Andrew would have to face at the next election. He knew their record backwards, admired virtue where he found it, and seemed acquainted with skeletons in closets not yet open for general viewing. Then, like he was skinning the day's quarry, he peeled back their skin to reveal the tender, weak spot that he would savage through counter-policy, rhetoric and ruthless, targeted mockery.

At length, he drew breath, and I remembered why I was actually here.

'You said you could explain things,' I ventured.

'Yes.' Andrew stood in front of the fire, looking down at his drink. 'The truth is, Charles, I've behaved rather badly towards you.'

It wasn't just out of character for Andrew to apologise; it was out of character for him even to admit a failing. I was so taken aback I nearly spilt my scotch.

'This whole business with Maldwyn . . . I was foolish to be cross about it. I mean, obviously, I still don't like the fact you went behind my back – but you were only trying to help. I see that now.'

I murmured something about it being unimportant, which was perhaps true, given recent developments. The announcement of the CPS pressing charges had only been made that week, and already I had observed Andrew's character and judgement increasingly being called into question by commentators. He had only just won the leadership contest. It was not a great start.

'Also they keep telling me that I still need you, so I've given in just to shut them up.' He gave a disconcerting grin.

'They? You mean Matt and Jane?'

Andrew waved my question away. Instead, he focused his

gaze on a hole in the rug between us that I didn't recall being there on my last visit. Clearly there was now a pet resident in Gilcaster Head. Perhaps Matt and Jane had told him to acquire a puppy, no doubt secreted away, in case there were any animal-friendly photo opportunities. But Andrew's thoughts were elsewhere.

'Do you know why I wanted to become leader, Charles?'

I shrugged. 'Well, of course. We talked about it for your profile. You want to move the party back towards the centre ground, reform the membership, get more women in—'

'No, I don't mean all that. Of course it's true, but I can assure you that reforming our party membership rules is not what drives me.'

'It was the chance to have a shot at the big job.'

He nodded. 'Yes. And the fact is, however much of an old friend he may be to both of us, we both know I'll do a better job than Maldwyn. I'm more likely to be invited by the country to do it too.'

I had come to Gilcaster Head in one of my rare pugnacious moods. Helpfully, the second large scotch on an empty stomach had loosened my tongue.

'You really think so? Why? Because you're facing criminal charges?'

A branch banged against the window – although that struck me as odd, because the nearest trees were at the end of the field. Andrew glanced sharply in the direction of the noise, then strode past me, and opened the sitting room door. I turned to see him checking the corridor, before closing the door again, firmly. Andrew dragged his chair over the torn rug nearer to mine, and spoke softly.

'I've never told anyone this before, Charles, and if you repeat a word of it outside this room, I'll send every lawyer in London after you with enough writs to sink the *Titanic* three times over—'

'Oh, come on, Andrew, if you can't trust me, who can you trust?'

His eyes caught the glow from the fire.

'What you've got to understand is that from a young age, I just knew I wanted to be prime minister. It's hard to explain to anyone who's never felt that way. I'm not just talking about ambition or vision, it's more than that. It's like it's in my DNA.'

'Well, if you still think I can help you articulate that to the electorate—' I began.

'Charles. Come on.' He cut me off. 'With all your nous, all your experience – you must know we're beyond the realms of articulation and spin now. One stupid mistake by a bird has been thrown out of all proportion and now I'm damaged goods.' Andrew bit his lip and scowled, as if the act of apology caused him physical pain. 'And I'm sorry for dragging you into it without warning the way I did – that was wrong too. At least . . . it was wrong not to have discussed it with you first.'

There was that sound at the window again. Andrew flinched, but didn't turn towards the noise.

'So why did you drag me into it?'

'Isn't it obvious?'

'I'm obviously being rather dim.' Although I felt far from dim – patronised and irritated perhaps; and wondering how soon I could make my escape from this increasingly oppressive drawing room. The heat from the fire seemed to be getting more intense, and I ran a finger around the inside of my collar. Andrew didn't seem to notice.

'We need actions now, not words. Focus on my ability to

act. That's how you can help me. Show how decisive I could be as prime minister – reclaim the narrative.'

I thought back to the think tank, the investment bank in Russia, to Caroline and to my recent abrupt dismissal, now apparently rescinded. Andrew was certainly decisive when it came to jettisoning projects or people, so I proceeded with caution.

'Yes. That is one definite advantage you have over your opponents.'

He leaned over and slapped my thigh, in an attempt to be either jovial or affectionate. It felt like neither, more like a physical warning.

'That's the idea, Charles. Now I need you to act with me, perhaps even act for me . . . But first, let's have something to eat.'

We sat at opposite ends of the polished table in the dining room, where a wood-burning stove was casting yet more heat into the room. I wondered if Andrew would think it eccentric if I removed my shirt. Sweat beaded my brow, and I dabbed at it continually with my damask napkin. Every flat surface – a mantelpiece, deep stone window sills, an eighteenth-century sideboard – was covered with framed photos of Andrew. Winning a charity rowing event for a global bank. Accompanying a trade delegation to China with the Mayor of London. Speaking at the last party conference. I was straining to see if I could spot a blurred Maldwyn in the corner of the latter when Mary bustled in and set down a steaming dish of pheasant casserole.

At least, I hoped it was pheasant. It was bony enough to be one of any number of birds, although I didn't dwell on the possibilities.

Andrew took a mouthful, then continued. 'So. You wouldn't believe me if I told you what's been going on . . .'

'I've read the papers.'

'It's not what's in the papers that's getting me down,' said Andrew, and with a gesture he raised the palms of both hands outwards as if dismissing the entire political world.

'So what is?'

He leaned back in his chair and glowered at me. I noticed that the scratches on his face seemed to have reddened by the fire, and a horrible thought occurred to me. 'It's the owls, isn't it? They're attacking you as well.'

He simply stared at me, the flicker of the candles on the table lending his eyes a hellish hue. As he held up his hand to silence any further conversation, it was not entirely clear what or who he was listening to. For the first time in our long acquaintance I began to doubt how secure his grip on sanity actually was.

'Have I ever told you about the history of this house?'

I shook my head. A dim memory floated into my mind of something Andrew had mentioned on our first fateful visit here. How his parents had sold up their family business, and bought this farm out in the middle of nowhere. But of the history of the house, I knew no more than what I could see around me: an overheated Cumbrian farmhouse bedecked in silk and tassels.

'I never told anyone at Oxford much about my past,' he said. 'I heard some people thought my parents owned a gold mine. I didn't start the rumour but I saw no harm in letting it go round either.' He picked up his fork and jabbed at his food savagely, as if it were to blame for the accident of his birth. 'Don't get me wrong, we were well-off enough but the only gold mine in my background was the one my parents spent on renovating this place.'

Andrew grinned at me. It was like his greeting at the station, an attempted display of warmth that ended up looking wolfish and vaguely alarming. 'Don't worry, I'm not about to tell you some sob story. If I had one of those, I would have given it to you for the campaign. Perhaps we should make one up for the election? I'd like to see the other side knock that.'

As if in echo of his words, there was another rap at the window, and we both started, the grin vanishing from his face.

'Probably just the wind,' I said.

'Yes, probably the wind . . .' he said bitterly, staring at the darkened glass. 'This place was nothing when my parents bought it, just a crude farmhouse with a couple of outbuildings. They sold their company for a very good price and spent a packet turning some peasant hovels into the grand building you see today. That facade as you come up the drive, the gabling, Georgian windows and porch – they were all lifted straight from the pages of a country magazine. And the land that came with the property was as wild as the moors we drove though just now. The wood beyond these windows used to come right up to the property, but my parents stripped it all back. A few of the locals got a bit upset, saying the wood was of historical importance, something to do with an ancient Roman settlement, but my father employed a very modern lawyer and that was the end of the matter.'

Andrew took a large gulp of his wine, his face flushed. He had never opened up to me in this way before, and I supposed I was meant to feel flattered. But there was an unsteady quality to his voice and movements, which were not so much those of a drunk man, more one trying to navigate the deck of a ship in troubled waters.

'By the time they'd finished, hardly a stone of the old outhouse was left, and the wood was reduced to the copse you see now. Of course, I gather there have been people farming this land in one way or another for centuries. This stone wall was built by so and so, that barn used to belong to Old Whatsisname, Farmer X once kept his flock in that field over there. All that. But you can thank my parents for the introduction of the telephone line, central heating and the refrigerator. Even the name is a post-war invention. I think it was called something like Little Gill when they bought it, but my father thought Gilcaster Head sounded more respectable.'

I had a brief vision of my long-dead genealogist uncle, Roland. Andrew emptied his glass and set it down on the table, his movements deliberate and wooden. 'They are as ungrateful as the electorate. We came here, we cleared the weeds, we landscaped the wood. We made changes so it was a better place to live. Then you make one tiny slip, and they go for you.'

'The locals or the owls?'

If Andrew heard my question, it didn't seem to register. Maybe, to someone like him, in this wind-blasted corner of remote countryside, they amounted to the same thing. 'They won't stop me. I have done nothing wrong. A bird flew into my windscreen and I did the humane thing. The right thing. They can flap all they like, it doesn't make any difference. Now I'm leader of the party I'll probably be spending most of my time in London. No danger of wretched owls there.'

It was the first time I had heard an owl referred to as a threat.

The conversation paused as Mary brought in a daunting pudding, which sank straight to the bottom of my stomach, and John poured out glasses of something treacly and viscous. The conversation now turned closer to home and to family. Andrew even summoned the grace to ask about Caroline. The mask of the political operator vanished for a moment, and he seemed to be genuinely curious as he enquired about her health and her work. Indeed his tone was verging on the wistful, which given his reputation as a man of decisive action made me nervous, so I steered us back to Helen. The enthusiasm faded from his face, and he gave closed, peremptory answers about her abandoned legal career and their child.

It occurred to me that this was the longest and most intimate conversation we had ever shared. John and Mary appeared to have retreated to some inner sanctum. Remarkably, given the media storm blowing a gale in London, Andrew kept his phone switched off so I had his full and undivided attention. Yet I was also aware that when the rich and powerful remove their mask, it often comes with a large price tag attached.

On some invisible signal, Mary returned to clear the dishes. Andrew produced a cigar from somewhere and offered me one, which I declined.

'I didn't know you smoked,' I said.

'This isn't smoking,' he said, puffing away, before examining the cigar. 'Filthy habit, I know. One of those things you more or less had to do after dinner with bankers in Russia. It's been a temptation ever since.'

Woody fumes filled the room. I was feeling drunk, hot, liverish and had the beginnings of a migraine.

'Can I ask you a leading question, Charles?' he said.

I nodded.

'Do you think I deserve this?'

'What – becoming prime minister or the criminal charges?'

'Don't be facetious, it doesn't suit you. I mean it, do you think I deserve this?' He blew another green cloud into the air. 'Do you think I'm good enough?'

'Why does that matter?'

'Because unless you do, why did you back me?' Andrew stood up and began to pace around the small dining room. For some reason I entertained anxious visions as he strode behind my chair, that at any moment, like a psychotic Groucho Marx, he might lean over and poke his burning cigar into my eye.

'I mentioned dreams earlier. It won't surprise you to learn that I've been having some very bad ones. This owl thing has really gone to my head, clearly. So many of them, circling and swooping, crying out. At times, I couldn't tell whether I was sleeping or waking or somewhere in between. In one they flew into my room and ripped apart my most expensive suits. And in another, you came in and cleared them away. Sometimes, it hasn't just been a dream, either. There are things happening, things I don't understand. Damage to the outside of the house, and inside too, for God's sake. One of the damn things must have got in through an open window or door. I gave John hell for that. But I've even been attacked in my own garden.'

He stopped pacing and stood at the table, cigar poised, staring at me. I could see the scratches and marks down one side of his face clearly now.

'It was just a dream, Andrew,' I muttered. 'These events are just unfortunate coincidences, unconnected . . .'

'No, they aren't,' he said. 'I know you can do it for me,

Charles. You can make this . . . owl problem disappear. You're the most trustworthy person I know, you always have been.'

Either the bird we had just consumed hadn't been cooked properly, or wasn't a bird fit for human consumption. I tried not to think about it, but it was hard not to. My stomach pitched and billowed with nausea. The dining room felt hotter than a ship's boiler room, the air as thick and smoky. I wished, too late, that I hadn't complicated matters further with the steamed pudding and dessert wine.

I stood up, unsteadily, clutching my chair.

'Well, Charles? Will you do it?'

'I'm sorry,' I mumbled. 'I must have picked something up in London, I'm not feeling terribly well . . .'

'Fine. Just answer me this one thing before you go,' Andrew said, without a shred of sympathy, stubbing his cigar out in the dregs of the wine. 'I know you believe in me. You are perceptive, you saw the same thing in me that I have known for years. The ability to put my mind to almost any activity and succeed. God knows I have failings in other areas, Charles, just ask Caroline or Helen. But succeeding has never been an issue for me. I have turned a boutique New York investment bank into a global giant. I can do the same for our great country, but not if the opportunity is denied to me because of some ridiculous misunderstanding over a bird of prey. You have been constant and loyal ever since we met. People who may not trust me will believe you. So will you do it for me, Charles? Will you make that sacrifice?'

He was beginning to rant, which did nothing for my nausea. Waving away the cigar smoke, I gingerly made my way towards the door. As I brushed past the heavy curtains, I noticed that the hems were completely shredded. With another heave of my stomach, I realised that no puppy or kitten could have caused such savage damage.

'If not for me, at least for the country,' Andrew called after me.

'Yes,' I turned. The migraine and nausea were so intense I could barely speak. 'Yes, Andrew, I'll do whatever it is you want. Don't worry, we'll get you out of this mess, I'm sure.'

He lifted his arms in silent triumph. I bolted for the ground floor lavatory, and was still throwing up when I heard him mount the stairs for bed.

The next morning I awoke with a ferocious hangover, and a vague sense of having agreed to do something I shouldn't have. I had received an apology of sorts, but as for assurances as to what would happen in the future, they felt very thin on the ground.

For a moment, I lay in bed, dry mouthed and immobile, as memories replayed themselves with a feverish intensity. Andrew in his Gothic coat at the station, his scratched face, then the flames leaping up the chimney, noises at the window, my host wielding his cigar like a lethal weapon.

With a great effort I got myself up and dressed. Drawing back the curtains, I sat on the bed and stared blankly out of the window. The bleak landscape of russets and greys stared blankly back. Except . . . I stood up, and pressed my face to the glass.

Something had changed.

Below my room lay an acre or so of patchy lawn, crudely bisected by a weed-strewn path. A peeling summer house and algae-filled pond completed the view. But beyond the ha-ha which bordered this idyll, the land looked different.

I could have sworn that before, there was at least another

acre of rough pasture between the garden and the wood. That was the memory from my last visit. So either the spruces had matured and grown since then, which seemed unlikely, or Minniver Wood had moved closer to the house.

My exhausted and fevered mind was doubtless confusing things. The last time I had seen the wood was at dusk, and we were drinking. Either way, the darkening aisles between them were gloomier than ever, even in the fresh light of day. The forest appeared to hover above the field, like a shadow of some far older place, a primeval echo. A movement caught my eye, and I started, but it was just the flap of a bird as it left a branch. Probably a wood pigeon.

I thought I would ask Andrew about this unusual phenomenon over breakfast, but when I came down, he was nowhere to be seen. Sitting alone in the farmhouse kitchen, while Mary busied herself behind me at the Aga, I poked at a boiled egg and studied the morning papers.

The furore over the owl was beginning to dominate the headlines. There was more commentary and opinion on the inside pages. Wildlife charities did battle with the motoring lobby over the ethics of what to do with roadkill, while legal experts explained the relevant Act in painstaking detail. The story was already being called Owlgate, which made my heart sink. I had agreed to do something with all this, but what?

The answer came, perhaps appropriately, by way of a text, pinging on to the phone next to my plate. 'I had to leave early to make an urgent shadow Cabinet meeting,' it read. 'Thank you again for being a true ally. Matt will be in touch re next steps.'

Again I felt a sense of unease about what I was being thanked for. I finished my breakfast, made my farewell to the ever silent Mary, grabbed my bag, and let John drive me to the station. I thought I would feel relieved to be out of the oppressive atmosphere of Gilcaster Head and to an extent, I was. But the echoes of my hangover were soon replaced by a far more troubling sensation.

It was slight and flickering, but persistent all the same. The very distinctive feeling that someone, or something, was following me.

2

We sped off towards the station in Andrew's car, with John at the wheel. I noticed that the windscreen had been repaired; all physical trace of the infamous collision was now gone. Sitting on the passenger seat with my overnight case perched on my lap, I wondered whether I should make some attempt at conversation. John and Mary had been nothing but courteous to Caroline and me when we had stayed, but I couldn't recall exchanging more than three words with them in as many months. Their English, as far as it went, seemed flawless, but I did not know how much further it went. And I knew nothing of their former lives, or how they had come to be working for the Landfords.

We approached a tight corner and John put his foot to the floor. We barrelled round, narrowly avoiding a collision with an agricultural digger, its great claw raised in alarm. A phone and some loose change tumbled out of the dashboard compartment on to the floor. My heart leapt into my mouth, but my driver seemed unconcerned, merely reaching down to retrieve his mobile.

I felt I should say something.

'I understand from Andrew that you were . . . in the Gurkhas.'

John gave a broad smile, shaking his wrinkled head. 'Oh yes.'

'What was that like, if you don't mind me asking?'

His smile vanished. 'It was difficult, but nothing compared to how tough life was before. I was a farmer, you see. Life was tough. We made very little money, yet we worked hard. Sometimes in one week we would earn less than . . . four pence?'

I nodded, slightly thrown by the detail and fullness of his answer.

'So I joined the Gurkhas. It was incredible training, only for the fittest. But it was hard, so many people dropped out. Then, I was in Borneo in the Sixties, with the Paras. That was unbelievable. Every day on your feet, in the jungle. We marched through swamps . . . climbed mountains . . . and our packs were heavy. You never knew when you would come under fire. I lost many friends.'

'That must have been awful,' I said dumbly. I hadn't quite realised how old he was.

'The most awful things you ever saw. Some of the nights were so long, I thought I would never see my family again. But all of that is nothing compared to what we face now. My wife and I have no money. We are in our seventies and we have to work like slaves every day of our life just to stay alive. So you ask was I in the Gurkhas? Sure I was. Yet now I can hardly believe that I ever fought for this country.'

I didn't know how to respond. My mind, still sluggish after the hallucinatory events of the previous night, grasped for something to fill the void. Unbidden, an image of something sharp flashed into my mind. I was determined not to make it an owl claw.

'Do you still have your kukri?'

John raised his eyebrows, as if I had asked him if he and his wife enjoyed Scottish dancing in the nude.

'Yes, but now I only use the knife for cooking.'

He shook his head, gnawing his lip, and we were both spared further communication by my phone vibrating in my pocket.

It was Matt Dilcombe. 'Charles, good to hear your voice. Now, where are you?'

'I'm in Gilcaster. I've just left Andrew and I'm on my way back to Newcastle—'

'Can you change your plans? We need you in London. Urgently.'

I tensed with irritation. Even when I was no longer in his employ, Andrew and his team treated me as if I was at their beck and call. What it must be like for the man sitting next to me in the car didn't bear thinking about.

'Can't it wait till tomorrow?'

'I've spoken to Andrew. We are all very grateful Charles, but I think the sooner we resolve this, the better. My PA has looked up some trains . . . there's a direct service to Euston leaving in half an hour. Shall I see you at my office at 6?'

He hung up before I could reply. Minutes later, John's car skidded into the station forecourt and he deposited me and my holdall on the pavement with a wide smile and a wave. The car screeched off before I could mutter a word of thanks. As it was, my mind was now preoccupied with how I was going to explain my delayed return to Caroline, and with something Matt had said. He was grateful, and it was unlike Matt to be grateful for anything. I was curious, so I took the train to London.

*

Matt's office was a small glass box stuffed into the corner of Andrew's open plan estate in St Stephen's Buildings. Most of it was occupied by a large circular wooden table, around which were squeezed Matt and a man in a dark suit wedged between two younger women, none of whom I recognised. The table was scattered with piles of documents, and plastic cups of coffee going cold. Owing to some quirk of the air conditioning, the room managed to be stifling hot and draughty at the same time. I manoeuvred myself into a seat with my back pressed against an internal window.

Matt pressed the door shut, which had the effect of creating an airlock.

'Thank you for coming at such short notice, Charles,' he said without any preamble. 'These guys are Andrew's lawyers.'

I felt constrained as it was, hardly able to move my arms and legs, but I felt my chest tighten even more at the mention of their profession. The man in the dark suit offered a heavy hand across the table.

'Keith Jackman,' he said. 'From Wuk, and these are my colleagues Joanna and Felicity, who will be drafting the paperwork.'

Law was not my field, but I knew 'Wuk' (spelt WK), or at least, I had found it hard to escape their expensive rebranding, the new name sprayed in luminous green over blue billboards wherever one looked. Previously Witheridge and Knight, a firm of solicitors which sounded like it might occupy a dusty Victorian parlour on a provincial high street, it was in fact now one of the largest law firms in the city, occupying a steel monolith in Canary Wharf. Jeremy and I had worked for them once or twice in the Nineties. I had heard the name mentioned again recently, but where exactly I couldn't recall.

Loose ends at some dinner party, no doubt. I did recollect that their clients ranged from petroleum multinationals to tech companies, hedge funds to foreign governments, but had only the vaguest idea why three of their highly paid representatives might be sitting in Matt's office waiting to talk to me.

I presumed it must have something to do with Andrew taking me on board again.

'I didn't know Wuk had an employment law department,' I said as breezily as I could manage.

Everyone stared at me.

'Charles,' said Matt, spreading his hands on the table, 'Keith isn't from employment law. He's on their criminal side.'

'Mr Fryerne,' said Keith Jackman, measuring his words, 'we represent Mr Landford in the matter of Regina v Andrew Landford.' He opened a glossy corporate folder in front of him, and smoothed the white pages down with a hairy hand.

I then realised where I had heard the name of WK more recently than my brush with them in the Nineties. Helen had worked for them. Before Andrew had scooped her up, transforming her into the million-pound haircut wife he had once envisaged Caroline being. He had insisted she give up her job in order to raise the one Landford child that no one ever saw. The last time I saw her, she had been drinking heavily, her breath sweet sour with Chardonnay.

Keith Jackman turned for a moment to Joanna, who whispered in his ear, and thumbed through the sheaf of documents, before laying a densely typed and highlighted page before him. Something about it seemed familiar, but I couldn't divine what. He glanced down at it, before continuing. He had sleepy eyes, which combined with the airless room, and his incantatory tone, left me feeling very drowsy.

'The Crown is preparing to drop the charges against Mr Landford.'

'Finally. About time, too.'

'But they are instead preparing a case against you.'

If I hadn't been so wedged in I would have leapt out of my seat.

'That's absurd. I had nothing to do with it.'

'That is what Mr Landford feels as well . . . it's just unfortunate that the CPS has been handed evidence at a late stage which has persuaded them to take another view. Which is why we need to have your testimony on record, before matters proceed.'

Felicity produced a small digital voice recorder, which she slid across the table towards me. I looked at Matt, my face flushed with bewilderment.

'We're all very grateful, Charles,' he said. 'Andrew is so grateful. He spoke so highly of your honesty and commitment. When all of this is over, you can be sure of a seat at the high table after the next election.'

So this was what I had agreed to, unsettled and drunk, over a dinner table in Cumbria. This was the decisive action Andrew had spoken of. I had moved from communicating the message to in effect being the message. A message of deflection. Suddenly all I wanted was to be very far away from this stifling room. Keith Jackman continued in his soporific drawl.

'The Crown is satisfied that Mr Landford killed the owl at your direction, and is preparing charges on that basis.'

A shot of real anger pulsed through me.

'On what bloody basis? The owl flew into the windscreen, and Andrew was furious that some bird had chipped his precious motor, so he dashed its brains to a pulp. I was a bystander, nothing more.'

Jackman peered down his nose at the page in front of him, and I realised why the blur of names and words seemed familiar.

'But on the 16 October, you were interviewed under caution at Carlisle police station, and said, "We couldn't think of what else to do."'

'So? I was trying to assist Andrew in a very difficult situation. I was going to be one of his advisers, which meant—'

'Andrew would take your advice on how to behave in such a critical situation?'

I could see where this was going.

'I don't think I'd like to say any more on this without my own lawyer present, if you don't mind.'

Keith's baggy face broke into its first smile of the afternoon.

'But Mr Fryerne, we are your lawyers now too. That's why we're here. Mr Landford has asked us to represent you. He's paying.'

By the time the meeting was over, it was past ten in the evening and the last train back to Newcastle had departed. Matt had offered to pay for a hotel, but I didn't want a penny more of Andrew Landford's money that day, if ever. I refused their offer of food and drink as well. I needed to think.

Under the guise of welcoming me back into the fold, oozing flattery over my ability to communicate his message, Andrew had laid a giant trap for me which I had leapt straight into. Keith Jackman had also offered me a very large amount of money, quite possibly a life-changing amount of money, to put myself in line for the criminal charges facing our future prime minister.

'The evidence is circumstantial,' he had drawled, 'but highly persuasive. In exchange for a guilty plea, the sentence may be very light, and if you're lucky, non-custodial. But it's a test case for Andrew's new law, so they're likely to want to set an example.'

'And if I refuse?'

'Then this conversation never happened.'

'How about if I accept?'

'Then this conversation still never happened, but please take this with Mr Landford's sincerest thanks for your trouble.' He pushed a thick cream envelope across the table. I knew what was inside, but I didn't even touch it.

They did not allow me to leave without signing several documents in triplicate, witnessed by Matt. If I didn't sign them, Andrew would sue me for breach of confidence over the Maldwyn deal. If I did sign, I wouldn't be able to tell anyone about the attempted bribe, whether I agreed to face the charges or not. If I signed them and changed my mind, they would sue me. In the end – whatever I did – Andrew would (unless the polls changed dramatically) fulfil his dream of running the country.

I wondered whether I should just obediently lie down and accept my role in the grander narrative. Did I believe a word of what I had written about Andrew for my profile of him? If I did, then I felt bound to support his political project, and play my part in its successful completion. My whole family history was predicated on a Fryerne lending critical aid to a usurper king at his time of need. True, he had not been obliged to sign a non-disclosure agreement amongst the corpses and gore of Bosworth Field, but perhaps as a backdrop, they were of a similarly persuasive nature. On the other hand, if I didn't believe a word of what I had written, then what little integrity I still possessed evaporated in a single weak puff before my eyes.

I was no Fryerne knight. But I was not prepared to accept my fate without a battle, either. My thoughts ablaze with feelings of betrayal and injustice, I hoped a walk would offer some relief. Winter was drawing in, the streets around Andrew's offices in Euston were blank and unlit. The trade union officials and civil engineering consultants who occupied the anonymous towers by day had long since departed for the shires or the pub, and only the odd rough sleeper remained, huddled under cardboard boxes and sleeping bags. Everything reeked of abandonment. Car parks, warehouses, a library. I hurried down avenues of garage shutters, security gates and blank walls. They seemed to be closing in on me, and at times I felt short of breath.

At the end of the street, a shadow soared in and out of the street lamp's arc. It could have been a large city crow or some less friendly bird.

I quickly turned the corner, and found myself wandering through a grid of grubby Edwardian terraces towards Mornington Crescent, where Caroline kept her basement studio. At a certain time of day sunlight flooded down through the railings and she could often be found on the greening steps, wrapped in a Persian shawl and sucking meditatively on a cigarette.

My hand rested for a moment on the flaking iron gate at the top of the steps. We had not spoken since I went to visit Andrew. We were only just speaking before I left. I felt that he was coming between us in a way he never had when she was actually living with him. All things considered, it had been a very bad idea for us to reconnect with him after all that time. Right from the moment he had collected us from the station on that night in his polished Range Rover, he had begun to cloud the very air we breathed.

The gate squeaked open, and I paused on the front step, looking behind me. Parked cars lined both sides of the road, and here and there were lighted front rooms. Further up the road I could hear a couple laughing as they walked along. I was being ridiculous. There were no angry owls in Mornington Crescent.

I hurried down the steps, and peered in, through a clay-smeared window, at the dimly lit silhouettes of Caroline's new sculptures, some still resting under cloth, ready to be fired and glazed. This must be for her new show, the one she had so obsessively kept secret from me.

It was Saturday and I knew she was back in Newcastle. But after the trap Andrew had laid the previous night, and the grim ambush of this afternoon, I needed to feel close to her in some way. I had a key. The door opened slowly, against a pile of junk mail. There was a musty smell about the place that I did not remember being there before. I wondered if Caroline had left something to rot in the small fridge she kept in the kitchen. It was unlikely, as normally the only thing to be found in there was a bottle of white burgundy.

I headed on into the studio, and as I did, I felt something under foot.

Something soft and brittle at the same time.

A draught from nowhere sucked the door shut behind me with a slam. When I looked down I saw that the floor was covered with feathers. The nausea I had been feeling over the last two days now threatened to overpower me completely, and fumbling for a light switch in the dark, I stumbled into one of the new statues arranged on the bench.

It was smooth and cold to the touch. As I stepped back, I saw with horror what it was.

An enormous owl, carved out of black stone, its wings raised, its eyes fixed in a furious glare. The work to make it must have been back-breaking. And, I saw now, all the new sculptures were of a similar turn. Owls. Sitting on a bench in a row and staring at me. I could see why Caroline had kept this new work hidden from me. For a moment, it was as if I had stumbled into an ancient temple. Hook-winged, beak-nosed, cold-eyed, they were a line of implacable judges, designed to sit in judgement for eternity.

By design or not, Andrew's single act of violence had now penetrated every corner of our lives. The birds demanded justice and would not be appeased until it was done.

3

The next day, I sat on the train to Newcastle checking my phone again and again for any news stories that might suggest it was I who had advised Andrew to kill the owl. It wouldn't be long before Matt Dilcombe made sure that the briefing was falling on to every editor's desk. Yet there was nothing. As I scrolled through various news sites by way of distraction, I came across other headlines. 'WHY ANDREW LANDFORD ISN'T FIT TO LEAD THE COUNTRY' turned out to be a disconnected series of mini-rants about Andrew's political beliefs and background. There was no coherent articulation of either his or Maldwyn's actual positions, and no mention of the dead owl, but there was, to my surprise, a mention of Merlin's.

'Landford was a member of the elite Oxbridge supper club Merlin's, which regularly caused thousands of pounds worth of damage to local businesses.'

I recalled that certainly being true of Merlin's, at least in the past, but as I had never seen Andrew at any of the dinners, blaming him for that behaviour seemed unfair. Merlin's had never held any real power in Oxford, and Andrew Landford's rise to the top was entirely of his own making. Blaming or giving credit for that rise to a self-important dining club seemed to be obscuring the issue. Maldwyn had never been a member. Andrew had joined purely for show but almost never attended. The source of their power lay quite outside its gilded halls, and refusing to acknowledge that seemed blinkered to me.

The more interesting story that I had once heard about Andrew and an accident with a punting pole seemed to have been swallowed up by history. Or erased from public view with clinical precision. I wondered if I was heading the same way.

Caroline opened the door to me in stockinged feet, a cigarette dangling from her hand. I kissed her, but found her stiff and unresponsive.

Without another word, she turned, and I followed her into the house, my bag trailing behind me.

Even by her standards, the house was a tip. Piles of plates, unwashed glasses, overflowing ashtrays and heaps of clothes lay everywhere. There was a smell in the air, an unlikeable combination of clay and cigarette smoke, as in her basement studio. No owl feathers covered the floor, at least, but I could not help noticing the sharp scratches down several of the tall windows.

She led me into the kitchen, where she sat and rested her feet on the table, still smoking. I dropped on to a small wooden chair opposite her and we regarded one another through the haze.

'Well, buddy?' she asked, finally.

I shrugged.

'Did you clear your name? Did you clear our name? Did you finally tell that bastard where to go?'

I didn't need to reply. I could barely look my own wife in the eye. She sighed.

'I thought as much. Because the owls sure as hell haven't

stopped.' She flicked a bit of ash in the direction of the scarred window. 'You know, I'm beginning to wonder whether you're capable of standing up for anything.'

'It's not that simple. It's hard when you don't know what to believe.'

Caroline snorted. 'What to believe? It's not very hard. He ran over an owl and bashed its brains out on a wall.'

'Well, firstly, that's not quite true . . . the owl flew into the windscreen first, he didn't run it over . . . but regardless of that, it's not what I believe about the owl. It's what I believe about Andrew.'

What I still believed, couldn't help believing, despite the way he had treated me. There was no denying that he was a master communicator, popular with the party, with a vision for the country that resonated with the electorate. That was the problem with being someone who had a reputation for telling the truth. Even when it wounded me directly, I could always see his strengths. I was baffled by self-delusion. I was turning into my father, who continued to believe in the institutions that had left him out to fester. Caroline gave an angry laugh.

'That he's a controlling, psychopathic monster who will stop at nothing to get into power?'

I shook my head. Caroline's analysis of Andrew was surely skewed by her personal history with him.

'Maybe he is controlling. But what if he actually is also a good thing for the country? Plenty of leaders are sociopaths to a degree. Look at Thatcher. Perhaps she needed to be. Andrew is strong. You've seen him work a crowd, work a room – the man has something. We have wave after wave of dull jobbing politicians who turn the voters off, and then someone comes along with that electrifying presence, the

ability to project charisma and vision, to bring about change
. . . and you think we should trash him for the sake of a
single bird? Is it worth throwing away that bigger truth for
a smaller one?' I could scarcely believe my own words, yet
out they tumbled. 'They're going to claim I killed the owl.
I know what you're going to say, but listen to me, it's one
small sacrifice for a grander aim—'

She cut me off with a wave of her arm, stubbed out her
cigarette and got up. 'I want to give up on you, Charlie boy.
I want to give up on you so bad. But the thing is I just can't
. . .' Her voice faltered and she left the room.

I seemed to spend the next week sitting at the same kitch-
en table, in a state of near-paralysis. I did leave the house,
several times, never for a good reason, but my memory is of
unseasonably strong November sunshine flooding through
the tall windows, the nicotine-stained kitchen reeking of
stale smoke, my head itching with sweat as my phone hopped
about angrily on the table, buzzing like an oversized beetle
bruising for a fight.

Matt and his team planted the seeds of my destruction
carefully. First, it was reported as rumour, radio reports
promising 'that we will learn later today', then the rumour
was confirmed through a press conference during which
Andrew dropped me in it with very little ceremony – although with no personal acrimony, at least – and finally
the story broadcast far and wide. As far as the world was
concerned, I was responsible for all the savagery formerly
attributed to Andrew. It was nothing short of a miracle that
they hadn't also suggested I arrange for the owl to fly into
the windscreen in the first place.

Anything resembling the facts of the case had receded so

far into the distance that it was impossible even to make out their outline. Facts had been replaced by something far more tempting and palatable. A plausible lie that people would want to swallow.

And swallow it they did, with relish.

I received so much abuse from assorted party loyalists and owl lovers, both electronically and physically, that I had to close various email accounts. I even felt the wrath of the distant Fryernes. A crumpled postcard in a stained envelope arrived from Alan Fryerne-Smith, the strange individual I had encountered at my father's funeral. He accused me in a spindly hand of 'bringing the Fryerne name into disrepute', and threatened to snub the next Fryerne gathering, which of all the many threats I received that week, was probably the most welcome.

Maldwyn, in typical low-key fashion, declined to exploit the revelations to his own advantage, merely issuing a statement alongside Andrew's that flatlined with non-judgemental disappointment. He didn't ring or email, and I didn't contact him. His non-statement said everything.

After a few days, Caroline and I stopped opening the post and let it pile up by the front door. This shoal of envelopes grew and grew, like a drift of autumn leaves, making it almost impossible to get out of the house.

Leaving the building was further complicated by the group of journalists and photographers now camped on the steps, who even if I went out to buy a pint of milk from the corner shop, flashed light bulbs and shouted questions in my face.

'Did you really kill the owl, Mr. Fryerne? Or are you covering for Landford?'

'Are you going to admit it in court, Charlie?'

'Is Landford paying you?'

In the early days of the story, they tailed me to our local police station, where I endured a day-long interview, going over the same ground so many times that I began to wonder whether the whole incident had been a dream. The Newcastle police were far more organised than their colleagues in Carlisle. Now they produced enlarged photographs of the stretch of road in question, snaps of the long-dead owl next to a tape measure. They also temporarily relieved me of my mobile phone and laptop, which was probably just as well – given the torrent of abuse flooding into them.

Andrew had a sudden change of heart over paying my legal fees, no doubt seeking to put as much legal and professional distance between us as possible. I learned this from Keith Jackson and his sharp-suited colleagues at Wuk via a very terse one-line email. So I faced the police officer's barrage of questioning with an amiable but clueless family solicitor by my side, recommended by a friend of Caroline. His main contribution to proceedings was to repeatedly offer me a fruit pastille and ask if I was feeling all right. Then Mr Barraclough of Barraclough's would sit with me in the breaks and rub a hand over his drooping features, and talk about how new all this Internet stuff was.

I returned to our house under another barrage of flash bulbs, but soon began to wonder if they might be preferable to the punishing silence I endured from Caroline indoors. She had chosen not to return to London, worried that the press hounding there would be even worse.

The only other time I left the house for any considerable amount of time during this purgatory was for a short but decisive meeting at the university, where a self-important panel of managers showered me with platitudes about dutiful service and appreciation before suspending me on full pay with immediate effect.

I took my cue and wrote a letter of regretful resignation to the Vice Chancellor, apologising for any damage I had caused the institution. It was an act of faith, implying that one day, I might not only want my job back but be in a position to take it.

In this alternative universe, it was not the strong and decisive leader of the Conservative Party who had mindlessly smashed out the brains of a defenceless owl. It was his 'so-called' communications adviser – which was in fact a title Andrew had invested me with only after the weekend in question, but now hung like a dunce's placard around my neck. My up and down employment record with Andrew only contributed to the impression that I was inflating my own importance. That notwithstanding, the same commentators who decried my level of importance in 'the Landford circle' never once doubted my ability to fatally influence him at a critical moment, when he held the life of a protected species in his hands.

In addition to contending with the plodding but insistent police investigation, and along with the shrill daily attacks from the wildlife lobby, the commentariat and the government, Andrew himself flung several flaming bolts at my head. He sweet-talked his neighbour Tom Gazelee into a tabloid 'Exclusive' in which Gazelee confirmed I had denied all knowledge of the accident at our chance meeting the following day. Apparently 'my silence spoke volumes'. Andrew's more vocal denials at the time were not mentioned. I also happened to notice in the same edition of the paper, buried in the back pages, a piece about the campaign Tom was organising to have a local Roman temple site properly excavated.

While this onslaught continued, Caroline finally decamped to London. Our muttered farewell in the hate-mail-strewn hallway was the only meaningful conversation we'd had for days. Despite the pressure, she looked more bright-eyed than she had in months. Perhaps it was the prospect of uninterrupted work in her London studio. Or being without me. Or both.

She gave a sad laugh, shaking her head.

'I've still got faith in you, believe it or not. I've got faith that one day you will finally understand what standing up for the truth actually involves.'

Then she was gone, dragging her bag down the steps to the click-clack chorus of cameras.

That evening I hauled myself into bed, pale-faced and twitchy from too much screen gazing. It was hard to resist when your own invented past and projected future was the subject of the drama. Pressure was mounting fast on the CPS to bring matters to a head. Senior party figures argued that it would be impossible to conduct a fair general election with any kind of cloud hanging over Andrew.

I lay back on my pillow and stared at the ceiling. Outside, the camera crews had packed up for the night and retreated to a nearby pub. Raindrops began to patter gently against the windows, the street lights casting them into a Morse code of dot and dash shadows over the floor. Wind rattled the crumbling sash frame. And then came another sound. Faint at first – it might have been a distant siren, or perhaps a passing drunk – but then the unmistakeable sound of hooting began to echo through the room.

Perhaps I was asleep, or having a waking dream. Perhaps my over-stimulated brain was suffering a hallucination. Either way, the effect was the same. I had grown used to beaks and claws scraping at the windows and the hooting in the night. But this time it was different. In my mind the birds seemed to be calling to me. They cried and screeched until I pulled the covers tight over my head, and somehow drifted off into a restless sleep.

The next morning, I awoke with new thoughts that formed slowly and inexorably in my head. The owls knocked, they called, but they never did *me* any harm, or even much lasting damage to the windows. They were not coming after me or Caroline.

There were other players in the drama who knew the truth after all, who had the most passionate cause to defend it. Perhaps, I thought, the owls were offering their help.

4

How exactly any form of assistance from my winged allies might materialise was less clear. But some form of aid was urgently required and I would take it from any quarter. The fevered media and political speculation was rising to a crescendo.

So it was not entirely a surprise when, a few days later, a sombre-suited Director of Public Prosecutions announced to a bouquet of microphones that after due consideration, there was 'ample and compelling evidence' that I should be tried on the new charge of 'inciting another to commit an offence against the Wildlife and Countryside Act'.

Perhaps I should have felt a sense of relief that the waiting was over. But in truth, I felt nothing. As is the modern way, I discovered the news via the public statement on television. The summons arrived later in the day by courier. I accepted without comment and withdrew into the house. The questions from the press mob on the doorstep no longer alarmed me, or seemed in any way unusual. They had become part of my daily routine, as the owls had made the night time their own.

I did what was required of me. I called Mr Barraclough who murmured his professional sympathies over the phone, and advised me not to book any holidays, before walking me through the court appearance that was to follow, and asking me for information which seemed both irrelevant and unlikely to change anything. I waited in vain for a call from the people who still mattered in my life. Caroline. Andrew. Maldwyn. But none came.

I discovered Andrew's view, of course, quite easily. He told the 'World at One' that 'it was a sad day for British politics and in particular, political advisers'. He also used the opportunity to call for reform to the system which provided advisers and vetted them, a system of which I was not previously aware. Batting away questions about his own culpability, I could almost hear him brandishing a rolled Wildlife and Countryside Act over the radio. The interview was followed by a short report on how this reversal of fortunes was gaining him traction amongst the undecided voters in the country, claiming that 'even those who disliked him on initial acquaintance will have changed their minds following Andrew Landford's superb handling of these ridiculous and unfounded allegations'.

Late one evening, as I was scraping the pallid remains of some ready meal into the bin, my phone rang. But it wasn't Caroline. It was Brad.

'Charles, how you holding up?' He was much older now, and thousands of miles away across the Atlantic, but his gravelly, soft voice purred out of the speaker as if we were sitting opposite each other in leather club armchairs, each clutching our scotch and soda. He didn't wait for my reply. 'Terrible business, if you ask me. We're all behind you, Charles, the whole clan. This thing stinks to high heaven. Is there anything I can do?'

'That's very kind of you Brad, but not really—'

'Leave it to me, Charlie. I'll make a few calls. Help out

where I can. And look on the bright side – you won't be the first Fryerne this has happened too.'

This was news. 'Really?'

'Ha! I knew you'd never read all of Uncle Roland's book. Well some of us have had more than a couple of transatlantic flights to fill over the years. You should perhaps read up on the first Charles Fryerne.'

My fragmented mind wasn't really up for a history tutorial, but somehow summoned up the founding images of the Fryerne clan. Bosworth Field. Henry Tudor.

'Yes . . . I remember now. There was a story about him helping the king on the battlefield or something. That's how our ancestors got the house and the name in the first place.'

Or at least, that's how I'd understood it. Like all such stories, I couldn't ever say whether I'd believed it or not. Uncle Roland's laboriously produced piece of private genealogy, full of generalised assertions backed up by highly selective interpretations of rolls and church registers, had never convinced on the facts.

'Well, to cut a long story short, I hired someone over here to look into the whole thing a while back.'

'In God's name, why?'

'No real reason. I guess I was curious. Too much time and too much money, Charles. Story of my life, you could say.'

'Who?'

'I can't remember now. Some old eagle from Harvard got me one of his brightest and best sophomores digging around . . . Anyhow, you'll never guess what they found.'

I trusted that my silence spoke volumes. Brad ploughed on.

'There was a Fryerne at Bosworth Field. He was recognised by the new king with a grant of land after the battle. But he didn't start the day fighting for Henry

Tudor. He was with the other guy, the hunchback.'

'Richard III?'

'Exactly. Except he stabbed him in the ribs when he saw which way the wind was blowing. Which is what I'm trying to tell you, Charlie. Loyalty and truth are fine, but they only get you so far in this game. Your old man would have approved of the way you're playing this. Hell, I approve. But you want to win in this game, you need to play dirty. I've got the number of a lawyer for you to call . . .'

Brad continued to talk but my mind was elsewhere, slipping off into the deep Atlantic waters. I had finished with lawyers, of any kind. I was playing what Brad described as a game the only way I knew how, and losing badly. His suggestion was not the answer, but he was right that I could not possibly win on my own. I made my excuses and hung up.

I tried Caroline a couple of times, at her studio and on the mobile, but got no answer. She had disappeared from my life with the same consummate grace and ease with which she had first entered it. Realising that made me miss her even more. I briefly considered an impulsive dash to London, but the thought faded before it had even begun. Perhaps she was working, or like me, festering in a trough of inaction. Wherever she was, I knew she would be waiting for me to find a way to redeem myself and rescue my name. My first court appearance was the following day, and somehow I didn't think redemption was amongst the likely outcomes.

The afternoon shadows behind me lengthened, and I could hear the edgeless noise of a radio from the flat next door. I contemplated calling Andrew once or twice, but thought better of it. He would either ignore me or box clever, and I was in no form to retaliate.

I realised that what I actually felt was an earnest and

heartfelt desire *not* to communicate. I had done little else for the last twenty years but investigate, articulate and communicate the views of others. Motivations had been laid bare, ambitions projected, visions encapsulated, arguments distilled. Suddenly, all I really wanted was peace.

The peace and stillness of the owl wood.

I pressed myself flat against the kitchen wall, and peered sideways out of the window, at the press pack camped outside, waiting to capture the moment of my downfall. But their flashlights and satellite dishes faded into a distant blur, and I was in another room – one that felt a world away. I was sitting amongst the polished oak chairs and tables of the Fryerne Arms, squinting through the bay window, across the car park at the row of drab post-war detached houses where Fryerne Court had once stood. My father was searching for his notes and getting to his feet. Caroline was standing, and beckoning me upstairs.

But I ignored them all. I dismissed my mother, reaching out for me. I even left Caroline standing at the bottom of the stairs. Instead, I walked out into the car park, under the sagging carvery banner and the blinking coloured bulbs. I looked across the road at the manicured asphalt drives and the neat pitched roofs where the house had once stood. There was not a trace of it left. Uncle Roland's book had been mostly conjecture. My parents now existed only in my memory. I was the last Fryerne of Fryerne Court.

It meant nothing, and yet I felt more committed to it now than ever before. There was, perhaps, some way to give the role meaning.

I could not rebuild the house, but I could at least do something worthy of the trust the family had placed in me.

I could start by telling the truth.

5

The magistrate's court in Newcastle was a monumental lump of grey and forbidding stone. A north-eastern December morning at its bleakest did nothing to favour the architecture.

I approached the building on foot, having asked the mini-cab driver to drop me a few streets away, as I wanted to get some air before being plunged into the chilly embrace of the justice system.

Air I certainly got, as I approached my every step was dogged by cameras and recording devices thrust into my face. 'Are you sorry for what you've done, Mr Fryerne?' 'Do you think you've wrecked Andrew Landford's election chances?' 'Do you like being cruel to animals, Charlie?'

I stretched out my hands in front of my eyes, like a man trying to shield himself from a distant explosion, and marched on. A young constable in a high-visibility jacket did his best to intervene, but his presence did little to mollify the press and the general hounding continued unabated.

Yet despite the cacophony, for the first time in weeks, I felt calm inside. I had no faith in trial by media, and only limited faith in trial by magistrate. But I had faith in something else. What exactly, I was struggling to comprehend. I only knew it had something to do with the winged creatures who had been haunting my dreams.

Then a different voice, which sounded out of key with the rest of the pack, said 'Do you regret betraying the family name, Charles?' It could have been my father, or my mother. Or Uncle Roland. Even Brad. I put down my hands and looked up, but there was only the same cameraman in a fleece I had seen everywhere, adjusting his focus, and the reporter who seemed barely out of school, adjusting his tie and asking me questions about animal rights.

The sheet taped to the peeling wall announced that my hearing was in just over an hour. Waiting in the vestibule, sitting on cheap furniture I stared at the wall, while Mr Barraclough wobbled his jowls through the depressing state of play. 'Not looking good I'm afraid . . . rather formidable witness statement by Mr Landford . . . highly respected politician, of course . . . his neighbour is none too keen on you and it rather looks like the local constabulary have now taken their MP's side as well . . . the RSPB is sending an expert witness . . . something of an owl crusader, it seems . . . in short, unless you have any rabbits in hats . . .'

I thought for a brief moment of mentioning my quasi-vision of the other night, but one look at Barraclough reminded me that he was not the sort of man who would regard hallucinations favourably. Shaking my head, I took a sip of coffee out of a thin plastic cup. 'What are we looking at, do you think – a fine or some kind of community sentence?'

I had, of course, tried to discuss this with him before over several fruit pastilles. But Mr Barraclough had fudged and fussed, endlessly deferring the matter, and now my optimistic fantasy of helping a team of young offenders to rescue baby owls was swept away by his first straight answer.

'Oh dear, Charles, I thought we'd . . . It's just that you're being charged with incitement, you see . . . Unfortunately that's rather more serious than if Landford had just run the thing over . . . In the eyes of the law – and this area is very much not my expertise, as you know – you inciting him to do it is as serious an offence as organising a dog fight. Then there's perverting the course of justice when you lied to the police. And this is something of a test case . . .'

The litany of punishment about to be brought down upon me rolled on and on.

I glanced around the echoing corridors and stairways of the court building for any sign of owls poised to fly to my aid, but there wasn't even a pigeon pecking on a window ledge. The only solution was to pretend that what happened today didn't matter, it was only the first step of many down a deep and winding staircase. There might be appeals. While I sat and contemplated my fate, my phone buzzed in my pocket. I glanced at the screen and saw I had several missed calls from an unidentified caller, and a voicemail from a Cumbria number I suspected might be the local police station. As I tried to check the message, my solicitor put his pink hand on my arm. 'They'll ask you to turn that off, I'm afraid. Not allowed.'

I obliged him, and shortly after, the main group of witnesses filed past us towards a waiting room. Then it was Andrew's turn. As he swept into the court building backlit by the same flashing lights as me, Andrew had never looked more presidential. He was surrounded by an entourage of advisers, including Matt Dilcombe, and wheeled past me towards the waiting room in a blur of pinstripe. I kept my head down, staring at the cooling coffee in my cup. Then, halfway down the corridor, Andrew stopped. Breaking free of his scrum, he came back and stood before me.

'I don't think I should be talking to you,' I said.

'No,' said Andrew. 'But I just wanted to let you know that I'm very grateful. We all are. For everything you've done.'

'Well. We'll see,' I muttered.

'I'm sorry we haven't had much of a chance to chat before now . . . but as you can imagine, it's been non-stop.'

I glanced up at him. Immersed in trying to shape my own impending future, I had almost forgotten about the political image I had once been hired to help manage. Andrew's hair was immaculate, his tie perfectly knotted, his suit pristine, but there was something in his face that alarmed me. He, or someone close to him, had tried to conceal them with make-up, but the scratches were still there. And there were more of them. He was about to return to his pack, but I called out after him.

'May I ask you one thing?'

He shrugged.

'They attacked you, didn't they? You know they will never rest until they get what they want.'

His eyes had never looked more cold. There was only the tiniest twitch at the edge of his mouth that let me know the truth.

'I'm afraid I don't know what you're talking about.'

Then he was gone, disappearing into a side room. Others followed. Helen, who tottered past with barely a frosty nod in my direction, leaving the very faintest scent of brandy in the air behind her. Tom Gazelee, wearing filthy farm boots, treading mud all over the place. The policemen from Cumbria. A wild-haired woman in a cable-knit jumper stomped past, who Barraclough revealed to me was the expert witness from the RSPB. There was also a motoring expert, whom we had summoned as a defence witness, and then . . .

She was the last to arrive.

The doors to the outside world slid open one final time and my heart skipped a beat as Caroline stepped in, removing a large hat and looking around, stamping her wet shoes on the entrance mat. She spoke briefly to the receptionist who pointed her in our direction. I looked over and waved, and her expression was one of such injury that I thought it was unlikely I would see or hear anything that pained me more over the next few hours, whatever was said in the courtroom.

Moments later, she stood before me, her winter coat fringed with drops of bright rain. There were bags under her eyes, and she had lost weight. Catching sight of my expression, she broke into a grimace.

'You aren't exactly an oil painting, yourself, Charlie.'

'I've missed you so much,' I said.

She nodded, eyeing the people drifting across the hallway.

'You're still seeing those damn birds, huh?'

'Andrew is too, but he won't admit it.'

'So what are you going to do in there that will make any of it stop?'

'I'm going to tell the truth.'

The words felt limp in my mouth, as I was no longer quite sure what telling the truth actually meant. Caroline clasped my hands. It wasn't so much a loving gesture as an act of desperation. 'Me too, Charlie. So make sure you do.'

I wanted to talk to her about so much suddenly – about her work, where she'd been staying, even the wretched owls – but she had already released me.

'You understand I can't . . . not till this is over,' she said, looking down at her boots. 'I want to be there for you. I am there for you. But I miss the old Charlie. The guy who said right out what he thought.'

'Yes, well . . . that seems to have got me into this mess in the first place.'

'And it can get you out of it,' she said, then she pecked me on the cheek before disappearing to wait with the other witnesses.

The waiting continued. 10 a.m., the allotted time for my appearance, came and went. Officials emerged from the courtroom, some stopping to have whispered conversations with Barraclough that he chose not to share with me. Landford dispatched a couple of earnest-faced young men from his encampment to find out what was going on, but they had no more luck than us. I looked meaningfully at Barraclough, who shrugged. 'I think there's some kind of delay,' he mouthed helpfully, before popping another sweet down his throat.

It didn't matter. I had made up my mind. Or rather, Caroline, the sight of her, the sound of her voice, her scent, had brought me to my senses.

'Mr Barraclough,' I began. 'I've changed my mind. In regards to the plea . . .'

But before I could make my grand declaration, the clerk of the court marched out from his lair, and summoned Barraclough into a huddle with the prosecuting solicitor. Mr Barraclough seemed to inflate majestically to twice his size, like a pinstriped barrage balloon, as he addressed them. Phrases drifted over towards me . . . 'New evidence . . . come to light . . . quite impossible . . .'

Something had happened, but I had no idea what.

Photographers began to hammer on the doors of the courthouse, held back by police, even jumping up and down trying to get a shot.

Barraclough sat down with a contented sigh, loosening his tie in satisfaction. 'Don't count your horses,' he beamed, 'but we might be looking at postponing till next week, to give us a chance to review the new evidence.'

I was about to ask him to explain further when, amid an explosion of protesting voices, Andrew shot out of the door further down the corridor and strode past us, the huddle of his praetorian guard marching alongside him. He didn't give me or Mr Barraclough a second glance, but headed straight for the exit, brushing aside the attempts of court officials and police to stop him.

As he vanished into the scrum outside, I heard a brief cry of 'Are you going to resign, Mr Landford?' Inside the court building, there was only shocked silence as the court staff gaped at one another in astonishment.

'Where does he think he's going?' my solicitor wheezed. 'He's a major witness!'

I didn't care whether it was allowed or not. I fired up my phone and skipped down some concrete steps to the gents, where standing on the seat in a cubicle and holding the device aloft, I managed to find a bar of signal.

The BBC website was tinted in garish blues and purples. But not so much that I couldn't see exactly what was going on. There was the now all too familiar scrum of microphones and cameras outside a building, which I soon recognised as the Cumbria police station where Andrew and I had given our interview. The scrum seemed to be swallowing two people, but eventually they were allowed to pass, their hands raised for protection. And there, blinking in the flashlights, were two people I had not given a moment's thought to since I last saw them.

John and Mary, the housekeepers at Gilcaster Head.

They had – as the rolling banner across the bottom of the screen, the texts and emails now swarming into my mobile all repeatedly informed me – sold their version of the story.

A version that could not be more different to the one Her Majesty's Leader of the Opposition had been preparing to swear to on oath in court.

6

John and Mary's story was told for the first time in painful detail to a tabloid reporter, who had been stalking them for some time. 'John', more properly known as Rai Thurpa, had served with the Gurkhas in Borneo in the early days, but a back injury had forced him into early retirement. On his return to Britain, he was rewarded with a fraction of the pension and benefits extended to other members of the military forces with comparable service. Without any other means to support himself and his wife, he decided to use what he had learned in his time in the camp kitchens and got work 'doing' for some retired military chiefs and their families.

Andrew and Helen had always had occasional staff, even when he was just starting out in Notting Hill. But when Gilcaster Head was acquired, they soon realised they would need someone to manage and maintain the property when they were not in residence. A chance meeting with Andrew's Uncle Gerald at a family birthday party had led to an introduction to 'Mary and John'. The Thurpas and the Landfords had got on well initially but this all changed as soon as they settled into Gilcaster Head. The reasons were now made all too clear in the Thurpas' confessional which was emblazoned on every front page in the land: 'Low pay, verbal harassment, racial abuse and unsatisfactory working conditions.' Their repayment in kind had been to eavesdrop on and record some of the more sensational conversations at Gilcaster Head using their phones. John had stood at the door and listened when Matt Dilcombe had asked us all to reveal any skeletons in our closets. Not only did he have all of that conversation on tape, but he also had Andrew confessing to the owl incident and seeking our counsel after the event. The indiscreet conversation I had had with Caroline while John was driving proved to be just that. Several noisy and drunken rows between the Landfords that I was unaware of were also alluded to, but most damaging of all, they had a recording of Helen yelling at Andrew, 'Why didn't you just take it to the vet like Charles suggested? Why do you never listen to anyone else?' Finally, there was a shaky video of our recent supper, with glimpses of Andrew pacing about with a cigar, promising me that I would be 'thanked'.

Until John and Mary had suggested otherwise, in the public view, Andrew Landford had only committed the sin of being caught up in a minor road traffic accident, the kind many people in Britain had every day. He had also been poorly advised, both at the time and since, by the kind of cynical media professionals who exerted too strong a grip on politics in general. Yet despite these unfortunate attacks on his character and good name, he had stayed strong. He had not ducked the questions in interviews, but faced them head-on. It was agreed that overall the entire saga had only highlighted the value of British wildlife and intensified public support for its protection; an outcome few could grumble at. The perseverance, strength and decisiveness he had shown were deemed to be the fundamental qualities required in a party leader and potential prime minister.

What Andrew hadn't counted on was how the public would react when the mask finally slipped.

Despite the dismay and shock rippling out from the large rock his former domestic servants had just lobbed into this pond of perfection, Andrew seemed oblivious as he once more addressed the press from the steps of Conservative Central Office. His face seemed redder and more inflamed than ever as he looked down the barrel of the lens. It was absurd, but I felt my pulse quicken, as if he were addressing me directly.

'You will be aware of the very serious allegations that have been made today against me and my wife by some former employees. Let me be very clear about one thing. I will contest their claims with every fibre of my being. I will not rest until they are defeated. However, I would like to thank the Thurpas for bringing to my attention the scandalous way in which brave Gurkhas are being treated by our country, and I will make improving their conditions a priority for any future Conservative government. But let us not allow gossip and rumour to divide us. I was recently elected to speak for a party which seeks to represent the whole nation, be you Gurkha or owl. We believe Britain can do better. I believe in our future success. If you want to be part of that success, come and join the Conservative Party. I have no further comment at this time.'

And with that, Andrew pocketed his notes and withdrew behind a glossy front door into the shadows. I wasn't sure if I had misheard the line about Gurkha or owl, but in the event, it was the last thing the listening journalists would pick up on.

It would also be the final time Andrew Landford spoke in public.

That was on a Friday. After that, Andrew declined all further opportunities to put his side of the story to the public. He was like a dog racing off with a bird in its mouth, refusing to listen to a single entreaty to drop the prize. Over the weekend, soundbites began to appear in the press from former loyalists in the party, with statements such as, 'I still have total confidence in Andrew,' which meant more or less that the game was up. In the lobbies and the tea rooms of the House, the leadership struggle seemed anything but settled by the recent contest, and members' allegiances were jumping to Maldwyn faster than iron filings to a magnet.

By Sunday morning, the crescendo of dismay over Andrew's treatment of his staff, and their all too audible proof of his true feelings had quite overwhelmed any lingering resonance his oratory may have had.

By Monday, calls for his immediate resignation were being publicly made, by those in the party and outside. On Monday afternoon, the CPS indicated that it was once again looking to press charges against him, on a number of fronts, from obstructing the course of justice to defrauding the Revenue.

But Andrew didn't resign.

He disappeared.

Calls to his phone went unanswered. He had not been seen at his office, his London flat, or Westminster.

As news of his disappearance spread, speculation began to fan out like wildfire, burning sense and reason in its path. He had gone to America. He had made some kind of defection to Russia. He was at the bottom of the Thames. The police made a brief and inconclusive search of both his homes, to no avail.

Which was when Maldwyn rang me. 'I'm assuming you haven't bumped him off for setting you up,' he began.

'I'm not really in the mood for jokes . . .'

'You rarely are. My finest lines are wasted on you. I need your help all the same. Your favourite owl murderer and mine has vanished off the face of the earth. Not answering his mobile, nor any landlines, nowhere to be seen in Westminster or Westmoreland. Even his worst enemies are worried.'

'I thought you'd be thrilled. He's probably cooling off somewhere. You know how . . . exercised he can get. Can't you take over the reins while he sorts his act out?'

There was an exasperated sigh at the end of the phone. 'That's precisely what I'm worried about. The last thing the party needs is the newly elected leader doing anything rash. I'm champing at the bit to take over but he does need to resign first. We have a mechanism to depose him, of course, but the worry is he'll do something reckless while he's still in office.'

'And what do you expect me to do about it?'

'He has always listened to you, Charles. I know that he must be your least favourite psychopathic former employer in the world right now, but won't you have a shot at bringing him to heel? Besides, as former members of that absurd dining club I would have thought you were sworn to help him by some Masonic oath or other. You've always been able to talk truth to power, that's why we love you so.'

'Go to hell, Maldwyn,' I said in my friendliest voice, and put down the phone.

But I knew what I had to do.

7

This time there was no Andrew to greet me at the station. I had tried several times to ring him from the train, but the house phone had rung and rung until a severe voice informed me that 'The other caller is not picking up'. His mobile voicemail was full, and his office appeared to have no idea where he was.

The last train to Carlisle was nearly deserted, and I spent most of the journey staring out at my reflection in the glass as the darkening countryside sped past. As soon as I stepped on to the platform, the cold air tore at my skin.

I shivered, and hurried out to the taxi rank.

We approached Gilcaster Head, speeding along the narrow road where this had all begun, the trees and peaks on the horizon shrouded in black. The taxi driver seemed to be in a hurry to get home, and I had to reach forward and tap him on the shoulder.

'Could you be careful along this road, please.'

The man grunted, but didn't slow down.

We didn't see any owls. In fact, we didn't see much at all, until the familiar gabled prow of Gilcaster Head rose up through the gloom like a ghost ship. There were no lights on apart from a solitary lamp above the porch. I paid the driver, and was left alone in the yard.

I knocked on the door, but no answer came.

I hammered louder.

'Andrew? It's Charles. We need to talk.'

His Range Rover was parked up behind me, so I knew he had to be nearby, even if the police hadn't had any joy finding him. Moving round the front of the house, I pressed my face against the windows. As I shone my phone through the panes, I was shocked to see what looked like the aftermath of a burglary. Bookcases were upended, their contents strewn over the floor. The expensive Mayfair curtains were half-torn off their poles, hanging in shreds at a lopsided angle. Plates and glasses lay smashed on the floor, and one of the intruders must have torn up some cushions or a pillow, because a light dusting of white feathers had settled over everything, a few still turning in the air.

A noise made me start. I turned around, but there was no one there. 'Hello?' I said again, to the empty house.

Then the noise came once more. It was carried on the wind, over the roofs and eaves of Gilcaster Head. A muffled cry, but whether human or animal, it was hard to tell. Fantasies of intruders having kidnapped Andrew for reasons yet mysterious flooded through my brain. Absurd, of course, but it felt as if the line between reality and fantasy was increasingly difficult to detect. The sound came again, a strangulated cry, from the other side of the house, towards Minniver Wood.

'Hang on, I'm coming!' I shouted.

Struggling to find my way around this unfamiliar part of Gilcaster Head, I tore my trousers on a barbed wire fence.

I kept reminding myself that I was not here to settle a score, or wreak revenge, but to try and get Andrew to see sense. As I stumbled through the rough grass and sheep mess of the field, I spotted a figure, waving his arms in the moonlight.

It was Andrew.

I approached him slowly, the torch beam sliding drunkenly as I navigated the slippery ground. He turned to face me, and I nearly dropped the phone.

How could this be the same man, the person I had first met striding out of the college chapel all those years ago? He was no longer recognisable as the enigmatic star, the College Swan. His hair stood up from his head in various different directions, his cheeks were scratched and inflamed, his beard coarse and unkempt. He was wearing a loose coat that seemed to be quite without warmth, his shirt and trousers in rags underneath.

Andrew stared at me for a moment, stretching out his arms – whether to repel me or beckon me towards him, I couldn't tell. The nails on his hands were long and encrusted with dried blood and grime.

'Charles,' he said hoarsely, shielding his eyes from the torchlight.

'I hope I'm not interrupting anything . . . it's just you hadn't returned any calls . . . People are worried . . .'

'I had to come back. They wouldn't let me sleep, you see.' He cocked his head, studying me. There was something jerky and unnerving about his movements, his natural poise gone. His eyes were rimmed red with either tears or exhaustion.

I extended a hand of my own.

'Come on. You'll freeze to death out here in that get-up. Why don't you come in, I'll pour us both a stiff drink and then you can tell me all about it.'

Andrew shook his head sadly, and backed away. 'You need

to see. How can you possibly understand what I've been through, if you don't see for yourself?'

I looked around obediently. In the inky blue of the night sky, Gilcaster Head seemed even more grand. The roofs and gables that yoked the old farm buildings together rose up through the darkness. Andrew snatched my phone and waved it about, casting a bright spotlight on window frames, doors, guttering and brickwork. Everywhere the light shone, I saw scratches and welts gouged out of paintwork and wood, turning them into livid raw wounds.

'And look,' he said, striding off down the field, pointing the light towards the ground. Beneath our feet, the rough pastures behind the house were covered not just with the leaves of years gone by, but with hundreds of white feathers. In some places they lay thick enough to form a kind of pelt that, away from the direct glare of the beam, looked like light snowfall.

Andrew strode through them, kicking up the soft down with his boots, as if such a sight was completely normal.

'They're everywhere. Look at this mess. No bloody escape.'

'How many of them are there, do you think?' I asked, staying where I was. My back still felt a glow of warmth from the heated house behind us. Meanwhile, the man who was, until only a few days ago, the bookmaker's favourite to become the next prime minister, disappeared behind a dusty cloud of owl feathers. He shouted something, but I don't think he was talking to me.

He was addressing the owls of Minniver Wood.

Standing there in the bitter cold, my breath freezing in the air, Andrew's shouts fading as he blundered into the thorny undergrowth, I too could think of nothing else. I could hear their cries, and in my mind, they swooped and pecked, their powerful wings beating in a fury.

For a moment, I paused.

This man had used me, smeared me, damaged my marriage and wrecked my career. I could simply walk away, and leave him to his fate, however grotesque that fate might be. Or perhaps I could use the phone in my hand to alert the police. Or the media. Even Andrew would struggle to spin his way out of this one.

Some instinct, perhaps long buried, told me that this was not the time to stick the knife into my old acquaintance, regardless of what he had done to me. I was the last Fryerne of Fryerne Court – a man who was by accident of birth, if not bound to believing in the truth, at least very strongly committed to it. The truth of this situation was that Andrew was in danger.

I hurried after him, my hand over my mouth, in an attempt not to inhale the trail of gritty feather dust he had kicked up. Standing on the edge of the wood, the thickets seemed to be even more wild and impenetrable than they had looked from the house. A strange cry came from within. I pushed my way past the briars.

Andrew stood a little way into the wood, in a sort of clearing, where twigs and yet more plumage lay all around, gleaming in a shaft of moonlight. His fists were clenched and he raised his head up to the sky, as if in some kind of exultation.

But, at first, there were no owls.

Then, as I stepped on a twig just behind him, he whirled round and signalled me to be quiet, a finger to his lips. Slowly, he inclined his head towards the circle of branches that enclosed us. I followed his gaze and found my stare returned by many others. A hundred or more pairs of eyes, blinking, watching us impassively. Wide discs of sulphurous yellow, each with a black and unyielding centre that seemed to follow our every breath. I stood and gazed back, to see if I could detect any message in their golden stares. And to my surprise, I found no malevolence, no animosity – only sorrow. Andrew began to mumble under his breath. At first I thought he was advising me what to do, how best to exit this owl grove we had stumbled into with minimum injury to either side. But gradually I realised that he was in fact making an appeal.

To the birds. That was when I also realised he had quite lost his mind. That he had been losing it for some time, I just hadn't understood it until now.

'Believe it or not,' he said, 'I really do think I can make a difference to this country. The party's in a state, the country's in a state, and you know that as well as I do. I may not have much in the way of Maldwyn's charm, and my contribution to the Wildlife and Countryside Bill Committee may go down in history as . . . unexpected, to say the least.'

I could have sworn that one of the watching owls gave a soft hoot at this. He then began to repeat what he had said to me the night I agreed to take the blame, followed by a condensed version of his leadership acceptance speech.

'I offer leadership, the kind that this country sorely needs. When I want to get something done, I make it happen. And I'm not going to let some wretched birds stop me.'

Now there was a distinct ruffling of feathers from the boughs around us. I didn't for a moment think they understood what Andrew was saying, but there was an unmistakeable sense of territorial transgression in the air, almost as if we had pulled back a veil on a sacred place, crossed a threshold that we should not have.

'Andrew, shall we take this conversation back indoors?'

'No. We need to leave this conversation exactly where it is, if you don't mind.'

'Why, for goodness' sake?'

'Because I need you to see these birds, to feel their power.' Suddenly, he clapped his hands. He might as well have fired both barrels of a shotgun. We ducked, covering our eyes and faces as the owls rose into the air around us with shrieks and wails, scratching and tearing where they could. For what seemed like an eternity they spun around our heads like winged Furies, before finally dissolving into the shadowy depths of the wood. I felt the hot trickle of blood on my left hand. Andrew lowered his guard, looking around.

His expression was not one of fear or relief, but wonder.

'I have never seen power like it. And I was in Russia when the oligarchs took over. Do you see now what I am up against? I see them in my dreams. I hear them scratching at the window. Even in London, I swore I could hear one clawing at the glass the other night. And that was when I realised. I don't understand how, but I realised then that they will never leave me alone. They are a waking nightmare from which I can never escape, unless I take radical action. The kind of action a leader is expected to take.' He turned to me, clasping my wounded hand in a rare show of physical intimacy. 'Help me. We can destroy them together. The party will thank me for it. The country will thank me for it.'

How could we destroy what we didn't understand? I had heard the birds calling to me, sensed their power in the night. I did not fully understand what the source of their power was, only that it was to be respected.

Caroline had seen the owls too. Whether the whole affair was a series of bizarre coincidences, some unexplained natural phenomena, or something more sinister, some long-buried elemental force reawakened, I no longer knew. Through its death, a single owl had created more devastation than it was possible to imagine. Andrew's career. My reputation. My marriage.

I felt a wave of sudden dizziness, and I wondered if I had been infected with something. It seemed unlikely. But then again, almost everything about this situation, standing in the black wood with Andrew, who clasped my hands in supplication while the icy wind nipped at our faces, seemed unlikely.

What I wished for more deeply than anything else in the world was for it all to cease. I wanted to be free of this man and his delusions of power. If I never saw Gilcaster Head again, I wouldn't regret it for a second. I wanted to be back with Caroline, in a house no longer battered by malevolent birds, our lives no longer in thrall to a tawdry tabloid drama played out on the national stage. Above all, I wanted to leave this wood before the owls returned. Maldwyn had sent me here to speak truth to power, but the real power in these woods could not be spoken to.

I tried to back out of the clearing, but Andrew gripped my hands more tightly.

'We can do something,' he said feverishly. 'Come and work for me. Come out of the cold.'

'I'm not the one who needs to get out of the cold, Andrew—' I began, but he was no longer listening.

'There's too much disorder in the world,' he said, letting go of my hands. 'Too much chaos, too much of this . . .' He swung his arm round at the haunted wood. 'We can sort it all out, Charles.'

Then he began to babble. Words were coming out of his mouth, but I could no longer make out what they were. He had stopped addressing me, and was talking instead to the trees, the sky, to the moon. Wrapping the remains of his coat around him, he wandered off into the shadows of the forest, mumbling as he went.

I did not follow. Instead I walked away, turning back through the trees towards the old house at the end of the field.

8

Andrew Landford would never see me again after that night. In fact, he never saw anyone.

It was Tom Gazelee who found him. He said he had been taking a walk in the field next door to the wood, although I suspect he might have been nosing around, looking for his ruins. Either way, that was when he heard the cries.

'Keening,' he said later, when I rang him up in an attempt to discover more. 'That's the only word I can use. A keening wail. I've never heard anything like it before or since. Like an animal caught in a trap, or worse. I thought . . . well, you know my views on the Landfords. We've never exactly seen eye to eye on country matters. I wondered if they'd put some totally unnecessary traps in the wood, and caught a fox or a deer.'

I winced. 'But did you see any feathers, any birds, anything at all of that nature?'

'No! I saw nothing like that. I saw a wild bit of woodland, at least, what was left of it after his parents cut it back to the stump of a thing it is today. I saw spruce and alder and hawthorn, holly bushes and drifts of leaves. The noise was getting louder and louder, and it was coming from the middle of the forest. The closer I got, the more it sounded like sobbing. And before you ask, I did see some blood. Flecks here and there on the bark of the trees, some on the ground. Similar to the kind of blood trail an animal in distress would leave, a lot of panicked and disorientated movement within a small space. And then I saw him. He was unrecognisable at first. His clothes were torn to shreds, and there were scratches all over his body . . .'

Tom's straightforward tone began to falter as he described what happened next.

'But I could see . . . it was Andrew. I mean, I recognised his hair, the shape of the body, you know. But I couldn't see his face, it was buried in his hands. What a sight. Fingers covered in blood, everything . . . it was awful. He was all huddled up in the middle of this clearing, shaking . . . making this horrific sound. "Andrew?" I asked him. "Is that you?" I had to be sure.

'He didn't reply at first. I had to ask him two or three times, then he just shook his head. I said "Are you all right, do you want me to call somebody?" You know, because I thought this might just be something he did . . . some weird ritual. He shook his head, violently this time, so I took that as a no. Then the boys came in, sniffing about as they do, so I shooed them away. I put my hand on Andrew's shoulder.

'"It's OK, Andrew. It's Tom. I'm here. Everything's going to be all right."'

There was a silence at the end of the line.

'That was when he dropped his hands. I never saw anything as horrible in my life. Why would anyone want to do that to somebody?'

No one was ever charged with the blinding of Andrew Landford. After he left hospital, where he would not receive visitors, not even Helen, and he retired from public life. Not just public life, but all life. He pulled one final disappearing trick and vanished. Gilcaster Head was sold in a private sale to a local charity, who announced their intention to convert it into a bird sanctuary, after a substantial donation from an anonymous donor. He never formally resigned as leader of the Conservative Party, but was removed from the post following an extraordinary motion put forward by a group of Maldwyn's backers. Maldwyn duly became acting leader then, following a vote of confidence, leader.

Last spring he was elected Britain's first openly gay prime minister, with a slim parliamentary majority. A reporter for a Sunday newspaper claimed to have tracked Andrew down for comment, supposedly hiding out in a mountain cave in northern Greece. But Matt Dilcombe, now employed as Maldwyn's director of communications, immediately saw to it that a huge increase in military spending was announced the same day the story broke, and the world moved on.

Caroline and I are together again, in our way. It is not perfect, but we have what we have. The winter after these events happened she finally exhibited her owl sculptures. They seemed to have been – and almost certainly were – produced with a visionary intensity. There they stood, high on their plinths, looking down on the viewer. She insisted the gallery spotlight and backlight them in the most dramatic way. Every curve of each beak, every line of the feathering, blazed not just with indignation and contempt for human folly, but with a mysterious otherness that I found hard to believe came from Caroline alone.

The show met with rapturous critical acclaim, of a kind she hadn't enjoyed for years, and several of the pieces sold for large amounts of money. Yet talking by ourselves, I found it hard to get her to talk about them. I knew, of course, that they had been conceived amid the tumult of the Landford scandal, but whether they were meant to be mythical creatures, or moral judges, or something else – she would not be drawn. Not on inspiration, not on meaning.

'You were there. You saw them too. How else was I meant to respond?' was all she said.

Caroline and I don't go back to London much now. She made enough money from her owl show to semi-retire, and we sold the studio. 'Quit while you're ahead, don't you think? We both should have done that a long time ago.' She still works though, selling the odd piece from a converted barn just inland from the coast at Bamburgh. Everything is in what we call her 'Northern style'. There are no more owls or toad princes: these sculptures are abstract, with jagged lines and intersecting planes that are constantly surprising. They carry the shape of the grey waves we see from our clifftop walks, the spikes of the reeds below, the undulating dunes, the scudding clouds. I think they are her finest work, and hardly anyone knows about them.

The last time I can remember either of us being back in the south was for a small family service, when we renewed our vows at St Mary's-Without. Indeed it was so small that, apart from the vicar, we were the only people there. For the first time, Brad was unable to make it over to a Fryerne gathering. He pleaded ill health and sent an overflowing bouquet of flowers, but I suspected that much like us, his heart was no longer in the Fryerne myth. Caroline and I shook hands with the bemused-looking vicar, and standing for a moment on the church path, we saw that the housing estate which had replaced Fryerne Court was itself being demolished. Some hoardings proclaimed the forthcoming arrival of

Fernlands, 'two hundred state-of-the-art investment opportunities. Penthouses available.'

Unless one felt inclined to see the allusion in Fernlands, no trace of our name remained. Not five minutes' drive away, the Fryerne Arms had also given way to a gardening centre. We exchanged some polite words with the vicar about the pace of change, got into our car, and didn't stop till we reached Newcastle.

I still have Uncle Roland's book, of course, gathering dust on a shelf somewhere. But neither of us is inclined to dwell much on the recent past.

We now find our comfort elsewhere.

Once or twice a year, if the weather is fine – on one of those crisp winter mornings, when the sky above the moors has the look of very thin air, the peaks on the horizon as sharp as a beak – we drive out towards Gilcaster Head. We try to arrive early, to avoid other visitors, rubberneckers or tourists, and we always leave before the light starts to fade. It's never a journey on which many words are exchanged, and we coast along the narrow roads, ever vigilant for any creature that might stray into our path.

Gilcaster Head itself is encased with scaffolding, shrouded in tarpaulin, as it is slowly being turned into a Visitor Centre for the bird sanctuary. We park in the drive, exactly as we did when we were guests. Entrance to the sanctuary, through the wilds of the Landfords' former garden, is free – although we leave something in the honesty box each time.

We take the path that winds over the bumpy field to Minniver Wood, which is already full of young trees in plastic sheaths, as the replanting of the reserve begins. If we get there early enough, we are normally the only ones there. A path has been hacked through the thicker parts of the wood, and laid with wood chips. Bordering the trail, laminated signs at knee height invite children to guess the age of a tree or identify the species by the leaf. Shrubs and bushes are labelled, as are several kinds of moss. There are also pictures of birds nailed to trunks – woodpeckers, hooded crows, terns and owls. There is rarely any sight of the birds themselves, although the nature trail marked along the path makes suggestions about the best time of year and day to see them.

We don't stick to the path. Once we are deep inside the wood, we step off the chippings and push aside prickly swathes of holly and gorse until we reach a small clearing, quite hidden from view. When we first came here, there were still discarded police gloves and scraps of incident tape stuck to the leaves, but all that is gone now. There is no trace of the horror that happened here.

We walk through the glade, to a wall I never noticed when I came here in the dark. A wall is not a fully accurate description; it is more the remains of a wall. Large slabs of weathered, yellowing stone, well over six feet high, trailing away to nothing on either side. This is what Tom Gazelee was campaigning about. Now the ruins have been found, he's chosen to leave them alone.

A wise decision.

For if you pull apart the strands of moss and bracken that cover the central slab, there is the faintest trace of carving, covering the entire section. It might be Roman, although no one knows how long the wall has been there. Following the shallow indentations with your finger, it is still just possible to make out the portrait of a goddess. She sits with a shield and a spear, as sharp as the claws of the owl perched on her shoulder. Some say she is Minerva, the Roman goddess of wisdom, and that Minniver Wood was a local corruption of her name. Others say that is pure speculation.

But whatever the time of year, whether there is frost hard on the ground, or there are bluebells spread out in the sun around us, when you place your hand on the stone, it is warm. The stone is still warm.